THE
VICTORIAN
CATALOGUE OF
HOUSEHOLD
GOODS

S. & F. NEW PREMISES, WOOD STREET, LONDON. S. & F.

S. & F. FURNITURE AND IRONMONGERY, LAMP, AND GASFITTINGS DEPARTMENTS. S. & F.

THE
VICTORIAN
CATALOGUE OF
HOUSEHOLD
GOODS

A Complete Compendium of over five
thousand items to Furnish and Decorate
the Victorian Home

INTRODUCTION BY
DOROTHY BOSOMWORTH

PORTLAND HOUSE
NEW YORK

The Victorian Catalogue of Household Goods was first published
by Silber and Flemming c. 1883 as *The Illustrated Catalogue of
Furniture and Household Requisites*.

Copyright © 1991 Studio Editions

This 1991 edition published by Portland House
distributed by Outlet Book Co, Inc.
a Random House Company
225 Park Avenue South
New York, New York 10003

The right of Dorothy Bosomworth to be identified as author of the
introduction has been asserted by her in accordance with the
Copyright, Designs and Patents Act, 1988.

Printed and bound in Czechoslovakia

ISBN 0-517-05396-9

8 7 6 5 4 3 2 1

Introduction

This illustrated anthology has been taken from a late nineteenth-century trade catalogue published by the firm of Silber & Fleming of London and Paris. Dating from the late 1880s (the exact date is not given in the original), it indicates the wide variety of decorative and useful goods in which the company traded. As such, it represents a remarkable insight into the true nature of taste among the late Victorian middle classes, revealing their fondness for ornament, their fascination with gadgets, and the vast proliferation of goods which they could buy. Such a prufusion of objects also indicates a clientele which had both the money and leisure to use and enjoy the items that they bought.

The Victorian era (1837–1901) witnessed a massive expansion in Britain's population, and in its economic fortunes. In the first half of the century, the population doubled from nine to eighteen million, and it kept on growing. Agriculture, already affected by the repeal of the Corn Laws in 1846, suffered a disastrous collapse in the 1870s, setting in train a massive exodus of rural people, either abroad to the colonies or into Britain's towns and cities, to seek alternative employment in commerce or industry. By the mid-century 54 per cent of the population was urban.

The 'Workshop of the World' and leader of the Industrial Revolution, Britain was also regarded as a nation of shopkeepers. Already its capitalist economy was well established: the Bank of England had been founded in 1694, and the London Stock Exchange chartered in 1698. The British banking system was arguably the best in Europe. The stock of the Bank of England was privately owned, and its management not controlled by the state, although it remained in close contact with the government, helping to stabilize public finance. Businessmen and entrepreneurs could thus develop their activities unhindered by fear of national bankruptcy or ruinous inflation.

The Great Exhibition of 1851, housed in the Crystal Palace, Hyde Park, marked the expansion of Britain's dominions: half the total length of 1,851 feet in the main nave was devoted to items from Britain and its colonies – the other half to the rest of the world. The industrial enterprise, commercial acumen and increased public demand for consumer goods which lay behind the successful organization of the Great Exhibition needed to be harnessed through an effective marketing and distribution system if there were to be a lasting economic benefit. It is against this background that in 1856 the London firm of Silber & Fleming was founded, as manufacturers, importers, warehousemen and agents.

Albert Marcius Silber was born in Schleswig Holstein in 1833, coming to England in 1854, where he became a naturalized subject in 1856. The same year, he established with N. H. Fleming (whose background is unknown) a small fancy goods warehouse at 60 Wood Street in the City of London. In addition to manufacturing its own products, the company also acted as importers, exporters and dealers in British and foreign fancy and leather goods, jewellery, silver and silver plate, china and glass, and ironmongery, and won contracts to supply 'Her Majesty's Government and most of the railway companies in Great Britain and Ireland', to quote the introduction to this volume of their catalogue. As their business grew, so their premises expanded, in handsome Italianate warehouses in Wood Street, off London Wall with a link to Bird Court, Philip Lane, to the rear.

In addition to its worldwide import–export trade, the company became well known for gas lighting, which was Albert Silber's special concern from about 1870 until his death in 1887. At separate but nearby premises at 40 Lower Whitecross Street and Beech Lane, he produced a wide variety of gas lamps, including signalling lanterns and carriage lamps for railways, as well as patenting a new form of gas burner, which the Silber Light Company (registered as a limited company in 1886) manufactured and exported through Silber & Fleming. An aggressive international marketing programme proved successful, and the company won awards at international exhibitions in Calcutta, Sydney, Melbourne and Adelaide.

A ten-volume run of Silber & Fleming catalogues survives in the National Art Library at the Victoria & Albert Museum, starting in 1872. From these it is clear that by that year the character and range of the business was already fully established. The title page of the 1872 edition announced 'Silber & Fleming, warehousemen and importers, British and foreign manufacturers' agents', giving their addresses as 56, 56½, 56a, 61 and 62 Wood Street, Cheapside, and Bird Court, Philip Lane, E.C., London, and 70 rue de paradis Poissonnière, Paris. The stock was summarized as follows: 'English and foreign gold, silver, and imitation jewellery, electroplating and japanned goods, pipes, leather goods, optical department, cabinet goods, stationery and foreign cabinet goods, fine art, haberdashery, beads, perfumery, Bohemian, French and flint glass and china, musical instruments, toys and games'. The second volume, dating from 1876–7, added watches, clocks and cutlery to the range listed above. A third volume, for the year 1878–89, included a section entitled 'Silber and Fleming: wholesale agents for the Silber Light Company'. Explaining Silber's achievements in developing gas lighting, it illustrated and itemized a variety of gas lamps and fittings.

By the early 1880s – after 1882, although the exact date is not clear – the company had expanded further, to include no. 71 Wood Street. For the first time the catalogue was published in two volumes and boasted a much more elaborate design, including a number of colour illustrations printed by chromolithography. A registered trademark appeared, showing a rope bow, with the initials 'A' and 'M' in the spaces within the bow's loops, and 'S' below, between the bow ends. New categories of stock included thermometers and lantern slides; and there were announcements of international trade exhibition awards for the Silber Light Company's moderator lamps; First Prize at Sydney in 1880, First Order of Merit at Melbourne in 1881 and a Gold Medal at Adelaide in 1882.

The company prided itself both on its ability to execute orders speedily, within twenty-four hours after receipt, and on the product knowledge and taste of its departmental managers. Clients were invited to submit general orders, specifying for example 'assorted goods' to a given price range. A complete furnishing service was also offered for private homes and hotels, again solely on a wholesale basis. The advantages of this were explained in the catalogue introduction: 'We are prepared to give you estimates for furnishing Private Houses or hotels throughout, if you give us the necessary details; and you will thus be enabled to supply your intending customer with everything he may require in the furnishing line at a moderate profit, as all the details of the execution of such an order will be done, when required, by us'. However, there is no indication in the separate introductions to the various sections as to whether they were indeed offering to supply all the furnishing requirements of a home on a regular basis.

Who, then, were their customers? Without surviving company records, it is impossible to form a detailed impression, but we can assume that they consisted both of retailers, such as department stores, furnishing shops and ironmongers, china, silver and glass specialists, and of corporate clients. Their dinner-ware, in the china section, includes a page of monogrammed and crested wares, with mottos and legends indicating that they had been made for the 'Royal Family Hotel, Poona' and the 'Grand Hotel de la Plage'. Other plates appear destined for military and naval messes.

The taste expressed in the Silber & Fleming catalogues is that of the fairly wealthy middle class, although without price lists, which were published separately from the main catalogues and have not survived, we cannot be precise about the costs involved. The impression of affluence is borne out by large and elaborate sections devoted to silver, electroplate and cutlery, and china and glass, as well as by the wide variety of mantel clocks. Items such as liqueur cabinets (nos. 14622–14632), cigar cabinets, workboxes and photograph albums also denote a clientele which had disposable income, and the time to enjoy it.

The luggage section features lawn tennis cases and a cricket bat bag (nos. 12846, 127847 and 12850) as well as tricyclist's valises, a game bag and a tourist's knapsack. Pages of dressing cases follow, many of them elaborately fitted, and referred to as 'patent', with an accompanying admonition warning that copyright infringement will be prosecuted.

Although decorative items which might be construed as small pieces of furniture are included, coal boxes or purdoniums, for example, cast iron umbrella stands and conservatory furniture, there is no mention of standard cabinet and upholstered furniture, tables, chairs and beds. Nor are there any textiles, whether in the form of curtains, bedding, carpets or napery. So we must assume that Silber & Fleming would liaise with other suppliers, to fulfil a complete interior decoration order as and when required. In this respect their catalogues are unlike the modern Habitat or Laura Ashley 'Home' catalogues. There are further points of difference also. The original volume on which this anthology is based includes domestic appliances, horse and carriage trappings, games and toys, and is thus more comparable to Littlewoods' or Universal Stores' current mail-order catalogues.

This volume begins with a section on silver and electroplate. Silber & Fleming describe themselves as manufacturing silversmiths, but rather than having their own full workshops and design studio, they probably subcontracted the silversmithing to jobbing firms, employing workmen directly to engrave monograms and initials. In addition to an extensive range of silver and electroplate, they also sold a wide selection of gold, silver and imitation jewellery, and even fans. The silver consists of presentation items, ranging from elaborate centrepieces, epergnes, tea and coffee services, to presentation spades, mallets and trowels, made to commemorate the laying of foundation stones. One elaborate silver spade duplicates an original given by the ladies of Dover to H.R.H. the Duchess of Connaught (no. 5608).

The design of the silver goods falls into three categories: historicist, naturalistic and Aesthetic, that is, with a degree of Japanese influence on the design. The historicist designs are typical of late nineteenth-century British silver, Classical in inspiration, mostly spun, with cast ornament, and engraved patterns in the case of flatware, such as cigarette and cigar cases. There are seven patterns of cutlery, mostly those with which we are still familiar today, such as fiddle pattern and King's pattern, although rat-tail is excluded in favour of two more elaborate patterns: Napier, and shaped Tudor pattern.

The electroplate section is extensive, the types of objects shown providing a wide variety of decorative holloware. Patents for electroplate and electrogilding had been taken out by George Richards Elkington and his cousin Henry Elkington in 1840, and developed in association with George Walker of the Sheffield firm of silversmiths and cutlers, Walker & Hall. The process enabled a fine skin of silver plate to be fused electrically onto a base metal object. The final appearance resembled sterling silver, but at a fraction of its price.

All the accoutrements of the affluent Victorian dining room and parlour are represented in this section of the catalogue, from tea and coffee services, claret jugs, cruet sets, cups, salvers and trays, to cake baskets, biscuit barrels, muffin dishes and entrée dishes. A glance through a copy of Mrs Beeton's cookery book would explain the need for such a plethora of items, when a dinner party could have as many as twelve courses.

The sections on glass and china are similarly wide-ranging. Consisting of both decorative items and table glass, the pieces are cut, engraved and pressed. The glass appears to be both foreign – Bohemian, French and Italian – and British, although no manufacturers' names are given. Silber & Fleming proudly boast that their stock is 'the largest held in this country', but stipulate a three-month order period for replacement in the event of great demand for particular items. There are strange anomalies in the design of certain pieces, as in the case of a number of double-handled vases, where the shape is of Etruscan inspiration, but the hand-painted decoration is naturalistic. The Victorian love of novelty and of fussy pattern is all too apparent in the decorative articles. Very rarely, simpler pieces are illustrated, but there is no sign in this section of more avant-garde work, such as Tiffany ware or the Clutha glass designed by Christopher Dresser.

Several flower stands are illustrated, suitably filled to give a good idea of late Victorian taste in flower arrangements (e.g. nos. 7501, 7503, 7507 and 7511). Roses, Sweet William, pansies, clematis, marguerites, harebells and lily of the valley are all present, along with ivy and ferns. The flower stands are of two types. One design consists of a central bowl, from which a principal tulip shaped vase rises, flanked by several shorter vases which splay out from a common base. The other form has a plateau base.

The extensive china section also includes both British and foreign goods. Dresden and Viennese porcelain, Bohemian and English majolica, Chinese and Japanese wares are all represented. The vast majority of the items, however, are middle of the range Staffordshire wares, probably unmarked, according to Jennifer Opie and Robin Hillyard of the Department of Ceramics, Victoria & Albert Museum. Some of the pieces may be German earthenware from Mettlach and possibly from Franz Mehlen's factory in Bonn.

The Victorians' love of animals is catered for by a wide range of clay models, many of them made in a frost-resistant impervious material. Intended as hall, conservatory and garden ornaments, brackets and saddlers' trade signs, they are convincingly life-like. They range from life-size models of deer, to miniatures of more exotic creatures such as bison, zebra and camels.

Silber & Fleming boast in their introduction to the china section of the original catalogue that they hold stock of most items and are thus able to despatch an order within a few hours of its receipt. Different combinations of dinner and tea services are quoted, as 'package' orders. A dinner service for 18 persons, the largest group quoted, consisted of no less than 168 pieces – 54 meat plates, 18 soup plates, 24 tart plates, 18 cheese plates, 1 20-inch gravy dish, 18 flat dishes, ranging in size between 9 and 20 inches, 1 soup tureen with ladle, 4 sauce tureens with ladles, 4 vegetable dishes, 4 pie dishes, 1 salad bowl, 1 cheese stand and 1 fish drainer. Small wonder that a Victorian household of any pretensions needed servants to be run properly!

Several designs are inspired by Japanese influences, either in the details of their transfer-printed decorations or in the shapes of certain pieces, for example, dinner services nos. 8773 and 8877. This is apparent in the disposition of the ornament, which uses an asymmetric collage effect, and in the details of the imagery, combining plants with birds and even a butterfly on the dinner plate of service no. 8877. Other patterns are more traditionally English in character, and may represent patterns still in production from current manufacturers such as Wedgwood, Minton, Royal Doulton and Royal Derby. A page of fish and game plates even includes 'best French china oyster plates'. The tea services all have cup shapes which flare only slightly, in contrast to the wider bowl shapes of earlier nineteenth-century china. Here again, designs vary enormously in elaboration, from the highly decorated to plainer pieces, which would have been cheaper.

A similar variety is available in the toilet services – essential items of equipment in Victorian houses, where bathrooms and plumbed-in basins were still very much novelties. Instead, cans of hot water would be brought up by a housemaid, and poured into a water jug, before being poured in turn into the bowl: a practice which persisted in the country, certainly until the First World War.

Warmth and cleanliness were two fundamental preoccupations in any Victorian household. A housemaid would be expected to rise at six or six-thirty, to open the shutters, clean the grates, lay the fires for the day, move all the furniture to sweep the carpets, move all the bric-à-bric to dust the furniture, and dust and polish that bric-à-bric. She would also be expected to take up the hot water for her employers to wash in, before laying the breakfast table, and serving the first meal of the day. All these functions are reflected in the catalogue. Whilst the contents stop short of fire surrounds, overmantels or mantel pelmets, brass fenders and fire irons are included at the start of the section on ironmongery. Fenders vary from the utilitarian to the decorative. like the other items of brassware in the catalogue, these would probably have been manufactured in Birmingham, the centre of the brass foundry industry in Britain, then as today.

For those house-owners with more modern plumbing, the company did offer a range of baths. Among these the *pièce de résistance* is undoubtedly the 'Healtheries' Combination Bath (no. 9725). Cased in wood, with a vertical section at the head of the bath, this offered douche, wave, spray, shower, plunge, sitz, cold and hot valves. Examples of these survive in a number of British country houses, where they are still in working order.

The fascination with patents and technical improvements, which is such a feature of the exterior appliances and machines featured in the catalogue, is also evident in the section on labour-saving machines and 'household requisites'. A variety of washing-machines, mangles and wringers would have helped the drudgery of the laundry, while in the kitchen meat cutters and mincers include, exceptionally, an American machine: the Enterprise Meat Chopper, manufactured by Crosscup & West of Philadelphia (no. 9849). The way in which this particular illustration is drawn, with the company credit appearing immediately beneath the skirt of the kitchen table to which the meat chopper is braced, suggests that it may have been 'lifted' directly from another catalogue, presumably that of the American manufacturers, without being redrawn.

Pages and pages of kitchen utensils and tools remind us of the complexities and drudgery of life below stairs. There is only one sign of any forerunner of the modern vacuum cleaner: 'The original champion carpet sweeper' (no. 10260), which appears alongside carpet brooms and whisks, billiard and bagatelle table brushes, even a bed brush!

Cheek by jowl with the brushes and equally utilitarian deed boxes and cash boxes, one suddenly finds a page of bird cages, including several wonderfully exotic creations, such as the 'Huntsman' pattern of ornamental wire canary cage, complete with miniature stag's head, affixed to the wire bars (no. 10299).

Silber & Fleming's tents and hammocks, illustrated in their ironmongery section, also suggest an international clientele. The 'Punjaub Hill Tent', no. 10844, is praised for its strong construction, with ropes stitched into the canvas. Yet this appears alongside patent bell tents, suitable for bathing and croquet parties at home.

Carriages and carts are included in the original catalogue, along with all the trappings of saddlery, but mechanical innovations appear too. Agricultural implements include mowers, binding harvesters, ploughs, rakes, reapers, turnip cutters, kibblers for oats, barley, malt, beans and peas. Dairy appliances are well represented, so too are carpenter's, builder's and engineer's tools.

The garden section ranges from an extensive array of garden tools and implements, to statuary and containers, and furniture for both outdoors and conservatory. There are recurrent emphases on 'the most modern improvements', to quote the caption for the 'Duplex Bee Hive' (no. 11087). Simplicity and practicality are continually stressed in the captions for farm and estate equipment, as in the new pheasant feeder, (no. 11088) or an improved poultry coop (nos. 11089 and 11090) designed by Mr Wragg, 'manager to Lady Gwydyr, a great authority on these matters'.

Sports and pastimes are represented by tennis racquets, croquet sets, cricket bats and stumps all included. There are even early versions of trainers in the lawn tennis shoes, with canvas, twill or kid uppers and corrugated 'Registered diamond' india-rubber soles. (This presumably refers to the india-rubber being stamped with a registered design sign which was diamond-shaped.) A number of bicycles, tandems and tricycles are included, from penny farthings to more technically sophisticated bicycles, such as the 'Coolie' Cycle, no. 16159, designed to accommodate four riders, two passengers sitting side by side on a bench seat in front, and two coolies sitting behind, pedalling to propel their passengers. Using the patent Cheylesmore automatic clutch gear, this was manufactured by the Coventry Machinists' Company, described in H. H. Griffin's book *Biclyes of the Year 1878* as the largest makers in the world, employing over 100 workmen in Coventry, with uncovered showrooms in London.

An early version of a folding push-chair, Trotman's patent, no. 16216, figures among a page of perambulators, while among an assortment of children's toys there is a clockwork horse omnibus, with a sign on the side: 'Louvre–Vincenn [*sic*], Bastille: Place de Trone: St. Mande, Compagnie Generale des Omnibus'. This is one of very few items in the catalogue which is obviously of French origin, imported through Silber & Fleming's French warehouse.

What can we learn from the design of the catalogue? Judging by the legends at the bottom of the original pages, it was printed in sections by several different printers, and then assembled for binding and publication. A clue to the identity of the Fleming of Silber & Fleming may come with the china section of the catalogue, where the words 'J. Fleming & Co., Lithographers, Leicester' appear on a number of pages. Other pages in this section were printed by Allbut & Daniel, Lithographers, Hanley, while in the metals sections much of the printing was done by Pawson & Brailsford of Sheffield. This method of assembly must have been dictated by the complexity of the compilation process, which entailed collating information and copying illustrations from a range of manufacturers' catalogues. Since the alternative would have been to assemble all the objects (a total of 11,128 items in the original of this volume) it is safe to assume that the piecemeal approach was adopted. Such a method would have also kept publication costs down, although there are a number of plates in colour, printed by chromolithography.

Even if the catalogue is a collation from other lists, rather than being specifically commissioned from artists, it still represents a considerable feat of art direction. The items illustrated are invariably shown in the round, rather than flat. Considerable thought has been given to the layout of each page, to make the displays look inviting. We must assume that the original drawings would have been done by jobbing illustrators, working directly for either Silber & Fleming or the printer concerned, much as a freelance illustrator would do today. The publication of the whole catalogue is thus likely to have been priced on a mixed basis of subcontracts and piece-work. We do not know if Silber & Fleming's customers would have been required to buy copies of the catalogue, rather than receiving them free: judging by present practice with pattern books, the former seems likely, although priority and prestige customers might have been exempted from paying.

What is to be gained from perusing a catalogue such as this? Lawrence B. Romaine, in his book *A Guide to American Trade Catalogs, 1744–1900* (R. R. Bowker & Co., New York, 1960, p. 35), asserts that 'the catalogs that actually sold the nation the inventions and improvements are the backbone of business history'. Kenneth L. Ames goes further. Writing an article entitled 'Meaning in Artefacts. Hall furnishings in Victorian America (*Journal of Interdisciplinary History*, vol. 9, no. 12, Summer 1978, p. 26), he explains that 'A modern-day interior designer or restoration consultant charged with reconstructing the inside of an old house cannot be said to have done an adequate job if he has not consulted trade catalogues of the same period. In a similar vein, reproduction of historic items should not be undertaken before considering the value the trade catalogue might lend to the project.'

For owners of Victorian houses, for location consultants in films and television, for museum curators and saleroom auctioneers, for nostalgia enthusiasts of any age, catalogues such as this give a fascinating window into our past.

DOROTHY BOSOMWORTH

STERLING SILVER GOODS,

𝔅ritish 𝔐anufacture.

HALL-MARKED.

ENGLISH AND FOREIGN

WATCHES,

CARD AND PENCIL CASES,

AND

GOLD AND SILVER JEWELLERY.

As almost every article represented herein is kept in stock by us, and can in most cases be dispatched within a few hours after receipt of order, you are placed in a position to execute the orders received from your customers at the shortest notice.

STERLING SILVER GOODS.

British Manufacture. Hall-Marked.

Drawings of special articles for Wedding and Birthday Presents, Presentations, Shooting, Rowing, Cricketing, or Bicycling Prizes, &c., are sent on application, and to customers who are well known to us, we sometimes send an assortment of goods to place before committees or others of their clients, which goods must of course be returned within seven days.

Monograms, Initials, and other Inscriptions engraved on any article, or on shields for attaching to same, at a few hours' notice, as we employ special workmen for that purpose.

All Sterling Silver Plate sold by us bears the Goldsmiths' Hall Mark, for which 1/6 per ounce is charged as Government duty, but when exported this duty is remitted. We credit our customers with the amount when returned to us by the authorities, after the goods have been shipped.

Special Designs submitted for Caskets, Epergnes, Salvers, and other articles suitable for presentation or prizes.

Sterling Silver Epergnes, Flower Vases, Fruit Dishes, &c., can be richly gilt with fine gold if desired.

ALL PRICES QUOTED IN OUR PRICE LIST ARE NETT.

As this Catalogue is specially compiled to illustrate goods suitable for Furnishing, we have only indicated by one page (336) our Departments of Real and Imitation Jewellery. Our assortment in these Departments is one of the largest and most varied shown in this country, and comprises the following goods :—

GOLD JEWELLERY, ETC.

Plain, or set with Diamonds or other Precious Stones.

Brooches.	Pen and Pencil Cases.
Bracelets.	
Bangles.	Rings.
Chains.	Scarf Pins.
Charms.	Sleeve Links.
Earrings.	Studs.
Head Ornaments.	Solitaires.
Lockets.	Sovereign Purses.
Masonic Jewellery.	Seals.
Necklets.	&c. &c.

REAL PEARLS AND PEARL JEWELLERY.

REAL CORAL BEADS AND JEWELLERY.

REAL ONYX BEADS AND JEWELLERY.

REAL AMBER BEADS AND JEWELLERY.

REAL AGATE BEADS AND JEWELLERY.

REAL GARNET BEADS AND JEWELLERY.

REAL JET GOODS.

SILVER JEWELLERY, ETC.

Brooches.	Pen and Pencil Cases.
Bracelets.	
Bangles.	Rings.
Chains and Charms.	Scarf Pins.
Earrings.	Sleeve Links.
Head Ornaments.	Studs and Solitaires.
Lockets.	Sovereign Purses.
Masonic Clothing.	Seals.
Necklets.	&c. &c.

Thimbles.	Whistles.
Smelling Bottles.	Cigar and Cigarette Cases.
Card Cases.	
Bells with Corals.	Purses.
Bouquet Holders.	Toothpicks and Pencils.
Dram Flasks.	

Fans.

Hand-painted and Embroidered Fans.
Bridal and Mourning Fans.
Fans made of fancy coloured Feathers.
Fans made of Ostrich Feathers, mounted with Real Tortoiseshell.
Fans made of Ostrich Feathers, mounted with Mother-of-Pearl.
Fans made of Ostrich Feathers, mounted with Ivory.

IMITATION JEWELLERY,

ENGLISH AND FOREIGN.

Black Cut Garnet Jewellery.

Vulcanite and Imitation Jet Jewellery.

Silvered and Gilt Jewellery.

Shell Goods.

Imitation Pearl Necklets.

Ivory Goods.

Aluminium Gilt Chains and Necklets.

Gold-cased Chains and Necklets.

Silver-plated Chains and Necklets.

Steel Chains.

Silk, Leather, and Hair Chains.

GOLD-PLATED JEWELLERY.
(*Will stand the test of acids.*)

COMBS AND OTHER HAIR ORNAMENTS, IN GILT, STEEL, REAL AND IMITATION TORTOISESHELL.

STERLING SILVER GOODS.

STERLING SILVER EPERGNES, FLOWER VASES, FRUIT DISHES, CANDELABRA, &c.,
CAN BE RICHLY GILT WITH FINE GOLD IF DESIRED.

No. 5502.—Sterling Silver Candelabrum, to match epergne, 3-arm, 4 lights. Height 20½ inches, diameter of base 8½ inches.
No. 5502A.—As No. 5502, but richly gilt.
No. 5502B.—As No. 5502, but silver plated on nickel silver.

No. 5502.—Sterling Silver Candelabrum, to match epergne, 3-arm, 4 lights. Height 23½ inches, diameter of base 8½ inches.
No. 5502A.—As No. 5502, but richly gilt.
No. 5502B.—As No. 5502, but silver plated on nickel silver.

No. 5503.—Sterling Silver Dessert Stand, with richly cut crystal glass bowl. Height 10¼ inches, diameter of base 6¼ inches, diameter of glass bowl 8½ inches.
No. 5503A.—As No. 5503, but richly gilt.
No. 5503B.—As No. 5503, but electro-silver plated on nickel silver.

No. 5500.—Sterling Silver Epergne, with one richly cut crystal glass dish and three saucers. Height 22¼ inches, width at base 8½ inches, diameter of top dish 8½ inches, diameter of saucer 5½ inches.
No. 5500A.—As No. 5500, but richly gilt.
No. 5500B.—As No. 5500, but electro-silver plated on nickel silver.

No. 5501.—Sterling Silver Plateau. Diameter of silver 12¾ inches, diameter of glass centre 9¾ inches, height 2½ inches.
No. 5501A.—As No. 5501, but richly gilt.
No. 5501B.—As No. 5501, but silver plated on nickel silver.

No. 5503.—Sterling Silver Dessert Stand, with richly cut crystal glass bowl. Height 10¼ inches, diameter of base 6¼ inches, diameter of glass bowl 8½ inches.
No. 5503A.—As No. 5503, but richly gilt.
No. 5503B.—As No. 5503, but electro-silver plated on nickel silver.

Special Designs submitted for Caskets, Epergnes, Salvers, and other articles, suitable for presentation, &c.

SILVERSMITHS.
A M S
TRADE MARK.

DOMINE DIRIGE NOS

ELECTRO PLATERS.
A M S
TRADE MARK.

STERLING SILVER GOODS.
THE FAMILY PLATE CHEST.

No. 5511.—Sterling Silver Fish Carvers, pearl handles, in silk and velvet-lined morocco leather case.

No. 5512.—Sterling Silver Cake Knife and Fork, ivory handles, in silk and velvet-lined morocco leather case.

No. 5513.—Sterling Silver Cake Knife and Fork, pearl handles, in silk and velvet-lined morocco leather case.

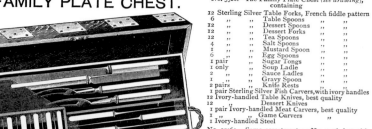

No. 68.

No. 5526.—The Family Plate Chest (see drawing), containing

12	Sterling Silver	Table Forks, French fiddle pattern		
6	,,	,,	Table Spoons	,,
12	,,	,,	Dessert Spoons	,,
12	,,	,,	Dessert Forks	,,
12	,,	,,	Tea Spoons	,,
4	,,	,,	Salt Spoons	,,
1	,,	,,	Mustard Spoon	,,
6	,,	,,	Egg Spoons	,,
1 pair	,,	,,	Sugar Tongs	,,
1 only	,,	,,	Soup Ladle	,,
2	,,	,,	Sauce Ladles	,,
1	,,	,,	Gravy Spoon	,,
2 pairs	,,	,,	Knife Rests	,,

1 pair Sterling Silver Fish Carvers, with ivory handles
12 Ivory-handled Table Knives, best quality
12 Dessert Knives
1 pair Ivory-handled Meat Carvers, best quality
1 ,, ,, Game Carvers ,,
1 Ivory-handled Steel

No. 5526A.—Same assortment as No. 5526, but with Spoons, Forks, &c., of Old English pattern.

No. 5526B.—Same assortment as No. 5526, but with Spoons, Forks, &c. of King's Shell, Rosette, Napier, Grecian, Tudor, and other fancy patterns.

The Canteen is of Oak, iron bound, with brass handles, lock and key, lined with blue cloth, contains sterling silver plate, hall-marked, and best ivory-handled cutlery.

Our Sterling Silver Spoons and Forks are wrought, hammered, and polished in the very best manner. See drawings, page 329.

No. 5514.—Sterling Silver Sugar Basin and Sugar Spoon, in silk and velvet lined morocco leather case.

No. 5516.—Sterling Silver Tea Pot, Sugar Basin, Cream Jug, and Sugar Tongs.

No. 5518.—Sterling Silver Sugar Basin and pair of Sugar Tongs, in silk and velvet-lined morocco leather case.

No. 5515.—Sterling Silver Salt Cellars and Spoons, in silk and velvet-lined morocco leather case.

No. 5517.—Sterling Silver Salt Cellars and Spoons, gilt lined, in silk and velvet-lined morocco leather case.

No. 5519.—Sterling Silver Soup Bowl and Spoon.

No. 5520.—Sterling Silver Sugar Basin, Cream Jug, and Sugar Tongs, in silk and velvet-lined morocco leather case.

No. 5521.—Sterling Silver Child's Mug, Fork and Spoon, in silk and velvet-lined morocco leather case.

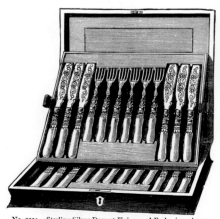

No. 5523.—Sterling Silver Dessert Knives and Forks, ivory handles, 12 pairs, in polished mahogany case, length of silver blade 4½ inches, length of ivory handle of knife 4 inches, length of 4-pronged fork 3¼ inches, length of handle of fork 3½ inches.

No. 5522.—Sterling Silver Fish Carver and Fork, in silk and velvet-lined morocco leather case.

No. 5524.—Sterling Silver Tea Pot, Sugar Basin, Cream Jug, and Sugar Tongs, in silk and velvet-lined morocco leather case.

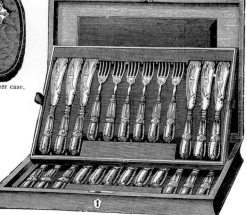

No. 5525.—Sterling Silver Fish Knives and Forks, 12 pairs, in polished mahogany case, length of knives 9 inches, length of forks 7½ inches.

A large variety of fancy Silver Goods, in handsome morocco leather cases, suitable for Wedding or Christening Presents.

S. & F.   S. & F.

STERLING SILVER GOODS.

TRADE MARK. AMS

TRADE MARK. AMS

No. 5527.—Sterling Silver Round Dessert Stand, Persian pattern, with richly cut crystal glass dish. Height 7 inches, diameter of base 4 inches, diameter of glass dish 6 inches.
No. 5527A.—As No. 5527, but richly gilt.

No. 5528.—Sterling Silver Round Jardinière, Grecian design, with richly cut crystal glass dish. Height 14¾ inches, diameter of base 7¾ inches, diameter of glass dish 11½ inches.
No. 5528A.—As No. 5528, but richly gilt.

No. 5529.—Sterling Silver Round Dessert Stand, Grecian design, with richly cut crystal glass dish. Height 11½ inches, diameter of base 6⅜ inches, diameter of glass dish 10 inches.
No. 5529A.—As No. 5529, but richly gilt.

No. 5530.—Sterling Silver Fruit and Flower Stand, with richly cut crystal glass bowl and flower vase. Extreme height 17½ inches.

No. 5531.—Sterling Silver Round Dessert Stand, Grecian design, with richly cut crystal glass dish. Height 8⅝ inches, diameter of base 4¾ inches, diameter of glass dish 8 inches.
No. 5531A.—As No. 5531, but richly gilt.

No. 5532.—Sterling Silver Oval Jardinière, richly embossed, Roman design, with finely cut crystal glass bowl. Height 13½ inches, length 16 inches, width 8 inches, diameter of base 8⅜ inches.
No. 5532A.—As No. 5532, but richly gilt.

No. 5533.—Sterling Silver Oval Dessert Stand, richly embossed, Roman design, with finely cut crystal glass bowl. Height 9¼ inches, length 11 inches, width 5¼ inches, diameter of base 6 inches.
No. 5533A.—As No. 5533, but richly gilt.

No. 5533.—Sterling Silver Oval Dessert Stand, richly embossed, Roman design, with finely cut crystal glass bowl. Height 9¼ inches, length 11 inches, width 5¼ inches, diameter of base 6 inches.
No. 5533A.—As No. 5533, but richly gilt.

No. 5536.

No. 5535.

No. 5536.

No. 5534.—Sterling Silver Round Dessert Stand, with richly cut crystal glass dish. Height 8⅜ inches, diameter of base 5 inches, diameter of glass dish 8 inches.
No. 5534A.—As No. 5534, but richly gilt.

No. 5535.—Sterling Silver Oval Jardinière, richly embossed, with fine cut crystal glass dish. Height 10⅝ inches, diameter of base 11¾ inches, length of glass dish 12½ inches.
No. 5535A.—As No. 5535, but richly gilt.

PLATEAU No. 5537.

No. 5537.—Sterling Silver Plateau, with mirror glass centre, 24 inches long (glass measure).
No. 5537A.—As No. 5537, but richly gilt.

No. 5536.—Sterling Silver Round Dessert Stand, richly embossed, with fine cut crystal glass dish. Height 5⅜ inches, diameter of base 3⅞ inches, diameter of glass dish 6 inches.
No. 5536A.—As No. 5536, but richly gilt.

No. 5538.—Sterling Silver Dessert Stand, with flower vase. Height 20 inches.

15

CAUTION. Any person infringing the Copyright of this Book will be prosecuted under the Act.

DOMINE DIRIGE NOS

STERLING SILVER
Dessert Knives and Forks.

A LARGE AND

Extensive Assortment

OF ALL THE

NEWEST DESIGNS,

WITH

Real Silver, Mother-of-Pearl, and Ivory Handles,

PLAIN OR CARVED,

Drawings of which can be had upon application.

—:o:—

STERLING SILVER
Fish Knives and Forks,

IN GREAT VARIETY OF

New and Choice Designs,

WITH

REAL SILVER, MOTHER-OF-PEARL, AND IVORY HANDLES.

These can be had in single pairs, or in cases of half-a-dozen, or one dozen pairs, drawings of which will be supplied upon application.

The following Goods are kept in stock, or can be supplied from the factories within two or three days after receipt of order:—

Sterling Silver Loving Cups.
,, ,, Rose-water Dishes.
,, ,, Egg Frames, 4, 6, or 8 cups.
,, ,, Crumb Scoops.
,, ,, Cream Ladles.
,, ,, Corner Dishes.
,, ,, Chop and Steak Dishes.
,, ,, Cheese Scoops.
,, ,, Butter Coolers.
,, ,, Ice Tongs.
,, ,, Sauce Tureens.
,, ,, Soup Tureens.
,, ,, Wine Strainers.
,, ,, Venison Dishes.
,, ,, Toddy Ladles.
,, ,, Toast Racks.
,, ,, Sugar Baskets.
,, ,, Spoon Warmers.
,, ,, Pickle Frames.
,, ,, Marrow Spoons.
,, ,, Soup Plates.
,, ,, Meat Plates and Dishes.
,, ,, Ice Pails, glass, silver mounted.
,, ,, Ice Pails, all silver.

Special Designs and Estimates supplied on application.

PRESENTATION PLATE
Made at very short Notice.

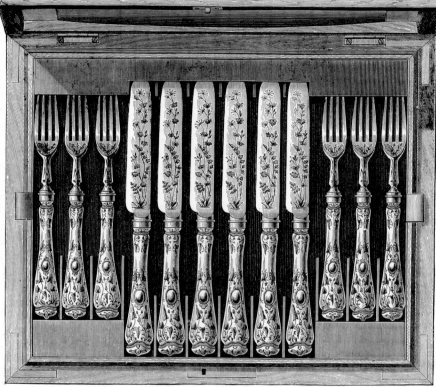

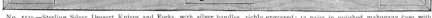

No. 5539.—Sterling Silver Dessert Knives and Forks, with silver handles, richly engraved; 12 pairs in polished mahogany case with cloth-lined movable tray.

EVERY DESCRIPTION OF
Sterling Silver Goods
MADE TO ORDER.

A LARGE VARIETY OF
TEA AND COFFEE
SERVICES
IN MODERN AND ANTIQUE DESIGNS.

SPECIAL DESIGNS IN
Communion Services,
MADE TO ORDER;
ALSO
POCKET
Communion Services,
IN CASES,
AT VARIOUS PRICES.

BISCUIT BOXES,
CAKE BASKETS,
AND
CRUETS,
In a great variety of Patterns.

PRIZE CUPS,
SUITABLE FOR
ATHLETIC SPORTS,
Horticultural Shows.
&c. &c.

EPERGNES,
Fruit and Flower Stands,
AND
CANDELABRA,
Made in various and choice designs, photographs of which can be had upon application.

LOVING CUPS,
Rose-water Dishes,
AND
EVERY DESCRIPTION OF
Presentation Plate,
MADE TO ORDER.

SPOONS AND FORKS,
Wrought, Hammered, and Polished
IN THE VERY BEST MANNER.

A LARGE VARIETY OF
FANCY SILVER GOODS,
IN
Handsome Morocco Leather Cases,
SUITABLE FOR
WEDDING
OR
Christening Presents.

No. 5540.—Sterling Silver Fish Knives and Forks, richly engraved, and with handsomely carved ivory handles; 12 pairs in polished oak case with cloth-lined movable tray.

16

STERLING SILVER GOODS.

No. 5541.—Sterling Silver Cake Basket, chased and engraved, 12 inches diameter.

No. 5548.—Sterling Silver Cruet Stand, length 10 inches, with eight handsomely cut glass bottles.

No. 5553.—Sterling Silver Cake Basket, beaded edge, 12 inches diameter.

No. 5542.—Sterling Silver Biscuit Box, hand engraved. Height 6¾ inches.

No. 5549.—Sterling Silver Tea Spoons and pair of Sugar Tongs in silk and velvet-lined morocco leather case.

No. 5554.—Sterling Silver Biscuit Box, hand engraved. Height 7 inches.

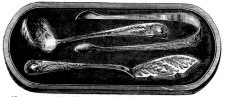

No. 5543.—Sterling Silver Sugar Sifter, Sugar Tongs, and Butter Knife, in silk and velvet-lined case.

No. 5555—Sterling Silver Sugar Sifter, Sugar Tongs, and Butter Knife, in silk and velvet-lined morocco leather case.

No. 5544.—Sterling Silver Fruit Spoons and pair of ivory-handled Nutcrackers, in silk and velvet-lined morocco leather case.

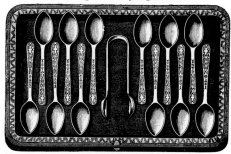

No. 5550.—Sterling Silver Grape Scissors, Sugar Sifter, and Cream Ladle, in silk and velvet-lined morocco leather case.

No. 5556.—Sterling Silver Knife, Fork, Spoon, and Napkin Ring, in silk and velvet-lined morocco leather case.

No. 5557.—Sterling Silver Fruit Spoons, in silk and velvet-lined morocco leather case.

No. 5546.—Sterling Silver Mug, Spoon, and Napkin Ring, in silk and velvet-lined morocco leather case.

No. 5551.—Sterling Silver Fruit Spoons and Sugar Sifter, in silk and velvet-lined morocco leather case.

No. 5545.—Sterling Silver Grape Scissors, in silk and velvet-lined morocco leather case.

No. 5547.—Sterling Silver Knife Rests, in silk and velvet-lined morocco leather case.

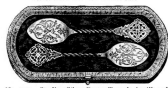

No. 5552.—Sterling Silver Butter Trowels, in silk and velvet-lined morocco leather case.

No. 5558.—Sterling Silver Knife Rest, in silk and velvet-lined morocco leather case.

No. 5559.—Sterling Silver Sugar Basin and Sugar Sifter, in silk and velvet-lined morocco leather case.

Biscuit Boxes, Cake Baskets, and Cruets in a great variety of patterns.

STERLING SILVER GOODS.

No. 5560.—Claret Jug, richly cut crystal glass body, sterling silver mounts.

No. 5561.—Claret Jug, richly cut crystal glass body, sterling silver mounts.

No. 5562.—Claret Jug, plain crystal glass body, sterling silver mounts.

No. 5563.—Claret Jug, richly cut crystal glass body, sterling silver mounts.

No. 5564.—Claret Jug, plain fluted crystal glass body, sterling silver mounts.

No. 5565.—Claret Jug, richly cut crystal glass body, sterling silver mounts.

No. 5566.—Claret Jug, richly cut crystal glass body, sterling silver mounts.

No. 5567.—Sterling Silver Tea Pot, Sugar Basin, and Cream Ewer, comprising a tête-à-tête set.

No. 5568.—Claret Jug, richly cut crystal glass body, sterling silver mounts.

No. 5569.—Claret Jug, richly cut and engraved crystal glass body, sterling silver mounts.

No. 5570.—Sterling Silver Child's Mug, engraved, gilt inside.

No. 5571.—Sterling Silver Child's Mug, engraved, gilt inside.

No. 5572.—Sterling Silver Child's Mug, gilt inside.

No. 5573.—Sterling Silver Child's Mug, gilt inside.

No. 5574.—Sterling Silver Child's Mug, gilt inside.

No. 5575.—Sterling Silver Child's Mug, gilt inside.

No. 5576.—Sterling Silver Child's Mug, engraved, gilt inside.

No. 5577. No. 5578. No. 5579. No. 5580. No. 5581. No. 5582. No. 5583. No. 5584. No. 5585. No. 5586. No. 5587. No. 5588.

Sterling Silver Napkin Rings.   **Sterling Silver Napkin Rings.**

No. 5590.—Sterling Silver Fruit Knife, with finely carved pearl handle.

No. 5591.—Sterling Silver Butter Knife with mother-of-pearl handle. (Drawn full size.)

No. 5592.—Sterling Silver Pickle Fork with mother-of-pearl handle. (Drawn full size.)

No. 5589.—Sterling Silver Muffineers, one pair in silk and velvet lined morocco leather case.

No. 5589.—Sterling Silver Muffineers, one pair in silk and velvet lined morocco leather case.

Loving Cups, Rose-water Dishes, and every description of Presentation Plate made to order.

CAUTION. Any person infringing the Copyright of this Book will be prosecuted under the Act.

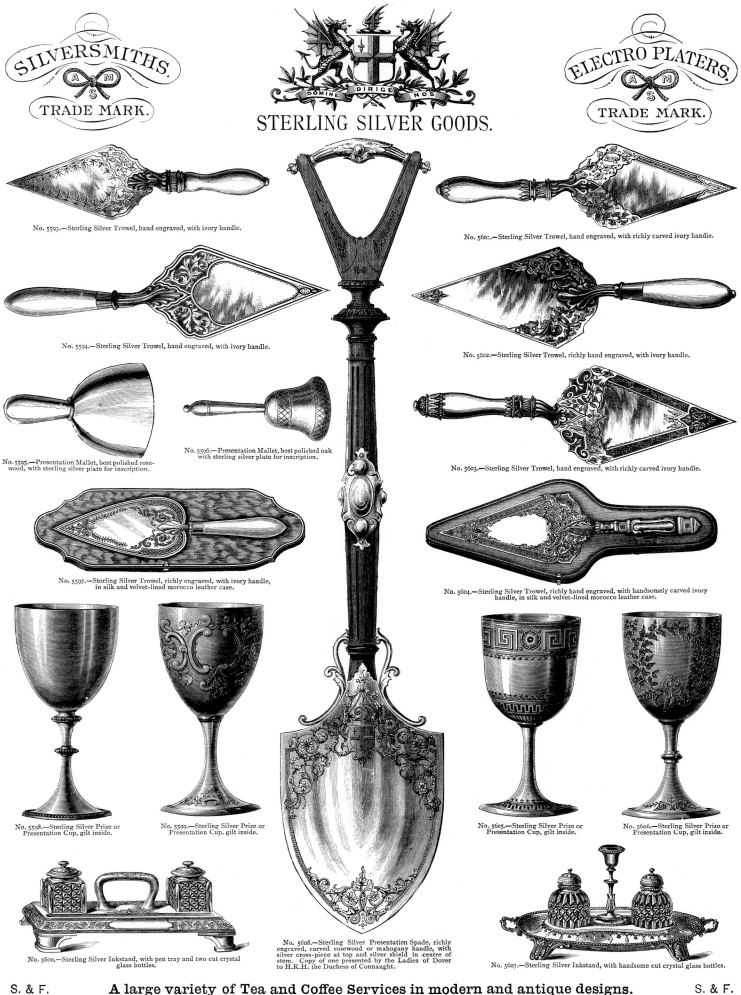

SILVERSMITHS. TRADE MARK.

DOMINE DIRIGE NOS

ELECTRO PLATERS. TRADE MARK.

STERLING SILVER GOODS.

No. 5593.—Sterling Silver Trowel, hand engraved, with ivory handle.

No. 5601.—Sterling Silver Trowel, hand engraved, with richly carved ivory handle.

No. 5594.—Sterling Silver Trowel, hand engraved, with ivory handle.

No. 5602.—Sterling Silver Trowel, richly hand engraved, with ivory handle.

No. 5595.—Presentation Mallet, best polished rosewood, with sterling silver plate for inscription.

No. 5596.—Presentation Mallet, best polished oak with sterling silver plate for inscription.

No. 5603.—Sterling Silver Trowel, hand engraved, with richly carved ivory handle.

No. 5597.—Sterling Silver Trowel, richly engraved, with ivory handle, in silk and velvet-lined morocco leather case.

No. 5604.—Sterling Silver Trowel, richly hand engraved, with handsomely carved ivory handle, in silk and velvet-lined morocco leather case.

No. 5598.—Sterling Silver Prize or Presentation Cup, gilt inside.

No. 5599.—Sterling Silver Prize or Presentation Cup, gilt inside.

No. 5605.—Sterling Silver Prize or Presentation Cup, gilt inside.

No. 5606.—Sterling Silver Prize or Presentation Cup, gilt inside.

No. 5600.—Sterling Silver Inkstand, with pen tray and two cut crystal glass bottles.

No. 5608.—Sterling Silver Presentation Spade, richly engraved, carved rosewood or mahogany handle, with silver cross-piece at top and silver shield in centre of stem. Copy of one presented by the Ladies of Dover to H.R.H. the Duchess of Connaught.

No. 5607.—Sterling Silver Inkstand, with handsome cut crystal glass bottles.

S. & F.   **A large variety of Tea and Coffee Services in modern and antique designs.**   S. & F.

CAUTION. Any person infringing the Copyright of this Book will be prosecuted under the Act.

19

SILVERSMITHS.
A M S
TRADE MARK.

DOMINE · DIRIGE · NOS

ELECTRO PLATERS.
A M S
TRADE MARK.

STERLING SILVER GOODS.

No. 5618.—Sterling Silver Butter Knife, pierced and engraved, in silk and velvet-lined morocco leather case.

No. 5611.—Sterling Silver Mounted Breakfast Cruet, with salt and mustard spoons complete.

No. 5612.—Sterling Silver, hall-marked, Cream Ewer, old English pattern.

No. 5619.—Sterling Silver Spoon and Napkin Ring, richly engraved, in silk and velvet-lined morocco leather case.

No. 5613.—Sterling Silver, hall-marked, Piano Candlestick.

No. 5614.—Sterling Silver, hall-marked, Muffineer, Queen Anne pattern.

No. 5615.—Sterling Silver, hall-marked, Piano Candlestick.

No. 5609.—Sterling Silver, hall-marked, Coffee Pot, hand engraved, fern pattern.

No. 5616.—Sterling Silver, hall-marked, Chased Cream Ewer.

No. 5617.—Sterling Silver, hall-marked, Chased Cream Ewer.

No. 5609A.—Sterling Silver, hall-marked, Teapot, hand engraved, fern pattern.

No. 5620.—Sterling Silver Fusee Case, Japanese engraved.

No. 5621.—Snuff Box, hall-marked sterling silver, richly engraved, with shield centre.

No. 5609B.—Sterling Silver, hall-marked, Sugar Basin, hand engraved, fern pattern.

No. 5622.—Cigarette Case, hall-marked sterling silver.

No. 5609C.—Sterling Silver, hall-marked, Cream Jug, hand engraved, fern pattern.

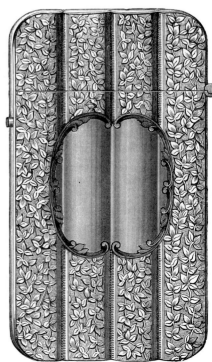

No. 5625.—Cigar Case, hall-marked sterling silver, richly engraved and fluted, with shield centre.

No. 5623.—Fusee Case, hall-marked sterling silver, strap and buckle pattern.

No. 5624.—Fusee Case, hall-marked sterling silver, with shield centre and ring top.

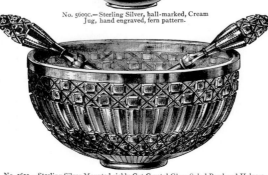

No. 5610.—Sterling Silver Mounted richly Cut Crystal Glass Salad Bowl and Helpers.

DOMINE DIRIGE NOS

STERLING SILVER GOODS.

No. 5629.—Sterling Silver Cream Jug, engraved
fluted Queen Anne pattern.

No. 5629.—Sterling Silver Tea Pot, engraved fluted
Queen Anne pattern.

No. 5629.—Sterling Silver Sugar Basin, engraved
fluted Queen Anne pattern.

No. 5629.—Sterling Silver Coffee Pot, engraved
fluted Queen Anne pattern.

No. 5633.—Sterling Silver Salver, richly engraved.

No. 5634.—Sterling Silver Salver, richly engraved.

No. 5635.—Sterling Silver Salver, Elizabethan,
richly engraved.

No. 5636.—Sterling Silver Asparagus Tongs.

No. 5637.—Sterling Silver Asparagus Servers.

No. 5638.—Sterling Silver Asparagus Tongs.

PATTERNS OF STERLING SILVER SPOONS, FORKS, &c.

No. 5639.—Napier
pattern.

No. 5640.—King's
pattern.

No. 5641.—Grecian
pattern.

No. 5642.—Tamworth
pattern.

No. 5643.—Shaped Tudor
pattern.

No. 5644.—Beaded Nurled
pattern.

No. 5645.—French Fiddle
pattern.

S. & F.   **Spoons and Forks wrought, hammered, and polished in the very best manner.**   S. & F.

STERLING SILVER GOODS.

No. 5646.—Child's Sterling Silver Rattle, with pearl handle. Drawn full size

No. 5647.—Child's Sterling Silver Rattle, with pearl handle. Drawn full size.

No. 5654. No. 5655. No. 5656. No. 5657. No. 5658.

No. 5654.—Richly Cut Crystal Eau de Cologne Bottle, with sterling silver screw top, 4½ inches long.
No. 5655.—Hall-marked Sterling Silver Eau de Cologne Bottle, 5¾ inches long.
No. 5656.—Richly Cut Crystal Eau de Cologne Bottle, with sterling silver screw top, 8 inches long.
No. 5657.—Hall-marked Sterling Silver Eau de Cologne Bottle, 5¾ inches long.
No. 5658.—Richly Cut Crystal Eau de Cologne Bottle, with sterling silver screw top, 4½ inches long.

No. 5648.—Child's Sterling Silver Rattle, with pearl handle. Drawn full size.

No. 5649.—Child's Sterling Silver Rattle, with pearl ring. Drawn full size.

STERLING SILVER AND SILVER GILT TOP SMELLING BOTTLES. *(Drawn full size.)*

No. 5650.—Bell Coral, hall-marked sterling silver, with one row of bells and imitation coral handle.

No. 5651.—Silver-mounted Whistle, hall-marked, with mother-of-pearl end and two bells, with ring for attaching to ribbon.

No. 5659.—Silver-mounted Union Smelling Bottle, with spring.

No. 5660.—Silver-mounted Union Smelling Bottle.

No. 5661.—Silver-mounted Union Smelling Bottle.

No. 5652.—Silver-mounted Whistle, hall-marked, with mother-of-pearl end, and ring for attaching to ribbon.

No. 5653.—Child's Sterling Silver Rattle, with pearl handle. Drawn full size.

No. 5662.—Silver-mounted Combination Bottle, with vinaigrette and silver thimble.

No. 5663.—Silver-mounted Union Smelling Bottle, flush top.

No. 5667.—Silver-mounted Smelling Bottle.

No. 5665.—Silver-mounted Smelling Bottle.

No. 5666.—Silver-mounted Smelling Bottle.

No. 5664.—Silver-mounted Smelling Bottle, flush top.

No. 5668.—Silver-mounted Smelling Bottle.

No. 5669.—Dram Flask, hall-marked sterling silver, richly engraved, with shield centre and patent cap.

STERLING SILVER GOODS.

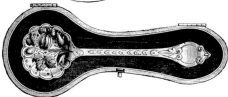

No. 5670.—Sterling Silver Sugar Sifter, richly chased, in silk and velvet-lined morocco leather case.

No. 5671.—Sterling Silver Butter Knife, Italian pattern engraved, in silk and velvet-lined morocco leather case.

No. 5672.—Sterling Silver Child's Spoon, richly engraved, in silk and velvet-lined morocco leather case.

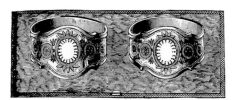

No. 5673.—Sterling Silver Napkin Rings, "Shield" pattern, in silk and velvet-lined and morocco leather case.

No. 5674.—Sterling Silver Ice Spoons, richly engraved, in silk and velvet-lined morocco leather case.

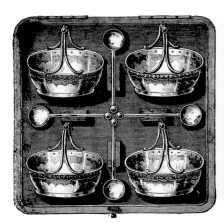

No. 5675.—Sterling Silver Salt Cellars and Spoons, in silk and velvet-lined morocco leather case.

No. 5676.—Sterling Silver Teaspoons and Sugar Tongs, in silk and velvet-lined morocco leather case,

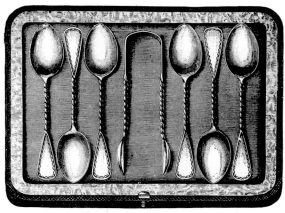

No. 5677.—Sterling Silver Salt Cellars and Spoons, in silk and velvet-lined morocco leather case.

No. 5678.—Sterling Silver Salt Cellars and Salt Spoons, fluted pattern, in silk and velvet-lined morocco leather case.

No. 5679.—Sterling Silver Mustard Pot and Spoon, Queen Anne's pattern, round shape.

No. 5680.—Sterling Silver Mustard Pot and Spoon, Queen Anne's pattern, square shape.

No. 5681.—Sterling Silver Mustard Pot and Spoon Queen Anne's pattern, oval shape.

No. 5682.—Sterling Silver Teaspoons, harlequin set of six different patterns in silk and velvet-lined morocco leather case.

No. 5683.—Sterling Silver Salt Cellars and Spoons, cradle pattern, in silk and velvet-lined morocco leather case.

MANUFACTURERS

OF

ENGLISH WATCHES.

DOMINE DIRIGE NOS

IMPORTERS OF

EVERY DESCRIPTION OF

FOREIGN WATCHES.

SILVER AND GOLD WATCHES.

ALSO WATCHES IN METAL CASES.

No. 5684.—Gentleman's Silver Open-face Centre Seconds or Stop Watch, horizontal movement, 8 holes jewelled.

No. 5685.—Lady's Silver Watch in hunting case, horizontal movement, 4 holes jewelled, engraved case, metal dome.

No. 5686.—Gentleman's Silver Open-face Keyless Chronograph Watch, registering to one-fifth of a second, cut crystal bevelled glass, visible chronograph at back.

No. 5687.—Lady's 18-carat Gold English Lever Watch, in hunting case, plain, engine-turned, or engraved, superior quality movement, rim capped and jewelled, white enamel or gold dial.

No. 5688.—Gentleman's Silver Open-face Watch, patent lever movement, jewelled in 10 holes, compensation balance, cut crystal bevelled glass, railway timekeeper's or ordinary dial.

S. & F.
MANUFACTURERS.

Superior Watches, in Gold Cases, richly painted and enamelled, set with Pearls, Diamonds, and other precious stones.

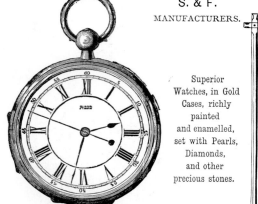

No. 5689.—Gentleman's Gold Open-face English Lever Watch, cut crystal bevelled glass, plain or engine-turned case, ¾-plate movement, with centre seconds, extra jewelled, and chronometer balance.

TRADE A M MARK.
S

PATENTEES,

MANUFACTURERS AND IMPORTERS,

CONTRACTORS TO

HER MAJESTY'S GOVERNMENT,

AND TO MOST OF THE

RAILWAY COMPANIES

IN

GREAT BRITAIN AND IRELAND.

HIGHEST AWARDS, "GOLD MEDALS."

Every Watch is carefully examined in our own Workshop before being despatched.

THE TRADE SUPPLIED WITH EVERY DESCRIPTION OF WATCH MATERIALS.

S. & F.
IMPORTERS.

Enamelling, Crests, Coats of Arms, Monograms, and Initials on the outside of the Cases can be executed in two or three days.

No. 5690.—Gentleman's Gold Keyless Chronograph Watch, white enamelled dial, sunk seconds, chronograph hands, registering to one-fifth of a second, fully jewelled movements compensated for any extreme of temperature; in 18-carat gold hunting or half-hunting case, either engine-turned or plain.

MINUTE REPEATING WATCH.

EVERY WATCH
IS DRAWN
FULL SIZE.

EVERY WATCH
IS DRAWN
FULL SIZE.

No. 5691.—Lady's 18-carat Gold Keyless Watch, in half-hunting case, plain, engine-turned, or engraved, with blue figures on opal enamelled ground, superior quality horizontal movement, jewelled in 8 holes.

No. 5692.—Lady's Metal Gilt Watch, in half-hunting case, keyless horizontal movement, 4 holes jewelled.

No. 5693.—Lady's Silver Keyless Open-face Watch, engraved, engine-turned, or plain cases, cut crystal bevelled glass, good quality horizontal movement, 8 holes jewelled.

No. 5694.—Lady's Silver Keyless Watch, in hunting case, good quality horizontal movement, 8 holes jewelled, richly engraved or engine-turned case, silver dome.

No. 5695.—Lady's Silver Keyless Watch, in half-hunting case, well finished horizontal movement, jewelled in 8 holes, richly chased case.

No. 5696.—Lady's Silver Open-face Watch, cut crystal bevelled glass, white enamelled dial, silver dome, good quality horizontal movement, 8 holes jewelled.

No. 5697.—Gentleman's Gold Keyless Repeater, in very strong 18-carat gold hunting or half-hunting case, lever movement fully jewelled, with compensated balance. When the slide on the rim of the case is moved the watch repeats the time. Repeating hours, half-hours, quarters, and minutes.

No. 5698.—Gentleman's 14-carat Gold Open-face Keyless Watch, sunk seconds, cut crystal bevelled glass, metal dome, plain or engine-turned case, very superior horizontal movement, jewelled in 8 holes.

No. 5699.—Lady's 14-carat Gold Open-face Watch, cut crystal bevelled glass, gilt dome and dial, good quality horizontal movement, jewelled in 4 holes.

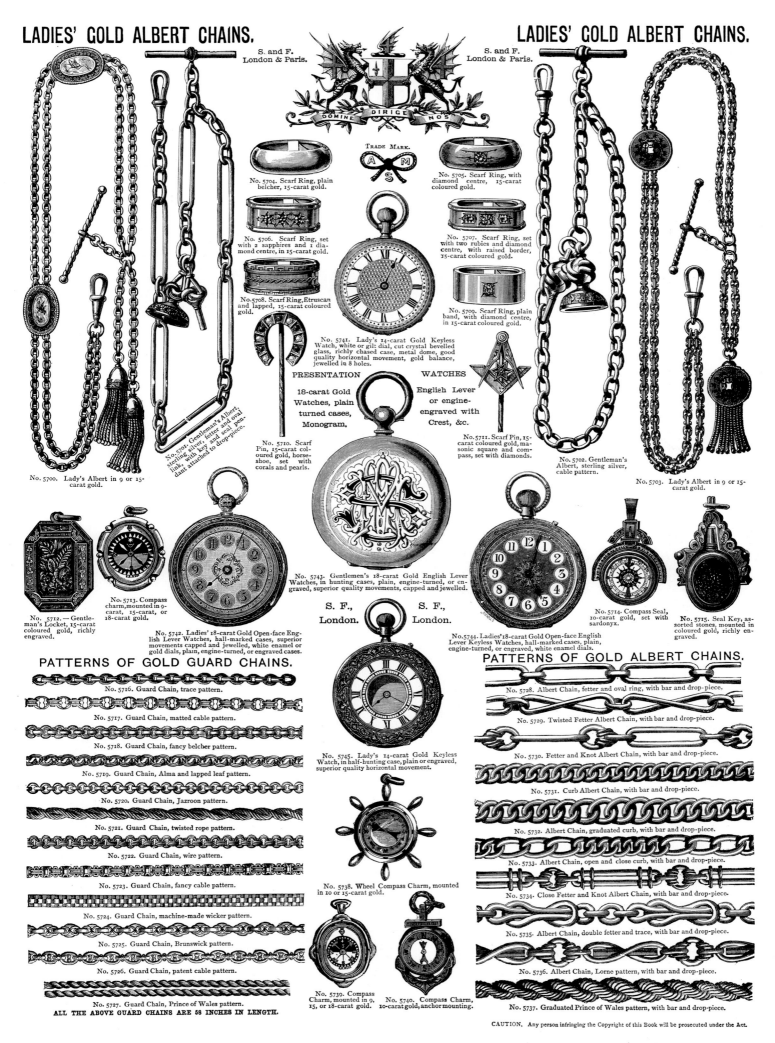

LADIES' GOLD ALBERT CHAINS.

LADIES' GOLD ALBERT CHAINS.

S. and F. London & Paris.

S. and F. London & Paris.

TRADE MARK.

DOMINE DIRIGE NOS

No. 5704. Scarf Ring, plain belcher, 15-carat gold.

No. 5705. Scarf Ring, with diamond centre, 15-carat coloured gold.

No. 5706. Scarf Ring, set with 2 sapphires and 1 diamond centre, in 15-carat gold.

No. 5707. Scarf Ring, set with two rubies and diamond centre, with raised border, 15-carat coloured gold.

No. 5708. Scarf Ring, Etruscan and lapped, 15-carat coloured gold.

No. 5709. Scarf Ring, plain band, with diamond centre, in 15-carat coloured gold.

No. 5700. Lady's Albert in 9 or 15-carat gold.

No. 5701. Gentleman's Albert, sterling silver, fetter and oval link, with key and seal pendant attached to drop-piece.

No. 5741. Lady's 14-carat Gold Keyless Watch, white or gilt dial, cut crystal bevelled glass, richly chased case, metal dome, good quality horizontal movement, gold balance, jewelled in 8 holes.

PRESENTATION

WATCHES

18-carat Gold Watches, plain turned cases, Monogram,

English Lever or engine-engraved with Crest, &c.

No. 5710. Scarf Pin, 15-carat coloured gold, horseshoe, set with corals and pearls.

No. 5711. Scarf Pin, 15-carat coloured gold, masonic square and compass, set with diamonds.

No. 5702. Gentleman's Albert, sterling silver, cable pattern.

No. 5703. Lady's Albert in 9 or 15-carat gold.

No. 5712.—Gentleman's Locket, 15-carat coloured gold, richly engraved.

No. 5713. Compass charm, mounted in 9-carat, 15-carat, or 18-carat gold.

No. 5743. Gentlemen's 18-carat Gold English Lever Watches, in hunting cases, plain, engine-turned, or engraved, superior quality movements, capped and jewelled.

No. 5742. Ladies' 18-carat Gold Open-face English Lever Watches, hall-marked cases, superior movements capped and jewelled, white enamel or gold dials, plain, engine-turned, or engraved cases.

No. 5714. Compass Seal, 10-carat gold, set with sardonyx.

No. 5715. Seal Key, assorted stones, mounted in coloured gold, richly engraved.

PATTERNS OF GOLD GUARD CHAINS.

No. 5716. Guard Chain, trace pattern.

No. 5717. Guard Chain, matted cable pattern.

No. 5718. Guard Chain, fancy belcher pattern.

No. 5719. Guard Chain, Alma and lapped leaf pattern.

No. 5720. Guard Chain, Jazroon pattern.

No. 5721. Guard Chain, twisted rope pattern.

No. 5722. Guard Chain, wire pattern.

No. 5723. Guard Chain, fancy cable pattern.

No. 5724. Guard Chain, machine-made wicker pattern.

No. 5725. Guard Chain, Brunswick pattern.

No. 5726. Guard Chain, patent cable pattern.

No. 5727. Guard Chain, Prince of Wales pattern.

ALL THE ABOVE GUARD CHAINS ARE 58 INCHES IN LENGTH.

S. F., London.

S. F., London.

No. 5744. Ladies' 18-carat Gold Open-face English Lever Keyless Watches, hall-marked cases, plain, engine-turned, or engraved, white enamel dials.

No. 5745. Lady's 14-carat Gold Keyless Watch, in half-hunting case, plain or engraved, superior quality horizontal movement.

No. 5738. Wheel Compass Charm, mounted in 10 or 15-carat gold.

No. 5739. Compass Charm, mounted in 9, 15, or 18-carat gold.

No. 5740. Compass Charm, 10-carat gold, anchor mounting.

PATTERNS OF GOLD ALBERT CHAINS.

No. 5728. Albert Chain, fetter and oval ring, with bar and drop-piece.

No. 5729. Twisted Fetter Albert Chain, with bar and drop-piece.

No. 5730. Fetter and Knot Albert Chain, with bar and drop-piece.

No. 5731. Curb Albert Chain, with bar and drop-piece.

No. 5732. Albert Chain, graduated curb, with bar and drop-piece.

No. 5733. Albert Chain, open and close curb, with bar and drop-piece.

No. 5734. Close Fetter and Knot Albert Chain, with bar and drop-piece.

No. 5735. Albert Chain, double fetter and trace, with bar and drop-piece.

No. 5736. Albert Chain, Lorne pattern, with bar and drop-piece.

No. 5737. Graduated Prince of Wales pattern, with bar and drop-piece.

SILVERSMITHS.
TRADE MARK.

DOMINE DIRIGE NOS

ELECTRO PLATERS.
TRADE MARK.

LADIES' STERLING SILVER TORTOISE-SHELL AND MOTHER-OF-PEARL CARD CASES.

MONOGRAMS AND CRESTS ENGRAVED TO ORDER.   A LARGE ASSORTMENT OF THE NEWEST DESIGNS ALWAYS IN STOCK.

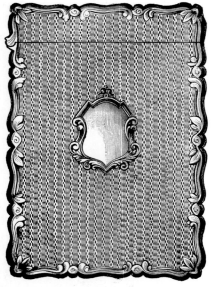

No. 5746.—Ladies' Card Case, hall-marked sterling silver, engine-turned, shield centre, in silk and velvet-lined morocco leather case.

No. 5747.—Ladies' Card Case, hall-marked sterling silver, richly engraved, in silk and velvet-lined morocco leather case.

No. 5748.—Ladies' Card Case, hall-marked sterling silver, book shape, richly engraved and inlaid with various colours of gold and oxydised birds, in silk and velvet-lined morocco leather case.

No. 5749.—Ladies' Card Case, hall-marked sterling silver, book shape, shield centre, in silk and velvet-lined morocco leather case.

No. 5750.—Tortoise-shell and Silver Card Case, book shape.

No. 5751.—Tortoise-shell and Silver Card Case, book shape.

No. 5752.—Mother-of-pearl and Silver Card Case, book shape.

GENTLEMEN'S

CARD CASES

IN STERLING SILVER,

TORTOISE-SHELL,

AND

MOTHER-OF-PEARL

IN GREAT VARIETY.

No. 5753.—Handsomely engraved Mother-of-pearl Card Case, book shape.

DRAWN FULL SIZE.

ALUMINIUM PEN AND PENCIL CASES.

No. 5754.—Aluminium Pencil, telescopic action, stone top, and reserve for leads.

No. 5755.—Aluminium Pencil, hexagon, sliding action, stone top, and reserve for leads.

No. 5756.—Aluminium Pencil, double telescopic action, ring top.

No. 5757.—Aluminium Pen and Pencil, fluted pattern, stone top, and reserve for leads.

No. 5758.—Aluminium Pencil, telescopic action, swivel top.

No. 5759.—Aluminium Pencil, telescopic action, with reserve for leads.

No. 5760.—Aluminium Pen and Pencil, telescopic action, ring top.

No. 5761.—Aluminium Pencil, telescopic action, ring top.

No. 5762.—Aluminium Pencil, spiral action.

No. 5763.—Aluminium Pencil, telescopic action, ring top.

TRADE MARK.

DRAWN FULL SIZE.

GOLD AND SILVER PEN AND PENCIL CASES.

No. 5764.—Pen and Pencil Case, bright gold, richly engraved, suitable for presentation.

No. 5765.—Pen and Pencil Case, coloured gold, richly engraved, with stone top.

No. 5766.—Pencil Case, bright gold, plain tube, chased top, set stone.

No. 5767.—Pencil Case, coloured gold, telescopic, with whistle and ring for chain.

No. 5768.—Pencil Case, bright gold, three-draw telescopic, engine-turned.

No. 5769.—Pencil Case, bright gold, three-draw telescopic, richly engraved.

No. 5770.—Pen and Pencil Case, silver, engraved, with stone top.

No. 5771.—Pen and Pencil Case, silver, engraved, with stone top.

No. 5772.—Pencil Case, silver, richly engraved, with stone top.

No. 5773.—Pencil Case, silver, fluted and engraved, with stone top.

STERLING SILVER AND SUPERIOR QUALITY ALUMINIUM PEN AND PENCIL CASES.

In Ebony Frame Cases, with Glass Tops. Suitable for the Counter.

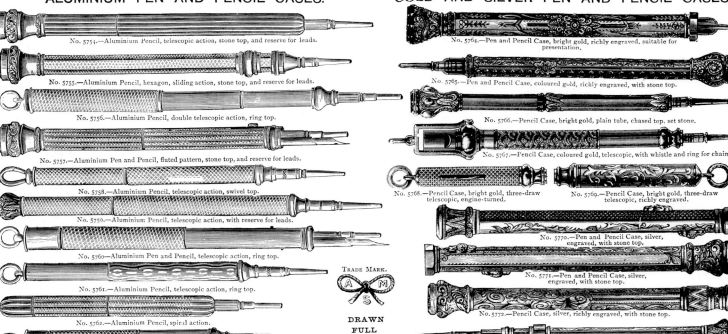

STERLING SILVER

Case 5785.—Containing 18 Sterling Silver Pen and Pencil Cases, from 3 inches to 5 inches in length, on movable velvet-covered tray.

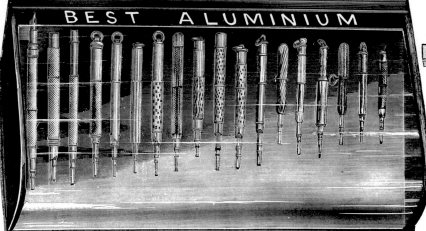

BEST ALUMINIUM

Case 5786.—Containing 18 best Aluminium Pen and Pencil Cases, from 2¾ inches to 5 inches in length, on movable velvet-covered tray.

No. 5774.—Pencil Case, whisky bottle, in sterling silver, 9-carat or 15-carat gold.

No. 5775.—Pencil Case, soda-water bottle, in sterling silver, 9-carat or 15-carat gold.

No. 5776.—Pencil Case, champagne bottle, in sterling silver, 9-carat or 15-carat gold.

No. 5777.—Sovereign Purse, hall-marked silver, to hold 5 sovereigns (closed).

No. 5777.—Sovereign Purse, hall-marked silver, to hold 5 sovereigns (open).

No. 5778.—Pencil Case, cannon, in sterling silver, 9-carat or 15-carat gold.

No. 5779.—Pencil Case, mallet, silver.

No. 5780.—Pencil Case, peg top, silver, plain, or chased.

No. 5781.—Pencil Case, boat, silver.

No. 5782.—Pencil Case, spirit level, silver.

No. 5783.—Pencil Case, owl, silver.

No. 5784.—Owl Whistle Charm, sterling silver.

GOLD BRACELETS, BANGLES, BROOCHES, AND SETS OF BROOCH AND EARRINGS,
CHASED, ENGRAVED, AND SET WITH DIAMONDS AND OTHER PRECIOUS STONES.

No. 5788.—Brooch, 15-carat colour-ed gold, round, plain centre.

No. 5789.—Brooch, 15-carat, coloured gold, with diamond centre.

DRAWN FULL SIZE.

No. 5796.—Bracelet, 15-carat coloured gold, with red and green gold wreath centre.

No. 5790.—Brooch, 15-carat coloured gold, oval Etruscan centre.

No. 5791.—Brooch, 15-carat coloured gold, lapped, with plain oval centre, set with ruby flower.

DRAWN FULL SIZE.

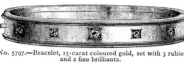

No. 5792.—Suite of Brooch and Earrings, 15-carat coloured gold, with plain centre, fancy lapped and shotted border.

No. 5793.—Suite of Brooch and Earrings, 15-carat coloured gold, raised round centre with rubies and diamonds.

No. 5797.—Bracelet, 15-carat coloured gold, set with 3 rubies and 2 fine brilliants.

No. 5798.—Bangle Bracelet, square centre, set with brilliant.

No. 5799.—Bracelet, 15-carat coloured gold, set with pink coral.

No. 5794.—Suite of Brooch and Earrings, with pearl and blue enamel centre.

No. 5795.—Suite of Brooch and Earrings, rose diamond centre, with filigree and lapped border.

LATEST NOVELTIES IN STERLING SILVER JEWELLERY.
DRAWN FULL SIZE.

No. 5800.—Bracelet, with raised gold fern leaves, and shotted edge.

No. 5808.—Brooch, richly engraved, raised centre, shotted ends.

No. 5809.—Brooch, tie pattern with engraved centre.

No. 5804.—Bracelet, flexible chain pattern.

No. 5801.—Bangle, with fancy lapped ends.

No. 5810.—Brooch, horseshoe, frosted with burnished nails.

No. 5812.—Locket, sterling silver, hall-marked, richly engraved.

No. 5811.—Brooch, engraved centre, with fancy filigree, and shotted border.

No. 5805.—Bracelet, engraved with flowers.

No. 5802.—Bangle, tie pattern.

No. 5806.—Bracelet, engraved leaf pattern.

No. 5803.—Bracelet, fire gilt, set with pearls and imitation diamonds and sapphires.

No. 5813.—Suite of Brooch and Earrings to match, plain centre, fancy border.

No. 5814.—Suite of Brooch and Earrings to match, plain frosted centre, with raised gold ornamentation, burnished gold rim, and shotted border.

No. 5807.—Bangle, with fancy engraved centre.

A Fully Illustrated Catalogue of Gold, Silver, and Imitation Jewellery can be sent on application.

ELECTRO-PLATED GOODS,

BRITISH OAK GOODS,

TABLE CUTLERY, POCKET CUTLERY, AND SCISSORS.

As almost every article represented herein is kept in stock by us, and can in most cases be dispatched within a few hours after receipt of order, you are placed in a position to execute the orders received from your customers at the shortest notice.

Our Illustrated Catalogue, published some time ago, of Electro-plated Goods and Cutlery contains a more complete selection of the goods sold by us in these Departments, and can be supplied on application.

ELECTRO-SILVER PLATED AND BRITANNIA METAL GOODS.

CUTLERY.

Our assortment of Electro-Silver Plated Goods, commencing at almost the lowest prices at which this class of goods is produced, and extending to the very highest quality and workmanship, offers to the purchaser the great advantage of finding goods suitable to his trade, and for any country. Most of our goods intended for export are kept in stock unplated, and are only finished and plated on receipt of order; we are thus enabled to execute almost any order within a few days of its receipt. The advantages to the purchaser are—that he receives the right goods at the right time, and at the right price, in good and fresh condition.

Electro-Silver Plated Goods are enveloped in a new paper which prevents oxydisation, and consequently discolouration, and even when placed in a damp or exposed position the goods will not tarnish.

The great progress which has taken place in this country of late years in the production of beautiful and correct designs, is shown most clearly when the Electro-Silver Plated Goods of the present day are compared with those produced ten years ago, even in articles of very moderate price. Many of the designs which we now bring under your notice are our own specialities, and the reasonable prices we are able to quote, considering the quality of the goods we deliver, will fairly meet any competition whether in this country or from across the Atlantic.

We draw your special attention to our Canteens, &c., on pages 322 and 381.

The Epergnes and Table Ornaments shown here serve but as an indication of the numerous designs we have constantly in stock, and we may add that Spoons and Forks, Cruets, &c., which have been purchased from us more than twenty years ago are still in use and in fair condition.

Our Cutlery Department shows a continuously increasing trade, which is the best proof that we give our customers good value for their money.

The following goods, not illustrated here, are kept in stock by us :—

Carving Knives and Forks, with Stag and Bone Handles.	Farriers' Knives.	Razor Strops.
	Glaziers' Diamonds.	Sailors' Knives.
Children's Knife, Fork, and Spoon, on card.	Nutcrackers.	Springless Knives.
Daggers in Sheaths.	Putty Knives, &c.	Shoe Knives.
Desk Knives.	Razors.	Swedish Knives.
Erasers.	Razor Cases.	Tailors' Shears.

Also a large and ever-varying assortment of Pen and Pocket Knives, Scissors, Corkscrews, Button Hooks, Whistles, &c., assorted one dozen each on attractive Show Cards, and generally retailed in this country at 4d., 6d., and 1s. each.

ALL PRICES QUOTED IN OUR PRICE LIST ARE NETT.

DOMINE DIRIGE NOS

ELECTRO-SILVER PLATED GOODS.

No. 5815.—Fruit Stand, silver plated on nickel silver, with richly cut glass dish. Height 7¾ inches.

No. 5816.—Fruit Stand, silver plated on nickel silver, richly chased, with cut crystal glass dish. Height 11¼ inches.

No. 5815.—Fruit Stand, silver plated on nickel silver, with richly cut glass dish. Height 7¾ inches.

No. 5817.—Fruit Stand, heavily silver plated on nickel silver, richly cut glass dish. Height 12 inches.

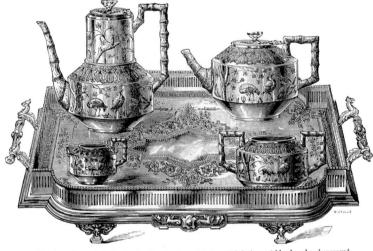

No. 5818.—Tea and Coffee Service, heavily silver plated on nickel silver, richly chased and engraved, consisting of 3-pint coffee pot, 2½-pint tea pot, gilt-lined sugar basin, and cream jug.
No. 5818s.—Salver, heavily silver plated on nickel silver, richly chased and engraved. Length 24 inches. Suitable for presentation.
The above Service can be made in hall-marked sterling silver.

No. 5819.—Fruit Stand, heavily silver plated on nickel silver, richly cut glass dish. Height 12 inches.

No. 5821.—Flower Vase, heavily electro-silver plated on nickel silver, satin finished, with richly cut glass. Height 11 inches.

No. 5820.—Table Ornament, consisting of centre Fruit Stand and two side Fruit Stands on plateau, heavily silver plated on nickel silver, with richly cut glass dishes. Height of centre 12½ inches, length of plateau 30 inches. Suitable for presentation.

No. 5821.—Flower Vase, heavily electro-silver plated on nickel silver, satin finished, with richly cut glass. Height 11 inches.

31

SILVERSMITHS. TRADE MARK.

DOMINE DIRICE NOS

ELECTRO PLATERS. TRADE MARK.

ELECTRO-SILVER PLATED GOODS.

No. 5822.—Side Fruit Dish, silver plated on nickel silver, with richly cut glass dish. Length 10½ inches, height 5½ inches.

No. 5823.—Centre Fruit Dish, silver plated on nickel silver, with richly cut glass dish. Length 13¾ inches, height 6½ inches.

No. 5822.—Side Fruit Dish, silver plated on nickel silver, with richly cut glass dish. Length 10½ inches, height 5½ inches.

No. 5824.—Fruit Stand, heavily electro-silver plated on nickel silver, satin finished, with richly cut glass dish. Height 11½ inches.

No. 5827.—Fruit Stand, silver plated on nickel silver, richly cut glass dish. Height 12 inches.

No. 5825.—Epergne, electro-silver plated on nickel silver, with richly cut crystal glass dishes. Height 19½ inches. The hanging baskets are movable and can be used separately.
No. 5826.—Plateau, electro-silver plated on nickel silver, with strong silvered plate glass centre. Diameter 13¼ inches.

No. 5828.—Assiette, silver plated on hard metal, cut glasses. Height about 22 inches.

No. 5829.—Fruit Stand, silver plated on nickel silver, with richly cut-glass dish. Height 18½ inches.

No. 5830.—Fruit Stand, electro-silver plated on nickel silver, with cut glass dish, height 18 inches.

No. 5831.—Fruit Stand, silver plated on nickel silver, with richly cut glass dish. Height on plateau, 22 inches.
No. 5831 P.—Plateau, silver plated on nickel silver, with strong silvered plate glass centre. Diameter 13 inches.

DOMINE DIRIGE NOS

ELECTRO-SILVER PLATED GOODS.

No. 5832.—Cream Jug, heavily silver plated on
nickel silver, richly hand engraved, gilt lined.

No. 5833.—"Queen Anne" Coffee Pot, heavily silver plated on nickel
silver, hand engraved, black handle, holding 3 pints.

No. 5834.—Cream Jug, electro-silver plated on nickel
silver, hand engraved, gilt inside.

No. 5832.—Sugar Basin, heavily silver plated on
nickel silver, richly hand engraved, gilt lined.

No. 5834.—Sugar Basin, electro-silver plated on
nickel silver, hand engraved, gilt inside.

No. 5832.—Tea Pot, heavily silver plated on nickel silver,
richly hand engraved, holding 2½ pints.

No. 5833.—"Queen Anne" Tea Pot, heavily silver plated on nickel
silver, hand engraved, black handle, holding 2½ pints.

. No. 5834.—Tea Pot, electro-silver plated on nickel silver, hand
engraved, holding 2 pints.

No. 5833.—"Queen Anne" Sugar Basin, heavily silver plated
on nickel silver, hand engraved, gilt lined.

No. 5832.—Coffee Pot, heavily silver plated on nickel silver,
richly hand engraved, holding 3 pints.

No. 5833.—"Queen Anne" Cream Jug, heavily silver plated on
nickel silver, hand engraved, gilt lined.

No. 5834.—Coffee Pot, electro-silver plated on nickel silver, hand
engraved, holding 2½ pints.

S. & F.
London.

The above patterns can be made in cheaper qualities when ordered in quantities.

S. & F.
London.

ELECTRO-SILVER PLATED GOODS.

SILVERSMITHS. TRADE MARK.

ELECTRO PLATERS. TRADE MARK.

DOMINE DIRIGE NOS

No. 5836.—Candelabrum, three-light, electro-silver plated on nickel silver. Height 18½ inches.

No. 5837.—Chamber Candlestick, electro-silver plated on nickel silver.

No. 5838.—Candelabrum, three-light, electro-silver plated on nickel silver. Height 20 inches.

No. 5840.—Chamber Candlestick, with shade, electro-silver plated on nickel silver.

TRADE MARK.

TRADE MARK.

No. 5841.—Candelabrum, four-light, electro-silver-plated on nickel silver. Height 21½ inches.

No. 5842.—Chamber Candlestick, electro-silver plated on nickel silver, with shade.

No. 5843.—Chamber Candlestick, electro-silver plated on nickel silver, Hotel pattern.

No. 5844.—Chamber Candlestick, electro-silver-plated on nickel silver.

No. 5839.—Pillar Candlestick, electro-silver plated, with shade. Height 8 in., 10 in., or 12 in.

No. 5845.—Pillar Candlestick, with shade, electro-silver plated. Height 8 in., 10 in., or 12 in.

No. 5846.—Piano Candlestick, electro-silver plated on nickel silver. Height 6¼ inches.

No. 5847.—Pillar Candlestick, electro-silver plated on nickel silver.

No. 5848.—Candelabrum, four-light, electro-silver-plated on nickel silver. Height 15½ inches.

No. 5849.—Pillar Candlestick, electro-silver plated on nickel silver.

No. 5850.—Piano Candlestick, electro-silver plated on nickel silver. Height 5½ inches.

S. & F.   **The above patterns can be made in cheaper qualities when ordered in quantities.**   S. & F.

DOMINE DIRIGE NOS

ELECTRO-SILVER PLATED GOODS.

No. 5851.—Cream Jug, electro-silver plated on nickel silver, handsomely engraved and embossed, gilt inside.

No. 5852.—Coffee Pot, electro-silver plated on nickel silver, hand engraved, holding 3 pints.

No. 5853.—Cream Jug, heavily silver plated on nickel silver, hand engraved, gilt inside.

No. 5851.—Sugar Basin, electro-silver plated on nickel silver, handsomely engraved and embossed, gilt inside.

No. 5852.—Tea Pot, electro-silver plated on nickel silver, hand engraved, holding 2½ pints.

No. 5853.—Sugar Basin, heavily silver plated on nickel silver, hand engraved, gilt inside.

No. 5851.—Tea Pot, electro-silver plated on nickel silver, handsomely engraved and embossed, holding 2 pints.

No. 5852.—Sugar Basin, electro-silver plated on nickel silver, hand engraved, gilt inside.

No. 5853.—Tea Pot, heavily silver plated on nickel silver, hand engraved, holding 2½ pints.

No. 5851.—Coffee Pot, electro-silver plated on nickel silver, handsomely engraved and embossed, holding 2½ pints.

No. 5852.—Cream Jug, electro-silver plated on nickel silver, hand engraved, gilt inside.

No. 5853.—Coffee Pot, heavily silver plated on nickel silver, hand engraved, holding 3 pints.

DOMINE DIRIGE NOS

ELECTRO-SILVER PLATED GOODS.

No. 5854.—Preserve Holder, silver plated on nickel silver, richly cut glass.

No. 5855.—Preserve Holder, silver plated on nickel silver, cut glass.

No. 5856.—Preserve or Jelly Stand, silver plated, crystal glass.

No. 5857.—Preserve Holder, silver plated on nickel silver, richly cut glass.

No. 5858.—Preserve Holder, silver plated, crystal glass.

No. 5859.—Preserve Holder, silver plated on nickel silver, richly cut glass.

S. & F.
London.

S. & F.
London.

No. 5863.—Tea and Coffee Service, consisting of 2½-pint Coffee Pot, 2-pint Tea Pot, and gilt-lined Sugar Basin and Cream Jug, heavily silver plated on nickel silver.
No. 5863s.—Salver, heavily silver plated on nickel silver, richly hand engraved. Length 24 inches.

No. 5860.—Preserve Holder, silver plated on nickel silver, richly cut glass.

No. 5861.—Jelly or Preserve Stand, silver plated on nickel silver, cut glass dish.

No. 5862.—Double Preserve Stand and Spoons, silver plated on nickel silver, crystal glasses.

No. 5864.—Preserve Holder, cut and engraved glass, mounts, lid, and spoon, electro-silver plated on nickel silver.

No. 5865.—Preserve Holder, silver plated, crystal glass.

No. 5866.—Sugar Basin, silver plated on nickel silver, ruby glass.

No. 5867.—Preserve Holder, silver plated on nickel silver, crystal glass.

No. 5868.—Preserve Holder, silver plated, cut crystal glass.

No. 5869.—Sugar Basket, engraved glass, with electro-silver plated mounts.

No. 5870.—Sugar Basin, silver plated on hard Britannia metal, hand engraved, gilt inside.

No. 5871.—Sugar Basin, silver plated on nickel silver, richly cut glass.

No. 5872.—Sugar Basin, silver plated on nickel silver, finely cut crystal glass.

ELECTRO-SILVER PLATED GOODS.

No. 5873.—Coffee Pot, silver plated on nickel silver, holding 3 pints.

No. 5873.—Tea Pot, silver plated on nickel silver, holding 2½ pints.

No. 5873.—Sugar Basin, silver plated on nickel silver, gilt inside.

No. 5873.—Cream Jug, silver plated on nickel silver, gilt inside.

The above pattern can be made silver plated on Britannia metal.

No. 5874.—Cream Jug, silver plated on Britannia metal, hand engraved, gilt inside.

No. 5874.—Sugar Basin, silver plated on Britannia metal, gilt inside.

No. 5874.—Tea Pot, silver plated on Britannia metal, hand engraved, holding 2 pints.

No. 5874.—Coffee Pot, silver plated on Britannia metal, hand engraved, holding 2½ pints.

No. 5875.—Coffee Pot, silver plated on Britannia metal, hand engraved, holding 2½ pints.

No. 5875.—Tea Pot, silver plated on Britannia metal, hand engraved, holding 2 pints.

No. 5875.—Sugar Basin, silver plated on Britannia metal, hand engraved, gilt inside.

No. 5875.—Cream Jug, silver plated on Britannia metal, hand engraved, gilt inside.

No. 5876.—Cream Jug, silver plated on nickel silver, hand engraved, gilt inside.

No. 5876.—Sugar Basin, silver plated on nickel silver, hand engraved, gilt inside.

No. 5876.—Tea Pot, silver plated on nickel silver, hand engraved, holding 2½ pints.

No. 5876.—Coffee Pot, silver plated on nickel silver, hand engraved, holding 3 pints.

No. 5877.—Coffee Pot, silver plated on nickel silver, holding 3 pints.

No. 5877.—Tea Pot, silver plated on nickel silver, holding 2½ pints.

No. 5877.—Sugar Basin, silver plated on nickel silver, gilt inside.

No. 5877.—Cream Jug, silver plated on nickel silver, gilt inside.

ELECTRO-SILVER PLATED GOODS.

No. 5879.—Butter and Double Preserve Stand, silver plated on nickel
silver, cut glasses. Length 13 inches.

No. 5891.—Oblong Fruit Dish, electro-silver plated on nickel
silver, with cut-glass dish.

No. 5878.—Double Preserve Stand, silver plated on nickel
silver, crystal glass.

No. 5885.—Sugar and Cream Stand, with two ladles,
electro-silver plated on nickel silver, cut glasses.

No. 5884.—Double Preserve Holder, electro-silver
plated, with two glasses.

No. 5882.—Custard Frame, electro-silver plated on nickel
silver, with six cut and engraved glasses.

No. 5880.—Double Preserve Stand and Spoons, silver
plated on nickel silver, hand engraved, cut glasses.

No. 5886.—Sugar and Cream Stand, with sugar sifters,
silver plated on nickel silver, cut glasses.

No. 5889.—Sugar and Cream Stand, silver plated on nickel silver
with richly cut glasses. Length 8½ inches.

No. 5887.—Sugar and Cream Stand, silver plated on
nickel silver, richly cut glass.

No. 5881.—Preserve Holder, with spoon,
electro-silver plated on nickel silver, satin
finished, cut glass dish.

No. 5888.—Custard Frame, silver plated on nickel silver,
6 cut glasses.

No. 5883.—Preserve Holder, silver plated
on nickel silver, cut glass dish.

No. 5890.—Custard Frame and Spoons, silver plated
on nickel silver, 6 cut glasses.

S. & F.   **The above patterns can be made in cheaper qualities when ordered in quantities.**   S. & F.

ELECTRO-SILVER PLATED GOODS.

No. 5893.—Tea Pot, electro-silver plated on hard Britannia metal, hand engraved.

No. 5894.—Tea Pot, electro-silver plated on hard Britannia metal, hand engraved.

No. 5895.—Tea Pot, electro-silver plated on Britannia metal, hand engraved.

No. 5896.—Tea Pot, electro-silver plated on hard Britannia metal, hand engraved.

No. 5897.—Tea Pot, electro-silver plated on hard Britannia metal, hand engraved.

No. 5898.—Tea Pot, electro-silver plated on hard Britannia metal, hand engraved.

No. 5899.—Tea Pot, electro-silver plated on hard Britannia metal, hand engraved.

No. 5900.—Tea Pot, electro-silver plated on hard Britannia metal, hand engraved.

No. 5901.—Tea Pot, electro-silver plated on hard Britannia metal, hand chased.

No. 5902.—Tea Pot, electro-silver plated on hard Britannia metal, hand engraved.

No. 5903.—Tea Pot, electro-silver plated on Britannia metal, hand engraved.

No. 5904.—Tea Pot, electro-silver plated on hard Britannia metal, hand engraved.

No. 5905.—Tea Pot, electro-silver plated on hard Britannia metal, hand engraved.

No. 5906.—Tea Pot, electro-silver plated on hard Britannia metal.

No. 5907.—Tea Pot, electro-silver plated on Britannia metal, hand engraved.

S. & F. **The above patterns can be made in cheaper qualities when ordered in quantities.** S. & F.

CAUTION. Any person infringing the Copyright of this Book will be prosecuted under the Act.

DOMINE DIRIGE NOS

ELECTRO-SILVER PLATED GOODS.

No. 5908.—Water or Ale Jug, electro-silver plated on nickel silver, satin finished, holding 2 pints.

No. 5909.—"Doric" Hot Water Jug, heavily silver plated on nickel silver.

No. 5910.—Water or Ale Jug, iced glass, electro-silver plated mounts, satin finished, holding 2 pints.

No. 5911.—Hot Water Jug, electro-silver plated on hard Britannia metal, hand engraved.

No. 5912.—Hot Water Jug, electro-silver plated on Britannia metal, hand engraved.

No. 5913.—Hot Water Jug, heavily silver plated on nickel silver, hand engraved, black handle.

No. 5914.—Hot Water Jug, electro-silver plated on Britannia metal, hand engraved.

No. 5915.—Hot Water Jug, electro-silver plated on Britannia metal, hand engraved.

BRITANNIA METAL GOODS, NOT PLATED.

No. 5916.—Tea Pot, Britannia metal.

No. 5917.—Tea Pot, best hard Britannia metal.

No. 5918.—Tea Pot, best hard Britannia metal.

No. 5919.—Tea Pot, best hard Britannia metal.

No. 5920.—Britannia Metal Hot Water Jug, with wicker-covered handle.

No. 5921.—Cruet Frame, Britannia metal not plated, four cut glass bottles. Suitable for hotel use.

No. 5922.—Coffee Pot, hard Britannia metal.

No. 5923.—Coffee Pot, hard Britannia metal, black handle.

S. & F.   The above patterns can be made in cheaper qualities when ordered in quantities.   S. & F.

SILVERSMITHS.

TRADE MARK.

ELECTRO PLATERS.

TRADE MARK.

DOMINE DIRIGE NOS

ELECTRO-SILVER PLATED GOODS.

No. 5924.—Claret Jug, cut crystal glass body, electro-silver plated on nickel silver mounts and lid. Height about 11 inches.

No. 5925.—Claret Jug, richly cut and engraved crystal glass body, mounts and lid electro-silver plated on nickel silver, hand engraved. Height about 11 inches.

No. 5926.—Claret Jug, richly cut crystal glass body, mounts and lid heavily plated on nickel silver, richly chased and engraved. Height 12 inches.

No. 5927.—Claret Jug, richly cut crystal glass body, mounts and lid electro-silver plated on nickel silver. Height 10 inches.

No. 5928.—Claret Jug, cut crystal glass body, mounts and lid electro-silver plated on nickel silver hand engraved. Height 12 inches.

TRADE MARK.

TRADE MARK

S. & F.

LONDON.

No. 5929.—Claret Jug, richly cut crystal glass body, mounts and lid electro-silver plated on nickel silver, hand engraved. Height 10 inches.

No. 5930.—Wine and Biscuit Stand, heavily silver plated on nickel silver, hand engraved, richly cut crystal glass. Length 18 inches.

No. 5931.—Claret Jug, richly cut crystal glass body, mounts and lid electro-silver plated on nickel silver, hand engraved. Height 11 inches.

No. 5932.—Claret Jug, cut crystal glass body, mounts and lid silver plated and gilt on hard metal, richly chased. Height 17 inches.

No. 5933.—Claret Jug, cut glass body, electro-silver plated mounts and lid. Height 10½ inches.

No. 5934.—Claret Jug, ruby glass body, hand painted, mounts silver plated on hard metal, richly gilt and chased. Height 12 inches.

No. 5935.—Claret Jug, cut glass body, electro-silver plated mounts and lid. Height about 12 inches.

No. 5936.—Claret Jug, peacock blue glass body, richly ornamented with flowers and foliage, mounts silver plated on hard metal, gilt and chased. Height 15 inches.

S. & F.

The above patterns can be made in cheaper qualities when ordered in quantities.

S. & F.

ELECTRO-SILVER PLATED GOODS.

No. 5938.—Cruet Frame, electro-silver plated on Britannia metal, 4 cut glass bottles.

No. 5939.—Cruet Frame, electro-silver plated on Britannia metal, 4 cut glass bottles.

No. 5940.—Cruet Frame, electro-silver plated on Britannia metal, 4 cut glass bottles.

No. 5941.—Cruet Frame, electro-silver plated on Britannia metal, 4 cut glass bottles.

TRADE MARK.

No. 5942.—Cruet Frame, electro-silver plated, 4 cut glass bottles.

No. 5943.—Cruet Frame, electro-silver plated on nickel silver 6 richly cut glass bottles.

No. 5944.—Cruet Frame, electro-silver plated on Britannia metal, 4 cut glass bottles.

No. 5945.—Cruet Frame, electro-silver plated on nickel silver, 6 cut glass bottles.

No. 5946.—Cruet Frame, electro-silver plated on nickel silver, 6 cut glass bottles.

No. 5947.—Cruet Frame, electro-silver plated on nickel silver, 6 cut glass bottles.

No. 5948.—Cruet Frame, electro-silver plated on hard metal, 4 richly cut glass bottles.

No. 5949.—Cruet Frame, electro-silver plated on nickel silver, 6 cut glass bottles.

S. & F.   **The above patterns can be made in cheaper qualities when ordered in quantities.**   S. & F.

DOMINE DIRIGE NOS

ELECTRO-SILVER PLATED GOODS.

No. 5950.—Cruet Frame, electro-silver plated on nickel silver, hand engraved and saw-pierced, six richly cut glass bottles.

No. 5951.—Cruet Frame, electro-silver plated on nickel silver, with six richly cut crystal glass bottles.

No. 5952.—Cruet Frame, electro-silver plated on nickel silver, hand engraved, six richly cut glass bottles.

No 5953.—Cruet Frame, electro-silver plated on nickel silver, with six cut glass bottles.

No. 5954.—Cruet Frame, electro-silver plated on nickel silver, richly saw-pierced and engraved, with six cut glass bottles.

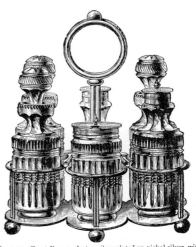

No. 5955.—Cruet Frame, electro-silver plated on nickel silver, with six superior cut glass bottles.

No. 5956.—Cruet Frame, electro-silver plated on nickel silver, with six richly cut crystal glass bottles.

No. 5957.—Cruet Frame, heavily plated on nickel silver, richly saw-pierced and engraved, with seven cut glass bottles.   Length 11½ inches.

TRADE MARK.

No. 5958.—Cruet Frame, electro-silver plated on nickel silver, with six richly cut crystal glass bottles.

S. & F.   **The above patterns can be made in cheaper qualities when ordered in quantities.**   S. & F.

CAUTION. Any person infringing the Copyright of this Book will be prosecuted under the Act.

SILVERSMITHS.
TRADE MARK.

DOMINE DIRIGE NOS

ELECTRO-SILVER PLATED GOODS.

ELECTRO PLATERS.
TRADE MARK.

No. 5959.—Breakfast Cruet, silver plated on nickel silver, 4 cut glasses.

No. 5960.—Cruet with Pickle Bottle, silver plated on nickel silver, cut glasses.

No. 5961.—Breakfast Cruet, electro-silver plated.

No. 5962.—Breakfast Cruet, with preserve or butter dish, silver plated on nickel silver, cut glasses.

No. 5963.—Breakfast Cruet, silver plated on nickel silver, cut glasses.

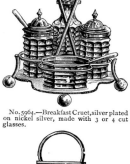

No. 5964.—Breakfast Cruet, silver plated on nickel silver, made with 3 or 4 cut glasses.

No. 5965.—Breakfast Cruet, silver plated on nickel silver, cut glasses.

No. 5966.—Breakfast Cruet, silver plated on nickel silver, cut glasses

No. 5967.—Breakfast Cruet, electro-silver plated on nickel silver, with cut glasses.

No. 5968.—Breakfast Cruet, electro-silver plated on nickel silver, with cut glasses.

No. 5969.—Breakfast Cruet, electro-silver plated on nickel silver, with cut glasses.

No. 5970.—Breakfast Cruet, electro-silver plated.

No. 5971.—Breakfast Cruet, electro-silver plated on nickel silver, with 4 cut glasses.

No. 5972.—Breakfast Cruet, silver plated on nickel silver, 5 cut glasses.

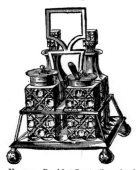

No. 5973.—Breakfast Cruet, silver plated on nickel silver, with cut crystal glass bottom and 4 cut glasses.

No. 5974.—Breakfast Cruet, silver plated on nickel silver, cut glasses.

No. 5975.—Breakfast Cruet, electro-silver plated on nickel silver, with 4 superior cut glasses and gilt-lined salt.

No. 5976.—Breakfast Cruet and Spoons, electro-silver plated on nickel silver, gilt-lined salt. Diameter 6¼ inches.

No. 5977.—Breakfast Cruet, silver plated on nickel silver, cut glasses.

No. 5978.—Breakfast Cruet, electro-silver plated on nickel silver, with cut and engraved glasses.

CAUTION. Any person infringing the Copyright of this Book will be prosecuted under the Act.

44

DOMINE DIRIGE NOS

ELECTRO-SILVER PLATED GOODS.

No. 5970.—Biscuit Box, glass body, electro-silver plated mounts and lid.

No. 5980.—Biscuit Box, cut crystal glass body, mounts and lid electro-silver plated on nickel silver.

No. 5981.—Biscuit Box, electro-silver plated on Britannia metal body, nickel silver lid, hand engraved.

No. 5982.—Biscuit Box, cut crystal glass body, mounts and lid electro-silver plated on nickel silver.

No. 5983.—Biscuit Box, cut crystal glass body, mounts and lid electro-silver plated on nickel silver.

No. 5984.—Biscuit Box, electro-silver plated on nickel silver.

5985.—Biscuit Box, electro-silver plated on nickel silver. Height 7¾ inches.

No. 5986.—Biscuit Box, cut crystal glass body, mounts and lid electro-silver plated on nickel silver. Height 7½ inches.

No. 5987.—Biscuit Box, cut crystal glass body, mounts and lid electro-silver plated on nickel silver.

No. 5988.—Biscuit Box, electro-silver plated on Britannia metal, nickel silver lid, hand engraved.

No. 5989.—Biscuit Box, electro-silver plated on Britannia metal, hand engraved. Length 8 inches.

No 5990.—Biscuit Box, electro-silver plated on nickel silver.

No. 5991.—Biscuit Box, electro-silver plated on Britannia metal, hand engraved. Length 8½ inches.

No. 5992.—Biscuit Box, electro-silver plated on Britannia metal, hand engraved. The handle of this box is so constructed that when pressed down it opens the lid on either side.

No. 5993.—Biscuit Box, electro-silver plated on Britannia metal, richly chased. Length 8 inches.

No. 5994.—Biscuit Box, electro-silver plated on nickel silver. Height 8 inches.

No. 5995.—Biscuit Box, electro-silver plated on Britannia metal, hand engraved. Length 8 inches.

ELECTRO-SILVER PLATED GOODS.

No. 5996.—Toast Rack, electro-silver plated on nickel silver. Length 8¼ inches.

No. 5997.—Toast Rack, electro-silver plated on nickel silver.

No. 5998.—Toast Rack, silver plated on nickel silver.

No. 5999.—Toast Rack, electro-silver plated on nickel silver.

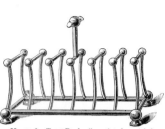
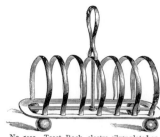

No. 6000.—Toast Rack, silver plated on nickel silver.

No. 6001.—Toast Rack, electro-silver plated.

No. 6002.—Toast Rack, electro-silver plated on nickel silver.

No. 6003.—Toast Rack, electro-silver plated on nickel silver.

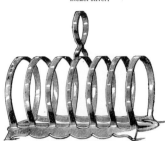

No. 6004.—Toast Rack, electro-silver plated on nickel silver.

No. 6005.—Toast Rack, electro-silver plated on nickel silver.

No. 6006.—Toast Rack and Butter Dish combined, electro-silver plated. Height 6¾ inches.

No. 6007.—Toast Rack, electro-silver plated on nickel silver.

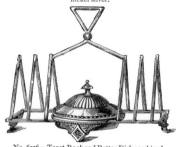

No. 6008.—Toast Rack and Butter Dish combined, electro-silver plated on nickel silver. Height 8 inches.

No. 6009.—Breakfast Cruet and Egg Frame combined, electro-silver plated on nickel silver, with gilt-lined Egg Cups and Spoons, cut glasses.

No. 6010.—Toast, Egg, and Salt Stand combined, electro-silver plated on nickel silver.

No. 6011.—Toast Rack, Butter Dish, and Bell combined, electro-silver plated on nickel silver.

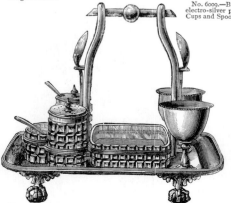

No. 6012.—Egg Frame, Breakfast Cruet, and Butter Dish combined, silver plated on nickel silver, cut glasses.

No. 6013.—Breakfast Cruet and Butter Dish combined, silver plated on nickel silver.

No. 6014.—Combination Set, consisting of Toast Rack, Butter and Marmalade Dishes, Pepper, Salt, and Mustard Cruets, and two gilt-lined Egg Cups and Spoons, electro-silver plated on nickel silver, cut glasses. Length 12½ inches.

DOMINE DIRIGE NOS

ELECTRO-SILVER PLATED GOODS.

No. 6016.—Afternoon Tea Set, silver plated on Britannia metal, hand engraved, consisting of 1-pint tea pot, gilt-lined sugar basin and cream jug.
Sugar Tongs, electro-silver plated on nickel silver.
China Cups and Saucers, blue Japanese decoration.
Tray, papier-maché, imitation walnut and ebony, ivory handles, with electro-silver plated mounts and ball feet.   Length 16 inches.

No. 6017.—Afternoon Tea Set, electro-silver plated on nickel silver, consisting of 1-pint tea pot, gilt-lined sugar basin and cream jug.
Kettle on stand, with spirit lamp, silver plated on nickel silver, 2 pints.
Sugar Tongs, electro-silver plated on nickel silver.
Tray, silver plated on nickel silver, with handles.   Length 16 inches.

No. 6018.—Afternoon Tea Set, silver plated on Britannia metal, hand engraved, consisting of 1-pint tea pot, gilt-lined sugar basin and cream jug.
Sugar Tongs, electro-silver plated on nickel silver.
China Cups and Saucers, blue Japanese decoration.
Tray, oval, electro-silver plated on nickel silver.   Length 16 inches.

No. 6019.—Egg Steamer, electro-silver plated on nickel silver.

No. 6020.—Egg Frame, electro-silver plated on nickel silver, gilt-lined cups and spoons.   Four or six cups.

No. 6021.—Revolving Breakfast Cruet, Egg Frame, and Toast Rack combined, silver plated on nickel silver, cut glasses, and gilt-lined spoons.

No. 6022.—Egg Steamer, electro-silver plated on nickel silver.

No. 6023.—Egg Frame, silver plated on nickel silver, gilt lined cups and spoons.   Four or six cups.

No. 6024.—Egg Frame, silver plated on nickel silver, gilt-lined cups and spoons.   Four or six cups.

No. 6025.—Egg Steamer, Egg Frame, and Spirit Lamp combined, silver plated on nickel silver, gilt-lined cups and spoons.

No. 6026.—Egg Frame, silver plated on nickel silver, gilt-lined cups and spoons.   Four or six cups.

No. 6027.—Egg Frame, with five cups and spoons, electro-silver plated on nickel silver, and handsomely decorated china plate.

No. 6028.—Egg Frame, silver plated on nickel silver, gilt-lined cups and spoons.   Four or six cups.

No. 6029.—Egg Frame, silver plated on nickel silver, gilt-lined cups and spoons.   Three, four, or six cups.

No. 6030.—Egg Frame and Egg Steamer combined, silver plated on nickel silver, gilt-lined cups and spoons.

ELECTRO-SILVER PLATED GOODS.

No. 6031.—Cake Basket, electro-silver plated on nickel silver, richly hand engraved and crewel work cloth. Length 12 inches.

No. 6032.—Card, Fruit, or Cake Basket, silver plated on nickel silver, richly hand engraved. Length 8½ inches.

No. 6033.—Cake Basket, electro-silver plated on nickel silver, crewel work cloth. Length 11 inches.

No. 6034.—Cake Basket, electro-silver plated on nickel silver. Length 12 inches.

No. 6035.—Card, Fruit, or Cake Basket, silver plated on nickel silver. Diameter 11 inches.

No. 6036.—Cake Basket, electro-silver plated on nickel silver. Length 13 inches.

No. 6037.—Cake Basket, electro-silver plated on nickel silver, hand engraved. Diameter 10½ inches.

No. 6038.—"Rustic" Card, Fruit, or Cake Basket, silver plated on nickel silver. Length 11 inches.

No. 6039.—Cake Basket, electro-silver plated on nickel silver. Diameter 12 inches.

No. 6040.—Biscuit Box, heavily silver plated on nickel silver, richly hand engraved, saw-pierced and gilt division inside. Length 10 inches. The handle is so constructed that when pressed down it opens the lid on either side.

No. 6041.—Biscuit Box, electro-silver plated on Britannia metal, hand engraved. Height 9 inches. The handle is so constructed that by simply lifting the knob, it falls and removes the lid.

No. 6042.—Biscuit Box, silver plated on nickel silver, hand engraved, with two compartments for plain and sweet biscuits; can also be used as a Cake or Fruit Basket. Length when open 11½ inches.

ELECTRO-SILVER PLATED GOODS.

No. 6043.—Kettle on Stand, with spirit lamp, electro-silver plated on nickel silver, holding 4 pints.

No. 6044.—Kettle on Stand, with spirit lamp, silver plated on Britannia metal, nickel silver bottom, hand engraved, holding about 4 pints.

No. 6045.—"Queen Anne" Kettle on Stand, silver plated on nickel silver, hand engraved, with spirit lamp, holding 3 pints.

No. 6046.—Kettle on Stand, with spirit lamp, silver plated on nickel silver, hand made, without seam, engraved, or quite plain, holding 3 pints or 4 pints.

No. 6048.—Kettle on Stand, with spirit lamp, richly hand engraved, heavily silver plated, ivory handle, holding about 4 pints.

No. 6049.—Kettle on Stand, with spirit lamp, electro-silver plated on nickel silver, holding 3 pints.

No. 6050.—Kettle on Stand, with spirit lamp, electro-silver plated on Britannia metal, holding 3 pints.

No. 6051.—Urn, electro-silver plated on nickel silver, with spirit lamp, holding 4 quarts.

No. 6052.—Kettle on Stand, with spirit lamp, silver plated on Britannia metal, hand engraved, holding 2 pints.

No. 6053.—Urn, electro-silver plated on nickel silver, with spirit lamp, holding 4 quarts.

S. & F.

S. & F.

ELECTRO-SILVER PLATED GOODS.

No. 6055.—Butter Dish, electro-silver plated on nickel silver, cut glass dish.

No. 6056.—Butter Dish, electro-silver plated on nickel silver, cut glass dish.

No. 6057.—Butter Dish, electro-silver plated on nickel silver, cut glass dish.

No. 6058.—Butter Dish, electro-silver plated on nickel silver, glass dish.

No. 6059.—Butter Dish, silver plated on nickel silver, hand engraved, cut glass slab, and butter knife.

No. 6060.—Butter Dish, silver plated on nickel silver, richly saw-pierced and engraved, cut crystal glass dish.

No. 6061.—Butter or Preserve Dish, silver plated on nickel silver, cut glass dish.

No. 6062.—Butter or Preserve Dish, silver plated on nickel silver, cut glass dish.

No. 6063.—Butter Dish, with revolving lid, silver plated on nickel silver, hand engraved. Length 8 inches.

No. 6064.—Revolving Butter Dish, electro-silver plated, hand engraved.

No. 6065.—Butter Dish, with revolving lid, silver plated on nickel silver, hand engraved.

No. 6066.—Butter Dish, with revolving cover, electro-silver plated on nickel silver.

No. 6067.—Butter Dish, silver plated on nickel silver, glass dish.

No. 6068.—Butter Dish, silver plated, cut glass dish, nickel silver lid.

No. 6069.—Butter Dish, silver plated on nickel silver, richly cut glass dish.

No. 6070.—Butter Dish, silver plated on Britannia metal, china dish, with light blue decoration.

No. 6071.—Butter Dish or Preserve Holder, silver plated on nickel silver, richly cut glass dish.

No. 6072.—Butter Dish, silver plated on nickel silver, glass dish.

No. 6073.—Butter or Preserve Dish, silver plated on nickel silver, richly cut glass dish.

No. 6074.—Butter Dish, silver plated on nickel silver, crystal glass dish.

ELECTRO-SILVER PLATED GOODS.

No. 6075.—Sardine Box, electro-silver plated on nickel silver, cut glass dish.

No. 6076.—Fruit Dish, electro-silver plated on nickel silver, richly cut glass dish. Length 14 inches.

No. 6077.—Sardine Box, electro-silver plated on nickel silver, cut glass dish.

No. 6078.—Pickle Frame, silver plated on nickel silver, cut glass bottles, ivory handle pickle forks.

No. 6079.—Cruet Frame, electro-silver plated on nickel silver, with six richly cut glass bottles.

No. 6080.—Pickle Frame, electro-silver plated on nickel silver, with cut glass bottles.

No. 6081.—Oil and Vinegar Frame, electro-silver plated on nickel silver, with cut glasses.

No. 6082.—Cruet Frame, electro-silver plated on nickel silver, with seven cut crystal glass bottles. Height 9½ inches.

No. 6083.—Pickle Frame, electro-silver plated on nickel silver, with two cut glass bottles.

No. 6084.—Oil and Vinegar Frame, silver plated on nickel silver, cut glass bottles.

No. 6085.—Cruet Frame, silver plated on nickel silver, six cut glass bottles.

No. 6086.—Oil and Vinegar Frame, electro-silver plated on nickel silver, with cut glasses.

SILVERSMITHS. TRADE MARK.

DOMINE DIRIGE NOS

ELECTRO PLATERS. TRADE MARK.

No. 6087.—Child's Mug, silver plated on Britannia metal, gilt inside, engraved with any name to order.

No. 6088.—Child's Mug, silver plated on nickel silver, gilt inside, hand engraved.

No. 6101.—Child's Mug, silver plated on nickel silver, hand engraved, gilt inside.

No. 6091.—Child's Mug, silver plated on nickel silver, hand engraved, gilt inside.

No. 6013.—Child's Mug, silver plated on nickel silver, gilt inside, satin finished.

No. 6092.—Child's Mug, silver plated on nickel silver, gilt inside, satin finished.

Special Designs for Presentation Plate made to order.

Initials, Monograms, Inscriptions, &c., engraved in superior style.

No. 6093.—Butter or Preserve Dish, silver plated on nickel silver, richly cut glass dish. Length 7 inches. Suitable for boating prize.

No. 6094.—Butter Dish, silver plated on nickel silver, richly cut glass dish. Length 10 inches. Suitable for Shooting prize.

PRIZES FOR BOATING, SHOOTING, AND ATHLETIC SPORTS.

PRIZES FOR AGRICULTURAL, HORTICULTURAL. AND CATTLE SHOWS.

No. 6095.—Boating Prize Cup, silver plated on nickel silver, richly hand engraved, gilt inside, satin finished. Height 11 inches.

No. 6096.—Child's Mug, silver plated on nickel silver, gilt inside.

No. 6097.—Presentation Cup, heavily silver plated on nickel silver, richly hand engraved, gilt inside, 3 pints. Height 16 inches.
This cup can be made with a plain knob, or with any of the figures as shown in drawing.

No. 6098.—Child's Mug, silver plated on Britannia metal, gilt inside.

No. 6099.—Prize Cup, silver plated on nickel silver, richly hand engraved, gilt inside. Height 12 inches.

For Christening Cups in Sterling Silver, see page 336.

For Prizes, Wedding & Birthday Presents in Sterling Silver, see pages 322, &c.

No. 6100.—Presentation Cup for shooting prize, silver plated on nickel silver, gilt decoration. Height 13 inches.

No. 6090.—Tankard, electro-silver plated on Britannia metal, gilt inside, holding 1 pint.

No. 6102. Prize Cup, electro-silver plated on nickel silver, hand engraved, gilt inside, holding 1 pint.

No. 6089.—Tankard, electro-silver plated on nickel silver, gilt inside, holding 1 pint.

No. 6104.—Presentation Cup, silver plated on nickel silver, richly engraved and gilt, holding 2 pints. Height 12 inches.

S. & F.　The above patterns can be made in cheaper qualities when ordered in quantities.　S. & F.

ELECTRO-PLATED GOODS.

No. 6105.—Prize Cup, electro-silver plated on nickel silver, gilt inside.

No. 6106.—Prize Cup, electro-silver plated on nickel silver, richly chased, gilt inside, holding 1 pint.

No. 6107.—Breakfast Cruets, silver plated on nickel silver, cut glass bottles. Suitable for tricycle race.

No. 6108.—Prize Cup, electro-silver plated on nickel silver, hand engraved, gilt inside, holding 1 pint.

No. 6109.—Prize Cup, electro-silver plated on nickel silver, gilt inside.

No. 6110.—Loving Cup, silver plated on nickel silver, richly chased, gilt inside, holding 1 pint.

No. 6111.—Loving Cup, made from ivory tusks, mounted in best nickel silver, heavily silver plated, holding about 2 pints.

No. 6113.—Loving Cup, with three handles, heavily silver plated on nickel silver, richly hand engraved, gilt inside, holding 2 pints.

No. 6114.—Presentation Cup, heavily silver plated on nickel silver, richly chased and engraved, gilt inside. Height 10 inches.

No. 6115.—Presentation Salad or Punch Bowl, richly hand chased, gilt inside, heavily silver plated on nickel silver, polished ebonised stand. Extreme height 12½ inches.

No. 6116.—Presentation Cup, silver plated on nickel silver, hand chased, gilt inside. Height 9½ inches.

No. 6117.—Fruit Stand, electro-silver plated on nickel silver, with cut glass dish. Height 15 inches.

No. 6118.—Fruit Stand, electro-silver plated on nickel silver, with cut and engraved glass dish. Height 9 inches.

No. 6119.—Fruit Stand, heavily electro-silver plated on nickel silver, satin finished, with richly cut glass dish. Height 11½ inches.

No. 6120.—Fruit Stand, electro-silver plated on nickel silver, with cut glass dish. Height 11½ inches.

S. & F. **The above patterns can be made in cheaper qualities when ordered in quantities.** S. & F.

CAUTION. Any person infringing the Copyright of this Book will be prosecuted under the Act.

DOMINE DIRIGE NOS

ELECTRO-SILVER PLATED GOODS.

No. 6121.—Salver, electro-silver plated on nickel silver, richly hand engraved, 8, 10, 12, 14, or 16 inches diameter.

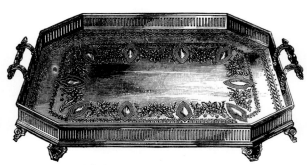

No. 6122.—Coffee Tray, electro-silver plated on nickel silver, 18, 20 22, 24, or 26 inches long.

No. 6123.—Rose-water Dish, electro-silver plated on nickel silver, richly embossed and gilt, 13 inches diameter.

No. 6124.—Liquor Frame, electro-silver plated on nickel silver, with cut glass bottles.

No. 6125.—Liquor Frame, electro-silver plated on nickel silver, superior cut glass bottles. Height about 13 inches.

No. 6126.—Liquor Frame, electro-silver plated on nickel silver. superior cut glass bottles. Height about 13 inches.

No. 6127.—Liquor Frame, electro-silver plated on nickel silver, cut glass bottles. Height about 13 inches.

No. 6128.—Soda Water Frame, electro-silver plated on nickel silver, made to hold 2, 4, or 8 bottles.

No. 6129.—Liquor Frame, heavily silver plated on nickel silver, richly cut glass bottles. Height 14½ inches. *Suitable for presentation.*

DOMINE DIRIGE NOS

ELECTRO-SILVER PLATED GOODS.

No. 6130.—Salver, electro-silver plated on nickel silver,
8, 10, 12, 14, and 16 inches.

No. 6131.—Salver, electro-silver plated on nickel silver,
richly chased, 8, 10, 12, 14, and 16 inches.

No. 6132.—Salver, electro-silver plated on nickel silver,
chased, 8, 10, 12, and 14 inches.

No. 6133.—Salver, electro-silver plated on nickel silver,
hand engraved, satin finished, 8, 10, 12, and 14 inches.

No. 6134.—Coffee Tray, heavily silver plated on nickel silver, richly hand engraved,
satin finished, 22, 24, and 26 inches.

No. 6135.—Salver, electro-silver plated on nickel silver,
satin finished, hand engraved, 8, 10, and 12 inches.

No. 6136.—Salver, electro-silver plated on nickel silver,
10, 12, 14, and 16 inches.

No. 6137.—Salver, electro-silver plated on nickel silver,
hand engraved, 8, 10, 12, and 14 inches.

No. 6138.—Salver, electro-silver plated on nickel silver,
8, 10, 12, and 14 inches.

SILVERSMITHS. TRADE MARK.

DOMINE DIRIGE NOS

ELECTRO PLATERS. TRADE MARK.

ELECTRO-SILVER PLATED GOODS SUITABLE FOR HOTELS, RESTAURANTS, ETC.

No. 6139.—Sauce Boat, silver plated on nickel silver.

No. 6140.—Vegetable Dish with division, silver plated on nickel silver. Diameter 6½ inches.

No. 6141.—Entrée Dish, round, electro-silver plated on nickel silver, movable handle. Diameter 9 inches.

No. 6142.—Meat Dish, silver plated on nickel silver, oval, 10, 12, 14, 16, and 18 inches.

No. 6143.—Sauce Boat, silver plated on nickel silver.

No. 6144.—Mustard Pot, silver plated on nickel silver.

No. 6145.—Wine Measure, silver plated on nickel silver.

No. 6146.—Tea Pot, silver plated on nickel silver, 1, 1½, 2, 2½, and 3 pints.

No. 6147.—Nut, Fruit, or Ice Bowl, silver plated on nickel silver, gilt inside. Height 9¾ inches.

No. 6148.—Ice Pail, silver plated on nickel silver.

No. 6149.—Cruet Frame, electro-silver plated on nickel silver, with four cut glass bottles. Height 9¾ inches.

No. 6150.—Ice Pail, silver plated on nickel silver, cut glass.

No. 6151.—Tankards, silver plated on nickel silver, 1 pint, ½ pint.

No. 6152.—Iced Water Jug, silver plated on hard Britannia metal, hand engraved.

No. 6153.—Vegetable Dish, with divisions and hot water reservoir, silver plated on nickel silver, ivory handle.

No. 6154.—Bride Cake Stand, heavily silver plated on nickel silver, with silvered plate glass top. Diameter 17 inches, height 4½ inches.

No. 6155.—Sandwich Stand, silver plated on nickel silver, glass cover. Height 15½ inches.

No. 6156.—Improved Wire Gauze Meat Cover, silver plated.

No. 6157.—Soup Tureen, electro-silver plated on nickel silver.
No. 6157A.—Soup Tureen, electro-silver plated on Britannia metal.
No. 6157B.—Soup Tureen, Britannia metal, not plated.

No. 6158.—Dish Cover, electro-silver plated on nickel silver.

ELECTRO-SILVER PLATED GOODS.

No. 6159.—Entrée Dish, electro-silver plated on nickel silver

No. 6160.—Breakfast Dish, silver plated on nickel silver, with hot water reservoir. Length 12 inches.

No. 6161.—Entrée Dish, silver plated on nickel silver, hand engraved.

No. 6162.—Spoon Warmer, electro-silver plated on nickel silver.

No. 6163.—Spoon Warmer, silver plated on hard Britannia metal, hand engraved.

No. 6164.—Muffin or Toast Dish, with revolving cover, silver plated on nickel silver, hand engraved satin finished.

No. 6165.—Spoon Warmer, silver plated on hard Britannia metal, hand engraved.

No. 6166.—Dish, with revolving cover, heavily silver plated on nickel silver, richly chased and engraved. Length 11 inches.

No. 6167.—Improved Dish, with revolving cover, silver plated on nickel silver, with loose dishes for chop or entrée, and movable bowl for soup. Length 11 inches.

No. 6168.—Dish, with revolving cover, silver plated on nickel silver, hand engraved, 9, 10, 11, and 12 inches.

No. 6169.—Improved Britannia Metal Dish Cover, extra strong, with silver-plated handle, 10, 12, 14, 16, and 18 inches.

No. 6173.—Salad Bowl and Servers, silver plated on nickel silver mounts, richly cut crystal glass.

No. 6171.—Dish Cover, hard Britannia metal, silver-plated handle, 10, 12, 14, 16, and 18 inches.

No. 6172.—Soup or Salad Bowl, silver plated on nickel silver, with movable lining. Height 11 inches.

No. 6170.—Dish Cover, heavily plated on nickel silver, richly hand engraved, 11, 12, 14, 16, and 18 inches.

No. 6174.—Soup Tureen or Salad Bowl, electro-silver plated on nickel silver, 3 quarts.

ELECTRO-SILVER PLATED GOODS.

No. 6175.—Tobacco Jar, electro-silver plated on nickel silver. Height 6¼ inches.

No. 6176.—"Roman Lamp" Cigar Lighter, electro-silver plated on nickel silver. Length 7 inches.

No. 6177.—Inkstand, electro-silver plated on nickel silver, hand engraved. Length 8 inches.

No. 6178.—Cigar Lighter, with spirit lamp, electro-silver plated on nickel silver.

No. 6180.—Tobacco Jar, electro-silver plated on Britannia metal.

No. 6181.—Cigar Stand, with taper, matches, and movable ash tray, silver plated on nickel silver. Height 7 inches.

No. 6182.—Snuff Box, polished ram's horn, electro-silver plated mounts, gilt inside.

No. 6183.—Cigar Stand, with tobacco jar, match holders, and movable ash tray, electro-silver plated on nickel silver, hand engraved. Length 9 inches.

No. 6184.—Inkstand, electro-silver plated on Britannia metal, hand engraved, cut glass bottles. Length 11 inches.

No. 6185.—Snuff Box, double ram's horn, electro-silver plated mounts, gilt inside. Length about 14 inches.

No. 6186.—Inkstand, electro-silver plated on Britannia metal, cut glass bottles. Length 7½ inches.

No. 6187.—Inkstand, electro-silver plated on nickel silver, stamp box and cut glass bottles. Length about 10 inches.

No. 6188.—Inkstand, electro-silver plated on nickel silver, with stamp box and cut glass bottles. Length 12 inches.

No. 6189.—Inkstand, electro-silver plated on nickel silver, cut glass bottles. Length 8½ inches.

No. 6190.—Inkstand, electro-silver plated on nickel silver, cut glass bottles. Length 14 inches.

No. 6191.—Inkstand, electro-silver plated on nickel silver, two cut glass bottles and stamp box. Length 14 inches.

No. 6192.—Inkstand, electro-silver plated on nickel silver, two cut glass bottles.

S. & F.   **The above patterns can be made in cheaper qualities when ordered in quantities.**   S. & F.

DOMINE DIRIGE NOS

ELECTRO-SILVER PLATED GOODS.

No. 6193.—Flagon, electro-silver plated on nickel silver.
No. 6194.—Flagon, electro-silver plated on Britannia metal.
No. 6195.—Flagon, Britannia metal, not plated.

No. 6196.—Communion Service, heavily silver plated on nickel silver, engraved with inscription, or plain.

No. 6199.—Presentation Mallet, best polished oak, with electro-silver plated plate for inscription.

No. 6200. — Presentation Mallet, best polished rosewood, with electro-silver plate for inscription.

No. 6197.—Flagon, electro-silver plated on nickel silver.
No. 6198.—Flagon, electro-silver plated on Britannia metal.

No. 6193.—Plate, electro-silver plated on nickel silver.
No. 6194.—Plate, electro-silver plated on Britannia metal.
No. 6195.—Plate, Britannia metal, 10-inch.

For other Trowels in Sterling Silver, with plain and carved ivory handles, see page

No. 6201.—Trowel, for presentation, electro-silver plated on nickel silver, hand engraved, ivory handle, length 12 inches.

No. 6202.—Trowel, for presentation, electro-silver plated on nickel silver, hand engraved, ivory handle, length 12 inches.

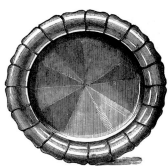

No. 6197.—Plate, electro-silver plated on nickel silver, 10-inch.
No. 6198.—Plate, electro-silver plated on Britannia metal, 10-inch.

No. 6193.—Paten, electro-silver plated on nickel silver.
No. 6194.—Paten, electro-silver plated on Britannia metal.
No. 6195.—Paten, Britannia metal.

TRADE MARK.

No. 6203.—Trowel, for presentation, electro-silver plated on nickel silver, hand engraved, carved ivory handle, length 14 inches.

No. 6204.—Trowel, for presentation, electro-silver plated on nickel silver, hand engraved, carved ivory handle, length 15 inches.

TRADE MARK.

No. 6197.—Paten, electro-silver plated on nickel silver.
No. 6198.—Paten, electro-silver plated on Britannia metal.

Communion Services in Sterling Silver, hall-marked, supplied at a few days' notice.

No. 6193.—Chalice, electro-silver plated on nickel silver, gilt lined, to hold 1 pint.
No. 6194.—Chalice, electro-silver plated on Britannia metal, gilt lined, to hold 1 pint.
No. 6195.—Chalice, Britannia metal.

No. 6205.—Pocket Communion Service; cup and plate, electro-plated on nickel silver, cut glass bottle, in silk and velvet-lined leather case.

No. 6206.—Alms Dish, brass, beaten work centre, engraved with inscription.

No. 6207.—Pocket Communion Service; cup and plate, electro-plated on nickel silver, cut glass bottle, in silk and velvet-lined leather case.

No. 6197.—Chalice, electro-silver plated on nickel silver, gilt lined, to hold 1 pint.
No. 6198.—Chalice, electro-silver plated on Britannia metal, gilt lined, to hold 1 pint.

Monograms and Inscriptions engraved in a superior style.

S. & F. **The above patterns can be made in cheaper qualities when ordered in quantities.** S. & F.

CAUTION. Any person infringing the Copyright of this Book will be prosecuted under the Act.

ELECTRO-SILVER PLATED GOODS.

No. 6208.—Wine Cork, electro-silver plated mounts (Drawn full size.)

No. 6209—Mustard Pot, electro-silver plated on nickel silver, glass lining.

No. 6210.—Wine Strainer, electro-silver plated on nickel silver.

No. 6211.—Wine or Spirit Label, electro-silver plated. (Drawn full size.)

No. 6212.—Fleming's Patent Lock Cork, with key. The advantages of this patent are that it forms a perfectly air-tight cork, and when locked in the bottle it cannot be removed without the key.

No. 6213.—Mustard Pot, electro-silver plated on nickel silver, glass lining.

No. 6215.—Wine Cork, electro-silver plated mounts, and pearl labels, assorted names. (Drawn full size.)

No. 6214.—Sauce Frame, electro-silver plated on nickel silver.

No. 6204A.—Tea Caddy, with lock and key, electro-silver plated on Britannia metal, holding 1 lb.

No. 6206C.—Biscuit Box, handsomely cut crystal glass, mounts and handle electro-silver plated on nickel silver. Height 10 inches.

No. 6215M.—Wine and Biscuit Stand, electro-silver plated on nickel silver, two richly cut and engraved crystal glass decanters, and four wine glasses. Length 19¾ inches.

No. 6205B.—Tea Caddy, with lock and key, electro-silver plated on Britannia metal, holding 1 lb.

No. 6207D.—Biscuit Box, electro-silver plated on Britannia metal.

No. 6208K.—Hot-water Plate, earthenware, Britannia metal mounted.

No. 6209F.—Cream Jug, electro-silver plated on Britannia metal, hand engraved.

No. 6210G.—Soup Bowl, electro-silver plated on nickel silver.

No. 6211H.—Britannia Metal Plate Cover, round, with silver-plated handle.

No. 6212J.—Hot-water Dish, al. Britannia metal.

No. 6213K.—Celery Stand, electro-silver plated on nickel silver, cut glass.

No. 6214N.—Hot-water Dish, earthenware, mounted in Britannia metal.

BRITISH OAK GOODS

with nickel silver mounts, electro
silver plated.

DOMINE DIRICE NOS

BRITISH OAK GOODS

with nickel silver mounts, electro
silver plated.

SILVERSMITHS & ELECTRO PLATERS.

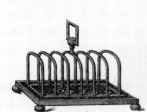

6216 Toast Rack, silver plated on nickel silver.

6217 Sugar Basin, with white china lining.

6218 Ice Pail, with white china lining.

6219 Biscuit Box, with white china lining.

6220 Butter Dish, with white china lining.

6221 Tankard, gilt lined, holding ½ pint or 1 pint.

6222 Breakfast Cruet, with 3 or 4 cut glasses.

TABLE GONGS.
SUITABLE FOR
HALL, DINING ROOM OR CLUB.

6223 Table Gong, nickel plated, polished walnut stand, height 13½ inches.

6224 Table Gong, Burmese metal, polished oak stand, height 11 inches.

6225 Table Bell, nickel plated, polished oak stand.

6226 Table Gong, nickel plated, polished oak stand.

6227 Table Gong, polished brass and polished oak stand, height 10 inches.

6228 Cruet Frame, with 4 or 6 cut glass bottles.

6229 Spirit Barrels on stand, gilt lined buckets.

6230 Cruet Frame, with 4 or 6 cut glass bottles.

6231 Table Gong, nickel plated, polished oak stand, height 12 inches.

6232 Salad Bowl, with white china lining and pair of servers.

6233 Salad Bowl, with white china lining and pair of servers.

6234 Salad Bowl, with white china lining and pair of servers.

6235 Salad Bowl, with white china lining and pair of servers.

6236 Lock-up Spirit Stand, polished oak, with nickel plated mounts and cut glass bottles.

6237 The "Sesame" Lock-up Spirit Stand, polished oak, with nickel plated mounts and cut glass bottles.
To unlock the Spirit Stand, simply turn the key, when the flaps that secure the stoppers of the bottles will be instantly released.
To re-lock, press down the plated flaps.

6240 Lock-up Spirit Stand, polished oak, silver plated on nickel silver mounts, with cut glass bottles.
To unlock, simply turn the key, when the cross bar and side handles will drop to lower part of frame, thus releasing the bottles.

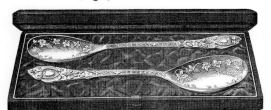

No. 6245   Fruit Spoons, silver plated on nickel silver, gilt bowls

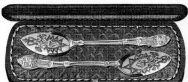

No. 6246   Jam Spoons, silver plated on nickel silver

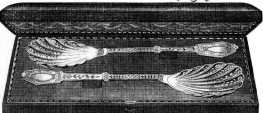

No. 6247   Fruit Spoons, silver plated on nickel silver, gilt bowls

No. 6248   Fruit Spoons, with gilt bowls, and Grape Scissors, silver plated on
nickel silver

No. 6249   Fruit Spoons with gilt bowls, and Grape Scissors, silver plated
on nickel silver, carved ivory mounts

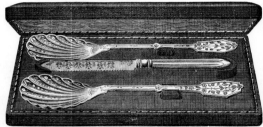

No. 6250   Fruit Spoons with gilt bowls, Lemon Saw with ivory handle,
silver plated on nickel silver

No. 10546   Nutcrackers, electro silver plated, carved ivory handles
No. 10547   Nutcrackers, as No. 10546, two pairs, in silk-lined leather-covered case
(For prices of above see price list of page 566).

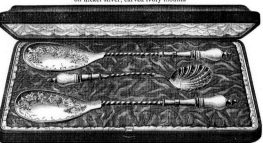

No. 6251   Fruit Spoons and Sugar Sifters, plated on nickel silver, gilt
bowls, ivory mounted

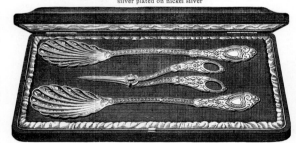

No. 6252   Fruit Spoons and Grape Scissors, silver plated on nickel silver,
gilt bowls to spoons

No. 10548   Improved Nutcrackers, electro silver plated, hand engraved
No. 10549   Nutcrackers, as No. 10548, two pairs, in silk-lined leather-covered case
For prices of above see price list of page 566).

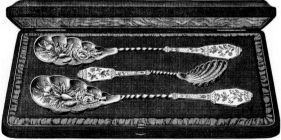

No. 6253   Fruit Spoons and Sugar Sifters, silver plated on nickel silver,
gilt-lined bowls

No. 6254   Fruit Spoons, silver plated on nickel silver, gilt bowls

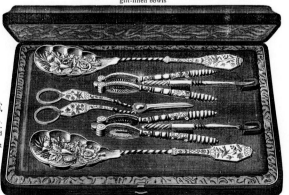

No. 6255   Fruit Spoons, Nutcrackers, Grape Scissors, Nutpeelers, silver plated,
gilt-lined bowls to spoons

S&F.
London.

SILVERSMITHS
AND
ELECTRO-PLATERS.

No. 6256   Fruit Spoons, Grape Scissors, Nutcrackers, and pearl-handled Nutpeelers, electro-silver plated, gilt-lined bowls to spoons

ENTERED AT STATIONERS' HALL.

ELECTRO PLATERS.
TRADE MARK.

DOMINE DIRICE NOS

COMBINATION CASES,
SUITABLE FOR PRESENTATION.

SILVERSMITHS.
TRADE MARK.

No. 6257   Dessert Knives and Forks, silver plated blades, ivory handles,
12 pairs, in leather-covered case

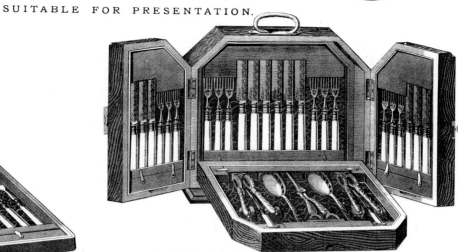

No. 6258 Gilt-mounted and inlaid polished Walnutwood Case, silk and velvet lined, with lock and
key, containing 12 pairs silver plated dessert knives and forks, with ivory handles ; 2 nutpeelers ;
2 fruit spoons with gilt bowls, silver plated on nickel-silver ; 1 grape scissor and 2 nutcrackers,
silver plated
No. 6259 As No. 6258, but with best pearl-handled dessert knives and forks

S&F.
London.

No. 6260 Polished Walnutwood Case, velvet lined, containing 6 pairs dessert knives and
forks, and 6 pairs fish knives and forks, silver plated on nickel-silver, ivory handles

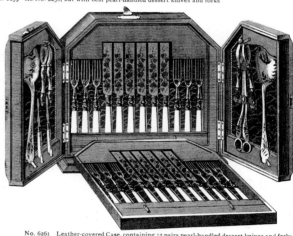

No. 6261 Leather-covered Case, containing 12 pairs pearl-handled dessert knives and forks ;
2 nutpeelers ; 2 fruit spoons, with gilt bowls ; 1 grape scissor and 2 nutcrackers, silver
plated

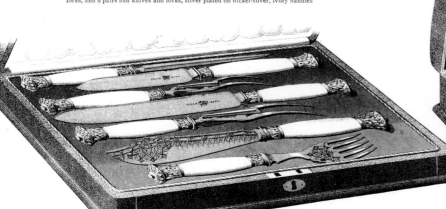

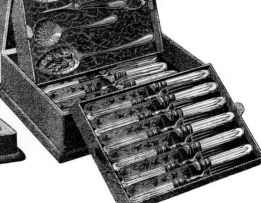

No. 6262 Morocco Leather-covered Case, silk and velvet lined, containing 1 pair best shear steel game carvers ; 1 pair
meat carvers, 1 steel, and 1 pair fish carvers, with nickel silver blades, heavily silver plated, all with best ivory handles,
and sterling silver caps and ferrules. Hall marked
No. 6263 As No. 6262, but with best stag handles

No. 6264 Morocco Leather-covered Case, silk lined, containing 12
pairs silver plated dessert knives and forks, with ivory handles ;
2 fruit spoons with gilt bowls ; 1 sugar sifter and 1 grape scissor,
silver plated

Initials, Crests, Monograms, Masonic and other devices engraved in a superior style. Replating and Repairing equal to new, at moderate charges.

CHILDREN'S CASES, CONTAINING KNIVES, FORKS, SPOONS, &c., AND CASES OF NUTCRACKERS.

No. 6268 Child's Knife, Fork and Spoon, electro-silver plated on nickel-silver, knife with pearl handle, in silk-lined leather case

No. 6269 Child's Knife, Fork and Spoon, electro-silver plated, knife with bone handle, in velvet-lined case

No. 6270 Child's Knife, Fork and Spoon, electro-silver plated on nickel silver, knife with ivory handle, in silk and velvet-lined leather case

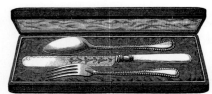

No. 6273 Child's Knife, Fork and Spoon, electro-silver plated, knife with carved bone handle, in silk-lined leather case

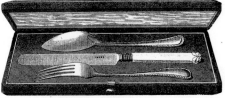

No. 6275 Child's Knife, Fork and Spoon, electro-silver plated on nickel-silver, knife with ivory handle, in silk-lined leather case

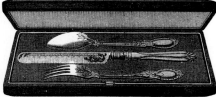

No. 6276 Child's Knife, Fork and Spoon, electro-silver plated on nickel-silver, knife with ivory handle, in silk-lined leather case

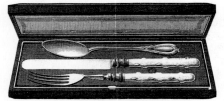

No. 6271 Child's Knife, Fork, Spoon and Napkin Ring, electro-silver plated on nickel-silver, knife with pearl handle, in silk and velvet-lined leather case

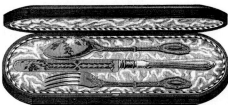

No. 6280 Nutcrackers and ivory handled Nut Peelers, electro-silver plated, in silk-lined leather case

S&F. London.

No. 6274 Child's Knife, Fork and Spoon, electro-silver plated on nickel-silver, knife with pearl handle, in silk-lined leather case

No. 6278 Child's Knife, Fork, Spoon and Napkin Ring, silver plated on nickel-silver, knife and fork with ivory handle, in silk-lined leather case

No. 6272 Children's School Sets, of Fork, Spoon, Tea Spoon and Napkin Ring, electro-silver plated on nickel-silver, and steel knife with ivory handle, in silk-lined leather case

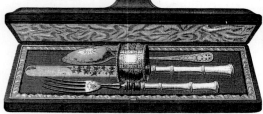

No. 6279 Nutcrackers, electro-silver plated, in silk-lined leather case

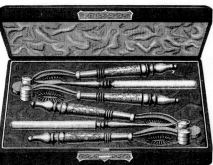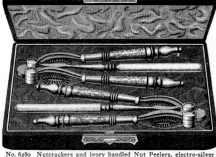

No. 6277 Presentation Set of Knife, Fork, Spoon and gilt-lined Cup, electro-silver plated on nickel-silver, knife with ivory handle, in silk-lined leather case

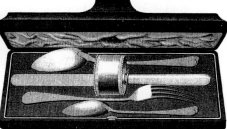

No. 6281 Nutcrackers, electro-silver plated, ebony handles, in silk-lined case

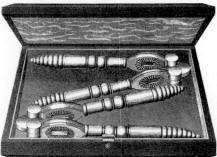

No. 6283 Nutcrackers and ivory handled Nut Peelers, electro-silver plated, in silk-lined leather case

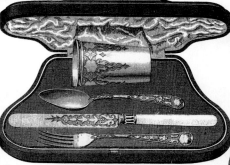

No. 6284 Nutcrackers and pearl handled Nut Peelers, electro-silver plated, in silk-lined leather case

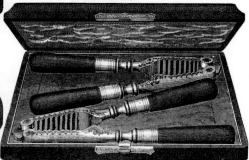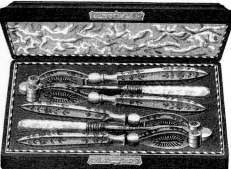

No. 6282 Nutcrackers, electro-silver plated, pearl handled Nut Peelers, in silk-lined leather case

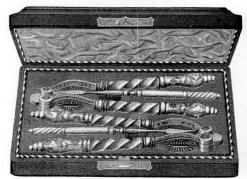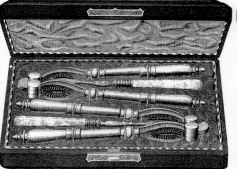

Initials, Crests, Monograms, Masonic and other devices engraved in a superior style. Replating and Repairing equal to new, at moderate charges.

Dawson & Brailsford lith Sheffield

ENTERED AT STATIONERS' HALL.

DOMINE DIRICE NOS

SALT CELLARS AND NAPKIN RINGS,
IN SILK AND VELVET-LINED LEATHER CASES.

S&F.
London.

No. 6285 Napkin Rings, silver plated on nickel silver, each ring engraved with a different bird, animal, or fish, in silk-lined leather case

No. 6286 Napkin Rings, silver plated on nickel silver, each ring engraved with a different flower, in silk-lined leather case

No. 6287 Napkin Rings, silver plated on nickel silver, engine-turned, in velvet-lined case

No. 6288 Napkin Rings, silver plated on nickel silver, hand engraved, in silk-lined fancy leather case

No. 6289 Napkin Rings, silver plated on nickel silver, in velvet-lined leather case

No. 6290 Salt Cellars and Spoons, silver plated on nickel silver, gilt lined, in silk-lined leather case

No. 6291 Salt Cellars and Spoons, silver plated on nickel silver, gilt lined, in silk-lined leather case

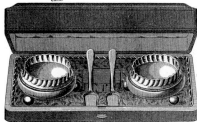

No. 6292 Salt Cellars and Spoons, silver plated on nickel silver, gilt lined, in silk-lined leather case

No. 6293 Salt Cellars and Spoons, silver plated on nickel silver, gilt lined, in velvet-lined leather case

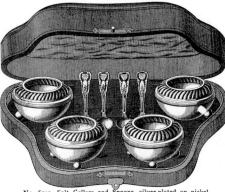

No. 6295 Salt Cellars and Spoons, silver plated on nickel silver, gilt lined, in velvet-lined leather case

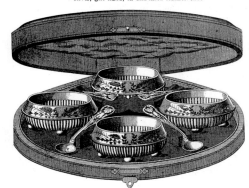

No. 6296 Salt Cellars and Spoons, silver plated on nickel silver, in velvet-lined case

No. 6297 Salt Cellars and Spoons, silver plated on nickel silver, gilt lined, in velvet-lined leather case

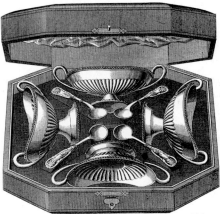

No. 6298 Salt Cellars and Spoons, silver plated on nickel silver, gilt lined, in velvet-lined leather case

No. 6298½ Salt Cellars and Spoons, silver plated on nickel silver, gilt lined, in velvet-lined leather case

Initials, Crests, Monograms, Masonic and other devices engraved in a superior style. Replating and Repairing equal to new, at moderate charges.

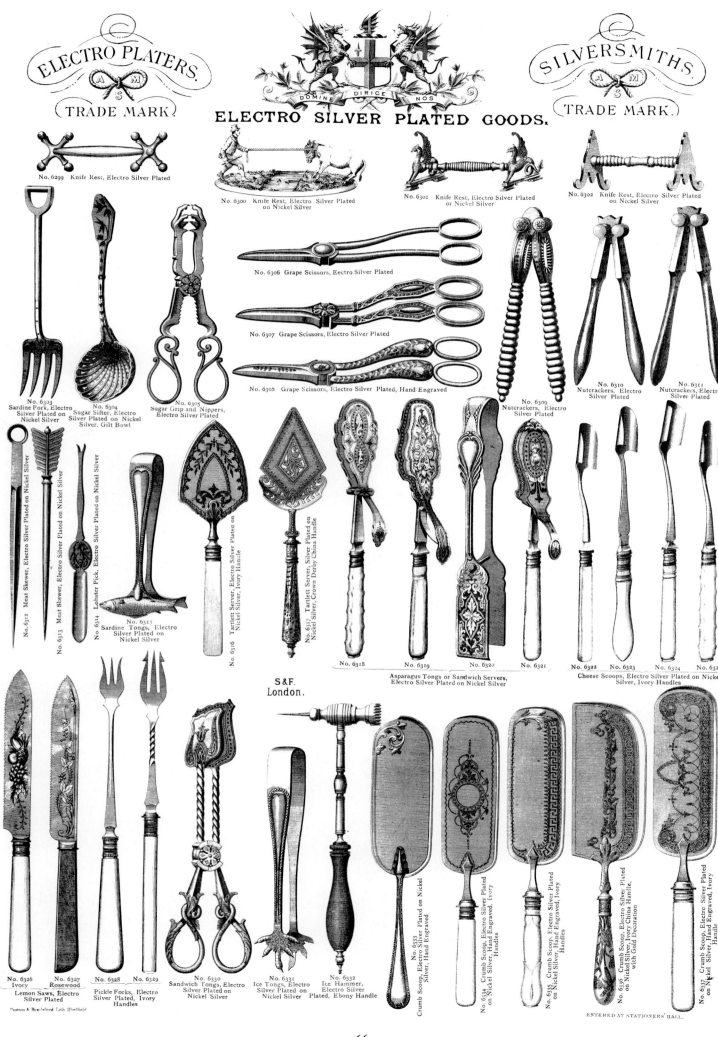

ELECTRO SILVER PLATED GOODS.

DOMINE DIRICE NOS

No. 6299 Knife Rest, Electro Silver Plated

No. 6300 Knife Rest, Electro Silver Plated on Nickel Silver

No. 6301 Knife Rest, Electro Silver Plated or Nickel Silver

No. 6302 Knife Rest, Electro Silver Plated on Nickel Silver

No. 6306 Grape Scissors, Eectro Silver Plated

No. 6307 Grape Scissors, Electro Silver Plated

No. 6308 Grape Scissors, Electro Silver Plated, Hand Engraved

No. 6309 Nutcrackers, Electro Silver Plated

No. 6310 Nutcrackers, Electro Silver Plated

No. 6311 Nutcrackers, Electro Silver Plated

No. 6303 Sardine Fork, Electro Silver Plated on Nickel Silver

No. 6304 Sugar Sifter, Electro Silver Plated on Nickel Silver, Gilt Bowl

No. 6305 Sugar Grip and Nippers, Electro Silver Plated

No. 6312 Meat Skewer, Electro Silver Plated on Nickel Silver

No. 6313 Meat Skewer, Electro Silver Plated on Nickel Silver

No. 6314 Lobster Pick, Electro Silver Plated on Nickel Silver

No. 6315 Sardine Tongs, Electro Silver Plated on Nickel Silver

No. 6316 Tartlett Server, Electro Silver Plated on Nickel Silver, Ivory Hanule

No. 6317 Tartlett Server, Silver Plated on Nickel Silver, Crown Derby China Handle

No. 6318   No. 6319   No. 6320   No. 6321

Asparagus Tongs or Sandwich Servers, Electro Silver Plated on Nickel Silver

No. 6322   No. 6323   No. 6324   No. 6325

Cheese Scoops, Electro Silver Plated on Nickel Silver, Ivory Handles

S&F. London.

No. 6326 Ivory   No. 6327 Rosewood

Lemon Saws, Electro Silver Plated

No. 6328   No. 6329

Pickle Forks, Electro Silver Plated, Ivory Handles

No. 6330 Sandwich Tongs, Electro Silver Plated on Nickel Silver

No. 6331 Ice Tongs, Electro Silver Plated on Nickel Silver

No. 6332 Ice Hammer, Electro Silver Plated, Ebony Handle

No. 6333 Crumb Scoop, Electro Silver Plated on Nickel Silver, Hand Engraved

No. 6334 Crumb Scoop, Electro Silver Plated on Nickel Silver, Hand Engraved, Ivory Handles

No. 6335 Crumb Scoop, Electro Silver Plated on Nickel Silver, Hand Engraved, Ivory Handles

No. 6336 Crumb Scoop, Electro Silver Plated on Nickel Silver, Ivory China Handle, with Gold Decoration

No. 6337 Crumb Scoop, Electro Silver Plated on Nickel Silver, Hand Engraved, Ivory Handle

Dawson & Brailsford Lith Sheffield

ENTERED AT STATIONERS' HALL.

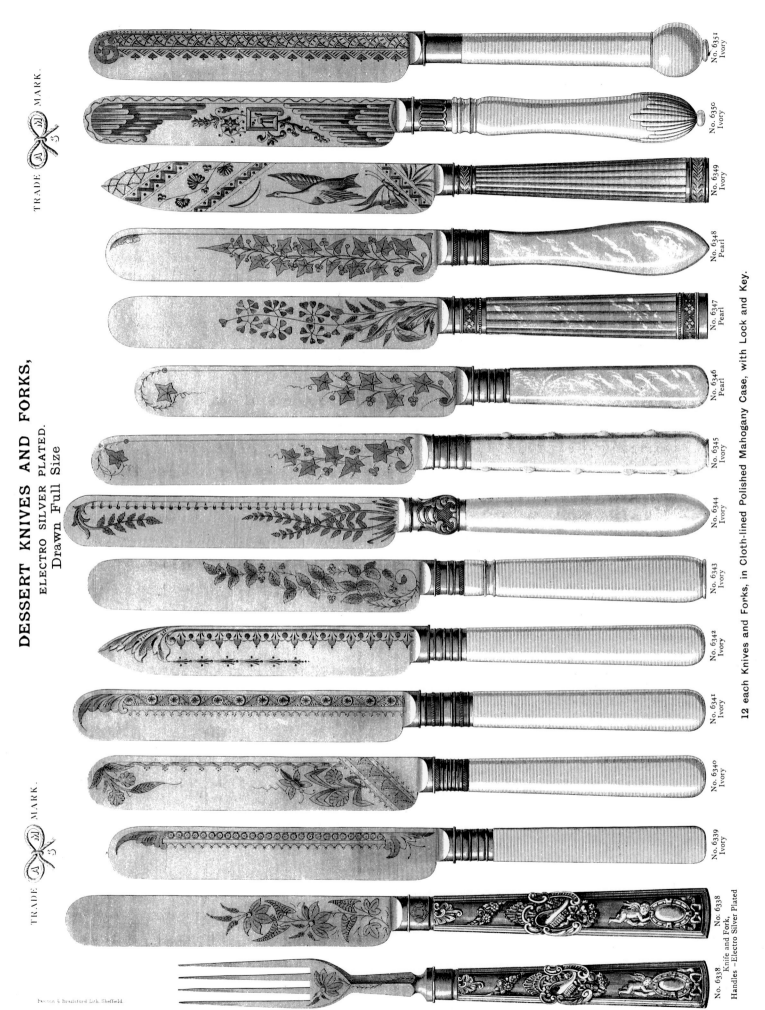

DESSERT KNIVES AND FORKS,
ELECTRO SILVER PLATED.
Drawn Full Size

No. 6351 Ivory
No. 6350 Ivory
No. 6349 Ivory
No. 6348 Pearl
No. 6347 Pearl
No. 6346 Pearl
No. 6345 Ivory
No. 6344 Ivory
No. 6343 Ivory
No. 6342 Ivory
No. 6341 Ivory
No. 6340 Ivory
No. 6339 Ivory
No. 6338 Knife and Fork, Handles—Electro Silver Plated

12 each Knives and Forks, in Cloth-lined Polished Mahogany Case, with Lock and Key.

Fawson & Brailsford Lith, Sheffield

Initials, Crests, Monograms, Masonic and other devices engraved in a superior style.   Replating and Repairing equal to new, at moderate charges.

CAUTION. Any person infringing the Copyright of this Book, will be prosecuted under the Act.

67

DOMINE DIRICE NOS

FISH CARVERS.
Drawn one-third size.

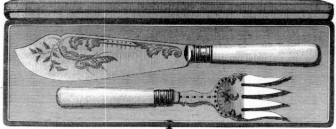

No. 6352   Fish Carvers, silver plated on steel, hard bone handles, in velvet-lined case

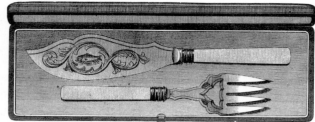

No. 6353   Fish Carvers, silver plated on nickel-silver, hand engraved, ivory handles, in
velvet-lined leather case

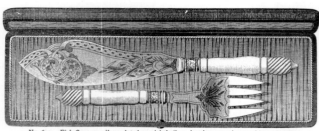

No. 6354   Fish Carvers, silver plated on nickel-silver, hand engraved, carved ivory handles,
in silk-lined leather case

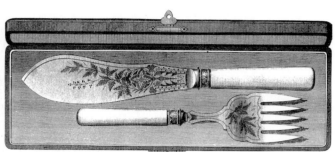

No. 6355   Fish Carvers, silver plated on nickel-silver, hand engraved, ivory handles, in
velvet-lined case

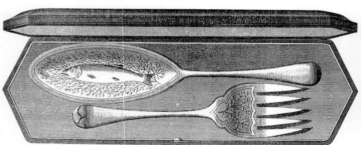

No. 6356   Fish Carvers, silver plated on nickel-silver, richly hand engraved, in velvet-lined
leather case

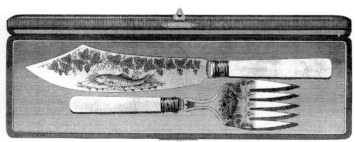

No. 6357   Fish Carvers, silver plated on nickel-silver, richly hand engraved, ivory handles,
in velvet-lined leather case

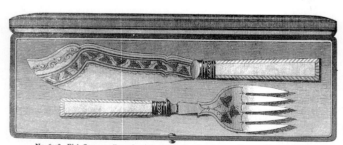

No. 6358   Fish Carvers, silver plated on nickel-silver, hand engraved, carved ivory handles,
in velvet-lined case

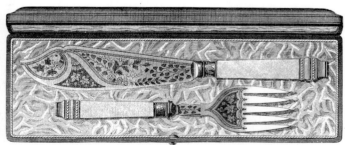

No. 6359   Fish Carvers, silver plated on nickel-silver, richly hand engraved, carved ivory
handles, in silk-lined leather case

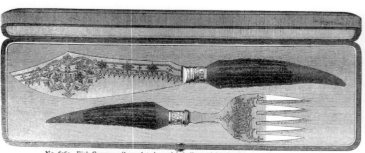

No. 6360   Fish Carvers, silver plated on nickel-silver. richly hand engraved, best German
stag horn handles, in velvet-lined case

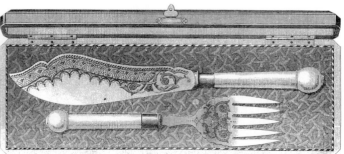

No. 6361   Fish Carvers, silver plated on nickel-silver, richly hand engraved, sterling silver
ferrules, carved ivory handles, in silk-lined polished oak case

Initials. Crests. Monograms, Masonic and other devices engraved in a superior style. Replating and Repairing equal to new, at moderate charges

FISH KNIVES AND FORKS,

ELECTRO SILVER PLATED ON NICKEL SILVER.

Drawn full size

No. 6372 Ivory

No. 6371 Ivory

No. 6370 Ivory

No. 6369 Ivory

No. 6368 Ivory

12 each Knives and Forks, in Cloth-lined Polished Mahogany Case, with Lock and Key.

No. 6367 Pearl

No. 6366 Ivory

No. 6365 Ivory

No. 6364 Ivory

No. 6363 Electro Silver Plated

No. 6362 Knife and Fork, Handles—Electro Silver Plated

Initials, Crests, Monograms, Masonic and other devices engraved in a superior style. Replating and Repairing equal to new, at moderate charges

CUTLERY MANUFACTURERS.
CARVERS,
IN SILK AND VELVET-LINED LEATHER CASES.
Drawn Quarter Size

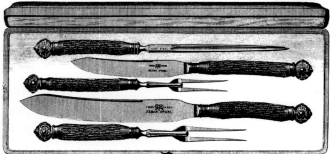

No. 6373   Carvers and Steel, in case, stag handles, sterling silver caps and ferrules

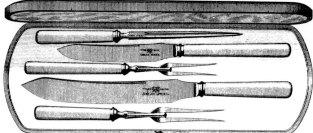

No. 6374   Carvers and Steel, in case, ivory handles

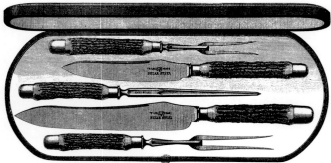

No. 6375   Carvers and Steel, in case, best stag handles, sterling silver caps and ferrules

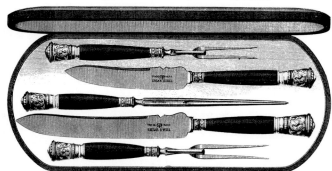

No. 6376   Carvers and Steel, in case, polished black horn, and ivory handles, silver plated caps and ferrules

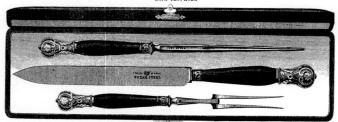

No. 6377   Carvers and Steel, in case, light horn handles, silver plated caps and ferrules

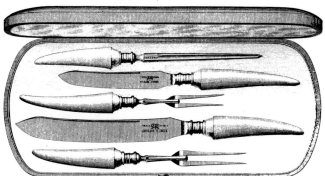

No. 6378   Carvers and Steel, in case, ivory handles, sterling silver ferrules

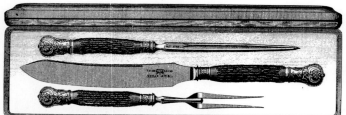

No. 6379   Carvers and Steel, in case, stag handles, electro silver plated caps and ferrules

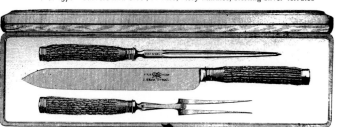

No. 6380   Carvers and Steel, in case, stag handles, electro silver plated caps and ferrules

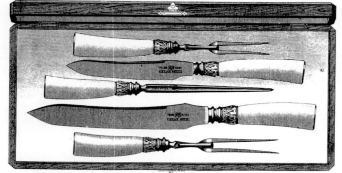

No. 6381   Carvers and Steel, best carved ivory handles, sterling silver Ferrules, in polished oak case

ENTERED AT STATIONERS' HALL.

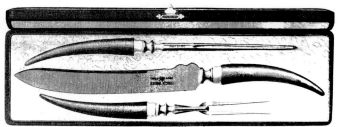

No. 6382   Carvers and Steel, in case, polished horn and ivory handles

Initials, Crests, Monograms, Masonic and other devices engraved in a superior style.   Replating and Repairing equal to new, at moderate charges.

DOMINE DIRICE NOS

SPOONS AND FORKS,
ELECTRO SILVER PLATED ON BEST NICKEL SILVER.

No. 6383   Fiddle Pattern.   Dessert Fork

No. 6384   Old English Pattern.   Dessert Spoon

No. 6385   Engraved Old English Pattern.   Dessert Fork

No. 6386   Rat Tail Pattern.   Dessert Spoon

No. 6387   Thread and Shell Pattern.   Dessert Fork

No. 6388   Beaded Pattern.   Table Spoon

No. 6389   King's Pattern.   Table Fork

No. 6389   King's Pattern.   Tea Spoon

Drawn full size.

S&F.
London.

Initials, Crests, Monograms, Masonic and other devices engraved in a superior style.   Replating and
Repairing, equal to new, at moderate charges.

S&F.
London.

SILVERSMITHS.

TRADE MARK.

DOMINE DIRICE NOS

CUTLERY MANUFACTURERS.

ELECTRO PLATERS.

TRADE MARK.

TRADE MARK
SHEAR STEEL

No. 6393 D.   Dessert Knife. Ivory Handle

Drawn full size.

No. 6390
Silver Plated
on
Nickel-Silver

No. 6391
Ivory

No. 6392
Ivory

No. 6393
Ivory

No. 6394
Ivory

No. 6395
Hotel Pattern,
Ivory

No. 6396
Silver Ferrule,
Ivory

No. 6397
Ivory

No. 6398
Carved Ivory

ENTERED AT STATIONERS' HALL.

IVORY, AND SILVER PLATED HANDLED TABLE KNIVES.

OAK CANTEENS.

CONTENTS OF No. 6399.
— AS SHEWN IN DRAWING. —

12 Ivory Handled Table Knives
12 Ivory Handled Dessert Knives
1 pr. Ivory Handled Meat Carvers
1 pr. Ivory Handled Game Carvers
1 Steel
12 Electro Silver Plated Table Forks
6 Electro Silver Pltd. Table Spoons
12 Electro Slvr. Pltd. Dessert Spoons
12 Electro Slvr. Pltd. Dessert Forks
12 Electro Silver Plated Tea Spoons
4 Electro Silver Plated Salt Spoons
1 Electro Slvr. Pltd. Mustard Spoon
6 Electro Silver Pltd. Egg Spoons
1 Electro Silver Pltd. Sugar Tongs
1 Electro Silver Pltd. Soup Ladle
2 Electro Silver Pltd. Sauce Ladles
1 Electro Silver Pltd. Gravy Spoon
2 prs. Electro Slvr. Pltd. Knife Rests
1 pairs Electro Silver Plated Fish
   Carvers, with Carved Ivory
   Handles

OAK CANTEEN.

CONTENTS OF No. 6400.

18 Ivory Handled Table Knives
18 Ivory Handled Dessert Knives
2 pr. Ivory Handled Meat Carvers
2 pr. Ivory Handled Game Carvers
2 Steels
18 Electro Silver Plated Table Forks
8 Electro Slvr. Pltd. Table Spoons
18 Electro Slvr. Pltd. Dessert Spoons
18 Electro Slvr. Pltd. Dessert Forks
18 Electro Silver Plated Tea Spoons
6 Electro Silver Plated Salt Spoons
2 Electro Silv. Pltd. Mustard Spoons
12 Electro Slvr. Pltd. Egg Spoons
1 Electro Silver Pltd. Sugar Tongs
1 Electro Silver Pltd. Soup Ladle
2 Electro Silver Pltd. Sauce Ladles
2 Electro Slvr. Pltd. Gravy Spoons
4 prs. Electro Slvr. Pltd. Knife Rests
1 prs. Electro Silver Plated Fish
   Carvers, with Ivory Handles

WALNUT CABINET.

CONTENTS OF No. 6403. (3 DRAWERS)

12 Ivory Handled Table Knives
12 Ivory Handled Dessert Knives
1 pr. Ivory Handled Meat Carvers
1 pr. Ivory Handled Game Carvers
1 Steel.
12 Electro Slvr. Pltd. Table Forks
12 Electro Slvr. Pltd. Dessert Forks
6 Electro Slvr. Pltd. Table Spoons
12 Electro Slvr. Pltd. Dessert Spoons
12 Electro Silver Plated Tea Spoons
6 Electro Silver Plated Egg Spoons
4 Electro Silver Plated Salt Spoons
2 Electro Slvr. Pltd. Mustard Spoons
1 Electro Silver Pltd. Sugar Tongs
2 Electro Silver Pltd. Sauce Ladles
1 Electro Silver Pltd. Soup Ladle
1 Electro Slvr. Pltd. Gravy Spoon
1 pair Electro Silver Plated Fish
   Carvers, Ivory Handles
2 Electro Silver Pltd. Pickle Forks
12 Electro Slvr. Pltd. Napkin Rings
2 prs. Electro Slvr. Pltd. Knife Rests
2 Electro Silver Plated Nutcrackers
2 Electro Silver Plated Nutpicks

These Canteens and Cabinets can be fitted with sterling silver Forks, Spoons, Fish Knives & Forks, etc.

For patterns, see pages 322 & 329

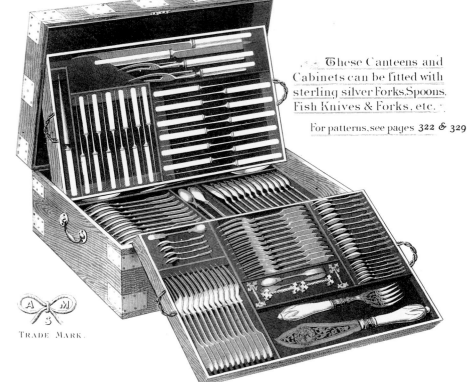

TRADE MARK.

No. 6399 OAK CANTEEN, IRON BOUND, BRASS HANDLES, LOCK AND KEY, LINED WITH BLUE CLOTH.

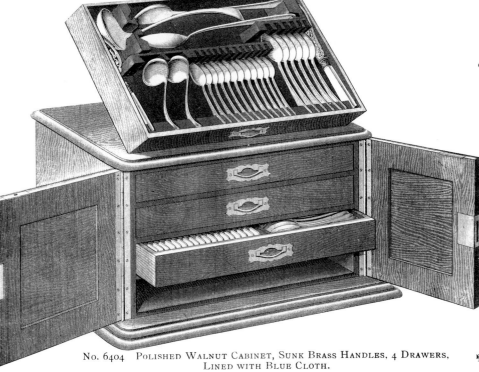

No. 6404 POLISHED WALNUT CABINET, SUNK BRASS HANDLES, 4 DRAWERS, LINED WITH BLUE CLOTH.

OAK CANTEENS.

CONTENTS OF No. 6401.

24 Ivory Handled Table Forks
24 Ivory Handled Dessert Knives
2 pair Ivory Handled Meat Carvers
2 pair Ivory Handled Game Carvers
2 Steels
24 Electro Silver Plated Table Forks
12 Electro Silver Pltd. Table Spoons
24 Electro Slvr. Pltd. Dessert Spoons
24 Electro Slvr. Pltd. Dessert Forks
24 Electro Silver Plated Tea Spoons
8 Electro Silver Plated Salt Spoons
2 Electro Slvr. Pltd. Mustard Spoons
12 Electro Silver Plated Egg Spoons
2 pr. Electro Slvr. Pltd. Sugar Tongs
2 Electro Silver Pltd. Soup Ladles
4 Electro Silver Pltd. Sauce Ladles
4 Electro Silver Pltd. Gravy Spoons
4 prs. Electro Slvr. Pltd. Knife Rests
1 prs. Electro Slvr. Pltd. Fish Carvers

OAK CANTEEN.

CONTENTS OF No. 6402.

36 Ivory Handled Table Knives
36 Ivory Handled Dessert Knives
3 pairs Ivory Handled Meat Carvers
2 pairs Ivory Handled Game Carvers
3 Steels.
36 Electro Silver Plated Table Forks
18 Electro Silver Pltd. Table Spoons
36 Electro Sivr. Pltd. Dessert Spoons
36 Electro Slvr. Pltd. Dessert Forks
36 Electro Silver Plated Tea Spoons
12 Electro Silver Plated Salt Spoons
3 Electro Slvr. Pltd. Mustard Spoons
18 Electro Silver Plated Egg Spoons
2 prs. Electro Slvr. Pltd. Sugar Tongs
2 Electro Silver Pltd. Soup Ladles
6 Electro Silver Pltd. Sauce Ladles
6 Electro Silver Pltd. Gravy Spoons
5 prs. Electro Slvr. Pltd. Knife Rests
1 prs. Electro Slvr. Pltd. Fish Carvers

WALNUT CABINET.

CONTENTS OF No. 6404, (4 DRAWERS)
AS SHEWN IN DRAWING.

12 Ivory Handled Table Knives
12 Ivory Handled Dessert Knives
1 pr. Ivory Handled Meat Carvers
1 pr. Ivory Handled Game Carvers
1 Steel
12 Electro Slvr. Pltd. Table Forks
12 Electro Slvr. Pltd. Dessert Forks
6 Electro Slvr. Pltd. Table Spoons
12 Electro Slvr. Pltd. Dessert Spoons
12 Electro Silver Plated Tea Spoons
4 Electro Silver Plated Salt Spoons
6 Electro Silver Plated Egg Spoons
2 Electro Slvr. Pltd. Mustard Spoons
1 Electro Slvr. Pltd. Sugar Tongs
2 Electro Silver Pltd. Sauce Ladles
1 Electro Slvr. Pltd. Soup Ladle
2 Electro Slvr. Pltd. Gravy Spoons
12 pairs Electro Silver Plated Fish
   Knives and Forks, Ivory
   Handles
1 pair Electro Silver Plated Fish
   Carvers, Ivory Handles
12 prs. Electro Silver Plated Dessert
   Knives and Forks, Ivory
   Handles
2 Electro Silver Plated Pickle Forks
   Ivory Handles
12 Electro Slvr. Pltd. Napkin Rings
2 prs. Electro Slvr. Pltd. Knife Rests
2 prs. Electro Slvr. Pltd. Nutcrackers
2 Electro Silver Plated Nutpicks

S. & F.
London.   Initials, Crests, Monograms, Masonic and other devices engraved in a superior style.   Replating and Repairing, equal to new, at moderate charges.

Pawson & Brailsford Lith. Sheffield

CUTLERY MANUFACTURERS.

No. 6413
Black Horn Handle
Drawn full size.

Handles — Solid Horn								
No. 6405	No. 6406 Bone	No. 6407 Bone	No. 6408 Bone	No. 6409 Bone	No. 6410 Bone	No. 6411 Black Horn	No. 6412 Black Horn	No. 6413 Black Horn

S&F.

Pawson & Brailsford, Lith. Sheffield.

S&F.

CUTLERY MANUFACTURERS.

Drawn full size.

TRADE MARK
SHEAR STEEL

TRADE MARK
SHEAR STEEL

TRADE MARK
SHEAR STEEL

TRADE MARK
SHEAR STEEL

TRADE MARK
SHEAR STEEL

TRADE MARK
SHEAR STEEL

TRADE MARK
SHEAR STEEL

TRADE MARK
SHEAR STEEL

| Handles— | No. 6414 Bone | No. 6415 Bone | No. 6416 Bone | No. 6417 Horn | No. 6418 Horn | No. 6419 Horn | No. 6420 Solid Black Horn | No. 6421 Stag Horn |

S&F.

S&F.

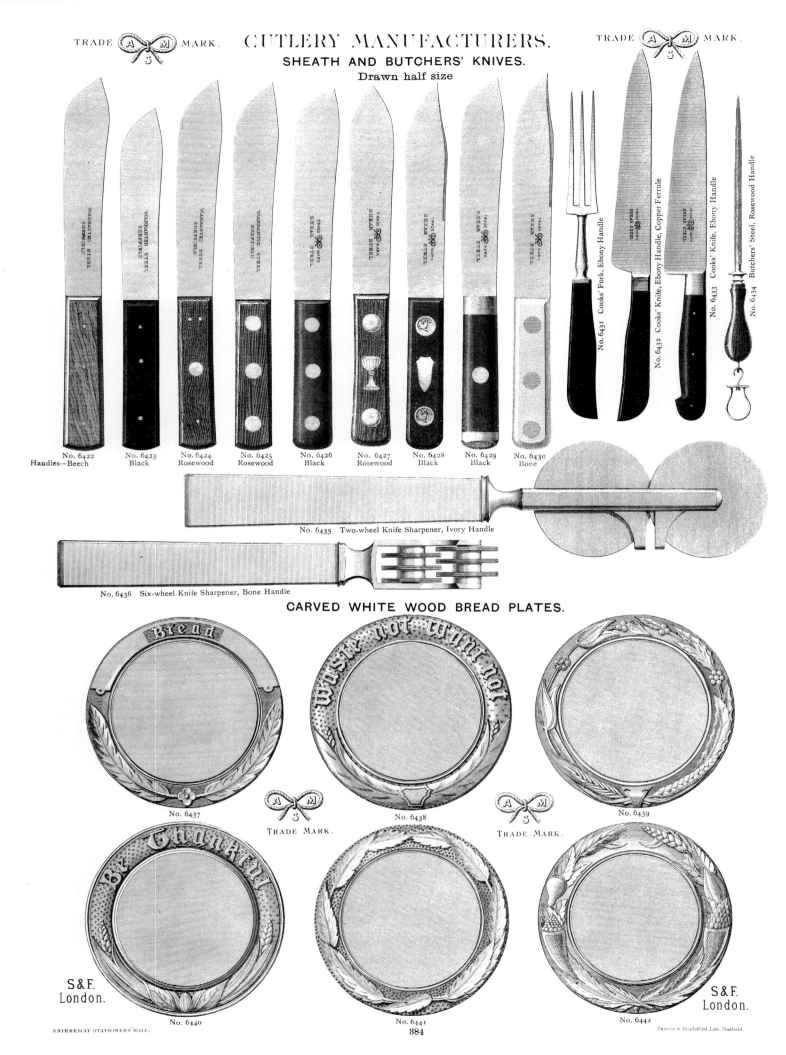

No. 6422
Handles—Beech

No. 6423
Black

No. 6424
Rosewood

No. 6425
Rosewood

No. 6426
Black

No. 6427
Rosewood

No. 6428
Black

No. 6429
Black

No. 6430
Bone

No. 6431 Cooks' Fork, Ebony Handle

No. 6432 Cooks' Knife, Ebony Handle, Copper Ferrule

No. 6433 Cooks' Knife, Ebony Handle

No. 6434 Butchers' Steel, Rosewood Handle

No. 6435 Two-wheel Knife Sharpener, Ivory Handle

No. 6436 Six-wheel Knife Sharpener, Bone Handle

CARVED WHITE WOOD BREAD PLATES.

No. 6437

TRADE MARK.

No. 6438

TRADE MARK.

No. 6439

S&F.
London.

No. 6440

No. 6441

No. 6442

S&F.
London.

Drawn full size.

No. 6443
Handles—Ivory

Pawson & Brailsford Lith. Sheffield.

No. 6444
Carved Ivory
Sterling Silver Ferrule

No. 6445
Horn and Ivory

No. 6446
Carved Wood

No. 6447
Carved Wood

No. 6448
Carved Wood
ENTERED AT STATIONERS' HALL.

CUTLERY MANUFACTURERS.

Drawn full size

TRADE MARK.

TRADE MARK.

No. 6450 Ivory

No. 6452 Smokers' Knife, Pearl

No. 6449 Pearl

No. 6451 Ivory

No. 6466 Nickel Silver

No. 6465 Ivory

No. 6464 Buffalo Horn

No. 6463 Pearl

No. 6462 Stag

No. 6461 Ivory

No. 6460 Tortoiseshell

No. 6459 Ivory

No. 6458 Stag

No. 6457 Ivory

No. 6456 Ivory

No. 6455 Stag

No. 6454 Ivory

No. 6453 Handles—Tortoiseshell

No. 6467 Hunting Knife, very superior quality, with 7½-inch blade and 4-inch horn handle, diamond cut. This Knife is so constructed that the blade can be folded into the handle, where it is locked by a spring, leaving exposed 4 inches of the blade, which is protected by a best solid leather sheath.

Drawn full size.

No. 6474 Stag

ENTERED AT STATIONERS' HALL.

S. & F.

No. 6473 Diamond-cut Horn

No. 6472 Stag

No. 6471 Ivory

No. 6470 Diamond-cut Horn

No. 6469 Ivory

No. 6468 Handles—Stag

S. & F.

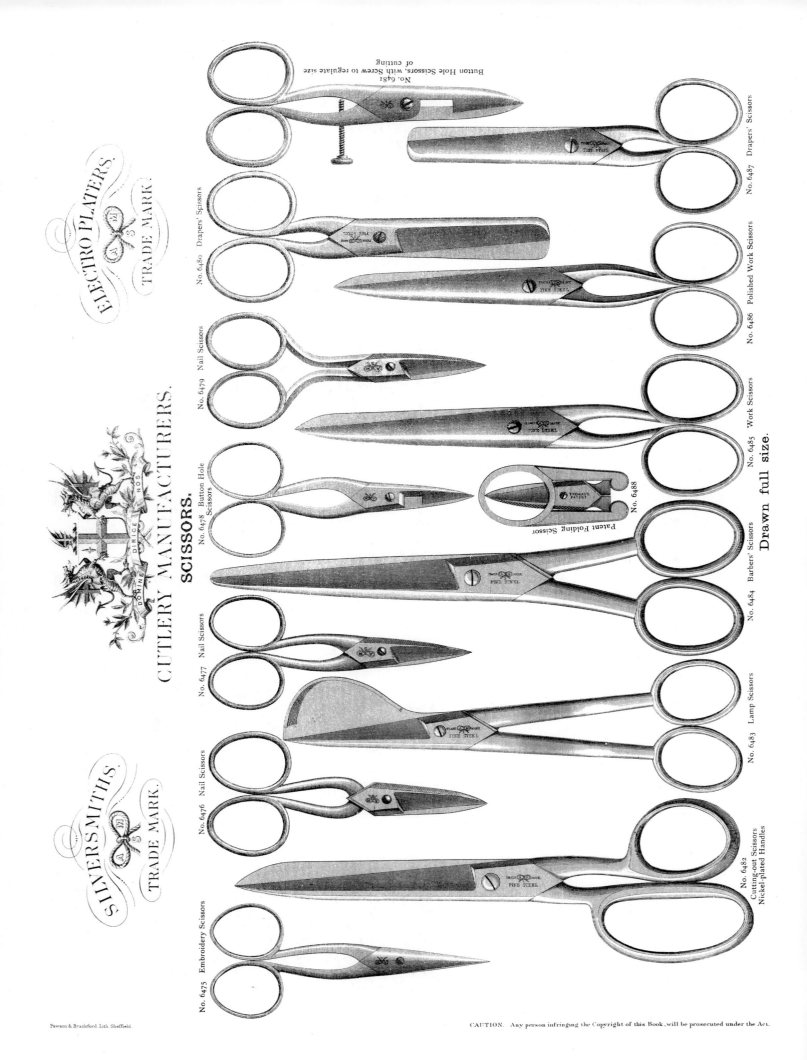

ELECTRO PLATERS. TRADE MARK.

SILVERSMITHS. TRADE MARK.

CUTLERY MANUFACTURERS.

SCISSORS.

No. 6481 Button Hole Scissors, with Screw to regulate size of cutting

No. 6487 Drapers' Scissors

No. 6480 Drapers' Scissors

No. 6486 Polished Work Scissors

No. 6479 Nail Scissors

No. 6485 Work Scissors

No. 6478 Button Hole Scissors

No. 6488 Patent Folding Scissor

No. 6484 Barbers' Scissors

No. 6477 Nail Scissors

No. 6483 Lamp Scissors

No. 6476 Nail Scissors

No. 6482 Cutting-out Scissors Nickel-plated Handles

No. 6475 Embroidery Scissors

Drawn full size.

MARBLE CLOCKS.

REAL AND IMITATION GILT CLOCKS,

PLAIN, OR ORNAMENTED WITH FINE PAINTINGS ON PORCELAIN.

HALL AND CHIMING CLOCKS,

CARRIAGE CLOCKS, REAL AND IMITATION BRONZE CLOCKS,

NICKEL, BRASS, AND CARVED WOOD CLOCKS,

CUCKOO AND SKELETON CLOCKS,

REAL AND IMITATION BRONZES,

REAL BRASS OR ORMOLU GOODS,

OPERA AND FIELD GLASSES, SPECTACLES AND EYE GLASSES,

TELESCOPES AND MICROSCOPES,

GRAPHOSCOPES AND STEREOSCOPES, MATHEMATICAL INSTRUMENTS,

MAGIC LANTERNS AND SLIDES,

PHOTOGRAPHIC APPARATUS, ELECTRIC APPARATUS,

MUSICAL BOXES, MECHANICAL FIGURES,

ETC.

☞ As almost every article represented herein is kept in stock by us, and can in most cases be dispatched within a few hours after receipt of order, you are placed in a position to execute the orders received from your customers at the shortest notice.

ENGLISH AND FOREIGN CLOCKS.

The Drawings of Clocks shown in the following pages will give but an indifferent idea of the large assortment regularly kept in stock by us, comprising—

Timepieces in wooden cases, square shaped.
Timepieces in wooden cases, fancy shaped.
Round Nickel Timepieces, with and without alarum.
Square Nickel Timepieces, with and without alarum.
American Round Dial Clocks, with and without drop.
French Brass Drum Clocks.
Fancy Carved Wood Timepieces, cylinder movement.
English Skeleton Clocks.
Carved Wood Cuckoo Clocks.
Carved Wood Sentry Clocks.
English Round Dial Clocks, with and without drop.
Railway Dial Clocks.
Marine Clocks.

Calendar Clocks.
Tell-Tale or Watchmen's Clocks.
Real Vienna Regulators.
Combination Clocks and Barometers, metal cases.
English Chiming Clocks.
Early English Clocks in wood and marble cases.
Carriage and Travelling Clocks.
Olive Wood Clocks.
Gilt Regulators under glass shades.
French Gilt Clocks under glass shades.
French Gilt and Alabaster Clocks under glass shades.
French Gilt and Porcelain Clocks under glass shades.

French Gilt and Porcelain Clocks under glass shades, with vases or candelabra to match.
Clocks in Dresden china cases, with candelabra to match.
Clocks in Barbotine china cases, with vases to match.
Real Bronze Gilt and Porcelain Clocks, with vases or candelabra to match.
Square Marble Clocks.
Scroll-shaped Marble Clocks.
Fancy-shaped Marble Clocks.
Fancy-shaped Marble Clocks with real bronze mounts.
Marble Clocks, with vases, &c., to match.
Clocks in solid " Californian" marble cases.
Clocks in Bronze cases, with vases to match.

Most of these Clocks are especially established by ourselves or made for us. Our large purchases enable us to sell these goods at very moderate prices.

Photographs and description of any style or size forwarded on application.

All Foreign Clocks are examined at our establishment in Paris by competent clockmakers, and they are again carefully examined in our London workshops before being dispatched to our customers.

We do not attempt to compete with the inferior class of goods of this kind, as we believe, and have found by experience, that our customers prefer to pay a small extra charge for movements of the very best kind, Clocks being of very little value when furnished with inferior and unreliable movements.

Estimates for Church, Turret, and other Clocks forwarded on application.

Presentation Clocks or Bronzes can be fitted with Brass, Silver, or Gold Inscription Plates at a few hours' notice.

As we employ only the best packers, the risk of damage or breakage is minimised.

REAL AND IMITATION BRONZES.
REAL ORMOLU AND BRASS GOODS, MODERN AND ANTIQUE.

The few illustrations which we now beg to submit to you represent but a very small part of our large and well-assorted stock of modern and antique Brass, Bronze, and Ormolu Goods. In this class of goods we look more to the finish of the articles than to cheapness in price, and every piece will be found to be properly finished, notwithstanding that many of our prices are extraordinarily moderate.

The patterns of these goods vary, or are modified and improved, from time to time; the older designs disappearing from our stock in consequence of not being replaced, and the latest novelties, therefore, being constantly introduced to our customers. When ordering, kindly take these facts into consideration, and allow us to substitute the latest patterns at about the same price as those illustrated should we not have the latter in stock. If particularly desired, the very article as shown and described can be forwarded; but if not in stock, from two to three months will be required for the execution of your orders.

Pedestals for Bronze Figures, &c., can be added in any height in Wood or Marble, black or coloured; or the marble foot can be replaced by an Oak, Mahogany, or Ebony Pedestal.

Presentation Bronzes can be fitted with Brass, Silver, or Gold Inscription Plates at a few hours' notice.

When sending for an assortment, please say whether we may add to your order, and state how many pieces and at about what prices; this will enable you to bring under the notice of your customers the latest novelties produced in Europe in this class of goods. Scarcely a season passes without some specialities being introduced into the trade, and you will no doubt agree with us that it is of great advantage to our clients, especially those who are not able to visit our warehouses regularly every season, to be kept well supplied with new patterns, it being a well-established fact that novelties not only attract customers, but leave a fair margin of profit.

Photographs can be sent of special large pieces to fit into recesses and alcoves, or for standing in halls, with or without arrangement for lighting by means of gas, oil, or petroleum.

OPTICAL GOODS.

OPERA AND FIELD GLASSES.
SPECTACLES, EYE GLASSES, AND EYE PRESERVERS.

TELESCOPES AND MICROSCOPES.
ANEROID AND MERCURIAL BAROMETERS.

THERMOMETERS.
MATHEMATICAL AND SURVEYING INSTRUMENTS.

MAGIC LANTERNS, SLIDES.
MODEL STEAM ENGINES.
ELECTRICAL APPARATUS, ETC.

COLOUR BOXES AND ARTISTS' MATERIALS.

The drawings herewith submitted to your inspection, considering the quality of the instruments we are known to deliver, will well compare with any goods of similar character yet introduced to the trade.

Our large stock, and the system in our establishment of executing almost every order within a few hours of its receipt, places our clients in a position to increase their trade without any increase of expense or capital; small and large orders receive equally good attention.

We have been compelled to omit from this Catalogue, through want of space, many articles in the Optical and Scientific Instrument trade, but any such goods can be supplied to order.

Every instrument is carefully examined and adjusted before being dispatched.

We employ only experienced packers, and the chance of damage in transit is thereby reduced to a minimum.

The Drawing Materials shown here are of the best kind only, and of English manufacture.

As our business extends to every part of the globe and to every class of traders, we are compelled to keep the lowest quality manufactured of many articles as well as the very highest class, but it is satisfactory to be able to record that we must have given satisfaction to our customers, as the increase in our Optical and Scientific Instrument trade has been in a much greater ratio than the general increase in our business.

MUSICAL BOXES, PLUMED SINGING BIRDS,
MECHANICALLY-MOVING FIGURES, WINDMILLS, ETC., WITH MUSIC,
MUSICAL CHAIRS, CIGAR STANDS, ALBUMS, ETC.

Being direct importers, and having these goods made especially to our order, we can guarantee all our Musical Boxes to be of first-class tone and perfect finish.

A large assortment, containing selections from the newest works of all the most eminent composers in operatic, dance, and vocal music, as well as sacred airs, always in stock.

In answer to frequent inquiries, it may be remarked that the durability of our Musical Boxes is equal to that of clock-work, and they are not liable to derangement, except through inattention to the very simple instructions for their management, which can be given with each instrument.

All our Musical Boxes are made of the choicest walnut or rosewood, plain or inlaid with tulip and other fancy woods representing Bouquets of Flowers, Flutes, Harps, &c.

Any published tune, whether of Sacred, Operatic, or Dance Music, can be adapted to any Musical Box at a small extra charge.

All Musical Boxes are carefully oiled before being packed.

BIRD BOXES AND BIRDS IN CAGES.

The mechanism and the finish of our Bird Boxes are of the highest order; the notes sung by the birds are such close imitations of nature that the best connoisseurs are frequently deceived.

Mechanical Novelties can be made to perform when a penny is dropped into the case from the outside at an extra cost of 20s. each; many hundreds have been made by us, especially for Exhibitions and places of public amusement.

We can also make any applicable subject our customers may desire, and shall be pleased to forward estimates and designs if required.

WATCH MATERIALS AND TOOLS
FOR
WATCHMAKERS, JEWELLERS, AND ENGRAVERS.

The arrangements we have made with some of the best—we may almost say the best—manufacturers of Watch Materials and Tools enable us to sell first-class articles at most reasonable prices. As the value of each article is comparatively small, it is, in all cases, to our interest, as well as that of those who use these goods, to supply only the best article procurable.

When perusing the pages of our Special Catalogue of Watch Materials and Tools, the complete assortment there illustrated and priced will most probably satisfy you that we have endeavoured to, and we be'' have succeeded in, showing and pricing all the articles requisite for the trader in these materials to properly assort his stock and supply his wants, and also to furnish every practical Watchmaker with every requisite of his trade.

ALL PRICES QUOTED IN OUR PRICE LIST ARE NETT.

S. & F.
London & Paris.

MANUFACTURERS AND IMPORTERS OF EVERY DESCRIPTION OF CLOCKS AND BRONZES.

S. & F.
London & Paris.

No. 6500.—Statuettes, French imitation bronze representing "Moorish Warriors." Height 24 inches.

No. 6502.—Pair of Marble Obelisks to match clock No. 6501. Height 22½ inches, width 7¼ inches, depth 5 inches.

No. 6501.—Black Marble Clock, richly engraved gilt and silvered lines, mounted with real bronze sphinx and Brèche marble sides, 15-day movement, striking the hours and half-hours on a deep-toned gong. Height to top of sphinx 18 inches, length 20 inches, depth 6¾ inches.

No. 6502.—Pair of Marble Obelisks to match clock No. 6501. Height 22½ inches, width 7¼ inches, depth 5 inches.

No. 6500.—Statuettes, French, imitation bronze, representing "Moorish Warriors." Height 24 inches.

All Kinds of Special Clocks and Bronzes made to order for presentations, at very short notice. Inscriptions engraved.

No. 6503.—Pair of Statuettes, French Imitation Bronze, representing "Summer" and "Winter." Height 22¾ inches.

No. 6504.—Black Marble Clock, gilt engraved lines, coloured marble reliefs, visible escapement, 15-day movement, striking the hours and half-hours, on deep-toned gong. Height 18 inches, length 18 inches, depth 6½ inches.

No. 6505.—Black Marble Clock, gilt engraved lines, Californian marble pillars and reliefs, real bronze mounts, 15-day movement, striking the hours and half-hours on deep-toned gong. Height 16½ inches, length 13 inches, depth 6¾ inches.

No. 6503.—Pair of Statuettes, French imitation bronze, representing "Summer" and "Winter." Height 22¾ inches.

TRADE MARK.

TRADE MARK.

No. 6506.—Black Marble Clock, gilt engraved lines, inlaid with marble of assorted colours, 15-day movement, striking the hours and half-hours. Height 14 inches, length 15¾ inches, depth 6½ inches.

No. 6507.—Black Marble Clock, gilt engraved lines, real bronze pillars and mounts, 15-day movement, striking the hours and half-hours on deep-toned gong. Height 19 inches, length 11½ inches, depth 6¾ inches.

No. 6508.—Black Marble Combination Clock, with gilt engraved lines, visible escapement, 15-day movement, striking the hours and half-hours, cut bevelled crystal glass in front showing pendulum, Calendar showing the days of the week, the date and name of the month, and the phases of the moon, also with Aneroid Barometer and Thermometer. Height 20 inches, length 20 inches, depth about 8 inches.

CAUTION. Any person infringing the Copyright of this Book will be prosecuted under the Act.

All Clocks are carefully examined in our own workshops on the premises before being despatched to our customers.

No. 6510.—French Gilt Clocks, assorted patterns, complete with glass shades and black wood stands, 8-day movements, white enamel dials. Height from base of stand to top of shade about 15 inches, length of base of stand about 14 inches.

No. 6511.—Fancy Gilt and Alabaster Clocks, superior finish and extra gilt mountings, complete with glass shades on black wood stands and extra velvet stand inside the shade, 8-day movements, long pendulum, white enamel dials, assorted patterns. Height from base of stand to top of shade about 17 inches, length of base of stand about 15 inches.

No. 6512.—"Dancer with Tambourine." Pair of Real Bronze Statuettes representing Dancers with Triangle and Tambourine. Height 21½ inches.

No. 6513.—Black Marble Clock, gilt engraved lines, with real bronze mounts, black marble dial, 15-day movement, striking hours and half-hours. Height 16 inches, width 8¾ inches.

No. 6513A.—Pair of Marble and Real Bronze Candelabra to match Clock No. 6513. Height 10¾ inches, width 8 inches.

No. 6513A.—Pair of Marble and Real Bronze Candelabra to match Clock No. 6513. Height 10¾ inches, width 8 inches.

No. 6512.—"Dancer with Triangle." Pair of Real Bronze Statuettes representing Dancers with Triangle and Tambourine. Height 22½ inches.

S. & F.

London

and

Paris.

S. & F.

London

and

Paris.

No. 6514.—Fancy Gilt and Alabaster Clocks, with painted medallions, superior finish, and richly gilt sides, 15-day movements, striking the hours and half-hours, complete with glass shades on black wood stands. Assorted patterns. Height from base of stand to top of shade about 18½ inches, length of base of stand about 18 inches.

No. 6515.—Fancy Gilt and Alabaster Clocks, assorted patterns, alabaster base, with gilt figures and ornaments, complete with glass shades and black wood stands, 8-day movements, white enamel dials. Height from base of stand to top of shade about 15 inches, length of base of stand about 13 inches.

No. 6516.—Fancy Gilt and Alabaster Clocks, assorted patterns, with painted medallions, superior finish, and richly gilt mountings, 15-day movements, striking the hours and half-hours, complete with glass shades on black wood stands, and with extra velvet stands inside the shades. Height from base of stand to top of shade about 19 inches, length of base of stand about 21 inches.

Patent 400-day
Clock.

PATENT 400-DAY CLOCK.

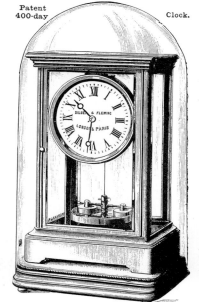

No. 6517.—Regulator Clocks, in square real bronze gilt cases, with bevelled crystal glass sides, 15-day movements, striking the hours and half-hours, visible escapements and mercurial pendulums, with glass shades on black wood stands.

No. 6518.—Patent 400-day Clock, with revolving pendulum, striking hours and half-hours. Height from base of stand to top of shade 15½ inches, width 10½ inches.
N.B.—This Clock requires winding only once in 400 days, and is an accurate timekeeper.

No. 6519.—Regulator Clocks, in oval real bronze gilt cases, with bevelled crystal glass sides, 15-day movements, striking the hours and half-hours, visible escapements and mercurial pendulums, with glass shades on black wood stands.

No. 6520.—Patent 400-day Clock, with revolving pendulum, in square real bronze gilt case with bevelled crystal glass sides, with glass shade and stand complete. Height from base of stand to top of shade 19 inches, width 12 inches.

CAUTION. Any person infringing the Copyright of this Book will be prosecuted under the Act.

S. & F.
London & Paris.

MANUFACTURERS AND IMPORTERS OF EVERY DESCRIPTION OF CLOCKS AND BRONZES.

S. & F.
London & Paris.

All clocks are carefully examined in our own workshops on the premises before being despatched to our customers.

No. 6521.—Real Bronze Bust, "Philopoemen." Height 11 inches. Suitable for standing upon marble clocks.

No. 6522.—Pair of Statuettes, French imitation bronze, on black wood stands, representing "Lansquenets." Height 21 inches.

No. 6522.—Pair of Statuettes, French imitation bronze, on black wood stands, representing "Lansquenets." Height 21 inches.

No. 6523.—Real Bronze Bust, "Ajax." Height 10½ inches. Suitable for standing upon marble clocks.

No. 6524.—Centre Piece, highly finished French imitation bronze, representing an "Albanian Horseman." Height from base of stand to top of gun 34 inches, length of base 24½ inches, depth of base 12 inches.

No. 6526.—"The Night Attack." Pair of Real Bronze Statuettes, on black marble stands. Height 19½ inches.

No. 6526.—"The Night Attack." Pair of Real Bronze Statuettes, on black marble stands. Height 19½ inches.

No. 6525.—Pair of 6-light Candelabra to match centre piece No. 6524, highly finished French imitation bronze. Height 36 inches.

No. 6525.—Pair of 6-light Candelabra to match centre piece No. 6524, highly finished French imitation bronze. Height 36 inches.

TRADE MARK.

TRADE MARK.

No. 6527A.—Tazzas to match clock No. 6527. Real Bronze Cup, mounted upon a black marble pedestal, engraved gilt lines. Height 16½ inches, breadth 7½ inches. No. 6528A.—Tazzas to match clock No. 6528. Height 13½ inches, breadth 5¾ inches.

No. 6527A.—Tazzas to match clock No. 6527. Real Bronze Cup, mounted upon a black marble pedestal, engraved gilt lines. Height 16½ inches, breadth 7½ inches. No. 6528A.—Tazzas to match clock No. 6528. Height 13½ inches, breadth 5¾ inches.

6527A.

6527A.

No. 6527.—Massive Black Marble Clock, engraved gilt lines, with real bronze fluted columns at side and bas-reliefs at top, black marble dial with gilt centre, 15-day movement, striking hours and half-hours on deep-toned gong. Height 20½ in., length 15½ in. No. 6528.—As No. 6527, but smaller size. Height of clock 16¼ inches, length 13¼ inches.

S. & F.
London & Paris.

S. & F.
London & Paris.

No. 6529.—Pair of Statuettes, French imitation bronze, representing "Reapers." Height 8½ inches.

No. 6530.—Pair of Statuettes, French imitation bronze, representing "Figaro" and "Rosine." Height 11½ inches.

No. 6531.—Pair of Statuettes, French imitation bronze, representing "The Departure" and "The Return." Height 13¾ inches.

No. 6532.—Pair of Statuettes, French imitation bronze, representing "Cavaliers." Height 11 inches.

No. 6533.—Pair of Statuettes, French imitation bronze, representing "Gladiators."

No. 6534.—Pair of French Imitation Bronzes, representing Ram and Goat, in green antique, brown, smoked, or dark bronze. Height 13¾ inches, length 10½ inches.

No. 6535.—Real Bronze "Marli" Horses, in either all dark bronze fumèe, or polished brass and bronze fumèe.

No. 6534.—Pair of French Imitation Bronzes, representing Ram and Goat, in green antique, brown, smoked, or dark bronze. Height 13¾ inches, length 10½ inches.

No. 6533.—Pair of Statuettes, French imitation bronze, representing "Gladiators."

TRADE MARK.

TRADE MARK.

No. 6536.—Pair of Statuettes, French imitation bronze, on black wood stands, representing "Byron" and "Scott." Height 20½ inches.

No. 6537.—French Imitation Bronze Equestrian Figures, on polished wood stands, in green antique, brown, smoked, and dark green bronze, representing Richard Cœur de Lion and Edward III.

No. 6538.—Imitation Bronze Figure on wood stand, representing Mercury. Height 32 inches, width 9 inches.

No. 6537.—French Imitation Bronze Equestrian Figures, on polished wood stands, in green antique, brown, smoked, and dark green bronze, representing Richard Cœur de Lion and Edward III.

No. 6536.—Pair of Statuettes, French imitation bronze, on black wood stands, representing "Byron" and "Scott." Height 20½ inches.

No. 6539.—Pair of Statuettes, French imitation bronze, on black wood stands, representing "Rubens" and "Rembrandt." Height 17 inches.

No. 6540.—Pair of Statuettes, French imitation bronze, representing "Duc de Guise" and "Montmorency." Height 20 inches.

No. 6541.—Pair of Statuettes, French imitation bronze, on black wood stands, representing "Shakespeare" and "Milton."

CAUTION. Any person infringing the Copyright of this Book will be prosecuted under the Act.

HALL AND CHIMING CLOCKS.

S. & F.
London and Paris.

S. & F.
London and Paris.

TRADE MARK.

TRADE MARK.

No. 6542.—English Chime Clock, in handsomely carved oak case, engraved silvered dial, very highly finished London made 8-day movement, chiming the quarters on the Cambridge or Westminster chimes and also upon 8 bells, and striking the hours on a cathedral-toned gong, with patent stop movement by which the clock can be made either striking or silent as desired. Height 23 inches, length 15 inches, depth 11 inches.

No. 6543.—English Chime Clock, in black wood case, with richly gilt mounts and mouldings, ornamental brass dial with silvered centre, very highly finished London made 8-day movement, chiming the quarters on the Cambridge or Westminster chimes and also upon 8 bells, and striking the hours on a cathedral-toned gong, with patent stop movement by which the clock can be made either striking or silent. Height 26 inches, length 16 inches, depth 12 inches.

No. 6544.—Massive Bracket Clock, in richly carved dark oak case, with real brass pillars and mountings, engraved silvered dial, 8-day movement, striking hours and half-hours on deep-toned gong. Height 27 inches, length 14 inches, depth 11 inches.

No. 6544.

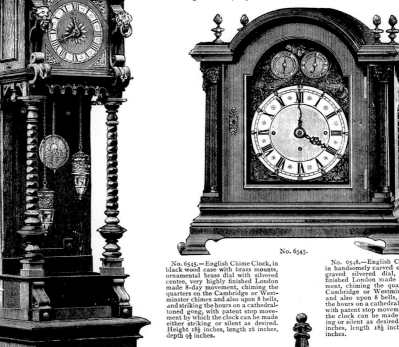

No. 6545.

No. 6545.—English Chime Clock, in black wood case with brass mounts, ornamental brass dial with silvered centre, very highly finished London made 8-day movement, chiming the quarters on the Cambridge or Westminster chimes and also upon 8 bells, and striking the hours on a cathedral-toned gong, with patent stop movement by which the clock can be made either striking or silent as desired. Height 18½ inches, length 16 inches, depth 9½ inches.

No. 6548.—English Chime Clock, in handsomely carved oak case, engraved silvered dial, very highly finished London made 8-day movement, chiming the quarters on the Cambridge or Westminster chimes and also upon 8 bells, and striking the hours on a cathedral-toned gong, with patent stop movement by which the clock can be made either striking or silent as desired. Height 30 inches, length 18½ inches, depth 11 inches.

No. 6546.—English Chime Clock, in black wood case, with richly gilt mounts and mouldings, fancy pierced and embossed gilt top, ornamental brass dial with silvered centre, very highly finished London made 8-day movement, chiming the quarters on the Cambridge or Westminster chimes and also upon 8 bells, and striking the hours on a cathedral-toned gong, with patent stop movement by which the clock can be made either striking or silent as desired. Height 26 inches, length 15 inches, depth 10 inches.

No. 6546.

No. 6547.—Massive Hall Clock, in richly carved dark oak case, with highly chased real brass mountings at top and fret-work in front of base, brass weights and chains, engraved and silvered dial, 8-day movement, striking hours and half-hours on deep-toned gong. Height 8 feet 9 inches, length 20½ inches, depth 12½ inches.

No. 6548.

No. 6549.—"**Lawn Tennis**" Clock in London-made nickelled and gilt metal case, 8-day cylinder movement, going in any position. Height 7¾ inches, width 6 inches.

No. 6550.—"**Grandfather**" Clock, in olive-wood case, 8-day cylinder movement, going in any position, Height 13¾ inches, width 3¾ inches.

No. 6551.—"**Splinter-bar Combination**" Clock in London-made nickelled and gilt metal case, 8-day cylinder movement, going in any position, and best quality aneroid barometer. Height 10 inches, width 10 inches.

No. 6552.—"**Lighthouse**" Clock, in real gilt ormolu case, with 8-day cylinder movement, aneroid barometer and two thermometers. The lantern portion above the balcony revolves by a separate movement. Height 19 inches, diameter of base 6 inches.

No. 6553.—"**Anchor**" Clock, in London-made nickelled and gilt metal case, 8-day cylinder movement, going in any position. Height 10 inches, width 5¾ inches.

No. 6554.—"**Wheel Clock**," in London-made nickelled and gilt metal case, 8-day cylinder movement, going in any position. Height 7¾ inches, width 8¼ inches.

No. 6555.—"**Shield Clock**," in gilt and nickelled metal case, pierced and engraved, 8-day cylinder movement, with silvered and engraved dial. Height 7¼ inches, width 7 inches.

No. 6557.—Fancy Clock, in London-made nickelled and gilt metal case, 8-day cylinder movement, going in any position. Extreme height 8 inches, extreme width 8 inches.

No. 6558.—Fancy Wood Timepiece, 8-day cylinder movement, 5-inch luminous dial which indicates the time by night as well as by day. Height to top of handle 7¾ inches, width 6¼ inches.

No. 6559.—French Drum Timepieces in brass cases, 8-day pendulum movements. Diameter 3¾ inches.

All Clocks are carefully examined by competent workmen on our own premises before being despatched to our customers.

The latest novelties in Clock Cases and all improvements in movements introduced.

No. 6556.—Fancy Wood Timepiece, with bevelled plate glass mirror and bracket in front, suitable for holding small china ornament, &c., 8-day French cylinder movement, going in any position. Length of case complete 21½ inches, width of case complete 8¼ inches, width of bracket shelf 7½ inches, depth of bracket shelf 2¾ inches. Can be supplied in either oak, walnut, or black wood cases.

Where Clocks are quoted at more than one price, corresponding value is given in the finish of the movements, but the style of the Clock is the same as shown in the drawing.

No. 6560.—Lever Timepiece, in nickelled metal case, 30-hour movement, going in any position, with alarum bell on top. Height to top of handle 6¼ inches.

No. 6561.—Carriage Clock, in nickelled metal case, with glass sides, 30-hour keyless lever movement, going in any position, plain white dial. Height to top of handle 8 inches, length of base 5 inches.

No. 6562.—Fancy Wood Timepiece, with brass handle on top, 8-day French cylinder movement, going in any position, fancy decorated dial, assorted woods, viz. oak, walnut, rosewood, and black. Height to top of handle 8½ inches, length of base 5¾ inches.

No. 6563.—Carriage Clock, in nickelled metal case, with glass sides, 30-hour keyless lever movement, going in any position. Height to top of handle 7⅜ inches, length 5 inches. With alarum.

No. 6564.—Carriage Clock in nickelled metal case, with glass sides, 30-hour keyless lever movement, going in any position, with alarum. Height to top of handle 7 inches, length of base 4¼ inches.

No. 6577a.—Pair of Tazzas to match
Clock No. 6577.
Height, 10 inches.
Length, 6½ inches.
Depth, 3½ inches.

No. 6577.—Black Marble Clock, with gilt engraved lines, inlaid with Brèche marble; visible
escapement, 15-day movement, striking the hours and half-hours. Height, 14½ inches;
length, 19½ inches; depth, 5½ inches.

No. 6577a.—Pair of Tazzas to match
Clock No. 6577.
Height, 10 inches.
Length, 6½ inches.
Depth, 3½ inches.

TRADE MARK.

TRADE MARK.

No. 6578a.—Marble and real Bronze
Jardinière to match Clock No. 6578.
Height, 15½ inches.
Length, 6½ inches.
Depth, 5 inches.

No. 6578.—Black Marble Clock, Gothic shape, with real bronze mounts and bas-reliefs;
fancy bronze dial, 15-day movement, striking the hours and half-hours on deep
toned gong. Height, 24 inches; length, 22½ inches; depth, 7½ inches.

No. 6578a.—Marble and real Bronze
Jardinière to match Clock No. 6578.
Height, 15½ inches.
Length, 6½ inches.
Depth, 5 inches.

No. 6579a.—Pair of Marble Tazzas to
match Clock No. 6579.
Height, 11½ inches.
Length, 8½ inches.
Depth, 5 inches.

No. 6579.—Black Marble Clock, richly gilt engraved lines, inlaid and relieved with Rouge Cerise Marble; visible escapement,
15-day movement, striking the hours and half-hours. Height, 17½ inches; length, 25½ inches; depth, 7 inches.

No. 6579b Clock, as No. 6579.
Height, 14½ inches; length,
21½ inches; depth 6 inches.

No. 6579c.—Pair of Tazzas to match
Clock No. 6579B.
Height, 10¼ inches.
Length, 7½ inches.
Depth, 4½ inches.

No. 6580a.—Pair of Marble and Bronze
Tazzas to match Clock No. 6580.
Height, 12½ inches.
Length, 6 inches.
Depth, 5 inches.

No. 6580.—Black Marble Clock, with real Florentine bronze reliefs, black and gilt dial; 15-day movement;
striking the hours and half-hours on a deep toned gong. Height, 15½ inches; length, 25½ inches; depth,
7½ inches. No. 6580b Clock, as No. 6580. Height, 11½ inches; length, 16 inches; depth, 6½ inches.

No. 6580c.—Pair of Marble and Bronze
Tazzas to match Clock No. 6580B.
Height, 9½ inches.
Length, 5½ inches.
Depth, 4½ inches.

S. & F.
LONDON
AND
PARIS.

S. & F.
LONDON
AND
PARIS.

TRADE MARK

TRADE MARK

No. 6581.—Black Marble Clock, gilt engraved lines, assorted colour marble reliefs, marble dial with gilt centre, 8-day silent movement, long pendulum. Height, 11 inches; length, 8¾ inches.

No. 6582.—Black Marble Clock, gilt engraved lines, assorted colour marble reliefs and pillars, fancy gilt dial, 15-day movement, striking the hours and half-hours on deep-toned gong. Height, 15½ inches; length, 13¾ inches.

No. 6583.—Black Marble Clock, gilt engraved lines, assorted colour marble reliefs, marble dial with gilt centre, 8-day silent movement, long pendulum. Height, 10½ inches; length, 10½ inches.

No. 6584.—Black Marble Clock, gilt engraved lines, assorted colour marble reliefs, white enamel dial, visible escapement, 15-day movement, striking the hours and half-hours. Height, 12 inches; length, 9 inches.

No. 6585.—Massive Black Marble Clock with real bronze bas-reliefs and pillars, white enamel dial, 15-day movement, striking the hours and half-hours on deep-toned gong. Height, 12¼ inches; length, 19 inches.

No. 6586.—Black Marble Clock, gilt engraved lines, assorted colour marble reliefs, marble dial with gilt centre, 8-day silent movement, long pendulum. Height, 14½ inches; length, 9 inches.

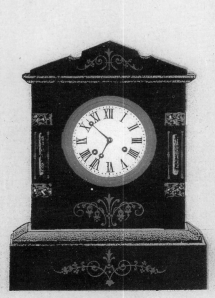

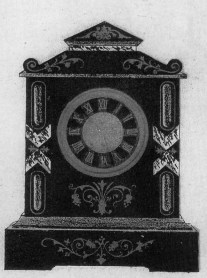

No. 6587.—Black Marble Clock, gilt engraved lines, assorted colour marble reliefs, white enamel dial, 15-day movement, striking the hours and half-hours. Height, 14 inches; length, 10 inches.

No. 6588.—Black Marble Clock, gilt engraved lines, assorted colour marble reliefs, marble dial with gilt centre, 15-day movement, striking the hours and half-hours on deep-toned gong. Height, 19 inches; length, 15½ inches.

No. 6589.—Black Marble Clock, gilt engraved lines, assorted colour marble reliefs, marble dial with gilt centre, 8-day silent movement, long pendulum. Height, 14 inches; length, 10½ inches.

S. & F.
LONDON
AND
PARIS.

S. & F.
LONDON
AND
PARIS

No. 6599a.—Pair of Vases to match Clock No. 6599. Height to top of shade, 16¼ inches.

No. 6599.—Clock in real bronze, gilt, with hand-painted porcelain dial plate and ornaments, coloured ground decorated with birds and flowers, best quality, 15-day movement, striking the hours and half-hours, with glass shade on black wood stand, and with extra gilt and velvet stand inside the shade. Height from base of stand to top of shade, 19 inches; length of black stand, 11 inches; width of ditto, 8¼ inches.

No. 6600.—Clock in real bronze, gilt, with hand-painted porcelain dial and ornaments, coloured ground with rich decoration of birds, butterflies, &c., best quality, 15-day movement, striking the hours and half-hours, with glass shade on black wood stand, and with extra gilt and velvet stand inside the shade. Height from base of stand to top of shade, 18 inches; length of black stand, 10½ inches; width of ditto, 7½ inches.

No. 6600a.—Pair of Vases to match Clock No. 6600. Height to top of shade, 16 inches.

No. 6601a.—Pair of Vases to match Clock No. 6601. Height to top of shade, 16 inches.

No. 6601.—Clock in real bronze, gilt and nickeled, with hand-painted porcelain dial and ornaments, coloured ground decorated with birds and flowers, best quality, 15-day movement, striking the hours and half-hours, on deep-toned gong, with glass shade on black wood stand, and with extra gilt and velvet stand inside the shade. Height from base of stand to top of shade, 18½ inches; length of black stand, 11½ inches; width of ditto 8 inches.

No. 6602.—Clock in real bronze, gilt and nickeled, with hand-painted porcelain dial and ornaments, coloured ground decorated with birds and flowers, best quality, 15-day movement, striking the hours and half-hours on deep-toned gong, with glass shade on black wood stand, and with extra gilt and velvet stand inside the shade. Height from base of stand to top of shade, 18½ inches; length of black stand, 11½ inches; width of ditto 8 inches.

No. 6602a.—Pair of Vases to match Clock No. 6602. Height to top of shade, 16 inches.

No. 6603a.—Pair of Vases to match Clock No. 6603. Height to top of shade, 15⅜ inches.

No. 6603.—Clock in real bronze, gilt, with hand-painted porcelain dial plate and ornaments, decorated in old Flemish style, best quality, 15-day movement, striking the hours and half-hours on deep-toned gong, with glass shade on black stand, and with extra gilt and velvet stand inside the shade. Height from base of stand to top of shade, 19 inches; length of black stand, 12 inches; width of black stand, 7¾ inches.

No. 6604.—Clock, in real bronze, gilt and nickeled, with hand-painted porcelain dial and ornaments, coloured ground decorated with birds and flowers, best quality, 15-day movement, striking the hours and half-hours on deep-toned gong, with glass shade on black wood stand, and with extra gilt and velvet stand inside the shade. Height from base of stand to top of shade, 24 inches; length of black stand, 14½ inches; width of black stand, 11 inches.

No. 6604a.—Pair of Vases to match Clock No. 6604. Height to top of shade, 18½ inches.

S. & F.
LONDON
AND
PARIS.

S. & F.
LONDON
AND
PARIS.

TRADE MARK.

No. 6619.—Pair of Vases to match. Height to top of shade, 15½ inches.

No. 6618.—French Gilt Clock, with hand-painted porcelain dial and ornaments, 15-day movement, striking the hours and half-hours, with glass shade on black wood stand, and with extra gilt and velvet stand inside the shade. Height, from base of stand to top of shade, 17½ inches; length of black stand, 13 inches; width of ditto, about 7 inches.

No. 6620.—French Gilt Clock, with hand-painted porcelain dial and ornaments, 15-day movement, striking the hours and half-hours, with glass shade on black wood stand, and with extra gilt and velvet stand inside the shade. Height from base of stand to top of shade, 19 inches; length of black stand, 11 inches; width of black stand, about 7 inches.

No. 6621.—Pair of Vases to match. Height to top of shade, 14 inches.

No. 6623.—Pair of Vases to match. Height to top of shade, 18½ inches.

No. 6622.—French Gilt Clock, with hand-painted porcelain dial and ornaments, 15-day movement, striking the hours and half-hours, with glass shade on black wood stand, and with extra gilt and velvet stand inside the shade. Height, from base of stand to top of shade, 21½ inches; length of black stand, 16½ inches; width of black stand, 9½ inches.

No. 6624.—French Gilt Clock, with hand-painted porcelain dial and ornaments, 15-day movement, striking the hours and half-hours, with glass shade on black wood stand, and with extra gilt and velvet stand inside the shade. Height, from base of stand to top of shade, 21 inches; length of black stand, 15 inches; width of black stand, about 8½ inches.

No. 6625.—Pair of Jugs to match. Height to top of shade, 19 inches.

No. 6627.—Pair of Vases to match. Height to top of shade, 20 inches.

No. 6626.—French Gilt Clock with hand-painted porcelain dial-plate and ornaments, 15-day movement, striking the hours and half-hours, with glass shade on black wood stand, and with extra gilt and velvet stand inside the shade. Height, from base of stand to top of shade, 26 inches; length of black stand, 14 inches; width of black stand, 10 inches.

No. 6628.—French Gilt Clock, with hand-painted porcelain dial and ornaments, 15-day movement, striking the hours and half-hours, with glass shade on black wood stand, and with extra gilt and velvet stand inside the shade. Height, from base of stand to top of shade, 21 inches; length of black stand, 13½ inches; width of black stand, 7½ inches

No. 6629.—Pair of Candelabra to match. Height to top of shade, 23½ inches.

S. & F.
LONDON
AND
PARIS.

S. & F.
LONDON
AND
PARIS

No. 6630.—Real Tortoiseshell Box, with enamelled and gilt door at top, which opens upon a spring being touched, and a miniature bird of exquisite plumage appears. The bird moves about, and opens and closes its wings and beak, singing in a most natural manner; at the end of its song returning into the box, the lid closing over it. Size, 3¼ inches by 2½ inches by 1½ inches. Fitted into a Morocco leather case, lined with silk velvet.

No. 6631.—Mechanical Singing Bird, as No. 6630, but in real silver box, richly gilt and engraved. Size, 3¾ inches by 2½ inches by 1¾ inches. Fitted into a Morocco leather case, lined with silk velvet.

No. 6632.—Mechanical Singing Bird, as No. 6631, but beautifully enamelled, with landscape, flowers, &c. Best quality mechanism. Size, 3½ inches by 2¼ inches by 1¾ inches. Fitted into a Morocco leather case, lined with silk velvet.

TRADE MARK

TRADE MARK

No. 6634.—Richly gilt cage, on gilt stand, with natural bird of brilliant plumage, stuffed, perched on a stand inside, and singing in perfect note. It opens its beak and moves its head and tail in a most natural manner. Height, 20½ inches; diameter of cage, 12 inches.

No. 6633.—Real Silver Box, engraved and parcel gilt in the Japanese style, with richly enamelled door at top, which opens upon a spring being touched, and two miniature birds of exquisite plumage appear, moving their wings, &c., in a most natural manner, and singing alternately as if in answer to each other's song.
DRAWN FULL SIZE.
Fitted into a Morocco leather case, lined with silk velvet

No. 6635.—Richly gilt cage, on gilt stand, very superior quality; containing two natural birds of the finest plumage, stuffed, which sing alternately in answer to each other's song. The works are most carefully made and well finished. Height, 21½ inches; diameter of cage, 12¼ inches.

No. 6636.—Musical Boxes in round japanned tin cases, fancy coloured and decorated, with handle, playing one tune; diameter, 3 inches.

No. 6644.—Large Musical Boxes, standing upon tables with four legs, and with a drawer in front for holding the extra barrels, inlaid walnut or rosewood cases.

No. 6638.—Musical Boxes, in fancy horn cases, assorted views at top; self-acting.

No. 6637.—Musical Boxes in square wood cases, decorated on top, with handle, playing one tune. Length, 3¼ inches; depth, 2¾ inches.

MUSICAL BOXES MADE TO ORDER TO PLAY ANY SPECIAL AIRS OF WHICH THE MUSIC IS OBTAINABLE IN THIS COUNTRY, SUCH AS HINDUSTANEE, CHINESE, RUSSIAN, TURKISH, ETC.

No. 6639.—Musical Boxes, in fancy wood cases, inlaid or carved, assorted colour woods; self-acting; best quality.

No. 6640.—Musical Boxes, in plain imitation rosewood cases, glass cover inside.

No. 6641.—Musical Boxes, in fancy inlaid rosewood cases, glass cover inside.

No. 6645.—Large Musical Boxes, standing upon tables with four legs, and with a drawer in front for holding the extra barrels, richly inlaid rosewood or walnut cases, best quality music, "Mandoline Expressive," with zither accompaniment.

No. 6642.—Musical Boxes, with visible drum, bells and castagnettes accompaniment.

ANY PUBLISHED TUNE, whether of SACRED, OPERATIC, or DANCE MUSIC, can be ADAPTED TO ANY MUSICAL BOX AT A SMALL EXTRA CHARGE.
ALL MUSICAL BOXES ARE CAREFULLY OILED BEFORE BEING PACKED.

No. 6643.—Musical Boxes, "Tremolo," with zither accompaniment, best quality music, and richly inlaid cases.

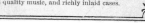

LATEST NOVELTIES IN MECHANICAL PIECES AND MOVING FIGURES.

No. 6646.—Mechanical Piece representing a Negro Fruit Seller, richly dressed in coloured satin. The figure is holding a tray, upon which are placed three kinds of fruit, viz. one apple which opens, displaying the head of a monkey which moves the mouth and eyes ; one pear which opens, showing two small figures waltzing ; and one peach which also opens, and exposes to view a white mouse running round. The figure itself bows and moves its head from side to side, and moves its eyes in a very natural manner. Two airs of music. Height 26½ inches.

No. 6647.—Musical Cigar Box, in carved wood, rustic case, representing a Swiss chalet. By lifting up the roof of the chalet and pushing it down again, a cigar is made to appear upon the top ledge, and the music commences to play. Height 8½ inches, length 9 inches, width 7¼ inches. Playing two airs.

No. 6648.— Mechanical Figure. Negress with Fan and Bouquet. Figure richly dressed in coloured satin and lace. In her right hand she holds a fan which she uses as if fanning herself, and occasionally moves the bouquet up to her face as if inhaling the perfume from the flowers. The figure also bows and moves her head from side to side, and also moves her eyelids. Two airs of music. Height 27 inches.

No. 6647.—Musical Cigar Box.

For **Watches**, 332 & 333
,, **Clocks,**
Bronzes, 391 to 412
&c.
,, **Optical**
Goods 413 to 418
See Pa

No. 6648.

No. 6649.—Mechanical Monkey Smoker. Figure richly dressed in coloured satin and velvet. In his right hand he holds a meerschaum cigarette holder, which he raises to and from his mouth, and from which, when a cigarette is put in, he smokes in a most perfect manner, moving it up and down to his mouth and puffing out the smoke ; in his left hand he holds a pair of eye-glasses, which he occasionally moves to and from his eyes. Height 26½ inches.

No. 6651.—Mechanical Piece representing " La Mascotte." Figure elaborately dressed in coloured velvet and satin. Suspended on her right arm is a wicker basket decorated with flowers, the lid of which opens and discloses to view a chicken which moves its head and chirps. In the left hand she has a bouquet which she raises at intervals to her face, as if inhaling the perfume from the flowers. She also bows and moves her head from side to side. Height 25 inches.

No. 6649.

No. 6651.

No. 6650.—Magnificent Musical Mechanical Piece representing French Huntsmen. The two figures are dressed in the characteristic style of French huntsmen, their costumes being of crimson and blue satin, faced with gold lace, their black hats adorned with real feathers. The imitation rock-work on which they stand is represented in the engraving as if embedded in rough foliage, which imparts to it a naturalness of appearance. Behind the figures are two trees, and within the base is a mechanical trumpet organ, which plays 6 hunting choruses. As the trumpet calls occur, the figures raise the horns to their mouths as if playing the instruments ; at the conclusion of each tune the figures move the horns from their mouths and turn their heads towards each other, bow, and move their eyelids as if in conversation. Height of figures 3 feet, height from base of stand to top of figures 6 feet 4½ inches, height from base of stand to top of trees 8 feet 3½ inches, length of base 4 feet 6 inches, depth of base 3 feet 1 inch.

No. 6652.—Mechanical Piece representing a Bird Charmer. Figure richly dressed in velvet and satin. In his right hand he holds a flute which he moves to and from his mouth, moving his fingers in time with the music. When he takes the flute from his mouth the music stops, and the bird, which is perched upon his left hand, immediately begins to sing the song of the nightingale, at the same time moving its head, beak, and wings. Two airs of music. Height 42 inches.

No. 6653.—Musical Smoker's Companion, in nickelled metal case. When the cigar cutter is pushed down the music commences to play. Height 6½ inches, diameter 9 inches. Playing two airs.

No. 6654.— Musical Revolving Cigar Stand, assorted coloured wood, with gilt mounts, playing two airs of music. Height 12 inches, width 7¼ inches.

No. 6655.—Musical Liqueur Stand, in carved wood frame, engraved crystal decanter and six glasses. When the decanter is lifted up the music commences to play. Height to top of decanter 14 inches, diameter 12 inches. Playing two airs.

No. 6656.—Mechanical Piece representing a Negro Flute Player. Figure richly dressed in coloured velvet and satin, standing upon an oval base covered with velvet. In his hands he holds a flute, which he raises to his mouth and plays in a most natural manner, moving the fingers in accordance with the music, which is an exact imitation of the tone of a real flute. When the air is finished, he raises his head and moves his eyes and mouth as if speaking. The piece plays 4 tunes. Height 53 inches, width of base 19¾ inches.

S. & F.
London & Paris.

MECHANICALLY-MOVING FIGURES, WINDMILLS, ETC.
WITH MUSIC.

S. & F.
London & Paris,

No. 6661.—Mechanical Piece, under glass shade, representing Lady at Sewing Machine. Richly dressed figure, moving its head, arms, and foot; the machine works in splendid imitation of a real sewing machine. Two airs of music. Height 26 in., length 16 in.

No. 6662.—Mechanical Piece, under glass shade, representing a Bootmaker's Saloon, surrounded by mirrors, and upholstered with crimson satin and gilt mouldings. The female figure is richly dressed in blue satin with white lace trimmings, and hat to match. The male figure is dressed in black silk with gilt buttons, and moves his head, eyes, and mouth, as if speaking to his customer; with his right hand he moves a bronzed leather shoe on and off the lady's foot when she raises it. Two airs of music. Height 26 inches, length 21 inches.

No. 6663.—Mechanical Piece, under glass shade, representing a Monkey Conjurer. Richly dressed figure standing behind a table, on which is a small glass shade with three dice. The figure places a small brass cover over the shade and then raises it, the numbers on the dice changing meanwhile. Two airs of music. Height 28 inches, length 19 inches.

TRADE MARK.

TRADE MARK.

No. 6664.—Mechanical Piece, under glass shade, representing Lady Preparing for a Ball. Two airs of music. Height 26½ inches, length 23 inches.

No. 6665.—Mechanical Piece, under glass shade, representing a Landscape with Flour Mill; one Ship sailing, which moves up and down on the imitation water; the mill-wheel revolves, the figure at foot turns the hand-wheel and causes the flour bags to ascend the lift and go into the room at the top of the house; a miller with a bag on his back comes out of the door on the left and walks to the other door, which opens at his approach and closes after him. Two airs of music. Height 26 inches, length 24 inches.

No. 6666.—Mechanical Piece, under glass shade, representing a Monkey Artist painting a landscape. The figure is richly dressed in dark velvet, embroidered with gold braid. The manner in which it takes the colour from the palette and then proceeds to paint is very natural. Two airs of music. Height 26½ inches, length 20 inches.

No. 6667.—Mechanical Piece, under glass shade with canopy of flowers, representing a Monkey Nurse with Baby. The nurse is dressed in blue and red satin, with white apron, and white lace cap, and is apparently feeding the baby with a feeding bottle. Two airs of music. Height 26 inches, length 20 inches.

No. 6668.—Mechanical Piece, under glass shade. Two Monkey Figures, richly dressed in coloured satin, seated at a table, in a saloon surrounded by mirrors, and upholstered in crimson satin, with black and gilt mouldings. Both figures move their heads, eyes, and mouths, as if speaking to each other. One has in its right hand a cigar, which it raises to its mouth, as if smoking, it also moves its left arm up and down. The other figure holds in its right hand a box, containing dice, which it raises, and throws the dice out on to the table; with its left hand it sweeps them off the table back again into the box, the numbers on the dice changing each time. Two airs of music. Height 26½ inches, length 24 inches.

No. 6669.—Mechanical Piece, under glass shade, representing a Lady Pianist, richly dressed in satin, with white lace and gold braid trimmings. Two airs of music. Height 26½ inches, length 20 inches.

No. 6670.—English Round Dial Clocks, in mahogany or oak cases, London - made movements, 8 - day silent, diameter of dial 12 inches.

No. 6671.—Carved oak frame, 24 inches high, combining calendar, 5-in. enamelled dial aneroid barometer, and an 8-day cylinder timepiece.

No. 6672.—Carved Oak Clock, silvered metal dial with black painted figures, superior quality movement, striking the hours and half-hours on a cathedral-toned gong. Height 22 inches, length 12½ inches.
No. 6672A, as No. 6672, but with superior quality movement, chiming every quarter-hour upon 8 bells, and striking the hours on a cathedral-toned gong.

No. 6673. - Carved oak "Wheat Ear" pattern frame, 22 inches high, combining a 5-in. enamelled dial aneroid barometer, hand - painted opal scale thermometer, and 8-day cylinder timepiece.

No. 6674.—Marine Clock, in bronzed metal case, 8-day silent London-made chain movement, lever escapement, going in any position, engraved and silvered metal dial showing seconds, solid brass ring and cut bevelled plate glass. Diameter of case 9½ inches.

No. 6671.

No. 6673.

No. 6675.—American Calendar Clock in rosewood case, 8-day striking movement, 12-inch dial, with calendar hand showing the date of the month.
No. 6675A.—American Clocks, with separate Calendar Dial, showing day of the week and date of the month, in rosewood cases.

S. & F. London.

S. & F. Paris.

Photographs and description of any style of Clock forwarded upon application.

Railway Dial Clocks.

No. 6676.—Railway Dial Clocks, in oak or mahogany cases, 8-day silent London - made chain movements, solid brass rings, with bevelled plate glasses.

Estimates given on application for Church, Turret, and Illuminated Dial Clocks.

Anglo-American Clocks.

No. 6677.—Anglo-American Clocks, in oak or mahogany cases, 12-inch dials with drop, 8-day striking movement, assorted patterns.

No. 6678.

No. 6679.

No. 6680.

No. 6681.

No. 6682.

No. 6683.

No. 6678.—Vienna Regulator, in richly carved walnutwood case, length 44 inches, superior quality 8-day silent movement.
No. 6679.—Vienna Regulator, in walnut and black wood case, length 46 inches, 8-day silent movement.
No. 6680.—Vienna Regulator, in stained rosewood case, length 47 inches, 8-day silent movement.

No. 6681.—New Clock Barometer, in bronzed metal case, 8-day lever movement, going in any position, best quality London-made aneroid barometer and thermometer. Length 28 inches, width 11 inches.
No. 6681A.—As No. 6681, but with best quality 8-day French cylinder movement, white enamel dial.

No. 6682.—Vienna Regulator, in carved walnut and black wood case, length 48 inches, 8-day silent movement.
No. 6682A.—As No. 6682, but striking on gong.
No. 6683.—Vienna Regulator, in richly carved walnut wood case, length 45 inches, superior quality, 8-day silent movement.
No. 6683A.—As No. 6683, but striking on gong.

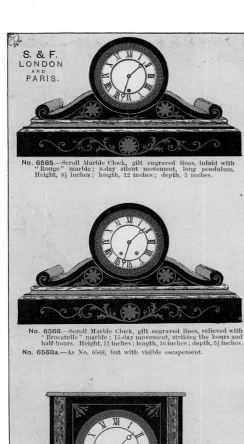

No. 6565.—Scroll Marble Clock, gilt engraved lines, inlaid with "Rouge" marble; 8-day silent movement, long pendulum. Height, 8½ inches; length, 12 inches; depth, 5 inches.

No. 6567.—Scroll Marble Clock, gilt engraved lines, relieved with green marble; visible escapement, 15-day movement, striking the hours and half-hours. Height, 11½ inches; length, 18 inches; depth, 5½ inches.

No. 6567a.—As No. 6567, but with plain dial.

No. 6566.—Square Marble Clock, gilt engraved lines, "Bleu Fleuri" marble pillars and relief; 8-day silent movement, long pendulum. Height, 10½ inches; length, 10 inches; depth, 6 inches.

No. 6566a.—As No. 6566, but with 15-day movement, striking the hours and half-hours.

No. 6566b.—As No. 6566A, but with visible escapement.

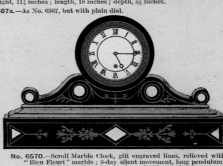

No. 6568.—Scroll Marble Clock, gilt engraved lines, relieved with "Brocatelle" marble; 15-day movement, striking the hours and half-hours. Height, 11 inches; length, 16 inches; depth, 5½ inches.

No. 6568a.—As No. 6568, but with visible escapement.

No. 6570.—Scroll Marble Clock, gilt engraved lines, relieved with "Bleu Fleuri" marble; 8-day silent movement, long pendulum. Height, 8½ inches; length, 14 inches; depth, 5 inches.

No. 6570a.—As No. 6570, but with 15-day movement, striking the hours and half-hours.

No. 6569.—Marble Clock, fancy shape, gilt engraved lines, inlaid "Malachite" reliefs; visible escapement, 15-day movement, striking the hours and half-hours. length, 16 inches; height, 10 inches; depth, 5½ inches.

No. 6571.—Square Marble Clock, gilt engraved lines, "Rouge Griotte" marble relief; 8-day silent movement, long pendulum. Height, 8½ inches, length, 8½ inches; depth, 4½ inches.

No. 6571a.—As No. 6571, but with 15-day movement, striking the hours and half-hours.

No. 6573.—Black Marble Clock, fancy shape, gilt engraved lines, Green marble pillars and relief; 8-day silent movement, long pendulum. Height, 13 inches; length, 10½ inches; depth, 6 inches.

No. 6573a.—As No. 6573, but with 15-day movement, striking the hours and half-hours.

No. 6573b.—As No. 6573A, but with visible escapement.

No. 6572.—Scroll Marble Clock, gilt engraved lines, relieved with "Rose" marble; visible escapement, 15-day movement, striking the hours and half-hours. Height, 12½ inches; length, 20 inches; depth, 5½ inches.

No. 6572a.—As No. 6572, but with plain dial.

No. 6574.—Massive Black Marble Clock, gilt engraved lines, assorted coloured marble pillars and reliefs, real bronze mounts; visible escapement, 15-day movement, striking the hours and half-hours upon a cathedral toned gong. Height, 17½ inches; length, 13¾ inches; depth, 7 inches.

No. 6575.—Fancy shape Black Marble Clock, gilt engraved lines, assorted coloured marble reliefs, real bronze mounts; visible escapement, 15-day movement, striking the hours and half-hours upon a cathedral toned gong. Height, 16¾ inches; length, 15 inches; depth, 7¼ inches.

No. 6576.—Fancy shape Black Marble Clock, gilt engraved lines, assorted coloured marble pillars and reliefs; visible escapement, 15-day movement, striking the hours and half-hours, Height, 14¾ inches; length, 12 inches; depth, 7 inches.

S. & F.
LONDON
AND
PARIS

S. & F.
LONDON
AND
PARIS.

TRADE MARK

TRADE MARK.

No. 6590.—French Gilt Clock, with hand-painted porcelain dial and ornaments, 15-day movement, striking the hours and half-hours, with glass shade on black wood stand, and with extra gilt and velvet stand inside the shade. In four subjects, viz., Industry, Agriculture, History and Commerce. Height from base of stand to top of shade, 18½ inches; length of black stand, 24 inches; width of ditto, about 8½ inches.

No. 6591.—French Gilt Clock, with hand-painted porcelain dial and ornaments, 15-day movement striking the hours and half-hours, with glass shade on black wood stand, and with extra gilt and velvet stand inside the shade. Height from base of stand to top of shade, 21 inches; length of black stand, 19½ inches; width of black stand, about 9 inches.

No. 6592.—French Gilt Clock, with hand-painted porcelain dial and ornaments, 15-day movement, striking the hours and half-hours, with glass shade on black wood stand, and with extra gilt and velvet stand inside the shade. Height from base of stand to top of shade, 21½ inches; length of black stand, 15 inches; width of ditto, about 8½ inches.

No. 6593.—French Gilt Clock, with hand-painted porcelain dial and ornaments, 15-day movement, striking the hours and half-hours, with glass shade on black wood stand, and with extra gilt and velvet stand inside the shade. In two subjects, viz., Hunting and Fishing. Height from base of stand to top of shade, 22 inches; length of black stand, 22 inches; width of ditto, about 9 inches.

No. 6594.—French Gilt Clock, with hand-painted porcelain dial and ornaments, 15-day movement, striking the hours and half-hours, with glass shade on black wood stand, and with extra gilt and velvet stand inside the shade. In four subjects, viz., Van Dyck, Etude, Coquette, Genie du Dessin. Height from base of stand to top of shade 16 inches; length of black stand, 13½ inches; width of ditto, about 7 inches.

No. 6595.—French Gilt Clock, with hand-painted porcelain dial and ornaments, 15-day movement, striking the hours and half-hours, with glass shade on black wood stand, and with extra gilt and velvet stand inside the shade. Height from base of stand to top of shade, 17½ inches; length of black stand, 15 inches; width of ditto, about 8 inches.

No. 6596.—French Gilt Clock, with hand-painted porcelain dial and ornaments, 15-day movement, striking the hours and half-hours, with glass shade on glass shade on black wood stand, and with extra gilt and velvet stand inside the shade. Height from base of stand to top of shade, 22½ inches; length of black stand, 14 inches; width of ditto, about 8½ inches.

No. 6597.—French Gilt Clock, with hand-painted porcelain dial and ornaments, 15-day movement, striking the hours and half-hours, with glass shade on black wood stand, and with extra gilt and velvet stand inside the shade. Height from base of stand to top of shade, 23½ inches; length of black stand, 19½ inches; width of ditto, about 8½ inches.

No. 6598.—French Gilt Clock, with hand-painted porcelain dial and ornaments, 15-day movement, striking the hours and half-hours, with glass shade on black wood stand, and with extra gilt and velvet stand inside the shade. Height from base of stand to top of shade, 22 inches; length of black stand, 14 inches; width of black stand, about 8½ inches.

S. & F.
LONDON
AND
PARIS.

S. & F.
LONDON
AND
PARIS.

No. 6605.—Square Carriage Timepiece in gilt metal case, with cut crystal bevelled glass sides, 8-day movement, horizontal escapement. Height, 4½ inches; length, 3 inches.

No. 6606.—Carriage Clock in real Ormolu and nickelled metal case, fancy porcelain dial plate, gilt ground with blue and white decoration; 8-day movement, lever escapement, compensation balance, striking the hours and half-hours on deep toned gong, with repetition. Height, 7¾ inches; width, 4½ inches.

No. 6607.—Carriage Clock in real Ormolu and nickelled metal case, fancy black and gilt dials with red figures; 8-day movement, lever escapement, compensation balance, striking the hours and half-hours on deep toned gong, with repetition and Alarum. Height, 7¾ inches; width, 4½ inches.

No. 6608.—Carriage Clock in real Ormolu and nickelled metal case, with richly painted porcelain dial plate and side plaques; 8-day lever movement, compensation balance, striking the hours and half-hours on deep toned gong, with repetition. Height, 7½ inches; width, 3½ inches.

No. 6609.—Carriage Clock in real Ormolu and nickelled metal case, gilt dial plate with fancy tinted enamel dial; 8-day movement, lever escapement, compensation balance, striking the hours and half-hours on deep toned gong, with repetition. Height, 8 inches; width, 4½ inches.

No. 6611.—Real Ormolu Clock, representing a Beam Engine, richly gilt and nickelled, standing upon a Black Marble Base; 15-day movement, striking the hours and half-hours. Height, 9½ inches; length, 10½ inches.

This Clock works similar to a Beam Engine, and is fitted with two pendulums, which work up and down into the cylinders at each side.

No. 6610.—Carriage Clock in real Ormolu case, richly enamelled in fancy colours upon all sides, 8-day movement, lever escapement, compensation balance, striking the hours and half-hours on deep toned gong, with repetition and Alarum. Height, 7½ inches; width, 4 inches.

No. 6612.—Fancy hand-painted Porcelain Plate Clock, richly decorated, with gilt hands and figures; 8-day silent movement. Height, 10 inches; width, 10 inches.

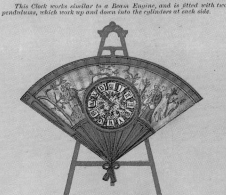

No. 6613.—Fancy hand-painted Porcelain Clock, representing a Fan, mounted upon a polished brass easel; 8-day silent movement. Height, 18½ inches; width, 18 inches.

No. 6614.—Fancy hand-painted Porcelain Plate Clock, with decoration representing a landscape with Church, the clock dial being placed in the steeple; 8-day silent movement. Height, 10 inches; width, 10 inches.

No. 6615.—Fancy hand-painted Porcelain Clock, representing a Palette, mounted upon a polished brass easel; 8-day silent movement. Height, 18 inches; width, 9½ inches.

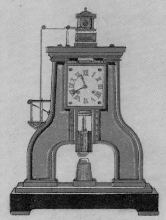

No. 6616.—Real Ormolu Clock, representing the Steam Hammer, richly gilt and nickelled, on Black Marble Base; 15-day movement, striking the hours and half-hours. Height, 18 inches; length, 11½ inches.

The pendulum of the Clock is in the shape of the Steam Hammer, and represents its movement.

No. 6617.—Fancy hand-painted Porcelain Plate Clock, with polished brass mountings; 8-day silent movement. Height, 18 inches; width, 11 inches.

LATEST NOVELTY.
ENGRAVED CRYSTAL TABLE GLASS,
FINEST QUALITY.

ORNAMENTED WITH GOLD, AND AS THE GOLD IS BURNT INTO THE CUTTING OR ENGRAVING IT IS ALMOST INDESTRUCTIBLE, AND SHOWS ON BOTH SIDES OF THE GLASSES ALIKE. MONOGRAMS, CRESTS, &c., CAN BE SUPPLIED.

No. 7513 Port   No. 7513 Sherry   No. 7513 Claret   No. 7513 Champagne   No. 7513 Liqueur

No. 7513 Custard

No. 7513 Decanter   No. 7513 Tumbler   No. 7513 Finger Basin   No. 7513 Jelly   No. 7513 Champange Tumbler   No. 7513 Claret Jug

Suite No. 7513

CHAMPAGNE TUMBLERS.

No. 7514 Champagne Tumbler   No. 7515 Champagne Tumbler   No. 7516 Champagne Tumbler   No. 7517 Champagne Tumbler   No. 7518 Champagne Tumbler   No. 7519 Champagne Tumbler

No. 7520 Port   No. 7520 Sherry   No. 7520 Claret   No. 7520 Champagne   No. 7520 Liqueur

No. 7520 Custard

No. 7520 Decanter   No. 7520 Tumbler   No. 7520 Finger Basin   No. 7520 Jelly   No. 7520 Champagne Tumbler   No. 7520 Claret Jug

Suite No. 7520

S&F.   MANUFACTURERS, IMPORTERS, WAREHOUSEMEN AND AGENTS.   **S&F.**

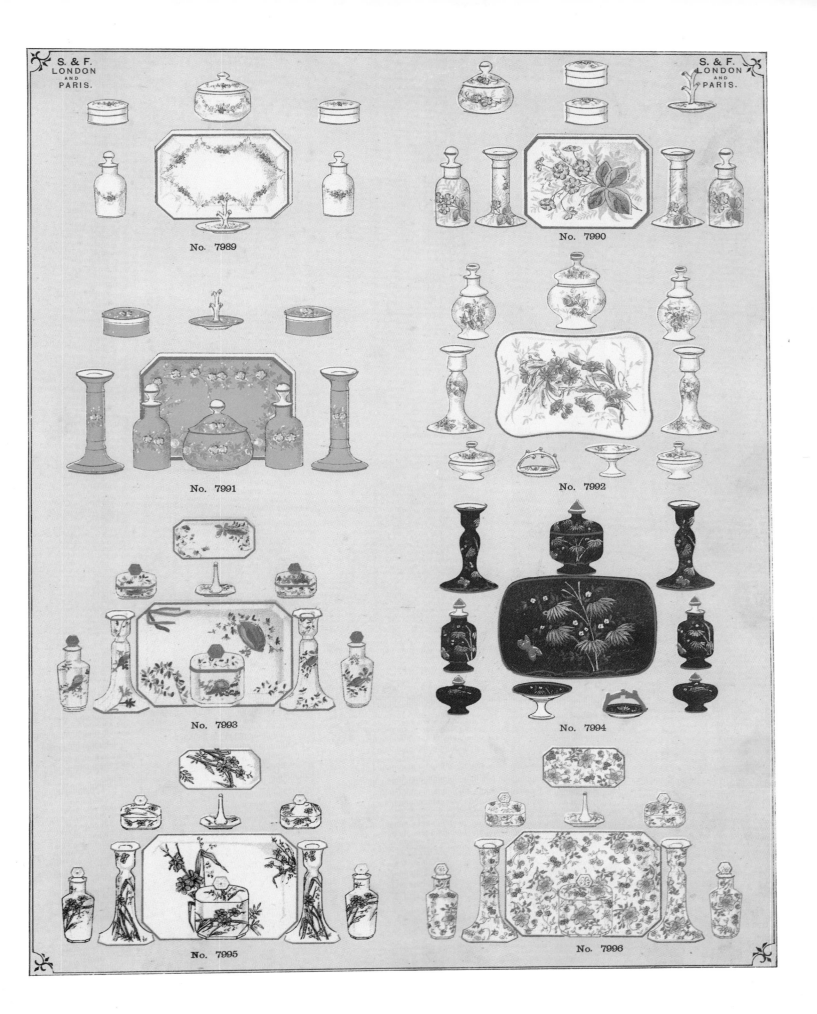

S. & F.
LONDON
AND
PARIS.

S. & F.
LONDON
AND
PARIS.

No. 7989

No. 7990

No. 7991

No. 7992

No. 7993

No. 7994

No. 7995

No. 7996

S. & F.
LONDON
AND
PARIS.

S. & F.
LONDON
AND
PARIS.

No. 8227

No. 8228

No. 8229

No. 8230

No. 8231

No. 8232

No. 8233

No. 8234

No. 8235

No. 8236

No. 8237

No. 8238

No. 8239

No. 8240

No. 8241

No. 8242

No. 8243

No. 8244

No. 8245

No. 8246

No. 8247

No. 8248

No. 8249

No. 8250

No. 8251

No. 8252

No. 8253

No. 8254

No. 8255

8401
8402
8402
8402
8403
8404
8405
8406
8407
8408
8409
8410
8411
8412
8413
8414
8415
8416
8417
8418
8419
8420

S. & F.
LONDON.

S. & F.
LONDON

UMBRELLA, WALKING STICK, OR FLOWER STANDS.

No. 9146
Fine Art Pottery, Umbrella or Flower Stand.

No. 9147
Fine Art Pottery, Umbrella or Flower Stand.

No. 9150
Fine Art Pottery, Umbrella or Flower Stand.
Real Japanese.

For Pampas Grass, &c. (see Price List).
  ,, Umbrellas, Sticks and Whips (see pages 668 to 671).

No. 9148
Fine Art Pottery, Umbrella or Flower Stand.

TRADE MARK

No. 9149
Fine Art Pottery, Umbrella or Flower Stand.

No. 6684.—Imitation Brass 5-light Candelabrum, highly finished and polished. Height to top of candelabrum 30½ inches, width 12½ inches.

No. 6686.—Imitation Brass Statuette Jardinière, with circular top, highly finished and polished. Height 37 inches, diameter at top 15½ inches, width of base 12¼ inches.

No. 6687.—Imitation Brass Statuette Jardinière, with circular top, highly finished and polished. Height 37 inches, diameter at top 15½ inches, width of base 12¼ inches.

No. 6685.—Imitation Brass 5-light Candelabrum, highly finished and polished. Height to top of candelabrum 30½ inches, width 12½ inches.

No. 6688.—Imitation Brass Pedestal, for vases, jardinières, statuettes, &c. Height 45½ inches, width at base 15 inches, width of top 11 inches. Also in smaller sizes, see price list.

No. 6689.—Ebonized Wood Pedestal, for vases, jardinières, statuettes, &c., with fluted column, handsomely carved at top of column. Height 45 inches, width at base 15¼ inches, width at top 13 inches.

No. 6690.—Ebonized Wood Pedestal, for vases, jardinières, statuettes, &c., with fluted column. Height 42 inches, width at base 11¼ inches, width at top 9½ inches.

No. 6691.—Ebonized Wood Pedestal, for vases, jardinières, statuettes, &c., with handsomely carved column. Height 43½ inches, width at base 12½ inches, width at top 11 inches.

No. 6692.—Imitation Brass Pedestal, for vases, jardinières, statuettes, &c. Height 48 inches, width at base 16¾ inches, width at top 13½ inches.

No. 6694A.—Pair of 5-light Candelabra to match Clock No. 6694. Height 21 inches.

No. 6694A.—Pair of 5-light Candelabra to match Clock No. 6694. Height 21 inches.

No. 6694.—Clock in real brass case, highly finished and polished, 15-day movement, striking hours and half-hours. Height 18½ inches, length 13 inches.

No. 6695.—Massive Clock, representing "Fortuna," highly finished French imitation bronze, 15-day movement, striking hours and half-hours on deep-toned gong. Height 26½ inches, length 15½ inches, depth 9 inches.

No. 6695A.—Pair of Vases to match Clock No. 6695, suitable for holding flowers, ferns, &c. Height to top of vase 12¾ inches, length 12¾ inches, depth 8 inches.

No. 6695A.—Pair of Vases to match Clock No. 6695, suitable for holding flowers, ferns, &c. Height to top of vase 12¾ inches, length 12¾ inches, depth 8 inches.

No. 6696.—Square Wood Timepiece, stained rosewood, with gilt mouldings, 30-hour movement. Height 9¼ inches, length 7 inches.

No. 6697.—Fancy Wood Timepiece, Early English style, gilt moulded front, with fancy blue and white dial, 30-hour movement. Height 11½ inches, length 7 inches.

No. 6698.—Fancy Wood Timepiece, walnut and black case, gilt engraved lines, 30-hour lever movement, going in any position. Height 8¾ inches, length 12 inches.

No. 6699.—Fancy Wood Timepiece, walnut case with gilt handle on top, 30-hour lever movement, going in any position. Height 9½ inches, length 7 inches.

No. 6700.—Wood Timepiece, fancy Gothic shape, black wood, with gilt decorations, fancy painted glass front, 30-hour movement. Height 10½ inches, length 6¼ inches.

No. 6701.—Square Wood Timepiece, in either walnut or mahogany case, 30-hour silent movement. Height 12 inches, length 8 inches.

No. 6702.—Wood Timepiece, octagon top walnut case, with decorated glass front, 30-hour pendulum movement. Height 10½ inches, width 7 inches.

No. 6703.—Wood Timepiece, horse shoe and stirrup, solid wood case, assorted colours, 30-hour lever movement, going in any position. Height 11¾ inches, width 7½ inches.

No. 6704.—Wood Timepiece, fancy mahogany case, with gilt moulding, decorated glass front, 30-hour pendulum movement. Height 11 inches, width 8¼ inches.

No. 6705.—Wood Timepiece, octagon top, stained rosewood case, with gilt mouldings, fancy coloured landscape at base, 30-hour movement. Height 16 inches, length 10¾ inches.

No. 6706.—Wood Clock, walnut case, with black reliefs, 30-hour movement, striking hours and half-hours. Height 19 inches, width 11 inches.

No. 6707.—Wood Timepiece, Gothic shape, gilt moulded front, with fancy coloured landscape at base, 30-hour movement. Height 12½ inches, length 8½ inches.

No. 6708.—Fancy Wood Clock, in either walnut or mahogany case, with front glass decorated in colours, visible pendulum, 30-hour striking movement. Height 18 inches, length 12 inches.

No. 6709.—Wood Timepiece, imitation rosewood case, with gilt mouldings, visible pendulum. Height 11¼ inches, length 7½ inches.

No. 6710.—Wood Clock, fancy carved walnut case, silvered metal dial, 8-day striking movement. Height 20¼ inches, width 11¼ inches.

No. 6711.—Fancy Wood Timepiece, gilt moulded front with fancy coloured landscape at base, 30-hour movement. Height 15½ inches, length 10 inches.

S. & F.
London & Paris.

No. 6712.—Wood Timepiece, fancy mahogany case with gilt beading, fancy decorated glass front, 30-hour pendulum movement. Height 16½ inches, width 9½ inches.

No. 6713.—Fancy-shape Walnut-wood Clock, 8-day striking movement, with visible registering pendulum. Height 22 inches, length 14½ inches.

No. 6714.—Square Wood Timepiece, in walnut and black case, gilt engraved lines, 30-hour lever movement, going in any position. Height 13½ inches, length 10¾ inches.

S. & F.
London & Paris.

No. 6715.—Carved Wood Cuckoo Clock, 30-hour striking movement, with weights. Height 14½ inches.

No. 6716. — Carved Wood Cuckoo Clock, 30-hour striking movement, with weights. Height 20 inches.

No. 6717.—Carved Wood Cuckoo Clock, with striking spring movement, without weights. Height 25 inches.

No. 6718.—Carved Wood Cuckoo Clock, 30-hour striking movement, with weights. Height 20 inches.
No. 6718A.—As No. 6718, but with the addition of a quail piping at each quarter-hour.

No. 6719.—Carved Wood Cuckoo Clock, 30-hour striking movement, with weights. Height 16½ inches.

No. 6720.—Carved Wood Cuckoo and Sentry Clock, with 30-hour movement, striking on deep-toned gong, with sentinel which walks to and fro continuously in front of the clock. Height 25 inches.

No. 6720.

No. 6721.—Carved Wood Cuckoo Clock, 30-hour spring movement. Height 10½ inches.

No. 6721.

No. 6722.—Fancy Timepiece, carved oak case, rustic pattern, 8-day French pendulum movement, with fancy coloured dial. Height 13¾ inches, length 9¼ inches.

No. 6722.

No. 6723.—Cuckoo Clock, in richly carved wood case, superior 8-day spring movement, striking the hours and half-hours upon a deep-toned gong. Height 21½ inches.

No. 6723.

No. 6724.—Wood Clock, Early English style, oak case, silvered metal dial, 8-day movement, striking hours and half-hours on deep-toned gong. Height 13½ in., width 7½ in.

No. 6724.

No. 6725.—Wood Clock, Early English style, oak case, white enamelled dial, 8-day movement, striking hours and half-hours on deep-toned gong. Height 16½ inches, width 9¾ inches.

No. 6725.

No. 6726.—Wood Clock, Early English style, oak case, with blue and white decoration porcelain dial and plaque, 8-day movement, striking hours and half-hours on deep-toned gong. Height 12¾ inches, width 7½ inches.

No. 6726.

No. 6727.—Wood Clock, Early English style, solid oak case, with blue and white decorated porcelain dial and plaques, 8-day movement, striking hours and half-hours on deep-toned gong. Height 16 inches, width 8 inches.

No. 6727.

No. 6728.—Eight-day English Brass Skeleton Clock, "Fuchsia" pattern, striking 1 blow at the hour, silvered and engraved dial, with shade and marble stand complete. Height from base of stand to top of shade 20½ inches, length of stand 12½ inches.

No. 6729.—Eight-day English Brass Skeleton Clock, Cathedral shape, pierced and silvered dial, chain movement, standing upon 4 gilt pedestals, striking 1 blow at each hour, with shade and marble stand complete. Height from base of stand to top of shade 22 inches, length of stand 15 inches.

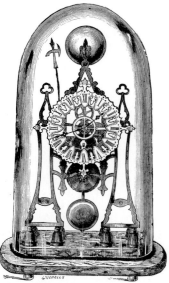

No. 6730.—Eight-day English Brass Skeleton Clock, pierced silvered dial, chain movement, standing upon 8 gilt feet, striking 1 blow at the hour, with shade and marble stand complete. Height from base of stand to top of shade 22 inches, length of stand 14 inches.

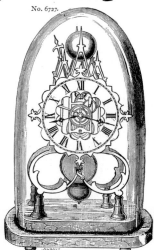

No. 6731.—Eight-day English Brass Skeleton Clock, striking 1 blow at the hour, with shade and marble stand complete. Height from base of stand to top of shade 17 inches, length of stand 11¾ inches.

No. 6732.—Polished Brass Inkstand. Height 3½ inches, length 10½ inches, width 5½ inches.

No. 6733. — Polished Brass Inkstand. Height 2½ inches, length 10½ inches, width 7 inches.

No. 6734.—Polished Brass Inkstand. Height 3½ inches, length 13½ inches, width 6 inches.

N). 6735.—Polished Brass Inkstand. Height 6 inches, length 12 inches, width 8½ inches.

No. 6736.—Polished Brass Inkstand, with candlesticks. Height 7¾ inches, diameter 6½ inches.

No. 6737.—Polished Brass Candlestick. Height 6¾ inches, base 2⅞ inches square.

No. 6739.—Massive 7-Light Candelabrum, real polished brass, very highly finished. Height of candelabrum 24 inches, diameter of base 7⅝ inches.
A large variety of Perforated Paper Candle Shades, with clips and holders and Venetian glass ornaments always kept in stock (as shown in drawing).

No. 6738.—Polished Brass Candlestick. Height 8½ inches, diameter of base 3¾ inches.

No. 6740.—Polished Brass Crumb Scoop and Brush. Length of scoop and brush 11 inches, width of scoop 6¾ inches.

No. 6740.

TRADE MARK.

No. 6741.—Polished Brass Library Suite, consisting of 1 inkstand, height 5⅝ ins., diameter 6 ins.; 1 pair candlesticks, height 7⅞ ins., diameter 4¼ ins.; 1 paper knife, length 8½ ins.; 1 pen tray, length 8½ ins., width 3¾ ins.

No. 6744.—Handsome Presentation Set, consisting of inkstand in rich burnished brass, with two bottles and bronze figure of archer in the centre, and two single-light candlesticks supported by bronze men-at-arms.

No. 6744.

No. 6746.—Polished Brass Candlestick, stork and tortoise. Height 14⅜ inches, length of tortoise 6½ inches, width of tortoise 3 inches.

No. 6742.—Polished Brass Candlestick. Height 5¾ in., diameter of base 3 in.

No. 6743.—Polished Brass Candlestick. Height 5¾ ins., diameter of base 2⅝ ins.

No. 6745. — Crystal Glass Flower Vase, mounted in polished brass, and ornamented with swinging owls, decorated in colours. Height 9¾ inches, diameter of base 3¼ inches.

No. 6746.

No. 6747.—Polished Brass Card and Flower Stand, with cut crystal glass centre, ornamented with swinging owls and cats, decorated in colours. Height 15 inches, diameter of tray 7½ inches.

No. 6748.—Handsome 5-Light Candelabrum, real polished brass, Early English style. Height 16 inches, width at base 6 inches.

No. 6749.—Flower Vase, frosted glass, ormolu mounted, with frosted and coloured glass feet. Height 7⅜ inches, width at feet 4⅝ inches.

No. 6761.—Opera Glass, black japanned body, in leather case, 15 and 19 lines.

No. 6762.—Opera Glass, leather-covered body, japanned mounts, large eye pieces, in leather case, 15 and 19 lines.

No. 6763.—Opera Glass, black morocco leather covered, japanned mounts, in leather case, 15, 17, 19, and 21 lines.

No. 6764.—Opera Glass, morocco leather covered body with gilt beaded mounts, in leather case, 15 and 17 lines.

No. 6770.—Opera Glass, pearl body, gilt mounts, in leather case, 12, 15, 17, and 19 lines.

No. 6772.—Opera Glass, ivory body, gilt mounts of superior quality, with 12 lenses, in leather case, 15, 17, and 19 lines.

No. 6771.—Opera Glass, ivory body, gilt mounts, in leather case, 11, 15, and 17 lines.

No. 6767.—Opera Glass, aluminium body, covered morocco leather, polished mounts, large eye pieces, very superior quality, 12 lenses, in leather case, 17 and 19 lines.

No. 6766.—Opera Glass, morocco leather-covered body, japanned mounts, superior quality, with 12 lenses, in leather case, 15, 17, 19, and 21 lines.

No. 6765.—Opera Glass, black morocco leather covered, japanned mounts, superior quality, with 12 lenses, in leather case, 12, 15, 17, 19, and 21 lines.

No. 6774.—Opera Glass, enamelled body inlaid pearls, with floral decorations in enamel, pearl heads, gilt mounts, in leather case, 11, 15 and 17 lines.

No. 6773.—Opera Glass, ivory body, decorated with ivory beaded mounts, gilt ornamented, in leather case, 13, 15, 17, and 19 lines.

No. 6769.—Opera or Field Glass, russia leather-covered body, with sunshades, 2 draws, japanned mounts, in leather case, 15 and 17 lines.

No. 6768.—Opera Glass, 3 changes, with separate eye pieces for marine, field, or theatre, morocco leather covered, japanned mounts, in leather case, 15, 17, 19, and 21 lines.

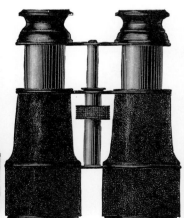

No. 6775.—Opera Glass, silvered body, richly decorated with painted birds, flowers, &c., gilt mounts, in leather case, 15 lines.

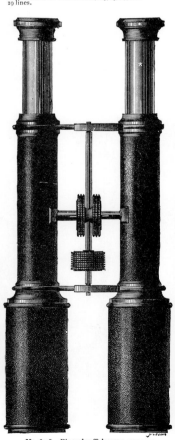

No. 6779.—Field Glass, 3 changes, with separate eye pieces for marine, field, and theatre, morocco leather-covered body, with japanned mounts, and 19, 21, 24, and 26 lines.

No. 6777.—Marine or Field Glass, 6 achromatic lenses, leather-covered body, japanned mounts, 15, 17, 19, 21, 24, and 26 lines.

No. 6776.—Marine Glass, non-achromatic, leather-covered body, japanned mounts, 19, 21, 24, and 26 lines.

Field and Marine Glasses are in solid leather cases, with shoulder strap complete.
All Opera Glasses shown are in flexible leather cases.
Sizes quoted are the diameters of the object glasses. 11 lines equal 1 inch.

No. 6778.—Binocular Telescope, morocco leather-covered body, japanned mounts, 11, 14, 16, 19, and 21 lines.

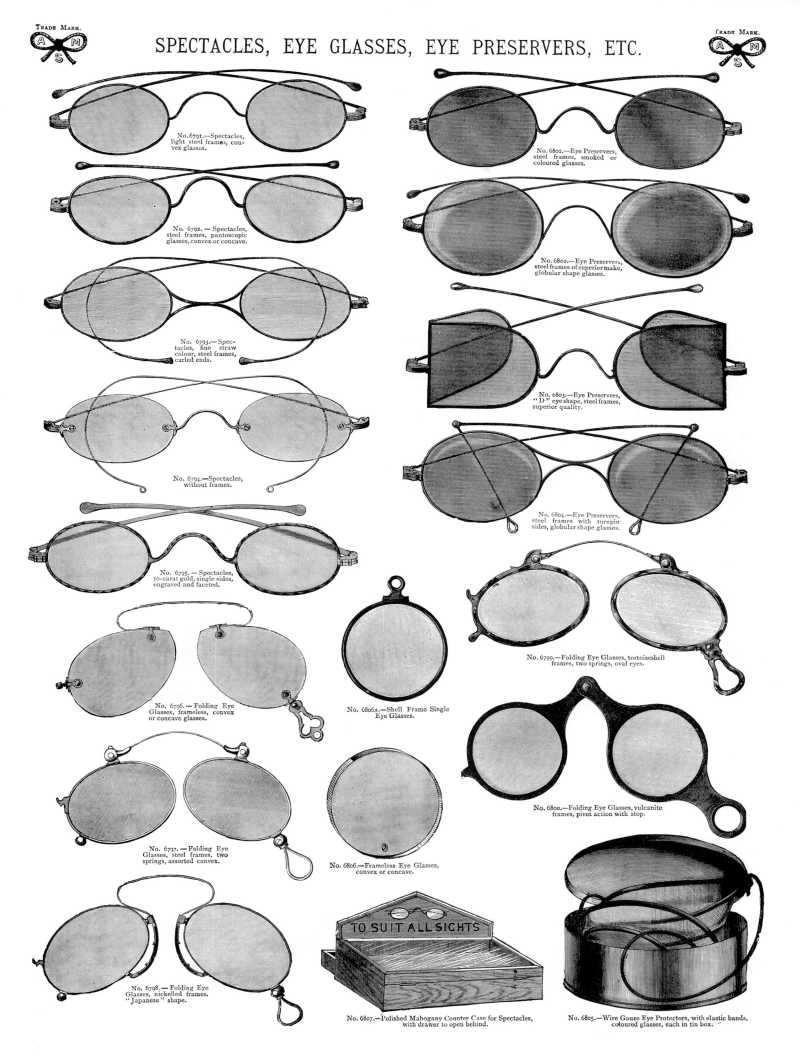

No. 6791.—Spectacles, light steel frames, convex glasses.

No. 6792.—Spectacles, steel frames, pantoscopic glasses, convex or concave.

No. 6793.—Spectacles, fine straw colour, steel frames, curled ends.

No. 6794.—Spectacles, without frames.

No. 6795.—Spectacles, 10-carat gold, single sides, engraved and faceted.

No. 6796.—Folding Eye Glasses, frameless, convex or concave glasses.

No. 6797.—Folding Eye Glasses, steel frames, two springs, assorted convex.

No. 6798.—Folding Eye Glasses, nickelled frames. "Japanese" shape.

No. 6801.—Eye Preservers, steel frames, smoked or coloured glasses.

No. 6802.—Eye Preservers, steel frames of superior make, globular shape glasses.

No. 6803.—Eye Preservers, "D" eye shape, steel frames, superior quality.

No. 6804.—Eye Preservers, steel frames with turnpin sides, globular shape glasses.

No. 6806A.—Shell Frame Single Eye Glasses.

No. 6806.—Frameless Eye Glasses, convex or concave.

No. 6799.—Folding Eye Glasses, tortoiseshell frames, two springs, oval eyes.

No. 6800.—Folding Eye Glasses, vulcanite frames, pivot action with stop.

TO SUIT ALL SIGHTS

No. 6807.—Polished Mahogany Counter Case for Spectacles, with drawer to open behind.

No. 6805.—Wire Gauze Eye Protectors, with elastic bands, coloured glasses, each in tin box.

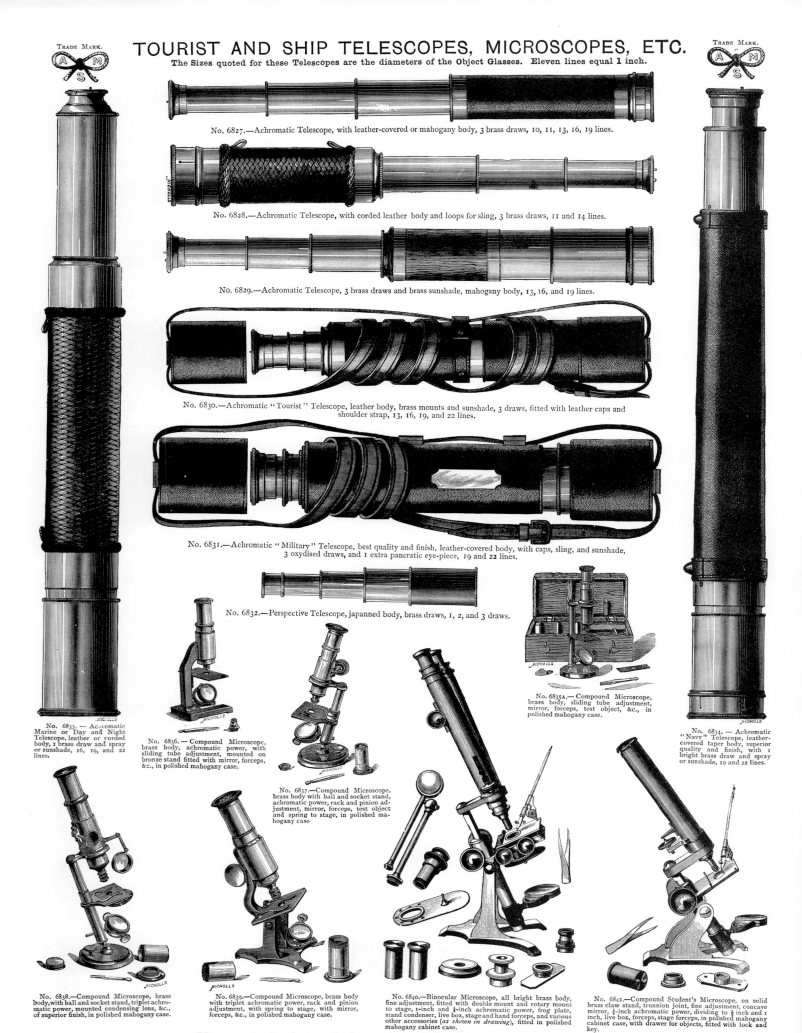

TOURIST AND SHIP TELESCOPES, MICROSCOPES, ETC.

The Sizes quoted for these Telescopes are the diameters of the Object Glasses. Eleven lines equal 1 inch.

No. 6827.—Achromatic Telescope, with leather-covered or mahogany body, 3 brass draws, 10, 11, 13, 16, 19 lines.

No. 6828.—Achromatic Telescope, with corded leather body and loops for sling, 3 brass draws, 11 and 14 lines.

No. 6829.—Achromatic Telescope, 3 brass draws and brass sunshade, mahogany body, 13, 16, and 19 lines.

No. 6830.—Achromatic "Tourist" Telescope, leather body, brass mounts and sunshade, 3 draws, fitted with leather caps and shoulder strap, 13, 16, 19, and 22 lines.

No. 6831.—Achromatic "Military" Telescope, best quality and finish, leather-covered body, with caps, sling, and sunshade, 3 oxydised draws, and 1 extra pancratic eye-piece, 19 and 22 lines.

No. 6832.—Perspective Telescope, japanned body, brass draws, 1, 2, and 3 draws.

No. 6835A.—Compound Microscope, brass body, sliding tube adjustment, mirror, forceps, test object, &c., in polished mahogany case.

No. 6833.—Achromatic Marine or Day and Night Telescope, leather or corded body, 1 brass draw and spray or sunshade, 16, 19, and 22 lines.

No. 6836.—Compound Microscope, brass body, achromatic power, with sliding tube adjustment, mounted on bronze stand fitted with mirror, forceps, &c., in polished mahogany case.

No. 6837.—Compound Microscope, brass body with ball and socket stand, achromatic power, rack and pinion adjustment, mirror, forceps, test object and spring to stage, in polished mahogany case.

No. 6834.—Achromatic "Navy" Telescope, leather-covered taper body, superior quality and finish, with 1 bright brass draw and spray or sunshade, 19 and 22 lines.

No. 6838.—Compound Microscope, brass body, with ball and socket stand, triplet achromatic power, mounted condensing lens, &c., of superior finish, in polished mahogany case.

No. 6839.—Compound Microscope, brass body with triplet achromatic power, rack and pinion adjustment, with spring to stage, with mirror, forceps, &c., in polished mahogany case.

No. 6840.—Binocular Microscope, all bright brass body, fine adjustment, fitted with double mount and rotary mount to stage, 1-inch and ¼-inch achromatic power, frog plate, stand condenser, live box, stage and hand forceps, and various other accessories (as shown in drawing), fitted in polished mahogany cabinet case.

No. 6841.—Compound Student's Microscope, on solid brass claw stand, trunnion joint, fine adjustment, concave mirror, ¼-inch achromatic power, dividing to ½ inch and 1 inch, live box, forceps, stage forceps, in polished mahogany cabinet case, with drawer for objects, fitted with lock and key.

Microscopic Apparatus, Instruments, and Sundries of every description.

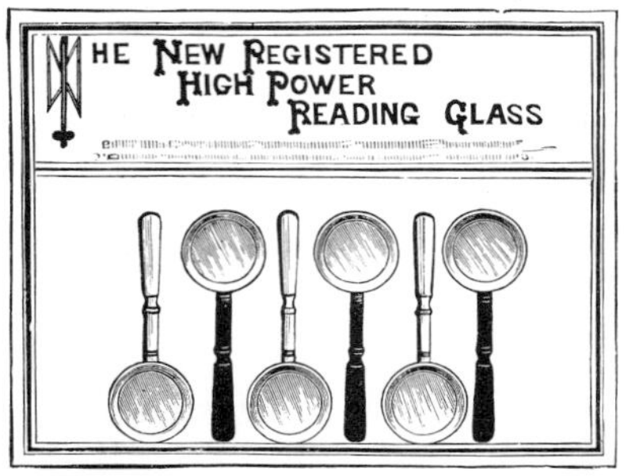

No. 6852.—Reading Glasses, $1\frac{1}{2}$ inches in diameter, assorted nickelled and brass frames, half-dozen on fancy show card.

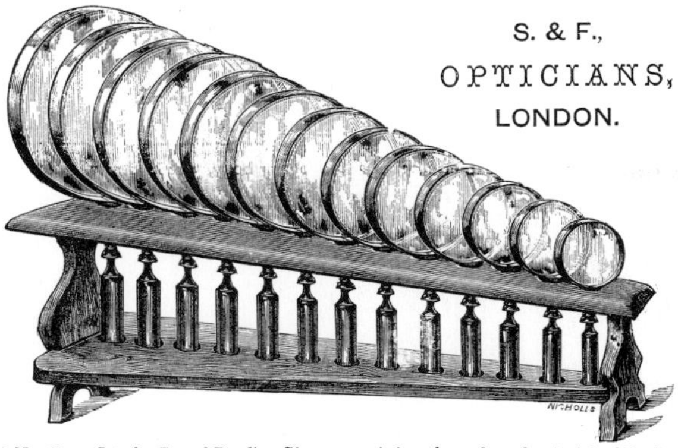

No. 6854.—Set of 13 Round Reading Glasses, consisting of one glass of each of the following sizes: $1\frac{5}{8}$, $1\frac{7}{8}$, $2\frac{1}{8}$, $2\frac{3}{8}$, $2\frac{5}{8}$, $2\frac{7}{8}$, $3\frac{1}{8}$, $3\frac{1}{2}$, $3\frac{3}{4}$, 4, $4\frac{1}{4}$, $4\frac{1}{2}$, $4\frac{3}{4}$ inches diameter. Lenses are of best quality, with German silver frames and black handles.

S. & F.,
OPTICIANS,
LONDON.

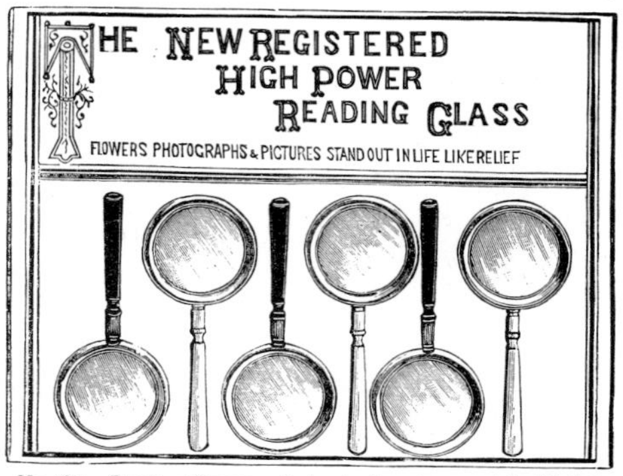

No. 6853.—Reading Glasses, 2 inches in diameter, assorted nickelled and brass frames, half-dozen on fancy show card.

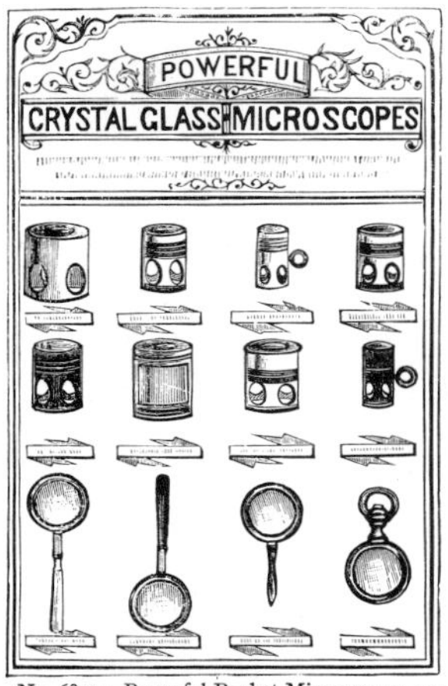

No. 6855.—Powerful Pocket Microscopes, assorted, one dozen various patterns on fancy show card.

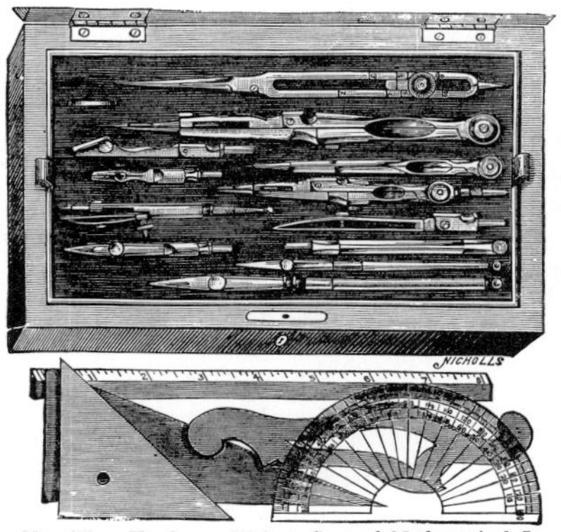

No. 6864.—Handsome Walnut Case of Mathematical Instruments, with lock and key, containing $6\frac{1}{2}$-inch bow compass, and $6\frac{1}{2}$-inch proportional brass compass with pen and pencil points, bar, divider, 2 drawing pens, and large protractor.

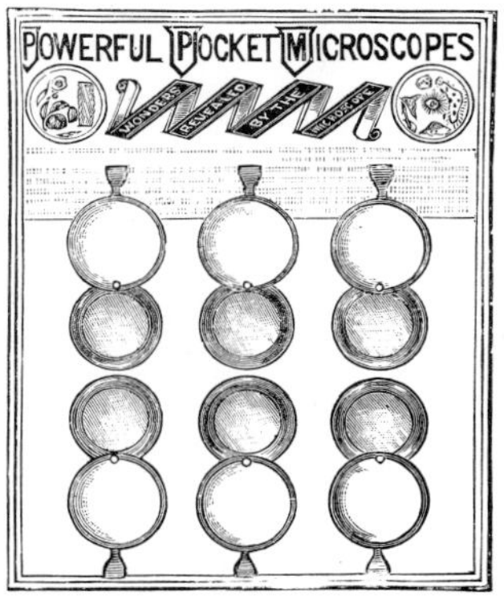

No. 6858.—Powerful Folding Pocket Microscopes, nickel-plated case, half-dozen on fancy show card.

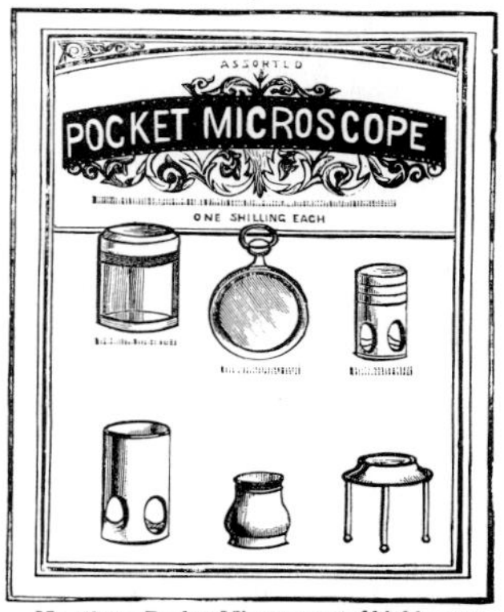

No. 6859.—Pocket Microscopes of highly magnifying power, assorted six patterns on fancy show card.

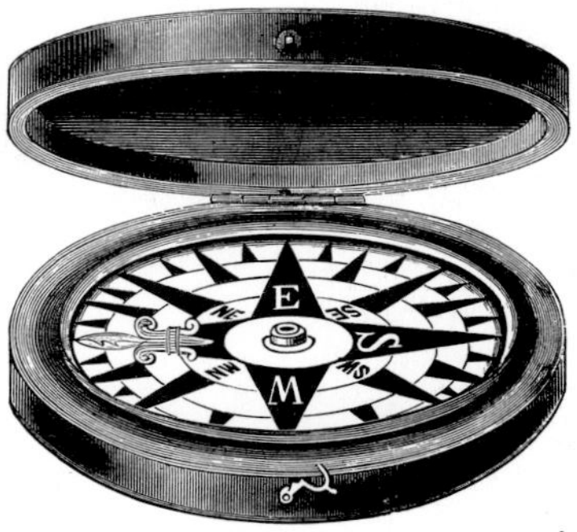

No. 6869.—Pocket Compass, ordinary or Singer's floating card dial, bevelled glass, in morocco case, $1\frac{1}{2}$, $1\frac{3}{4}$, 2, $2\frac{1}{4}$, and $2\frac{1}{2}$ inches in diameter.

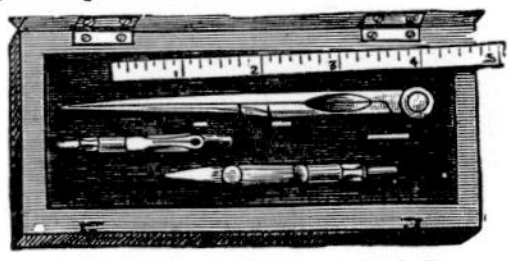

No. 6863.—Rosewood Case of Mathematical Instruments, containing a $6\frac{1}{2}$-inch screw-jointed compass, with pen and pencil points, bar, divider, drawing pen, and protractor, well finished box; with lock and key.

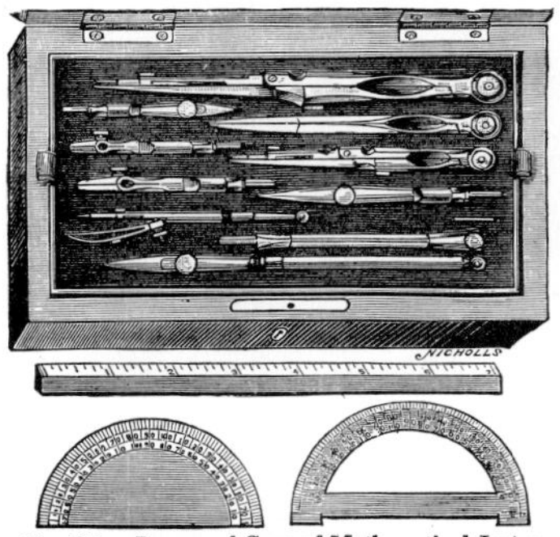

No. 6861.—Case of Mathematical Instruments, containing $5\frac{1}{2}$-inch needle-bow, compass, pen and pencil points, lengthening bar, $4\frac{1}{2}$-inch divider, drawing pen, pencil holder, and protractor, with tray to rosewood box.

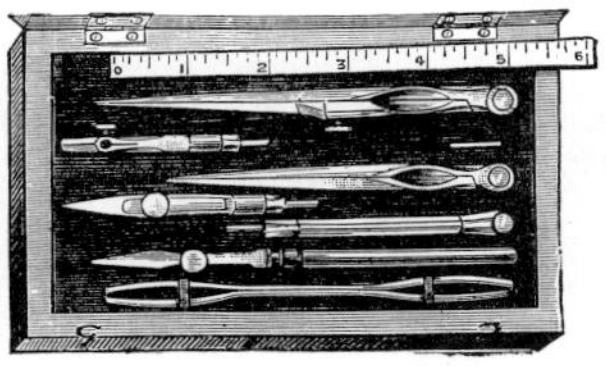

No. 6865.—A 7-inch case of Electrum Mathematical Instruments, consisting of a square walnut or oak case, electrum bound, lined with silk velvet, containing the following extra-finished instruments: 6-inch proportional compass, engine divided, 6-inch compass, with improved needle points, ink and pencil points, and lengthening bar; improved hair divider, ink and pencil bows, with improved needle points; three needle spring bows, 2 drawing pens, pricker, knife key; set of 3 ivory architect's scales, or sector, protractor, and parallel.

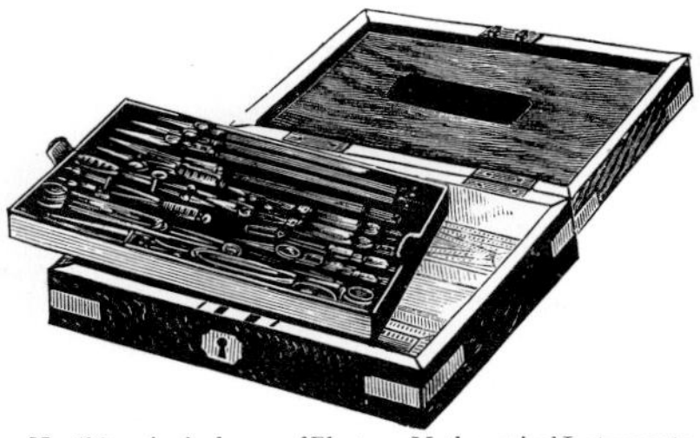

No. 6860.—Case of Mathematical Instruments, containing 4-inch brass compass, with pen and pencil points, and pencil holder.

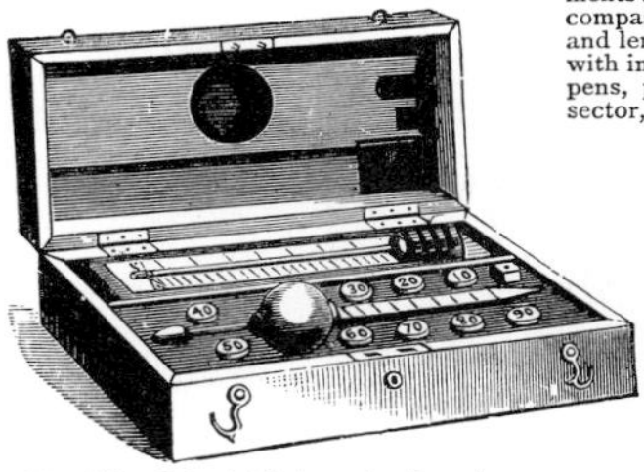

No. 6866.—Sykes's Hydrometer, in mahogany case, 1st quality, best electro-gilt or pure nickel plated, with proof, valuation, and mixing rules, ivory scale thermometer, book of tables and instructions, and trial glass, complete.

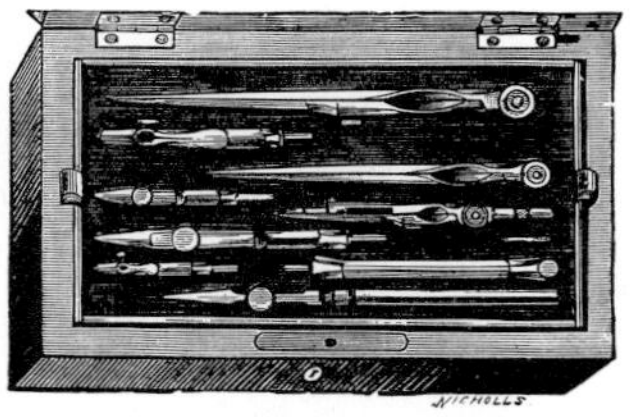

No. 6862.—Rosewood Case of Mathematical Instruments, containing $6\frac{1}{2}$-inch bow compass, with pen and pencil points, bar, divider, drawing pen, and protractor, with tray and lock to case.

No. 6856.—Tripod Microscope, nickel-plated body, with screw adjustment, $1\frac{1}{2}$, $1\frac{3}{4}$, and 2 inches in diameter.

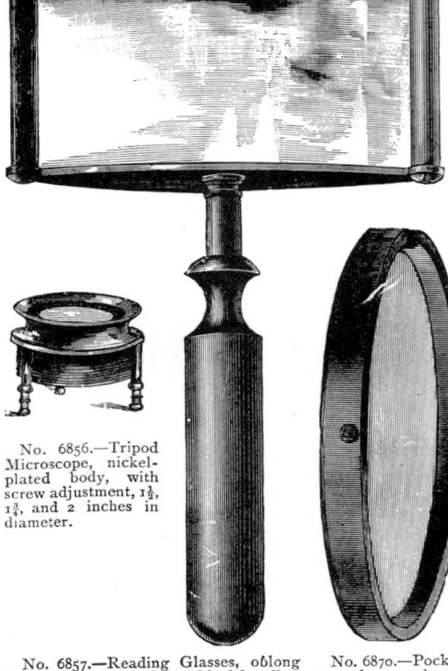

No. 6857.—Reading Glasses, oblong lens, German silver frame, black handles, $2\frac{5}{8}$, $2\frac{7}{8}$, $3\frac{1}{8}$, $3\frac{1}{2}$, and $3\frac{3}{4}$ inches in diameter.

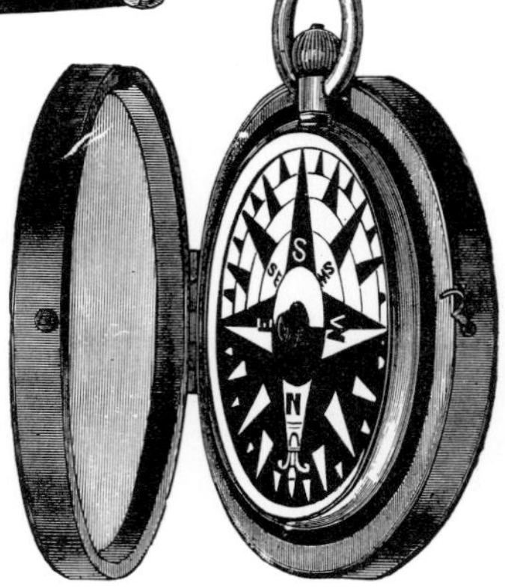

No. 6870.—Pocket Magnetic Compass, in morocco case, best made gilt case, with pearl dial, Singer's patent; best hardened and tempered bar-needle, jewelled cap, keyless action stop, $1\frac{1}{4}$, $1\frac{1}{2}$, $1\frac{3}{4}$, and 2 inches in diameter.

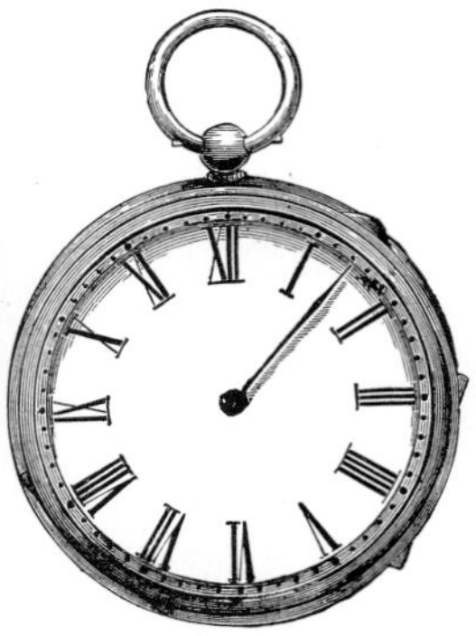

No. 6871.—Pedometer. This instrument, when carried in the pocket, accurately measures the distance walked by the wearer. Nickel-plated case, crystal glass front, in morocco case.

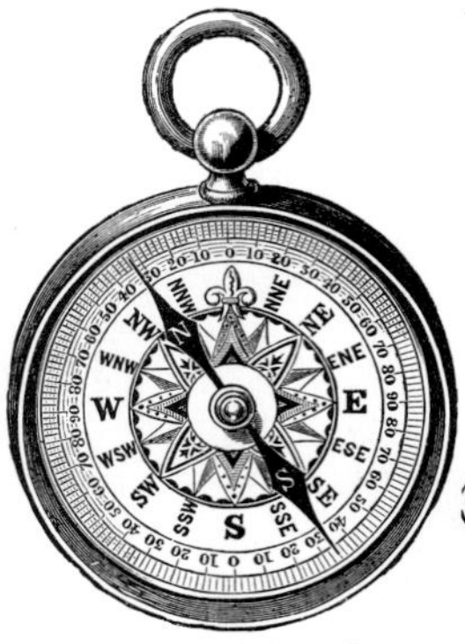

No. 6868.—Watch Form Compass, in wash-leather bag, gilt case, card dial, brass cap, blued needle, $1\frac{1}{4}$, $1\frac{1}{2}$, $1\frac{3}{4}$, and 2 inches in diameter.

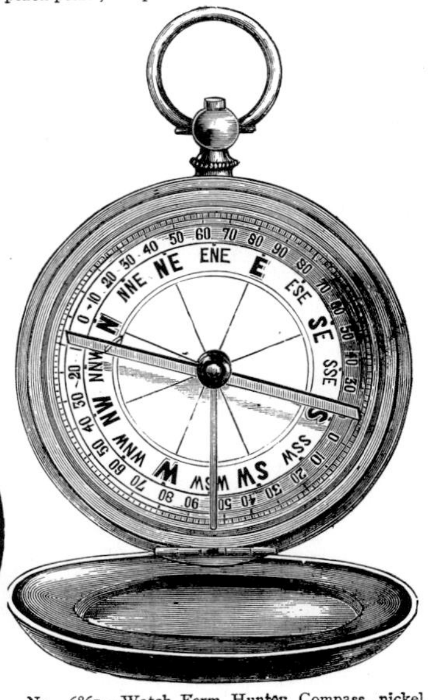

No. 6867.—Watch Form Hunter Compass, nickel plated, secret spring, enamelled card dial, best hardened and tempered edge bar needle, jewelled cap, self-acting stop, $1\frac{1}{2}$, $1\frac{3}{4}$, and 2 inches in diameter.

STEREOSCOPES, GRAPHOSCOPES, MAGNETIC MACHINES, &c.

Cabinet Stereoscope.

Graphoscope, with Large Lens.

Revolving Stereoscope.

TRADE MARK.

No. 6893.—Grapho-scope, with large lens for viewing photographs and large pictures. Also small lenses for viewing opaque or transparent stereo-scopic slides.

No. 6883.—Monocle and Stereoscope com-bined. The Stereoscope is fitted with opera eye pieces and side screw adjustment, ebon-ized and engraved body, very superior finish, 6½-inch lens.

No. 6884.—Monocle, for viewing photographs, &c., large size, ebonized and engraved body, very superior finish.

No. 6893.

No. 6885.—Very handsome solid rosewood or walnut Revolving Cabinet Stereo-scope, to hold 200 slides, fitted with screw adjustment to eye pieces, mounted with massive brass handles.

No. 6882.—Cabinet Stereoscope, fitted with large lens, in addition to the stereo-scopic eye pieces, screw adjustment. The body is of ebonized wood, very richly en-graved, mounted on castors, with massive brass handles on sides ; to hold 200 slides.

No. 6889.—Stereoscope, with fixed opera eye pieces, maho-gany body.

No. 6892.—Stereoscope, with opera eye pieces and side screw adjustment, mahogany body.

No. 6891.—Stereoscope, with large opera eye pieces and screw to adjust focus, maho-gany body.

No. 6888.—Mahogany Stereo-scope, with glass reflector.

No. 6890.—Stereoscope with opera top, and screw to adjust focus, mahogany body.

No. 6901.—Galvanic Machine, superior quality, in superior mahogany case, 8 ins. by 7 ins. by 6 ins.

No. 6897.—Magneto-Electric Machine, superior quality, in polished mahogany box with lock and key.

No. 6899.—Magneto-Electric Machine, in polished pinewood box, best quality and finish, silvered wheel.

No. 6886.—Revolving Stereo-scope, walnut or rosewood body, bevelled edge with moulded top, to hold 50 views. Height 18 inches.

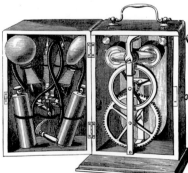

No. 6895.—Magneto-Electric Machine in polished deal box.

No. 6895.

THE NEW POCKET MAGNETO-ELECTRIC MACHINE.

No. 6894.—Pocket Magneto-Electric Ma-chine, in polished mahogany case, 5½ ins. by 3 ins. by 2¾ ins., fitted with lock and key.

No. 6896.—Magneto-Electric Machine, superior finish, in imitation mahogany box.

No. 6900.—Cabinet Magneto-Electric Machine, in upright mahogany case with brass handle and lock and key, fitted with all necessary appliances.

TRADE MARK.

No. 6887.—Monocle, for viewing photo-graphs, &c., mahogany case, carte-de-visite size.

No. 6898.—Magneto-Electric Machine, fitted with registering dial to indicate strength of current (*as shown in drawing*).

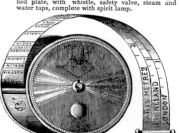

No. 6906.—Miniature Brass Locomotive, on four brass flanged wheels, bronzed ends to boiler, bright bed plate, with whistle, safety valve, steam and water taps, complete with spirit lamp.

No. 6903.—Patent Spring Measure in brass case, fitted with spring stop, linen tape. Sizes, 3, 4, 5, 6, 9, 12, and 18 feet

No. 6902.—Patent Spring Measure in brass case with linen tape. Sizes, 3, 4, 5, and 6 feet.

No. 6904.—Spring Measure with Three Measurements on one side, and the ells, &c., of various countries on the other, brass case, fitted with patent spring stop, linen tape. Sizes, 3, 4, 5, and 6 feet.

No. 6905A.—In Leather Case, with folding handle, ⅝-inch linen tape, marked on both sides. Sizes, 24, 33, 40, 50, 66, 75, and 100 feet.

All Magic Lanterns in this List are of the best manufacture, with the latest improvements. Care is taken that they are sent out complete with accessories, and in good working order.

No. 6993.—The Improved New Mineral Oil Russian Iron Lantern, 4-inch condenser, with improved all brass stage, and special rack achromatic portrait front lens, and fitted with the improved new three-wick lamps, in case.

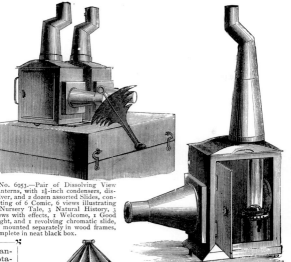

No. 6953.—Pair of Dissolving View Lanterns, with 1⅜-inch condensers, dissolver, and 2 dozen assorted Slides, consisting of 6 Comic, 6 views illustrating a Nursery Tale, 3 Natural History, 3 views with effects, 1 Welcome, 1 Good Night, and 1 revolving chromatic slide, all mounted separately in wood frames, complete in neat black box.

No. 6984.—The Polytechnic Lantern and Slides, comprising a new form of lantern to burn mineral oil, with 3-inch condenser, and 24 superior slides, consisting of Nursery Tales, Riddles, Comic Slipping Slides, and Views, complete in neat box.

Every description of Lantern Apparatus and adaptations, including Gas Bags, Pressure Boards, Aphengescopes, Generators, Purifiers, Lime Cylinders, Screens, Screen Stands, Carrier Frames, &c., can be supplied at the shortest notice.

No. 6937.—Magic Lantern, with 3-inch lens, brass front and solar argand lamp, in neat black box.

TRADE MARK.

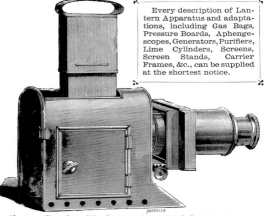

No. 6997.—Cheap form of New Lantern in japanned tin body, with 3½-inch condensing lenses, and the improved new lamp, in box complete.

No. 6975.—Bi-Unial Lantern, with polished mahogany body, lined with tin, with 3½-inch condensers.

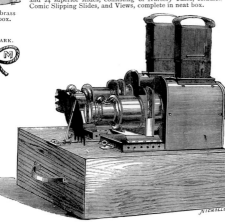

No. 6994.—Pair of the Improved New Mineral Oil Russian Iron Lanterns, 4-inch condensers, with improved all brass stage, and special rack achromatic portrait front lens, and fitted with the improved new 3-wick lamps, complete in case.

No. 7002.—Photographic Slides for Magic Lanterns, plain or coloured.

No. 6688. — Best Tin Japanned Body Magic Lantern, to burn paraffin oil, of improved shape, brass front and nozzle, brass paraffin lamp and brass chimney, in neat box, with directions.

No. 6932.—Magic Lantern, with brass jacket and sliding front, rack and pinion adjustment to lamp.

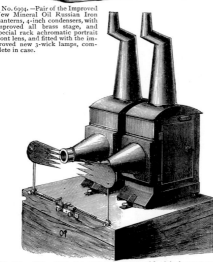

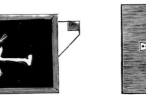

No. 7006.—Changing Comic Slides in great variety of amusing subjects.

No. 6979.—The "Gem" sets of Lanterns and Slides, complete in box, in various sizes, consisting of a superior Magic Lantern and 1 dozen best quality Slides, comprising 4 superior Comic, 4 Nursery Tales, and 4 Movable Slides.

No. 6961.—Pair of Dissolving View Lanterns, with 3½-inch compound condensers, and rack dissolver, complete in box with lock and key.

No. 7006.—Changing Comic Slides in great variety of amusing subjects, such as—

Boy stealing Jam.
Man swallowing Rats.
Dentist drawing Teeth.
Parson driving Pig.
Tightrope Dancer.
Cobbler at Work.
Scotchman taking Snuff.
Lady on Kicking Donkey, &c., &c.

No. 7003.—Chromatropes and Moving Slides of every description.

No. 7004.—Illustrated Jokes, Conundrums, Hymns, &c.

No. 7005.—Lever-action Slides in great variety of newest subjects, such as—

Lady Riding. Swan Drinking.
Donkey-riding Extraordinary, &c., &c.

Every description of Slides, Scriptural Subjects, Astronomical, Panoramic, Dioramic, Rackwork, Mechanical, &c., supplied at shortest notice.

No. 7001.—Magic Lantern Slides, Comic, Nursery Tales, and Natural History, in great variety.

PHOTOGRAPHIC APPARATUS AND ACCESSORIES, DRY PLATES, Etc.

SQUARE FOLDING BELLOWS CAMERAS.

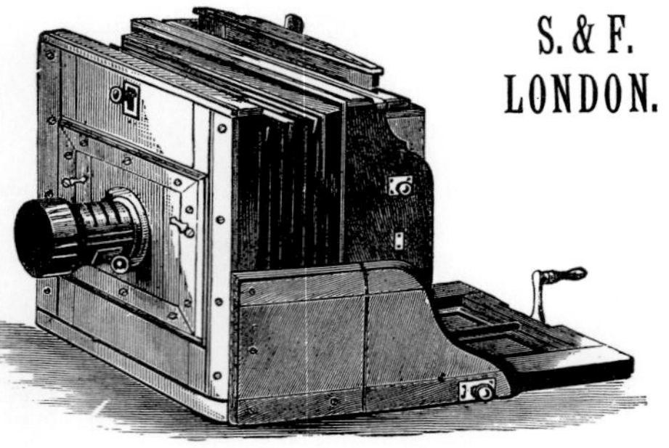

No. 7033.—Square Folding Bellows Cameras. Specially suited for professional use and where they are likely to have rough usage, being the strongest form of camera made. Each fitted with leather bellows, swing-back, folding baseboard, and 2 hinged side wings, which make it perfectly rigid when set up for use. Can be had in all sizes, and each camera being square, takes its plate either horizontally or vertically. Sizes, 6½ by 4¾ inches, 8½ by 6½ inches, 10 by 8 inches, 12 by 10 inches, and 15 by 12 inches.

RAPID DOUBLET LENSES.

No. 7037.—Rapid Doublet Lenses for Groups and Views. Suitable for cameras Nos. 7033, 7034, and 7041. Each complete with Waterhouse diaphragms.

Sizes.		Focus.
4¼ by 3¼ inches	... ...	4½ inches
5 ,, 4 ,,	... ...	5½ ,,
6½ ,, 4¾ ,,	... ...	7½ ,,
8½ ,, 6½ ,,	... ...	10 ,,
10 ,, 8 ,,	... ...	12 ,,
12 ,, 10 ,,	... ...	15 ,,

FOLDING TRIPOD STANDS,

Suitable for Large and Small Cameras.

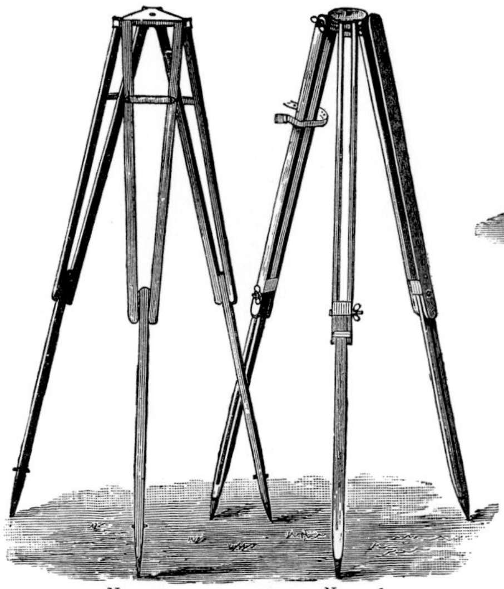

No. 7035. No. 7036.

No. 7035.—Tripod Stand, with sliding legs to adapt to uneven ground. Sizes of tops, 4, 6, and 8 inches.

No. 7036.—Best Ash Tripod, brass top, covered in leather, rigid legs. The strongest pattern folding tripod made. Sizes of tops, 4, 6, 8, and 10 inches.

LIGHT PORTABLE TOURISTS' CAMERAS.

Specially for Dry Plate Work.

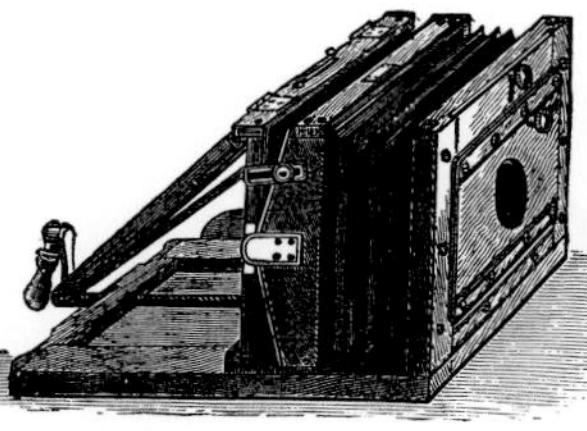

7034 (open).

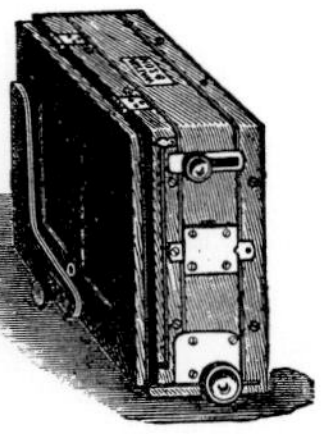

7034 (closed).

No. 7034.—Light Portable Tourists' Cameras, specially for dry dry plate work. The lightest and most compact form of camera that can be made perfectly rigid. It has leather bellows body, rising and sliding front, swinging back, and folding baseboard. These cameras are horizontal, but are arranged that they may screw to the tripod on their side when required for upright pictures. Each camera is supplied complete with 3 double dark slides. Sizes, 4¼ by 3¼ inches, 5 by 4 inches, 6½ by 4¾ inches, 7½ by 5 inches, 8 by 5 inches, 8½ by 6½ inches, 10 by 8 inches, and 12 by 10 inches.

Note.—The focussing adjustment may be either by screw, as illustrated, or by rackwork at side.

SINGLE LANDSCAPE LENSES.

No. 7039.—Single Landscape Lenses, of highest quality, for fine landscape work, giving a more brilliant picture than any other kind of lens. Suitable for cameras Nos. 7033, 7034, and 7041.

Sizes.		Focus.
4¼ by 3¼ inches	... ...	4½ inches
5 ,, 4 ,,	... ...	5 ,,
6½ ,, 4¾ ,,	... ...	7 ,,
7½ ,, 5 ,,	... ...	8 ,,
8½ ,, 6½ ,,	... ...	9 ,,
10 ,, 8 ,,	... ...	10 ,,
12 ,, 10 ,,	... ...	11 ,,

UNIVERSAL STUDIO CAMERA.

Trade Mark.

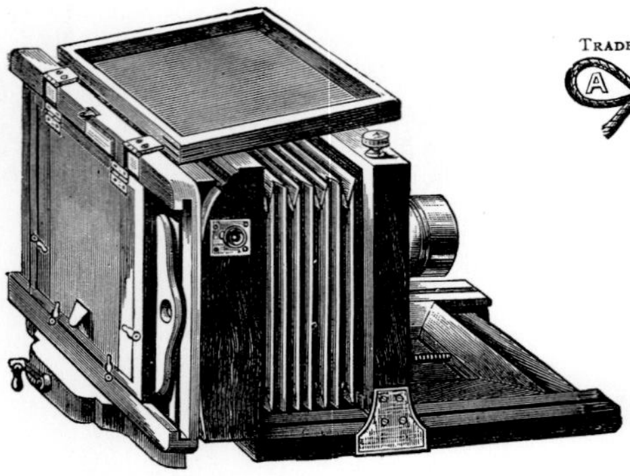

No. 7040.—Universal Studio Camera, having double extension, and giving sufficient range of focus to use for copying if required. Fitted with leather bellows body, rigid base, and arranged with repeating back to take 2 pictures on the full-size plate of camera, or of any size smaller. These cameras are square, to take their plates either horizontally or vertically. If desired may have double-swing back at extra cost. For plates 6½ by 4¾ inches, 8½ by 6½ inches, 10 by 8 inches, and 12 by 10 inches.

INSTANTANEOUS DROP SHUTTER.

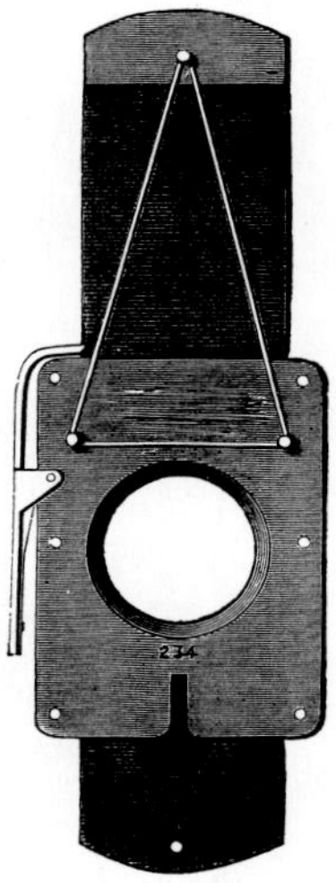

No. 7038.—Instantaneous Drop Shutter, for large or small lenses, to fit on hood of lens. In ordering, please quote exact size of hood of lens.

LIGHT FOLDING TOURIST CAMERA.

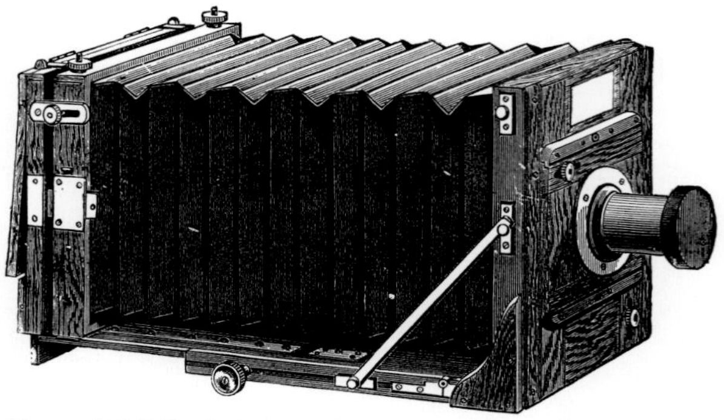

No. 7041.—Light Folding Tourist Camera of an improved construction, having double extension to focus, and giving most extreme range possible for each sized camera, with leather bellows body, rackwork adjustment to focus, double-swing back, double-action front, reversing frame to allow of taking either horizontal or upright pictures without turning the camera; combining every improvement required for the modern practice of photography. They are the highest class instrument made. In all sizes, each complete, with 3 double dark slides. Sizes 5 by 4 inches, 6½ by 4¾ inches, 7½ by 5 inches, 8 by 5 inches, 8½ by 6½ inches, 10 by 8 inches, 12 by 10 inches, and 15 by 12 inches.

NON-ACTINIC LANTERNS.

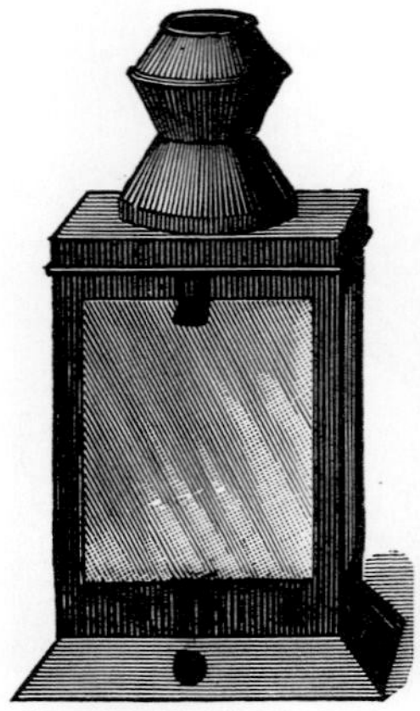

No. 7042.—Non-Actinic Lantern, large size, to burn paraffin oil.

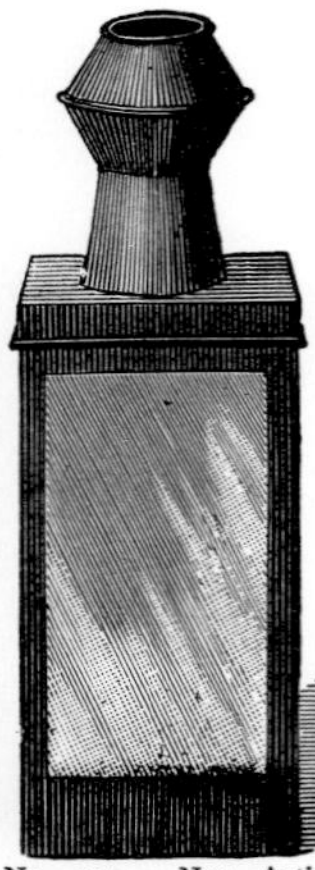

No. 7043.—Non-Actinic Lantern, medium size, for candle.

For Magic Lanterns and Slides, Opera and Field Glasses, Spectacles, &c., see Pages 413 to 418.

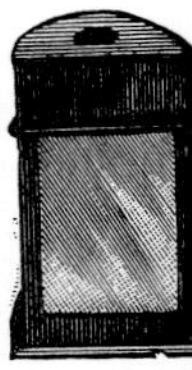

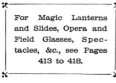

No. 7044.—Non-Actinic Lantern, small size, for travelling.

CAMERA STAND.

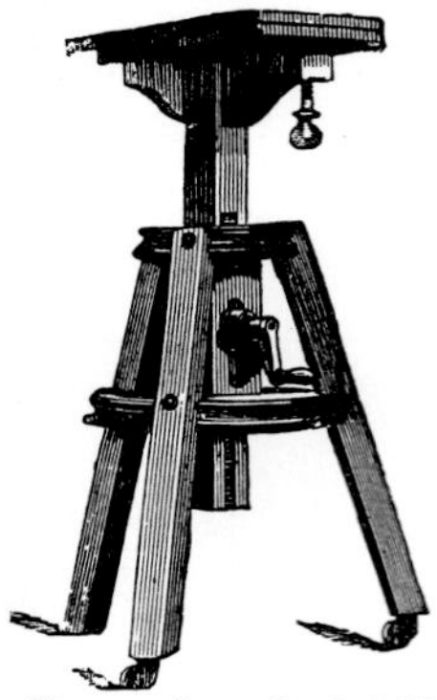

No. 7045.—Camera Stand. Solid stands for indoor use, with rackwork to raise or lower, and screw to tilt. In polished pine, ash, or oak.

SENSITIVE DRY PLATES.

No. 7046.—Sensitive Dry Plates, rapid and extra rapid, packed in cases of one dozen in the following sizes :—

4¼ by 3¼ inches
5 ,, 4 ,,
6½ ,, 4¾ ,,
7½ ,, 5 ,,
8 ,, 5 ,,
8½ ,, 6½ ,,
9 ,, 7 ,,
10 ,, 8 ,,
12 ,, 10 ,,
15 ,, 12 ,,

Ready sensitive paper. Pyrogallic acid.

QUICK ACTING PORTRAIT LENSE.

No. 7047.—Quick Acting Portrait Lense, suitable for use with Studio Camera No. 7040, with rack and pinion to focus, and fitted with a case of Waterhouse stops.

Sizes.	Focus.
Carte-de-visite	4½ inches
Cabinet	7 ,,
8½ inches by 6½ inches	10 ,,
10 ,, ,, 8 ,,	14 ,,

New Complete Students' Sets of Photographic Apparatus.

No. 7049.—Complete Students' Sets of Photographic Apparatus, consisting of light folding bellows camera, with rackwork to focus, swing back, 3 double dark slides, rapid doublet lens with Waterhouse diaphragms, and folding tripod stand, for working following sizes of plates: 4¼ by 3¼ inches, 5 by 4 inches, 6½ by 4¾ inches, 7½ by 5 inches, 8½ by 6½ inches, and 10 by 8 inches.

No. 7050.—Complete Photographic Chests, iron bound, for travelling, containing 2 dozen dry plates, 1 quire sensitive paper, printing frames, developing trays, non-actinic lantern, scales and weights, and full supply of chemicals for the dry plate process, for working following sizes of plates: 4¼ by 3¼ inches, 5 by 4 inches, 6½ by 4¾ inches, 7½ by 5 inches, 8½ by 6½ inches, and 10 by 8 inches.

QUOTATIONS GIVEN FOR PURE CHEMICALS AND PREPARATIONS USED IN THE VARIOUS PROCESSES OF THE PHOTOGRAPHIC ART.

COLOURED AND DECORATED GLASS WARE.

TABLE GLASS, CUT, ENGRAVED, AND PRESSED

TABLE GLASS,
RICHLY CUT AND DECORATED WITH GOLD.

GLASS AND STONE FILTERS AND AQUARIA.

COLOURED AND DECORATED GLASSWARE.

Coloured and Decorated Glassware, which, as an article of commerce in this country, was scarcely known half a century ago, when but a few common glasses and ornamental vases, &c., were made and introduced here, has undergone such improvements in its manufacture, that not only all modern fine colours, but also the most carefully studied ancient and modern designs of Vases, Lustres, Baskets, Flower Stands, and many other articles, are produced.

These improvements, combined with the now celebrated hand-painted decorations and moderate prices, have given this Coloured and Decorated Glassware a high rank amongst articles of luxury designed for the ornamentation of Rooms, Halls, &c., and have made it almost an article of necessity.

The patterns which we herewith bring under your notice are but a small representation of an assortment of many thousands of different shapes and decorations, of which we hold stock. To keep pace with the constant changes which take place in the shapes and style of decoration, as also in all other manipulations to which this Glass is subjected, we are compelled to change our assortment very frequently so as to be enabled to supply our customers with the latest novelties.

We have selected, therefore, as illustrations, such patterns as we consider will find a ready sale for a number of years; but at the same time, for reasons stated above, we recommend our customers not to confine their orders strictly to the illustrated patterns, but, to some extent, to leave it with us to send a similar article to the one ordered.

Although our stock of Coloured and Decorated Glassware is by far the largest held in this country, yet it may occur that, through the great demand for certain patterns, the stock of these becomes exhausted, in which case it requires at least three months to replace. When, therefore, strict adherence to patterns is required, kindly allow that time for the delivery of such articles as are not in stock when the order is received.

In a Supplementary Catalogue we submit list of assortments of this Glass in Cases. More than thirty years' experience as manufacturers, importers, and traders with all parts of the globe, places us in a favourable position to prepare assortments suited to stock a shop or warehouse, either in this country or the various countries where coloured and decorated glass finds a ready sale.

The prices for original packages are considerably lower than for goods already opened out for stock, on account of the saving, in our warehouse, of the cost of labour of unpacking and re-packing, and the consequent risk of breakage.

The advantage, therefore, in purchasing assortments ready packed at the manufactory is evident.

ENGLISH AND FOREIGN TABLE GLASS AND TABLE ORNAMENTS.

The following articles are required to make a complete assortment for Table use :—

Wine Glasses, Port.	Champagne Tumblers.	Claret Jugs.	Round Dishes.
,, ,, Sherry.	Goblets.	Carafes and Tumblers.	Oval ,,
Claret ,,	Custard Glasses.	Water Bottles.	Butter ,,
Champagne Glasses.	Jelly ,,	Water Sets.	Marmalades.
Liqueur ,,	Finger Basins.	Pickle Jars.	Sugar Basins.
Soda-water Tumblers.	Decanters, quart.	Salt Cellars.	Cream Jugs.
Tumblers, half-pint.	,, pint.	Comports.	Celery Glasses.

Our purchases of every description of Flint Glass being on a large scale, enable us very often to sell at cheaper prices than the ordinary prices quoted by the manufacturers.

All Goods are carefully examined, and only Glass of good colour sent. Each Tumbler, Wine Glass, &c., of the better quality is carefully wrapped in paper.

When comparing prices per dozen with those quoted per case, the advantage to the purchaser will be found very considerable.

All prices are subject to fluctuation.

Foreign Glass is packed in Cases, but Glass of English manufacture can be packed in either Cases or Casks. No charge is made for original foreign Cases; English Glass is generally packed in Casks, which are charged at moderate prices.

Strong sound Cases or Casks only are used for packing Glassware, and great care is taken that the Cases are properly filled up with hay or straw to prevent breakage.

Monograms, Crests, Masonic or other devices, engraved on each Glass at a very moderate charge.

Cut, Engraved, or Moulded Glass of every description made to order and to any practicable design required.

Most of the patterns illustrated in the Catalogue can be executed in inferior Glass when ordered in quantities.

The large stock which we hold of Flint Glass of every description enables us to execute most orders intrusted to us within a few days after their receipt.

All Glass is packed by the most skilful packers in the trade.

FOR ASSORTED GLASSWARE IN ORIGINAL CASES, see Supplementary Catalogue.

ALL PRICES QUOTED IN OUR PRICE LIST ARE NETT.

COLOURED AND DECORATED GLASS.

S & F.
London & Paris.

S & F.
London & Paris.

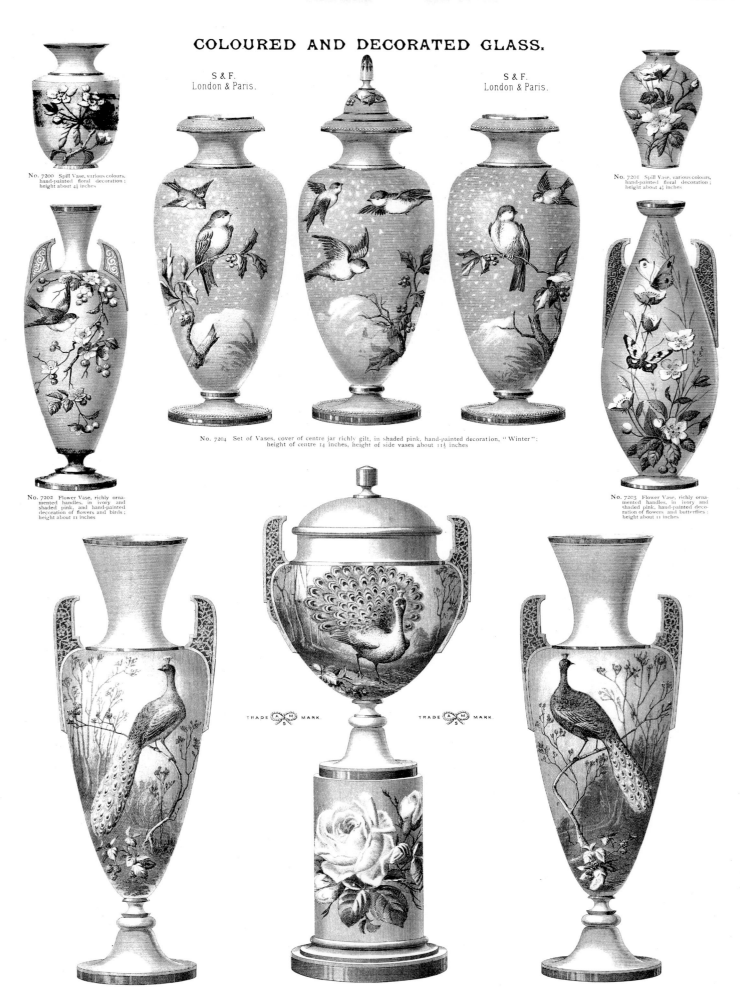

No. 7200 Spill Vase, various colours, hand-painted floral decoration; height about 4½ inches

No. 7201 Spill Vase, various colours, hand-painted floral decoration; height about 4½ inches

No. 7204 Set of Vases, cover of centre jar richly gilt, in shaded pink, hand-painted decoration, "Winter"; height of centre 14 inches, height of side vases about 11½ inches

No. 7202 Flower Vase, richly ornamented handles, in ivory and shaded pink, and hand-painted decoration of flowers and birds; height about 11 inches

No. 7203 Flower Vase, richly ornamented handles, in ivory and shaded pink, hand-painted decoration of flowers and butterflies; height about 11 inches

TRADE MARK

TRADE MARK

No. 7205 Set of Vases, with richly ornamented and gilt handles, in pink or ivory colour, fine hand-painted decoration of landscape and peacocks; the pedestal of centre bowl is richly decorated with flowers; height of centre 21 inches, height of side vases about 17 inches

Paxton & Bradsford Lith Sheffield

MANUFACTURERS, IMPORTERS, WAREHOUSEMEN AND AGENTS. ENTERED AT STATIONERS' HALL.

COLOURED AND DECORATED GLASS.

No. 7206 Jar, with cover, and richly gilt handles, in pink or ivory color, decorated with hand-painted flowers and birds; height about 14 inches

No. 7207 Flower Vase, richly gilt handles, in pink, the shield a pale blue color, hand-painted decoration; height about 12 ins.

No. 7208 Flower Vase, richly decorated and gilt handles, in ivory color or pink, hand-painted decoration of birds and landscape; height about 12 inches

No. 7209 Jar, with cover, cylinder shape, with richly gilt handles, in ivory color, hand-painted decoration of bird and ferns; height about 13½ inches.

TRADE MARK.

No. 7210 Flower Vase, in ivory color, richly gilt handles, fine hand-painted decoration of landscape with deer; height about 17 inches. Covered Bowl to match, as No. 7205, to make set of three

S & F.
London & Paris.

S & F.
London & Paris.

No. 7211 Flower Vase, chamois color ground, with two richly decorated and gilt handles, neck and foot, fine hand-painted decoration of landscape and bird; height about 21 inches

TRADE MARK.

No. 7210 Flower Vase, in ivory color, richly gilt handles, fine hand-painted decoration of landscape with deer; height about 17 inches. Covered Bowl to match, as No. 7205, to make set of three

ENTERED AT STATIONERS' HALL. MANUFACTURERS, IMPORTERS, WAREHOUSEMEN AND AGENTS. Pawson & Brailsford Lith Sheffield

COLOURED AND DECORATED GLASS WARE.

S. & F.
London & Paris.

S. & F.
London & Paris.

No. 7212 Bouquet Holder with gilt handles, assorted colors, hand-painted floral decoration; height about 5¼ inches

No. 7214 Bouquet Holder with gilt handles, assorted colors, hand-painted floral decoration; height about 5¼ inches

No. 7213 Bouquet Holder with gilt handles, assorted colors, hand-painted floral decoration; height about 5¼ inches

No. 7216 Set of Vases, centre jar with handles richly enamelled and gilt, on pink color ground, fine hand-painted decoration of ferns and birds; height of jar about 13 inches, height of vases 11 inches.

No. 7215 Bouquet Holder with gilt handles, assorted colors, hand-painted floral decoration; height about 5½ inches

TRADE MARK.

TRADE MARK.

No. 7217 Jar with cover, handles richly gilt, on chamois or pink color ground, hand-painted enamelled decoration of flowers and butterfly; height about 17 inches. Vases to match about 13½ inches high

No. 7218 Flower Vase, richly gilt and decorated handles, on pink or chamois colored ground, hand-painted decoration of birds and foliage; height about 21 inches

No. 7219 Jar with cover, richly gilt handles, chamois colored ground, hand painted landscape and bird decoration; height about 14 inches. Vases to match 11½ inches high

ENTERED AT STATIONERS' HALL. MANUFACTURERS, IMPORTERS, WAREHOUSEMEN AND AGENTS. Pawson & Brailsford, Lith. Sheffield.

121

COLOURED AND DECORATED GLASS.

No. 7220   Liqueur Set, 9 pieces, (1 bottle, 7 glasses and 1 tray) optic glass richly decorated with gilt and enamel flowers, &c. in gold, amber, aquamarine or ruby color

No. 7226   Set of Vases, pink or chamois colored ground; decorated with fine hand-painted landscape mountain scenery; handles cut, richly gilt and ornamented.   Height of centre jar, about 17 inches, height of vases about 13 inches

No. 7223   Card Tray, pink or canary-colored glass, oblong shaped and cut, varied decoration of flowers, birds, &c., richly gilt; length about 10½ inches

No. 7224   Canteen, crystal glass, richly engraved floral decoration.   The barrel is inlet to the stand, and can be revolved.   Glass dish, diameter about 11 inches

No. 7221   Liqueur Set, 9 pieces, (1 jug, 7 glasses and 1 tray) transparent optic glass, amber color with crystal ornamentation, or aqua color with amber ornamentation, stopper, and feet

S & F.
London & Paris.

S & F.
London & Paris.

No. 7222   Flower Vase, black or chamois colored ground.   The hand-painted decoration of foliage and birds is of a high class.   Height of vase about 17 inches

No. 7227   Set of Vases, optic glass, in aqua or ruby color; richly ornamented with hand-painted classical designs.   Height of centre jar 28 inches, height of side vases about 22 inches.

No. 7225   Flower Vase, jet colored glass. The decoration, representing Cupids surrounded with ornamental design, is hand-painted.   Height of vase about 17 inches.

No. 7228   Flower Vase, hand-painted decoration of flowers, birds, &c. on grey, ivory, canary, pink, or celadon colored ground.   Height about 12 inches.

No. 7229   Flower Vase, hand-painted decoration of begonia leaves, flowers, &c. on ivory or canary-colored ground. Height about 14½ inches.

TRADE MARK.   TRADE MARK.

No. 7230   Flower Bowl, pink or ivory-colored ground, decorated with hand-painted animals, landscape, &c.   The handles are richly gilt and ornamented.   Extreme height about 17 inches, diameter of bowl about 8 inches.   These bowls are painted in pairs, the subjects facing each other.   Vases to match this Flower Bowl of same shape as No. 7222, height about 17 inches

No. 7231   Jars with cover, black, opal or ivory-colored ground, handsomely decorated with views of summer and winter; feet and handles cut, richly ornamented and gilt.   Height about 14 inches.

MANUFACTURERS, IMPORTERS, WAREHOUSEMEN AND AGENTS.   Pawson & Brailsford, Lith. Sheffield

"IVORINE" VASES, FLOWER BASKETS &C.

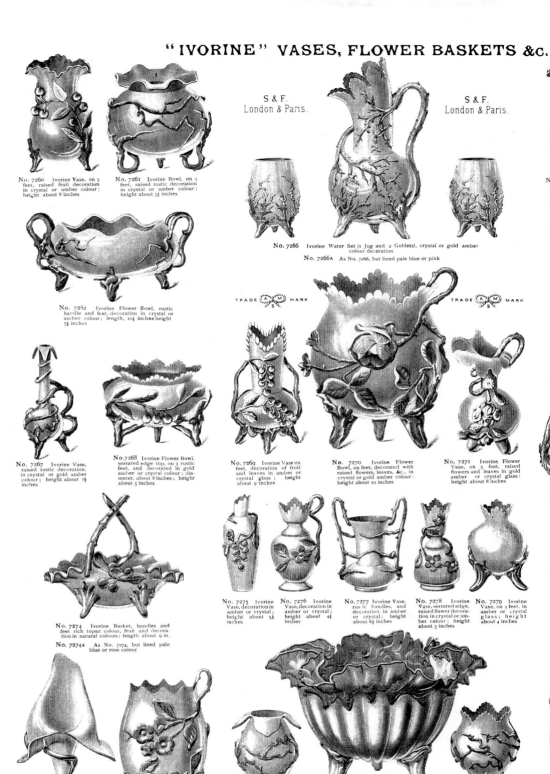

S & F.
London & Paris.

S & F.
London & Paris.

No. 7260 Ivorine Vase, on 3 feet, raised fruit decoration in crystal or amber colour; height about 8 inches

No. 7261 Ivorine Bowl, on 3 feet, raised rustic decoration in crystal or amber colour; height about 5½ inches

No. 7262 Ivorine Flower Bowl, rustic handle and feet, decoration in crystal or amber colour; length, 10¼ inches height 5¼ inches

No. 7266 Ivorine Water Set (1 Jug and 2 Goblets), crystal or gold amber colour decoration

No. 7266A As No. 7266, but lined pale blue or pink

No. 7263 Ivorine Vase, in ivory, pale blue, or pale green colour, with ribbon round neck, edge round top, and feet of contrasting colours; height about 7½ inches

No. 7264 Ivorine Vase in ivory, pale blue, or pale green colour, with ribbon round neck, edge round top, and feet of contrasting colours; height about 7½ in.

No. 7265 Ivorine Fruit Dish, on 4 feet, rustic decorations in gold amber colour; rich gold rim round edge of dish; length about 10½ inches; height, 5 inches

TRADE MARK   TRADE MARK

No. 7267 Ivorine Vase, raised rustic decoration, in crystal or gold amber colour; height about 7½ inches

No. 7268 Ivorine Flower Bowl, serrated edge top, on 3 rustic feet, and decorated in gold amber or crystal colour; diameter, about 8 inches; height about 5 inches

No. 7269 Ivorine Vase on feet, decoration of fruit and leaves in amber or crystal glass; height about 9 inches

No. 7270 Ivorine Flower Bowl, on feet, decorated with raised flowers, leaves, &c., in crystal or gold amber colour; height about 10 inches

No. 7271 Ivorine Flower Vase, on 3 feet, raised flowers and leaves in gold amber or crystal glass; height about 8 inches

No. 7272 Ivorine Tripod Basket, handles, feet and decoration in gold amber or crystal glass; height about 9 in.

No. 7272A As No. 7272, but lined light blue or rose colour

No. 7273 Ivorine Vase, with crystal or amber decoration; height about 10 inches

No. 7274 Ivorine Basket, handles and feet rich topaz colour, fruit and decoration in natural colours; length about 9 in.

No. 7274A As No. 7274, but lined pale blue or rose colour

No. 7275 Ivorine Vase, decoration in amber or crystal; height about 5½ inches

No. 7276 Ivorine Vase, decoration in amber or crystal; height about 4½ inches

No. 7277 Ivorine Vase, rustic handles, decoration in amber or crystal; height about 6½ inches

No. 7278 Ivorine Vase, serrated edge, raised flower decoration in crystal or amber colour; height about 5 inches

No. 7279 Ivorine Vase, in amber or crystal glass; height about 4 inches

No. 7280 Ivorine Bowl, on 3 feet, raised crystal or natural colour fruit decoration; diameter about 9½ inches

No. 7281 Ivorine Vase, foot and stem gold amber colour; height 7, 9 or 12 inches

No. 7282 Ivorine Vase, raised flower decoration, in crystal amber or natural colours; height about 9 inches

No. 7283 Ivorine Bowl, rustic decoration, in crystal or gold amber colour; height about 6½ inches

No. 7284 Ivorine Flower Bowl, fluted crinkled edge, lined pale blue or pink, with edges of contrasting colour, and topaz feet; diameter about 11 inches; height about 8 ins.

No. 7284A Dish, similar to No 7284, but shallower and without feet

No. 7285 Ivorine Bowl, rustic decoration, and feet, in amber or crystal glass; height about 6½ inch

No. 7286 Ivorine Vase, on 3 topaz feet, raised flower and leaf decoration, in natural colours; height about 9 inches

No. 7286A As 7286, but lined pink, blue or primrose colour

No. 7287 Ivorine Vase, raised fruit and leaf decoration, in amber or crystal glass; height about 9 inches

No. 7288 Ivorine Flower Basket, on 4 feet, handles and decoration in amber or crystal glass; height about 10 inches

No. 7289 Ivorine Vase, rustic handles and raised flower decoration, in gold amber colour; height about 12 ins.

No. 7290 Ivorine Flower Bowl, on twisted amber stem, decoration of fruit and flowers in natural colours, lined pink; height about 12 inches

No. 7289 Ivorine Vase, rustic handles and raised fruit decoration, in gold amber colour; height about 12 ins.

No. 7291 Ivorine Flower Basket, lined blue or rose colour, handles and feet in topaz or crystal; length about 9 inches; height about 7 inches

ENTERED AT STATIONERS' HALL.   MANUFACTURERS, IMPORTERS, WAREHOUSEMEN AND AGENTS.   Pawson & Brailsford, Lith. Sheffield.

123

No. 7292   Toilet Table Set, 3 pieces, alabaster coloured, pink or crysopas ground, richly gilt, cut stoppers
No. 7292A   6 pieces, comprising 2 scent bottles, 1 puff box, 2 small boxes and ring stand

No. 7302   Toilet Table Set, 9 pieces, hand-painted floral and bird decoration, on ivory, celadon, pink, or canary coloured ground
No. 7302A   6 pieces only, comprising 2 scent bottles, 1 puff box, 2 small boxes, and 1 ring stand

No. 7295   Toilet Table Set, 6 pieces, hand-painted floral decoration on drab, celadon, alabaster coloured, black, or celest blue ground

No. 7293   Toilet Table Set, 3 pieces, hand-painted on opal, celadon, grey, celest blue, or drab ground

No. 7296   Flower Holder, opal glass, hand-painted yellow rose decoration, pink foot and gold lines; height about 5 inches
No. 7297   Flower Holder, opal glass, hand-painted yellow rose decoration, pink foot and neck; height about 4½ inches
No. 7298   Flower Holder, opal glass, hand-painted bird and flower decoration, various coloured neck; height about 5 ins.

No. 7294   Toilet Table Set, 3 pieces, hand-painted on opal, celadon, grey, celest blue, or drab ground

No. 7303   Toilet Table Set, 9 pieces, hand-painted decoration on drab, celadon, or canary coloured ground
No. 7303A   6 pieces only, comprising 2 scent bottles, 1 puff box, 2 small boxes, and 1 ring stand

No. 7299   Flower Holder, shaded ruby, blue and green opaline hand-painted decoration; height about 5 inches
No. 7300   Flower Holder, celadon, ivory or canary coloured ground, hand-painted bird decoration; height about 4 inches
No. 7301   Flower Holder, opal, celadon, ivory or canary coloured ground, hand-painted decoration; height about 5 inches

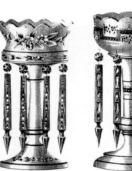 

No. 7305   Lustre, hand-painted floral decoration on ivory coloured, celadon, black or drab ground; height about 10 inches, with 7 cut drops
No. 7306   Lustre, hand-painted decoration, various subjects, on celadon, ivory coloured, celest blue or ruby ground; height about 10 inches, with 7 cut drops

No. 7304   Toilet Table Set, 9 pieces, hand-painted robin red, breast and holly decoration, on ivory or celadon coloured ground
No. 7304A   6 pieces only, comprising 2 scent bottles, 1 puff box, 2 small boxes, and 1 ring stand

No. 7307   Lustre, hand-painted scroll decoration on black, blue, ivory, celadon or canary coloured ground; height about 10½ inches, with 7 cut drops
7308   Lustre, crystal glass, the bowl, stem and foot richly cut; height about 11 inches, with 8 cut drops

    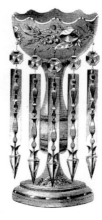 

No. 7309   Lustre, ROSA DU BARRY colour, with rich gilt decoration; height about 10½ inches, with 8 cut drops
No. 7310   Lustre, crystal glass, bowl, stem and foot richly cut; height about 13 inches, with 15 fancy cut drops
No. 7311   Lustre, hand-painted floral decoration and gilt lines, in ruby, ivory, celadon, canary, black or brown coloured ground; height about 13 inches, with 8 cut drops.   Same in 9, 10, 11, 12 inches
No. 7312   Lustre, hand-painted rich floral decoration in six colours; height about 14 inches, with 8 cut drops; also in ROSA DU BARRY colour
No. 7313   Lustre, hand-painted lily decoration, on black, ivory, canary or blue coloured ground; height about 13½ inches, with 10 cut drops
No. 7314   Lustre, hand-painted, on ivory, black, celadon or pink ground, about 11 inches high; 10 finely cut drops

"IVORINE" BASKETS AND FLOWER HOLDERS.

TRADE  MARK.

TRADE  MARK.

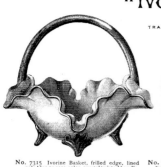

No. 7315 Ivorine Basket, frilled edge, lined pale blue or rose color, crystal twisted handle. Height about 7 inches, diameter 9 inches

No. 7316 Flower Vase, ivory color, lined blue or rose, with vandyke top. Height about 5½ inches

No. 7327 Ivorine Flower Bowl, lined pale blue or rose color, with transparent decoration and feet. Height about 6 inches, diameter 6½ inches

No. 7327A Also in optic glass, assorted colors

No. 7321 Flower Vase, ivory color, lined blue or rose, with crystal edges. Height about 5¼ inches

No. 7322 Ivorine Basket, frilled edge, lined pale blue or rose color, with crystal leaf handle, and feet. Height about 9 inches, diameter 8 inches

No. 7317 Flower Bowl, frilled edge on crystal feet, assorted colors, lined with contrasting colors, diameter about 6½ inches

No. 7318 Flower Vase, frilled top, ivory color, lined blue or rose, with raised cherry and leaf decoration. Height about 6 inches

No. 7323 Ivorine Flower Vase, with topaz rustic handle, flower and leaf decoration in natural colors. Height about 6½ inches

No. 7324 Ivorine Vase, flat oval shape, with rustic handles, leaf and flower decoration in natural colors. Height about 5½ inches

No. 7319 Ivorine Flower Vase, flat oval shape, lined blue or rose color, with handles and raised crystal leaf decoration, on four topaz colored feet

No. 7320 Ivorine Vase, with threaded neck in ruby, blue, or topaz color. Height about 5 inches

No. 7328 Ivorine Bowl, fluted and turn over edge, lined light blue or pink. Height about 8 inches, diameter about 8 inches, on three gold amber feet

TRADE  MARK.

No. 7325 Flower Vase, flat oval shape, ivory color; lined rose with topaz edges and rustic feet, rich gold and silver decoration. Height about 6½ inches

No. 7326 Ivorine Vase, lined pale blue or rose color, with crystal or topaz leaf and fruit decoration, and feet. Height about 7½ inches

S & F.
London & Paris.

S & F.
London & Paris.

No. 7329 Flower Vase, ewer shape, in ivory, canary, celadon or pink, with hand-painted decoration of birds and flowers. Height about 12 inches

No. 7330 Flower Vase, cut top, in ivory color, with hand-painted decoration of flowers and bird. Height about 9 or 11 inches

No. 7331 Flower Vase, optic indented glass, crystal and amber color feet. Height about 6 inches

No. 7332 Flower Vase, ivory color, with feet, in assorted color transparent glass. Height about 5 inches

No. 7332A As 7332, but decorated with raised cherries and leaves

No. 7333 Flower Vase, rosine optic indented glass, with crystal icicle decoration. Height about 6½ inches

No. 7334 Flower Vase, ruby optic indented glass, with crystal icicle decoration. Height about 4½ inches

No. 7335 Ivorine Bowl, transparent rope handles and frilled edge, assorted colors, hand-painted decoration of birds, flowers, &c. and gilt lines. Height about 4 inches

No. 7336 Purpurine Vase, assorted colors, with pink lining. Height about 5 inches

No. 7337 Flower Vase, with handles, assorted colors, hand-painted decoration of birds and flowers. Height about 9 inches

No. 7338 Flower Vase, pink or canary color, hand-painted orchid decoration, and richly gilt. Height about 10½ inches

No. 7339 Flower Vase, hand-painted floral and bird or floral decoration, on pink, black or celadon ground. Height about 13 inches

No. 7340 Flower Vase, canary, black or celadon color, hand-painted decoration of birds and flowers. Height about 12½ inches

No. 7341 Flower Vase, fluted, black, celadon, ivory, or canary colored vase, on black square foot. Extreme height about 10½ inches

No. 7342 Jar with Cover, pink, black, ivory, canary or celadon color, hand-painted decoration of birds and flowers. Height about 12½ or 14½ inches

No. 7343 Flower Vase, opal body, pink or blue neck, hand-painted decoration of birds and flowers. Height about 10½ inches

No. 7344 Flower Vase, richly gilt handles, in ivory or canary colored ground, hand-painted arabesque decoration. Height about 12 inches

No. 7345 Flower Vase, pink or chamois colored ground, hand-painted. Height about 13 inches

COLOURED AND DECORATED GLASS.

No. 7346 Vase, hand-painted lily decoration, ivory, blue, celadon. black or brown coloured ground : height about 8½ inches ; also in ROSE DU BARRY colour.

No. 7347 Vase, alabaster colour, raised gold and enamel decoration ; height about 9, 10, or 12 inches.

No. 7362 Vase, assorted colours and shapes, decorated with hand - painted flowers and gilt lines; height about 8, 9, 11, or 12 inches

No. 7363 Vase, assorted colours and shapes, decorated with hand - painted flowers and gilt lines; height about 8, 9, 11 or 12 inches

No. 7364 Vase, assorted colours and shapes, decorated with hand - painted flowers and gilt lines ; height about 8, 9, 11, or 12 inches

No. 7354 Vase, assorted painted decoration of flowers, &c., on ivory, brown, celadon, black, or blue colour ground; height about 9 inches

No. 7355 Vase, hand - painted rose decoration, on ivory, canary, blue, black, or celadon coloured ground ; height about 9 inches

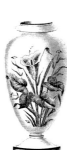

No. 7348 Vase, frilled top, decorated with painted flowers, &c.; blue, black, celadon, or ivory coloured ground ; height about 8 in.

No. 7349 Vase, gilt handles, painted floral decoration on ivory, blue, celadon or black ground ; height about 9 inches.

No. 7356 Vase, flat oval shape, hand-painted floral and bird decoration on ivory, black, or celadon coloured ground ; height about 8½ inches

No. 7357 Vase, raised gilt and enamel decoration on blue, ivory, black, celadon, or canary coloured ground ; height about 9 inches

No. 7350 Vase, alabaster colour, raised gilt and enamel decorations ; height about 9, 10, or 12 inches.

No. 7351 Vase, alabaster colour, hand-painted floral decorations, cut top; height about 9, 10, or 12 inches.

No. 7365 Set of Vases, hand-painted decoration on pink, ivory, black, or celadon ground; height of centre jar 11 inches, height of vases about 9 inches

No. 7358 Vase, hand-painted floral decoration, assorted colours ; height about 8½ inches

No. 7359 Vase, alabaster colour, raised gilt decoration on shaded ground ; height about 9½ or 11½ in.

No. 7352 Vase, painted floral decoration on blue, ivory, black, celadon, or canary colour ground ; height about 11 inches

No. 7353 Vase, hand-painted floral decoration on black, ivory, celadon, or canary colour ground ; height about 9½ inches

No. 7366 Set of Vases, hand-painted decoration on ivory, black, celadon, or canary coloured ground ; height of centre jar about 15 inches, height of side vases about 11 inches

No. 7360 Vase, hand-painted floral decoration on assorted coloured ground ; height about 11 inches

No. 7361 Vase, hand-painted yellow rose decoration on pink black, ivory, canary, or celadon coloured ground ; height about 11 inches

No. 7367 Flower Vase, hand painted rose decoration on pink, ivory, celadon, black, or canary coloured ground ; height about 11 or 12 inches

No. 7368 Flower Vase, richly hand painted decoration of begonia leaves, flowers, &c., on canary, brown, celadon, or pink ground ; height about 11 inches

No. 7369 Flower Vase, hand-painted floral decoration on black, blue, or canary coloured ground ; height about 11 inches

No. 7370 Flower Vase, rich hand-painted floral decoration on ivory, brown, black, celadon, or canary coloured ground ; height about 13 in.

No. 7371 Flower Vase, hand-painted flower and bird decoration and gilt lines, on ivory, black, or celadon coloured ground ; height about 11 inches

No. 7372 Flower Vase, hand-painted decoration of roses, &c., on ivory, brown, canary, or celadon coloured ground ; height about 10 or 12 inches

TRADE MARK. TRADE MARK.

No. 7375 Flower Tube, amberine, with gold amber colour feet; height about 6 inches

No. 7376 Flower Tube, in crystal glass, richly engraved and best gilt decoration, assorted shapes; height about 6½ inches

No. 7377 Flower Tube, optic glass, in amber, blue, or gold amber colour; height about 6½ inches, with raised snake of contrasting colour

No. 7378 Flower Tube, optic glass, crystal foot and ring, blue, amber, or crystal colour tube; height about 6 inches

No. 7379 Flower Tube, optic glass, crystal foot and ball, amber, blue, or crystal tube; height about 6 inches

No. 7380 Flower Holder, transparent or opaque glass, assorted colours, decorated with ornamentation in raised white and gold; height about 7 inches

No. 7381 Flower Tube, crystal optic glass, richly engraved; height about 7 inches Assorted shapes

No. 7373 Flower Tube, crystal glass, richly enamelled decorations in white; height about 7 inches

No. 7374 Flower Tube, crystal or blue coloured glass, cut top, with floral decoration in white; height about 7 inches

No. 7382 Flower Tube, crystal glass, engraved with flowers, and gilt; height about 6½ inches

No. 7383 Flower Tube, opaque glass in opal, canary, celadon, or ivory colour, hand-painted various decorations; height about 6½ inches

No. 7384 Flower Holder, optic glass in gold amber, crystal, or aqua colour, with handles of contrasting colour; height about 3½ inches

No. 7385 Flower Holder, optic glass, on 3 shell feet, in a variety of colours; height about 4 inches

No. 7386 Flower Vase, ivory, canary, or celadon colour, richly decorated with silver and gold flowers; height about 4½ inches

No. 7387 Flower Vase, in optic or crackled glass, blue, amber, crystal, or gold amber colour, with ribbon and feet of contrasting colour; height about 7 inches; also in ruby colour

No. 7388 Flower Vase, ivory, canary, celadon, brown, or blue colour, richly enamelled hand painted decoration of flowers; height about 5 inches

No. 7389 Flower Bowl, gold, amber, iris colour, inlaid with silver flakes; diameter about 6½ ins.
No. 7389 A As No. 7389, but in aqua, or amber optic and rosine

No. 7390 Flower Bowl, in optic or crackled glass, amber, blue, crystal, or gold amber colour; height about 3 inches

No. 7391 Flower Holder, opaque glass, in celadon, ivory, canary, black or brown colour, decorated with hand-painted flowers, &c.; height about 4½ inches

No. 7392 Flower Vase, opal glass, decorated in Japanese style in blue, gold, and silver; height about 7½ inches

No. 7393 Flower Tube, in assorted colour, clear glass, on 3 ball feet; height about 5 inches

No. 7394 Flower Holder, in amberine, optic, or crackled hammered glass, in four shapes; height about 5½ inches

No. 7395 Flower Holder, optic glass, in aqua, amber, or aurora colour, with raised roses & 3-leaf feet of contrasting colour; height about 6 inches

No. 7396 Flower Holder, optic hammered glass, amber, aqua, crystal, or gold amber colour; height about 5½ inches. Also in ruby colour

No. 7397 Flower Holder, opaque glass, in celadon, canary, or ivory colour, decorated with hand-painted flowers, &c.; height about 6 in.

No. 7398 Flower Holder, amberine, crackled, or optic glass; height about 5½ inches

No. 7399 Flower Holder, opaque glass, in celadon, canary, brown, black, or ivory colour, decorated with painted flowers, &c.; height about 5 inches

No. 7400 Mug, optic glass, in amber, crystal, or aquamarine colour, hand-painted floral decoration; height about 4 inches

No. 7401 Flower Tube, pink, green or yellow ground, hand-painted decoration; height about 5½ inches

No. 7402 Flower Tube, opaque glass, in ivory, torquoise, canary, or citron colour, decorated with painted begonia leaves; height about 5 inches

No. 7403 Flower Tube, opaque glass, assorted in five colours, hand-painted decoration; height about 6½ inches

No. 7404 Flower Tube, opaque glass, assorted in five colours, decorated with hand-painted flowers, &c.; height about 7 inches

No. 7405 Flower Holder, opaque glass, assorted in 4 colours, decorated with hand-painted flowers, &c.; height about 5 inches

No. 7406 Flower Holder, opaque shaded glass, assorted in four colours, with hand-painted floral decoration; height about 5 inches

No. 7407 Bouquet Holder, opaque glass, assorted in 5 colours, hand-painted floral decoration; height about 5½ inches

No. 7408 Mug, optic hammered glass, in amber, green, aqua, crystal, or gold amber colour; height about 4½ inches

S. & F.
London & Paris.

S. & F.
London & Paris.

No. 7409 Flower Stand, crystal optic glass, richly engraved with ferns, flowers, &c.; diameter of bowl 9 inches, height about 16 inches

No. 7410 Flower Stand, crystal glass, richly engraved and cut; diameter of bowl 10½ inches, height about 14 inches

No. 7411 Flower Stand, 2 dishes, richly engraved and gilt; diameter of bowl 8½ inches, height about 16 inches

No. 7412 Flower Stand, crystal glass, engraved star and Greek key pattern; diameter of bowl 7½ inches, height about 12 inches

No. 7413 Flower Stand, crystal glass, richly engraved with cut tulip top stem; diameter of bowl 8½ inches, height about 15 inches

MANUFACTURERS, IMPORTERS, WAREHOUSEMEN AND AGENTS. Pawson & Brailsford, Lith. Sheffield

No. 7414.   Water Set (1 jug and 2 goblets), optic indented glass, in aqua, topaz, or ruby colour.   Jug to hold about 2 pints

No. 7415   Water Jug, square-edge barrel shape, optic indented glass, in gold amber, aqua, or ruby colour, with shell handle of contrasting colour; to hold about 1, 2, or 3 pints

No. 7416   Water Jug (to hold about 1½ pints) and tumblers, waved or optic glass, amber, crystal, or aqua colour.   The handle and feet of the jug, and the feet of the tumblers in contrasting colours.   Per set of 1 jug and 2 tumblers, or separately

No. 7417   Wine or Spirit Bottle (to hold about 1½ pints) transparent glass, optic or waved, flat shaped, in light-blue or amber colour

No. 7418 Finger Bowl, transparent glass, optic or waved, light blue, crystal, amber, or rose colour

No. 7419 Finger Bowl, transparent crackled glass, light blue crystal, amber, or rose colour

No. 7420 Water Jug, iced (or frosted) glass, gilt edge around rim; sizes about 1, 2, 3 or 4 pints

No. 7421 Water Jug, iced (or frosted) glass; sizes about 1 or 2 pints

No. 7422 Water Jug, tankard-shape, optic or crackled glass, in light-blue, crystal, amber, or ruby colour, with handle of varying colours
Also in barrel shape

No 7423   Candle Ring, crystal glass, plain or with gilt edge; diameter 2½ and 3 inches

No. 7424   Candle Ring, crystal glass, engraved, in a variety of decorations; diameter 3 ins.

No. 7425   Water Bottle and Tumbler, crackled, or optic, crystal, light blue, amber, and rose colour

No. 7426   Dish, iced (or frosted) glass, oblong-shaped and fluted; diameter about 6, 7, 8, 9 or 10 inches

No. 7429   Tumbler, crackled glass, light blue, crystal, amber, or rose colour; sizes about ½ or 1 pint

No. 7430 Tumbler, transparent glass, optic, crystal, light blue, amber, or rose colour; sizes about ½ or 1 pint

No. 7432 Ice Shell, leaf-shaped, iced (or frosted) glass, richly gilt; length about 3½ inches

No. 7434   Goblet, iced (or frosted) glass, gilt band round rim; size about 1-5th quart

No. 7427   Fruit Dish, 3 compartments, iced (frosted), or crackled glass, crystal colour, richly gilt
No. 7427A   Fruit Dish as No. 7427, but with 2 compartments

No. 7428   Ice Pail, iced (frosted) or crackled glass, Height about 5½ inches, diameter about 5 inches

TRADE MARK

No. 7431   Water Set (1 jug and 2 goblets); jug to hold about 2 pints, in optic glass, aquamarine, crystal, amber, or ruby colour, with handles of contrasting colour.   Jug or goblets may he had separately

No. 7433 Comport Stand, iced (or frosted) glass, rose coloured glass snake, richly gilt

No. 7435   Tumbler, iced (or frosted) glass; sizes about ½ or 1 pint

No.7436 Carafe and Up, optic glass, in aqua, crystal, amber or ruby colour

No. 7437 Jug, optic indented glass, amberine colour (ruby shading into amber).to hold about 2 pints

No.7438 Carafe and Up, in transparent glass, crackled or optic, crystal, light blue, amber, or rose colour

No. 7441   Water Jug, barrel shape, optic indented glass, amberine colour, with shell handle in rich topaz colour; to hold 1, 2 or 3 pints; also in tankard shape

No. 7442   Water Jug, barrel shape, optic glass, ruby colour, with crystal rope handle; to hold 1 or 2 pints

No. 7439   Water Set (1 jug and 2 tumblers), shaded crystal and reseda, or crystal and ruby, richly decorated with hand-painted flowers, and gilt edges. Jug to hold 1 or 2 pints; also in tankard shape

No. 7440   Filter (ready for use) crackled glass, also iced or frosted, in assorted colours Height about 22 inches, diameter 8 inches

No. 7443   Strawberry Set, comprising tray, cream jug and covered sugar box; celadon or chamois coloured glass, with hand-painted flowers and gilt lines; length of tray about 11 inches, width about 9½ inches; or in iced (or frosted) glass, decorated with gold

No. 7470.—Flower Stand, tinted opalescent glass, topaz ornamentation, three flower holders and centre vase; fitted with silver-plated screws and sockets on a silvered, cut, and bevelled glass plateau, metal mounted. Height 13 inches. diameter 10 inches.

No. 7471.—Flower Stand, opalescent glass, three flower holders and centre vase; fitted with silver-plated sockets and screws on silvered and bevelled glass plateau, metal mounted. Height 9½ inches, diameter 6 inches.

No. 7472.—Flower Stand, pink and opal glass, engraved, three flower holder sand centre vase; fitted with silver-plated screws and sockets on a silvered and bevelled glass plateau, metal mounted. Height 9½ inches, diameter 6 inches.

No. 7473.—Flower Stand, tinted opalescent glass, topaz ornamentation, three flower holders and centre vase; fitted with silver-plated screws and sockets on a silvered cut and bevelled glass plateau, metal mounted. Height 11 inches, diameter 10 inches.

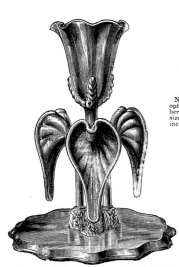

No. 7474.—Flower Stand, leaves of natural colour, centre vase pink opalescent; fitted with silver-plated screws and sockets on a silvered and escalloped glass plateau, metal mounted. Height 13 inches, diameter 10 inches.

No.7474½.—Flower Holder, optic frilled glass, blue, amber, and flint, made in three sizes. Height 6 inches, 7½ inches, 9½ inches.

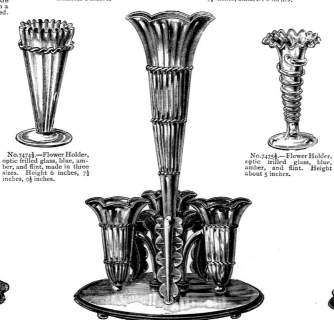

No.7475½.—Flower Holder, optic frilled glass, blue, amber, and flint. Height about 5 inches.

No. 7475.—Flower Stand, optic and frilled crystal glass, three side vases, three leaves and centre vase; fitted with silver-plated screws and sockets on a silvered and bevelled glass plateau, metal mounted. Height 18 inches, diameter 12 inches.

No. 7476.—Flower Stand, leaves of natural colour centre vase ivor and pink; fitted with silver-plated screws and sockets on a silvered and escalloped glass plateau, metal mounted. Height 12 inches, diameter 12 inches.

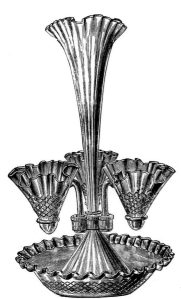

No. 7477.—Flower Stand, optic glass, made in three colours, viz. blue, amber, and ruby, three side vases and large centre vase; fitted with silver-plated screws and sockets on a dish. Height 18 inches, diameter 11 inches.

S. & F.
London
and
Paris.

No. 7478.—Flower Stand, tinted opalescent glass, three baskets hanging from arms; fitted with silver-plated screws and sockets on a frilled dish, made in three colours, viz. blue, citron and ruby. Height 19 inches, diameter 10 inches.

S. & F.
London
and
Paris.

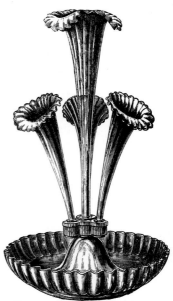

No. 7479.—Flower Stand, tinted opalescent glass, three side vases and one large centre vase; fitted with silver-plated screws and sockets on a frilled dish, made in three colours, viz. blue, citron, and ruby. Height 19 inches, diameter 11 inches.

No. 7495.—Flower Stand, threaded and optic crystal glass. Height 12 inches, diameter 8 inches.

No. 7496.—Wall Bracket, cut silvered glass, mounted on peacock blue, crimson, or gold-coloured plush velvet. Size 17 by 8 inches, depth of shelf 4½ inches.

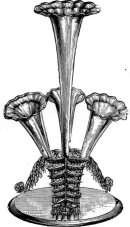

No. 7497.—Flower Stand, optic crystal glass. Height 14 inches, diameter 7 inches.

No. 7498.—Wall Bracket, cut silvered glass mounted on peacock blue, crimson, or gold coloured plush velvet. Size 14 by 8 inches, depth of shelf 4 inches.

No. 7499.—Flower Stand, threaded and frilled crystal glass. Height 15 inches, diameter 9 inches.

No. 7500.—Mirror Wall Bracket, silvered cut glass, mounted on maroon velvet. Size 25 by 18½ inches.

No. 7501.—Flower Stand, threaded and frilled crystal glass. Height 20 inches, diameter 10 inches.

No. 7502.—Preserve Dish, engraved best crystal; made in four sizes.

No. 7503.—Flower Stand, plain crystal glass, three side vases and one large centre vase, screw-on dish. Height 16½ inches, diameter of dish 9 inches.

No. 7504.—Wall Bracket, silvered, bevelled, and cut glass mirror, mounted on maroon velvet. Size 21 by 13 inches, depth of shelf about 6 inches.

No. 7505.—Wall Mirror, silvered and bevelled glass, handsomely engraved, fitted with brass sconce, mounted on peacock blue, crimson, or gold-coloured plush velvet. Size 10 inches diameter.

No. 7506.—Flower Stand, threaded and frilled crystal glass on cut silvered glass plateau. Height 19 inches, diameter of plateau 12 inches.

No. 7507.—Flower Stand, plain crystal glass, silver-plated fittings. Height 24 inches, diameter of dish 11 inches

No. 7508.—Flower Stand, engraved optic crystal glass. Height 18 inches, diameter 10 inches.

No. 7509.—Wall Mirror, silvered and bevelled glass, handsomely engraved, fitted with two brass sconces, mounted on peacock blue, crimson, or gold plush velvet. Size 12½ inches diameter.

TRADE MARK.

S. & F.
London.

No. 7510.—Wall Mirror, silvered and bevelled glass, handsomely engraved, fitted with three-light brass sconces, mounted on peacock blue, crimson, or gold-coloured plush velvet. Size 15 inches diameter.

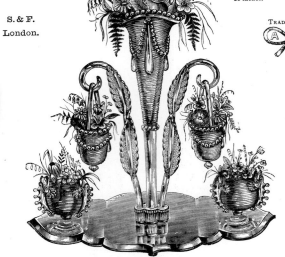

No. 7511.—Flower Stand, threaded and ornamented, various colours on crystal glass, viz. ruby and topaz, turquoise and topaz, flint and topaz, fancy shaped plateau. Height 19 inches, plateau 18 by 12 inches.

No. 7512.—Wall Mirror silvered and bevelled glass, handsomely engraved, mounted on peacock blue, crimson, or gold-coloured plush velvet. Size 15 inches diameter.

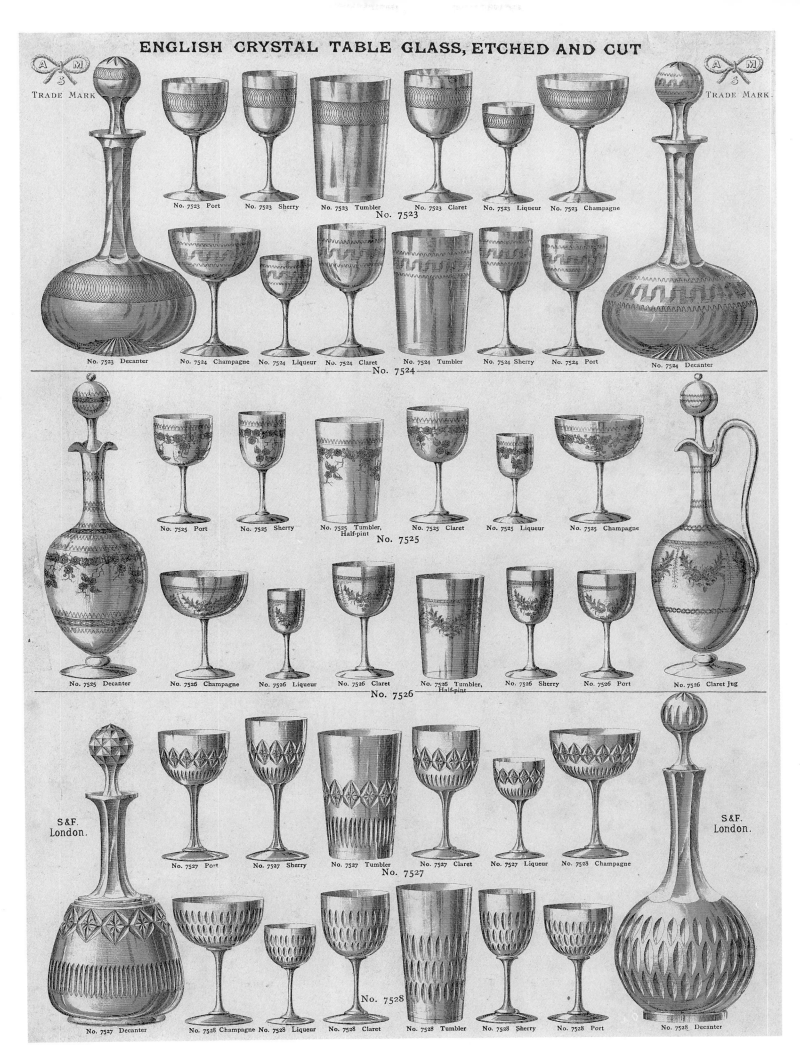

No. 7523 Port No. 7523 Sherry No. 7523 Tumbler No. 7523 Claret No. 7523 Liqueur No. 7523 Champagne

No. 7523

No. 7523 Decanter No. 7524 Champagne No. 7524 Liqueur No. 7524 Claret No. 7524 Tumbler No. 7524 Sherry No. 7524 Port No. 7524 Decanter

No. 7524

No. 7525 Port No. 7525 Sherry No. 7525 Tumbler, Half-pint No. 7525 Claret No. 7525 Liqueur No. 7525 Champagne

No. 7525

No. 7525 Decanter No. 7526 Champagne No. 7526 Liqueur No. 7526 Claret No. 7526 Tumbler, Half-pint No. 7526 Sherry No. 7526 Port No. 7526 Claret Jug

No. 7526

No. 7527 Port No. 7527 Sherry No. 7527 Tumbler No. 7527 Claret No. 7527 Liqueur No. 7528 Champagne

No. 7527

No. 7527 Decanter No. 7528 Champagne No. 7528 Liqueur No. 7528 Claret No. 7528 Tumbler No. 7528 Sherry No. 7528 Port No. 7528 Decanter

No. 7528

Trade Mark. Trade Mark.

S&F. London. S&F. London.

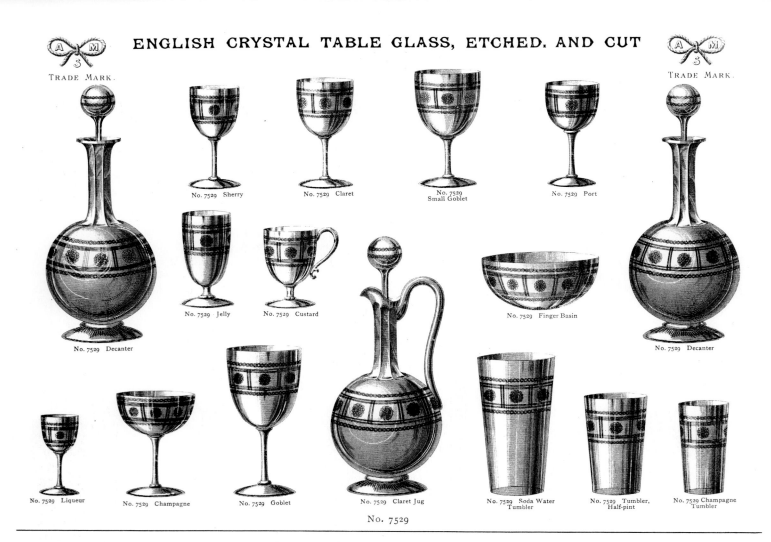

TRADE MARK.

TRADE MARK.

No. 7529 Sherry

No. 7529 Claret

No. 7529 Small Goblet

No. 7529 Port

No. 7529 Jelly

No. 7529 Custard

No. 7529 Finger Basin

No. 7529 Decanter

No. 7529 Decanter

No. 7529 Liqueur

No. 7529 Champagne

No. 7529 Goblet

No. 7529 Claret Jug

No. 7529 Soda Water Tumbler

No. 7529 Tumbler, Half-pint

No. 7529 Champagne Tumbler

No. 7529

No. 7530 Sherry

No. 7530 Claret

No. 7530 Small Goblet

No. 7530 Port

S&F. London.

No. 7530 Decanter

No. 7530 Jelly

No. 7530 Custard

No. 7530 Finger Basin

No. 7530 Decanter

No. 7530 Champagne Tumbler

No. 7530 Tumbler, Half-pint

No. 7530 Soda Water Tumbler

No. 7530 Claret Jug

No. 7530 Goblet

No. 7530 Champagne

No. 7530 Liqueur

No. 7530

Pawson & Brailsford Lith Sheffield.

MANUFACTURERS, IMPORTERS, WAREHOUSEMEN AND AGENTS.

TRADE MARK.

No. 7531   The Brighton Fern Case

No. 7532   The Cottage Roof Fern Case

No. 7533   Oblong Aquarium

No. 7534   Oblong Fern Case (round roof)

No. 7535   Globe Aquarium

No. 7536   The Albert Fern Case

No. 7537   The Alexandra Fern Case

No. 7538   The Princess of Wales' Fern Case

No. 7539   Fern Stand

No. 7540   Window Conservatory

No. 7541   The Harrogate Fern Case

TRADE MARK

No. 7542   Fernery and Aquarium

No. 7543   The Hexagon Fern Case

No. 7544   Window Conservatory

No. 7545   Rustic Fern Stand

No. 7546   Round Shades

No. 7547   Aquarium

No. 7548   Oval Shades

No. 7549   Terra Cotta Fern Stand

No. 7550   Propagating Glasses

No. 7551   Square Shades

No. 7552   Fish Globe

No. 7553   Round Shades

No. 7554   Bee Glass

No. 7555   Rustic Fern Stand   No. 7556   Black Stands

No. 7557   Rustic Fern Stand

No. 7558   Rustic Fern Stand

S&F.
London.

No. 7559   Real Wedgwood Tile

No. 7560   Real Wedgwood Tile

Aquaria, Fern Cases, Window Conservatories, &c., can be made in any size or shape. For full description and sizes, see Price List. Stands for Aquaria and Fern Cases in metal, green or light bronze always in stock.

MANUFACTURERS, IMPORTERS, WAREHOUSEMEN AND AGENTS.

ENTERED AT STATIONERS' HALL.

Paxton & Bradleford Lith. Sheffield

No. 7561.—Champagne. No. 7561.—Liqueur. No. 7561.—Claret. No. 7561.—Tumbler, half-pint. No. 7561.—Sherry. No. 7561.—Port.

No. 7562.—Decanter, quart. No. 7562.—Port. No. 7562.—Sherry. No. 7562.—Tumbler, half-pint. No. 7562.—Claret. No. 7562.—Liqueur. No. 7562.—Champagne. No. 7561.—Claret Jug.

No. 7563.—Champagne. No. 7563.—Liqueur. No. 7563.—Claret. No. 7563.—Tumbler, half-pint. No. 7563.—Sherry. No. 7563.—Port.

No. 7563.—Decanter, quart. No. 7564.—Port. No. 7564.—Sherry. No. 7564.—Tumbler, half-pint. No. 7564.—Claret. No. 7564.—Liqueur. No. 7564.—Champagne. No. 7564.—Claret Jug.

No. 7565.—Champagne. No. 7565.—Liqueur. No. 7565.—Claret. No. 7565.—Tumbler, half-pint. No. 7565.—Sherry. No. 7565.—Port.

No. 7565.—Decanter, quart. No. 7566.—Port. No. 7566.—Sherry. No. 7566.—Tumbler, half-pint. No. 7566.—Claret. No. 7566.—Liqueur. No. 7566.—Champagne. No. 7566.—Claret Jug.

No. 7567.—Carafe and Tumbler, plain demi-crystal glass.

No. 7568.—Carafe and Tumbler, demi-crystal, moulded narrow flutes.

No. 7569.—Carafe and Tumbler, demi-crystal, engraved vine pattern.

No. 7570.—Carafe and Tumbler, one row cut hollows, demi-crystal.

No. 7571.—Carafe and Tumbler, demi-crystal, engraved fern pattern.

No. 7572.—Carafe and Tumbler, English crystal glass, cut neck, cut star bottom.

No. 7573.—Carafe and Tumbler, English crystal glass, engraved star and wreath, cut neck.

No. 7574.—Carafe and Tumbler, demi-crystal, engraved fern pattern.

No. 7575.—Carafe and Tumbler, crystal glass, one row cut hollows, and cut neck.

No. 7576.—Carafe and Tumbler, demi-crystal, engraved stars.

No. 7577.—Carafe and Tumbler, plain demi-crystal.

No. 7578.—Carafe and Tumbler, English crystal glass, fancy cut pattern.

No. 7579.—Toilet Bottle, English crystal glass, richly cut.

No. 7580.—Toilet Bottle, English crystal glass.

No. 7581.—Water Set (1 jug and 2 goblets) English crystal glass, handsomely engraved, with crystal decoration.

No. 7582.—Toilet Bottle, English crystal glass, richly cut.

No. 7583.—Toilet Bottle, English crystal glass, richly cut.

No. 7584.—Glass Jug, engraved ivy pattern, three sizes, viz. 1 pint, 2 pints, 3 pints.

No. 7585.—Glass Jug, plain, tankard-shaped, three sizes, viz. 1 pint, 1½ pint, 2 pints.

No. 7586.—Jug, crystal glass, engraved wreath, four sizes, ½ pint, 1, 2, and 3 pints.

No. 7587.—Jug, crystal glass, plain, four sizes, ½ pint, 1, 2, and 3 pints.

No. 7588.—Glass Jug, demi-crystal, engraved, three sizes, viz. 1, 1½, and 2 pints.

No. 7589.—Jug, crystal glass, engraved fern pattern, three sizes, viz. 1, pint, 2 pints, 3 pints.

No. 7590.—Water Bottle, cut neck, demi-crystal.

No. 7591.—Water Bottle, engraved fern pattern, English crystal glass.

No. 7592.—Water Bottle, demi-crystal, cut neck, cut star bottom.

No. 7593.—Water Bottle, engraved body, cut neck.

No. 7594.—Water Bottle, heavy, demi-crystal, cut neck, and cut star bottom.

ENGRAVED TABLE GLASS.

No. 7601.—Soda Water Tumbler.

No. 7601.—Tumbler, ½ pint, thin.

No. 7601.—Champagne Tumbler.

No. 7601.—Liqueur.

No. 7601.—Port.

No. 7601.—Sherry.

No. 7601.—Claret.

No. 7601.—Champagne.

No. 7601.—Tumbler, ½ pint, heavy.

No. 7601.—Custard.

No. 7601.—Jelly.

No. 7601.—Honey.

No. 7601.—Butter Dish, three pieces.

No. 7601.—Butter Dish, two pieces.

No. 7601.—Finger Basin.

No. 7601.—Covered Sugar.

No. 7601.—Cream Jug.

No. 7601.—Oval Dish, 6, 7½, 9, 10, 11 inches.

TRADE MARK.

No. 7601.—Decanter, quart.

No. 7601.—Claret Jug.

No. 7601.—Decanter, pint.

No. 7601.—Comport, 7, 8, 9 inches.

No. 7601.—Sugar Basin.

No. 7601.—Carafe and Tumbler.

No. 7601.

No. 7602.—Soda Water Tumbler.

No. 7602.—Tumbler, ½ pint, thin.

No. 7602.—Champagne Tumbler.

No. 7602.—Liqueur.

No. 7602.—Port.

No. 7602.—Sherry.

No. 7602.—Claret.

No. 7602.—Champagne.

No. 7602.—Tumbler, ½ pint, heavy.

No. 7602.—Round Dish, 6, 7, 8, 9, 11 inches.

No. 7602.—Tankard Jug, ½, 1, 2, 3, 4 pints.

No. 7602.—Salt.

No. 7602.—Finger Basin.

No. 7602.—Sugar Basin.

No. 7602.—Cream Jug.

No. 7602.—Butter Dish, three pieces.

No. 7602.—Butter Dish, two pieces.

No. 7602.—Carafe and Tumbler.

No. 7602.—Goblet.

No. 7602.—Decanter, pint.

No. 7602.—Claret Jug.

No. 7602.—Decanter, quart.

No. 7602.—Pickle Jar.

No. 7602.—Sweetmeat.

No. 7602.—Celery.

No. 7602.

WINE GLASSES, CLARETS, CHAMPAGNES, GOBLETS, &c.

WINE GLASSES.

No. 7603.—Port, plain demi-crystal.　No. 7604. — Sherry, plain demi-crystal.　No 7605.—Sherry, engraved.　No. 7606.—Sherry, engraved.　No. 7607.—Sherry, cut hollows.　No. 7608.—Sherry, cut 2 row mirrors.　No. 7609.—Sherry, cut 1 row hollows.　No. 7610.—Sherry, cut flutes.　No. 7611.—Sherry, cut flat flutes.　No. 7612.—Sherry, plain thin crystal.　No. 7613.—Port, cut flat flutes.

HOCK OR CLARET GLASSES.　CHAMPAGNE GLASSES.　HOCK OR CLARET GLASSES.

No. 7614.— Hock or Claret Glass, green bowl, plain crystal stem.　No. 7615.— Hock or Claret Glass, ruby bowl cut crystal stem.　No. 7616.—Champagne Glass, plain demi-crystal.　No. 7617.—Champagne Glass, demi-crystal, cut one row hollows.　No. 7618.—Champagne Glass, engraved fern pattern, demi-crystal.　No. 7619.—Champagne Glass, cut hollow stem.　No. 7620.— Hock or Claret Glass, green bowl, cut crystal stem.　No. 7621.— Hock or Claret Glass, ruby bowl plain crystal stem.

CHAMPAGNE TUMBLERS.

No. 7622.—Champagne Tumbler, plain, demi-crystal.　No. 7623.—Champagne Tumbler, demi-crystal, cut flat flutes.　No. 7624.— Champagne Tumbler, demi-crystal cut splits.　No. 7625.—Champagne Tumbler, demi-crystal, engraved fern pattern.　No. 7626.—Champagne Tumbler, demi-crystal, engraved border.　No. 7627.— Champagne Tumbler, demi-crystal, engraved stars and dots.　No. 7628. — Champagne Tumbler, plain, thin crystal.　No. 7629.—Champagne Tumbler, crystal, cut flat flutes.　No. 7630.— Champagne Tumbler, crystal, cut 1 row hollows.

GOBLETS.

No. 7631.—Goblet, plain, tall, about 5 to quart.　No. 7632.—Goblet, cut broad flat flutes, full half-pint.　No. 7633.—Goblet, cut flat mirrors, about 5 to quart.　No. 7634.— Goblet, cut hollows, about 5 to quart.　No. 7635.— Goblet, cut "Brushfield" shape, about 5 to quart.　No. 7636.—Goblet, "Elgin" shape, cut stem, about 5 to quart.　No. 7637.—Goblet, tall, cut reverse flutes, about 5 to quart.

No. 7638. — Goblet, for spirits, diamond cut stem, about 8 to quart.　No. 7639.—Goblet, 1 row cut hollows, about 8 to quart.　No. 7640.—Goblet, plain, about 8 to quart.　No. 7641. — Goblet, plain, lemon bowl shape, about 5 to quart.　No. 7641½.—Goblet, plain, lemon bowl shape, about 8 to quart.　No. 7642. — Goblet, plain, squat shape, about 8 to quart.　No. 7643. — Goblet, plain stem, "Lady" shape, about 6 to quart.　No. 7644.—Goblet, for spirits, cut flat flutes, about 8 to quart.

No. 7645.—Goblet, "Sensation" shape, plain, about 5 to quart.　No. 7646.—Goblet, plain egg bowl shape, about 5 to quart.　No. 7647. — Goblet, "Sensation" shape, engraved stars and band, about 5 to quart.　No. 7648.—Goblet, plain, "Elgin" shape, about 5 to quart.　No. 7649.—Goblet, cut stem, "Lady" shape, about 6 to quart.　No. 7650.—Goblet, cut stem, "Elgin" shape, about 5 to quart.　No. 7651.—Goblet, plain, heavy, about 5 to quart.　No. 7652.—Goblet, plain, heavy, about half-pint.

137

GLASS, STONE, DOULTON WARE, TERRA-COTTA, AND MAJOLICA FILTERS.

GLASS FILTERS.

GLASS FILTERS.

No. 7693.—Glass Filter, plain, cut star bottom, fitted with carbon block.

No. 7694.—Filter, transparent glass, optic (or waved), light blue, amber, or rose colour, fitted with carbon block.

No. 7695.—Engraved Glass Filter, fitted with carbon block.

No. 7695½.—Engraved Glass Filter, with handle, fitted with carbon block.

No. 7696.—Engraved Glass Filter, with handle, fitted with carbon block.

No. 7697.—Filter, transparent glass, optic (waved), light blue, amber, or rose colour, fitted with carbon block.

No. 7698.—Engraved Glass Filter, fitted with carbon block.

TRADE MARK. A M S

TRADE MARK. A M S

No. 7699.—Filter, iced (frosted) glass, also crackled, or optic in crystal, blue, or amber colour, fitted with carbon block and silver-plated tap. Height about 22 inches, diameter 8 inches.

No. 7700. — Cylindrical Glass Filter, engraved key pattern, fitted with carbon block, and silver-plated tap.

No. 7701.—Glass Filter, plain, fitted with carbon block.

> The great advantage of the use of these table filters is that water for drinking purposes is purified directly under the supervision of the user, and not left to the care of servants.

No. 7702.—Filter, cylinder shaped, ivory-coloured glass, decorated with hand-painted flowers, &c., fitted with carbon block and silver-plated tap. Height about 15 inches, diameter about 7 inches.

No. 7703. — Cylindrical Glass Filter, engraved stars, fitted with carbon block, and silver-plated tap.

No. 7704.—Filter, ivory-coloured glass, with hand-painted decorations, flowers, fern, foliage, &c., fitted with carbon block and silver-plated tap. Height about 22 inches, diameter about 8 inches.

No. 7705.—Vase-shape Table Filter, holding 1 quart, in Doulton ware or silicon ware.

No. 7706.　　No. 7707.

Nos. 7706 and 7707.—Table or Dining Room Filters, highly decorative in appearance, combined with perfect filtration, in Doulton ware, silicon or figured glazed wares. Made in two sizes, 1 gallon or 5 pints.

No. 7708.—Table Filter, holding 3 quarts, in Doulton, silicon, ivory glaze, or green silicon ware.

No. 7709.—Stand for Filters assorted designs.

No. 7710.—Dining Room Filter, made in red Wedgwood ware, or black with gold lines.

No. 7711.—Table Filter, in terra-cotta ware, just sufficiently porous to allow water to ooze through. The rapid evaporation that takes place in tropical climates cools the water considerably.

No. 7712.—Vase-shape Table Filter, in enamelled stoneware, as shown in illustration, holding 1 quart filtered water. The block is screwed to the bottom of the vase, and by means of ground surfaces the joint is perfectly watertight.

S. & F.
London & Paris.

TRADE MARK

No. 7713.—Filter in majolica ware. This filter is made with movable lining, as shown in section No. 7734, on page 449.

No. 7714.—Gothic Vase Filter, capable of purifying 25 gallons per day.

No. 7715.—Filter in Doulton Ware or enamelled ornamental stoneware, capable of purifying 12 gallons per day.

No. 7716.—Filter in Doulton Ware or enamelled ornamental stoneware, capable of purifying 15 gallons per day.

No. 7717.—Filter in majolica ware. This filter is made with movable lining, as shown in section No. 7734, on page 449.

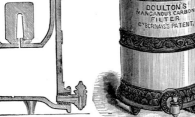

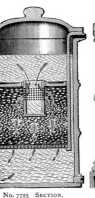

No. 7723
ENAMELLED STONEWARE FILTER.

No. 7723 SECTION.

BROWN STONEWARE FILTER.

Nos. 7723 and 7724 SMALL, capacity 2 galls. MEDIUM, capacity 4 galls. LARGE, capacity 7 galls.

The Patent Manganous Carbon of this Filter is compressed into the form of a block, which is screwed to the bottom of a Stoneware basket, and by means of ground surfaces the junction is absolutely water-tight. This screwed joint admits of the simple and easy removal and replacement of the block; *and the arrangement is such that every part of the Filter can be separated, examined and cleansed without the slightest hindrance.*

No. 7725 DOMESTIC STONEWARE FILTER.

This rapid Water Filter will purify the most offensive, stagnant, or other waters with astonishing rapidity. The most efficient Filter which has yet been invented. The effect of this Filter upon even the foulest Thames water is surprising, and chemical analysis fails to detect the least trace of organic matter in the water that has once passed through it.

No. 7725 ELEVATION.   **No. 7725 SECTION.**   **No. 7726 SECTION.**

SILICATED CARBON FILTER
With patent movable block.

No. 7727 SPONGY IRON FILTER.

DESCRIPTION.

The unfiltered Water is supplied by means of Ball-cock (B) with glass ball (G) and screw valve (V); the latter serves to shut off the water in any emergency. The Ball-cock requires no fixing to a wall, but is fastened to the side of the filter case by thumb screws (R); it is connected with the water supply or cistern by ⅜-bore india rubber or other tubing (P). The connection with the ordinary water supply is mostly very simple, and can be made, if desired, by the Company's plumber.

The water passes through the several layers of filtering materials, which are enclosed between the removable perforated plates (C, C', C''). It is next collected in a small well, or regulator bowl, and thence passes into a tin tube, provided at its outer end with screw cap (A). The lateral opening (X) in the side of the tube forms the only communication between the upper part of the filter and the reservoir for filtered water. The flow of water is thus controlled by the size of such opening, and the contact between the water and the filtering materials regulated.

If the unfiltered water contains much **muddy suspended matter**, a small stoneware vessel may be placed into space (U) so as to surround the ball of Ball-cock, allowing it to play. The remaining part of (U) should then be filled with sand, to be washed and replaced periodically when it becomes choked. This greatly tends to prevent choking of the filtering materials underneath.

No. 7727 SECTION WITH BALL-COCK COMPLETE.

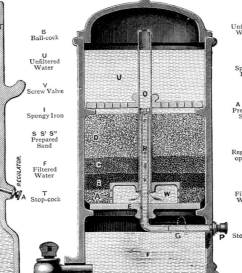

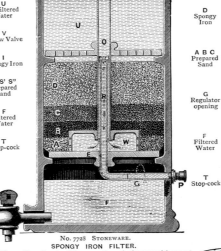

Figures corresponding to the Packages for charging.

B   Ball-cock

U   Unfiltered Water

V   Screw Valve

I   Spongy Iron

S S' S''   Prepared Sand

F   Filtered Water

T   Stop-cock

No. 7728 STONEWARE.

SPONGY IRON FILTER.

The unfiltered water (U) passes through the several layers of filtering materials into the collecting well (W), and thence in the direction indicated by arrows in the section. Tube (R) is fixed in partition (E), and provided underneath at (G) with a small lateral opening. This forms *the only communication between the upper part of the Filter and the reservoir for filtered water.* The flow of water is thus controlled by the size of such opening.

U   Unfiltered Water

D   Spongy Iron

A B C   Prepared Sand

G   Regulator opening

F   Filtered Water

T   Stop-cock

THE STONE CISTERN FILTER.

AIR PIPE

OUTLET   **No. 7729 SECTION SHOWING A STONE FILTER INSIDE CISTERN.**

No. 7729

Purifying 40 gallons per day.

Larger and less sizes in proportion.

The Porous Stone Filters for Cisterns, Ship Tanks, Water Butts, &c., are made any size or shape to suit different hydraulic arrangements.

The water passes through the Porous Stone to an inside Chamber, which holds a reserve of filtered water.

No. 7730 STONE REFRIGERATIVE FILTER.

This Filter is made of porous stone, in the shape of a bottle, and, on account of its simplicity in use, will be found invaluable in hot climates, or where it is difficult to obtain pure water.

When filtered water is required, it is only necessary to place the Filter EMPTY even in the most dirty water, ponds, rivers, &c., when the water will filter through the sides into the bottle, from whence it can be used in a purified state.

To keep the water in the Filter, a cork tightly inserted into the neck will prevent it oozing through, consequently it is especially adapted for travelling purposes.

By slightly raising the cork the water will gently ooze through the sides, and the rapid evaporation from the surface, which always takes place in hot climates, will produce a most refreshing and delightful coolness in the water.

To clean it, it is sufficient to brush the exterior with a hard brush, or to blow into the interior, in order to open the holes in the stone.

When the Filter is new or long out of use, the first two or three filterings should be thrown away.

No. 7730

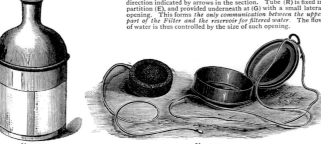

No. 7731

This consists of a block of pure "Compressed Charcoal," with cork, into which is fitted a stout glass tube, and attached to this is a long flexible india rubber tube, manufactured from the purest rubber that can be obtained. The whole fits into a neat, portable, japanned case.

No. 7732

THE TRAVELLERS' FILTER.

The necessity for a portable Filter which shall be compact and unbreakable, is met in the 'Travellers' Filter, which is made of white metal, coated with an impervious enamel. It is about 8½ inches high, is fitted with a carbon block, and, placed on an ordinary decanter, will filter a pint of water in a very few minutes.

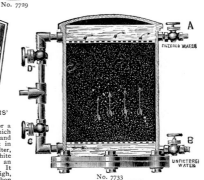

No. 7733

IMPROVED FILTER
For High-Pressure or Main Service supply.
Purifying from 100 to 5,000 gallons per hour, according to size.

No. 7734 Stoneware Filter.   Showing interior of No. 7734

This Filter is manufactured in hard Vitrified Stoneware, and fitted with a movable lining, a special feature to which we would direct particular attention. Every part is accessible, and may therefore be kept perfectly fresh and wholesome. The filtering medium is a solid block of Carbon, and the perfect filtration of every drop of water which may pass into the pure water chamber is ensured.

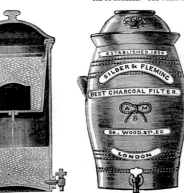

No. 7735 The Ship Filter for ships' use.

Nos. 7735 and 7736 For scientific arrangement and durability of wear, these Filters maintain their reputation as thorough purifiers of water in almost any condition, whether from river, rain, or pond.

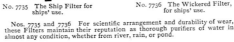

No. 7736 The Wickered Filter, for ships' use.

No. 7737 White Ironstone China Filter, fluted and marbled, decorated with Grecian figures. Holding 2 gallons.

No. 7738 Terra Cotta Ware Filter, just sufficiently porous to allow water to ooze through. The rapid evaporation that takes place in tropical climates cools the water considerably.

Pawson & Brailsford, Typ., Sheffield

TRADE MARK.

TRADE MARK.

No. 7792 Cream Jug, pressed glass; height about 3½ inches, diameter about 2½ inches

No. 7792 Sugar Basin, pressed glass; height about 3 inches, diameter about 5½ inches

No. 7795 Cream Jug, pressed glass; height about 4½ inches, diameter about 3 inches

No. 7793 Sugar Basin, pressed glass; height about 3 inches, diameter about 5½ inches

No. 7793 Cream Jug, pressed glass; height about 3½ inches, diameter about 2½ inches

No. 7794 Sugar Basin, pressed glass; height about 5 inches, diameter about 6 inches

No. 7794 Cream Jug, pressed glass; height about 4½ inches, diameter about 2½ inches

No. 7795 Sugar Basin, pressed glass; height about 4½ inches, diameter about 5½ inches

No. 7796 Cream Jug, pressed glass; height about 4½ inches, diameter about 3 inches

No. 7796 Sugar Basin, pressed glass; height about 5½ inches, diameter about 5½ inches

S&F. London.

S&F. London.

No. 7797 Sugar Basin, with Plate and Cover, three pieces, pressed glass, height about 6 inches, diameter of plate, 6½ inches

No. 7798 Sugar Basin, with Plate and Cover, three pieces, pressed iced glass, height about 7½ inches, diameter of plate about 7 inches

No. 7799 Sugar Basin, with Plate and Cover, three pieces, pressed iced glass, height about 6 inches, diameter of plate about 6½ inches

No. 7800 Sugar Basin, plain, clear glass; height about 3½ inches, diameter about 5½ inches

No. 7800 Cream Jug, plain, clear glass; height about 4 inches, diameter about 2½ inches

No. 7803 Cream Jug, English crystal glass, richly cut; height about 5 inches, diameter 3 inches

No. 7801 Cream Jug, cut 1 row hollows; height about 4 inches, diameter about 2½ inches

No. 7801 Sugar Basin, cut 1 row hollows; height about 3½ inches diameter about 5½ inches

No. 7802 Sugar Basin, cut 1 row hollows; height about 6 inches, diameter about 5½ inches

No. 7802 Cream Jug, cut 1 row hollows; height about 4 inches, diameter about 2½ inches

No. 7803 Sugar Basin, English crystal glass, richly cut; height about 5½ inches, diameter about 5 inches

No. 7804 Cream Jug, engraved fern pattern; height about 4 inches, diameter about 2½ inches

No. 7804 Sugar Basin, engraved fern pattern; height about 6 inches, diameter about 5½ inches

ENTERED AT STATIONERS' HALL. **MANUFACTURERS, IMPORTERS, WAREHOUSEMEN AND AGENTS.**

TRADE MARK.

TRADE MARK.

No. 7805 Butter Dish and Cover, pressed glass, diameter about 6 inches

No. 7806 Oval Dish, pressed glass, made in five sizes; length, 6 inches, 7½ inches, 9 inches, 10½ inches, and 12 inches
Round Dish, to match, in five sizes; diameter, 5 inches, 6 inches, 7½ inches, 9 inches, 10½ inches, and 12 inches

No. 7807 Butter Dish and Cover, pressed glass, diameter about 6½ inches

No. 7808 Butter Dish and Cover, cut one row hollows, diameter about 6½ inches

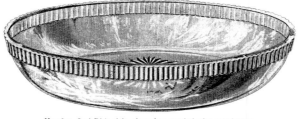

No. 7809 Oval Dish, plain, clear glass, notched edge, star bottom, made in seven sizes; length, 5 inches, 6 inches, 7 inches, 8 inches, 9 inches, 10 inches, and 11 inches
Round Dish, to match, in seven sizes; diameter, 5 inches, 6 inches, 7 inches, 8 inches, 9 inches, 10 inches, and 11 inches

No. 7810 Butter Dish and Cover, engraved, diameter about 6½ inches

No. 7811 Butter Dish and Cover, pressed iced glass, extreme width about 8 inches

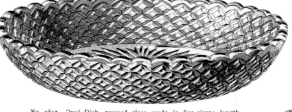

No. 7812 Oval Dish, pressed glass, made in five sizes; length, 6 inches, 7½ inches, 9 inches, 10½ inches, and 12 inches

No. 7813 Butter Dish and Cover, pressed glass, diameter about 7½ inches

S&F.
London.

No. 7814 Butter Dish and Cover, frosted ground, cut stars, diameter about 7 inches

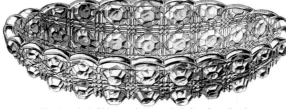

No. 7815 Oval Dish, pressed glass, made in four sizes; length, 6¾ inches, 7½ inches, 9 inches, and 10½ inches
Round Dish, to match, made in five sizes; diameter, 5 inches, 6½ inches, 8¼ inches, 9½ inches, and 10½ inches

S&F.
London.

No. 7816 Butter Dish and Cover, oval, perforated edge, pressed glass, length about 7 in.

No. 7817 Butter Dish and Cover, pressed glass, diameter about 6½ inches

No. 7818 Oval Dish, pressed glass, made in seven sizes; length, 6 inches, 7 inches, 8 inches, 9 inches, 10 inches, 11 inches, and 12 inches
Round Dish, to match, made in eight sizes; 5 inches, 6 inches, 7 inches, 8 inches, 9 inches, 10 inches, 11 inches, and 12 inches.

TRADE  MARK.

No. 7819 Butter Dish and Cover, pressed glass, diameter about 7 inches

MANUFACTURERS, IMPORTERS, WAREHOUSEMEN AND AGENTS.

No. 7820 Pickle Jar, moulded, diamond pattern; height about 5½ inches, diameter about 2¾ inches

No. 7821 Pickle Jar, cut flat flutes; height about 6½ inches, diameter about 3 inches

No. 7822 Pickle Jar, engraved and cut, crystal glass; height 6½, diameter 3¼ ins.

No. 7823 Pickle Jar, cut English crystal glass; height about 5½ inches, diameter about 2¾ inches

No. 7824 Pickle Jar, engraved; height about 6¾ inches, diameter about 3 inches

No. 7825 Pickle Jar, cut English crystal glass; height about 4½ inches, diameter about 4½ inches

No. 7826 Comport, tall, engraved fern pattern; diameter 7½ inches, height 4½ inches

No. 7827 Piano Insulator, pressed glass, made in three colours, viz., green, canary and flint

No. 7828 Comport, tall, pressed glass, made in five sizes; diameter 5 inches, 6 inches, 7½ inches, 9 inches and 10½ inches; height in proportion

No. 7829 Piano Insulator, pressed glass, made in three colours, viz., green, canary and flint

No. 7830 Comport, tall, cut one row hollows; diameter 7½ inches, height 4½ inches

No. 7831 Comport, tall, engraved fern pattern, made in five sizes; diameter 6 inches, 7 inches, 8 inches, 9 inches and 10 inches; height in proportion

No. 7832 Comport, low, cut one row hollows; diameter 6½ inches, height 2½ inches

No. 7833 Comport, tall, pressed glass, made in four sizes; diameter 5½ inches, 8½ inches, 10 inches, and 11½ inches; height in proportion

No. 7834 Comport, low, engraved; diameter 6½ inches, height 2½ inches.

No. 7835 Comport, tall, plain clear glass, made in 5 sizes; diameter 6 inches, 7 inches, 8 inches, 9 inches and 10 inches; height in proportion

S&F.
London.

S&F.
London.

No. 7836 Celery Glass, pressed; height about 8½ inches, diameter about 5 inches

No. 7837 Celery Glass, pressed; height about 7½ inches, diameter about 4½ inches

No. 7838 Celery Glass, pressed; height about 8½ inches, diameter about 4½ inches

No. 7839 Celery Glass, pressed; height about 7½ inches, diameter about 4½ inches

No. 7840 Celery Glass, plain, clear glass; height about 10 inches, diameter about 5 inches

FINE ART POTTERY,
CHINA, AND EARTHENWARE,
LAVA AND MAJOLICA GOODS,

THE LATEST PRODUCTIONS

FROM THE BEST-KNOWN MANUFACTURERS IN ENGLAND AND ON

THE CONTINENT, AS WELL AS FROM CHINA AND JAPAN,

ALL CLASSES AND QUALITIES OF GOODS,

FROM THE CHEAPEST TO THE VERY BEST,

FINE ART POTTERY.

Our stock of Glass, China, and Earthenware, as exhibited in our Show Rooms, represents the largest and most varied assortment held by any house in this trade.

As it is almost impossible to illustrate more than a limited number of patterns of the Goods kept in stock by us, we solicit the favour of an early visit to our Warehouses; should this not be possible, please note that we sell almost every article produced in China and Earthenware, whether made in Europe, China, or Japan.

Our great experience and intimate acquaintance with the taste of the various markets, enable us to select only such patterns as will find a ready sale at a fair profit.

Any particular pattern or style required for your special trade that you may intrust to our care will receive immediate attention and be executed in the shortest possible time, and at the lowest prices.

A very great number of the articles shown in this department are designed and made for us exclusively, and cannot, therefore, be purchased elsewhere.

When ordering Art Pottery, please allow us to send samples of the latest novelties, stating the amount to which you limit your order.

Almost every article represented in the following pages of this Catalogue is kept in stock by us, and can in most cases be dispatched within a few hours after the receipt of order; you will thus be enabled to supply your customers with the goods at the shortest notice.

Most of the patterns of Vases, Figures, and other Goods illustrated in this Catalogue can, when ordered in quantities, be supplied of an inferior quality, that is, with the painting or other decoration less elaborately finished, at lower prices than those quoted in our Price List. As we do not keep these qualities in stock, two or three months are required to execute such orders.

We do not hold ourselves responsible for breakage of, or damage to, goods in transit, but we employ none but well-trained and experienced packers, thus guaranteeing freedom from breakage to some extent, unless caused by extreme rough usage or accident, such as a case falling from a wagon, &c.

All prices are quoted free at our Warehouse.

ALL PRICES QUOTED IN OUR PRICE LIST ARE NETT.

No. 7897

No. 7898

No. 7899

No. 7900

No. 7901

No. 7902

No. 7903

No. 7904

No. 7906

No. 7908

No. 7909

S. & F.
LONDON
AND
PARIS.

S. & F.
LONDON
AND
PARIS.

No. 7905

No. 7907

TRADE MARK

TRADE MARK

Nos. 7910 & 7911

No. 7912

Nos. 7913 & 7914

No. 7917

No. 7918

No. 7919

No. 7920

No. 7923

No. 7924

No. 7925

No. 7926

Nos. 7915 & 7916

No. 7927

No. 7928

No. 7929

No. 7930

Nos. 7921 & 7922

145

No. 7931

No. 7932

No. 7933

No. 7934

No. 7935

No. 7936

No. 7937

No. 7938

No. 7939

No. 7940

No. 7941

No. 7942

No. 7943

No. 7944

No. 7945

No. 7946

No. 7947

No. 7948

No. 7949

No. 7950

No. 7951

No. 7952

No. 7953

No. 7954

No. 7955

No. 7956

No. 7957

No 7958

No. 7959

No. 7960

No. 7961

No. 7962

No. 7963

No. 7964

No. 7965

No. 7966

No. 7967

No. 7968

No. 7969

S. & F.
LONDON
AND
PARIS.

S. & F.
LONDON
AND
PARIS.

No. 7971

No. 7972

No. 7973

No 7974

No. 7975

No. 7976

No. 7977

No. 7978

No. 7979

No. 7980

No. 7981

No. 7982

No. 7983

No. 7984

No. 7985

No. 7986

No. 7987

No. 7988

No. 8178. Vienna China Plaque, decorated with hand-painted figures, representing The departure of Hagar, in rich colours. The border is exquisitely painted and relieved with floral designs, in burnished gold. Diameter, about 9½ in. These plates are suitable for mural decorations.

No. 8179.—Vienna China Vase, with gilt handles, moveable cover and base, decorated with hand-painted figures, representing "Cleopatra and Alexander," and on the reverse side "Venus, Helen and Paris." The borders are of raised floral designs in burnished gold, on pale green ground, the foot of vase and plinth are relieved with floral designs, in burnished gold on maroon ground. Height, 16½ inches; extreme diameter, 9 inches.

No. 8180.—Vienna China Plaque, decorated with hand-painted figures, representing "Appelles, Alexander and Campaspe," in rich colours, the border being exquisitely painted and relieved with floral designs, in burnished gold, on violet coloured ground. diameter, about 9½ inches.

No. 8182.—Vienna China Vase with cover, fluted, richly decorated with floral designs in burnished gold, on coloured ground, pink and blue, the cover, neck and foot is of dull gold. Height, 5¾ inches; diameter, 2½ inches.

No. 8181.—Real Dresden China Vase with cover, decorated with hand-painted landscapes, in colours on white ground, floral designs, &c., on pink, green, black or yellow ground, and heavily gilt borders. Height, 17½ inches; extreme diameter, 8 ins.

No. 8183.—Vienna China Vase with cover, decorated with hand-painted figures, blue medallions, and burnished gold floral designs, on pink coloured ground. Height, 6 inches; diameter, 2½ inches.

No. 8184.—Vienna China Cup and Saucer with cover, exquisitely decorated with hand-painted figures, burnished gold floral designs, &c., on dark red ground, with pink border, the handle and feet of Cup is heavily gilt. Height of cup, 5 inches; diameter of saucer, 5¾ inches.

No. 8186.—Vienna China Vase with Cover, richly decorated with burnished gold, floral designs in relief, blue medallions, &c., on pink ground. Height, 6 ins.; diam., 2½ ins.

No. 8187.—Vienna China Ewer, on movable plinth, exquisitely decorated with hand-painted figures, in rich colours, burnished gold floral designs in relief on green ground, the neck and handle heavily gilt. Height, about 21 inches; extreme diameter, about 12 inches; diameter of base, about 7½ inches.

No. 8188.—Real Dresden China Vase with Cover, decorated with hand-painted figures, "Watteau," on white ground, and floral designs on blue ground, richly gilt borders. Height, about 11 inches; diameter, about 7½ inches.

No. 8185.—Vienna China Inkstand on movable plateau, decorated with hand-painted figures, representing "Cupid Captive," &c., in rich colours, burnished gold floral designs, on red ground, with ivory and gilt edge. Extreme height, 6½ inches; extreme diameter, 8 inches.

No. 8189.—Real Dresden China Vase bottle shaped, decorated with hand-painted figures "Watteau," on white ground, floral designs, &c., on blue, pink or green grounds, the borders are richly gilt. Height, 14 inches; extreme diameter, 6½ inches.

No. 8190.—Vienna China Plaque, richly decorated with hand-painted figures, representing "Cleopatra and Augustus," burnished gold floral designs, on light green ground, relieved with maroon panels. Diameter, about 9½ inches.

No. 8191.—Real Dresden China Coffee Pot on plateau, decorated with hand-painted battle scenes in colours, in gilt medallions, floral designs, &c., on green ground, richly decorated spout and handle. Height, 13½ inches; diameter of plateau, 11 inches.

No. 8192.—Vienna China Plaque, exquisitely decorated with hand-painted figures, representing "Ariadne" burnished gold floral designs, in pink and white medallions, on dark blue ground. Diameter, 9½ inches.

This Real Dresden and Vienna China is of the highest class and finish, painted in the best style by well-known Artists, and is most suitable for Wedding and Birthday Presents.

MANUFACTURERS, IMPORTERS, WAREHOUSEMEN, AND AGENTS.

S. & F. LONDON AND PARIS.

S. & F. LONDON AND PARIS.

No. 8193.—China Figure, painted in colours. Height, 3½ inches diameter, 1¼ inches.

No. 8194.—China Figure, painted in colours. Height, 3½ ins.; diameter, 1½ ins.

No. 8195.—China Figure, decorated in colours. Height, 3½ ins.; diameter, 1½ ins.

No. 8196.—China Figure and Lion, decorated in colours. Height 3 ins.; length, 3 ins.

No. 8197.—China Figure, decorated in colours. Height, 3½ ins.; diameter, 1½ ins.

No. 8198.—China Group of Figures, decorated in colours. Height, 3 inches; width, 2 inches.

No. 8199.—China Figure, decorated in colours. Height, 4 inches; diameter, 1½ inches.

No. 8193 to No. 8206, when packed in one case, offer a nice assortment for any shop. 26 gross fill a good package.

When ordering China Ornaments, kindly allow us to add the latest novelties to such an amount as you may choose to name.

No. 8200.—China Figure, decorated in colours. Height, 3½ ins.; diameter, 1½ ins.

No. 8201.—China Vase, decorated with painted flowers, &c. Height, 3½ ins.; width, 1½ ins.

No. 8202.—China Mug, decorated with blue floral designs on white ground. Height, 1½ ins.; diameter, 1¾ ins.

No. 8203.—China Figure and Elephant, decorated in colours. Height, 3 ins.; length, 3 ins.

No. 8204.—China Basket with two Figures, decorated in colours. Height, 2 inches; length, 2¾ inches.

No. 8205.—China Jug, decorated in colours. Height, 3 ins.; diameter, 1½ ins.

No. 8206.—China Bird with Whistle, decorated in colours. Height, 2 ins.; length, 1½ ins.

No. 8207.—China Figure holding basket for flowers, decorated with raised coloured flowers, &c. Height, 4 ins.; diameter, 3 ins.

No. 8208.—China Figure Match Holder, decorated in colours and gilt. Height, 4 ins.; diameter, 2¾ ins.

No. 8209.—China Owl Cruet, painted in natural colours. Height, 4 ins.; diameter, 3½ ins.

No. 8210.—China Vase, decorated with dogs, flowers, &c., in relief. Height, 2¾ ins.; diameter, 2 ins.

No. 8211.—China Figure, holding tube for flowers, decorated in colours. Height, 4 ins.; diameter, 2 ins.

No. 8212.—China Cruet, with loose pepper box, decorated with gilt lines on white ground. Height, 3½ ins.; diameter, 5 ins.

No. 8213.—China Egg Set, with 4 movable cups, decorated with gilt lines on white ground. Height, 4 ins.; diameter, 6 ins.

No. 8214.—China Cruet, decorated with gilt lines on white ground. Height, 4 ins.; diameter, 4½ ins.

No. 8215.—China Cruet, with movable pepper, salt and mustard pot, decorated with floral designs in red, blue, and gilt on white ground; old Derby style. Height, 4 ins.; diameter, 5½ ins.

No. 8216.—China Mustard Pot, decorated with blue floral designs on white ground. Height, 3½ ins.; extreme diameter, 4 ins.

No. 8217.—China Salt Scuttle, decorated painted flowers, blue bands, &c., on white ground. Length, about 3½ ins.

No. 8218.—China Wheelbarrow for salt, in olive green. Length, about 4 ins.

No. 8219.—China Mustard Pot, white and gold, representing a bunch of grapes, with coloured vine leaf cover. Height, about 3½ ins.; diameter 2½ ins.

No. 8220.—China Egg Cup, white with gilt lines. Height, about 2½ inches.

No. 8221. China Cruet, decorated with blue and gilt designs on white ground Height, 3 ins., diameter, 5 ins.

No. 8222.—China Cream Jug. Height, 4 ins.; diameter, 3½ ins.

No. 8223.—China Cream Jug, fluted, painted flowers, gilt lines, &c., on white ground. Height, 5 ins.; diam., 4½ ins.

No. 8224.—China Toast Rack, white and gold. Height, 5 inches; length 7 inches.

No. 8225.—China Cream Jug. Height, 4½ ins.; diam., 2½ ins. painted flowers, gilt lines and mottoes, on white ground.

No. 8226. China Cream Jug, gilt rope designs and gilt lines on white ground. Height, 5½ ins.; diam., 3½ ins.

MANUFACTURERS, IMPORTERS, WAREHOUSEMEN, AND AGENTS.

S. & F.
LONDON
AND
PARIS.

S. & F.
LONDON
AND
PARIS

No. 8256

No. 8257

No. 8258

No. 8259

No. 8260

No. 8261

No. 8262

No. 8263

No. 8264

No. 8265

No. 8266

No. 8267

No. 8268

No. 8269

No. 8270

No. 8271

No. 8272

No. 8273

No. 8274

No. 8275

No. 8276

No. 8277

No. 8278

No. 8279

No. 8280

No. 8281

No. 8282

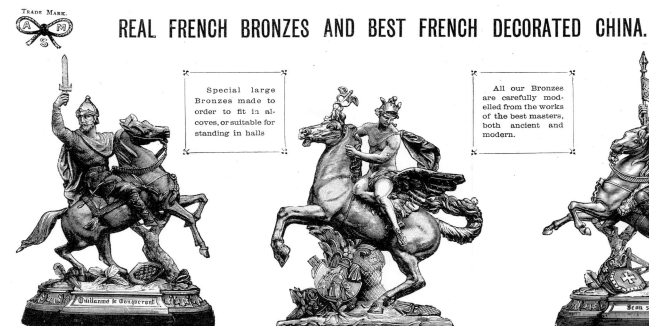

Special large Bronzes made to order to fit in alcoves, or suitable for standing in halls

All our Bronzes are carefully modelled from the works of the best masters, both ancient and modern.

No. 8284.—"William the Conqueror." Pair of Real Bronze Equestrian Figures, on black wood stands, representing William the Conqueror and John Lackland. Height 23 inches, length 16 inches.

No. 8286.—"Mercury upon Pegasus." Pair of Real Bronze Equestrian Figures representing Mercury upon Pegasus, and Renown. Height 42 inches.

No. 8284.—"John Lackland." Pair of Real Bronze Equestrian Figures, on black wood stands, representing William the Conqueror and John Lackland. Height 23 inches, length 16 inches.

S. & F.
London.

S. & F.
London.

No. 8287.—French China Bust representing "Summer." Of superior make, very richly decorated with raised and coloured flowers, the head-dress is beautifully modelled, and is of a pale pink colour relieved with bows of pale blue, and raised coloured flowers. A "fichu" or scarf is loosely thrown over the shoulders, decorated with hand-painted and enamelled floral designs on white ground, and richly gilt. The base is covered with dull gold, relieved with a spike design border in bright gold. Height 28½ inches, extreme width 13 inches, width of base 6½ inches.

No. 8280.—French China Group, "Love Declaration in Brittany." Of very superior make, most elaborately decorated with hand-painted and enamelled floral designs in pink and blue, and heavily gilt. The stand on which the female figure is sitting represents a rock, and is painted in natural colours. Height 23½ inches, extreme length 17½ inches, length of base 14 inches, width of base 9 inches.

No. 8288.—French China Bust representing "Winter." Of superior make, with drapery thrown loosely over the head and shoulders, very richly decorated with hand-painted and enamelled floral designs in blue and white, rich pink lining, and heavily gilt. The base is covered with dull gold, relieved with a spike design border in bright gold. Height 26½ inches, extreme width 13½ inches, width of base 6½ inches.

No. 8290.—"St. Louis." Pair of Real Bronze Equestrian Figures representing St. Louis and Godfrey de Bouillon. Height 25½ inches, length 22 inches.

No. 8286.—"Renown." Pair of Real Bronze Equestrian Figures representing Mercury upon Pegasus, and Renown. Height 42 inches.

No. 8290.—"Godfrey de Bouillon." Pair of Real Bronze Equestrian Figures representing St. Louis and Godfrey de Bouillon. Height 25½ inches, length 22 inches.

REAL PARIAN STATUETTES, Etc.

S. & F.
London.

Trade Mark

No. 8304.

No. 8304.—Parian Figure, "Young England," by Halse. Height 14½ inches, diameter of base 5¾ inches. (Nos. 8304 and 8305 form a pair.)

No. 8305. — Parian Figure, "Young England's Sister," by Halse. Height 14½ inches, diameter of base 5¾ inches. (Nos. 8304 and 8305 form a pair.)

No. 8306.—Parian Group, "Emily and White Doe," after Miller. Height 18 inches, length 13½ inches, width 9½ inches.

No. 8307. — Parian Figure, "Market Boy." Height 14½ inches, diameter of base 5½ inches. (Nos. 8307 and 8308 form a pair.)

No. 8308. — Parian Figure, "Market Girl." Height 14½ inches, diameter of base 5½ inches. (Nos. 8307 and 8308 form a pair.)

No. 8308.

ON THE SEA SHORE

No. 8309. Parian Figure, "On the Sea Shore — Calm," by Durham, R.A. Height 19½ ins., diameter of base 8½ inches. (Nos. 8309 and 8313 form a pair.)

No. 8310. — Parian Figure, "River Side," by Owen Hale. Height 18½ inches, diameter of base 5¾ inches. (Nos. 8310 and 8312 form a pair.)

No. 8311.—Parian Centrepiece, "Vintage." Height 25 inches, diameter of dish 13½ inches, diameter of base 10 inches.

No. 8312. — Parian Figure, companion to "River Side," by Owen Hale. Height 18½ inches, diameter of base 5¾ inches. (Nos. 8310 and 8312 form a pair.)

ON THE SEA SHORE

No. 8313. Parian Figure, "On the Sea Shore — Storm," by Durham, R.A. Height 19½ ins., diameter of base 8½ inches. (Nos. 8309 and 8313 form a pair.)

No. 8314.—Parian Figure, "Trysting Tree." Height 20 inches, diameter of base 8½ inches. (Nos. 8314 and 8316 form a pair.)

No. 8314.

No. 8315.—Parian Basket, Vine pattern. Height 6 inches, length 11 inches.

No. 8316.—Parian Figure, "Trysting Tree." Height 20 inches, diameter of base 8½ inches. (Nos. 8314 and 8316 form a pair.)

No. 8316.

S.& F.
London.

No. 8319.—Parian Centrepiece, "Spring." Height 10 inches, diameter 8 inches. Nos. 8319 and 8321 form a pair.

No. 8320.—Parian Centrepiece, Rustic Basket. Height 9¾ inches, length 13½ inches, width 7 inches.

No. 8321.—Parian Centrepiece, "Summer." Height 10 inches, diameter 8 inches. Nos. 8319 and 8321 form a pair.

SABRINA

No. 8323.—Parian Centrepiece, "Sabrina." Height 10 inches, length 17 inches, width 9 inches.

No. 8322.—Parian Figure, "Miss Ellie," by J. Durham, R.A. Height 20 inches, diameter 8½ inches. Nos. 8322 and 8324 form a pair.

MASTER TOM

No. 8324.—Parian Figure, "Master Tom," by J. Durham, R.A. Height 20 inches, diameter of base 8½ inches. Nos. 8322 and 8324 form a pair.

No. 8325.—Parian Bust, "Summer," by Hale. Height 17½ inches, length of base 8 inches, width 6 inches.

No. 8326.—Parian Bust, "Winter," by Hale. Height 17½ inches, length of base 8 inches, width 6 inches. Also "Spring" and "Autumn," making a set of 4. Always in stock.

The Statuettes, &c., represented on this page and on page No. 470 have been executed by the best modellers, and are of superior finish.

No. 8327.—Parian Figure, "Young Naturalist." Height 15¾ inches, diameter of base 6 inches. Nos. 8327 and 8329 form a pair.

No. 8328.—Parian Figure, "Before the Ball." Height 15 inches, length of base 19 inches, width of base 10 inches.

No. 8329.—Parian Figure, companion to "Young Naturalist." Height 15¾ inches, diameter of base 6 inches. Nos. 8327 and 8329 form a pair.

No. 8330.—Real Dresden China Cup and Saucer "King's Shape," decorated with hand-painted figures and flowers in colours, and richly gilt. Height of cup 2⅜ inches, diameter of saucer 5 inches.

No. 8331.—Real Dresden China Cup and Saucer, ship shape, decorated with painted swans and shell designs in relief, on white ground, and richly gilt. Height of cup 2½ inches, length 3 inches, diameter of saucer 5 inches.

No. 8332.—Capo di Monti Cup and Saucer, decorated with fruit and floral designs, mythological figures in coloured relief on white ground, and richly gilt. Height of cup 2½ inches, diameter of saucer 4½ inches.

No. 8333.—Real Dresden China Cup and Saucer, with cover, decorated with hand-painted marine views in colours, and richly gilt. Height of cup 3 inches, diameter of saucer 4 inches.

No. 8334.—Real Dresden China Moustache Cup and Saucer, decorated with hand-painted figures (Watteau subjects), flowers, &c., in colours, and richly gilt. Height of cup 3½ inches, diameter of saucer 6 inches.

No. 8335.—Real Dresden China Cup and Saucer, oval-shaped, decorated with hand-painted figures and flowers in colours, and richly gilt. Height of cup 3⅜ inches, length of saucer 5¼ inches.

No. 8336.—Real Dresden China Cup and Saucer, decorated with hand-painted flowers in colours on white ground and gilt lines. Height of cup 1½ inches, diameter of saucer 3 inches.

No. 8337.—China Framed Mirror, bevelled edge, decorated with raised and coloured roses and lilies, and richly gilt, with two Cupid figures at base holding wreath of flowers; made to hang against wall or stand upon table or bracket. Height about 9½ inches, width about 5¼ inches.

No. 8338.—China Framed Mirror, bevelled edge, decorated with raised and coloured flowers, and richly gilt, two Cupid figures at the top holding flowers and ferns; made to hang against wall or stand on table or bracket. Height about 9½ inches, width about 5½ inches.

No. 8339.—Real Dresden China Bowl, decorated with hand-painted figures and flowers in colours, and richly gilt. Height 3 inches, extreme diameter 5½ inches, diameter of base 3 inches.

No. 8340.—Real Dresden China Cup and Saucer, oval-shaped, decorated with hand-painted figures and flowers in colours, and richly gilt. Height of cup 1¼ inch, length of saucer 3 inches.

No. 8341.—Real Dresden China Cup and Saucer, decorated with hand-painted figures and flowers in colours, and richly gilt. Height of cup 2½ inches, diameter of saucer 4½ inches.

No. 8342.—Real Dresden China Mug and Saucer, decorated with hand-painted figures in colours, and richly gilt. Height of mug 1½ inches, diameter of saucer 3 inches.

No. 8343.—Real Dresden China Vase, with movable dome-shaped cover, leaf handles and square base, very richly decorated with hand-painted figures and flowers in colours, and heavily gilt. Height 20½ inches, extreme diameter 8½ inches, width of base 6 inches.

No. 8344.—Real Dresden China Mug and Saucer, decorated with hand-painted figures in colours on white ground, coloured edge, and gilt. Height 1½ inches, diameter 3 inches.

No. 8345.—China framed Mirror, bevelled edge, old Dresden style, with handsome scroll-shaped frame, very richly gilt, and decorated with sprays of raised and coloured roses and leaves, and figure of Cupid holding wreath of flowers, fitted with three movable branches for candles. Height about 19 inches, width about 11 inches.

No. 8346.—Real Dresden China Jug, decorated with hand-painted figures and flowers, and richly gilt neck and borders. Height 6 inches, diameter of base 3 inches.

No. 8347.—Real Dresden China Dish, octagon shaped, richly decorated with hand-painted figures and flowers, heavily gilt. Length 11 inches, width 8 inches.

S. & F.
London.

No. 8348.—Real Dresden China Tray, shell-shaped, decorated with hand-painted figures and flowers in colours, and richly gilt. Diameter 7½ inches.

No. 8349.—Real Dresden China Vase, bottle-shaped, flat, with stopper, very handsomely decorated with figures, trees, and flowers painted in colours, and richly gilt. Height 17 inches, width 7 inches.

No. 8350.—Real Dresden China Plate, decorated with hand-painted figures and flowers in colours, and richly gilt. Diameter 9½ inches.

No. 8351.—Real Dresden China Watering Pot, decorated with hand-painted figures and flowers in colours, and richly gilt. Height 7 inches, extreme length 9 inches, width 3 inches.

No. 8352.—Real Dresden China Vase, with cover, very richly decorated with hand-painted figures and flowers in colours, and richly gilt. Height 15 inches, extreme diameter 8 inches, diameter of base 5 inches.

8353 Vase, black with red handles,
Height 2½ inches, diameter 1½ inches,

8354 Vase, black with red handles,
Height 2¾ inches, diameter 1½ inches,

Ewer, black
Height
diameter

with red handles,
2½ inches,
1½ inches.

8355

Ewer, black
Height
diameter

with red handles,
2½ inches,
1¾ inches.

8356

Vase, with
views, floral
in colours
ground
diameter

hand-painted
designs, &c.,
on black
Height 4-in.,
3 inches.

8357

Vase, with
and floral
on black
diameter

hand-painted views,
designs in colours,
ground. Height 4-in.,
2 inches.

8358

Ewer and Plateau, grotesque
in imitation of green bronze ;
on rough gilt ground.
Diameter of Plateau

heads and floral designs,
Mermaids, &c., in relief
Height 21½ inches,
14½ inches.

8359

Vase, hand-painted views
in colours on black ground
diameter

floral designs, &c.,
Height 4 inches,
2 inches.

8360

Ewer, hand-painted
designs, &c., in
black ground,
diameter

views, floral
colours on
Height 4½ in.
1¾ inches.

8360a

Vase, in imitation
floral scroll on
Height 3¾ inches.

8361

of green bronze,
rough gilt ground.
Diameter 4½ inches.

Vase, hand-painted,
on blue ground, and
ground. Height
diameter

Babylonish designs
gilt tracing on black
4½ inches, extreme
4½ inches.

8365

Vase, on feet, raised figures and flowers
in colours, on black ground. Height 7½ in.
Diameter 4½ inches.

8362

Figure, decorated in imitation of brown bronze,
relieved with silver. Height 15 inches, diameter
of base 5½ inches. Nos. 8363 and 8363a form a pair.

8363

Vase, grotesque figure
of green bronze, with
wreaths of fruit, flowers,
Height 24 inches,
12 inches, diameter of

handles in imitation
heads, figures,
&c., on black ground.
Extreme diameter
base 8 inches.

8364

Figure, decorated in imitation of brown bronze, relieved with
silver. Height 15 inches, diameter of base, 5 inches.
Nos. 8363 and 8363a form a pair.

8363a

Vase, raised coloured figures, &c., on
black ground. Height 6-in., diameter 3-in.

8366

Vase, in imitation of green bronze, with leaf designs,
wreaths of flowers, &c., on black ground. Height
14 in., extreme diameter 8-in., diameter of base 4-in.

8367

Vase, with figures,
floral designs, &c.,
relief, on black
ground. Height
7 inches, diameter
4 inches.

8368

grotesque heads,
in copper coloured
ground. Height 12½ in.
4 inches.

Centrepiece, (with glass
brown bronze. Height
base 7½ inches, diameter

dish,) in imitation of
17 inches, diameter of
of glass dish 11 inches.

8369

Vase, in imitation of
floral designs, &c., in
ground. Height
extreme diameter
diameter of base

green bronze, shells,
relief, on black
12¾ inches,
6½ inches,
4 inches.

8370

Vase, with figures,
and rich floral
coloured relief, on
Height 14 inches,
of base

grotesque heads,
designs, in copper
black ground,
extreme diameter
4½ inches.

8371

8372   8372   8373   8373   8374   8374

8375   8375   8378   8378

8376   8376   8377   8377   8379   8379

8380   8380   8381   8381   8382   8382

8383   8383   8384   8385   8386   8384   8387   8387

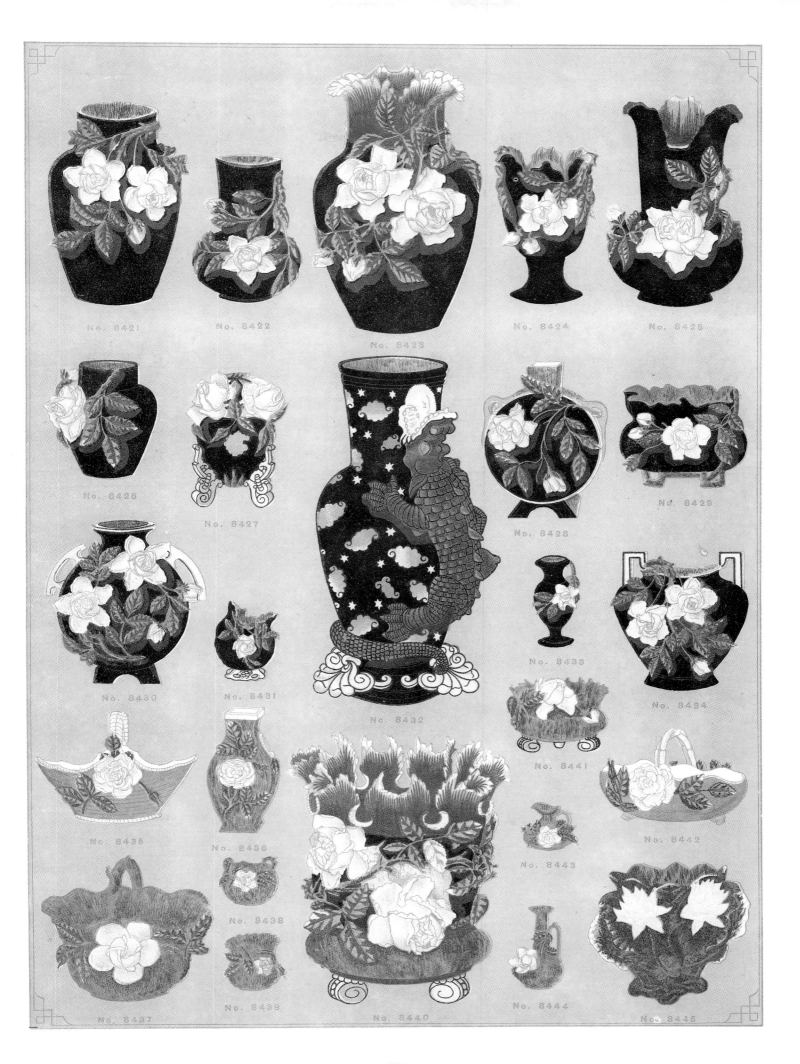

No. 8421   No. 8422   No. 8423   No. 8424   No. 8425

No. 8426   No. 8427   No. 8428   No. 8429

No. 8430   No. 8431   No. 8432   No. 8433   No. 8434

No. 8435   No. 8436   No. 8441   No. 8442

No. 8437   No. 8438   No. 8439   No. 8440   No. 8443   No. 8444   No. 8445

No. 8446

No. 8447

No. 8448

No. 8449

No. 8451

No. 8450

No. 8452

No. 8456

No. 8455

No. 8457

No. 8458

No. 8459

No. 8460

No. 8454

No. 8453

No. 8461

No. 8462

No. 8463

No. 8464

No. 8466

No. 8467

No. 8469

No. 8468

No. 8470

No. 8465

No. 8475

No. 8471

No. 8472

No. 8473

No. 8474

No. 8476

8477   8478   8479   8480   8481

8482   8482½   8483   8484   8484½   8485   8485½

8486   8486   8487   8488   8488½

S. & F.
LONDON.

S. & F.
LONDON.

8489   8489½   8490   8491   8492

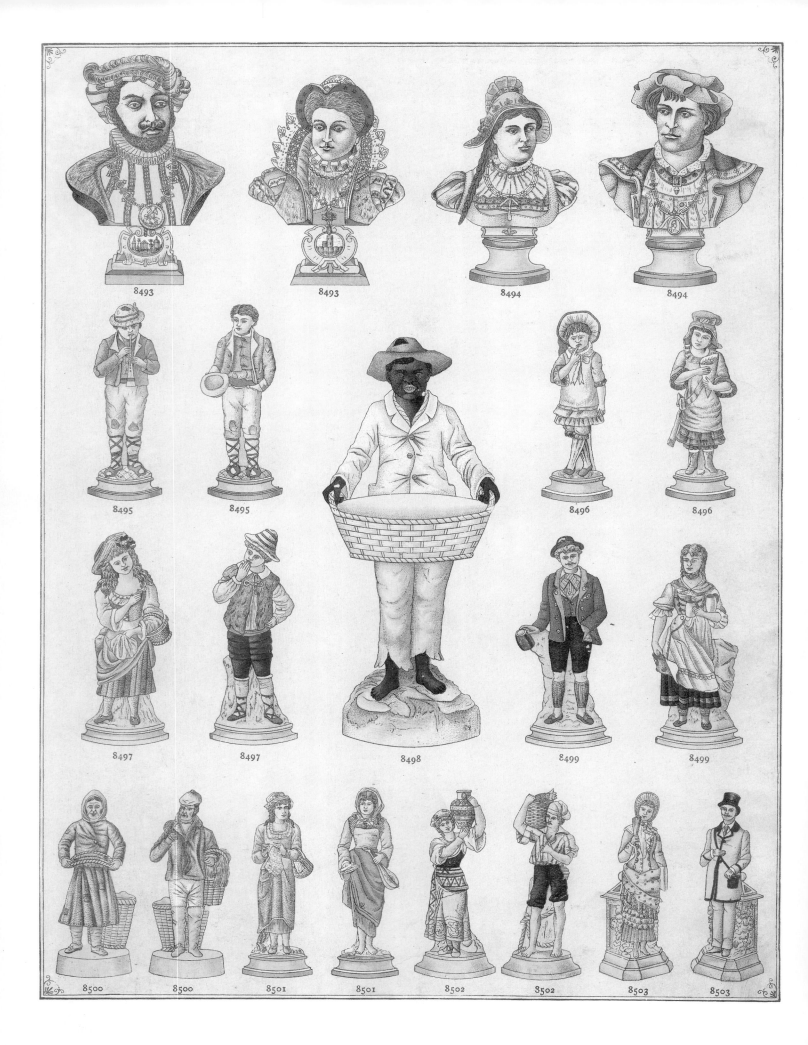

8493   8493   8494   8494

8495   8495   8496   8496

8497   8497   8498   8499   8499

8500   8500   8501   8501   8502   8502   8503   8503

HALL, CONSERVATORY, AND GARDEN ORNAMENTS AND BRACKETS, AND SADDLERS' TRADE SIGNS.

These Animals and Heads are made of a Ware which will bear exposure to the atmosphere. They are carefully modelled, and painted in exact imitation of the Animals they represent. A great variety of Animals and Birds always in stock.

TRADE MARK.

TRADE MARK.

No. 8538. — Bracket, Wild Boar's Head. Height about 14 inches, diameter about 13 inches, projection about 15 inches.

No. 8539.—Carriage Dog. Extreme height about 9 inches, extreme length about 16 inches.

No. 8540.—Bracket, Ram's Head, with real horns. Height about 12 inches, width about 9 inches, extreme height about 16 inches, extreme width about 19 inches.

No. 8542.—Fox, on coloured stand. Length of stand about 28 inches, width about 15 inches, extreme height about 19 inches, extreme length about 29 inches.

No. 8543.—Pug Dog, grey, with collar. Extreme height about 15 inches, extreme length about 18 inches.

No. 8541.—Stag, on stand. Length of base 15½ inches, width 7 inches, extreme height about 21 inches, length about 18 inches.

No. 8544.—Dog (Otter Hound). Extreme height about 7½ inches, length about 8 inches.

No. 8544.

No. 8548.—Rabbit. Extreme height about 11½ inches, length about 7½ inches.

No. 8549.—Cat. Extreme height 8 inches, length about 7 inches.

No. 8545.—Bracket, Horse's Head, chesnut (saddler's sign). Height about 22 inches, diameter about 10 inches, extreme height about 26 inches, projection 24 inches.

No. 8547.—Bracket, Hare's Head. Height 6 inches, diameter 5 inches, extreme height 10 inches.

No. 8546.—Bracket, Stag's Head. Height 6½ inches, diameter 5 inches, extreme height 14 inches.

No. 8548.

These Animals are painted in correct imitation of the natural colour of their skin hair, eyes, and horns.

No. 8550. — Bracket, Spaniel's Head, with 4 hooks. Height about 5 inches, width about 4½ inches, width across hooks, about 8 inches.

No. 8551. — Bracket, Dog's Head (King Charles), with 2 hooks. Height about 7 inches, width about 6 inches.

No. 8552.—Hare sitting. Extreme height about 20½ inches.

No. 8553.—Monkey sitting, holding an orange. Height about 14 inches.

No. 8554.—Bull Dog. Extreme height about 22 inches, extreme width about 17½ inches.

No. 8555.—Bracket, Pug Dog's Head, with 4 hooks. Extreme height about 6½ inches, width across hooks 8 inches.

No. 8556.—Bracket, Carriage Dog's Head, with 4 hooks. Extreme height about 6½ inches, width across hooks about 8 inches.

No. 8552.

MANUFACTURERS, IMPORTERS, WAREHOUSEMEN, AND AGENTS.

No. 8557.—Group of White Mice, drawn full size.

No. 8558.—Group of Swans, white, drawn full size.

No. 8559.—Group of Cats, tabby, drawn half size.

No. 8560.—Group of Dogs, white, drawn full size.

No. 8561.—Group of Cats, assorted colours, drawn full size.

No. 8562.—Group of Dogs, brown and white, drawn full size.

No. 8563.—Group of Sheep, white, drawn full size.

No. 8564.—Group of Kangaroos, brown and white, drawn full size.

No. 8565.—Group of Pug Dogs, grey, drawn full size.

No. 8566.—Group of Owls, painted in natural colours. Height 2 inches, length 2¼ inches.

No. 8567.—Owl (extinguisher), painted in natural colours. Height 2⅜ inches diameter 1¼ inches.

No. 8568.—Group of Rabbits, white, drawn full size.

No. 8569.—Group of Pigs, white with black spots, drawn full size.

No. 8570.—Group of Elephants, brown and white, drawn full size.

No. 8571.—Group of Pug Dogs, grey, drawn half size.

No. 8572.—Group of Rabbits, white, drawn half size.

Packed each Family in a box.   Drawn full size, excepting Nos. 8559, 8566, 8567, 8571, and 8572, which are drawn smaller.   Packed each Family in a box.

MANUFACTURERS, IMPORTERS, WAREHOUSEMEN, AND AGENTS.

No. 8573.—Tiger, painted in natural colours. Height 4 inches, length 5½ inches.

No. 8574.—Lion, painted in natural colours. Height 4½ inches, length 5½ inches.

No. 8575.—Polar Bear, painted in natural colours. Height 4¼ inches, length 5 inches.

No. 8576.—Camel, painted in natural colours. Height 1⅛ inches, length 2 inches.

No. 8577.—Fox, painted in natural colours. Height 1½ inches, length 2½ inches.

No. 8578.—Zebra, painted in natural colours. Height 1½ inches, length 1¾ inches.

No. 8579.—Bison, painted in natural colours. Height 1⅝ inches, length 2 inches.

No. 8580.—Cat, with ball, painted in natural colours. Height 3½ inches, length 8 inches.

No. 8582.—Roebuck, reclining, with real, movable horns, painted in natural colours. Height 25 inches, length 40 inches, width 20 inches, height to top of horns 41 inches, width across horns 37 inches.
This animal is made of a ware which will bear exposure to the atmosphere.

No. 8583.—Kangaroo, painted in natural colours. Height 4 inches, length 3½ inches.

No. 8581.—Walrus, painted in natural colours. Height 1¼ inches, length 2 inches.

No. 8584.—Roe, reclining, with real, movable horns, painted in natural colours. Height 25 inches, length 38 inches, width 19 inches, height to top of horns 29 inches, width across horns 30 inches.
This animal is made of a ware which will bear exposure to the atmosphere.

No. 8585.—Dog, "King Charles," painted in natural colours. Height 1¾ inches, length 2⅜ inches.

S. & F.
London.

No. 8586.—Squirrel, holding nut, painted in natural colours. Height 2½ inches, length 2 inches.

No. 858 7.—Dog (Setter), painted in natural colours. Height 2 inches, length 3¼ inches.

No. 8588.—Reindeer, painted in natural colours. Extreme height 5 inches, length 5 inches.

No. 8589.—Rabbit, sitting, painted in natural colours. Height 2 inches, width 1 inch.

No. 8590.

No. 8590.—Mule, painted in natural colours. Height 3 inches, length 4 inches.

No. 8591.—Rhinoceros, painted in natural colours. Height 2½ inches, length 3½ inches.

S. & F.
LONDON.

TRADE MARK.

No. 8592.—Stag reclining. Extreme height about 25 inches, extreme length about 29 inches, width about 13 inches.

No. 8594.—Hind reclining. Extreme height 24 inches, extreme length 28 inches, width about 12 inches.

No. 8593.—Leopard sitting. Height 26½ inches, length 27 inches, width across fore paws 13½ inches.

No. 8595.—Cat. Extreme height about 14½ inches, extreme width about 7 inches, diameter of base 7 inches.

No. 8596.—Cat. Extreme height about 12½ inches, diameter of base 6½ inches.

No. 8598.—Cat. Extreme height about 12½ inches, diameter of base 6½ inches.

No. 8599.—Cat. Extreme height about 12½ inches, diameter of base 6½ inches.

No. 8597.—Cow.—Extreme height about 12½ inches, extreme length about 20 inches.

No. 8600.—Cat. Extreme height about 12½ inches, diameter of base 6½ inches.

No. 8601.—Cat. Extreme height about 12½ inches, diameter of base 6½ inches.

No. 8602.—Leopard reclining. Height 18½ inches, extreme length 43 inches, extreme width 19½ inches.

No. 8603.—Cat Group. Extreme height about 15 inches, length of base about 15 inches, width about 9 inches.

No. 8604.—Monkey. Extreme height about 9 inches, extreme width about 5 inches.

No. 8605.—Weasel. Extreme height about 8½ inches, extreme width about 6½ inches.

No. 8606.—Tiger. Height 19 inches, extreme length 49 inches, extreme width about 19 inches.

No. 8607.—Squirrel. Extreme height about 9 inches, extreme width about 8 inches.

No. 8608.—Dog. Extreme height about 8½ inches, extreme width about 6 inches.

No. 8609.—Dog.—Extreme height about 12½ inches, extreme width about 7 inches.

TRADE MARK

No. 8610.—Lion.—Extreme height about 21 inches, extreme length about 49½ inches, width about 19½ inches.

No. 8611.—Dog. Extreme height about 13 inches, extreme width about 11½ inches.

These Animals are made of a ware which will bear exposure to the atmosphere. They are carefully modelled, and painted in exact imitation of the Animals they represent. A great variety of Animals and Birds always in stock.

DINNER, DESSERT,
TEA, AND BREAKFAST SERVICES,

IN CHINA AND EARTHENWARE.

ENGLISH AND FOREIGN MANUFACTURE.

DINNER SERVICES.

Dinner Service for 6 persons, 54 pieces, comprises :—

12 Meat Plates.	1 Dish, 10 inch.
12 Tart ,,	2 ,, 9 ,,
12 Cheese ,,	2 Vegetable Dishes.
1 Dish, 16 inch.	2 Sauce Tureens, with Ladles and
1 ,, 14 ,,	Stands complete.
1 ,, 12 ,,	

Dinner Service for 8 persons, 73 pieces, comprises :—

12 Meat Plates.	1 Dish, 10 inch.
12 Soup ,,	2 ,, 9 ,,
12 Tart ,,	1 Soup Tureen, with Ladle and Stand
12 Cheese ,,	complete.
1 Dish, 18 inch.	2 Sauce do. do.
1 ,, 16 ,,	2 Vegetable Dishes.
1 ,, 14 ,,	2 Butter Boats.
1 ,, 12 ,,	

Dinner Service for 12 persons, 120 pieces, comprises :—

36 Meat Plates.	2 Flat Dishes, 10 inch.
24 Tart ,,	2 ,, ,, 9 ,,
12 Cheese ,,	1 Soup Tureen, with Ladle and Stand
12 Soup ,,	complete.
1 Gravy Dish, 18 inch.	2 Sauce do. do.
1 Flat ,, 18 ,,	4 Vegetable Dishes.
1 ,, ,, 16 ,,	1 Salad Bowl.
2 ,, ,, 14 ,,	3 Pie Dishes.
2 ,, ,, 12 ,,	1 Fish Drainer.

Dinner Service for 18 persons, 168 pieces, comprises :—

54 Meat Plates.	4 Flat Dishes, 9 inch.
18 Soup ,,	1 Soup Tureen, with Ladle and Stand
24 Tart ,,	complete.
18 Cheese ,,	4 Sauce do. do
1 Gravy Dish, 20 inch.	4 Vegetable Dishes.
1 Flat ,, 20 ,,	2 Pie Dishes, 9 inch.
1 ,, ,, 18 ,,	2 ,, ,, 11 ,,
2 ,, ,, 16 ,,	1 Salad Bowl.
2 ,, ,, 14 ,,	1 Cheese Stand.
4 ,, ,, 12 ,,	1 Fish Drainer.
4 ,, ,, 10 ,,	

The number of Pieces comprising Services can be altered to suit purchasers.

N.B.—No Ladles are supplied with Real China Dinner Services.

Every single article counts as a "piece;" thus a Soup or Sauce Tureen comprises and counts four pieces, viz., Tureen, Cover, Stand, **and** Ladle; a Vegetable Dish comprises and counts two pieces, viz., Dish and Cover.

Extra pieces, as Hot-water Plates, Vegetable Drainers, Cheese Stands (with or without covers), Butter Boats, Pickle Trays, Hash Dishes (with hot-water pans), or Beef Steak Dishes, can be made to match any Service.

DESSERT SERVICES.

A Dessert Service of 18 pieces comprises :—

12 Plates.	4 Low Comports.	2 Tall Comports.

The number of pieces comprising Services can be altered to suit purchasers. Centre pieces can be made to match any Service.

TEA AND BREAKFAST SERVICES.

A Tea Service of 28 pieces comprises :—

12 Tea Cups.	1 Cream Jug.
12 ,, Saucers.	2 Bread Plates.
1 Slop Basin.	

A Tea Service of 35 pieces comprises :—

12 Tea Cups.	1 Slop Basin.
12 ,, Saucers.	2 Bread Plates.
8 Coffee Cups.	

A Tea Service of 40 pieces comprises :—

12 Tea Cups.	1 Slop Basin.
12 ,, Saucers.	1 Cream Jug.
12 Small Plates.	2 Bread Plates.

A Breakfast Service of 29 pieces comprises :—

6 Breakfast Cups.	1 Slop Basin.
6 ,, Saucers.	1 Sugar Basin.
6 Plates, 7 inch.	1 Milk Jug.
6 Egg Cups.	2 Bread Plates.

A Breakfast Service of 55 pieces comprises :—

12 Breakfast Cups.	1 Sugar Basin.
12 ,, Saucers.	1 Milk Jug.
12 Plates, 7 inch.	1 Covered Muffin Dish.
12 Egg Cups.	2 Bread Plates.
1 Slop Basin.	

The number of Pieces comprising Services can be altered to suit purchasers.

Every single article counts as a "piece;" thus there are two pieces in a Cup and Saucer.

Extra pieces, such as Tea Pots, Sugar Boxes, Butter Dishes, Toast Racks, Dishes, and Egg Stands, can be made to match any Service.

Monograms, Crests, and Masonic Devices, Regimental, Hotel, and other Badges, printed or painted in one or more colours on each piece of ware, to order.

Every single Article is charged at a fixed rate, according to the price of the Service.

We beg to draw your special attention to the great advantage of ordering a sufficient quantity of one pattern to make a package, as given in the Price List.

Each package can be assorted with Services of any number of pieces to suit the convenience of the purchaser, but all must be of one pattern.

The prices for English Services in packages are understood as being at the potteries, and of French China Services at our warehouse in London; the packages are charged as low as possible.

Almost every article represented in the following pages is kept in stock by us, and can in most cases be dispatched within a few hours after the receipt of order, you will thus be enabled to supply your customers with the goods at the shortest notice.

Most of the Services illustrated in the following pages of this Catalogue can be supplied of an inferior or mixed quality, when ordered in quantities, at lower prices than those quoted in our Price List. As we do not keep these qualities in stock, we shall require two or three months for the execution of such orders.

We do not hold ourselves responsible for breakage of, or damage to, goods in transit; but we employ experienced packers, thus minimising risk of breakage.

All prices are quoted free at our warehouse, excepting where special quotations are given for original packages delivered at the potteries.

ALL PRICES QUOTED IN OUR PRICE LIST ARE NETT.

No. 8768

No. 8768

No. 8768

No. 8769

No. 8769

No. 8769

No. 8770

No. 8770

No. 8770

No. 8771

No. 8771

No. 8771

S. & F.
LONDON
AND
PARIS.

BEST ENGLISH STONEWARE,

S. & F.
LONDON
AND
PARIS.

No. 8772

No. 8773

No. 8773

No. 8774

No. 8772

No. 8773

No. 8774

No. 8775

No. 8776

No. 8777

No. 8775

No. 8776

No. 8777

No. 8750

No. 8752

No. 8750

No. 8751

No. 8752

No. 8753

No. 8751

No. 8754

No. 8756

No. 8755

No. 8756

No. 8757

No. 8755

No. 8757

BEST ENGLISH CHINA

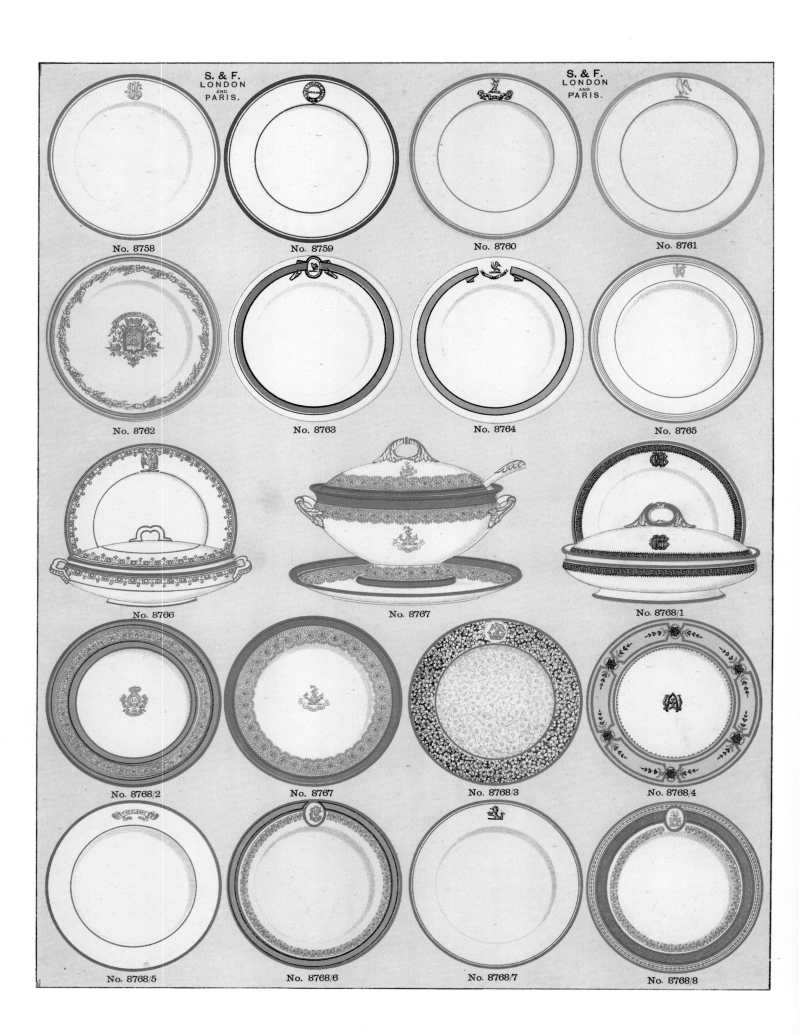

S. & F.
LONDON
AND
PARIS.

S. & F.
LONDON
AND
PARIS.

No. 8758

No. 8759

No. 8760

No. 8761

No. 8762

No. 8763

No. 8764

No. 8765

No. 8766

No. 8767

No. 8768/1

No. 8768/2

No. 8767

No. 8768/3

No. 8768/4

No. 8768/5

No. 8768/6

No. 8768/7

No. 8768/8

No. 8805

No. 8807

No. 8805

No. 8806

No. 8807

No. 8808

No. 8806

No. 8809

No. 8811

No. 8810

No. 8811

No. 8812.

No. 8810

No. 8812.

S. & F.
LONDON
AND
PARIS.

S. & F.
LONDON
AND
PARIS.

No. 8917

No. 8918

No. 8919

No. 8920

No. 8921

No. 8922

No. 8923

No. 8924

No. 8925

No. 8926

No. 8927

No. 8928

No. 8929

No. 8930

No. 8931

S. & F.
LONDON
AND
PARIS.

No. 8946

No. 8947

S. & F.
LONDON
AND
PARIS.

No. 8948

No. 8946

No. 8947

No. 8948

No. 8949

No. 8949/1

No. 8950

No. 8951

No. 8952

No. 8953

No. 8951

No. 8952

No. 8953

S. & F.
LONDON
AND
PARIS.

ENGLISH CHINA WARE.

S. & F.
LONDON
AND
PARIS.

No. 8979

No. 8980

No. 8981

No. 8982

No. 8983

No. 8984

No. 8985

No. 8986

No. 8987

No. 8988

No. 8989

No. 8990

No. 8991

No. 8992

No. 8993

S. & F.
LONDON
AND
PARIS.

ENGLISH CHINA WARE.

S. & F.
LONDON
AND
PARIS

No. 9039

No. 9040

No 9041

No. 9042

No. 9043

No. 9044

No. 9045

No. 9046

No. 9047

No. 9048

No. 9049

No. 9050

No. 9051

No. 9052

No. 9053

No. 9157

No. 9158

No. 9160

No. 9161

No. 9162

No. 9163

No. 9164

No. 9165

No. 9166

No. 9167.

S. & F.
LONDON
AND
PARIS.

BEST ENGLISH STONEWARE.

S. & F.
LONDON
AND
PARIS.

No. 8778

No. 8779

No. 8780

No. 8778

No. 8779

No. 8780

No. 8781

No. 8783

No. 8781

No. 8782

No. 8783

No. 8781

No. 8782

No. 8783

BEST ENGLISH STONEWARE.

S. & F.
LONDON
AND
PARIS.

S. & F.
LONDON
AND
PARIS.

No. 8784

No. 8785

No. 8786

No. 8785

No. 8784

No. 8785

No. 8787

No. 8788

No. 8789

No. 8789/1

No. 8789/2

No. 8789/3

No. 8789/1

No. 8789/2

No. 8789/3

S. & F.
LONDON
AND
PARIS.

BEST ENGLISH STONEWARE.

S. & F.
LONDON
AND
PARIS.

No. 8796

No. 8798

No. 8796

No. 8797

No. 8798

No. 8799

No. 8797

No. 8802

No. 8800

No. 8801

No. 8802

No. 8803

No. 8801

ENGLISH STONEWARE.

No. 8803

No. 8813   Cane Rice Dishes.

No. 8814   Sponge Rice Dishes.

No. 8815   Painted Rice Dishes.

No. 8816   Cane Pudding Bowls.

No. 8817   Cane Bakers.

No. 8818   Pheasant Bakers.

No. 8819   Oval Bakers White

No 8820   Sponged Bakers.

No. 8821   Plain Bowls.

No 8822   Pressed Bowls, white lined.

No 8823   Pressed Lip Bowls, white lined.

No. 8824   Cane Jelly Jars,

No. 8825   White Jelly Jars.

No. 8826   Covered Cane Sugar Pot.

TRADE MARK

TRADE MARK

No. 8827   Butter Pot.

No. 8828   Stew Pot.

No. 8829   Stock Jar, with handles.

No. 8830   Stock Jar, plain.

No. 8831   Stock Jar, Dutch shape.

No. 8832   Cane Rice Jar.

No. 8833   Cane Covered Jar.

No. 8834   Cane Porter Mug.

No. 8835   Cane Mug.

No. 8836   Cane Butter Pot.

No. 8837   Cane Foot Bath, white lined.

No. 8838   Cane Stool Pan, white lined.

No. 8839   Cane Bed Pan.

No. 8840   Cream-Coloured Stoneware.

No. 8840   Showing Interior.

No. 8842   The Ship Filter, for Ship's use.

No. 8843   The Wickered Filter, for Ship's use.

No. 8844   Made of White Ironstone China, Fluted and Marbled, decorated with Grecian Figures, holding two gallons.

No. 8845   Made of Terra-Cotta Ware just sufficiently porous to allow water to ooze through. The rapid evaporation that takes place in tropical climates cools the water considerably.

For scientific arrangement and durability of wear, these Filters maintain their reputation as thorough purifiers of water in almost any condition, whether from river, rain, or pond.

No. 8846   Pickle Jar, wicker covered.

No. 8847   Patent Air-tight Jar.

No. 8848   Spirit Bottle.

No. 8849   Spirit Bottle, wicker covered.

No. 8850   Round Spirit Barrel.

No. 8851   Spirit Barrel, white, with maroon, green or pink lines and lettering, ½, 1, 2, 3, 4 and 6 gallons.

No. 8852   Spirit Barrel, white, with gilt lines, gilt border and lettering, ½, 1, 2, 3, 4, and 6 gallons.

S. & F. LONDON.

No. 8853

No. 8854

No. 8855

No. 8856

No. 8857

No. 8858

No. 8859

No. 8860

No. 8861

No. 8859

No. 8862

No. 8863

No. 8864

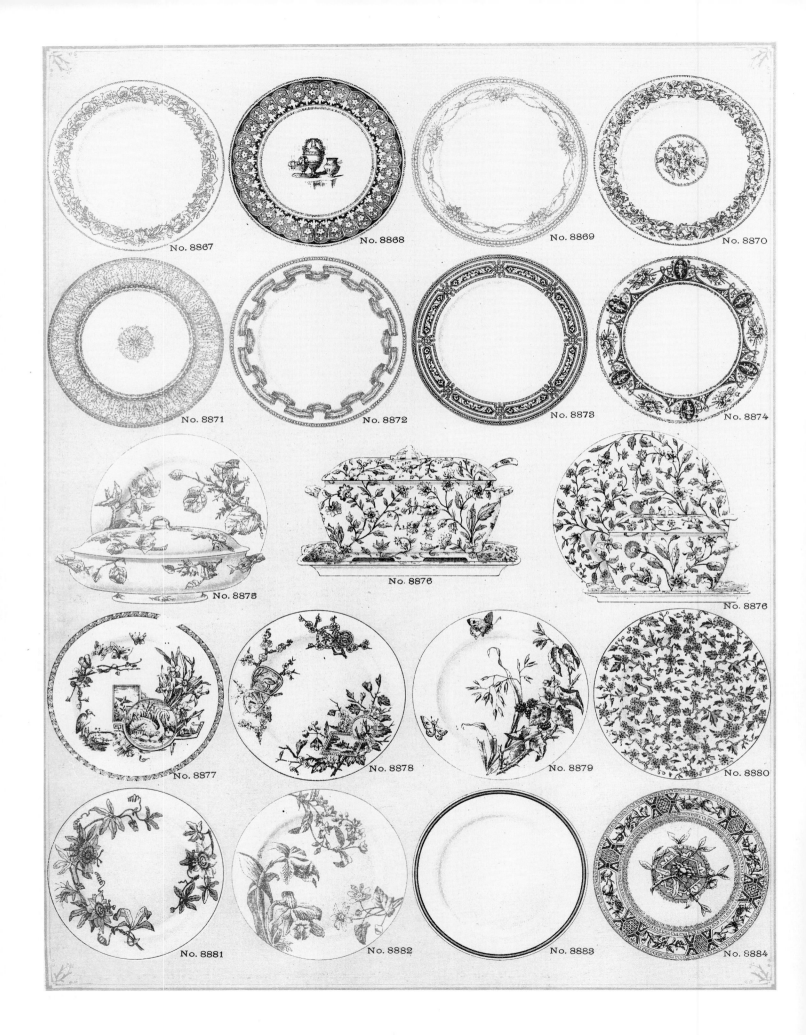

No. 8867

No. 8868

No. 8869

No. 8870

No. 8871

No. 8872

No. 8873

No. 8874

No. 8875

No. 8876

No. 8876

No. 8877

No. 8878

No. 8879

No. 8880

No. 8881

No. 8882

No. 8883

No. 8884

BEST ENGLISH STONEWARE.

No. 8885

No. 8886

No. 8887

No. 8888

No. 8889

No. 8890

No. 8891

No. 8891

No. 8892

No. 8892

No. 8893

No. 8893

No. 8894

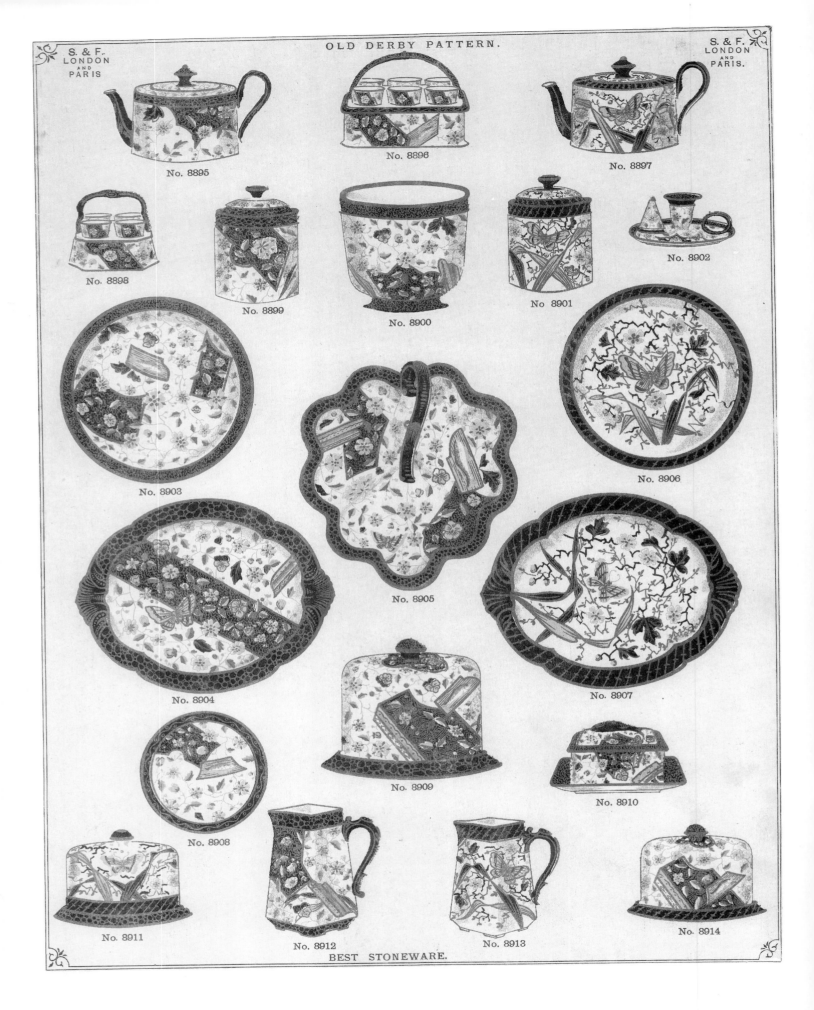

No. 8895

No. 8896

No. 8897

No. 8898

No. 8899

No. 8900

No 8901

No. 8902

No. 8903

No. 8905

No. 8906

No. 8904

No. 8907

No. 8908

No. 8909

No. 8910

No. 8911

No. 8912

No. 8913

No. 8914

BEST STONEWARE.

S. & F.
LONDON
AND
PARIS.

S. & F.
LONDON
AND
PARIS.

No. 8932

No. 8933

No. 8934

No. 8932

No. 8933

No. 8934

No. 8935

No. 8936

No. 8937

No. 8935

No. 8936

No. 8937

S. & F.
LONDON
AND
PARIS.

S. & F.
LONDON
AND
PARIS

No. 8938

No. 8933

No. 8939

A M
S
TRADE MARK

A M
S
TRADE MARK

No. 8940

No. 8940

No. 8941

No. 8942

No. 8942

No. 8943

No. 8944

No. 8945

No. 8945

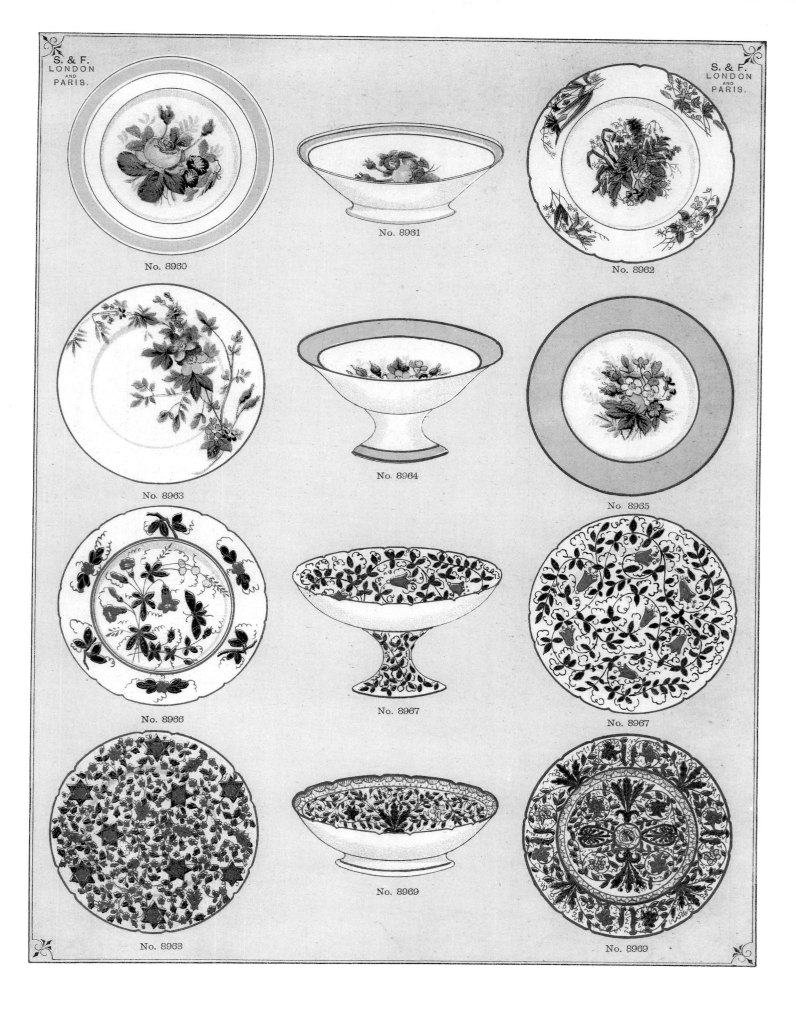

S. & F.
LONDON
AND
PARIS.

S. & F.
LONDON
AND
PARIS.

No. 8960

No. 8961

No. 8962

No. 8963

No. 8964

No. 8965

No. 8966

No. 8967

No. 8967

No. 8968

No. 8969

No. 8969

S. & F.
LONDON
AND
PARIS.

ENGLISH CHINA WARE.

S. & F.
LONDON
AND
PARIS

No. 8994

No. 8995

No. 8996

No. 8997

No. 8998

No. 8999

No. 9000

No. 9001

No. 9002

No. 9003

No. 9004

No. 9005

No. 9006

No. 9007

No. 9008

S. & F.
LONDON
AND
PARIS

ENGLISH CHINA WARE,

S. & F.
LONDON
AND
PARIS,

No. 9009

No. 9010

No. 9011

No. 9012

No. 9013

No. 9014

No. 9015

No. 9016

No. 9017

No. 9018

No. 9019

No. 9020

No. 9021

No. 9022

No. 9023

No. 9024

No. 9025

No. 9026

No 9027

No. 9028

No. 9029

No. 9030

No. 9031

No. 9032

No. 9033

No. 9034

No. 9035

No. 9036

No. 9037

No. 9038

No. 9053

No. 9054

No. 9055

No. 9056

No. 9057

No. 9058

No. 9059

No. 9060

No. 9061

No. 9062

No. 9063

No. 9064

No. 9065

No. 9066

No. 9067

No. 9069

No. 9070

No. 9071

No. 9072

No. 9073

No. 9074

No. 9075

No. 9076

No. 9077

No. 9078

No. 9079

No. 9080

No. 9081

No. 9082

No. 9083

No. 9084. No. 9085 No. 9086 No. 9087

No. 9088 No. 9089 No. 9090 No. 9091

No. 9092 No. 9093 No. 9094 No. 9095

No. 9096 No. 9097 No. 9098 No. 9099 No. 9100

No. 9101 No. 9102 No. 9103 No. 9104 No. 9105

No. 9106 No. 9107 No. 9108 No. 9109 No. 9110

No. 9111 No. 9112 No. 9113 No. 9114 No. 9115

No. 9116　　No. 9117　　No. 9118　　No. 9119　　No. 9120

No. 9121　　No. 9122　　No. 9123　　No. 9124　　No. 9125

No. 9126　　No. 9127　　No. 9128　　No. 9129　　No. 9130

No. 9131　　No. 9132　　No. 9133　　No. 9134　　No. 9135

No. 9136　　No. 9137　　No. 9138　　No. 9139　　No. 9140

No. 9141　　No. 9142　　No. 9143　　No. 9144　　No. 9145

TOILET SERVICES

IN

CHINA AND EARTHENWARE.

———•———

SANITARY WARE.

TOILET SERVICES,

IN CHINA, EARTHENWARE, Etc.

———— · ◆ · ————

A Toilet Service of 5 pieces comprises :—

    1 Ewer and Basin.   1 Soap Box.

    1 Chamber.   1 Brush Tray.

A Toilet Service of 6 pieces comprises :—

    1 Ewer and Basin.   1 Soap Box.

    2 Chambers.   1 Brush Tray.

A Double Service of 9 pieces comprises :—

    2 Ewers and Basins.   1 Soap Box.

    2 Chambers.   1 Brush Tray.

                 1 Sponge Bowl.

The number of pieces comprising Services can be altered to suit purchasers.

———— · ◆ · ————

Extra pieces, such as Slop Jar, Foot Bath, Supply Jug, Cover to Chamber, or Small Mouth Ewer and Basin, can be made to match any Service.

We beg to draw your special attention to the great advantage of ordering a sufficient quantity of one pattern to make a package, as given in the Price List.

Each Cask or Crate can be assorted with sets of five, six, or nine pieces to suit the convenience of the purchaser, but all must be of one pattern.

The prices for goods in packages are understood as being at the potteries. The packages are charged as low as possible.

SANITARY WARE, Etc.

———— · ◆ · ————

The arrangements we have made for the delivery of White Earthenware and Sanitary Ware of every description are such that we are enabled to execute the orders of our customers at very short notice.

We beg to draw your special attention to our illustrations of—

    BATHS AND BATH ROOM FITTINGS, on pages 544 to 546.

    JAPANNED TOILET WARE, on page 247, Volume I.

    LAVATORY FURNITURE, on page 248, Volume I.

    ENGLISH AND JAPANESE SCREENS, on page 93, Volume I.

Almost every article represented in the following pages is kept in stock by us, and can in most cases be dispatched within a few hours after the receipt of order; you will thus be enabled to supply your customers with the goods at the shortest notice.

Most of the patterns of Toilet Services illustrated in this Catalogue can be supplied of an inferior or mixed quality, when ordered in quantities, at lower prices than those quoted in our Price List. As we do not keep these qualities in stock, we shall require two or three months for the execution of such orders.

We do not hold ourselves responsible for breakage of, or damage to, goods in transit; but we employ experienced packers, thus minimising risk of breakage.

All prices are quoted free at our warehouse, excepting where special quotations are given for original packages delivered at the potteries.

ALL PRICES QUOTED IN OUR PRICE LIST ARE NETT.

No. 9304

No. 9304

No. 9305

No. 9304

TRADE MARK

No. 9305

No. 9306

No. 9306

No. 9307

S. & F.
LONDON.

No. 9306

No. 9307

S. & F.
LONDON
AND
PARIS.

ENGLISH STONEWARE.

S. & F.
LONDON
AND
PARIS.

No. 9308

No. 9309

No. 9308

No. 9309

No. 9310

No. 9311

No. 9309

No. 9310

No. 9312

No. 9311

No. 9313

No. 9312

No. 9313

S. & F.
LONDON
AND
PARIS.

S. & F.
LONDON
AND
PARIS.

No. 9292

No. 9291

No. 9291

No. 9292

No. 9293

No. 9293

No. 9294

No. 9294

No. 9295

No. 9295

No. 9296

No. 9296

WHITE EARTHENWARE.

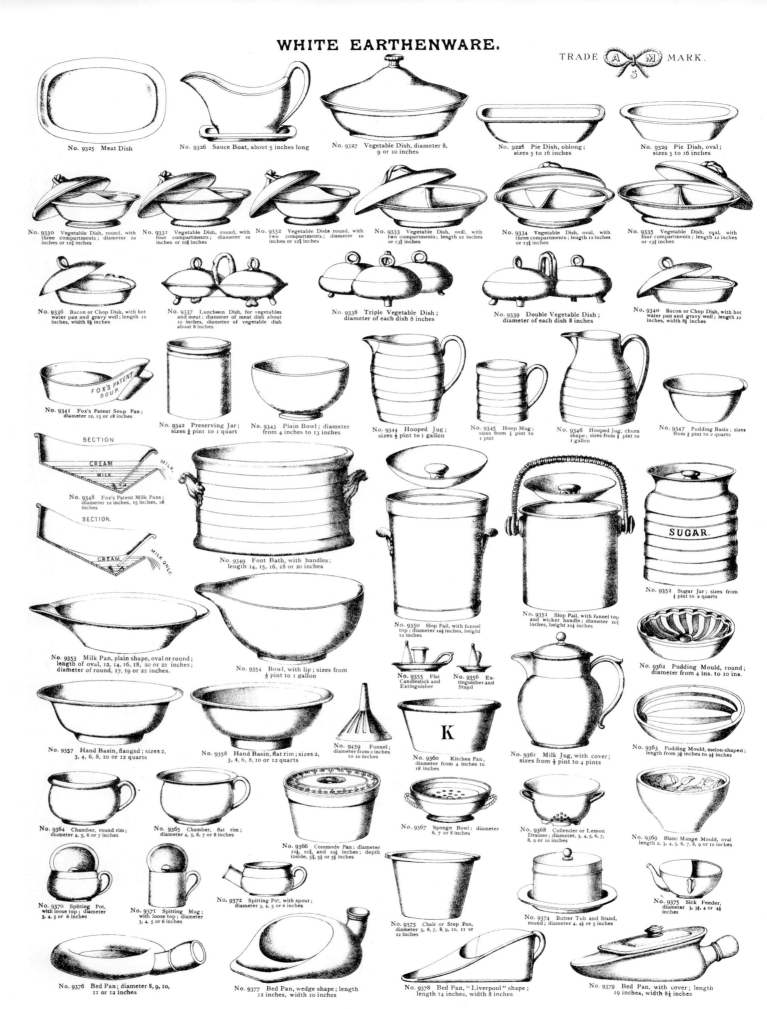

No. 9325 Meat Dish

No. 9326 Sauce Boat, about 5 inches long

No. 9327 Vegetable Dish, diameter 8, 9 or 10 inches

No. 9228 Pie Dish, oblong; sizes 5 to 16 inches

No. 9329 Pie Dish, oval; sizes 5 to 16 inches

No. 9330 Vegetable Dish, round, with three compartments; diameter 10 inches or 12½ inches

No. 9331 Vegetable Dish, round, with four compartments; diameter 10 inches or 12½ inches

No. 9332 Vegetable Dish, round, with two compartments; diameter 10 inches or 12½ inches

No. 9333 Vegetable Dish, oval, with two compartments; length 12 inches or 13½ inches

No. 9334 Vegetable Dish, oval, with three compartments; length 12 inches or 13½ inches

No. 9335 Vegetable Dish, oval, with four compartments; length 12 inches or 13½ inches

No. 9336 Bacon or Chop Dish, with hot water pan and gravy well; length 12 inches, width 8½ inches

No. 9337 Luncheon Dish, for vegetables and meat; diameter of meat dish about 10 inches, diameter of vegetable dish about 8 inches

No. 9338 Triple Vegetable Dish; diameter of each dish 8 inches

No. 9339 Double Vegetable Dish; diameter of each dish 8 inches

No. 9340 Bacon or Chop Dish, with hot water pan and gravy well; length 12 inches, width 8½ inches

No. 9341 Fox's Patent Soup Pan; diameter 12, 15 or 18 inches

No. 9342 Preserving Jar; sizes ½ pint to 1 quart

No. 9343 Plain Bowl; diameter from 4 inches to 13 inches

No. 9344 Hooped Jug; sizes ½ pint to 1 gallon

No. 9345 Hoop Mug; sizes from ½ pint to 1 pint

No. 9346 Hooped Jug, churn shape; sizes from ½ pint to 1 gallon

No. 9347 Pudding Basin; sizes from ½ pint to 2 quarts

SECTION — CREAM — MILK — MILK.

No. 9348 Fox's Patent Milk Pans; diameter 12 inches, 15 inches, 18 inches

SECTION. — CREAM — MILK ONLY.

No. 9349 Foot Bath, with handles; length 14, 15, 16, 18 or 20 inches

No. 9350 Slop Pail, with funnel top; diameter 10½ inches, height 12 inches

No. 9351 Slop Pail, with funnel top and wicker handle; diameter 10½ inches, height 10½ inches

SUGAR.

No. 9352 Sugar Jar; sizes from ½ pint to 2 quarts

No. 9353 Milk Pan, plain shape, oval or round; length of oval, 12, 14, 16, 18, 20 or 22 inches; diameter of round, 17, 19 or 22 inches.

No. 9354 Bowl, with lip; sizes from ½ pint to 1 gallon

No. 9355 Flat Candlestick and Extinguisher

No. 9356 Extinguisher and Stand

No. 9362 Pudding Mould, round; diameter from 4 ins. to 10 ins.

No. 9357 Hand Basin, flanged; sizes 2, 3, 4, 6, 8, 10 or 12 quarts

No. 9358 Hand Basin, flat rim; sizes 2, 3, 4, 6, 8, 10 or 12 quarts

No. 9459 Funnel; diameter from 2 inches to 10 inches

No. 9360 Kitchen Pan; diameter from 4 inches to 18 inches

K

No. 9361 Milk Jug, with cover; sizes from ½ pint to 4 pints

No. 9363 Pudding Mould, melon-shaped; length from 3½ inches to 9½ inches

No. 9364 Chamber, round rim; diameter 4, 5, 6 or 7 inches

No. 9365 Chamber, flat rim; diameter 4, 5, 6, 7 or 8 inches

No. 9366 Commode Pan; diameter 11½, 10½, and 10½ inches; depth inside, 5¾, 5½ or 5½ inches

No. 9367 Sponge Bowl; diameter 6, 7 or 8 inches

No. 9368 Cullender or Lemon Drainer; diameter, 3, 4, 5, 6, 7, 8, 9 or 10 inches

No. 9369 Blanc Mange Mould, oval length 2, 3, 4, 5, 6, 7, 8, 9 or 10 inches

No. 9370 Spitting Pot, with loose top; diameter 3, 4, 5 or 6 inches

No. 9371 Spitting Mug; with loose top; diameter 3, 4, 5 or 6 inches

No. 9372 Spitting Pot, with spout; diameter 3, 4, 5 or 6 inches

No. 9373 Chair or Step Pan, diameter 5, 6, 7, 8, 9, 10, 11 or 12 inches

No. 9374 Butter Tub and Stand, round; diameter 4, 4½ or 5 inches

No. 9375 Sick Feeder; diameter 3, 3½, 4 or 4½ inches

No. 9376 Bed Pan; diameter 8, 9, 10, 11 or 12 inches

No. 9377 Bed Pan, wedge shape; length 12 inches, width 10 inches

No. 9378 Bed Pan, "Liverpool" shape; length 14 inches, width 8 inches

No. 9379 Bed Pan, with cover; length 19 inches, width 8½ inches

MANUFACTURERS, IMPORTERS, WAREHOUSEMEN AND AGENTS.

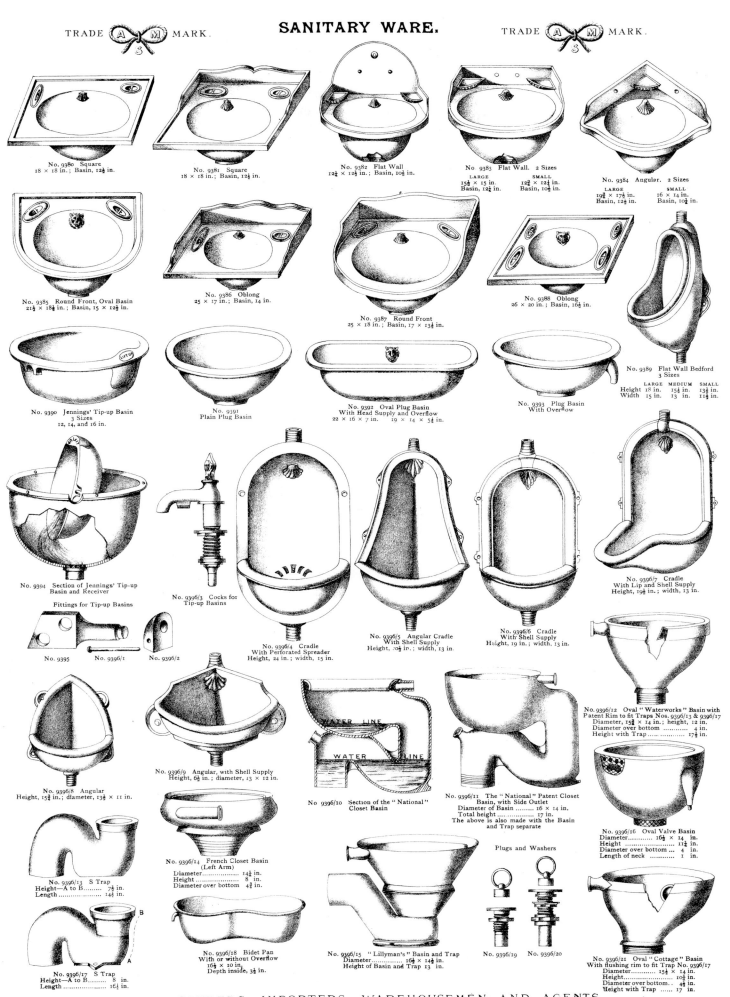

No. 9380 Square
18 × 18 in.; Basin, 12½ in.

No. 9381 Square
18 × 18 in.; Basin, 12½ in.

No. 9382 Flat Wall
12½ × 12½ in.; Basin, 10½ in.

No. 9383 Flat Wall. 2 Sizes

	LARGE	SMALL
	15½ × 15 in.	12½ × 12½ in.
	Basin, 12½ in.	Basin, 10½ in.

No. 9384 Angular. 2 Sizes

	LARGE	SMALL
	19½ × 17½ in.	16 × 14 in.
	Basin, 12½ in.	Basin, 10½ in.

No. 9385 Round Front, Oval Basin
21½ × 18½ in.; Basin, 15 × 12½ in.

No. 9386 Oblong
25 × 17 in.; Basin, 14 in.

No. 9387 Round Front
25 × 18 in.; Basin, 17 × 13½ in.

No. 9388 Oblong
26 × 20 in.; Basin, 16½ in.

No. 9389 Flat Wall Bedford
3 Sizes

	LARGE	MEDIUM	SMALL
Height	18 in.	15½ in.	13½ in.
Width	15 in.	13 in.	11½ in.

No. 9390 Jennings' Tip-up Basin
3 Sizes
12, 14, and 16 in.

No. 9391
Plain Plug Basin

No. 9392 Oval Plug Basin
With Head Supply and Overflow
22 × 16 × 7 in.   19 × 14 × 5½ in.

No. 9393 Plug Basin
With Overflow

No. 9394 Section of Jennings' Tip-up
Basin and Receiver

No. 9396/3 Cocks for
Tip-up Basins

No. 9396/4 Cradle
With Perforated Spreader
Height, 24 in.; width, 15 in.

No. 9396/5 Angular Cradle
With Shell Supply
Height, 20½ in.; width, 13 in.

No. 9396/6 Cradle
With Shell Supply
Height, 19 in.; width, 13 in.

No. 9396/7 Cradle
With Lip and Shell Supply
Height, 19½ in.; width, 13 in.

Fittings for Tip-up Basins

No. 9395   No. 9396/1   No. 9396/2

No. 9396/8 Angular
Height, 15½ in.; diameter, 13½ × 11 in.

No. 9396/9 Angular, with Shell Supply
Height, 6½ in.; diameter, 13 × 12 in.

No. 9396/10 Section of the "National"
Closet Basin

WATER LINE

WATER LINE

No. 9396/11 The "National" Patent Closet
Basin, with Side Outlet
Diameter of Basin .... 16 × 14 in.
Total height .... 17 in.
The above is also made with the Basin
and Trap separate

No. 9396/12 Oval "Waterworks" Basin with
Patent Rim to fit Traps Nos. 9396/13 & 9396/17
Diameter, 15½ × 14 in.; height, 12 in.
Diameter over bottom .... 4 in.
Height with Trap .... 17½ in.

No. 9396/13 S Trap
Height—A to B ...... 7½ in.
Length .... 14½ in.

No. 9396/14 French Closet Basin
(Left Arm)
Diameter................ 14½ in.
Height.................. 8 in.
Diameter over bottom.... 4¾ in.

No. 9396/16 Oval Valve Basin
Diameter.......... 16½ × 14 in.
Height .... 11¼ in.
Diameter over bottom ... 4 in.
Length of neck .... 1 in.

No. 9396/17 S Trap
Height—A to B ...... 8 in.
Length .... 16½ in.

No. 9396/18 Bidet Pan
With or without Overflow
16½ × 10 in.
Depth inside, 3½ in.

No. 9396/15 "Lillyman's" Basin and Trap
Diameter................ 16½ × 14½ in.
Height of Basin and Trap 13 in.

Plugs and Washers

9396/19   9396/20

No. 9396/21 Oval "Cottage" Basin
With flushing rim to fit Trap No. 9396/17
Diameter............ 15½ × 14 in.
Height .... 10½ in.
Diameter over bottom... 4½ in.
Height with Trap ...... 17 in.

MANUFACTURERS, IMPORTERS, WAREHOUSEMEN AND AGENTS.

No. 9397

No. 9398

No. 9399

No. 9400

No. 9400

No. 9401

No. 9400

No. 9401

No. 9402

No. 9403

No. 9403

No. 9404

No. 9404

No. 9405

No. 9405

No. 9406

No. 9406

No. 9407

No. 9407

No. 9408

No. 9408

No. 9409

No. 9409

No. 9410

No. 9410

No. 9411

No. 9411

No. 9412

No. 9412

No. 9413

No. 9413

No. 9414

No. 9415

No. 9414

No. 9415

No. 9415

No. 9414

No. 9415

No. 9415

No. 9416

No. 9416

No. 9417

No. 9417

IRONMONGERY GOODS,

FENDERS AND FIRE-IRONS, COPPER URNS, COAL BOXES,

TRAYS, JAPANNED TOILET SETS, BATHS,

LABOUR-SAVING MACHINERY,

REFRIGERATORS, ICE-MAKING MACHINES, SODA-WATER MACHINES,

KNIFE CLEANERS, WEIGHING, CHOPPING, AND MIXING MACHINES,

TOOLS,

COFFEE MILLS, ROASTERS, AND HOUSEHOLD REQUISITES,

BREAD CUTTERS, SUGAR CHOPPERS, ENAMELLED IRON WARE,

COPPER HOUSEHOLD GOODS, TINNED IRON WARE,

DISH COVERS AND HOT-WATER DISHES,

GROCERS' CANISTERS AND OTHER FITTINGS,

COPPER, TINNED, AND ENAMELLED IRON COOKING UTENSILS,

TURNED WOOD AND OTHER HOUSEHOLD GOODS,

HOUSEHOLD BRUSHES,

BIRD CAGES,

CASH BOXES AND SAFES,

UMBRELLA STANDS, WASHING STANDS,

JAPANNED TRAVELLING TRUNKS,

SPOONS, FORKS, CRUETS, CORKSCREWS, Etc.

TRADE MARK

TRADE MARK

Nos. 9523 to 9534   Fire Irons, polished steel

Nos. 9535 to 9537 Fire Irons, black, with brass head

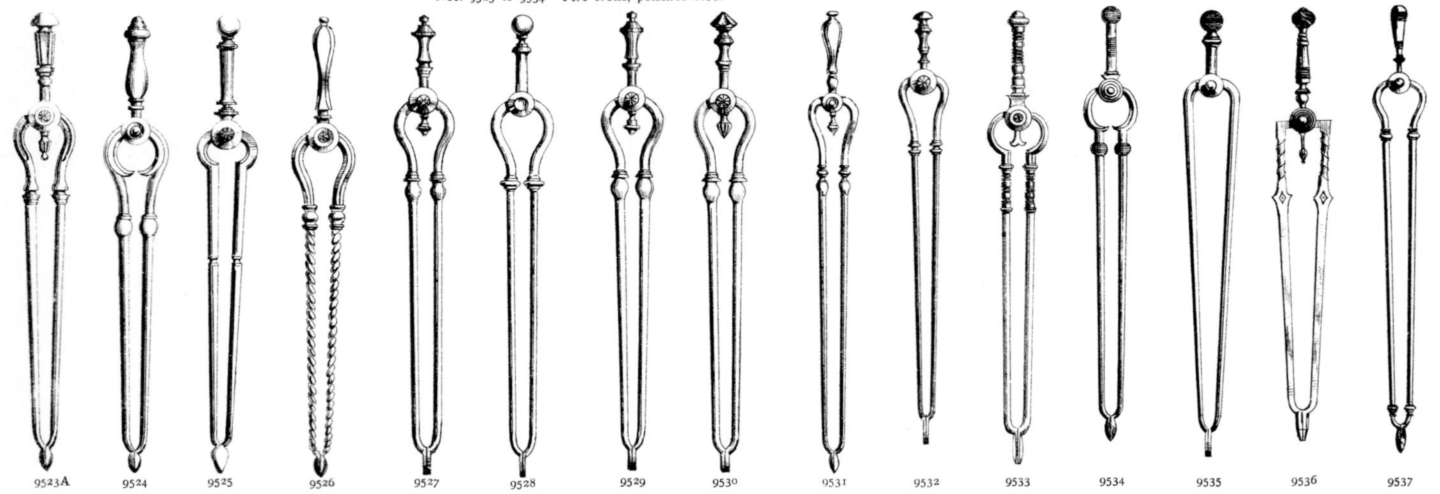

9523A   9524   9525   9526   9527   9528   9529   9530   9531   9532   9533   9534   9535   9536   9537

No. 9538 Fire Iron Rest, black and brass

S&F. London

No. 9539 Fire Iron Rest, all brass

No. 9540 Fire Iron Rest, all brass

No. 9541 Fire Iron Rest, all brass

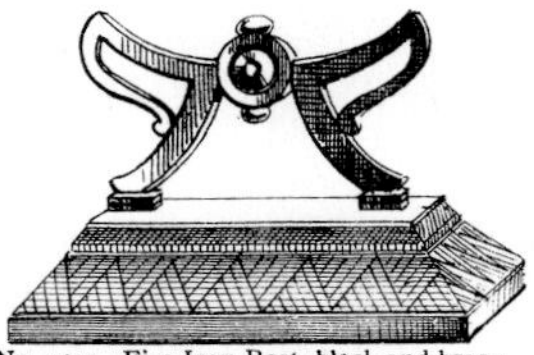

No. 9542 Fire Iron Rest, black and brass

No. 9543 Fire Iron Rest, all brass

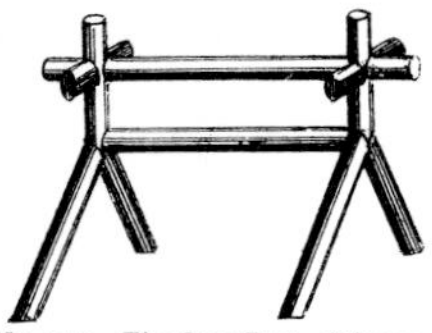

No. 9544 Fire Iron Rest, all brass

No. 9545 Fire Iron Rest, all brass

No. 9546 Fire Iron Rest, all brass

No. 9547 Fire Iron Rest, all brass

No. 9548 Fire Iron Rest, black and bright steel

No. 9549 Fire Iron Rest, all brass

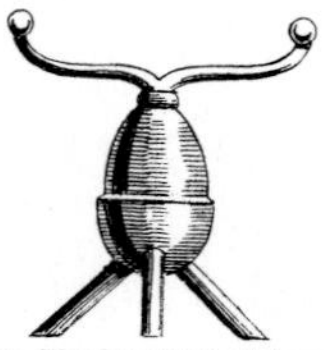

No 9550 Fire Iron Rest, all brass

No. 9551 Fire Iron Rest, all brass

No. 9552 Fire Iron Rest, all brass

No. 9553 Fire Iron Rest, black and bright steel

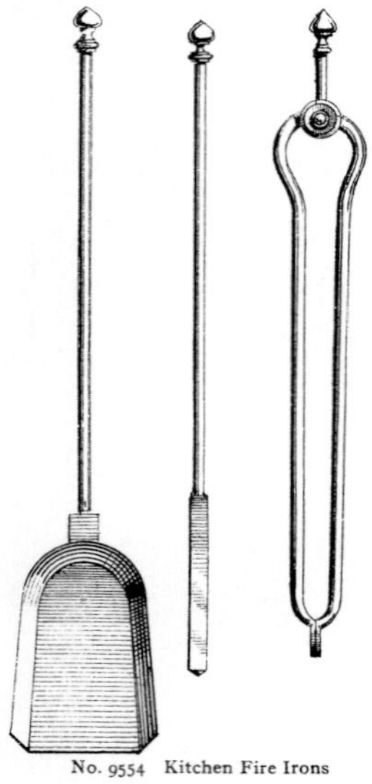

No. 9554 Kitchen Fire Irons

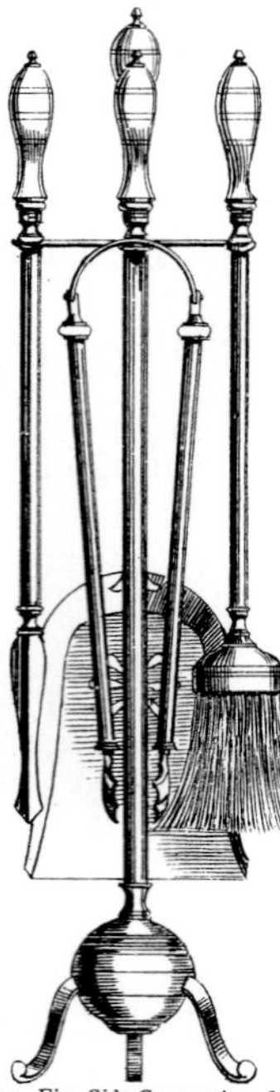

No. 9555 Fire Side Companion, fitted complete, polished brass, ebony handles

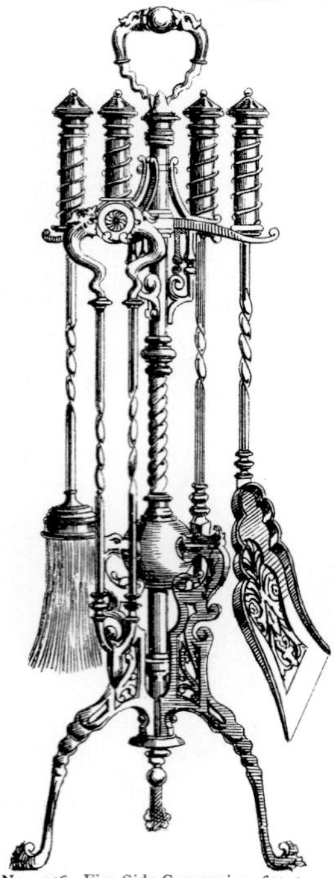

No. 9556 Fire Side Companion, fitted complete, polished brass

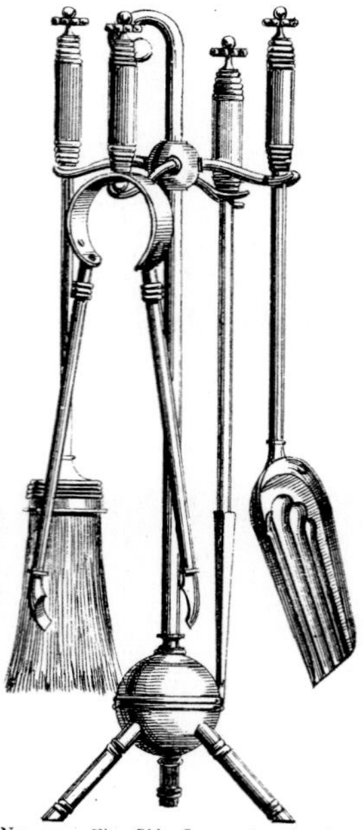

No. 9557 Fire Side Companion, fitted complete, polished brass, ebony handles

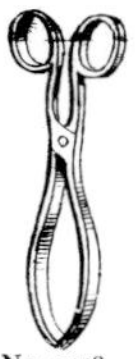

No. 9558 Coal Box Tongs, bronzed or black

No. 9559 Coal Box Tongs, polished brass

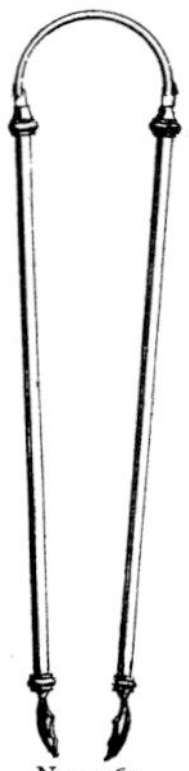

No. 9560 Coal Box Tongs, brass, spring bow

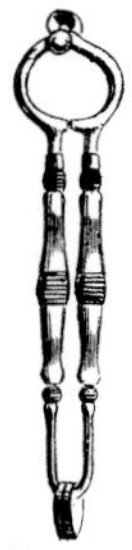

No. 9561 Coal Box Tongs, ebony and brass

S&F.

S&F.

ENTERED AT STATIONERS' HALL.   MANUFACTURERS, IMPORTERS, WAREHOUSEMEN AND AGENTS

Pawson & Brailsford, Lith. Sheffield.

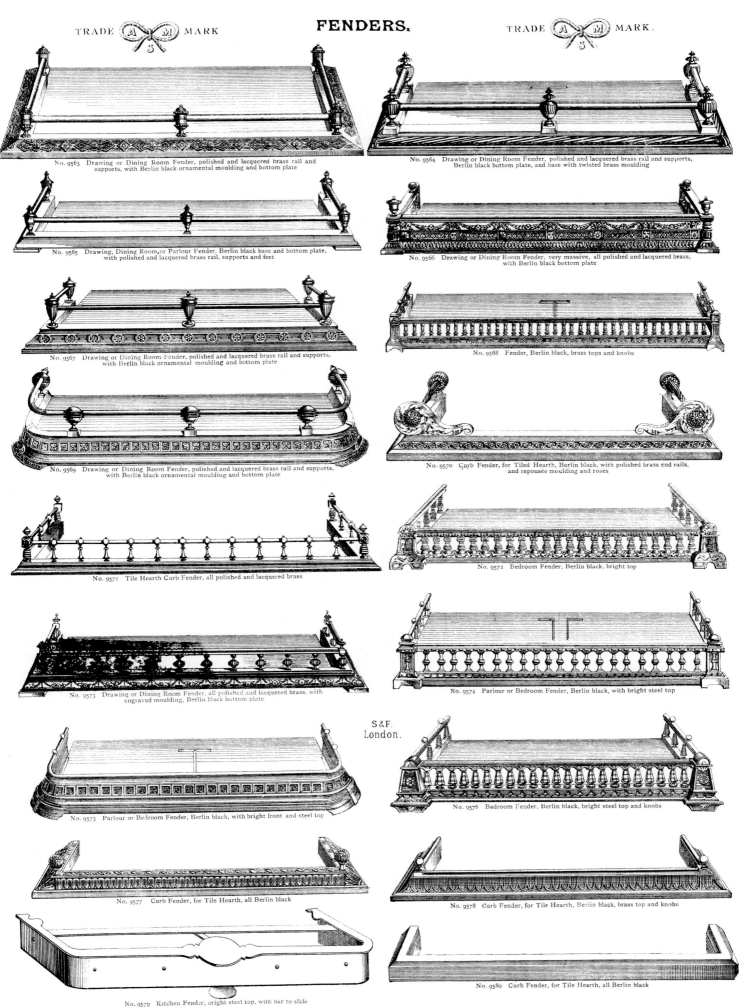

TRADE MARK

TRADE MARK

No. 9563   Drawing or Dining Room Fender, polished and lacquered brass rail and supports, with Berlin black ornamental moulding and bottom plate

No. 9564   Drawing or Dining Room Fender, polished and lacquered brass rail and supports, Berlin black bottom plate, and base with twisted brass moulding

No. 9565   Drawing, Dining Room, or Parlour Fender, Berlin black base and bottom plate, with polished and lacquered brass rail, supports and feet

No. 9566   Drawing or Dining Room Fender, very massive, all polished and lacquered brass, with Berlin black bottom plate

No. 9567   Drawing or Dining Room Fender, polished and lacquered brass rail and supports, with Berlin black ornamental moulding and bottom plate

No. 9568   Fender, Berlin black, brass tops and knobs

No. 9569   Drawing or Dining Room Fender, polished and lacquered brass rail and supports, with Berlin black ornamental moulding and bottom plate

No. 9570   Curb Fender, for Tiled Hearth, Berlin black, with polished brass end rails, and repoussée moulding and roses

No. 9571   Tile Hearth Curb Fender, all polished and lacquered brass

No. 9572   Bedroom Fender, Berlin black, bright top

No. 9573   Drawing or Dining Room Fender, all polished and lacquered brass, with engraved moulding, Berlin black bottom plate

No. 9574   Parlour or Bedroom Fender, Berlin black, with bright steel top

S&F.
London.

No. 9575   Parlour or Bedroom Fender, Berlin black, with bright front and steel top

No. 9576   Bedroom Fender, Berlin black, bright steel top and knobs

No. 9577   Curb Fender, for Tile Hearth, all Berlin black

No. 9578   Curb Fender, for Tile Hearth, Berlin black, brass top and knobs

No. 9579   Kitchen Fender, bright steel top, with bar to slide

No. 9580   Curb Fender, for Tile Hearth, all Berlin black

MANUFACTURERS, IMPORTERS WAREHOUSEMEN AND AGENTS

No. 9584 Oval Tea Kettle and Stand, with spirit lamp complete, made entirely of polished and lacquered brass, with ebony knob and handle

No. 9585 Round Tea Kettle & Stand, with spirit lamp, polished and lacquered brass, with repoussé border, ebony knob and handle

No. 9586 Octagon Tea Kettle & Stand, with spirit lamp, polished and lacquered brass, repoussé ornamentation and beaded, ebony knob and handle

No. 9587 Globe Tea Kettle and Stand, with spirit lamp, polished and lacquered brass, repoussé border and beaded, ebony knob and handle

No. 9588 Round Tea Kettle & Stand, with spirit lamp, polished and lacquered brass or nickel silver plated, with ebony handle

No. 9589 Round Toddy Kettle, polished and lacquered brass, with opal or crystal glass handle

No. 9590 Toilet or Hot Water Can, made of polished and lacquered brass, and lined inside with tin

No. 9591 Sausage Warmer. The body is made of brass, polished and lacquered; the cover of block tin. It has a tinned copper lining for containing hot water, with a lip for filling or drawing off. It is also provided with an enamelled iron dish for holding the sausages, and is heated by gas underneath

No. 9592 "Criterion" Cafetière, nickel silver, with ebonized handle
No. 9592A As No. 9592, but entirely of block tin

No. 9593 Round Tea Kettle, polished copper, or polished and lacquered brass, with plain opal or crystal glass handle

No. 9594 Hot Water or Shaving Jug, polished and lacquered brass, lined with tin

No. 9595 Pillar Candlestick, polished and lacquered brass

No. 9596 Chamber Candlestick, flat or bell shape, polished and lacquered brass, with extinguisher and socket to take out

No. 9597 Short Pillar Candlestick, polished and lacquered brass, richly ornamented

No. 9598 Chamber or Kitchen Candlestick, polished and lacquered brass, with handle and extinguisher

No. 9599 Ornamental Pillar Candlestick, polished and lacquered brass

No. 9600 Hot Water Jug, with cover, polished brass or browned copper

No. 9601 Coal Scoop, polished and lacquered brass, with handsome repoussé hood and ebony handle, with hand scoop

No. 9602 Helmet Coal Scoop, polished and lacquered brass, with repoussé ornamentation, and lined with zinc

No. 9603 Coal Box, also suitable for logs of wood; made of polished and lacquered brass, with handsome repoussé ornamentation, and lined inside with zinc; with brass hand scoop complete. Length 22 ins., width 13½ ins., height 12 ins.

No. 9604 Helmet Coal Scoop, polished copper or polished & lacquered brass

No. 9605 Coal Box, all polished and lacquered brass, repoussé panel, with loose coal container, and brass hand scoop with ebony handle

TRADE MARK

S. & F., London

No. 9606 Swing Kettle on hinged stand, with pin, and spirit lamp, browned copper, or nickel silver plated, with china knob and handle

No. 9607 Rustic Kettle and Stand, with spirit lamp, made in browned copper, with china knob on cover

No. 9608 Gipsy Kettle and Rustic Stand, with spirit lamp, made in browned copper, with china knob on cover

No. 9609 Swing Kettle on Stand, with spirit lamp, browned copper, with china knob and handle

ENTERED AT STATIONERS' HALL

No. 9615.—Browned Copper Coffee Roasting Machine and Spirit Lamp, with filler and funnel, on hard wood stand.

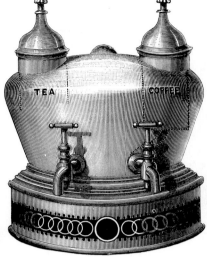

No. 9616.—Browned Copper Counter Urn, with nickel silver mounts.

No. 9617. — Napierian Coffee Machine. Directions for use.—Put the ground coffee into the jar; then pour over it as much boiling water as is required; put a teacupful of hot water into the bottle, and light the spirit lamp. Then fit the syphon tightly into the bottle, allowing the perforated end to rest on the bottom of the jar, and when the air is expelled from the bottle (which will be known by the commotion in the jar subsiding), extinguish the flame and the coffee will pass through the syphon into the bottle, from which it may be poured into the cups as required.

No. 9619.—Browned Copper Wine or Beer Muller and Water Urn, with nickel silver mounts.

No. 9621.—Browned Copper Cafetière, with polished black handle.

No. 9620.—Browned Copper Coffee Machine with white earthenware lining, spirit lamp, and extinguisher, cut glass lid.

No. 9622.—Browned Copper Coffee Roasting Machine and Spirit Lamp, with filler and funnel.

No. 9618.—Browned Copper Egg Steamer, with spirit lamp and silver-plated knob.

No. 9623.—Browned Copper Egg Steamer, for cooking one egg, with reservoir for spirit, fitting inside.

No. 9624.—Browned Copper Cafetière, with black handle.

No. 9625.—Browned Copper Coffee Machine, with spirit lamp and extinguisher, cut glass lid.

No. 9626.—Platow's Patent Coffee Urn. Directions for use.—Pour the water (the hotter the better) into the lower vessel, screw the upper vase tight, throw in the required quantity of coffee, and place the lamp underneath. When the water has risen into the upper vessel, let it simmer for about two minutes, then withdraw the lamp, without loosening the screw. The coffee will be immediately filtered clear into the urn, and on relaxing the screw may be drawn off for use.

No. 9627.—Counter Urn, copper, brown planished, nickel silver mounted, fitted with 3 best named taps, bag rings, and fixed stand, 2 stone jars, water circulation all round, handsomely engraved at back.

No. 9628.—Tea Urn, copper, brown planished, electro-silver plated tap.

No. 9629.—Tea Urn, copper, brown planished, with loose heater case, and electro-silver plated tap.

No. 9630.—Tea Urn, copper, brown planished, with loose heater case, and electro-silver plated tap.

No. 9631.—Tea Urn, copper, brown planished, electro-silver plated tap.

No. 9632.—Tea Urn, copper, brown planished, with loose heater case, and electro-silver plated tap.

No. 9633.—Tea Urn, copper, brown planished, with loose heater case, and electro-silver plated tap.

No. 9634.—Old English Tea or Coffee Urn, with spirit lamp.

COAL BOXES,

JAPANNED IRON, BRASS FRONT, AND WOOD, WITH REMOVABLE INTERIORS.

No. 9635.—The "Kensington" Coal Box, japanned, with brass repoussé or hand-painted panel, and brass mounts.

No. 9636.—The "Oxford" Coal Box, japanned, with raised brass or hand-painted panel, and brass mounts.

No. 9637.—The "Kent" Coal Box, japanned (any colour), with all brass engraved front and brass mounts.

No. 9638.—The "Kent" Coal Box, japanned, with hand-painted raised panel and brass mounts.

No. 9639.—The "Brighton" Coal Box, japanned, fancy border, dome, and centre, with bronzed handle.

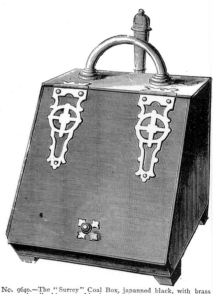

No. 9640.—The "Surrey" Coal Box, japanned black, with brass handle, hinges, and knob, and china-handled scoop.

No. 9641.—The "Bromley" Wood Coal Box, with brass handle, hinges, knob, and hand scoop.

No. 9642.—The "Dublin" Wood Coal Box, very strong, with brass handle, and hand scoop.

No. 9643.—The "Litchfield" Wood Coal Box, well made, with brass handle, and hand scoop.

WOOD COAL BOXES, BRASS MOUNTED, WITH MOVABLE COAL CONTAINERS.

No. 9644.—The "Surrey" Whatnot Coal Box, with carved panel and brass mounts.

No. 9645.—The "Savoy" Whatnot Coal Box, with patent folding doors, to be opened or closed by moving handle.

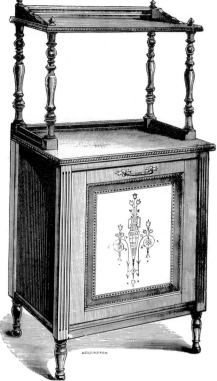

No. 9646.—The "Salisbury" Whatnot Coal Box, with inlaid satin wood panel.

No. 9647.—The "Savoy" Coal Box, with patent folding doors and repoussé brass panels.

No. 9648.—The "Belfast" Coal Box, wood handle and carved panel.

No. 9649.—The "Adam" Coal Box, with engraved brass hinge, beaded panel and sides.

TRADE MARK.

S. & F.
London.

No. 9650.—The "Ely" Coal Box, with repoussé brass panel.

No. 9651.—The "Japanese" Coal Box, with hand-painted panel and ornamental brass handle.

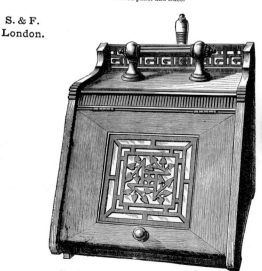

No. 9652.—The "Rochester" Coal Box, with fret work and brass panel.

S. & F.
London.

JAPANNED AND WOOD TEA TRAYS OR WAITERS, CABINET AND WHATNOT COAL BOXES.

S. & F.
London.

No. 9653.—Tea Tray or Waiter, oval, japanned iron, best quality, with hand-painted gold border, various designs, in sets of three sizes, 16-inch, 24-inch, and 28-inch. Any size can be had separately, from 12 to 30 inches.

No. 9654.—Tea Tray or Waiter, oval, japanned iron, hand-painted ornamental design, best quality, in sets of three sizes, 16-inch, 24-inch, and 28-inch. Any size can be had separately, from 12 to 30 inches.

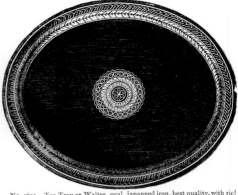

No. 9655.—Tea Tray or Waiter, oval, japanned iron, best quality, with rich gold border and centre, painted by hand, in sets of three sizes, 16-inch, 24-inch, and 28-inch. Any size can be had separately, from 12 to 30 inches.

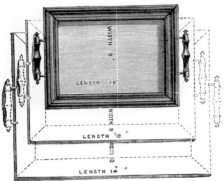

No. 9656.—Fancy Trays or Waiters, oak, ebonized sides, square corners, with nickel-plated and ebonized handles, strongly made of well-seasoned wood, and put together with screws, will stand any climate. In sets of seven, sizes—10 inches by 8 inches, 12 inches by 9 inches, 14 inches by 10 inches, 16 inches by 12 inches, 18 inches by 14 inches, 20 inches by 15 inches, 22 inches by 16 inches.

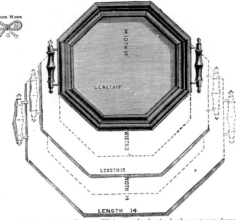

No. 9657.—Fancy Trays or Waiters, oak, ebonized sides, octagon shape, nickel-plated and ebonized handles, strongly made of well-seasoned wood, and put together with screws will stand any climate. In sets of three, sizes—10 inches by 10 inches, 12 inches by 12 inches, 14 inches by 14 inches.

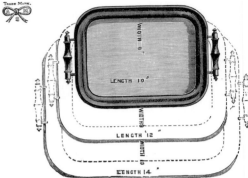

No. 9658.—Fancy Trays or Waiters, oak, ebonized sides, round corners, nickel-plated and ebonized handles, strongly made of well-seasoned wood, and put together with screws, will stand any climate. In sets of seven, sizes—10 inches by 8 inches, 12 inches by 9 inches, 14 inches by 10 inches, 16 inches by 12 inches, 18 inches by 14 inches, 20 inches by 15 inches, 22 inches by 16 inches.

No. 9659.—Cabinet Coal Box, with fall-front door, made in Mahogany, Oak, Walnut or Ebonized wood, with galvanized coal container and brass hand scoop.

No. 9660.—Cabinet Coal Box, with fall-front door, made in Mahogany, Oak, Walnut, or Ebonized wood, with carved panel, &c., with coal container and brass hand scoop.

No. 9661.—Ottoman Coal Box, with upholstered top, made in Mahogany, Oak, Walnut, or Ebonized wood, carved fall-front, with brass handle, with coal container and hand scoop.

No. 9662.—Cabinet Coal Box, made in Mahogany, Oak, Walnut, or Ebonized wood, fall-front, with brass handle and mounts, with coal container and hand scoop.

No. 9663.—Cabinet Coal Box and Whatnot, with patent folding doors, made in Mahogany, Oak, Walnut, or Ebonized wood, with coal container and scoop.

No. 9664.—Cabinet Coal Box and Whatnot, with fall-front, made in Mahogany, Oak, Walnut, or Ebonized wood, with coal container and scoop.

No. 9665.—Cabinet Coal Box and Whatnot, with carved fall-front, made in Mahogany, Oak, Walnut, or Ebonized wood, with coal container and hand scoop.

No. 9666.—Cabinet Coal Box and Whatnot, rotary action cover, with brass repoussé panel and drawer, with coal container and hand scoop.

JAPANNED IRON AND PAPIER-MACHÉ TEA TRAYS AND WAITERS, CRUMB TRAYS AND BRUSHES.

These Tea Trays are made up in Sets of three, including a 16-inch, 24-inch, and 28-inch Tray. Single Trays can be had from 12 inches to 30 inches. Round or Octagon Waiters are made to match Trays, sizes, 8, 10, and 12 inches.

No. 9671.—Oval Tea Tray or Waiter, japanned iron or papier-maché, japanned in various colours, with ornamental borders, centres, and designs.

No. 9672.—The "Douglas" Tea Tray or Waiter, japanned iron or papier-maché in various colours and designs, with nickel silver-plated handles, containing Tea and Coffee Service, silver-plated on Britannia metal, hand engraved.

No. 9673.—The "Elgin" Tea Tray or Waiter, japanned iron or papier-maché, in various colours, handsomely decorated borders and centres or designs.

No. 9674.—Round Crumb Tray or Waiter, with best hair Brush, japanned iron or papier-maché, in various colours and designs.

No. 9675.—"Combination" Tea Tray or Waiter, made of light wood which will stand any climate and not warp, japanned fancy colour grounds and handsomely decorated borders, centres, and designs, with nickel-plated galleries, handles, and feet. Very suitable for use in public buildings, such as hotels, clubs, &c., and also for private houses.

No. 9676.—Crumb Tray, with best hair Brush, japanned iron or papier-maché, fancy coloured grounds, with hand-painted designs, borders, and centres.

No. 9677.—The "Regent" Tea Tray or Waiter, japanned iron or papier-maché, in various colours and ornamental designs.

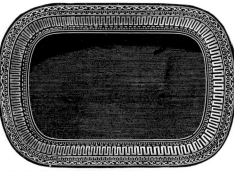

No. 9678.—The "Norfolk" Tea Tray or Waiter, japanned iron or papier-maché, in various coloured grounds, with handsome hand-painted borders, centres, and designs.

No. 9679.—The "Granville" Tea Tray or Waiter, japanned iron, in various coloured grounds, with fancy borders, centres, and ornamental designs, hand painted.

No. 9680.—The "Canton" Tea Tray or Waiter, japanned iron, in various coloured grounds, with handsome decorated borders, centres, and designs.

No. 9681.—The "Queen Anne" Tea Tray or Waiter, japanned iron, fancy coloured grounds, with handsome hand-painted ornamental borders, centres, and designs.

No. 9682.—The "Club" Tea Tray or Waiter, japanned iron or papier-maché, various coloured grounds, with handsome ornamental borders, centres, and designs.

No. 9683.—The "Carlton" Breakfast or Five o'clock Tea Tray, 22 inches long, japanned iron or papier-maché, in various colours and designs.

For Electro-Plated Salvers and Waiters, see page 363.

For Sterling Silver Salvers and Waiters, see page 329.

No. 9684.—The "Club" Breakfast or Five o'clock Tea Tray, 22 inches long, japanned iron or papier-maché, in various colours and designs.

WATER HEATERS WITH SPECIAL MERITS, ENAMELLED IRON BATHS, AND LAVATORIES.
THE CALIFONT (PATENT).

EXPLANATION OF SECTION.

The cold water first falls (from any convenient tap) into the basin A, and overflows into the outer jacket or chamber B B. As soon as this chamber is full, and the water runs over the inner ring, it flows into the top tray C (which is always marked 4) as shown in the Interior Elevation. From this tray the water percolates through holes in the bottom to the next tray D (3), and thence to E (2) and F (1), out of which it flows into the inverted cone G, and thence on to the top of the dome H. Here it collects until it overflows through the spout I.

It will readily be seen that in falling from A to H the water is repeatedly brought into contact with the heat from the gas ascending, as shown by the arrow marks, while at the same time the heat is repeatedly driven, by the obstruction of the tray, against the inner ring of the jacket. By means of this double action, the heat is almost entirely absorbed into the water, and the escape which takes place round the basin A is cooler than the water which is poured out at the spout I.

No. 9699 is made of stout tinned or galvanised iron, the outside being neatly japanned. With Bunsen* Burner (swing-out) warms one gallon per minute 60 to 90 degrees, or a warm bath (30 gallons) in half-an-hour.

No. 9699A, similar to No. 9699, warms the water at the rate of two gallons per minute, or warm bath in a quarter of an hour.

No. 9699B, best quality, is made of copper,† with brass ring burner (swing-out) and jets same as used for lighting, warms one and a half gallons per minute, or warm bath in twenty minutes.

No. 9699C, best quality, similar to No. 9699B, warms three gallons per minute, or warm bath in ten minutes.

* Though we are obliged to use the Bunsen Burner for the cheapest heaters (the fittings required for the white flame being so much more costly) we yet do not advise the use of the Bunsen Burner in bath rooms, because, however carefully made, it will (after using some time if not at first) smell unpleasantly; and still more because the blue flame is likely to allow an escape of carbon oxide, which is highly dangerous The white flame as used in our best heaters is the same as used for lighting, and is quite free from smell, and quite safe.

† N.B.—The best quality, Nos. 9699B and 9699C are made *entirely* of copper and brass, without any iron whatever in any part of them. If there is *any* iron (whether black japanned, tinned, or galvanised) it is of little use that the other parts are of copper, as when the iron rusts through the apparatus is put out of order.

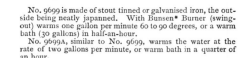

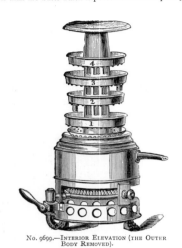

No. 9699.—Interior Elevation (the Outer Body Removed).

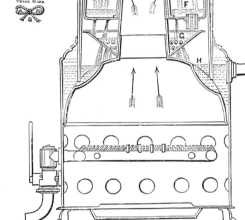

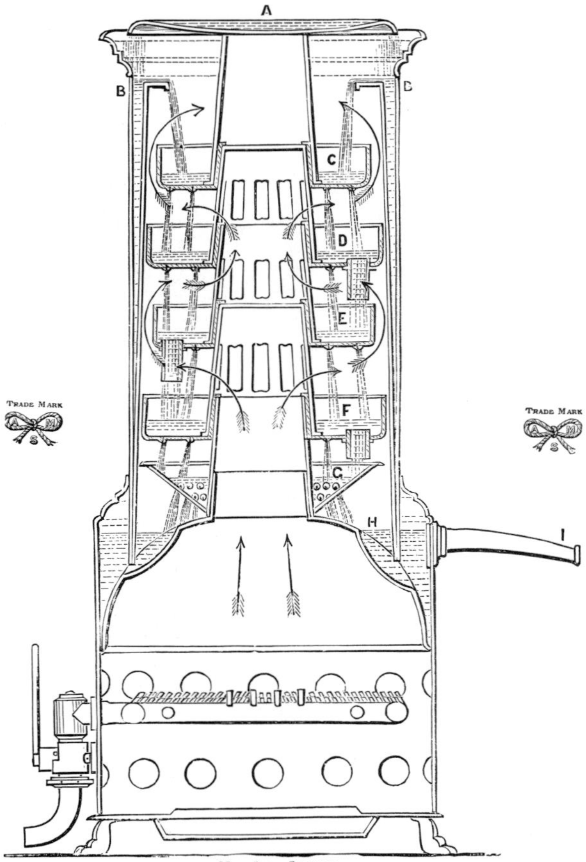

No. 9699.—Section.

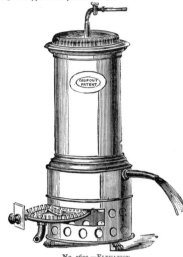

No. 9699.—Elevation.

No. 9700.—Lift-up Enamelled Iron Lavatory, with two Basins, complete, with nickel-plated taps.

This Lavatory is specially adapted for use in hotels, clubs, warehouses, schools, &c. It requires very little fixing. It is perfectly clean, the slab and basins being enamelled. After use the basin is raised from the front, and the contents are carried away by a pipe which is connected with waste pipe. Cannot get out of order.

No. 9703.—Lift-up Lavatory, single basin, cast iron, enamelled inside basin and top, with silver-plated tap.

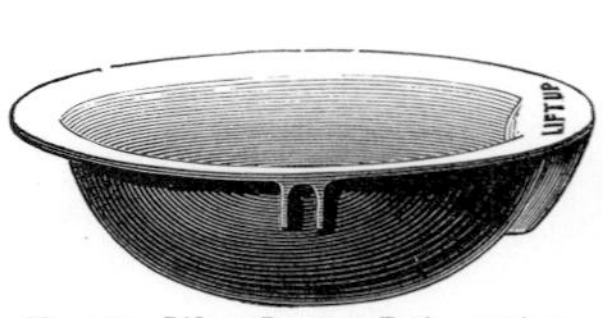

No. 9702.—Lift-up Lavatory Basin, cast iron, enamelled white inside.

PORTABLE TURKISH HOT AIR AND VAPOUR BATHS.

No. 9706.—Apparatus for use under chair, with best cloak. Tinned iron supports, in box complete.

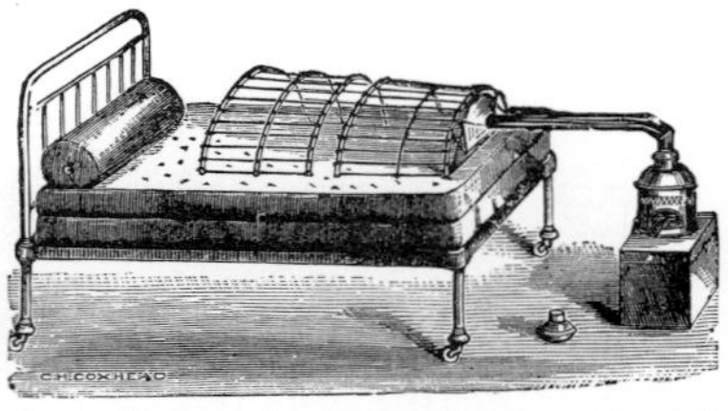

No. 9707.—Apparatus complete in wood box, with pair of wicker frames and foot-plate.

This apparatus will give a hot-air or vapour bath, a medicated or mercurial bath. For general or local application, it is acknowledged the best yet introduced for portability, cheapness with durability, and thorough efficiency.

PATENT FLANGED BATH.
(FOR WOOD CASING.)

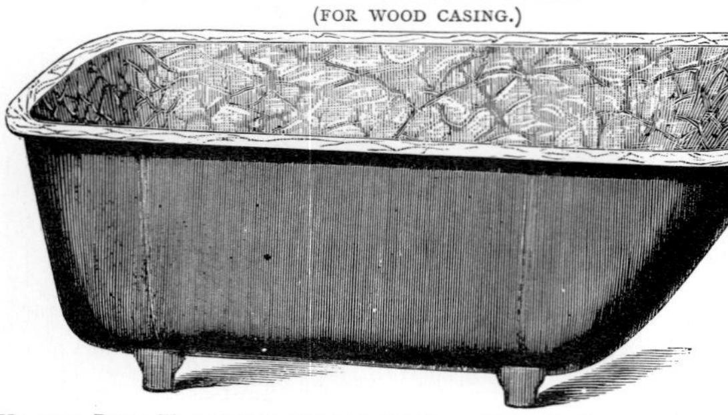

No. 9701.—The New Crown Boiler, for cooking, heating water for baths, and general purposes, possesses the following advantages :—

The interior is of stout copper, tinned.

The outer casing is of polished brass.

It contains no iron to rust, nor paint to wear off.

The flame, being visible, can be easily lighted and regulated.

A stream of **boiling** water can be procured in 3½ minutes, a stream of **warm** water in ½ a minute.

A warm bath can be obtained in temperate weather at a cost of three farthings.

PATENT BEADED-EDGE BATH.
(NO WOODWORK REQUIRED.)

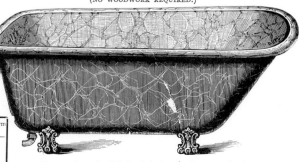

No. 9704.—Patent Flanged Bath, with hole at bottom, suitable for plug or washer. Made of tinned steel or copper, japanned white Sienna or other marbles or colours.

Size of Pipe.	Warmed per Minute.	Time for a Warm Bath.
⅜ inch.	3 quarts.	40 minutes.
½ ,,	1 gallon.	30 ,,
⅝ ,,	1½ ,,	23 ,,
¾ ,,	2 ,,	15 ,,
⅞ ,,	3 ,,	10 ,,
1 ,,	5 ,,	6 ,,

No. 9705.—Patent Beaded-edge Bath, tinned steel or strong tinned copper, japanned white Sienna or other marbles inside, green marbles or other colours outside, fitted with 1¼-inch brass plug, union and overflow, and cast-iron feet.

TIN BATHS, JAPANNED IMITATION OAK OUTSIDE, AND WHITE INSIDE.

No. 9739.—Oxford Hip Bath.

No. 9742.—Child's Bath, equal ends.

No. 9740.—Travelling Hip Bath, with lock and strap.

No. 9741.—Athenian Hip Bath.

No. 9743.—Sitz Bath.

No. 9744.—Travelling Bath, with lock and strap.

No. 9745.—Bed Bath.

No. 9747.—Sponging Bath, with inverted rim to prevent water splashing over.

No. 9746.—Sponging Bath, wire edge.

No. 9748.—Nursery Bath, on stand.

No. 9749.—Sponging Bath, beaded.

No. 9750.—Equal End Bath.

No. 9751.—Slipper Bath.

No. 9752.—Taper Bath.

S. & F.
London.

No. 9753.—Oval Bath, galvanized iron.

No. 9757.—Bath Thermometer, tin case, mercury column.

No. 9755.—Thermometer, boxwood, spirit column.

No. 9754.—Improved Patent Self-acting Gas Bath.

No. 9756.—Hip and Shower Bath combined, japanned oak, with brass raising main, brass pump, valves, cock, and copper waterways, with curtain complete.

"Royal" Washer.

TRADE MARK.

Improved "Premier" Box Mangle.

TRADE MARK.

"Royal" Washer.

No. 9759.—"Royal" Washer, Wringer, and Mangle combined, with elliptical spring giving an equal pressure to the rollers.

No. 9760.—Improved "Premier" Box Mangle.

No. 9761.—"Royal" Washer, Wringer, and Mangle combined, double screw pressure.

Self-Acting Washer.

The "Surprise" Wringer.

Improved Wringing and Mangling Machine.

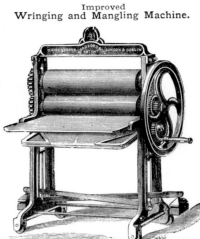

No. 9762.

No. 9763.—The "Surprise" Wringer and Mangle combined, with bow top and elliptical spring.

No. 9764.—Improved Wringing and Mangling Machine, with lever and weight pressure.

The "Royal" Washer.

Washing, Wringing, and Mangling Machine Combined.

No. 9762. — Self - Acting "Fountain" Washer. The washer should be placed in the centre of copper half filled with water, and the clothes placed in such a manner that they form a thick mass on the perforated flange of the washer. The clothes should remain in from 20 to 30 minutes after the water boils, when they should be taken out and cold water thrown upon them; the washing process will then be completed.

The "Princess" Royal.

No. 9765.—The "Royal" Washer, with india-rubber wringer.

Washing Machine.

No. 9766.—Washing, Wringing, and Mangling Machine combined. The pressure upon the rollers is obtained by self-adjusting levers that require no care on the part of the user.

"Marvel" Wringer.

No. 9767.—The "Princess" Royal Wringer and Mangle combined. A very strong machine with elliptical spring and 6-in. rollers.

Wringing Machine.

No. 9768.—Washing Machine, compact, portable, and a very efficient washer. The above drawing represents the washing machine with wringing machine attached.

The "Imperial."

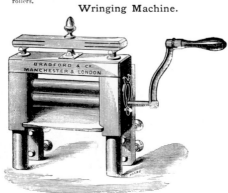

No. 9769.—The "Marvel" Wringer and Mangle combined, with lever and weight pressure.

No. 9770.—Wringing Machine, with best vulcanised india-rubber rollers and patent pressure link, which relieves both rollers and linen from undue strain.

No. 9771.—The "Imperial" India-rubber Wringer, self-adjusting and self-fixing, for fixing on to tub or washing machine.

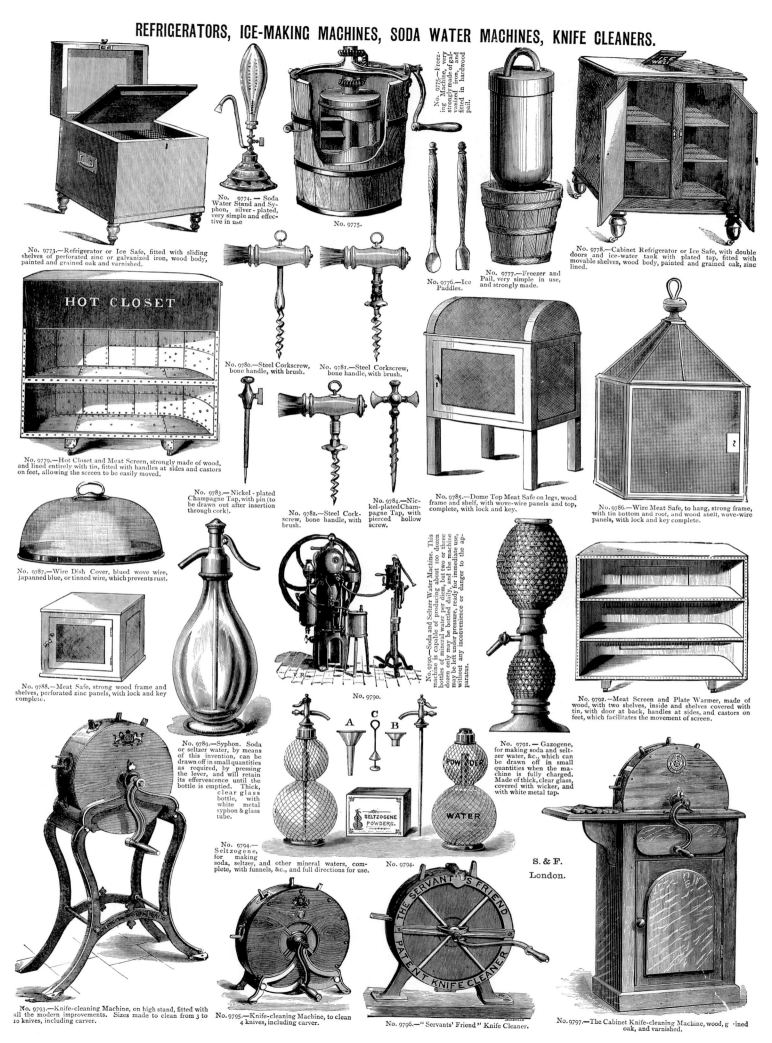

No. 9774.— Soda Water Stand and Syphon, silver-plated, very simple and effective in use.

No. 9775.

No. 9775.—Freezing Machine, very strongly made of galvanized iron, and fitted in hardwood pail.

No. 9773.—Refrigerator or Ice Safe, fitted with sliding shelves of perforated zinc or galvanized iron, wood body, painted and grained oak and varnished.

No. 9776.—Ice Paddles.

No. 9777.—Freezer and Pail, very simple in use, and strongly made.

No. 9778.—Cabinet Refrigerator or Ice Safe, with double doors and ice-water tank with plated tap, fitted with movable shelves, wood body, painted and grained oak, zinc lined.

HOT CLOSET

No. 9779.—Hot Closet and Meat Screen, strongly made of wood, and lined entirely with tin, fitted with handles at sides and castors on feet, allowing the screen to be easily moved.

No. 9780.—Steel Corkscrew, bone handle, with brush.

No. 9781.—Steel Corkscrew, bone handle, with brush.

No. 9782.—Steel Corkscrew, bone handle, with brush.

No. 9783.—Nickel-plated Champagne Tap, with pin (to be drawn out after insertion through cork).

No. 9784.—Nickel-plated Champagne Tap, with pierced hollow screw.

No. 9785.—Dome Top Meat Safe on legs, wood frame and shelf, with wove-wire panels and top, complete, with lock and key.

No. 9786.—Wire Meat Safe, to hang, strong frame, with tin bottom and roof, and wood shelf, wove-wire panels, with lock and key complete.

No. 9787.—Wire Dish Cover, blued wove wire, japanned blue, or tinned wire, which prevents rust.

No. 9788.—Meat Safe, strong wood frame and shelves, perforated zinc panels, with lock and key complete.

No. 9789.—Syphon. Soda or seltzer water, by means of this invention, can be drawn off in small quantities as required, by pressing the lever, and will retain its effervescence until the bottle is emptied. Thick, clear glass bottle, with white metal syphon & glass tube.

No. 9790.—Soda and Seltzer Water Machine. This machine is capable of producing about 100 dozen bottles of mineral water per diem, but two or three dozen only may be bottled daily, and the machine may be left under pressure, ready for immediate use, without any inconvenience or danger to the apparatus.

No. 9790.

No. 9791.—Gazogene, for making soda and seltzer water, &c., which can be drawn off in small quantities when the machine is fully charged. Made of thick, clear glass, covered with wicker, and with white metal tap.

No. 9792.—Meat Screen and Plate Warmer, made of wood, with two shelves, inside and shelves covered with tin, with door at back, handles at sides, and castors on feet, which facilitates the movement of screen.

A C B

SELTZOGENE POWDERS.

POWDER WATER

No. 9794.—Seltzogene, for making soda, seltzer, and other mineral waters, complete, with funnels, &c., and full directions for use.

No. 9794.

S. & F. London.

No. 9793.—Knife-cleaning Machine, on high stand, fitted with all the modern improvements. Sizes made to clean from 3 to 10 knives, including carver.

No. 9795.—Knife-cleaning Machine, to clean 4 knives, including carver.

THE SERVANT'S FRIEND
PATENT KNIFE CLEANER

No. 9796.—"Servants' Friend" Knife Cleaner.

No. 9797.—The Cabinet Knife-cleaning Machine, wood, grained oak, and varnished.

No. 9803.—Set of Household Tools.

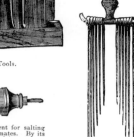

No. 9804.—Lemon Squeezer, with china bowl.

No. 9805.—Weighing Machine, with Bronzed Platform and Set of Weights.

No. 9806.—White Wood Lemon Squeezers.

No. 9807.—Set of Kitchen Utensils.

No. 9808.—Salting Instrument for salting meat in hot weather or hot climates. By its use a joint of meat can be salted in one hour fit for use or keeping. Full directions for use sent with each machine. Made in 2 sizes, packed in case complete.

No. 9809.—Set of Steel Skewers.

No. 9810.—Counter Weighing Machine.

No. 9811.—Brass Pocket Balance.

No. 9812.—Iron Lemon Squeezer, with China Bowl.

No. 9813.—Whisk and Mixing Machine.

No. 9814.—Meat and Vegetable Chopping Machine.

No. 9815.—Family Scale.

No. 9816.—Crimping Machine.

No. 9817.—Meat and Vegetable Chopper.

No. 9818.—Apple-paring Machine.

No. 9819.—Cucumber and Vegetable Slicer.

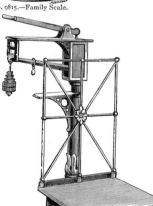

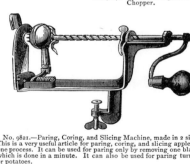

No. 9821.—Paring, Coring, and Slicing Machine, made in 2 sizes. This is a very useful article for paring, coring, and slicing apples at one process. It can be used for paring only by removing one blade, which is done in a minute. It can also be used for paring turnips or potatoes.

No. 9822.—Brawn or Tongue Presser.

No. 9823.—Meat Saw.

No. 9820.—Platform Weighing Machine.

No. 9824.—Chopping Board and Knife.

No. 9825.—Meat Chopper.

No. 9826.—Box Iron.

No. 9827.—Set of Smoothing Irons, patent handle.

No. 9828.—Flat Iron and Stand.

No. 9829.—Charcoal Box Iron.

COFFEE MILLS, ROASTERS, MINCING MACHINES, BREAD CUTTERS, SUGAR CHOPPERS, FRUIT DRESSERS, PAINT MILLS, &c.

Bronzed Coffee Mill.
As fixed to Table.

No. 9833.—Bronzed Coffee Mill, for grinding coffee, pepper, spice rice, &c.

Counter Coffee Mill.

No. 9834.—Counter Coffee Mill, on iron stand, with gun-metal bushes.

Counter Coffee Mill.

No. 9835.—Counter Coffee Mill, with 2 fly-wheels, with bronzed or brass hopper.

Bronzed Coffee Mill.
As fixed to Wall.

No. 9836.—Bronzed Coffee Mill, for grinding coffee, pepper, spice, rice, &c., can also be fixed on table.

Square Box Coffee Mill.

Oak Pepper Mill.

No. 9838.—Oak Pepper Mill, with electro-plated mounts.

No. 9837.—Square Box Coffee Mill, with brass hopper.

Patent Bread Cutter.

No. 9839.—Patent Bread Cutter.

Automatic Coffee Roaster.

No. 9840.—Automatic Coffee Roaster, to hang before the fire.

Flanged Coffee Mill.

S. & F.
London.

Sugar Mill.

Currant Dressing and Cleansing Machine.

No. 9841.—Newly Improved Centrifugal Patent Currant Dressing and Cleansing Machine.

No. 9842.—Flanged Coffee Mill, with fly-wheel.

No. 9843.—Sugar Mill, to lay on Cask.

Meat Cutter.

No. 9844.—Meat Cutter, top half removed to show interior.

Bread-cutting Machine.

No. 9845.—Bread-cutting Machine.

Hand Paint Mill.

No. 9846.—Hand Paint Mill.

Mincing Machine.

No. 9847.—Mincing Machine.

Hale's Patent Mincer.

No. 9848.—Hale's Patent Mincer.

Enterprise Meat Chopper.

TRADE MARK.

No. 9849.—Enterprise Meat Chopper.

Compound Mincer and Sausage Filler.

No. 9850.—Compound Mincer and Sausage Filler.

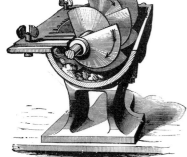

ENAMELLED IRON-WARE, WHITE INSIDE AND GREY OUTSIDE.

No. 9853 Ewer

No. 9854 Vegetable Dish, round, with cover

No. 9855 Soup Plate

No. 9856 Bell-shape Cup and Saucer

No. 9857 Tumbler

No. 9858 Poultry Fountain

No. 9859 Bowl-shape Cup and Saucer

No. 9860 Pudding Cup

No. 9861 Drinking Cup

No. 9862 Dinner Plate

No. 9863 Beer or Water Can, with cover

S. & F., London

No. 9864 Fluted Gridiron with reservoir for gravy

No. 9865 Mulling Pot

No. 9866 Flat Candlestick

No. 9867 Spittoon

No. 9868 Hand Bowl, with wood handle

No. 9869 Round Soup Tureen

No. 9870 Oblong Vegetable Dish, with cover

No. 9871 Funnel

No. 9872 Chamber Utensil, with cover

No. 9873 Chamber Utensil

No. 9874 Spitting Cup

No. 9875 Wash Bowl

No. 9876 Round Frying Pan, with straight handle

No. 9877 Egg Frying Pan

No. 9878 Round Omelet Pan

No. 9879 Brush Tray, with cover

No. 9880 Basting Ladle

No. 9881 Skimmer

No. 9882 Soup Ladle

No. 9883 Oval Frying Pan

No. 9884 Wash-hand Basin, with plug-hole

No. 9885 Deep Stew Pan, with bright tin cover

No. 9886 Soap Dish, to hang

No. 9887 Round Baking Dish

TRADE MARK

TRADE MARK

No. 9888 Square Baking Pan

No. 9889 Ob'ong Baking Pan

No. 9890 House Pail

No. 9891 Chamber Pail

No. 9892 Oblong Pie Dish

No. 9893 Oblong Meat Dish

No. 9894 Milk Pan

No. 9895 Flange Basin, with plug-hole

No. 9896 Preserving Pan

COOKING UTENSILS.

ECONOMY, CLEANLINESS & EXPEDITION, BY USING PERKINS'S PATENT COVERED FRYING PANS.

PAN WITH COVER DOWN.

COVER OPEN.

No. 10001

COVER BEING REMOVED.

COVER AS PLATE.

In introducing the above to notice, we eel we are offering an article much wanted, as nothing is more vexing to the careful housewife than to have her tidy Gas Stove or hot Plate bespattered all over with grease when frying, causing the Stove to smell, whether cooking or not; or to have soot suddenly fall into her pan when the contents are almost ready for the table.

The Patent covered Pans will be found also to cook quicker and brown better than the ordinary pans without

cover; and the cover may be lifted up to examine the contents of the pan and replaced, or lifted entirely off, using the cooking fork for either operation. For camping out the Cover may be used as a plate.

The Patent Pans are made in all sizes, both round and oval; also they are coated with pure tin, instead of the dangerous mixture containing lead, with which common Frying Pans are covered, and which the medical profession so strongly condemn; while the prices are very little higher than those charged for the common pans.

No. 10002 Cast-iron Digestor, tinned inside

No. 10003 Cast-iron Oval Boiler, tinned inside, bail or end handles

No. 10004 Iron Saucepan and tin steamer

No. 10005 Tea Kitchen, cast-iron, tinned inside, with brass tap

No. 10006 Wrought-iron Tea Kettle, tinned inside

No. 10007 Batchelor's Broiler, stamped tinned iron

No. 10008 (When used for Boiling)

No. 10008 (When used for Steaming)
No. 10008 Block-tin Potato Saucepan, for boiling or steaming potatoes, with tin drainer

No. 10009 Batchelor's Broiler, stamped tinned-iron

No. 10010 Best London wrought-iron Tea Kettle, tinned inside, & tinned handle, & cover

No. 10011 Stewpan, best wrought-iron, tinned inside and bright handle

No. 10012 Iron Saucepan, tinned inside, with cover

No. 10013 Stewpan, cast-iron, tinned inside, with cover

No. 10014 Omelet Pan, wrought-iron, tinned inside, with bright handle

No. 10015 Wrought-iron Fish Fryer, tinned inside, with wire drainer

No. 10016 Oval tinned-iron Frying Pan

No. 10017 Block-tin Steamer, to fit iron saucepan

No. 10018 Round tinned-iron Frying Pan

No. 10019 Wrought-iron Stock Pot, tinned inside, with brass tap, and strainer

No. 10020 Tin Game Oven, with dish

No. 10021 Wrought-iron Saucepan, tinned inside

No. 10022 Wrought-iron Bain Marie Pan, tinned inside, with tray

No. 10023 Block-tin Mackerel Saucepan, with drainer inside

No. 10024 Dutch Oven, with movable grid and pan

No. 10025 "Capt. Warren's" Tin Cooking Saucepan

No. 10026 Fluted Gridiron, all bright, with gravy receiver

No. 10027 "Capt. Warren's" Cooking Pot, oval, tin

No. 10028 Iron Gridiron, with adjustable receiver for gravy, and hooks

No. 10029 "Capt. Warren's" Fish Kettle

"Capt. Warren's" utensils prevent viands coming in contact with water or steam, and save 12½ per cent. They also render burning, over-boiling and smoking impossible

TRADE MARK.

TRADE MARK.

No. 10043.—Tin Oblong Baking Pan.

No. 10044.—Tin Round Baking Pan.

No. 10068.—Carpenter's Oiler.

No. 10070.—Double Knife Tray, japanned black, with gold lines.

No. 10002.—Dish Cover, block tin, with Britannia metal handle.

No. 10071.—Dirty Knife Basket, wicker work, tin lined.

No. 10042.—Double Reading Lamp, japanned, brown or green.

No. 10045.—Tin Spoon Drip.

No. 10069.—Improved Oil Filler, with sunk top and guard.

No. 10072.—Knife Tray, japanned black, with gold lines.

No. 10046.—Hot Water Dish, earthenware, with tin body.

No. 10063.—Dish Cover, block tin, with Britannia metal handle.

No. 10073.—Hot Water Dish, made entirely of best block tin, with metal handles.

No. 10048.—Tin Breakfast Dish, with earthenware drainer and divisions.

No. 10047.—Tin "Etna," with spirit measure.

No. 10976.—Round Tin Chop, Covers.

No. 10049.—Patent Machine Oiler.

No. 10074.—Gas Kettle, with iron handle.

No. 10064.—Dish Cover, extra deep and strong, block tin, with silver-plated handle.

No. 10077.—Block Tin Plate Cover, with metal knob.

No. 10050.—Tin Oil Kettle.

No. 10051.—Block Tin Seasoning Box.

No. 10052.—Tin Funnel.

No. 10078.—Hot Water Soup Plate and Cover.

No. 10053.—Bread and Meat Grater.

No. 10065.—Dish Cover, block tin, with Britannia metal handle.

No. 10075.—Ale Warmer, strong tin.

No. 10079.—Hot Water Plate, block tin body, earthenware plate.

No. 10054.—Sliding Plate Hanger, all bright steel.

No. 10055.—Knife Scalder, japanned brown.

No. 10081.—Japanned String Box, weighted.

No. 10080.—Hot Water Plate, tin body, with lip.

No. 10057.—Hand Bowl, wood handle.

No. 10066.—Dish Cover, best block tin, with silver-plated handle and Britannia metal edge.

No. 10059.—Gravy Strainer, with wood handle.

No. 10084.—Conical Tea Strainer, tin.

No. 10056.—Tin Beer Can.

No. 10058.—Hand Bowl, strong tin.

No. 10082.—Covered Milk Can, tin.

No. 10083.—Boiler Filler, japanned mottled.

No. 10085.—Tin Hand Scoop.

FLOUR

No. 10060.—Slop Pail, japanned.

No. 10061.—Galvanised Bucket.

No. 10067.—Dish Cover, best block tin, silver-plated handle, and Britannia metal edge.

No. 10086.—Tin Cake Pan.

No. 10087.—Flour Bin, japanned blue, with black bands.

No. 10101.—Counter Machine, with tin scoop, for flour.

No. 10102.—Iron Bar Weight.

No. 10103.—Flour Scoop, block tin.

No. 10104.—Biscuit Box, japanned with any name or colour.

ALBERTS

No. 10106.—Tea or Flour Scoop, block tin.

No. 10107.—Sugar or Soda Scoop, galvanized iron.

No. 10108.—Snuff or Mustard Scoop.

No. 10105.—Stand Scales, japanned and gilt beam, china or copper pan.

No. 10109.—Tea Scales, brass or iron beam, with copper pans.

No. 10110.—Sugar Mill, to lay on cask. *For Coffee Mills, &c., see page 550.*

No. 10111.—Loaf Sugar Chopper, with fly-wheel and treadle action.

No. 10112.—Loaf Sugar Chopper, with single cross knife.

S. & F. LONDON.

No. 10113.—Brass Bell Pattern Weight.

SHAG

No. 10114.—Tobacco Jar, japanned with any colour or name.

COFFEE

No. 10115.—Coffee Box, japanned any colour, with 3 divisions.

RETURNS

No. 10116.—Tobacco Jar, japanned with any colour or name.

12

No. 10117.—Tea Canister, japanned with any colour or number.

No. 10118.—Oil Drum, strong, iron.

No. 10119.—Tea Mixer, very strong, japanned, 30 inches diameter.

No. 10120.—Oil Cisterns, with brass tap, japanned any colour.

GOLDEN SYRUP

No. 10121.—Treacle or Golden Syrup Can, with tap, japanned any colour.

No. 10122.—String Box, wood or japanned.

No. 10123.—String Reel, to stand on counter, japanned.

No. 10124.—Oil Drainer, with loose grating, strong tin.

No. 10125.—Treacle Pot.

No. 10126.—Ham Stand, block tin, weighted.

No. 10127.—Oatmeal Measure, wood.

No. 10128.—Corn Measure, wood.

No. 10129.—Measure, galvanized iron, very strong, with handles at sides.

No. 10130.—Oil Jack, with hoops and straps, gauged inside, very strong tin.

TRADE MARK.

No. 10131.—Paraffin Measure, strong tin.

No. 10132.—Oil Measure, strong tin, with hoops.

No. 10133.—Paint Strainer, strong tin, with perforated or gauze bottom.

No. 10134.—Benzoline Funnel, tin, with screw for fixing into drum.

No. 10140A.—Oil Pump, with elbow, strong tin.

No. 10135.—Paint Kettle, tin or galvanized iron.

No. 10136.—Wood Sack Truck, very strong, with wrought-iron mounts.

No. 10137.—Portable Boiler, wrought-iron, with galvanized pan, elbow, and 2 feet of pipe.

No. 10138.—Washing Copper, galvanized iron or copper.

No. 10139.—Sack Truck, wrought iron, with cast-iron wheels.

No. 10140.—Oil Bottles, tin, also with screw stopper.

No. 10141.—Block Tin Tea or Coffee Urn, with brass tap.

No. 10142.—Block Tin Coffee Pot.

No. 10143.—Coffee or Tea Urn with earthenware lining.

No. 10144—Block Tin Cafetière.

No. 10145.—Block Tin Percolator.

No. 10146.—Loysel's Patent Coffee Urn.

No. 10152.— Block Tin Candlestick.

No. 10153.—Japanned Candle Box.

No. 10147.—Block Tin Dustpan.

No. 10148.—Block Tin Bread Mould.

No. 10149.—Block Tin Tea Kettle, with iron spout and handle.

No. 10150.—Block Tin Tea Pot.

No. 10151.—Block Tin Bronchitis Kettle, with spreader.

No. 10154.—Block Tin Range Kettle, with copper bottom and well.

No. 10155.—Japanned Square Sugar Box.

No. 10156.—Wash-hand Basin.

No. 10157.—Basting Ladle.

No. 10158.—Fish Slice, with iron handle.

No. 10159.—Egg Slice, with iron handle.

No. 10160.—Oval Baking Pan.

No. 10161.—Japanned Tea Canister.

No. 10162.—Tin Nutmeg Grater.

No. 10163.—Tin Flour Dredger.

No. 10165.—Block Tin Dripping Pan and Well.

No. 10164.—Block Tin Turbot Kettle.

No. 10167.—Improved Egg Poacher.

No. 10168.—Milk Saucepan, with china lining.

No. 10166.— Round Sugar Box.

No. 10169.—Roasting Jack with Hooks and Flywheel.

No. 10171.—Double Range Pan, with meat grid.

No. 10170.—Japanned Spice Box, round.

No. 10172.—Block Tin Fish Fryer with Wire Drainer.

No. 10173.—Colander.

No. 10174.—Oval Tin Boiler.

No. 10175.—Meat Screen, with Dripping Pan.

No. 10176.—Fish Kettle with Drainer.

No. 10177.—Improved Broiler to slide, with hanger.

No. 10181.—Kitchen Bellows.

No. 10182.—Windsor Chair.

No. 10183.—Kitchen Table, with drawer and hinged leaf.

No. 10184.—Windsor Chair with Arms.

No. 10185.—Dover Egg Whisk.

No. 10186.—Wire Egg Whisk, with wooden handle.

No. 10187.—Hard Wood Steak Beater.

No. 10188.—Cast-iron Glue Pot, with tinned lining, and brush.

No. 10189.—Wooden House Pail.

No. 10190.—Set of Cooks' Sieves.

No. 10191.—Oak Salt Box.

No. 10192.—Improved Rolling Pin, white wood.

No. 10193.—Egg Stand.

No. 10194.—Servants' Lantern, wove wire.

No. 10195.—Washing Tray and Stool.

No. 10196.—Dirty Plate Basket, tin lined.

No. 10197.—Wooden Soap Box.

No. 10198.—Wedgewood Pestle and Mortar.

No. 10199.—Coal Hammer, with hard wood handle.

No. 10200.—Jack-towel Roller, with brackets.

No. 10201.—Galvanized Soap Tray, to stand, hang inside pail, or on wall.

No. 10202.—Hard Wood Chopping Tray.

No. 10203.—Jelly Bag and Wooden Stand.

No. 10204.—Wicker Plate Carrier, tin lined.

No. 10205.—Japanned Hand Scoop, flat.

No. 10206.—Japanned Hand Scoop, round back, wooden handle.

No. 10207.—Japanned Wrought-iron Wine Bin.

No. 10208.—Plate Rack.

No. 10209.—Clothes Horse, 3 fold.

No. 10210.—Housemaid's Steps.

No. 10211.—Wooden Beer Tap.

No. 10212.—Hard Wood Potato Masher.

No. 10213.—Butler's Tray and Stand.

No. 10214.—Iron Shovel, with holes.

No. 10215.—Iron Coal Shovel.

No. 10216.—Wooden Tubs.

No. 10217.—Cinder Sieve, galvanized wire bottom.

No. 10218.—Wrought-iron Cask Stand.

No. 10219.—Wrought-iron Cask Stand, to fold.

No. 10220.—Wooden Cask Stand, with Screw Lever for tilting.

No. 10221.—Linen Press, with Drawer.

No. 10222.—Cinder Shovel, galvanized wire.

No. 10223.—Wooden Spoon.

No. 10225.—Beetle Trap.

No. 10227.—Rocking Cinder Sifter, wood.

No. 10224.—The "Perpetual" Mouse Trap.

No. 10226.—Housemaid's Box, wood.

No. 10228.—"Break Back" Mouse or Rat Trap.

No. 10229.—Rat Trap, galvanized wire.

HOUSEHOLD BRUSHES.

Broom Head.

No. 10231.—Superior quality, all hair.

Baluster Brush.

No. 10232.—All hair.

Bass Broom Heads.

No. 10234.—Set or Glued.

No. 10235.—Drawn.

SCRUBBING BRUSHES.

FLAT BACK SCRUBBING BRUSH.

No. 10239.

SOLID BACK SCRUBBING BRUSH.

No. 10240.

SOLID BACK VICTORIA SCRUBBING BRUSH.

No. 10241.

SOLID BACK ADELAIDE SCRUBBING BRUSH.

No. 10242.

DECK SCRUB.

No. 10254.

STOCKING BRUSH.

No. 10255.

Double Baluster Brush.

No. 10236.

Sweeps' Brush.

No. 10237.

Whisk Baluster Brush.

No. 10238.

Set Carpet Whisk Broom.

No. 10256.

Round Carpet Brooms.

No. 10258.

STOVE BRUSHES.

BENT STOVE BRUSH.

No. 10243.

PORCUPINE STOVE BRUSH.

No. 10246.

REGISTER STOVE BRUSH.

No. 10248.

BENT OVAL STOVE BRUSH.

No. 10245.

CONVEX STOVE BRUSH.

No. 10247.

VICTORIA STOVE BRUSH.

No. 10249.

Adelaide Carpet Broom.

No. 10257.

Round Black Lead Brushes.

No. 10250.

Hearth Brushes.

No. 10253.

No. 10252.   No. 10251.

American Carpet Brooms.

No. 10259.

The "Original Champion" Carpet Sweeper.

No. 10260.

India-rubber Squeegees.

No. 10261.

Flesh Brushes.

No. 10263.—With handles.

No. 10262.—Straps.

Feather Dusters.

No. 10265.

No. 10266.

Flue Brushes.

No. 10267.

Furniture Brushes.

No. 10270.—Cater cornered.

No. 10269.—Round.

Crumb Brushes.

No. 10268.

Lamp Brushes.

No. 10272.

Billiard and Bagatelle Table Brushes.

No. 10273.

Plate Brushes.

Bent.

No. 10274.

Straight.

No. 10275.

Turk's Head.

No. 10276.

Mats.

No. 10282.—Wool bordered, Vandyke.

SINNOT MATS.

No. 10281.

India-rubber Mats.

No. 10288.

Shoe Brushes.

No. 10277.

Bed Brush.

No. 10280.

ORNAMENTAL WIRE CANARY CAGES, BRIGHTON CAGES, PARROT CAGES, PAROQUET CAGES, PARROTS' STANDS.

Trade Mark.

Trade Mark.

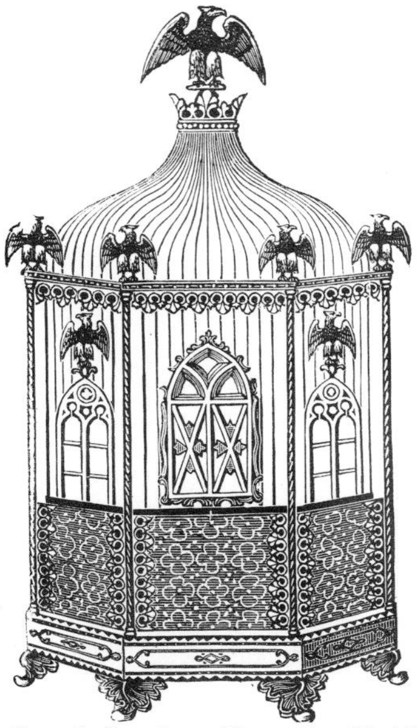

No. 10296.—Fancy Japanned Sexagon Cage, "Eagle" pattern, with drawer and frosted glass panels. Diameter 10½ inches.

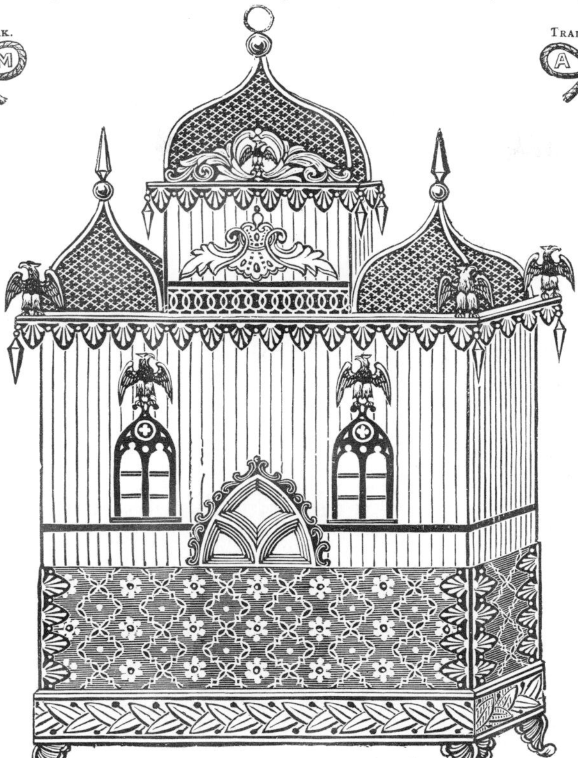

No. 10297.—Fancy Japanned Cage, "Eagle" pattern, with frosted glass panels and drawer. Size, 13 inches by 9 inches.

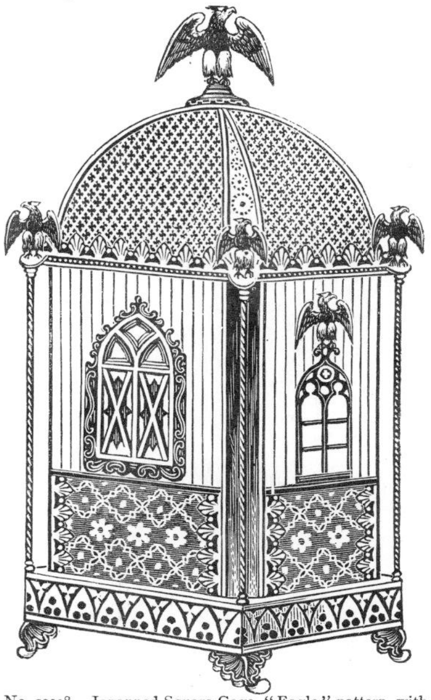

No. 10298.—Japanned Square Cage, "Eagle" pattern, with drawer and frosted glass panels. Size, 9 inches square.

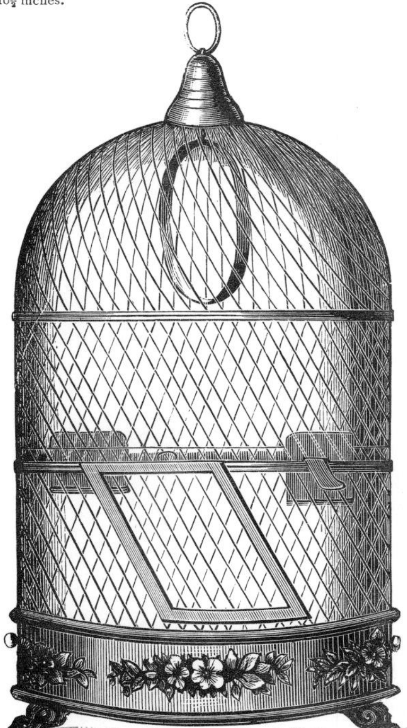

No. 10307C.—Parrot Cage, ordinary painted zinc bottom, brass bands, tinned wire.

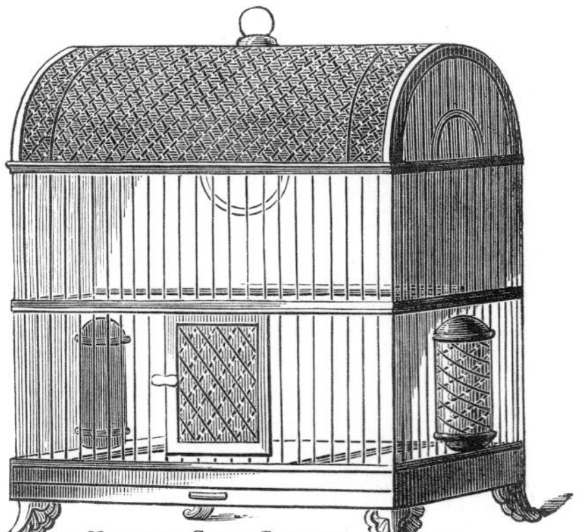

No. 10300.—Canary Cage, waggon shape, with drawer.

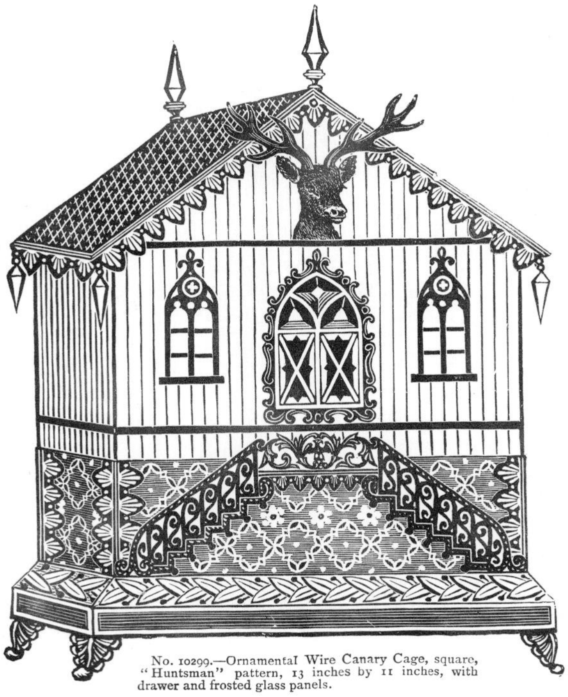

No. 10299.—Ornamental Wire Canary Cage, square, "Huntsman" pattern, 13 inches by 11 inches, with drawer and frosted glass panels.

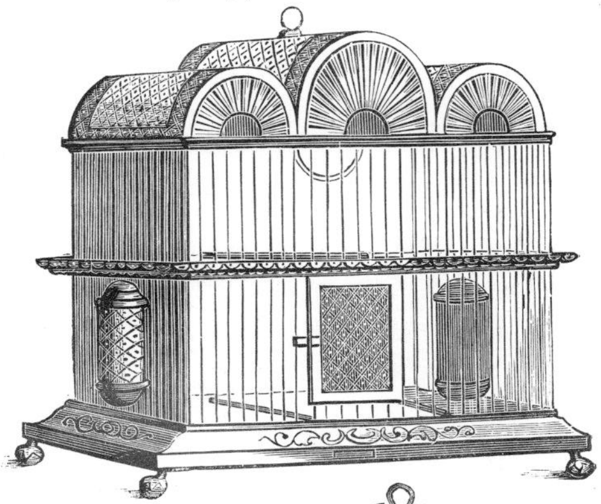

No. 10301. — Ornamental Wire Canary Cage, Crystal Palace pattern, with drawer.

No. 10309.—Paroquet Cage, with drawer and frosted glass panels.

No. 10309.

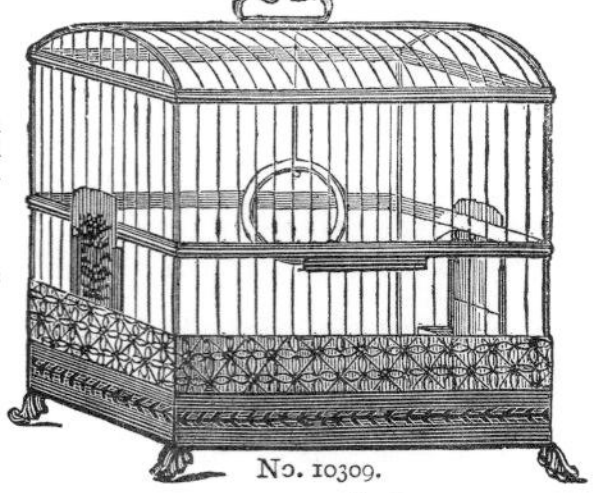

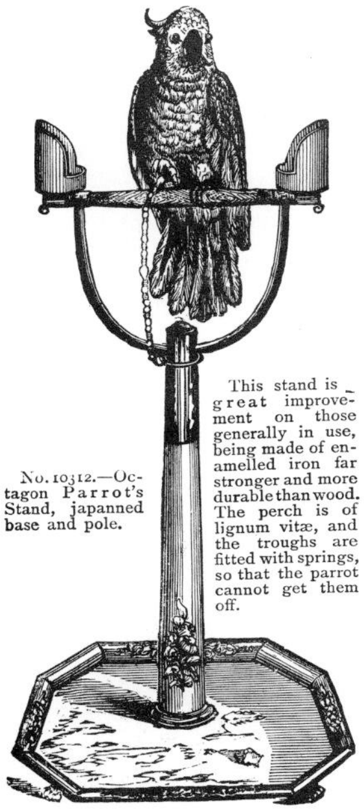

No. 10312.—Octagon Parrot's Stand, japanned base and pole.

This stand is a great improvement on those generally in use, being made of enamelled iron far stronger and more durable than wood. The perch is of lignum vitæ, and the troughs are fitted with springs, so that the parrot cannot get them off.

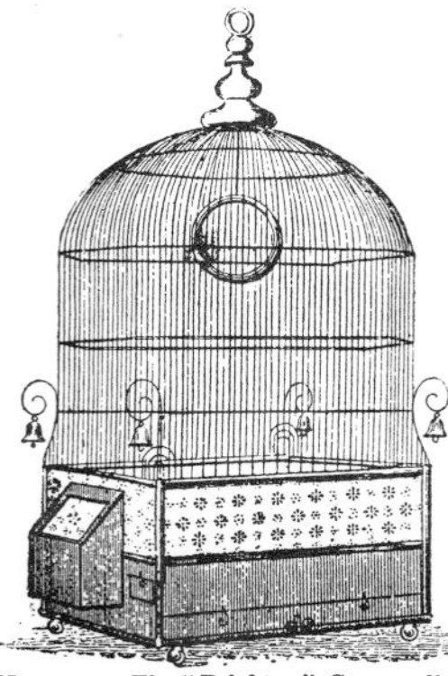

No. 10303.—The "Brighton" Cage, polished pine, tinned wire, dome top and bells.

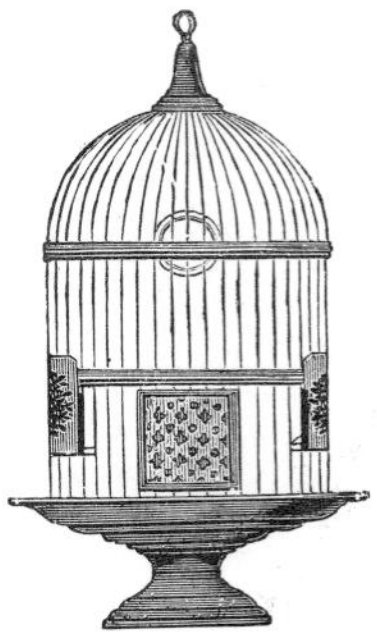

No. 10305.—Wire Canary Cage, round.

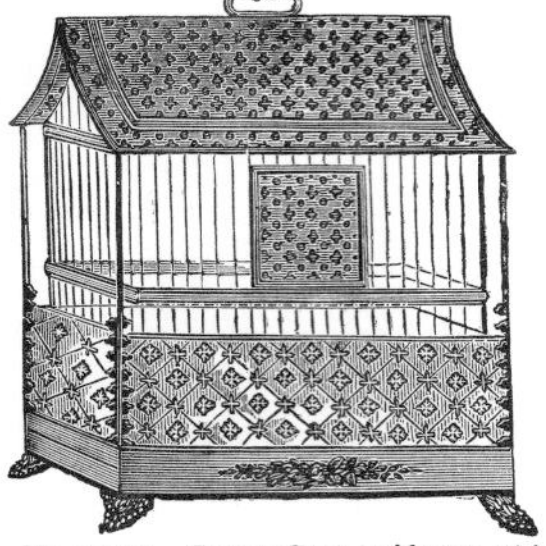

No. 10304A.—Canary Cage, gable top, with drawer and frosted glass panels.

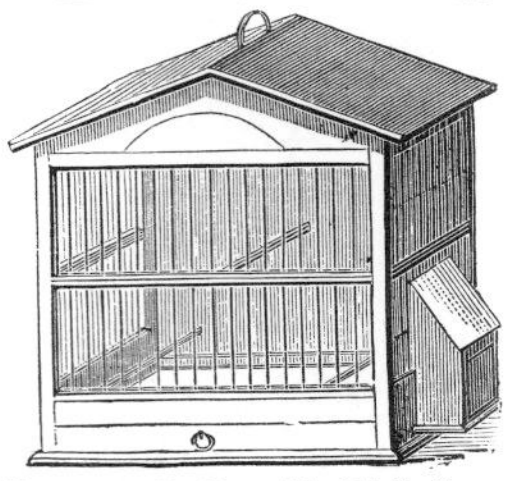

No. 10326.—Lark's or Blackbird's Cage, painted green or brown.

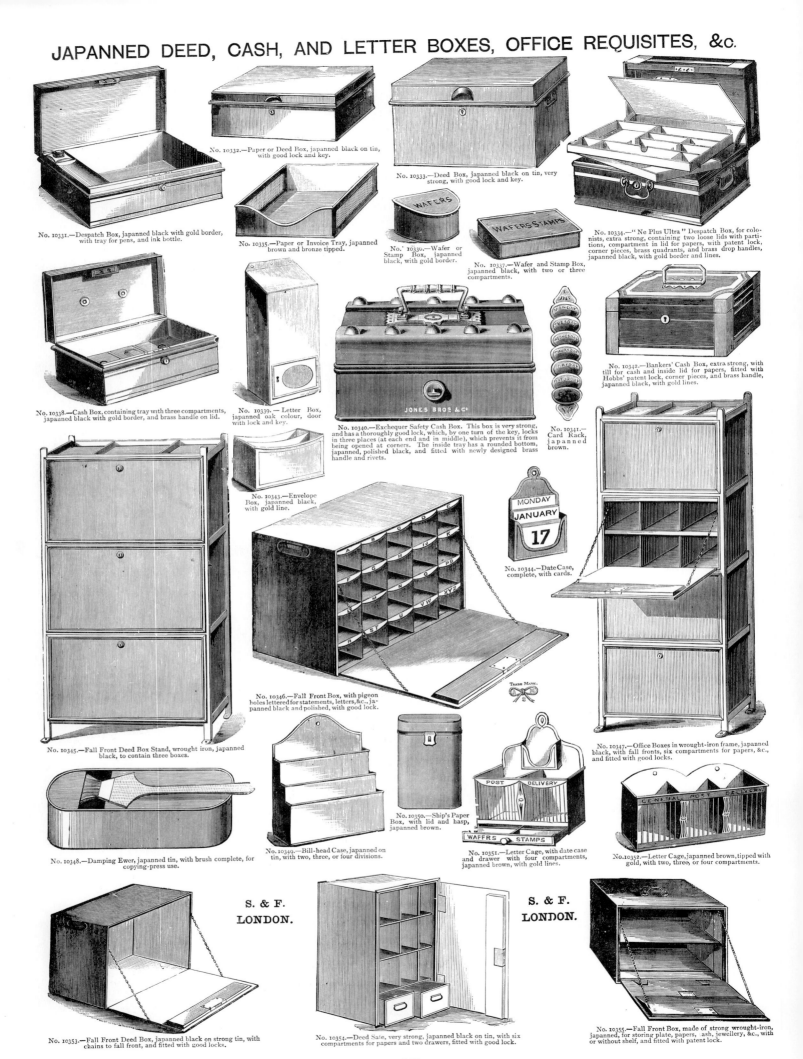

No. 10331.—Despatch Box, japanned black with gold border, with tray for pens, and ink bottle.

No. 10332.—Paper or Deed Box, japanned black on tin, with good lock and key.

No. 10335.—Paper or Invoice Tray, japanned brown and bronze tipped.

No. 10333.—Deed Box, japanned black on tin, very strong, with good lock and key.

No. 10330.—Wafer or Stamp Box, japanned black, with gold border.

No. 10337.—Wafer and Stamp Box, japanned black, with two or three compartments.

No. 10334.—"Ne Plus Ultra" Despatch Box, for colonists, extra strong, containing two loose lids with partitions, compartment in lid for papers, with patent lock, corner pieces, brass quadrants, and brass drop handles, japanned black, with gold border and lines.

No. 10338.—Cash Box, containing tray with three compartments, japanned black with gold border, and brass handle on lid.

No. 10339.—Letter Box, japanned oak colour, door with lock and key.

No. 10340.—Exchequer Safety Cash Box. This box is very strong, and has a thoroughly good lock, which, by one turn of the key, locks in three places (at each end and in middle), which prevents it from being opened at corners. The inside tray has a rounded bottom, japanned, polished black, and fitted with newly designed brass handle and rivets.

No. 10341.—Card Rack, japanned brown.

No. 10342.—Bankers' Cash Box, extra strong, with till for cash and inside lid for papers, fitted with Hobbs' patent lock, corner pieces, and brass handle, japanned black, with gold lines.

No. 10343.—Envelope Box, japanned black, with gold line.

No. 10344.—Date Case, complete, with cards.

No. 10345.—Fall Front Deed Box Stand, wrought iron, japanned black, to contain three boxes.

No. 10346.—Fall Front Box, with pigeon holes lettered for statements, letters, &c., japanned black and polished, with good lock.

No. 10347.—Office Boxes in wrought-iron frame, japanned black, with fall fronts, six compartments for papers, &c., and fitted with good locks.

No. 10348.—Damping Ewer, japanned tin, with brush complete, for copying-press use.

No. 10349.—Bill-head Case, japanned on tin, with two, three, or four divisions.

No. 10350.—Ship's Paper Box, with lid and hasp, japanned brown.

No. 10351.—Letter Cage, with date case and drawer with four compartments, japanned brown, with gold lines.

No. 10352.—Letter Cage, japanned brown, tipped with gold, with two, three, or four compartments.

S. & F. LONDON.

S. & F. LONDON.

No. 10353.—Fall Front Deed Box, japanned black on strong tin, with chains to fall front, and fitted with good locks.

No. 10354.—Deed Safe, very strong, japanned black on tin, with six compartments for papers and two drawers, fitted with good lock.

No. 10355.—Fall Front Box, made of strong wrought-iron, japanned, for storing plate, papers, cash, jewellery, &c., with or without shelf, and fitted with patent lock.

No. 10391 Hall or Restaurant Table, painted and bronzed cast-iron, top painted imitation marble. Can be had with marble top

No. 10392 Hall or Restaurant Table, painted and bronzed cast-iron, with marble top, or can be had with ornamental iron or imitation marble top

No. 10393 Hall, Restaurant or Ladies' Work Table, Berlin black or painted and bronzed iron, with japanned iron top

No. 10394 Hall or Restaurant Table, painted and bronzed, with ornamental cast-iron top

No. 10395 Hall or Restaurant Table, painted and bronzed, cast-iron top painted imitation marble, or with marble slab

No. 10397 Door Porter, japanned cast-iron, height 7½in.

No. 10396 Door Porter, japanned cast-iron, height 3½in.

No. 10398 Door Porter, japanned cast-iron, height 7½in.

No. 10399 Door Porter, japanned cast-iron, height 1ft 2½in.

No. 10400 Door Porter, polished and lacquered brass, weighted, 8½in. high

No. 10401 Hall Chair Mahogany or Oak well-finished

No. 10402 Hall Chair, black Walnut or Oak, solid seat and back, well-finished

No. 10403 Scraper with Pan, japanned black or bronze; size of pan, 8½in. by 11¾in.

No. 10404 Scraper with Brushes and loose Pan, japanned black or bronze

No. 10405 Garden Scraper, japanned black, width 7½in., height 19¾in.

No. 10406 Scraper with Pan, japanned black or bronze

No. 10407 Scraper with Pan, japanned black or bronze

No. 10408 Umbrella Stand, polished and lacquered brass supports and top, japanned iron base, with loose pan

No. 10409 Umbrella Stand, all polished and lacquered brass; height 23 in., dia. 9 in., with loose pan, japanned white

No. 10410 Umbrella Stand, polished and lacquered brass supports and top, japanned iron base, with loose pan; height 23 in., length at base 15½ in. width 5 in.

No. 10411 Umbrella Stand, made entirely of bronzed iron, with loose zinc pan

No. 10412 Umbrella Stand, polished and lacquered brass supports and arched top, japanned iron base, with loose pan

No. 10413 Umbrella Holder or Rail, for pews, &c., to fold, all polished and lacquered brass, 10½ in. long, 4 in. wide

No. 10414 Umbrella Pan for pews, &c., to lift up for removing water, suitable for rail above, japanned cast-iron, 5½in. long, 3½in. wide.

No. 10415 Umbrella Stand, bronzed cast-iron, with loose scalloped pan

No. 10416 Umbrella Stand, bronzed cast-iron height 30 in., width of base 15 in., standing out 8 in.

No. 10417 Umbrella Stand, bronzed cast-iron, with loose pan; height 30 in., width at base 15 in., standing out 8 in.

No. 10418 Hat and Umbrella Stand for hall, bronzed cast-iron, with mirror, marble slab, and 2 loose pans; height 6 ft. 4 in., width at base 2 ft. 1 in.

No. 10419 Hat and Umbrella Stand, handsome ornamental bronzed cast-iron, with mirror, marble slab, and 2 loose pans

No. 10420 Umbrella Stand, bronzed cast-iron with loose pan; height 32 in., width 17½ in.

S&F. London.

S&F.

JAPANNED IRON WASHSTANDS, TRUNKS AND BONNET BOXES, JAPANNED TIN COLLAR BOXES, &C.

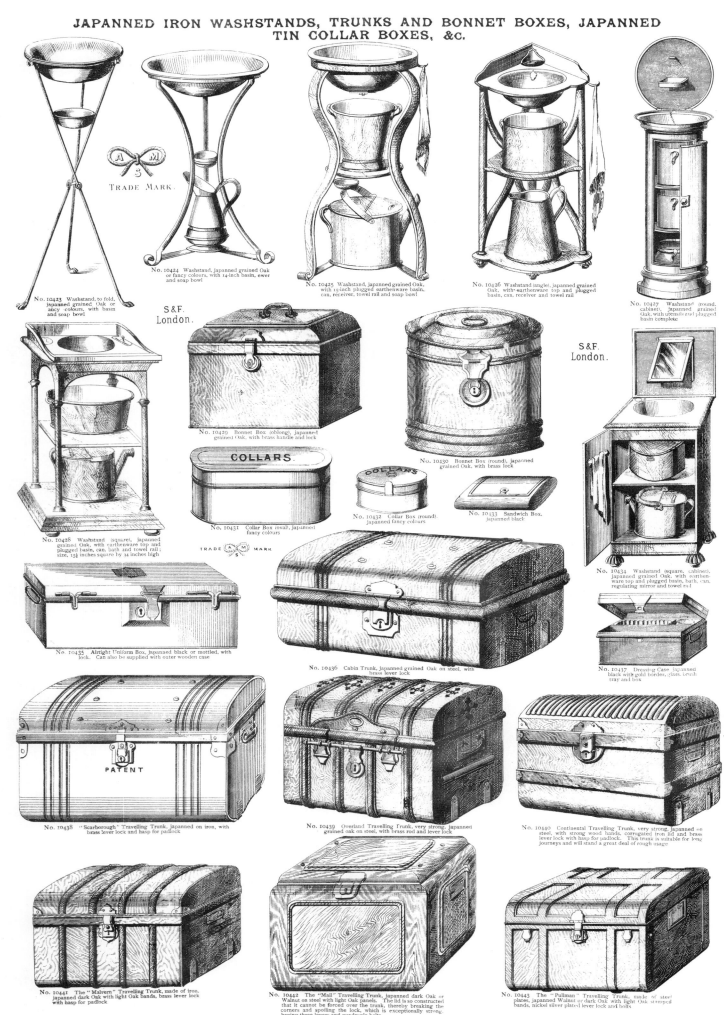

TRADE MARK.

S&F. London.

S&F. London.

No. 10423 Washstand, to fold, japanned grained Oak or fancy colours, with basin and soap bowl

No. 10424 Washstand, japanned grained Oak or fancy colours, with 14-inch basin, ewer and soap bowl

No. 10425 Washstand, japanned grained Oak, with 15-inch plugged earthenware basin, can, receiver, towel rail and soap bowl

No. 10426 Washstand (angle), japanned grained Oak, with earthenware top and plugged basin, can, receiver and towel rail

No. 10427 Washstand (round, cabinet), japanned grained Oak, with utensils and plugged basin complete

No. 10428 Washstand (square), japanned grained Oak, with earthenware top and plugged basin, can, bath and towel rail; size, 15½ inches square by 34 inches high

No. 10429 Bonnet Box (oblong), japanned grained Oak, with brass handle and lock

COLLARS.

No. 10430 Bonnet Box (round), japanned grained Oak, with brass lock

No. 10431 Collar Box (oval), japanned fancy colours

No. 10432 Collar Box (round), japanned fancy colours

No. 10433 Sandwich Box, japanned black

No. 10434 Washstand (square, cabinet), japanned grained Oak, with earthenware top and plugged basin, bath, can, regulating mirror and towel rail

TRADE MARK

No. 10435 Airtight Uniform Box, japanned black or mottled, with lock. Can also be supplied with outer wooden case

No. 10436 Cabin Trunk, japanned grained Oak on steel, with brass lever lock

No. 10437 Dressing Case, japanned black with gold border, glass, brush tray and box

PATENT

No. 10438 "Scarborough" Travelling Trunk, japanned on iron, with brass lever lock and hasp for padlock

No. 10439 Overland Travelling Trunk, very strong, japanned grained oak on steel, with brass rod and lever lock

No. 10440 Continental Travelling Trunk, very strong, japanned on steel, with strong wood bands, corrugated iron lid and brass lever lock with hasp for padlock. This trunk is suitable for long journeys and will stand a great deal of rough usage

No. 10441 The "Malvern" Travelling Trunk, made of iron, japanned dark Oak with light Oak bands, brass lever lock with hasp for padlock

No. 10442 The "Mail" Travelling Trunk, japanned dark Oak or Walnut on steel with light Oak panels. The lid is so constructed that it cannot be forced over the trunk, thereby breaking the corners and spoiling the lock, which is exceptionally strong, having three levers and quadruple bolts

No. 10443 The "Pullman" Travelling Trunk, made of steel plates, japanned Walnut or dark Oak with light Oak stamped bands, nickel silver plated lever lock and bolts

MANUFACTURERS, IMPORTERS, WAREHOUSEMEN AND AGENTS.

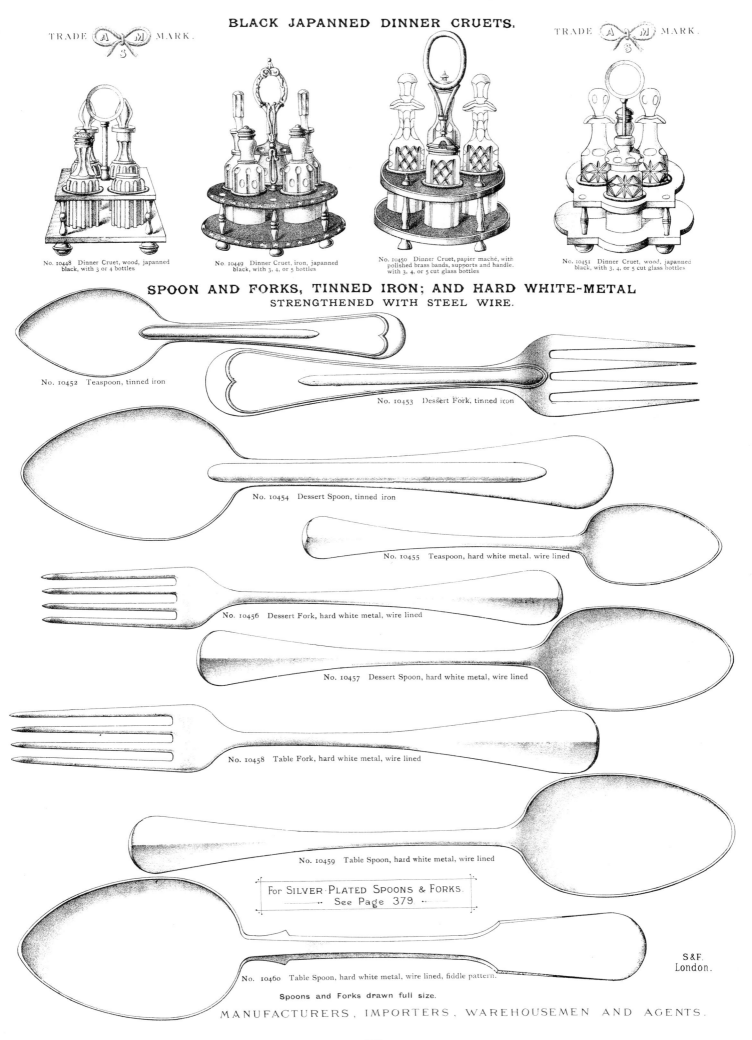

BLACK JAPANNED DINNER CRUETS.

TRADE MARK.

TRADE MARK.

No. 10448 Dinner Cruet, wood, japanned black, with 3 or 4 bottles

No. 10449 Dinner Cruet, iron, japanned black, with 3, 4, or 5 bottles

No. 10450 Dinner Cruet, papier maché, with polished brass bands, supports and handle, with 3, 4, or 5 cut glass bottles

No. 10451 Dinner Cruet, wood, japanned black, with 3, 4, or 5 cut glass bottles

SPOON AND FORKS, TINNED IRON; AND HARD WHITE-METAL
STRENGTHENED WITH STEEL WIRE.

No. 10452 Teaspoon, tinned iron

No. 10453 Dessert Fork, tinned iron

No. 10454 Dessert Spoon, tinned iron

No. 10455 Teaspoon, hard white metal, wire lined

No. 10456 Dessert Fork, hard white metal, wire lined

No. 10457 Dessert Spoon, hard white metal, wire lined

No. 10458 Table Fork, hard white metal, wire lined

No. 10459 Table Spoon, hard white metal, wire lined

For SILVER-PLATED SPOONS & FORKS. See Page 379.

No. 10460 Table Spoon, hard white metal, wire lined, fiddle pattern.

S&F. London.

Spoons and Forks drawn full size.

MANUFACTURERS, IMPORTERS, WAREHOUSEMEN AND AGENTS.

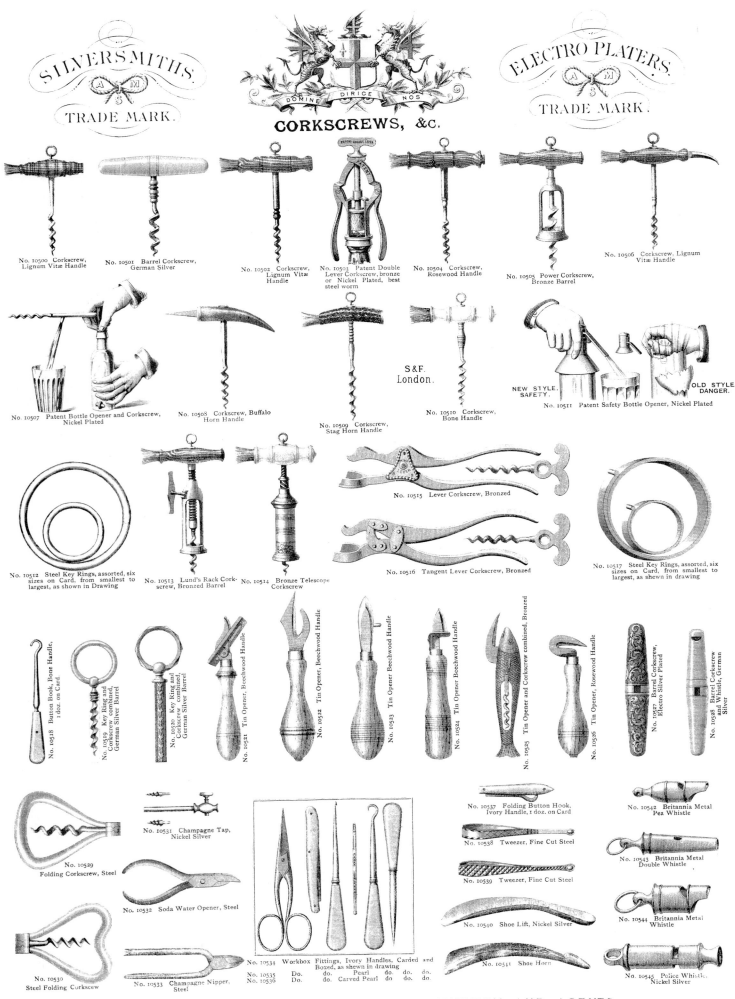

No. 10500 Corkscrew, Lignum Vitæ Handle

No. 10501 Barrel Corkscrew, German Silver

No. 10502 Corkscrew, Lignum Vitæ Handle

No. 10503 Patent Double Lever Corkscrew, bronze or Nickel Plated, best steel worm

No. 10504 Corkscrew, Rosewood Handle

No. 10505 Power Corkscrew, Bronze Barrel

No. 10506 Corkscrew. Lignum Vitæ Handle

No. 10507 Patent Bottle Opener and Corkscrew, Nickel Plated

No. 10508 Corkscrew, Buffalo Horn Handle

No. 10509 Corkscrew, Stag Horn Handle

S. & F. London.

No. 10510 Corkscrew, Bone Handle

NEW STYLE. SAFETY.

OLD STYLE. DANGER.

No. 10511 Patent Safety Bottle Opener, Nickel Plated

No. 10512 Steel Key Rings, assorted, six sizes on Card, from smallest to largest, as shown in Drawing

No. 10513 Lund's Rack Corkscrew, Bronzed Barrel

No. 10514 Bronze Telescope Corkscrew

No. 10515 Lever Corkscrew, Bronzed

No. 10516 Tangent Lever Corkscrew, Bronzed

No. 10517 Steel Key Rings, assorted, six sizes on Card, from smallest to largest, as shewn in drawing

No. 10518 Button Book, Bone Handle, 1 doz. on Card.

No. 10519 Key Ring and Corkscrew combined, German Silver Barrel

No. 10520 Key Ring and Corkscrew combined, German Silver Barrel

No. 10521 Tin Opener, Beechwood Handle

No. 10532 Tin Opener, Beechwood Handle

No. 10523 Tin Opener Beechwood Handle

No. 10524 Tin Opener Beechwood Handle

No. 10525 Tin Opener and Corkscrew combined, Bronzed

No. 10526 Tin Opener, Rosewood Handle

No. 10527 Barrel Corkscrew, Electro Silver Plated

No. 10528 Barrel Corkscrew and Whistle, German Silver

No. 10529 Folding Corkscrew, Steel

No. 10531 Champagne Tap, Nickel Silver

No. 10532 Soda Water Opener, Steel

No. 10530 Steel Folding Corkscrew

No. 10533 Champagne Nipper, Steel

No. 10534 Workbox Fittings, Ivory Handles, Carded and Boxed, as shewn in drawing
No. 10535 Do. do. Pearl do. do.
No. 10536 Do. do. Carved Pearl do. do.

No. 10537 Folding Button Hook, Ivory Handle, 1 doz. on Card

No. 10538 Tweezer, Fine Cut Steel

No. 10539 Tweezer, Fine Cut Steel

No. 10540 Shoe Lift, Nickel Silver

No. 10541 Shoe Horn

No. 10542 Britannia Metal Pea Whistle

No. 10543 Britannia Metal Double Whistle

No. 10544 Britannia Metal Whistle

No. 10545 Police Whistle, Nickel Silver

AGRICULTURAL IMPLEMENTS

AND

MACHINERY,

HORTICULTURAL TOOLS,

LAWN MOWERS, GARDEN ROLLERS, WATER TANKS,

GARDEN PUMPS, SYRINGES, AND FOUNTAINS,

STABLE FITTINGS,

POULTRY HOUSES AND DOG KENNELS,

ORNAMENTAL IRON GATES AND PALISADES,

CONSERVATORIES, GREENHOUSES,

PLANT PRESERVERS,

TENTS AND HAMMOCKS,

GARDEN SEATS, EDGINGS, AND ORNAMENTS,

DAIRY FARM FURNITURE.

No. 10600.—Wire Flower Stand, 2 ft. high.

No. 10601.—Hanging Flower Basket.

No. 10602.—Strong Wire Flower Stand to stand against wall, 3 ft. high and 3 ft. to 4 ft. wide.

No. 10603.—Wrought-iron Tree Guard.

No. 10604.—Strong Wire Flower Stand, 2 ft. 6 ins. to 3 ft. high and 2 ft. 6 ins. to 3 ft. 6 ins. wide.

No, 10605.—Flower Basket, to hang.

No. 10606.—Wire Flower Stand, 3 ft. 4 ins. high, 12 ins. wide at top.

No. 10607.—Strong Wire Flower Stand, 2 ft. 9 ins. to 3 ft. 6 ins. high and 2 ft. 6 ins. to 3 ft. 6 ins. wide.

No. 10608.—Wrought-iron Garden Chair, with steel spring back and seat, japanned.

No. 10609.—Wire Bordering, 10 ins. high.

No. 10610.—Scroll Bordering, 10 ins. high.

No. 10611.—Wire Bordering, 10 ins. high.

No 10612.—Japanned Garden Chair, with steel spring seat and back, and wrought-iron frame and arms.

No. 10613—Garden Seat and Table combined, 6 feet long, made of best pitch pine. Without loosening the screw or bolt this garden seat can be converted, by a simple movement, into a table and seat combined, as shown in drawing No. 10614.

For further Illustrations of Garden Seats, see pages 575 and 576.

No. 10614.—Garden Seat and Table combined, the same description as No. 10613, but with awning, complete.

S. & F. LONDON, *Manufacturers,* IMPORTERS, Warehousemen, AND AGENTS.

No. 10616.—Strong Wire Flower Stand, to stand against wall, ornamental design.

No. 10618.—Galvanised Wire Netting, with wrought-iron fencing, for lawn-tennis ground, &c.

TRADE MARK.

No. 10615.—Very strong Wire Garden Arch, made in two halves, and connected with bolts and nuts.

No. 10619.—Galvanised Wire Pea or Seed Protectors.

No. 10620.—Galvanised Wire Netting, diamond mesh.

No. 10617.—Galvanized Wire Netting for Croquet Lawns, with pins.

No. 10621.—Cast-iron Dog Trough, with partition.

No. 10622.—Circular Iron Trough, for dogs.

No. 10623.—Circular Cast-iron Pig Trough, with cross rods.

No. 10624.—Double Pig Trough, with cross rods to prevent waste.

No. 10625.—Pig Trough, with inverted rim and wrought-iron cross bars or partitions.

No. 10626.—Circular Poultry Trough with five compartments, and centre one for water.

No. 10627.—Single Pig Trough, with cross bars to prevent waste.

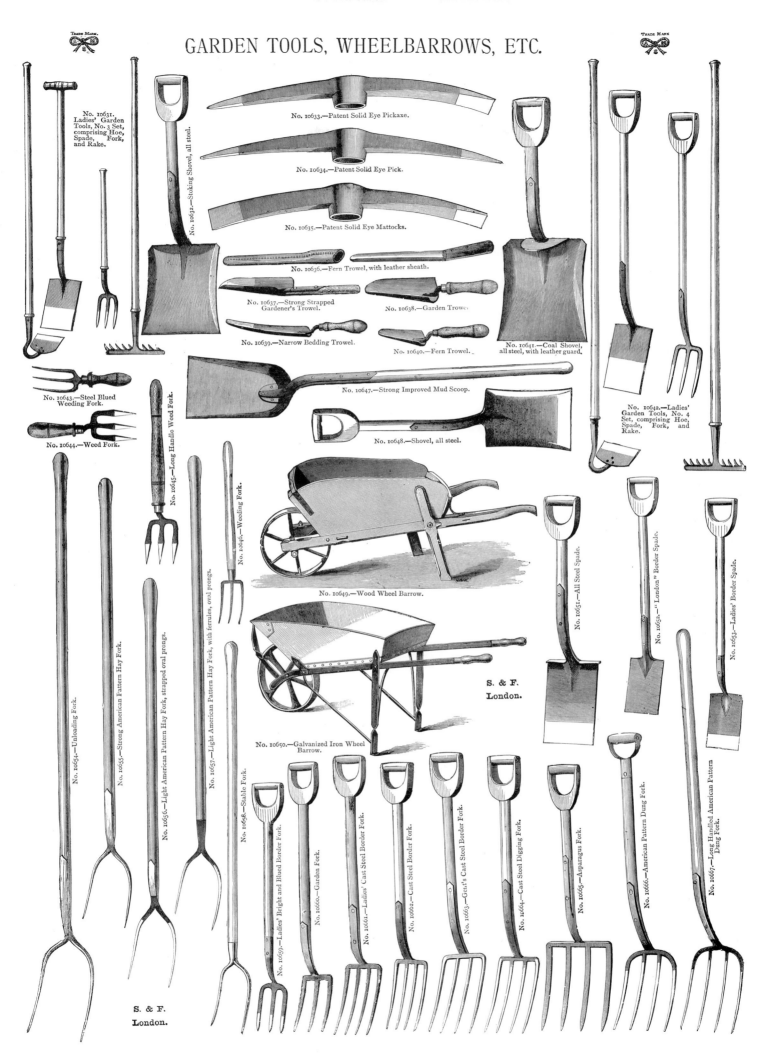

No. 10631.—Ladies' Garden Tools, No. 3 Set, comprising Hoe, Spade, Fork, and Rake.

No. 10632.—Stoking Shovel, all steel.

No. 10633.—Patent Solid Eye Pickaxe.

No. 10634.—Patent Solid Eye Pick.

No. 10635.—Patent Solid Eye Mattocks.

No. 10636.—Fern Trowel, with leather sheath.

No. 10637.—Strong Strapped Gardener's Trowel.

No. 10638.—Garden Trowel.

No. 10639.—Narrow Bedding Trowel.

No. 10640.—Fern Trowel.

No. 10641.—Coal Shovel, all steel, with leather guard.

No. 10642.—Ladies' Garden Tools, No. 4 Set, comprising Hoe, Spade, Fork, and Rake.

No. 10643.—Steel Blued Weeding Fork.

No. 10644.—Weed Fork.

No. 10645.—Long Handle Weed Fork.

No. 10646.—Weeding Fork.

No. 10647.—Strong Improved Mud Scoop.

No. 10648.—Shovel, all steel.

No. 10649.—Wood Wheel Barrow.

No. 10650.—Galvanized Iron Wheel Barrow.

S. & F. London.

No. 10651.—All Steel Spade.

No. 10652.—"London" Border Spade.

No. 10653.—Ladies' Border Spade.

No. 10654.—Unloading Fork.

No. 10655.—Strong American Pattern Hay Fork.

No. 10656.—Light American Pattern Hay Fork, strapped oval prongs.

No. 10657.—Light American Pattern Hay Fork, with ferrules, oval prongs.

No. 10658.—Stable Fork.

No. 10659.—Ladies' Bright and Blued Border Fork.

No. 10660.—Garden Fork.

No. 10661.—Ladies' Cast Steel Border Fork.

No. 10662.—Cast Steel Border Fork.

No. 10663.—Gent's Cast Steel Border Fork.

No. 10664.—Cast Steel Digging Fork.

No. 10665.—Asparagus Fork.

No. 10666.—American Pattern Dung Fork.

No. 10667.—Long Handled American Pattern Dung Fork.

S. & F. London.

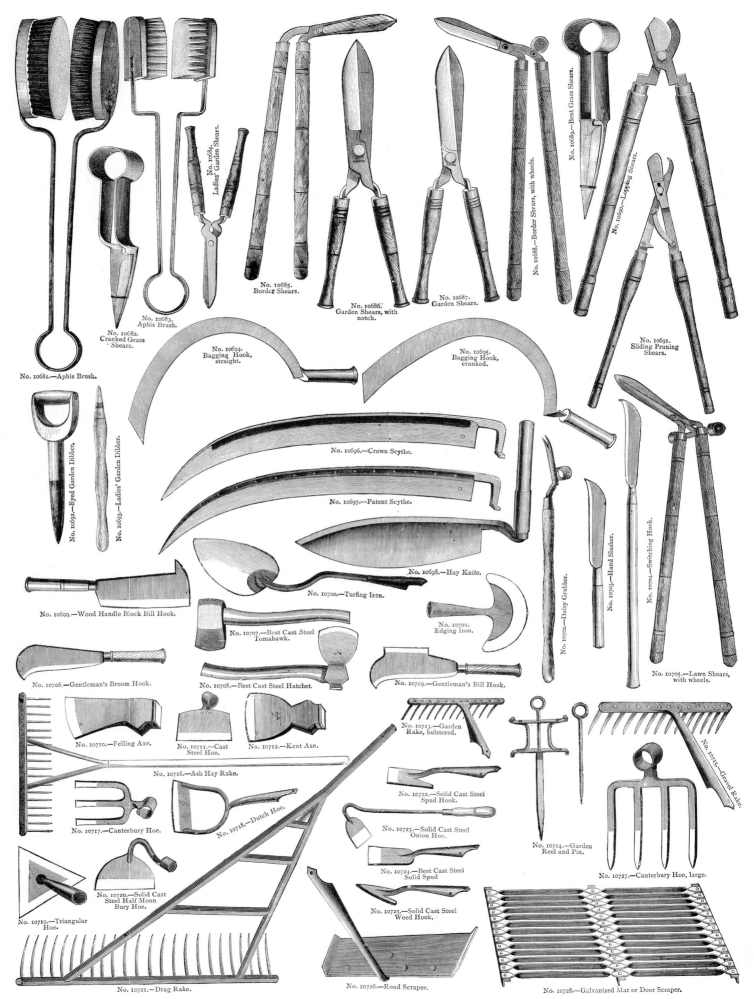

No. 10684.—Ladies' Garden Shears.

No. 10685.—Border Shears.

No. 10686.—Garden Shears, with notch.

No. 10687.—Garden Shears.

No. 10688.—Border Shears, with wheels.

No. 10689.—Bent Grass Shears.

No. 10690.—Lopping Shears.

No. 10683.—Aphis Brush.

No. 10682.—Cranked Grass Shears.

No. 10681.—Aphis Brush.

No. 10691.—Sliding Pruning Shears.

No. 10692.—Eyed Garden Dibber.

No. 10693.—Ladies' Garden Dibber.

No. 10694.—Bagging Hook, straight.

No. 10695.—Bagging Hook, cranked.

No. 10696.—Crown Scythe.

No. 10697.—Patent Scythe.

No. 10698.—Hay Knife.

No. 10700.—Turfing Iron.

No. 10702.—Daisy Grubber.

No. 10703.—Hand Slasher.

No. 10704.—Switching Hook.

No. 10701.—Edging Iron.

No. 10699.—Wood Handle Block Bill Hook.

No. 10707.—Best Cast Steel Tomahawk.

No. 10705.—Lawn Shears, with wheels.

No. 10706.—Gentleman's Broom Hook.

No. 10708.—Best Cast Steel Hatchet.

No. 10709.—Gentleman's Bill Hook.

No. 10710.—Felling Axe.

No. 10711.—Cast Steel Hoe.

No. 10712.—Kent Axe.

No. 10713.—Garden Rake, bolstered.

No. 10715.—Gravel Rake.

No. 10716.—Ash Hay Rake.

No. 10717.—Canterbury Hoe.

No. 10718.—Dutch Hoe.

No. 10722.—Solid Cast Steel Spud Hook.

No. 10723.—Solid Cast Steel Onion Hoe.

No. 10714.—Garden Reel and Pin.

No. 10727.—Canterbury Hoe, large.

No. 10719.—Triangular Hoe.

No. 10720.—Solid Cast Steel Half Moon Bury Hoe.

No. 10724.—Best Cast Steel Solid Spud.

No. 10725.—Solid Cast Steel Weed Hook.

No. 10721.—Drag Rake.

No. 10726.—Road Scraper.

No. 10728.—Galvanized Mat or Door Scraper.

GARDEN EDGING, GARDEN SEATS, FLOWER BOXES FOR WINDOWS, FLOWER POTS, BRACKETS, GARDEN VASES, AND FOUNTAINS.

GARDEN EDGING IN EITHER GLAZED STONEWARE OR BUFF TERRA-COTTA.

No. 10741.—9 inches long.

No. 10742.—9 inches long.

No. 10743.—12 inches long and 6 inches long.

No. 10744.—9 inches long.

No. 10745.—9 inches long.

No. 10746.—Glazed Garden Seat, 19½ inches high.

No. 10748.—Set of Window Boxes, in Doulton ware. Each division is separate and removable, and measures 7½ inches wide and 7 inches high.

No. 10747.—Glazed Garden Seat, 19½ inches high.

No. 10753/1.—Terra-cotta Flower Pot, 7 inches high.

No. 10749.—Set of Window Boxes, in Doulton ware. Each Box is separate. By the insertion of more middle pieces longer sets may be obtained. 3 feet long.

No. 10753/2.—Terra-cotta Flower Pot, 19 inches high.

No. 10752.—Flower Pot, 9½ inches high, in red or brown Silicon ware.

No. 10750.—Window Box, in terra-cotta. This is in one piece, 3 feet long. Can be had with or without pendant knobs.

No. 10753.—Flower Pot, 13 inches high, in terra-cotta.

No. 10753/3.—Terra-cotta Flower Pot, 9½, 10½ inches high.

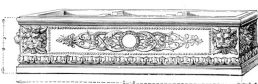

No. 10751.—Window Box, in terra-cotta. This is in one piece.

No. 10753/4.—Terra-cotta Flower Pot, 17 inches high.

No. 10754.—Terra-cotta Pendant, in two sizes, 7 inches diameter, and 13½ inches diameter.

No. 10756.—Terra-cotta Wall Bracket, 6 inches high.

No. 10757.—Stoneware Flower Ring, in three sizes, 6 inches, 9 inches, and 12 inches diameter.

No. 10758.—Terra-cotta Wall Bracket, 7 inches high.

No. 10755.—Terra-cotta Pendant, 10½ inches diameter.

No. 10759.—Terra-cotta Vase, 1 foot 4 inches high.

S. & F.
LONDON.

S. & F.
LONDON.

No. 10753/6.—Terra-cotta Flower Pot, 8½ inches high.

No. 10762.—Terra-cotta Vase, 1 foot 4 inches high.

No. 10753/5.—Terra-cotta Flower Pot, 7½ inches high.

Trade Mark

No. 10760.—Terra-cotta Vase, in two sizes, 28 inches high and 22 inches high.

No. 10761.—Fountain, in terra-cotta. Upper reservoir is 2 feet diameter, lower reservoir is 2 feet 8 inches diameter, crane standard is 2 feet 1 inch high.

Trade Mark.

No. 10763.—Terra-cotta Vase, 2 feet 4 inches high.

BOXING GLOVES.

No. 10766.—Buff Chamois, without fingers, set of four.
No. 10767.—Buff Chamois, stuffed with Indian grass, set of four.
No. 10768.—Buff Chamois, stuffed with Indian grass, elastic round the wrist, set of four.
No. 10769.—Buff Chamois, half hair and half Indian grass, set of four.
No. 10770.—Buff Chamois, all hair, set of four.
No. 10771.—Buff Chamois, all hair, ventilated, set of four.
No. 10772.—White Chamois, all hair, set of four.
No. 10773.—White Chamois, all hair, ventilated, set of four.
No. 10774.—White Chamois, all hair, ventilated, leather piping, set of four.
No. 10775.—White Kid, all hair, ventilated.
No. 10776.—The Thumbless, ventilated, set of four.

THE "CHAMPION" GLOVE.

Nos. 10777 to 10782.

ASHANTEE HAMMOCKS.

HAMMOCK PACKED IN CASE WITH STRAP TO HANG OVER SHOULDER. SIZE OF PARCEL 10 × 5 × 5 IN. WEIGHT FROM 1½ LBS TO 4 LBS.

No. 10780.—Ashantee Hammock, made of twine, and packed in waterproof case (as drawing).

QUOITS.

No. 10783.—Quoits, Black or Bright Weights, 3½, 4, 4½, 5, 5½, 7, 7½, 8, 9, or 10 lbs. per pair.
No. 10784.—Pins, Split, to hold paper, in pairs.

No. 10803.—THE NEW FRENCH HAMMOCK, with adjustable stand, can be used both in and out of doors without the assistance of any peg, hook, or cord. It is very portable for travelling. Weight 18 lbs.

The "Champion" Glove is so arranged that the padding is brought over from the back of the hand to the inside of the fingers, passing over the tips and extending to above the second joints of the same; the thumb is padded in same manner. The fingers being protected by the padding, all danger of injury is entirely avoided.

No. 10777.—The "Champion" Glove, buff chamois, all hair, set of four.
No. 10778.—The "Champion" Glove, buff chamois, all hair, ventilated, set of four.

No. 10779.—The "Champion" Glove, white chamois, set of four.
No. 10780.—The "Champion" Glove, white chamois, ventilated, set of four.

No. 10781.—The "Champion" Glove, white chamois, ventilated, and red leather piping, set of four.
No. 10782.—The "Champion" Glove, white kid, all hair, ventilated, very superior, set of four.

No. 10804.—GYMNASTIC, complete. Can be put up and fixed in 30 minutes.

No. 10805.—FRENCH MANILLA HAMMOCKS, with Wood Stretchers.
No. 10806.—FRENCH MANILLA HAMMOCKS, with Folding Metal Stretchers.
No. 10807.—FRENCH MANILLA HAMMOCKS (as drawing), with Bent Wood Stretchers.

FOOT BALLS.

No. 10788.—Basil Foot Balls.
No. 10789.—The "Association" Foot Ball, superior hide leather.

No. 10790.—The "Rugby" Foot Ball, superior hide leather.

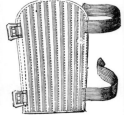

No. 10791.—Crown Association Foot Ball. These are made in eight pieces, cut from cowhide, lined with india-rubber to keep them waterproof and to prevent the oil from destroying the rubber. They are also stitched at the ends to keep them from bursting. They have double lace holes and extra strong bladders.
No. 10792.—Crown Rugby Foot Ball. These are made in four pieces, cut from cowhide, lined with waterproof sheeting, with double lace holes and ends made extra strong.

FOOT BALL SHIN GUARDS.

No. 10793.—Buff Leather Shin Guard, with cane, and fastened with elastic and buckless rim, light, and great protection, can be worn under the stocking, weighing under 5 oz. per pair.
No. 10794.—As No. 10793, but in white chamois.
No. 10795.—As No. 10793, but in brown Cape leather.

FOOT BALL INFLATORS.

No. 10796.—Superior Brass Foot Ball Inflators.
No. 10797.—Pocket Foot Ball Inflator.

No. 10798.—Foot Ball Goals, Rugby, 4 poles, 14 feet, painted in one colour, 2 cross bars, 18½ feet.
No. 10799.—Four Poles with Cross Bar complete (New Regulation).
No. 10800.—Foot Ball Belts, 3-inch webbing, very strong.
No. 10801.—Ditto, 1½-inch leather, and plated snake fastening.
No. 10802.—Foot Ball Players' Bag, suitable for carrying uniform.

SINGLE STICKS AND BASKETS.

No. 10785.—Ash Single Sticks.
No. 10786.—Fencing Baskets, Wicker.
No. 10787.—Fencing Baskets, Cane.

MARQUEES, TRAVELLING, ENGINEERS', BOATING, PUNJAUB HILL, REGULATION BELL, AND UMBRELLA TENTS.

Marquee.

No. 10840.
Sizes.
A, 18ft. by 12 ft.
B, 22 ft. „ 14 ft.
C, 30 ft. „ 16 ft.
D, 40 ft. „ 20 ft.
E, 50 ft. „ 25 ft.
F, 50 ft. „ 30 ft.

Each tent is furnished with poles, ropes, pegs, and mallet complete.

Marquee.

Travelling Tents.

No. 10841.
Sizes.
A, 6ft. by 4ft. 6in.
B, 6 ft. „ 6 ft.
C, 9 ft. „ 7 ft.
D, 12 ft. „ 7 ft.
E, 13 ft. „ 10 ft.
F, 15 ft. „ 12 ft.

These are made with socketed poles, roped ridge, and every facility for transport, and can be fitted with an inner lining for use in the Tropics, allowing a free draught between the outer and inner roofs.

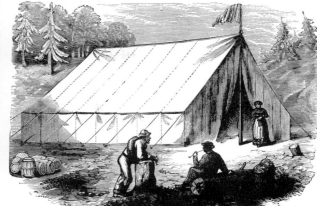

Travelling Tent.

Boating Tent.

No. 10842.
Sizes.
A, 7 ft. by 6 ft.
B, 9 ft. „ 6 ft.
C, 12 ft. „ 7 ft.

This Tent is very suitable for Boating Excursions, the smallest size weighing only 17 lbs., and can be had packed in bag complete, measuring 30 inches by 12 inches. Ground Sheets made to fit interior.

Boating Tent.

TRADE MARK.

Engineers' Tent.

No. 10843.
Sizes.
A, 6ft. by 4 ft. 6in.
B, 6 ft. by 6 ft.
C, 9 ft. „ 7 ft.
D, 12 ft. „ 7 ft.
E, 13 ft. „ 10 ft.
F, 15 ft. „ 12 ft.

Engineers' Tent.

Panjaub Hill Tent.

No. 10844.
Sizes.
A, 9 ft. by 9 ft.
B, 11 ft. „ 11 ft.
C, 13 ft. „ 13 ft.

This Tent is most suitable for travelling, being made with strong socketed poles (of which there are three), and ropes stitched to the canvas. It can be erected in the most boisterous weather by pegging the canvas to the ground at the four corners, and then adjusting the centre poles.

Panjaub Hill Tent.

Regulation Bell Tent.

No. 10845.
The British Government Regulation Bell Tent, 40 feet circumference, with socketed pole complete. Full instructions are given with each Tent.

British Government Regulation Bell Tent.

PATENT UMBRELLA TENTS.

Patent Umbrella Tent.

No. 10846.
The Patent Umbrella Tent. Of plain materials, for Bathing and Seaside purposes. Size, 6 feet diameter at roof, and 10 feet diameter at base.

Patent Umbrella Tent.
Plain.

Patent Umbrella Tent.

No. 10847.
Striped Tents for Croquet Parties, Lawn Tennis, &c. Size, 6 feet diameter at roof, and 10 feet diameter at base.

Patent Umbrella Tent.
Striped.

The chief characteristics of this Tent are extreme portability and facility of erection, as no lines, ropes, or wall poles are required. The principal feature of the patent is in the roof, which is suspended upon arms closing upwards, the reverse to an umbrella, and being erected opens out of the way of everybody. It is destined to supersede all kinds of Umbrella Tents. A special space for its stowage during winter is not required, as a box with folding legs (forming a seat) can be had, into which the whole fittings can be packed, and which will at all times be found useful.

TRADE MARK.

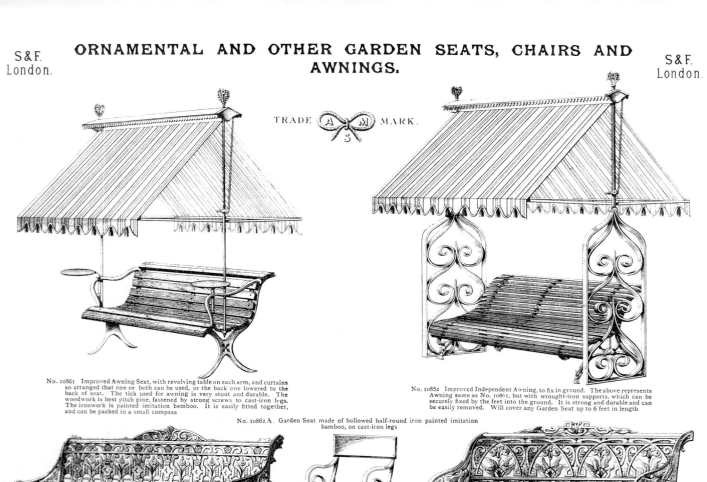

No. 10861 Improved Awning Seat, with revolving table on each arm, and curtains so arranged that one or both can be used, or the back one lowered to the back of seat. The tick used for awning is very stout and durable. The woodwork is best pitch pine, fastened by strong screws to cast-iron legs. The ironwork is painted imitation bamboo. It is easily fitted together, and can be packed in a small compass

No. 10852 Improved Independent Awning, to fix in ground. The above represents Awning same as No. 10861, but with wrought-iron supports, which can be securely fixed by the feet into the ground. It is strong and durable and can be easily removed. Will cover any Garden Seat up to 6 feet in length

No. 10862 A. Garden Seat made of hollowed half-round iron painted imitation bamboo, on cast-iron legs

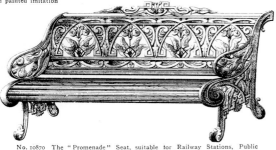

No. 10863 The "Park Seat," suitable for Promenades, Railway Stations, Public Grounds, Squares or Gardens; back, arms and legs of massive ornamental bronzed iron, and seat of well-seasoned wood, painted and grained oak

No. 10867 Garden Chair with Arms. The woodwork is of pitch pine, stained and varnished, painted green or grained oak; the framework of wrought-iron painted green. Can easily be taken apart for packing

No. 10870 The "Promenade" Seat, suitable for Railway Stations, Public Grounds, Squares, Gardens, &c.; back, arms and legs of massive ornamental bronzed iron, and seat of well-seasoned wood, painted and grained oak

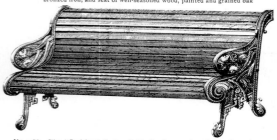

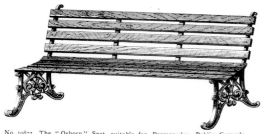

No. 10864 The "Parisian" Seat, suitable for Promenades, Public Grounds, Squares or Gardens; arms and legs of massive ornamental bronzed iron, and seat of well-seasoned wood, painted and grained oak This seat can be easily taken apart, and will occupy little room in packing

No. 10868 Garden Chair. Very light and comfortable to sit in. The wood work can be had as No. 10867 above; the wrought-iron work painted green

No. 10871 The "Osborn" Seat, suitable for Promenades, Public Grounds, Squares, Gardens, &c.; supports and legs of strong bronzed iron, seat of well-seasoned wood, painted and grained oak. Can be easily fixed or taken apart for packing

No. 10865 The "Windsor" Seat, suitable for Promenades, Public Grounds, Squares or Gardens; back and seat of well-seasoned wood, painted and grained oak, ends of bronzed iron, very durable

No. 10869 Garden Chair to fold for packing. By simply lifting the back of seat, this chair can be made to fold as shewn below, so that a great number can be packed in a small space. The material is of the same description as No. 10867

No. 10872 Lounge Garden Seat with Arms, back and seat of pitch pine stained and varnished, or can be had painted green or grained. The framework is of wrought-iron painted green. Can be easily taken apart and packed

(OPEN)

No. 10866 Garden Seat with Arms, very strong and durable. The seat and back are of pitch pine stained and varnished, or can be had painted green or grained oak. The framework is of wrought-iron painted green. The whole can be easily fixed together and takes up very little room in packing

No. 10869 (CLOSED)

No. 10873 The "Sandringham" Seat, suitable for Promenades, Public Grounds, Squares or Gardens; made entirely of wrought-iron, painted green

S. & F.
LONDON
AND
PARIS.

S. & F.
LONDON
AND
PARIS

REAL DRESDEN DECORATION.
HAND-PAINTED.

No. 9280

No. 9281

No. 9282

No. 9283

No. 9282

No. 9283

No. 9282

No. 9280

No. 9283

TRADE MARK

No. 9282

BEST STONEWARE.

No. 9283

241

S. & F.
LONDON
AND
PARIS.

S. & F.
LONDON
AND
PARIS

No 9285

No. 9284

No. 9284

No. 9285

No. 9237

No. 9288

No. 9237

No. 9288

No. 9286

No. 9286

No. 9287

No. 9288

No. 9290

No. 9289

No. 9289

No. 9289

No. 9290

S. & F.
LONDON
AND
PARIS.

ENGLISH STONEWARE.

S. & F.
LONDON
AND
PARIS.

No. 9297

No. 9298

No. 9297

No. 9298

No. 9299

No. 9301

No. 9299

No. 9301

No. 9300

No. 9300

No. 9299

No. 9302

No. 9301

No. 9302

No. 9303

No. 9303

No. 9303

S. & F.
LONDON
AND
PARIS.

S. & F.
LONDON
AND
PARIS.

No. 9314

No. 9315

No. 9316

No. 9314

No. 9315

No. 9317

No. 9318

No. 9316

No. 9317

No. 9318

No. 9316

No. 9317

No. 9318

No. 9418   No. 9419   No. 9420   No. 9421   No. 9422   No. 9423   No. 9424

No. 9425   No. 9426   No. 9427   No. 9428   No. 9429   No. 9430

No. 9431   No. 9432   No. 9433   No 9434   No. 9435   No. 9436   No. 9437   No. 9438

No. 9439   No. 9440   No. 9441   No. 9442   No. 9443   No. 9444   No. 9445

No. 9446   No. 9447   No. 9448   No. 9449   No. 9450   No. 9451   No. 9452   No. 9453

No. 9454   No. 9455   No. 9456   No. 9457   No. 9458   No. 9459   No. 9460

No. 9461   No. 9462   No. 9463   No. 9464   No. 9465

No. 9466   No. 9467   No. 9468   No. 9469   No. 9470   No. 9471   No. 9472

PLUNGE BATHS, WATER HEATERS, ETC.

PLUNGE BATH,
Without Casing or Feet.

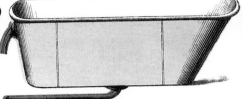

No. 9719.—Taper Plunge Bath, beaded, 21 inches deep, to stand without casing. These baths are made either in copper, zinc, tinned iron, or galvanized iron. They can be had flanged or beaded, as shown. The beaded baths are japanned, grained oak outside and white or marble inside; but when flanged for casing they are only painted with a plain coat outside.

COPPER, ZINC, OR IRON BATH,
With one Pipe, for Casing.

No. 9720.—Taper Bath, flanged, without feet, for casing. Fitted with copper overflow at end, copper well, a d 1-inch copper pipe from centre to end. Made in copper, tinned iron, galvanized iron, and three qualities of zinc. Japanned white or marble inside. These baths can also be had beaded and with feet, to order.

BEADED BATH,
To stand without Casing.

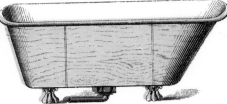

No. 9721.—Taper Plunge Bath, beaded, with feet, to stand without casing, and is fitted with ornamental cast-iron feet and waste plug with bent union. It can also be supplied with overflow pipe at end. Made in tinned iron and zinc. Japanned grained oak outside, white or marble inside.

ZINC OR IRON BATH,
With three Pipes, for Casing.

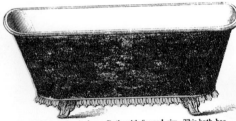

No. 9722.—Taper Plunge Bath, with flanged rim for wood casing. This bath is fitted with copper hot and cold water pipes, overflow pipe at end, and waste pipe. Made in copper, tinned iron, galvanized iron, and three qualities of zinc. Japanned white or marble inside. Can be supplied beaded, instead of flanged, to order.

THE "HEALTHERIES"
SPRAY AND SHOWER BATH.

ASYLUM BATH,
Extra Strong, with Standard Fittings.

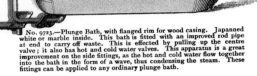

No. 9723.—Plunge Bath, with flanged rim for wood casing. Japanned white or marble inside. This bath is fitted with an improved rod pipe at end to carry off waste. This is effected by pulling up the centre valve; it also has hot and cold water valves. This apparatus is a great improvement on the side fittings, as the hot and cold water flow together into the bath in the form of a wave, thus condensing the steam. These fittings can be applied to any ordinary plunge bath.

SEMI ROMAN BATH.

No. 9724.—Roman Semi-plunge Bath, with flanged rim. This bath has a bronzed iron ornamental border at bottom, and stands on bronzed iron feet, requiring no fixing. It is made of tinned copper, tinned iron, or extra thick copper. Japanned white marble inside and grained oak outside, or Sienna marble inside and green marble outside. Can be had without feet for casing.

THE "BIJOU" GAS BATH.

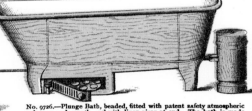

No. 9726.—Plunge Bath, beaded, fitted with patent safety atmospheric gas burner underneath, and with linen airer at end. The bath is made of tinned iron with copper heating plate. Japanned white marble inside and grained oak outside. Can also be made of thick zinc or copper with copper bottom. This bath is suitable for asylums, hospitals, or for private houses where the water is required to be heated in a short time.

HOSPITAL BATH,
Copper or Iron.

No. 9727.—Hospital Bath, on wheels. These baths are specially adapted for use in hospitals, asylums, &c. They are fitted with cast-iron wheels with india-rubber tyres, and can easily be moved from one ward to another, without trouble or noise. They are also fitted with brass tap at end for drawing off waste. Made in copper, tinned iron, or zinc. Japanned white or Sienna marble inside and grained oak or green marble outside.

ROMAN BATH.

No. 9728.—Roman Plunge Bath, with bold flanged rim. This bath requires 1 o fixing, as it stands on massive ornamental bronzed cast-iron feet and border. It is made in copper, tinned iron, or extra thick zinc. Japanned Sienna marble inside and green marble outside. Can be supplied with any of the pipes and fittings illustrated on this page.

No. 9725.—The "Healtheries" Combination Bath. The special feature of this bath is that by pulling out the various valves eight different baths can be obtained, as enumerated below—

 1. Douche Bath.

 2. Wave   ,,

 3. Spray   ,,

 4. Shower   ,,

 5. Plunge   ,,

 6. Sitz   ,,

 7. Cold   ,,

 8. Hot   ,,

THE "CHALLENGER,"
Combined Bath and Boiler.

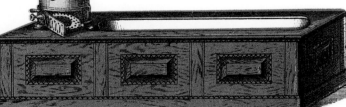

No. 9729.—Combined Plunge Bath and Gas Water Heater. By this arrangement a Hot Bath can be had in ten minutes after lighting the gas; the trouble and expense of connection with kitchen boiler is thus saved. The bath is made of tinned iron or copper. Japanned white or marble inside and grained oak or fancy marble outside. With cast-iron feet. The boiler is made of tinned copper and cased in polished brass. The bath fitted with standard waste and overflow.

CASED BATH,
With Boiler.

No. 9730.—Cased Bath with Boiler. This bath and heater is of similar description to No. 9729, but the bath is made of copper either tinned and polished, or japanned and polished; fitted with improved waste and overflow. The case is made in Mahogany or Walnutwood. The bath and casing can be supplied with water heater, and can be fitted with hot and cold water supply and waste as No. 9723.

WROUGHT-IRON ENAMELLED COOKING & OTHER UTENSILS.

No. 9901 Bowl-shaped Cup and Saucer

No. 9902 Tumbler

No. 9903 Teapot

No. 9904 Can, with hinged cover

No. 9905 Coffee Pot

No. 9906 Drinking Mug

No. 9907 Bell-shaped Cup and Saucer

No. 9908 Deep Milk Pan

No. 9909 Soup Plate

No. 9910 Dinner Plate

No. 9911 Shallow Milk Pan

No. 9912 Drinking Mug

No. 9913 Drinking Mug, with spout

No. 9914 Round Washbasin

No. 9915 Oblong Soap Dish, with drainer

No. 9916 Bowl, with side handles

No. 9917 Chamber Utensil

No. 9918 Straight Pot, with side handle

No. 9919 Round Range Kettle

No. 9920 Range Kettle, with well

No. 9921 Funnel, with handle

No. 9922 French Tea Kettle

No. 9923 Ewer and Basin

No. 9924 Round-bellied Pot, with end handles

No. 9925 Oval-bellied Pot, with side handles

No. 9926 Round-bellied Pot, with bail handle

No. 9927 Oval-bellied Pot, with end handles

No. 9928 Straight Saucepan, with end handles

No. 9929 Round Frying Pan

TRADE MARK

No. 9930 Round Egg Roaster

No. 9931 Bellied Saucepan, with lip

No. 9932 Water or Milk Bucket, with iron handle

No. 9933 Oval Dish Washer

No. 9934 Stewpan, with cover

TRADE MARK

No. 9935 Bucket, with foot and wood handle

No. 9936 Oblong Baking Pan

No. 9937 Oblong Pie Dish, deep

No. 9938 Fluted Gridiron, with well

No. 9939 Round Vegetable Dish, with foot and cover

No. 9940 Round Soup Tureen, with cover

No. 9941 Dinner Plate, with lines

No. 9942 Dinner Plate, with fancy border and centre

No. 9942/1 Dinner Plate, with floral border and centre

No. 9942.2 French Pattern Jug and Basin, with lines

No. 9943 Round Jelly Mould

No. 9944 Oval Jelly Mould

No. 9945 Oval Jelly Mould

No. 9946 Round Border Mould

No. 9947 Round Preserving Pan

No. 9948 Egg Bowl

No. 9954 Parisian Water Jug, brass or copper

No. 9949 Saucepan, with cover, tinned, iron handle

No. 9950 Soup Ladle

No. 9951 Omelet Pan

No. 9952 Canton Water Jug

No. 9953 Bain Marie Pan, with cooking vessels

No. 9955 Frying Pan

No. 9956 Saucepan, with lip, and polished wood handle

No. 9157 Sugar or Butter Saucepan

No. 9958 Stock Pot and cover, with brass tap and inside strainer

No. 9959 Tea Kettle, with barrel handle

No. 9960 Turbot Kettle and cover

No. 9961 Jack or Carp Pan and cover

No. 9962 Oval Stewpan, with cover

No. 9963 Brazing Pan, with plate and cover

No. 9964 Round Stewpan, with cover

No. 9965 Cutlet or Sauté Pan

S.&F. London.

No. 9966 Fish Fryer, with wire drainer

No. 9967 Stewpan, with fire cover

No. 9968 Fish or Egg Slice, tinned

No. 9969 Dripping Pan, with well, on legs

No. 9970 Brass Beer Tap, with loose key

No. 9971 Brass Beer Tap, with fixed key

No. 9972 Baking Sheet

No. 9973 Foot Warmer, desk shape

No. 9974 Foot Warmer, D shape

No. 9975 Carriage Foot Warmer, brass ends, solid screw and handle, covered with carpet

No. 9976 Bed Airer for hot water

No. 9977 Bed Warmer, bottle shape

No. 9978 Potato Knife, wood handle

No. 9980 Garnishing Knife, ebony handle

No. 9981 Cook's Knife, small, ebony handle

No. 9982 Chopping Knife, ebony handle

No. 9979 Onion Knife, wood handle

No. 9988 Larding Pin

No. 9989 Trussing Needle

No. 9683 French Cook's Knife, ebony handle

No. 9990

No. 9996

No. 9984 Lard Knife, ebony handle

No. 9991

No. 9997

No. 9985 Cook's 3-prong Fork, ebony handle

No. 9992

No. 9998

No. 9993

No. 9999

No. 9986 Dishing-up Fork, 2-prong

No. 9994

No. 10000

No. 9995

Nos. 9990 to 9995 Vegetable Scoops, steel, with ebony handles, assorted patterns

Nos. 9996 to 10000 Vegetable Cutters, steel, with ebony handles

No. 9987 Dishing-up Fork, 3-prong

No. 10877 Folding Chair, strongly made and well finished; the wood-work is of polished birch and the carpet is fastened with brass-headed nails

No. 10878 Rustic Flower Stand, strongly made of well-seasoned wood, stained and varnished; nailed

No. 10879 Rustic Garden Table, strongly made of well-seasoned wood, stained and varnished;

No. 10880 Rustic Flower Stand, strongly made of well-seasoned wood, stained and varnished; nailed

No. 10881 Folding Arm Chair, strongly made and well finished, wood-work of polished birch, carpet back and seat, brass nailed

No. 10882 Rustic Garden Seat, with arms and straight back, very strongly made of well-seasoned wood, stained and varnished, and well nailed together

No. 10883 Rustic Stool, made of well-seasoned wood, stained and varnished; nailed

No. 10884 Rustic Garden Seat, with arms, very strongly made of well-seasoned wood, stained and varnished, and firmly nailed together

No. 10885 Folding Garden Seat. This seat can be made to fold as shown in drawing at side; the frame-work is of wrought-iron, japanned green, and the wood-work can be had in pitch pine stained and varnished, also painted green or grained oak

S&F. London.

No. 10885 As folded

S&F. London.

No. 10886 Rustic Garden Seat, with arms, very strongly made of well-seasoned wood, stained and varnished, and firmly nailed together

No. 10887 Wrought-iron Garden Seat, with arms, made entirely of wrought-iron, painted green and varnished

TRADE MARK.

No. 10888 Folding Garden Seat. The back of this seat is made to fold as shewn below; it is very strong, the frame-work is of wrought-iron, painted green, the back of zinc with wood splines, and seat of pitch pine, varnished, painted green or grained oak

No. 10889 The "Parade" Seat, suitable for promenades, public grounds, &c.; the standards are of massive iron, painted; the seat and back of well-seasoned pitch-pine, stained and varnished

No. 10890 Portable Foot Rest, made of well-seasoned wood, painted green or grained oak and varnished

No. 10888 This illustration represents the seat above with back folded on the seat. By this means the seat is protected from dust and rain, and so rendered very durable

No. 10891 The "Lounge" Chair, with leg rest; the seat and back of this chair are made of tinned spiral wire, the frame-work is of wrought-iron, painted green

No. 10892 Garden Chair. The frame-work is of wrought-iron, painted green, the splines are of pitch pine varnished; can also be had painted green with lines of different colour, or grained oak

No. 10893 Circular Seat, with back, made entirely of wrought-iron, in halves, to bolt together round trunk of a tree, painted green and varnished; can also be had without back

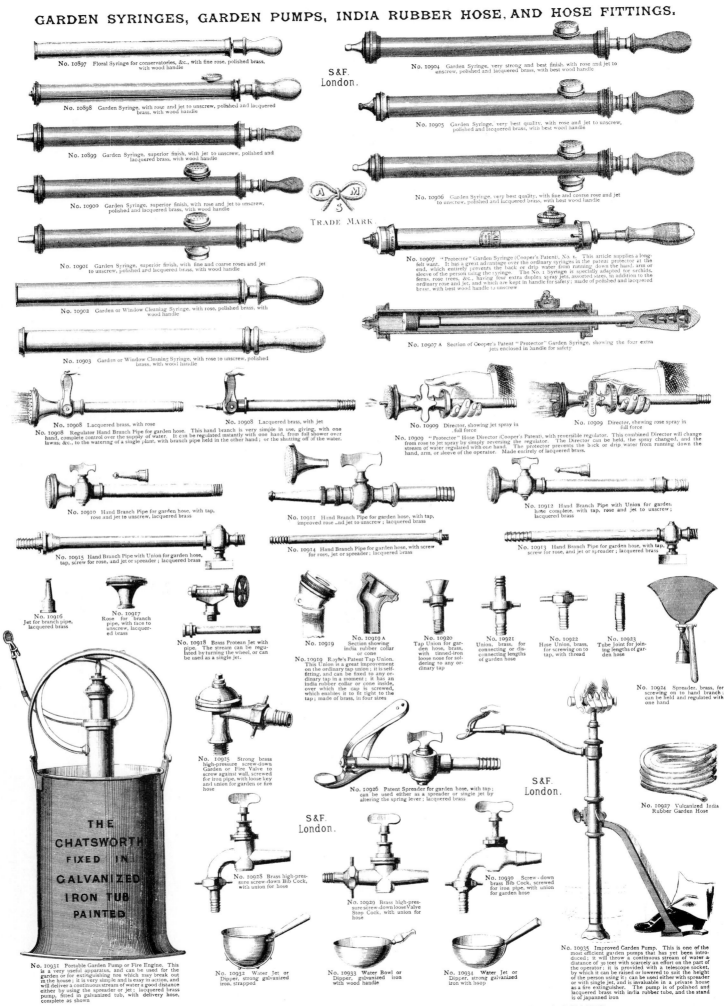

No. 10897 Floral Syringe for conservatories, &c., with fine rose, polished brass, with wood handle

No. 10898 Garden Syringe, with rose and jet to unscrew, polished and lacquered brass, with wood handle

No. 10899 Garden Syringe, superior finish, with jet to unscrew, polished and lacquered brass, with wood handle

No. 10900 Garden Syringe, superior finish, with rose and jet to unscrew, polished and lacquered brass, with wood handle

No. 10901 Garden Syringe, superior finish, with fine and coarse roses and jet to unscrew, polished and lacquered brass, with wood handle

No. 10902 Garden or Window Cleaning Syringe, with rose, polished brass, with wood handle

No. 10903 Garden or Window Cleaning Syringe, with rose to unscrew, polished brass, with wood handle

S&F. London.

TRADE MARK.

No. 10904 Garden Syringe, very strong and best finish, with rose and jet to unscrew, polished and lacquered brass, with best wood handle

No. 10905 Garden Syringe, very best quality, with rose and jet to unscrew, polished and lacquered brass, with best wood handle

No. 10906 Garden Syringe, very best quality, with fine and coarse rose and jet to unscrew, polished and lacquered brass, with best wood handle

No. 10907 "Protector" Garden Syringe (Cooper's Patent), No. 1. This article supplies a long-felt want. It has a great advantage over the ordinary syringes in the patent protector at the end, which entirely prevents the back or drip water from running down the hand, arm or sleeve of the person using the syringe. The No. 1 Syringe is specially adapted for orchids, ferns, rose trees, &c., having four extra duplex spray jets, assorted sizes, in addition to the ordinary rose and jet, and which are kept in handle for safety; made of polished and lacquered brass, with best wood handle to unscrew

No. 10907 A Section of Cooper's Patent "Protector" Garden Syringe, showing the four extra jets enclosed in handle for safety

No. 10908 Lacquered brass, with rose   No. 10908 Lacquered brass, with jet
No. 10908 Regulator Hand Branch Pipe for garden hose. This hand branch is very simple in use, giving, with one hand, complete control over the supply of water. It can be regulated instantly with one hand, from full shower over lawns, &c., to the watering of a single plant, with branch pipe held in the other hand; or the shutting off of the water.

No. 10909 Director, showing jet spray in full force   No. 10909 Director, shewing rose spray in full force
No. 10909 "Protector" Hose Director (Cooper's Patent), with reversible regulator. This combined Director will change from rose to jet spray by simply reversing the regulator. The Director can be held, the spray changed, and the stream of water regulated with one hand. The protector prevents the back or drip water from running down the hand, arm, or sleeve of the operator. Made entirely of lacquered brass.

No. 10910 Hand Branch Pipe for garden hose, with tap, rose and jet to unscrew, lacquered brass

No. 10911 Hand Branch Pipe for garden hose, with tap, improved rose and jet to unscrew; lacquered brass

No. 10912 Hand Branch Pipe with Union for garden hose complete, with tap, rose and jet to unscrew; lacquered brass

No. 10915 Hand Branch Pipe with Union for garden hose, tap, screw for rose, and jet or spreader; lacquered brass

No. 10914 Hand Branch Pipe for garden hose, with screw for rose, jet or spreader; lacquered brass

No. 10913 Hand Branch Pipe for garden hose, with tap, screw for rose, and jet or spreader; lacquered brass

No. 10916 Jet for branch pipe, lacquered brass

No. 10917 Rose for branch pipe, with face to unscrew, lacquered brass

No. 10918 Brass Protean Jet with pipe. The stream can be regulated by turning the wheel, or can be used as a single jet.

No. 10919   No. 10919 A Section showing india rubber collar or cone
No. 10919 Royle's Patent Tap Union. This Union is a great improvement on the ordinary tap union; it is self-fitting, and can be fixed to any ordinary tap in a moment; it has an india rubber collar or cone inside, over which the cap is screwed, which enables it to fit tight to the tap; made of brass, in four sizes

No. 10920 Tap Union for garden hose, brass, with tinned-iron loose nose for soldering to any ordinary tap

No. 10921 Union, brass, for connecting or disconnecting lengths of garden hose

No. 10922 Hose Union, brass, for screwing on to tap, with thread

No. 10923 Tube Joint for joining lengths of garden hose

No. 10924 Spreader, brass, for screwing on to hand branch; can be held and regulated with one hand

No. 10925 Strong brass high-pressure screw-down Garden or Fire Valve to screw against wall, screwed or iron pipe, with loose key and union for garden or fire hose

No. 10926 Patent Spreader for garden hose, with tap; can be used either as a spreader or single jet by altering the spring lever; lacquered brass

S&F. London.

S&F. London.

No. 10927 Vulcanized India Rubber Garden Hose

THE CHATSWORTH FIXED IN GALVANIZED IRON TUB PAINTED

No. 10928 Brass high-pressure screw-down Bib Cock, with union for hose

No. 10929 Brass high-pressure screw-down loose Valve Stop Cock, with union for hose

No. 10930 Screw-down brass Bib Cock, screwed for iron pipe, with union for garden hose

No. 10931 Portable Garden Pump or Fire Engine. This is a very useful apparatus, and can be used for the garden or for extinguishing fire which may break out in the house; it is very simple and is easy in action, and will deliver a continuous stream of water a good distance either by using the spreader or jet; lacquered brass pump, fitted in galvanized tub, with delivery hose, complete as shown

No. 10932 Water Jet or Dipper, strong galvanized iron, strapped

No. 10933 Water Bowl or Dipper, galvanized iron, with wood handle

No. 10934 Water Jet or Dipper, strong galvanized iron with hoop

No. 10935 Improved Garden Pump. This is one of the most efficient garden pumps that has yet been introduced; it will throw a continuous stream of water a distance of 30 feet with scarcely an effort on the part of the operator; it is provided with a telescope socket, by which it can be raised or lowered to suit the height of the person using it; can be used either with spreader or with single jet, and is invaluable in a private house as a fire extinguisher. The pump is of polished and lacquered brass with india rubber tube, and the stand is of japanned iron

FOUNTAIN JETS.

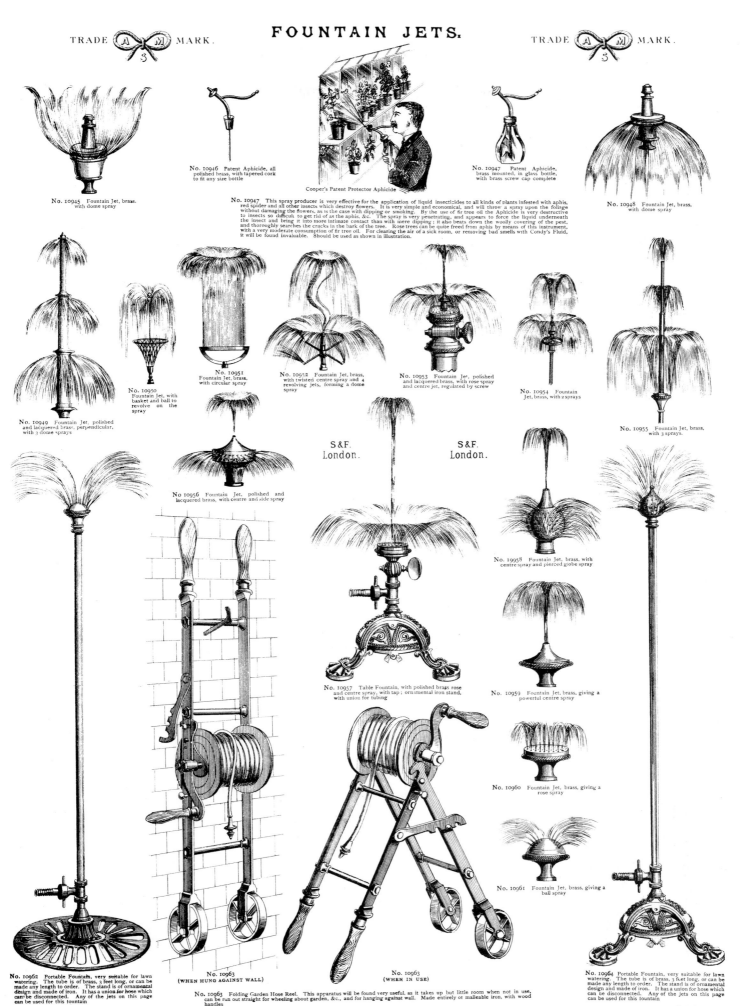

No. 10945 Fountain Jet, brass, with dome spray.

No. 10946 Patent Aphicide, all polished brass, with tapered cork to fit any size bottle

Cooper's Patent Protector Aphicide

No. 10947 Patent Aphicide, brass mounted, in glass bottle, with brass screw cap complete

No. 10947 This spray producer is very effective for the application of liquid insecticides to all kinds of plants infested with aphis, red spider and all other insects which destroy flowers. It is very simple and economical, and will throw a spray upon the foliage without damaging the flowers, as is the case with dipping or smoking. By the use of fir tree oil the Aphicide is very destructive to insects so difficult to get rid of as the aphis, &c. The spray is very penetrating, and appears to force the liquid underneath the insect and bring it into more intimate contact than with mere dipping; it also beats down the woolly covering of the pest, and thoroughly searches the cracks in the bark of the tree. Rose trees can be quite freed from aphis by means of this instrument, with a very moderate consumption of fir tree oil. For clearing the air of a sick room, or removing bad smells with Condy's Fluid, it will be found invaluable. Should be used as shown in illustration.

No. 10948 Fountain Jet, brass, with dome spray

No. 10949 Fountain Jet, polished and lacquered brass, perpendicular, with 3 dome sprays

No. 10950 Fountain Jet, with basket and ball to revolve on the spray

No. 10951 Fountain Jet, brass, with circular spray

No. 10952 Fountain Jet, brass, with twisted centre spray and 4 revolving jets, forming a dome spray

No. 10953 Fountain Jet, polished and lacquered brass, with rose spray and centre jet, regulated by screw

No. 10954 Fountain Jet, brass, with 2 sprays

No. 10955 Fountain Jet, brass, with 3 sprays.

No. 10956 Fountain Jet, polished and lacquered brass, with centre and side spray

S&F. London.

S&F. London.

No. 10957 Table Fountain, with polished brass rose and centre spray, with tap; ornamental iron stand, with union for tubing

No. 10958 Fountain Jet, brass, with centre spray and pierced globe spray

No. 10959 Fountain Jet, brass, giving a powerful centre spray

No. 10960 Fountain Jet, brass, giving a rose spray

No. 10961 Fountain Jet, brass, giving a ball spray

No. 10962 Portable Fountain, very suitable for lawn watering. The tube is of brass, 3 feet long, or can be made any length to order. The stand is of ornamental design and made of iron. It has a union for hose which can be disconnected. Any of the jets on this page can be used for this fountain

No. 10963 (WHEN HUNG AGAINST WALL)

No. 10963 (WHEN IN USE)

No. 10963 Folding Garden Hose Reel. This apparatus will be found very useful, as it takes up but little room when not in use, can be run out straight for wheeling about garden, &c., and for hanging against wall. Made entirely of malleable iron, with wood handles

No. 10964 Portable Fountain, very suitable for lawn watering. The tube is of brass, 3 feet long, or can be made any length to order. The stand is of ornamental design and made of iron. It has a union for hose which can be disconnected. Any of the jets on this page can be used for this fountain

MANUFACTURERS, IMPORTERS, WAREHOUSEMEN AND AGENTS. S&F.

Pawson & Brailsford, Lith. Sheffield

ENTERED AT STATIONERS' HALL.

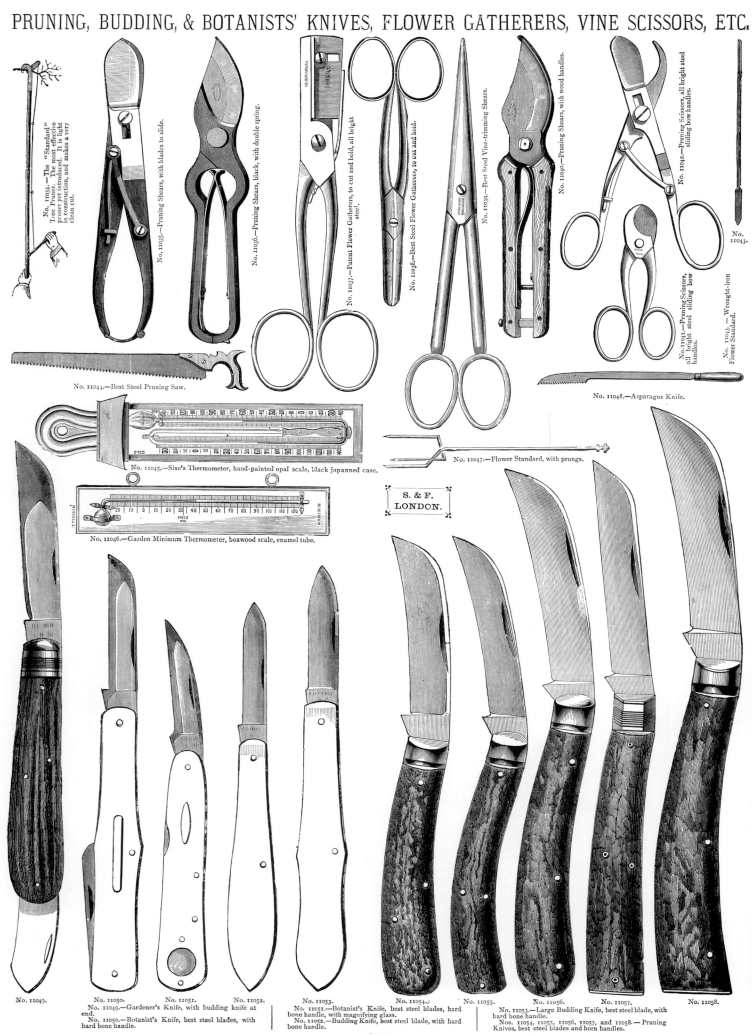

No. 11034.—The "Standard" Tree Pruner. The most effective pruner yet introduced. It is light in construction, and makes a very clean cut.

No. 11035.—Pruning Shears, with blades to slide.

No. 11036.—Pruning Shears, black, with double spring.

No. 11037.—Patent Flower Gatherers, to cut and hold, all bright steel.

No. 11038.—Best Steel Flower Gatherers, to cut and hold.

No. 11039.—Best Steel Vine-trimming Shears.

No. 11040.—Pruning Shears, with wood handles.

No. 11041.—Pruning Scissors, all bright steel sliding bow handles.

No. 11042.—Pruning Scissors, all bright steel sliding bow handles.

No. 11043.—Wrought-iron Flower Standard.

No. 11044.—Best Steel Pruning Saw.

No. 11048.—Asparagus Knife.

No. 11045.—Sixe's Thermometer, hand-painted opal scale, black japanned case.

No. 11046.—Garden Minimum Thermometer, boxwood scale, enamel tube.

No. 11047.—Flower Standard, with prongs.

S. & F. LONDON.

No. 11049.

No. 11050.—Gardener's Knife, with budding knife at end.
No. 11050.—Botanist's Knife, best steel blades, with hard bone handle.

No. 11051.

No. 11052.

No. 11053.

No. 11051.—Botanist's Knife, best steel blades, hard bone handle, with magnifying glass.
No. 11052.—Budding Knife, best steel blade, with hard bone handle.

No. 11054.

No. 11055.

No. 11056.

No. 11053.—Large Budding Knife, best steel blade, with hard bone handle.
Nos. 11054, 11055, 11056, 11057, and 11058.—Pruning Knives, best steel blades and horn handles.

No. 11057.

No. 11058.

TERRA-COTTA TERMINALS, PEDESTALS, VASES, AND TAZZAS, FOR GARDENS, Etc.

TRADE MARK.

S. & F.
LONDON.

No. 11059.—Terra-cotta Vase Terminal.
Height 2 feet 8½ inches, width 1 foot 5 inches.

No. 11060. — Terra-cotta
Obelisk Terminal. Height
2 feet 1½ inches, width 8¾
inches

No. 11061.—Terra-cotta Vase Terminal. Height
3 feet 1¼ inches, width 11¼ inches.

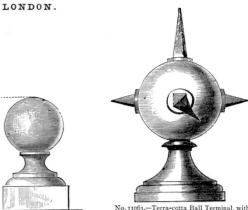

No. 11062. — Terra-cotta Ball
Terminal. Height 1 foot 7 inches,
width 10 inches.

No. 11063.—Terra-cotta Ball Terminal, with
top and side spikes. Height 2 feet 9 inches.
No. 11063A.—As No. 11063, but with top
spike only.
No. 11063B.—As No. 11063, but without
spikes.

PEDESTALS.

No. 11064.—Terra-cotta Pedestal.
Height 24 inches, width 10¾ inches.

No. 11065.—Terra-cotta Pedestal. Height 20 inches, width
10¾ inches.

No. 11066.—Terra-cotta Pedestal, 10½ inches by 16 inches.
No. 11066A.—As No. 11066, but
smaller size, viz. 8½ inches by
15 inches.

No. 11067.—Terra-cotta Pedestal.
Height 19 inches, width 9½ inches.

No. 11068.—Terra-cotta Pedestal.
Height 2 feet 7 inches, width 15½ inches.

No. 11069.—Terra-cotta Vase. Height 16
inches.
No. 11069A.—Terra-cotta Pedestal. Height
14 inches.

No. 11070.—Terra-cotta Tazza. Height 18 inches.
No. 11070A—Terra-cotta Pedestal. Height 29
inches.

No. 11071.—Terra-cotta Tazza. Height 4 feet.

No. 11072.—Terra-cotta Vase. Height 34 inches.
No. 11072A.—As No. 11072, but without handles.
No. 11072B.—Terra-cotta Vase, as No. 11072, but
smaller size. Height 25 inches.
No. 11072C.—As No. 11072B, but without handles.

No. 11073.—Terra-cotta Vase. Height 2 feet
10½ inches.

TRADE MARK.

No. 11074.—Terra-cotta Vase. Diameter 3 feet 6 inches, height 2 feet.

TRADE MARK.

No. 11075.—Terra-cotta Vase. Height 2 feet 5 inches.

No. 11080.—Galvanized Iron Water Bucket, riveted sides.

No. 11081.—Improved Swing Water Barrow, with shafts for pony or donkey. The above is very strong, the cistern being made of riveted wrought iron, galvanized after completion. The spokes are of oval iron, and the axles made on an improved principle. By raising the shafts the tank may be detached from the carriage.

No. 11082.—Galvanized Wrought-iron Tank on wheels, very strong, and specially adapted for removing kitchen refuse, mixing pigs' food, or conveying water, or liquid manure to gardens, &c.

For Garden Hose, Syringes, &c., see page 577.

No. 11083.—Garden Hose Reel, strongly made of wrought iron, galvanized after it is made.

No. 11084.—Improved Swing Water Barrow, with wrought-iron frame and wood tank. The framework of above is made very strong, and the axles are on an improved principle. The tank is made of well-seasoned oak and painted with three coats of good oil colour.

S. & F. LONDON.

No. 11085.—Improved Wrought-iron Swing Water Barrow. These barrows are by far the best value of any in the trade, being extremely strongly made and well finished. The wrought wheels have improved flanged spokes, and the bearings are on the improved principle. The cisterns are galvanized after being made, and are very durable.

CISTERN.

No 11086.—Very strong riveted Wrought-iron Cistern, galvanized after it is made.

No. 11087.—"Duplex" Bee Hive. This hive is constructed with the most modern improvements. It is suitable for either winter or summer. It has nine bar frames for lateral super, which are interchangeable. The super is so arranged as to avoid the risk of taking surplus honey. It is furnished with sliding floor board, and provision is made for supering in roof case. Made of pitch pine, varnished, with white wood lining and fittings.

For further Illustrations of Poultry Houses, &c., see page 586.

TRADE MARK.

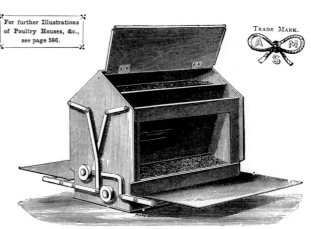

No. 11088.—New Pheasant Feeder. This feeder is so constructed that nothing but pheasants can feed from it. It is sheltered from rain, and is vermin proof. It is very simple and cannot get out of order, and causes no waste. Can be had double or single, painted green, with glass panels, which can be removed for the purpose of cleaning.

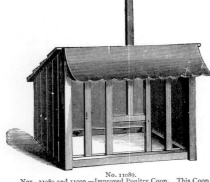

No. 11089.

No. 11090.

Nos. 11089 and 11090.—Improved Poultry Coop. This Coop has been designed by Mr. Wragg, manager to Lady Gwydyr, a great authority on these matters, and is without doubt the very best of its kind. Part of the roof is removable, in order to facilitate the removal of the birds. The illustration No. 11089 shows the coop with the hood on for protection from rain: No. 11090 shows it with the hood taken away, and the shutter let down in front for the night. It is made of pitch pine, varnished, and is very strong.

No. 11091.—Poultry House on Wheels. The framework is made of deal, with varnished pitch pine match boarding for sides and ends, and corrugated galvanized iron roof. It has six separate nest boxes and brood roosting bar, and is capable of housing 12 fowls. The door at side allows easy access to the interior for the purpose of cleaning the house and collecting the eggs, and can be locked at night time, for which purpose a padlock is provided.

No. 11091.

No. 11092.—Wrought-iron Enclosure for Dogs. This enclosure is suitable for fixing against brick kennels, or can be used in conjunction with wood kennels, as shown in engraving.

GARDEN ROLLERS, LAWN MOWERS, WATER TANKS AND CARTS, WATER POTS.

No. 11100.—Rotary Garden Fumigator. By turning the handle the blower sends a continuous current of sulphur, contained in cup, into plants, killing insects, &c. Japanned bronze green.

No. 11102.—Garden Watering Pot, strong, japanned red or green.

No. 11101.—Garden Fumigating Drencher, sulphur contained in tin handle.

No. 11104.—Strawberry Watering Pot, strong, japanned red or green, with hood.

No. 11103.—Watering Pot, with long spout, and brass rose to unscrew, japanned green or red, strongly made.

No. 11105.—The Coventry Lawn Mower, specially adapted for cutting long or short grass, will turn in its own width, and very easy to work.

No. 11106.—Improved Geared Lawn Mower, with patent silent ratchet. This machine is suitable for cutting grass which is very rough and coarse. The wheels are contained in a box, which deadens the noise usually accompanying geared machines.

No. 11108.—Improved Garden Roller, with shafts for horse, pony, or donkey. Double Cylinder. Being made in two parts, these rollers are free to turn on their own axis, and obviates the dragging motion produced on gravel or grass by the single cylinder roller.

No. 11109.—Double Cylinder Garden Roller, with balance handles.

No. 11107.—Single Cylinder Garden Roller, with balance handles.

No. 11110.—Swing Water Barrow with Improved Hand Pump, complete, with lever, spreader, and 18 inches of delivery hose, capable of throwing a jet of water 40 feet.

No. 11111.—Improved Galvanized Wrought-iron Tank on Wheels, with shafts for pony or horse, with pump and 10 feet suction hose, galvanized, wired inside.

S. & F.
London.

TRADE MARK

No. 11112.—Galvanized Tank on Wheels, with shafts for a pony or horse, suitable for conveying water or liquid manure to gardens, &c. This barrow is remarkably compact, will turn in its own length, and will pass through any garden door of ordinary width.

No. 11113.—Galvanized Wrought-iron Tank, on wood wheels, with valve and spreader.

CHAFF AND TURNIP CUTTERS, CORN CRUSHERS, AND OIL CAKE MILLS.

Kibbler for Beans and Peas.

No. 11208.—Kibbler for Beans and Peas. The cutting barrels of this machine consist of single castings with chilled cutting edges, which will kibble either hard or soft beans. The sample is regulated by a set screw.

Improved Circular Chaff Cutter.

No. 11209.—Improved Circular Chaff Cutter. The above is a very durable machine, and is strongly recommended for gentlemen's stables. It is mounted on an open cast-iron column, and will occupy very little room.
No. 11209A as No. 11209, but fitted on strong wooden legs with cast-iron feet.

Chaff Cutter.

No. 11210.—Chaff Cutter, with rising mouth 8¼ by 3½ inches. Cuts two lengths, viz. ¼ inch and 7/16 inch. These lengths can be altered by substituting other outside wheels. It is strong and well made, and can easily be worked by one man. The gearing is protected by a wrought-iron cover.

Kibbler for Oats, Barley, and Malt.

No. 11211.—Kibbler for Oats, Barley, and Malt. The kibbling parts of this mill consist of 2 grooved rollers of unequal diameters, which are case-hardened. The degree of fineness of the sample is easily adjusted by means of a regulating screw.

Improved Oil Cake Mill.

No. 11212.—Improved Oil Cake Mill. This machine is, with the exception of the sides of the spout, made entirely of iron, and can be regulated to break 7 different sizes by means of an eccentric. The mouth is 12 inches wide, and can be made larger by removing the slip plate.

New Pattern Kibbler.

No. 11213.—New Pattern Kibbler. This machine is for kibbling oats, beans, maize, &c. The roller and cutting plate are of hardened steel, they can be easily removed, and the feed adjusted without the aid of a spanner. It is machine finished, and will produce a fine and regular sample.

Improved Disc Turnip Cutter.

No. 11214.—Improved Disc Turnip Cutter. This is a new machine for cutting finger pieces, and is mounted on a strong iron frame with wooden legs. It is fitted with a single concave knife, and cuts finger pieces (⅜ by ¾ inch) for sheep. By the addition of a slicing knife it can be made to cut pieces for cattle. It is also provided with a shield, by means of which it is enabled to effectually cut the last piece.

Improved Oil Cake Mill.

No. 11215.—Improved Oil Cake Mill. This is a similar machine to No. 11212, but much larger and stronger. It breaks seven different sizes, and can be easily worked by one man. Two handles are sent with the machine, which can thus be worked by two lads. The mouth is 16 ins. wide.

Improved Barrel Pulper.

No. 11216.—Improved Barrel Pulper. This machine is suitable for horse, steam, or water power, and will pulp from 4 to 5 tons of roots per hour. It has brass bearings and a large hopper. The barrel is 20 inches in length and 12 inches in diameter.

Gardner's Single-Action Turnip Cutter.

S. & F.
London.

TRADE MARK

No. 11217.—Gardner's Single-Action Turnip Cutter. This machine has 30 knives, and cuts finger pieces (⅜ inch by ¾ inch) for sheep. It has a large hopper. The frame is of iron, with wrought-iron grate, and stands on wooden legs. It is so constructed as to effectually cut the last piece.

Corn, Seed, and Malt Crusher, with Kibbler attached.

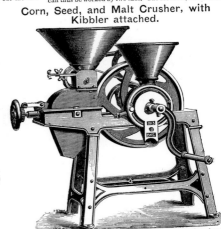

No. 11218.—This machine is adapted for crushing corn, seed, and malt by hand, horse, or steam power. By regulating the feed in the hopper, it will crush from 1 to 50 bushels per hour, according to the quality of the grain and the power applied. It is fitted with an extra large kibbler for splitting beans, peas, and maize.

Chaff Cutter, Circular.

No. 11219.—Chaff Cutter, Circular. Fitted on strong wooden legs with cast-iron feet.

Two-Horse Gear Driving Machine.

No. 11220.—This engraving shows a Two-Horse Gear and Single Gear Intermediate Motion, arranged for driving a chaff cutter and root pulper. A corn crusher or other machine can be driven at the same time. These gears are made in four different sizes, viz. for 1, 2, 3, and 4 horses, and are also adapted for driving thrashing machines. It has a covered wheel, and is fitted with an improved safety clutch, to prevent the poles from running on to the horses when stopped. The pinion shaft of the gear revolves at a speed of 7 turns to one of the horses, and by means of the separate intermediate the speed can be increased to either 19, 22, 26, 32, or 38 revolutions.

Pulper, Stripper, Slicer, or Turnip Cutter.

No. 11221.—This machine can be adapted for any of the above purposes by altering the different discs. The cast-iron cover prevents waste. In ordering it will be necessary to state for which purpose and what discs are required.

No. 11221.

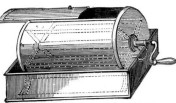

No. 11221A.—"Sussex" Butter Churn, of simple construction, made entirely of strong block tin, with sliding lid and wood handle, fitted in block tin tray. In 5 sizes, to make from 2½ to 28 lbs. of butter.

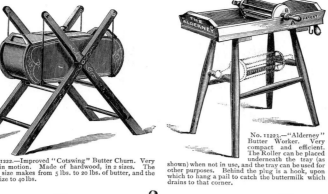

No. 11222.—Improved "Cotswing" Butter Churn. Very simple in motion. Made of hardwood, in 2 sizes. The smaller size makes from 5 lbs. to 20 lbs. of butter, and the larger size to 40 lbs.

No. 11223.—"Alderney" Butter Worker. Very compact and efficient. The Roller can be placed underneath the tray (as shown) when not in use, and the tray can be used for other purposes. Behind the plug is a hook, upon which to hang a pail to catch the buttermilk which drains to that corner.

No. 11224.—Butter Worker or Kneading Machine. This machine has a revolving table, the butter being worked *upwards* by a differential motion of the fluted roller, which effects a rapid and efficient working of the butter.

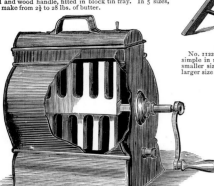

No. 11225.—"London" Butter Churn, of block tin, with sycamore wood beaters, loose tin cover with vent. In 3 sizes, to make 4, 7, or 12 lbs. Very simple in construction.

No. 11226.—Improved Egg Beater. This machine is fixed to an earthenware jar, which can be removed for cleaning purposes. Very simple and efficacious.

No. 11227.— Improved Box Butter Churn. Made of highly seasoned sycamore wood, in various sizes, to churn from 2½ to 25 quarts of milk. Full directions for use supplied with each churn.

No. 11228.— Patent Egg Beater, for beating small quantities of eggs or batter, fitted to an earthenware beating bowl. Directions are supplied with above, giving the proper quantities of ingredients for cake, salad, sauce, &c.

A.—Warm Milk Receiver.
B.—Refrigerator.
C.—Milk Outlet.
D.—Water Inlet.
E.—Water Outlet.

No. 11229.—Patent Capillary Milk Refrigerator. By the aid of this refrigerator, the milk intended for transit or for making of butter or cheese, may be cooled as soon as it leaves the cow, and before any injurious change can possibly have taken place. By passing warm water through the refrigerator the temperature of the milk can be raised to any degree required, which in cold weather is a great advantage in cheesemaking.

TRADE MARK.

CREAM SEPARATOR.

No. 11231.

"De Laval's" Cream Separator. The following are some of the advantages of the separator:—

1. The cream can be separated from the milk immediately after it leaves the cow.

2. From 15 to 20 per cent. more butter can be obtained than by the "setting systems."

3. Great saving in space, time, and labour.

4. Improved quality of butter by this means.

No. 11230.—The "Diaphragm" Butter Churn, octagonal, with unequal sides, the interior perfectly plain, a large perfectly water-tight lid, a solid end piece under each lid, and between these two end pieces a "diaphragm" slides in for churning either milk or cream. Made in hardwood or best oak, in various sizes.

NEW MILK
CREAM.
SKIMMED MILK.

No. 11231.

No. 11232.—Improved Revolving Disc Milk Pan Stand. The revolving discs or tables allow of skimming each pan without having to move from one position. It is very portable, and can be placed in any position desired for ventilation, &c. Made of iron, painted, or hardwood, to hold 6 enamelled iron or earthenware pans.

No. 11233.— The "Ovifer" or Spring Egg Carrier. This useful invention provides an economical, clean, quick, and safe method of packing large or small quantities of eggs, which are securely held between wire springs fixed into tin trays, placed in cases, baskets, &c., for removal.

No. 11234.—"Ovifer" Tray, tin, with handles for placing in cases, &c., to hold 12 eggs.

No. 11235.—"Ovifer" Tin Tray, with sides, to hold 12 eggs.

No. 11236.—Butter Weighing Machine, japanned iron, with gold lines, and earthenware plate.

No. 11237.—Egg Collecting Basket (open or covered), to contain 1 or 2 dozen eggs.

No. 11238.—Tin Hand Case, japanned, with "ovifers," to contain 1 or 2 dozen eggs.

No. 11239.— Milk Can and Carriage. The can is made of strong tin, planished, in various sizes. The carriage is of wrought iron, mounted on iron or wood wheels, and fitted with india-rubber springs to prevent oscillation. Made in various sizes.

No. 11240.—Milk Can Carriage, with 1 or 2 cans. The cans are of strong tin, planished, and the carriage of wrought iron, mounted on wood wheels, fitted with india-rubber springs to prevent oscillation; with name boards complete.

No. 11241.—Milk Can Perambulator. This machine is made very strong and durable. The framework is of wrought iron, the sides and bottom of wood, and mounted on wood wheels, well finished and painted, will carry a supply can and a number of hand cans.

No. 11242.—Milk Cart for Pony or Donkey, of best workmanship, painted, lined, and varnished. To contain 12 gallons, strong tin milk can, with brass bands and tap, and movable box for fixing can, with provision for carrying butter, &c.

No. 11245.—Milk Measure, block tin, with tin or brass over-handle and hook.

No. 11246.—Milking Pail, extra strong tin, with bands and tinned iron bottom rim.

No. 11247.—Hand Milk Can, oval, strong tin, with tin or brass bands and mounts.

No. 11248.—Milk or Cream Bottle, strong tin, with hasp for padlock.

No. 11249.—Milk Kettle, strong tin, with planished cover.

No. 11250.—Milk or Cream Can, strong tin. Can also be had with bail handle and band.

No. 11251.—Milk Measure, strong tin, with tin handle, or brass handle and band.

No. 11252.—Milk Strainer, on legs, block tin, with pierced or brass gauze wire bottom.

No. 11253.—Milk Strainer, extra strong tin, with strong handle and hook, and brass gauze wire bottom.

No. 11254.—Butter Mould, hard wood, assorted patterns.

No. 11255.—Cream Skimmer, strong tin, with round handle.

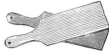

No. 11257.—Butter Slices, sycamore or boxwood.

No. 11260.—Cream Pan, strong tin, half covered, with side lip.

No. 11256.—Cream Skimmer, strong tin, with long handle.

No. 11258.—Butter Beaters, sycamore or boxwood.

No. 11266.—Butter Runner or Roller, assorted patterns.

No. 11261.—Butter Cooler, zinc, with cloth covering, sunk rim to be kept filled with water, ventilated at top.

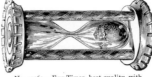

No. 11262.—Egg Timer, best quality, with boxwood ends.

No. 11263.—Butter Crease, boxwood, for forming butter into shape.

No. 11264.—"Signal" Egg Timer, with brass bell, will regulate to 2, 3, or 4 minutes.

No. 11259.—Butter Pats or "Scotch Hands," sycamore or boxwood.

No. 11265.—Milk Saver. This apparatus entirely prevents milk burning or boiling over the saucepan. The milk when boiling rushes up the middle and spreads over the top of the apparatus.

No. 11267.—Butter Print in case, hard wood, assorted patterns.

No. 11269.—Butter Board, hard wood, round.

No. 11271.—Butter Block, for counter, polished marble, well screwed together, with marble or slate bed or slab. Can also be had in black japanned slate.

No. 11272.—Butter Stand, round, china.

No. 11273.—Butter Stand, round, china, with foot.

No. 11274.—Butter Tub, in oak, round, with handles.

No. 11268.—Butter Print, hard wood, assorted patterns.

No. 11270.—Butter Forcer, with four assorted patterns.

No. 11275.—Milk Pan, round, stamped, tinned or enamelled iron, with flanged rim.

No. 11276.—Yoke for carrying milk cans or pails, hard wood, plain ends.

No. 11277.—Yoke for carrying milk cans or pails, hard wood, with ferrules and turned ends.

No. 11278.—Milk Pan, round, stamped, tinned or enamelled iron, wired rim and at bottom.

No. 11279. Drenching Bottle, strong tin, for giving medicine to cows, &c.

No. 11280.—Milking Pail, strong tin, with bail handle, open or with cover.

No. 11281.—Milk Churn, for conveyance by rail, strong tinned iron, with tin or iron bands, and tinned iron side-handles.

No. 11282.—Milk Churn, for dairyman's window, extra strong tin, with brass bands, engraved plate, and brass handles.

No. 11283.—Milk Churn, for conveyance by rail, strong tinned iron or steel without bands, malleable iron top.

No. 11284.—Milk Pan, for counter, extra strong tin, with brass bands and handles.

TRAVELLING REQUISITES,

TRUNKS, PORTMANTEAUS,

HAT AND BONNET BOXES, LADIES' BAGS, TRAVELLING BAGS,

LADIES' AND GENTLEMEN'S FITTED BAGS,

FLASKS, FITTED PICNIC BASKETS,

DOG COLLARS, BASKETS.

TRAVELLING REQUISITES.

TRUNKS, PORTMANTEAUS, HAT AND BONNET BOXES, LADIES' BAGS, TRAVELLING BAGS.

When, more than a quarter of a century ago, we introduced these goods—to the manufacture of which we have always paid special attention—they soon found a ready sale in all markets to which they were introduced. Our customers soon satisfied themselves that, making allowance for the solidity and careful finish of our Leather Goods, they were the best market value obtainable.

The sale of our Leather Goods at the present moment is sufficient evidence that our endeavours to give the best value have been successful.

FITTED DRESSING BAGS,
From 18s. to £250 each.

We beg to draw your attention to the illustrations on pages 651 to 654, which will give some idea of the various shapes, sizes, and qualities of Bags introduced by us.

FITTED PICNIC BASKETS, CANTEENS, AND FLASKS.

The great variety of these goods shown on pages 659 to 661 and 692 justifies us in thinking that a larger assortment has not yet been shown, especially at the low prices quoted.

LADIES' AND GENTLEMEN'S FITTED DRESSING CASES.
From 2s. 9d. to 100 Guineas each.

The illustrations and descriptions on pages 655 and 656 give an indication of the assortment we always keep in stock.

ALL PRICES QUOTED IN OUR PRICE LIST ARE NETT.

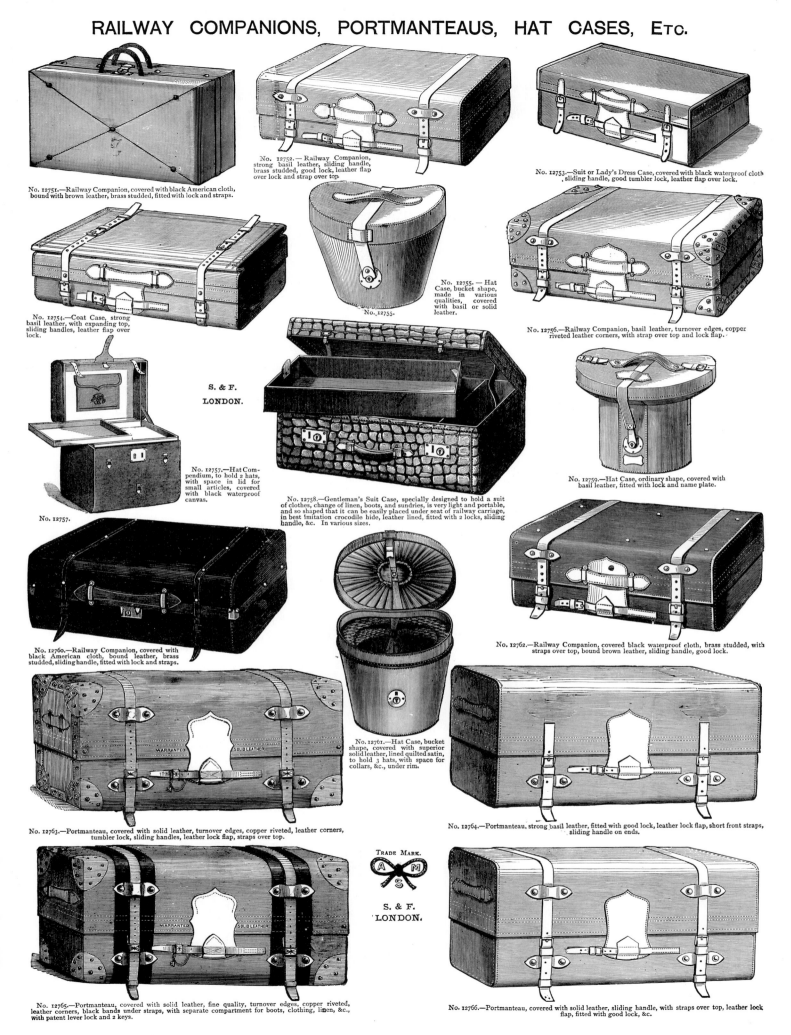

No. 12751.—Railway Companion, covered with black American cloth, bound with brown leather, brass studded, fitted with lock and straps.

No. 12752.—Railway Companion, strong basil leather, sliding handle, brass studded, good lock, leather flap over lock and strap over top.

No. 12753.—Suit or Lady's Dress Case, covered with black waterproof cloth, sliding handle, good tumbler lock, leather flap over lock.

No. 12754.—Coat Case, strong basil leather, with expanding top, sliding handles, leather flap over lock.

No. 12755.—Hat Case, bucket shape, made in various qualities, covered with basil or solid leather.

No. 12755.

No. 12756.—Railway Companion, basil leather, turnover edges, copper riveted leather corners, with strap over top and lock flap.

S. & F.
LONDON.

No. 12757.—Hat Compendium, to hold 2 hats, with space in lid for small articles, covered with black waterproof canvas.

No. 12757.

No. 12758.—Gentleman's Suit Case, specially designed to hold a suit of clothes, change of linen, boots, and sundries, is very light and portable, and so shaped that it can be easily placed under seat of railway carriage, in best imitation crocodile hide, leather lined, fitted with 2 locks, sliding handle, &c. In various sizes.

No. 12759.—Hat Case, ordinary shape, covered with basil leather, fitted with lock and name plate.

No. 12760.—Railway Companion, covered with black American cloth, bound leather, brass studded, sliding handle, fitted with lock and straps.

No. 12761.—Hat Case, bucket shape, covered with superior solid leather, lined quilted satin, to hold 3 hats, with space for collars, &c., under rim.

No. 12762.—Railway Companion, covered black waterproof cloth, brass studded, with straps over top, bound brown leather, sliding handle, good lock.

WARRANTED SOLID LEATHER

No. 12763.—Portmanteau, covered with solid leather, turnover edges, copper riveted, leather corners, tumbler lock, sliding handles, leather lock flap, straps over top.

No. 12764.—Portmanteau, strong basil leather, fitted with good lock, leather lock flap, short front straps, sliding handle on ends.

WARRANTED SOLID LEATHER

TRADE MARK.
S. & F.
LONDON.

No. 12765.—Portmanteau, covered with solid leather, fine quality, turnover edges, copper riveted, leather corners, black bands under straps, with separate compartment for boots, clothing, linen, &c., with patent lever lock and 2 keys.

No. 12766.—Portmanteau, covered with solid leather, sliding handle, with straps over top, leather lock flap, fitted with good lock, &c.

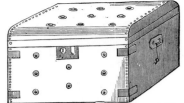

No. 12767.—School or Dress Box, covered black enamel cloth, oval top, studded brass nails, with tray inside, fitted with lock and key.

No. 12768.—Ladies' American Dress Trunk, very superior quality, covered with hide, fitted with patent lock and bolts, brass bound, inside tray, &c.

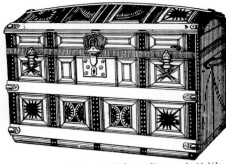

No. 12769.—Ladies' Saratoga Trunk, best quality, covered with hide, fitted with patent lock and bolts, iron bound, lined holland, with various trays and compartments inside.

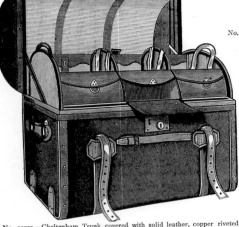

No. 12770.—Cheltenham Trunk, covered with solid leather, copper riveted, sliding handles, ash battens on bottom, 2 straps round, tray fitted with various compartments, as shown in drawing, lever lock, 2 keys.

No. 12771.—Ladies' Saratoga Trunk, very superior quality, covered with hide, fitted with patent lock and bolts, brass bound, inside fitted with various trays and compartments, as shown in drawing.

No. 12772.—American Dress Trunk, flat top, with japanned iron fittings, oak battens, inside tray.

No. 12773.—French Dress Trunk, covered with brown canvas, fitted with patent lock and bolts, japanned iron fittings, oak battens, inside tray.

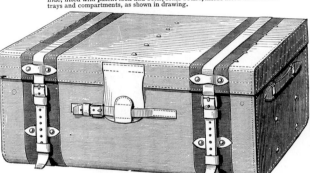

No. 12774.—Ladies' Dress Trunk, covered with solid leather, extra quality and finish, fitted with movable tray, lever lock, 2 keys, straps round, with black painted bands under straps, as shown in drawing.

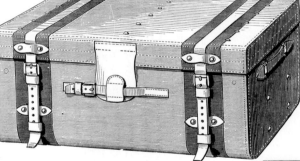

No. 12775.—Ladies' Dress Trunk, covered with black leather cloth, flat top, iron bound, oak battens, fitted with patent lock and bolts, movable tray.

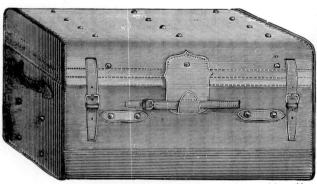

No. 12776.—Dress Trunk, dull waterproof canvas, copper riveted, space in lid, separated by partition, with leather pocket, movable tray, &c.

TRADE MARK.

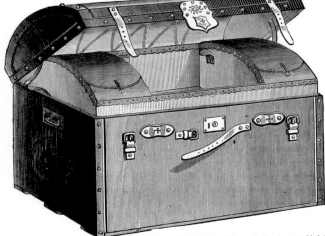

No. 12777.—Overland Trunk (regulation size), covered with dull canvas, bound with brown leather, brass studded, good lock, and straps.

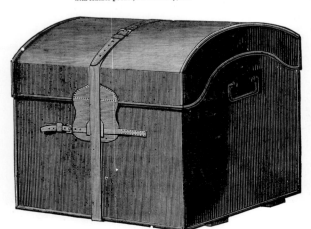

No. 12778.—Ladies' Basket Trunk, covered dull canvas, bound black leather, fitted with tray, good lock, straps, &c.

No. 12779.—Ladies' Cheltenham Trunk, covered with enamelled cloth, bound brown leather, brass studded, fitted with good lock and straps, movable tray, with partitions, as shown in drawing.

GLADSTONE, BRIEF, AND TRAVELLING BAGS, BONNET BOXES, Etc.

S. & F.
LONDON.

No. 12780.—Brief Bag, enamel duck, cloth lined.

No. 12793.—Travelling Bag, best roan leather, lined cloth, nickel mounts.

No. 12781.—Brief Bag, black or brown cowhide, in various qualities.

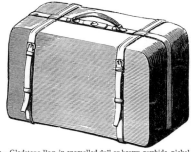

No. 12787.—Gladstone Bag, in enamelled dull or brown cowhide, nickel furniture, superior quality and finish, 16, 18, 20, 22, 24 inches.

No. 12794.—Travelling Bag, roan leather, square top, lined cloth, fitted with nickel lock and clips.

No. 12782.—Expanding Travelling Bag, imitation morocco leather, cloth lined.

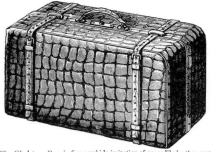

No. 12788.—Gladstone Bag, in fine cowhide imitation of crocodile leather, very superior finish, with nickel mounts and clamps, complete, with straps 16, 18, 20, 22, 24 inches.

No. 12795.—Travelling Bag, expanding gussets, French morocco leather, nickel-plated mounts, with straps round.

No. 12783.—Square-mouth Travelling Bag, in black, brown, or enamel cowhide.

No. 12789.—Gentleman's Handy Travelling Bag, in black cowhide, with nickel lock and clips, 18 and 20 inches.

No. 12796.—Travelling Bag, best roan leather, square top, outside pocket, lined leather, fitted with nickel lock and clips.

No. 12784.—Travelling Bag, enamelled leather, in various qualities and sizes.

No. 12790.—Travelling Bag, French morocco leather, nickel mounts and clips, outside pocket, straps round, 13, 14, 15, 16 inches.

No. 12797.—Travelling Bag, in black or brown cowhide lined leather, with nickel lock and clips.

S. & F.
LONDON.

Manufacturers,
Importers,
AND
Warehousemen.

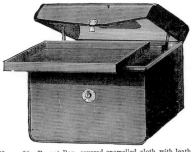

No. 12785.—Carpet Bag, leather bottoms, made in various sizes.

No. 12791.—Bonnet Box, covered enamel cloth, leather handle, fitted with lock and key, in nests of 6 various sizes.

No. 12798.—Venetian Carpet Bag, leather bottom and gussets, made in various sizes.

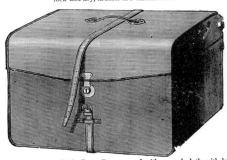

No. 12786.—Bonnet Box, covered enamelled cloth, with leather handle, superior lock and key, inside tray, made in various sizes.

No. 12792.—Bonnet or Light Dress Box, covered with enamel cloth, with leather handle, superior lock and key, inside tray, strap round, in nests of 5 various sizes.

No. 12799.—Ladies' Cap Cases, covered enamelled cloth, with leather handle and gilt lock, in nest of 3 sizes.

No. 12800.—Ladies' Bag, shaped, with gusset, plain calf leather.

No. 12801.—Ladies' Bag, block shaped, calf leather, nickel frame, leather lined.

No. 12802.—Ladies' Bag, block shaped, imitation Russia leather, lined cloth.

No. 12803.—Ladies' Bag, soft gussets, lined leather, with purse inside, calf leather, nickel frame.

No. 12804.—Ladies' Bag, morocco leather, leather lined, gilt frame with ivory mounts.

No. 12805.—Ladies' Bag, flat shape, expanding gusset, with handkerchief pocket outside, in calf leather, lined leather.

No. 12806.—Ladies' Bag, flat shape, expanding gusset with handkerchief pocket outside, imitation crocodile leather, lined leather.

No. 12809.—Ladies' Bag, flat shape, with expanding gusset, handkerchief pocket outside, in chequered Russia leather, lined leather.

No. 12807.—Ladies' Bag, flat shape, expanding gusset with outside pocket, calf leather, lined leather.

No. 12808.—Ladies' Bag, flat shape, with expanding gusset, in chequered Russia leather, lined leather.

No. 12810.—Ladies' Square Top Bag, roan leather, cloth lined, nickel lock.

No. 12812.—Ladies' Bag, square shape, morocco leather, lined leather.

No. 12811.—Ladies' Square Top Bag, roan leather, lined leather, with outside pocket, nickel-plated lock and fittings.

No. 12813.—Ladies' Bag, square shape, calf leather, lined leather, nickel-plated lock and frame.

No. 12814.—Ladies' Bag, square shape, with outside pocket, in calf leather, leather lined.

S. & F.
LONDON.

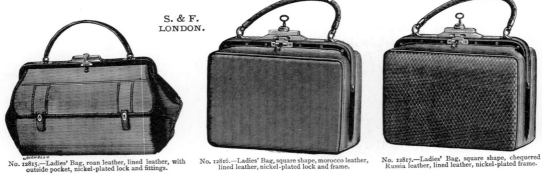

No. 12815.—Ladies' Bag, roan leather, lined leather, with outside pocket, nickel-plated lock and fittings.

No. 12816.—Ladies' Bag, square shape, morocco leather, lined leather, nickel-plated lock and frame.

No. 12817.—Ladies' Bag, square shape, chequered Russia leather, lined leather, nickel-plated frame.

No. 12818.—Ladies' Bag, Russia leather, leather lined, with outside pocket, nickel-plated mounts.

No. 12819.—Ladies' Bag, leather, with outside pocket, lined cloth, nickel mounts, lock and key. 9, 10, 11, and 12 inches.

No. 12820.—Ladies' Bag, chequered Russia leather, lined leather, with outside pocket, nickel-plated frame and mounts.

No. 12821.—Ladies' Bag, roan leather, leather lined, with outside pocket with floral decoration on flap, nickel-plated lock and mounts. 9, 10, 11, and 12 inches.

LADIES' FANCY PLUSH AND LEATHER HAND BAGS, FITTED WORK BAGS.

No. 12822.—Ladies' Handkerchief Bag, in assorted colours of plush, nickel frame, silk lined.

No. 12823.—Ladies' Bag, in best silk plush, stamped to imitate crocodile leather, nickel-plated frame, leather lined.

No. 12824.—Ladies' Bag, flat shape, expanding gusset, best silk plush, nickel-plated frame, handkerchief pocket outside.

No. 12825.—Ladies' Bag, flat shape, expanding gusset, roan leather, lined with leather, nickel-plated frame.

No. 12826.—Ladies' Bag, in assorted colours of plush, leather lined, nickel-plated frame.

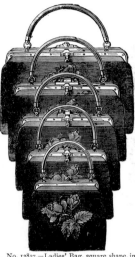

No. 12827.—Ladies' Bag, square shape, in best silk plush, with embossed floral decoration on front, leather lined, nickel-plated frame, $4\frac{1}{2}$, $5\frac{1}{2}$, $6\frac{1}{2}$, $7\frac{1}{2}$, $8\frac{1}{2}$ inches.

No. 12828. — Ladies' Square-top Bag, imitation russia leather, leather lined, with outside pocket, assorted colours, nickel-plated frame, 9, 10, 11, 12 inches.

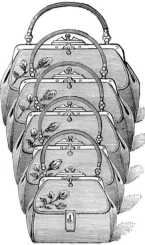

No. 12829.—Ladies' Handkerchief Bag, silk plush, leather lined, with outside pocket, decorated with inlaid coloured flower on flap, $4\frac{1}{2}$, $5\frac{1}{2}$, $6\frac{1}{2}$, $7\frac{1}{2}$, $8\frac{1}{2}$ inches.

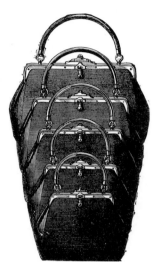

No. 12830.—Ladies' Handkerchief Bag, in assorted colours of plush, leather lined, nickel-plated frame.

No. 12831.—Ladies' Fitted Work Bag, calf leather, lined with satin, fitted with instruments, as shown in sketch.

Ne. 12832. — Ladies' Fitted Work Bag, roan leather, lined with leather, nickel-plated frame, fitted with instruments, as shown in drawing.

No. 12833.—Ladies' Fitted Work Bag, calf leather, lined with leather, with nickel frame and handle, fitted with various instruments, scent bottle, &c.

No. 12834.—Ladies' Fitted Work Bag, square shape, russia leather, lined with satin, and fitted with instruments, as shown in drawing.

No. 12835.—Ladies' Fitted Work Bag, calf leather, lined with leather, nickel-plated frame, and fitted in outside pocket with various instruments, sewing silks, needles, &c.

S. & F.
London.

TRADE MARK

Manufacturers,
Importers,
Warehousemen,
and Agents.

No. 12836.—Ladies' Fitted Standard Work Bag, square shape, russia leather, lined with satin, lift-out instrument board in centre, fitted with instruments for work, two scent bottles, memorandum book, and card case.

No. 12837.—Ladies' Bag and Purse combined, flat shape, with expanding gusset, handkerchief pocket outside, purse inside, morocco leather, lined with leather, nickel-plated frame.

No. 12838.—Ladies' Fitted Standard Work Bag, square shape, calf leather, lined with satin, lift-out instrument board in centre, fitted with instruments for work, two scent bottles, memorandum book, and card case.

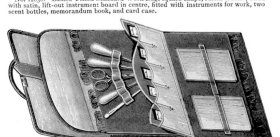

No. 12839.—Ladies' Fitted Carriage Case, in calf leather, lined with leather and satin, fitted with various work instruments, needles, sewing silks, memorandum book, and card case.

No. 12840.—Ladies' Fitted Companion, bag shape, calf leather, lined with satin, fitted with various work instruments, note book, mirror, &c.

COURIER, LAWN TENNIS, AND CRICKET BAGS; SATCHELS, KNAPSACKS, BICYCLE SATCHELS, Etc.

No. 12841.—School Satchel, fancy tweed, leather bound, and with stout leather shoulder strap.

No. 12842.—Courier Bag, fancy tweed, with outside pocket. leather bound, with strong shoulder strap.

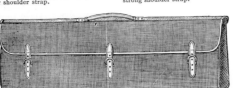

No. 12846.—Lawn Tennis Case, in canvas, brown, slate colour, or blue, leather bound, with leather handle and straps.

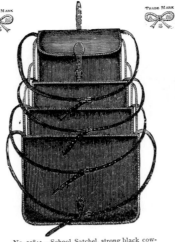

No. 12843.—School Satchel, strong black cowhide, with shoulder strap, 10, 11, 12, and 13 inches.

No. 12844.—Courier Bag, brown waterproof canvas, leather-covered frame, gilt lock and fittings, with shoulder strap.

No. 12845.—Courier Bag, best roan leather, lined leather, nickel-plated lock and fittings, ticket pocket on outside flap, with shoulder strap.

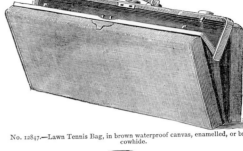

No. 12847.—Lawn Tennis Bag, in brown waterproof canvas, enamelled, or brown cowhide.

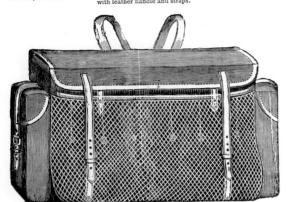

No. 12848.—Game Bag, tanned canvas, leather lined, with network front, leather binding and straps.

No. 12849.—Brown Hide Satchel or Courier Bag, with binding and strong shoulder strap, 7½, 8½, 9½, 10½, 11½, and 12½ inches.

No. 12850.—Cricket Bat Bag, in best Brussels carpet, with pattern, or in plain colours.

No. 12851.—Tourist's Knapsack, waterproof check, drab, or brown material, outside pockets, bound leather, with stout shoulder straps, &c.

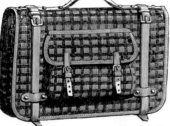

No. 12852.—The "Comfortable" Travelling Bag, waterproof tweed, leather binding, straps, and handle, with numerous pockets.

No. 12853.—Cyclist's Wallet, solid leather. Made in four sizes.

No. 12854.—Tricyclist's Luggage Valise, made in brown canvas, fitted with straps, &c. A thoroughly strong and reliable article.

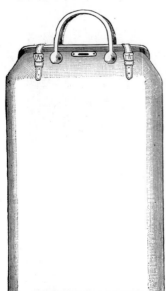

No. 12858.—Brown Canvas Soiled Linen Bag, for use on board ship, &c. Three sizes, 24 by 30 inches, 24 by 36 inches, and 24 by 42 inches.

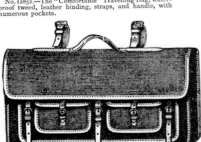

No. 12855.—Tricyclist's Valise, "Multum in Parvo," made in brown waterproof canvas, and fitted complete with straps, &c.

No. 12856.—Yorkshire Water Keg, with shoulder strap and lock, wooden or glass ends.

No. 12857.—Manilla Market Bag. best make. Sizes 12, 14, 16, and 18 inches.

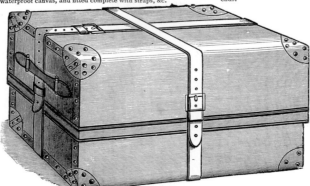

No. 12859.—Sample Cases, solid leather, for carpets or heavy woollen goods, copper riveted, sliding handles, straps, &c.

No. 12860.—Brown Hemp Market Bag, with twisted handle and tassels. Sizes 8½, 9½, and 10½ inches.

No. 12861.

No. 12861.—Ladies' Fitted Dressing Bag, 12½ inches long, in Morocco leather, with outside pocket, nickel-plated double-action lock and fasteners, lined with leather, fitted with glass tooth brush roller, glass soap case, and glass scent bottle, with electro-silver plated mounts, hair, tooth, and nail brushes, comb, mirror, and instrument board furnished with nail scissors, button hook, stiletto, and tweezers.

No. 12862.—Ladies' Fitted Dressing Bag, as No. 12861, but lined with blue watered silk, with additional fittings, viz. leather writing case and patent ink and match cases.

No. 12863.—Ladies' Fitted Dressing Bag, as No. 12862, but with additional fittings, viz. glass powder jar with electro-plated top, clothes brush, and paper knife.

No. 12865.

No. 12864.—Ladies' Fitted Dressing Bag, 12 inches long, in best French roan leather, lined leather, with nickel-plated lock and fittings, containing glass tooth brush roller, glass powder jar with nickel-plated tops, hair brush, tooth brush, and comb.

No. 12865.—Ladies' Fitted Dressing Bag, as No. 12864, but 13 inches long, and with additional fittings, viz. glass scent bottle with nickel-plated top and paper knife.

No. 12866.—Ladies' Fitted Dressing Bag, as No. 12865, but 14 inches long.

> Waterproof Covers can be supplied to any Bag in our list.
> Monograms, Crests, and Engraving of every description on Silver and Ivory.

No. 12867.

No. 12867.—Ladies' Fitted Dressing Bag, 14 inches long, in best French Morocco, with outside pocket, engraved, gilt, or nickel-plated double-action lock and fasteners, lined watered silk, and containing glass soap jar, glass tooth and nail brush roller, glass pomade jar, and glass scent bottle (all with engraved "hall-marked" sterling silver mounts), ivory-backed hair and cloth brushes, ivory glove stretchers, ivory shoe lift, ivory paper knife, tooth and nail brushes, mirror, comb, leather writing case, patent ink and match cases, and instrument board containing nail scissors, button hook, tweezers, crotchet hook, and stiletto, all with pearl handles.

No. 12868.—Ladies' Fitted Travelling Dressing Bag, as No. 12867, but with plated tops to bottles, and wooden back brushes instead of ivory.

LADIES' PATENT TOP DRESSING BAGS.

The fittings in these Bags are arranged in the top or shoulder of the Bag, leaving the whole of the lower part free for clothes, &c.

The fittings can be made either fixed in the Bag or to take out and place on the dressing table (*as shown in sketch*) at the option of the purchaser.

When ordering, please state whether fixed or movable fittings are required.

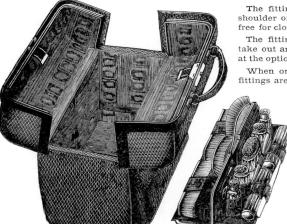

No. 12872 (WITH FITTINGS TAKEN OUT).

No. 12869.—Ladies' Patent Top Dressing Bag, 14 inches long, dead gilt or nickelled, double-action lock and fastenings, in Morocco leather, with outside pocket, containing writing book, patent ink and match cases. Bag lined with silk, and fitted with glass soap and pomade jars, tooth and nail brush, glass, and scent bottle, with engraved electro-plated tops, hair brush, clothes brush, mirror, and instrument board containing nail scissors and four other instruments (with pearl handles), comb, paper knife, and card case.

No. 12870.—As No. 12869, but with sterling silver mounts to bottles, ivory brushes, and thread book extra.

No. 12871.—As No. 12870, but 15 inches long, and with additional fittings, viz. extra scent bottle, ivory-backed velvet brush, and glove stretcher.

No. 12872.—As No. 12871, but in chequered Russia leather, lined with best watered silk, with expanding outside pocket fitted with separate lock. The leather fittings of this Bag are also in Russia leather.

No. 12872 (WITH FITTINGS CLOSED UP).

No. 12873.

No. 12873.—Ladies' Fitted Dressing Bag, 15 inches long, in Morocco leather, with outside pocket, dull gilt or nickel-plated lock and fastenings, lined with leather, fitted with glass soap case, glass pomade jar, glass tooth and nail brush roller, and glass scent bottle (all with plain or engraved electro-silver plated tops), leather writing book, patent ink and match cases, mirror, and instrument board fitted with nail scissors, button hook, tweezers, nail file, and stiletto (all with pearl handles), ivory paper knife, comb, and wood-backed hair and clothes brushes.

No. 12874.—Ladies' Fitted Travelling Dressing Bag, as No. 12873, but with "hall-marked" sterling silver mounts to bottles.

No. 12875.—Ladies' Fitted Travelling Dressing Bag, as No. 12874, but with sterling silver mounts to bottles, ivory-backed brushes and glove stretchers, and one extra glass bottle.

S. & F.
London.

No. 12876.

No. 12876.—Ladies' Fitted Dressing Bag, 14 inches long, in Morocco leather, patent wide opening frame, dead gilt or nickelled double-action lock and fastenings, lined with watered silk, containing glass soap case, glass tooth and nail brush roller, glass pomade jar, glass oil and scent bottles with plain or engraved electro-plated tops, good hair and clothes brushes, tooth and nail brush, leather writing case, patent ink and match cases, thread case, card case, mirror, comb, paper knife, glove stretcher, and instrument board containing nail scissors and four pearl-handled instruments.

No. 12877.—Ladies' Fitted Dressing Bag, as No. 12876, but with sterling silver "hall-marked" tops to bottles.

No. 12878.—Ladies' Fitted Dressing Bag, as No. 12877, but with ivory-backed brushes and superior leather fittings.

**MANUFACTURERS,
IMPORTERS,
WAREHOUSEMEN,
& AGENTS.**

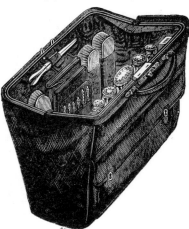

No. 12879.

No. 12879.—Ladies' Fitted Travelling Dressing Bag, 15 inches long, in dark green chequered Russia leather, with engraved and gilt Bramah lock and fastenings, lined with superior watered silk, and fitted with glass soap case, glass pomade jar, glass screw-top powder jar, glass tooth and nail brush roller, and glass scent bottle (all with engraved "hall-marked" sterling silver mounts), ivory-backed hair and cloth brushes, ivory glove stretcher, and paper knife, leather writing book, bevelled-edged mirror, tooth and nail brushes, and instrument board containing nail scissors, button hook, nail file, crotchet hook, and stiletto (all with engraved pearl handles), patent ink and match cases, comb, &c.

No. 12880.—Ladies' Fitted Travelling Dressing Bag, as No. 12879, but with inside leather fittings, writing book, &c., in chequered Russia leather, and card case, thread book and long silver-top scent bottle extra.

LADIES' DRESSING BAGS.

Ladies' Dressing Bags,
WITH FITTINGS ON MOVABLE STAND.

The fittings of these Bags are arranged on a stand in the centre of the Bag, which can be removed and placed on the dressing table.

They also have the advantage of being more easily packed than any others.

The stand can be removed, and the Bag used as an ordinary Travelling Bag, as shown in drawing.

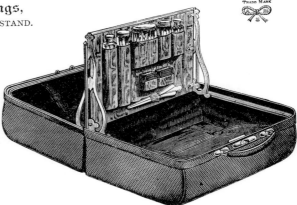

No. 12883 (SHOWING STAND WITH FITTINGS REMOVED).

No. 12883 (SHOWING STAND WITH FITTINGS PLACED IN BAG).

No. 12881.—Ladies' Fitted Dressing Bag, 15 inches long, Morocco leather, lined leather, with gilt or nickelled stand and pockets for fittings, nickelled or gilt lock and fastenings; fitted, on movable stand, with glass soap dish, tooth brush glass, pomade and scent bottles, long oil bottle (all with electro-silver plated tops), wood-backed hair and clothes brushes, tooth and nail brushes, ivory paper knife, writing book, mirror, and instrument board containing nail scissors and four pearl-handled instruments, patent ink and match cases, card case, and comb.

No. 12882.—As No. 12881, but 16 inches long, with inside flaps, bottles with sterling silver tops, hair and clothes brushes of best African ivory, and ivory glove stretchers.

No. 12883.—As No. 12882, but in best chequered Russia leather, lined throughout with best watered silk. The leather fittings are of real Russia, the bag is of the best quality, and highly finished.

> We shall be pleased to submit special Estimates for PRESENTATION and other high-class Dressing Bags free of charge.
>
> Waterproof Covers can be supplied to any Bag at an additional cost, according to size.

Ladies' Dressing Bags,
WITH FITTINGS ON MOVABLE STAND.

No. 12885 (SHOWING STAND WITH FITTINGS PLACED IN BAG).

No. 12885 (SHOWING STAND WITH FITTINGS REMOVED).

No. 12884.—Ladies' Fitted Dressing Bag, 16 inches long, Morocco leather, lined with best watered silk, fitted with Bramah lock. The workmanship in this bag is of a very superior quality. The fittings are the same as in bag No. 12882.

No. 12885.—As No. 12884, but in Russia leather, plain or chequered. The leather fittings of this bag are also in Russia leather; it is fitted with extra stout sterling silver tops to bottles, and thick African ivory brushes.

No. 12886.—Ladies' Dressing Bag, in real Crocodile hide, with fittings on movable standard, as in bag No. 12884, but with the following extra fittings, viz., a screw powder jar with sterling silver top, ivory back velvet brush, thread board, bevelled-edged mirror, instrument board containing two pairs of scissors, five pearl-handled instruments, and tortoiseshell comb.

No. 12895.—Gentlemen's Fitted Dressing Bag, 14 inches long, in black enamelled Cowhide, with outside pocket, lined with leather, double-action lock and fastenings, glass soap dish, glass pomade jar, glass tooth and nail brush roller, and glass scent bottles (all with electro-silver plated tops), writing case, mirror, and instrument board containing nail scissors, pair of razors, button hook, nail file, hair, cloth, tooth, nail, and shaving brushes, patent ink and match cases, comb and strop.

GENTLEMEN'S DRESSING BAGS.

No. 12888.—Gentlemen's Fitted Dressing Bag, 13 inches long, in best French roan, leather lined, nickel-plated lock and clips, containing glass tooth brush roller, glass shaving brush case, glass pomade jar (all with electro-silver plated tops), hair brush, tooth and shaving brushes, comb, strop, razor, paper knife, hand mirror, &c.

No. 12889.—Gentlemen's Fitted Dressing Bag, 14 inches long, in best French roan, leather lined, nickel-plated lock and clips, fittings as in Bag No. 12888.

No. 12890.—Gentlemen's Fitted Dressing Bag, 12 inches long, in best French roan, leather lined, nickel-plated lock and clips, bag with outside pocket, containing glass tooth brush roller, glass pomade jar, glass shaving brush case (all with nickel-plated tops), hair, tooth, and shaving brushes, comb, strop, razor, and hand mirror.

No. 12891.—Gentlemen's Fitted Dressing Bag, as No. 12890, but 13 inches long, and with paper knife extra.

No. 12892.—Gentlemen's Fitted Dressing Bag, as No. 12891, but 14 inches long.

No. 12893.—Gentlemen's Fitted Dressing Bag, as No. 12892, but containing leather writing case and patent ink and light case extra.

No. 12894.—Gentlemen's Dressing Bag, 14 inches long, Morocco leather, with outside pocket, nickel-plated double-action lock and fastenings, lined with black leather, fitted with hair, cloth, tooth, and nail brushes, soap dish, pomade and scent bottles (with electro-silver plated tops), mirror, writing case, shaving brush, razor, nail scissors, button hook, comb, ink and match boxes.

No. 12896.—Gentlemen's Fitted Dressing Bag, 14 inches long, in green Morocco leather, fitted with glass soap dish, glass pomade jar, glass tooth and nail brush roller, glass scent bottle (all with electro-silver plated tops), leather writing case, mirror, and instrument board containing nail scissors, pair of razors, button hook, and nail file, hair, cloth, shaving, tooth, and nail brushes, comb, strop, and patent ink and match cases.

No. 12897.—Gentlemen's Fitted Dressing Bag, as No. 12896, but with sterling silver "hall-marked" tops to bottles, and with ivory-backed hair and cloth brushes.

No. 12887.—Gentlemen's Fitted Dressing Bag, 12 inches long, in best French roan, leather lined, nickel-plated lock and clips, containing glass tooth brush roller, glass shaving brush case, glass pomade jar (all with electro-silver plated tops), hair, tooth, and shaving brushes, comb, strop, razor, and hand mirror.

No. 12898.—Gentlemen's Patent Top Dressing Bag, Morocco leather, fully fitted, electro-silver plated tops to bottles, wooden-backed brushes; with outside pocket, containing leather writing case, and patent ink and match cases.

GENTLEMEN'S FITTED DRESSING BAGS.

GENTLEMEN'S DRESSING BAGS,
With fittings on Movable Stand.

The fittings of these Bags are arranged on a movable stand in the centre, which can be taken out and placed on the dressing table.

They also have the advantage of being more easily packed than any others.

The Stand can be removed and the Bag used as an ordinary Travelling Bag, as shown in sketch.

S. & F.
London.

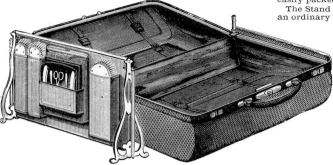

No. 12906 (SHOWING BAG WITH FITTINGS REMOVED).

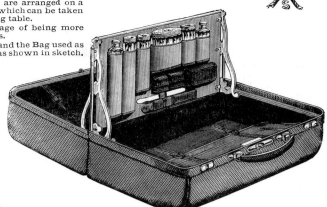

No. 12906 (SHOWING BAG WITH FITTINGS PLACED).

No. 12899.—Gentlemen's Dressing Bag, 18 inches long, in black Morocco leather, lined with leather, nickel or gilt lock and fastenings, with patent end clips to frame, containing the following fittings on movable stand: glass tooth and nail brush jars, glass shaving brush case, glass soap dish, glass powder jar and scent bottle (all with best electro-plated tops), leather writing case, leather-covered mirror, patent ink and match cases, razor strop, paper knife, comb, card case, metallic book, scissors, two razors, button hook, nail file, and corn knife, hair, cloth, and hat brushes (all best make, with wooden backs), and shaving brush.

No. 12900.—Gentlemen's Dressing Bag, as No. 12899, but 20 inches long, and with extra bottle for oil, with electro-plated top.

No. 12901.—Gentlemen's Dressing Bag, fitted as No. 12899, but with sterling silver "hall-marked" tops to bottles, instead of electro-plated.

No. 12902.—Gentlemen's Dressing Bag, as No. 12901, but with ivory backs to brushes instead of wood.

No. 12903.—Gentlemen's Dressing Bag, as No. 12900, 20 inches long, but with sterling silver "hall-marked" silver tops to bottles instead of electro-plated.

No. 12904.—Gentlemen's Dressing Bag, as No. 12903, but with ivory backs to brushes instead of wood.

No. 12905.—Gentlemen's Dressing Bag, in dark green Morocco leather, fitted as No. 12900, but with sterling silver "hall-marked" tops to bottles, and with extra fittings, viz. railway key, barrel corkscrew, and thread board.

No. 12906.—Gentlemen's Dressing Bag, as No. 12903, but in chequered Russia leather, and with ivory backs to brushes instead of wood.

GENTLEMEN'S GLADSTONE DRESSING BAGS.

The fittings of these Bags can be removed at pleasure, as shown in the drawing. They are made in enamelled and brown Cowhide, also in Morocco, are very strong and durable, and well suited for travellers' use.

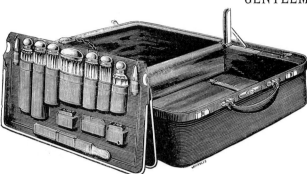

No. 12911 (SHOWING BAG WITH FITTINGS REMOVED).

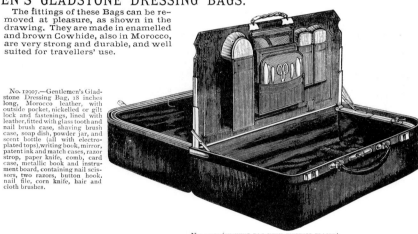

No. 12911 (SHOWING BAG WITH FITTINGS PLACED).

No. 12907.—Gentlemen's Gladstone Dressing Bag, 18 inches long, Morocco leather, with outside pocket, nickelled or gilt lock and fastenings, lined with leather, fitted with glass tooth and nail brush case, shaving brush case, soap dish, powder jar, and scent bottle (all with electro-plated tops), writing book, mirror, patent ink and match cases, razor strop, paper knife, comb, card case, metallic book and instrument board, containing nail scissors, two razors, button hook, nail file, corn knife, hair and cloth brushes.

No. 12908.—Gentlemen's Gladstone Dressing Bag, as No. 12907, but with sterling silver "hall-marked" tops to bottles instead of electro-plated.

No. 12909.—Gentlemen's Gladstone Dressing Bag, as No. 12908, but with ivory backs to brushes instead of wood.

No. 12910.—Gentlemen's Gladstone Dressing Bag, as No. 12907, but 20 inches long, and with extra bottle for oil, with electro-plated top.

No. 12911.—Gentlemen's Gladstone Dressing Bag, as No. 12910, but with sterling silver "hall-marked" tops to bottles, and superior fittings and finish.

GENTLEMEN'S DRESSING BAGS.

No. 12912.—Gentlemen's Fitted Dressing Bag, 16 inches long, in best Morocco leather, lined with leather, nickel-plated lock and fittings, and containing glass soap dish, glass powder jar, and glass tooth and nail brush roller (all with electro-plated tops), hair brush, clothes brush, tooth, nail, and shaving brushes, leather writing case, leather-covered mirror, instrument board containing two razors and one pair of nail scissors, razor strop, patent ink and light cases, and ivory paper knife. The whole of these fittings are conveniently arranged in the outside pocket of the bag, leaving the whole of the interior free for packing.

No. 12913.—Gentlemen's Dressing Bag, 15 inches long, in green or red chequered Russia leather, with outside pocket lined dark blue roan, gilt lever lock and fastenings, fitted with glass tooth brush case, shaving brush case, and soap case, pomade jar and scent bottle (all with engine-turned sterling silver mounts), with screw wood-back hair, cloth, and hat brushes, writing case, bevelled edge mirror, instrument board containing nail scissors, two ivory-handled razors, button hook, nail file, and corn knife, patent ink and match case, razor strop, paper knife, and comb.

No. 12914.—As No. 12913, but with extra fittings, viz. long scent bottle, thread book, card case, best African ivory brushes, ivory-handled razor strop, and ivory comb. The leather fittings of this Bag are covered with Russia leather.

No. 12915.—Gentlemen's Fitted Dressing Bag, in Cowhide, stamped in imitation of crocodile, 22 inches long, leather lined, with outside pocket, strap, and nickel-plated lock and fittings. The fittings are arranged on a movable board, which can be readily taken from the bag and placed upon the dressing table, and consist of glass soap dish, glass tooth brush roller, glass shaving brush roller, glass powder jar (all with dome-shape electro-plated tops), hair brush, hat and cloth brush, tooth, nail, and shaving brushes, comb, razor strop, and ivory paper knife, patent ink and light case, leather writing case, leather-covered mirror, and instrument board containing two razors, button hook, nail file, and pair of nail scissors.

No. 12916.—Gentlemen's Gladstone Dressing Bag, best Cowhide, 18 inches long, containing hair, tooth, nail, and shaving brushes, comb, strop, pair of razors, nail scissors, mirror, soap case, &c.

No. 12917.—Gentlemen's Gladstone Dressing Bag, best Cowhide leather, with strong lock and sliding clips, lined with stout cloth, completely fitted, cut glass bottles, good serviceable brushes, and superior English cutlery, &c., 16 inches, 18 inches, and 20 inches long.

No. 12918.—As No. 12917, but lined throughout with leather.

No. 12912.

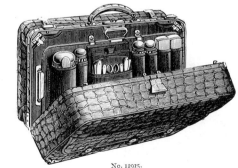

No. 12915.

No. 12913

No. 12916.

GENTLEMEN'S FITTED DRESSING BAGS.

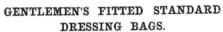

GENTLEMEN'S DRESSING BAGS,
With Fittings on Movable Stand.

The fittings of these Bags are arranged on a movable Stand in the centre, which can be taken out and placed on the dressing table.

They also have the advantage of being more easily packed than any others.

The Stand can be removed and the Bag used as an ordinary Travelling Bag, as shown in sketch.

S. & F.
LONDON.

No. 12919.

No. 12921.

GENTLEMEN'S FITTED STANDARD DRESSING BAGS.

No. 12919.—Gentleman's Fitted Standard Dressing Bag, 18 inches long, made in chequered Russia leather, and containing cut glass soap jar, glass shaving brush case, glass tooth and nail brush case, scent bottle, oil bottle, screw-top powder jar (all with sterling silver "hall-marked" tops), plated cork-screw and railway key, tooth, nail, and shaving brush, two ivory-backed hair brushes, ivory-backed clothes brush, ivory-backed hat brush, fitted housewife, card case and note book in Russia leather to match the bag, Russia leather covered mirror, razor strop, comb, and paper knife, and cutlery board which contains two razors, pair of nail scissors, button hook, nail file, and corn knife. In the outside pocket is a Russia leather writing case, and patent ink and light case, also covered in Russia leather.

No. 12920.—Gentleman's Fitted Standard Dressing Bag as No. 12919, but 20 inches long.

GENTLEMEN'S GLADSTONE DRESSING BAGS.

Fitted with movable Stand in centre, which always remains upright when in the Bag.

No. 12921.—Gentleman's Gladstone Dressing Bag, 18 inches long, in Morocco leather, with outside pocket, nickelled or gilt lock and fastenings, lined leather, containing glass tooth and nail brush case, shaving brush case, tooth powder jar, and scent bottle (all with electro-plated tops), hair and cloth brushes, writing book, mirror, patent ink and match cases, razor strop, paper knife, comb, card case, metallic book, and instrument board containing nail scissors, two razors, button hook, nail file, and corn knife.

No. 12922.—Gentleman's Gladstone Dressing Bag, as No. 12921, but with sterling silver "hall-marked" tops to bottles.

No. 12923.—Gentleman's Gladstone Dressing Bag, as No. 12921, but with sterling silver "hall-marked" tops to bottles, and best *ivory-backed* brushes.

No. 12924.—Gentleman's Gladstone Dressing Bag, as No. 12921, but 20 inches long, and fitted with extra perfume bottle and hat brush.

No. 12925.—Gentleman's Gladstone Dressing Bag, as No. 12924, but with sterling silver "hall-marked" tops to bottles.

No. 12926.—Gentleman's Gladstone Dressing Bag, as No. 12924, but with sterling silver "hall-marked" tops to bottles, and best *ivory-backed* brushes.

No. 12931.
(SHOWING BAG WITH FITTINGS CLOSED UP.)

No. 12927.

GENTLEMEN'S FITTED GLADSTONE DRESSING BAGS.

No. 12927.—Gentleman's Fitted Gladstone Dressing Bag, 20 inches long, in enamelled, brown, or dull cowhide, with nickel-plated lock and fittings, outside straps, &c., and containing metal soap case, cut glass tooth and nail brush roller, glass shaving brush roller, glass powder jar, and perfume bottle (all with electro-plated tops), wooden-backed hair and clothes brushes, tooth, nail, and shaving brushes, leather-covered mirror, comb and razor strop, and cutlery board containing two razors and pair of nail scissors.

No. 12928.—Gentleman's Fitted Gladstone Dressing Bag, 18 inches long, in enamelled, brown, or dull cowhide, with nickel-plated lock and fittings, outside straps, &c., and containing metal soap case, cut glass tooth and nail brushes roller, glass shaving brushes roller, glass powder jar (all with electro-plated tops), wooden-backed hair and clothes brushes, tooth, nail, and shaving brushes, leather-covered mirror, comb and razor strop, and cutlery board containing two razors and pair of nail scissors.

No. 12931.
(SHOWING FITTINGS OPEN READY FOR USE.)

No. 12929.

GENTLEMEN'S STANDARD DRESSING BAGS.

No. 12929.—Gentleman's Fitted Standard Dressing Bag, in real crocodile hide, 18 inches long, with pocket outside, Bramah lock, folio lock on outside pocket, lined best blue roan, and containing cut glass soap jar, glass shaving brush case, glass tooth and nail brush case, scent bottle, oil bottle, screw-top powder jar (all with sterling silver "hall-marked" tops), plated corkscrew and railway key, tooth, nail, and shaving brushes, two hair brushes, cloth and hat brushes, fitted housewife, card case and note book, leather-covered mirror, razor strop, comb, and paper knife, leather writing case and patent ink and light cases, and cutlery board which contains two razors, pair of nail scissors, button hook, nail file, and corn knife.

No. 12930.—Gentleman's Fitted Standard Dressing Bag, as No. 12929, but 20 inches long, and with *ivory-backed* brushes.

No. 12940.
(WITH FITTINGS CLOSED UP.)

GENTLEMEN'S PATENT TOP DRESSING BAGS.

The fittings in these Bags are arranged in the top or shoulder of the Bag, leaving the whole of the bottom part free for Linen, &c.

The fittings can be removed and the Bag used as an ordinary Travelling Bag.

GENTLEMEN'S PATENT TOP DRESSING BAGS.

The fittings in these Bags are arranged in the top or shoulder of the Bag, leaving the whole of the bottom part free for Linen, &c.

No. 12931.—Gentleman's Patent Top Dressing Bag, 14 inches long, in Morocco leather, lined with leather, with nickelled or gilt lock and fastenings, outside pocket, containing writing case and ink and match cases, fitted with glass tooth and nail brush cases, soap dish, pomade jar, and scent bottle (all with electro-plated tops), hair, cloth, tooth, nail, and shaving brushes, mirror, razor strop, paper knife, and comb, and instrument board containing two razors, nail scissors, button hook, and nail file.

No. 12932.—Gentleman's Patent Top Dressing Bag, as No. 12931, but with sterling silver "hall-marked" tops to bottles.

No. 12933.—Gentleman's Patent Top Dressing Bag, as No. 12932, but with ivory-backed hair and cloth brushes, ivory-handled razors, and separate lock to outside pocket.

No. 12934.—Gentleman's Patent Top Dressing Bag, as No. 12931, but 16 inches long, and with extra scent bottle and hat brush.

No. 12935.—Gentleman's Patent Top Dressing Bag, as No. 12934, but with sterling silver "hall-marked" tops to bottles.

No. 12936.—Gentleman's Patent Top Dressing Bag, as No. 12935, but with ivory-backed hair and cloth brushes, ivory-handled razors, and separate lock to outside pocket.

No. 12937.—Gentleman's Patent Top Dressing Bag, as No. 12931, but 16 inches long, and containing extra glass brush case and scent bottle (with electro-plated tops), and hat brush.

No. 12938.—Gentleman's Patent Top Dressing Bag, as No. 12937, but with sterling silver "hall-marked" tops to bottles.

No. 12939.—Gentleman's Patent Top Dressing Bag, as No. 12938, but with ivory-backed hair and cloth brushes, ivory-handled razors, and with separate lock to outside pocket.

No. 12940.
(WITH FITTINGS TAKEN OUT.)

No. 12940.—Gentleman's Patent Top Dressing Bag, 15 inches long, in best chequered Russia leather, lined with leather, fitted with lever lock and separate lock to outside pocket, and containing glass tooth and nail brush case, soap dish, tooth powder jar, and scent bottle (all with sterling silver "hall-marked" tops), mirror, hair, cloth, hat, tooth, nail, and shaving brushes, razor strop, comb, and paper knife, and instrument board containing two razors, nail scissors, button hook, and nail file. The outside pocket contains a leather writing case and patent ink and match cases.

No. 12941.—Gentleman's Patent Top Dressing Bag, as No. 12940, but 16 inches long.

No. 12942.—Gentleman's Patent Top Dressing Bag, as No. 12941, but with *ivory-backed* brushes.

LADIES' AND GENTLEMEN'S LEATHER-COVERED DRESSING CASES.

No. 12963 Gentlemen's Dressing Case, containing razor, strop, comb and tooth brush; size 6¼ by 3½ by 1 inch

No. 12964 As No. 12963, but fitted for Ladies' use.

No. 12965 Gentlemen's Dressing Case, containing 2 razors, razor strop, comb, tooth and shaving brushes and mirror; size 6½ by 4½ by 1½ inch

No. 12966 As No. 12965, but fitted for Ladies' use

No. 12967 Gentlemen's Dressing Case, containing looking glass, 2 razors, razor-strop, hair, hat and shaving brushes; size 7 by 3½ by 2 inch

No. 12968 Gentlemen's Dressing Case, containing hair brush, metal soap dish, mirror, tooth, nail, and shaving brushes, razor, strop and comb; size 7 by 3 by 2¼ inch

No. 12969 As No. 12968, but fitted for Ladies' use

S&F. London.

No. 12970 Gentlemen's Dressing Case, containing hair, cloth, tooth and nail brushes, shaving brush, mirror, metal soap dash, razor, strop and comb; size 6½ by 4½ by 2½ inch

No. 12971 As No. 12970, but fitted for Ladies' use

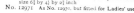

No. 12972 Gentlemen's Dressing Case, containing hair, tooth, nail and shaving brushes, comb, 2 razors, razor strop, metal soap box, scissors and mirror; size 7½ by 5½ by 2½ inch

No. 12973 Gentlemen's Dressing Case, containing hair, cloth, tooth and nail brushes, turn-back shaving brush, 2 razors, razor strop, comb, mirror and metal soap box; size 7⅞ by 5 by 3½ inch

No. 12974 As No. 12973, but fitted for Ladies' use

No. 12975 Gentlemen's Dressing Case, containing hair, tooth, nail and shaving brushes, tooth powder box, 2 razors, razor strop, comb, scissors, soap box and mirror; size 7 by 6 by 3½ inch

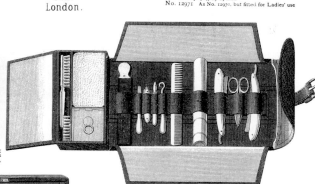

No 12976 Gentlemen's roll-up Dressing Case, containing hair, tooth, nail and shaving brushes, soap box, bone roller, 2 razors, razor strop, comb, scissors, penknife, nail cleaner, button hook and tweezers; size 7¼-in. long, 6-in. wide, and 3½-in. thick

TRADE MARK.

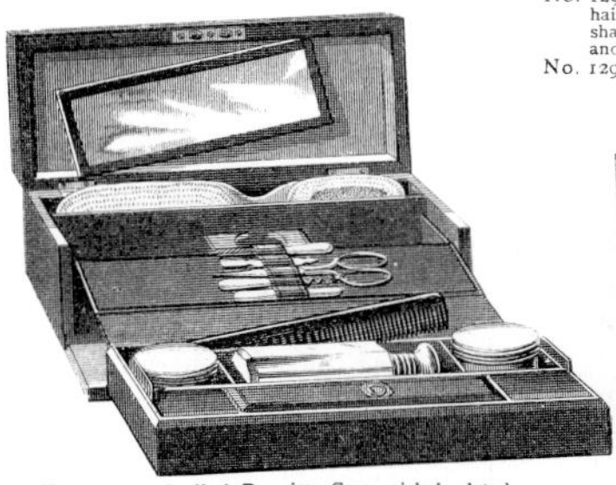

No. 12977 Ladies' Dressing Case, nickel plated handle on top, containing hair, cloth, tooth and nail brushes, cut glass scent bottle, and 2 glass jars with plated tops, comb, scissors, penknife, corkscrew, nail file, scoop, and mirror, with velvet-lined partition for jewellery; size 11 by 6 by 4½ in.

No. 12978 As No. 12977, but fitted for Gentlemen's use

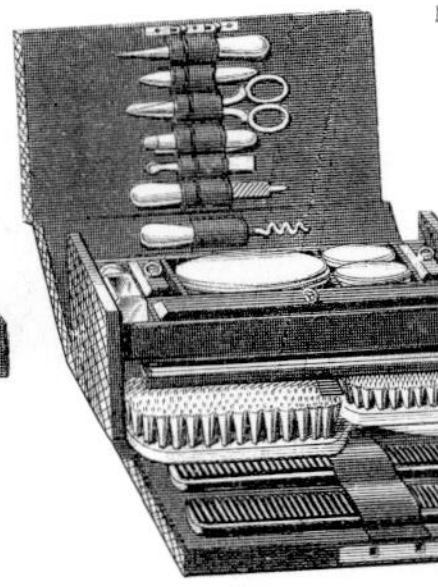

No. 12979 Gentlemen's Dressing Case, covered with Russian leather, handle on top, containing cloth, hair, hat, tooth, nail and shaving brushes, 2 razors, razor strop, comb, 2 pairs scissors, cork-screw, button hook, knife, nail cleaner, tweezers, soap jar, scent bottle and 2 glass jars with plated tops, looking glass and small compartment for rings, &c.; size 8½ by 6½ by 4½ inch

No. 12980 As No. 12979, but fitted for Ladies' use

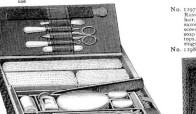

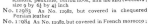

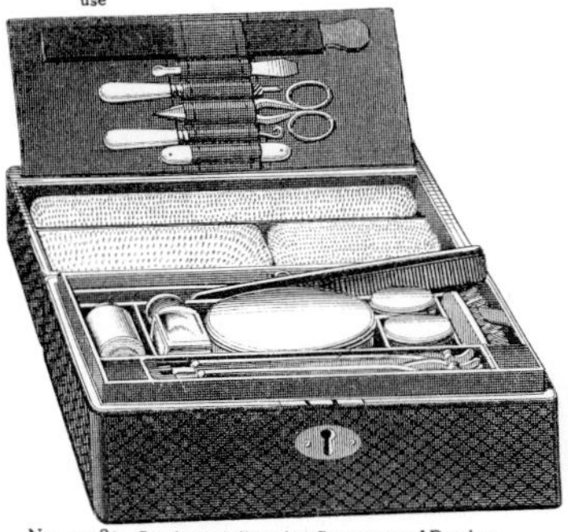

No. 12982 Gentlemen's Dressing Case, covered Russian leather, sunk handle, containing glass soap dish and 2 pomade pots with plated tops, scent bottle, shaving brush, tooth and nail brushes, comb and pair of best razors; hair, cloth and nail brushes, razor strop, nail scissors, penknife, button hook, nail file and tweezers; size 9 by 6½ by 4½ inch

No. 12983 As No. 12982, but covered in chequered Persian leather

No. 12984 As No. 12982, but covered in French morocco; Dressing Cases Nos. 12982, 12983, and 12984 can be had fitted for Ladies' use at the same prices

No. 12985 Gentlemen's Dressing Case, covered chequered Persian leather, containing glass soap dish, and 2 pomade jars with plated tops, hair, cloth, tooth, nail and shaving brushes, 2 razors, comb and strop, with mirror in lid; size 8 by 7 by 4½ inch

No. 12986 As No. 12985, but fitted for Ladies' use

No. 12981 Ladies' Dressing Case, covered Russian leather, lined with leather, nickel plated handle on lid, bevelled mirror, containing hair, velvet and cloth brushes, tooth and nail brushes in glass jar, soap dish, 2 jars and 2 scent bottles with electro-plated tops, comb, 2 pairs scissors, knife, button hook and compartment for jewellery; size 12 by 7 by 5½ inch

No. 12987 Gentlemen's Dressing Case, covered chequered Persian leather, containing glass soap dish, 2 pommade jars, glass roller for shaving brush, glass tooth and nail roll with plated tops, hair, cloth, tooth, nail and shaving brushes, comb, razor strop, 2 razors and bevelled edge mirror; size 10 by 7½ by 4 inch

No. 12988 As No. 12987, but fitted for Ladies' use

S&F. London.

No. 12989 Gentlemen's Dressing Case, covered chequered Persian leather, containing glass soap dish, 2 pommade jars, glass roller for shaving brush, glass tooth and nail roll and perfume bottle with plated tops, hair, cloth, hat, tooth, nail and shaving brushes, comb, strop, 2 razors, 2 pairs of scissors, penknife, tweezers, button hook, nail file and bevelled edge mirror; size 10 by 7 by 5½ inch

No. 12990 As No. 12989, but fitted for Ladies' use

No. 12991 Gentlemen's Dressing Case, covered Russian leather, engraved sunk gilt handle on lid, mirror in head, and containing 2 large cut glass bottles, oval jar, soap tray, nail and tooth brush trays, 2 small jars and shaving brush in plated and engraved case; all tops are best electro-plated and richly engraved; strop, comb and partition for jewellery; hair, hat and cloth brushes; the cutlery is contained in a spring drawer at side of case, and consists of 1 pair of razors, corn knife, nail file, button hook, tweezers and corkscrew, all with ivory handles, and 2 pairs scissors; size 11 by 9 by 7 inch

No. 12991a As No. 12991, but fitted for Ladies' use, containing 2 large hair brushes, comb, mirror, 5 long cut glass jars and bottles, cut glass trays for tooth and nail brushes, soap dish and 2 small jars, all with electro-plated and richly engraved tops; velvet block, containing scissors, penknife, nail file, and button hook with pearl handle, bodkin, and case for jewellery; size 11 by 8½ by 6½ inch

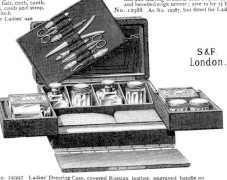

No. 12992 Ladies' Dressing Case, covered Russian leather, engraved handle on lid, reversible mirror in head, containing glove stretchers, 2 pairs scissors, fluted pearl handle knife, tweezers, corkscrew, stiletto, button hook, 4 long jars and bottles, hair and velvet brushes, comb, tooth and nail brushes; 2 cut glass jars and nail brush tray; large perfume bottle and soap dish; all tops are best electro-plated and richly engraved; size 10¼ by 8 by 5½ inch

No. 12992a As No. 12992, but fitted for Gentlemen's use; containing reversible mirror, 2 best razors, 2 pairs scissors, corn knife, button hook, nail file, tweezers, corkscrew; 4 long bottles, hair and hat brushes, tooth and nail brushes, comb and strop; badger-hair shaving brush and soap tray; 2 glass jars and nail brush tray; all tops are best electro-plated and richly engraved

No. 12993 Ladies' Dressing and Jewel Case combined, covered Persian leather, fall-down front, swinging bevelled edge mirror in velvet frame inside lid, nickel plated handle on top, containing hair, hat, tooth and nail brushes, comb, scissors, stiletto, button hook, crochet hook, tweezers, cut glass scent bottle and 2 glass jars with plated tops, and 2 jewel drawers lined with velvet and satin; size of case 9¾ by 7 by 8½ inch

MANUFACTURERS, IMPORTERS, WAREHOUSEMEN AND AGENTS.

SOLID-LEATHER DRESSING CASES.

TRADE MARK.

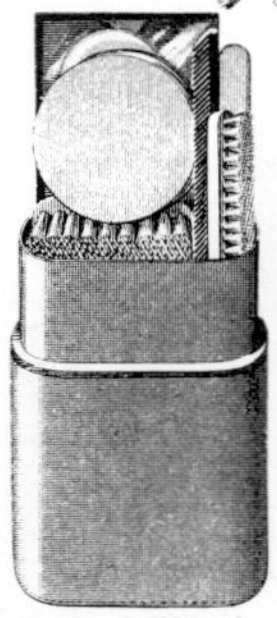

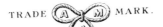

No. 12994 Solid-leather Dressing Case, containing hair, tooth and nail brushes, comb, mirror and metal soap box; size, $7 \times 3\frac{3}{4} \times 1\frac{1}{2}$ in.

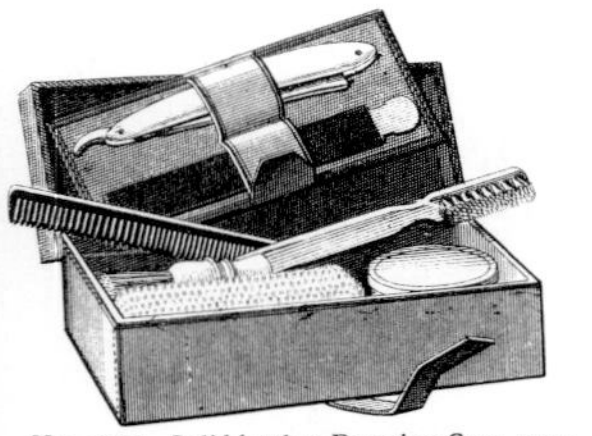

No. 12995 Solid-leather Dressing Case, containing hair, tooth and shaving brushes, razor, strop, comb and metal soap box; size, $7\frac{1}{2} \times 3\frac{1}{2} \times 2$ in.

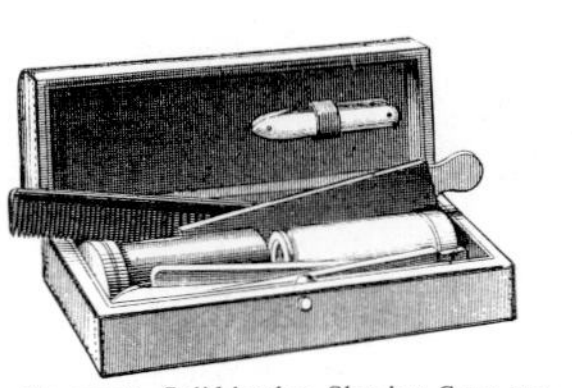

No. 12996 Solid-leather Shaving Case, containing 1 pair razors, comb, razor strop, turn-back shaving brush, metal case to hold Pears's shaving stick, and penknife; size, $6\frac{3}{4} \times 3 \times 1\frac{3}{4}$ in.

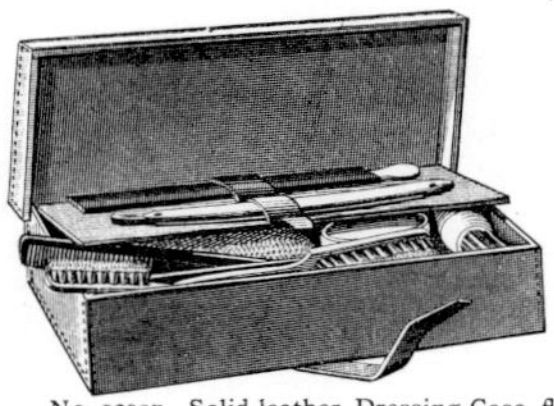

No. 12997 Solid-leather Dressing Case, flat, containing hair, tooth and nail brushes in metal case, metal soap box, comb, mirror, nail scissors, button hook and nail trimmer; size, $7\frac{1}{2} \times 4 \times 2$ in.

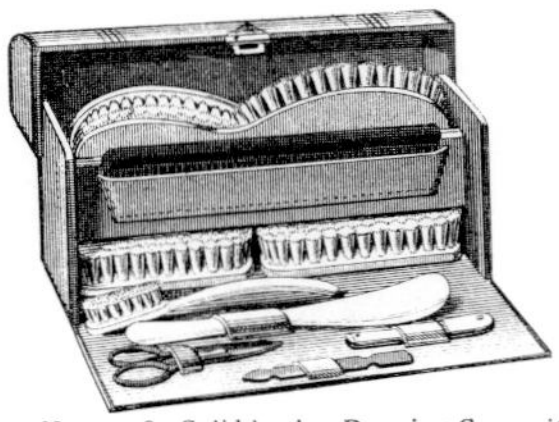

No. 12998 Solid-leather Dressing Case, with nickel-plated lock, containing 1 pair long handle hair brushes, comb, cloth and hat brushes, nail scissors, penknife, shoe lift, and nail trimmer; size, $9 \times 2\frac{3}{4} \times 4\frac{1}{4}$ in.

S&F.
London.

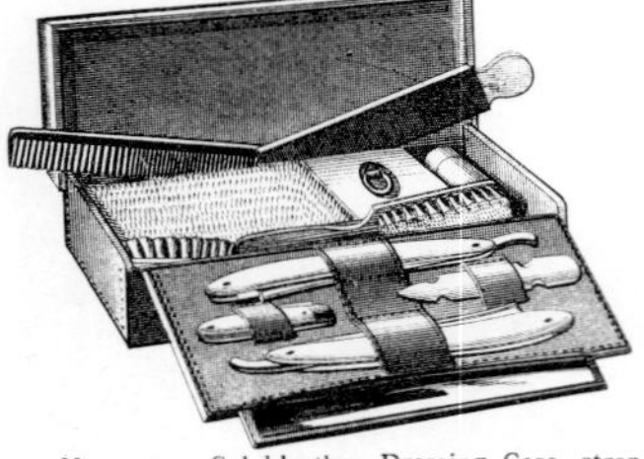

No. 12999 Solid-leather Dressing Case, strap round, containing hair, shaving, tooth and nail brushes in metal tray, metal soap box, razor strop, comb, mirror, 2 razors, penknife and nail trimmer; size, $8\frac{1}{4} \times 4 \times 2$ in.

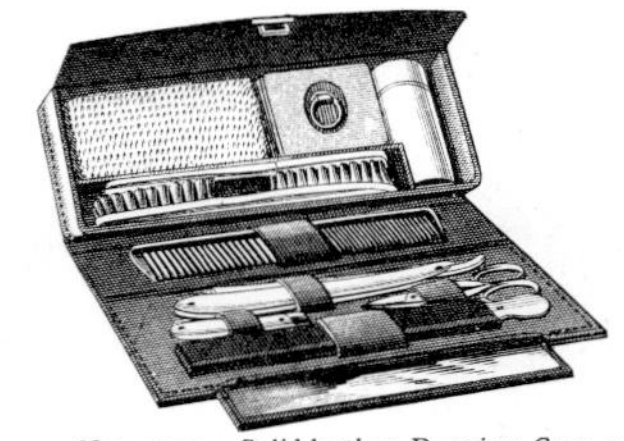

No. 13000 Solid-leather Dressing Case, with nickel-plated lock, containing hair, shaving, tooth and nail brushes in metal tray, metal soap box, comb, razor, razor strop, nail scissors, penknife and mirror; size, $8\frac{1}{4} \times 4\frac{1}{4} \times 2$ in.

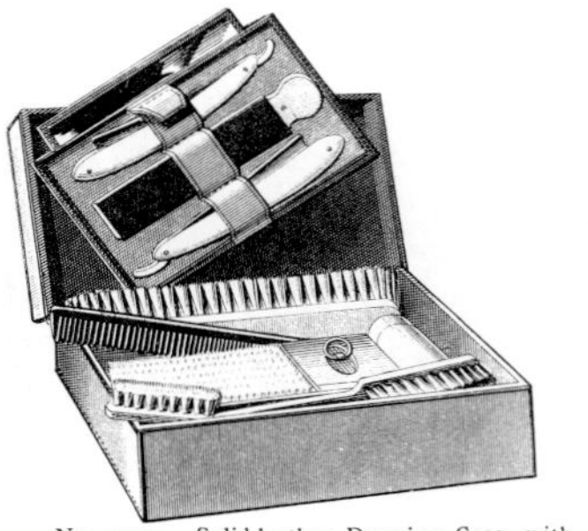

No. 13001 Solid-leather Dressing Case, with strap round, containing hair and cloth brushes, tooth and nail brushes in metal case, metal soap case, shaving brush, pair razors, razor strop, comb and mirror; size, $8 \times 5\frac{1}{2} \times 2\frac{3}{4}$ in.

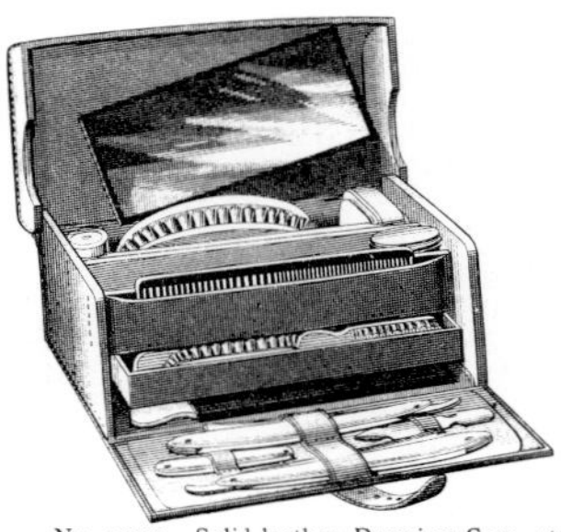

No. 13002 Solid-leather Dressing Case, strap round, containing 1 pair military hair brushes, cloth and shaving brushes, tooth and nail brushes in metal case, razor strop, comb, 1 pair razors, penknife and nail trimmer; size, $8 \times 5\frac{1}{4} \times 3\frac{1}{2}$ in.

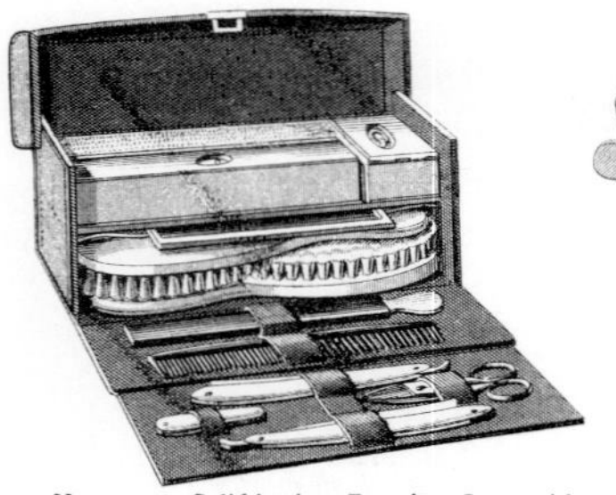

No. 13003 Solid-leather Dressing Case, with nickel-plated lock, sliding handle, containing 1 pair long handle hair brushes, cloth brush, tooth, nail and shaving brushes in metal case, metal soap box, mirror, pair razors, razor strop, comb, nail scissors and penknife; size, $10\frac{1}{4} \times 4 \times 4\frac{1}{4}$ in.

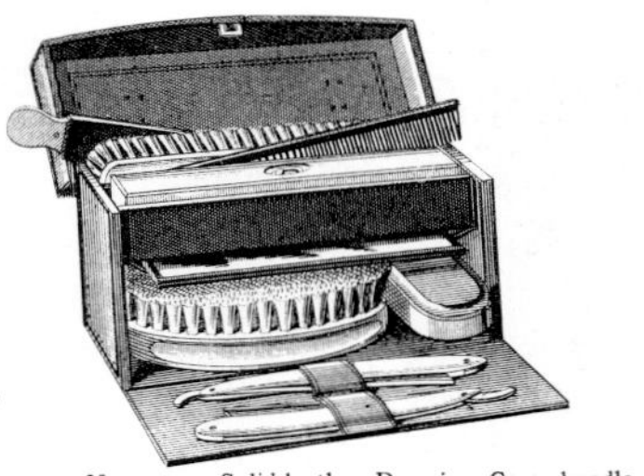

No. 13004 Solid-leather Dressing Case, handle on top, with nickel-plated lock, containing screw-back military hair brush, cloth brush, tooth, nail and shaving brushes in metal case with lid, razor strop, comb, metal soap box, mirror and 1 pair razors; size, $8\frac{1}{4} \times 4\frac{1}{4} \times 3\frac{1}{2}$ in.

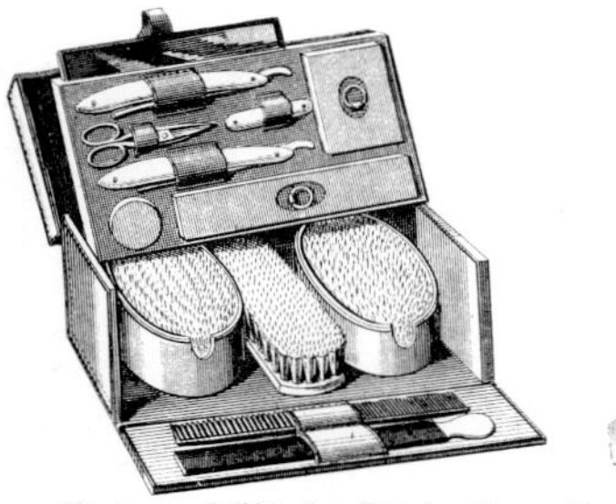

No. 13005 Solid-leather Dressing Case, with nickel-plated lock, sliding handle on top, containing 1 pair military hair brushes, hat brush, comb, strop, mirror, tooth and nail brushes in metal case, plated-top pomade jar, 1 pair razors, nail scissors and penknife; size, $10\frac{1}{2} \times 6\frac{1}{4} \times 3\frac{1}{2}$ in,

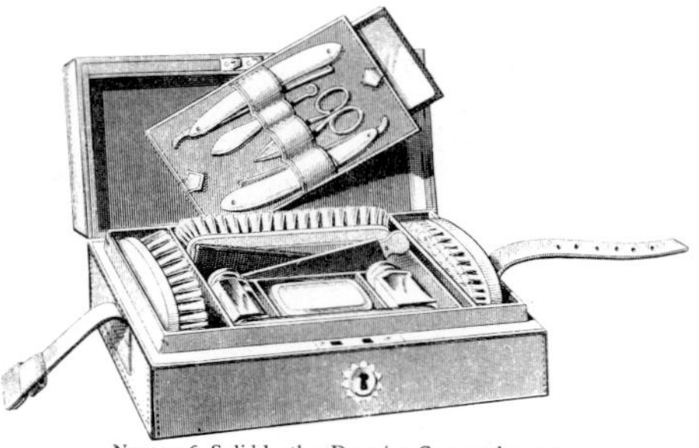

No. 13006 Solid-leather Dressing Case, mahogany lined, strap across top, tumbler lock, containing 1 pair military hair brushes, cloth, hat and shaving brushes, tooth and nail brushes in metal tray, metal soap box, razor strop, comb, mirror, plated-top scent bottle and pomade jar, 1 pair razors, nail scissors and trimmer; size, $11 \times 6\frac{3}{4} \times 3\frac{1}{4}$ in.

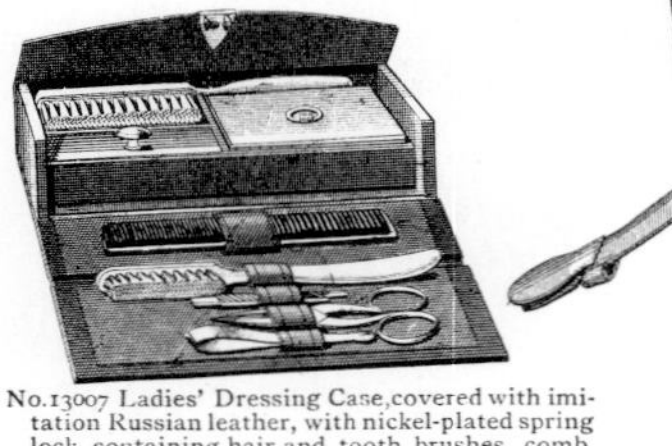

No. 13007 Ladies' Dressing Case, covered with imitation Russian leather, with nickel-plated spring lock, containing hair and tooth brushes, comb, scissors, nail file, tweezers, metal soap box and small partition for rings, &c.; size, $6\frac{3}{4} \times 5 \times 2$ in.

No. 13008 As No. 13007, but fitted for Gentlemen's use, containing hair, tooth and shaving brushes, comb, scissors, razor and metal soap box.

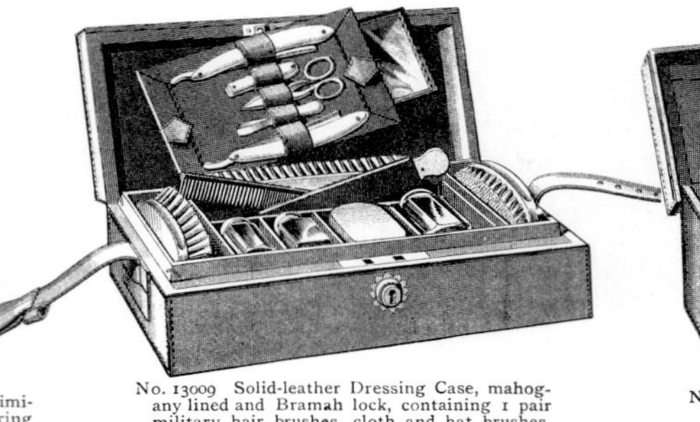

No. 13009 Solid-leather Dressing Case, mahogany lined and Bramah lock, containing 1 pair military hair brushes, cloth and hat brushes, tooth and nail brushes in metal case, shaving brush, metal soap box, 2 pomade jars and scent bottle with plated tops, razor strop, comb, 2 razors, nail scissors, penknife, tweezers, corkscrew, nail trimmer and mirror; size, $12\frac{1}{4} \times 7\frac{3}{4} \times 3\frac{1}{2}$ in.

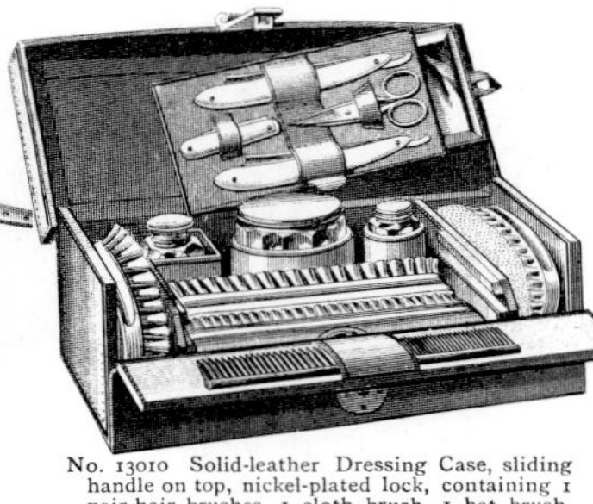

No. 13010 Solid-leather Dressing Case, sliding handle on top, nickel-plated lock, containing 1 pair hair brushes, 1 cloth brush, 1 hat brush, tooth, nail, and shaving brushes in metal case, razor strop, comb in leather case, bevelled mirror, 2 razors, nail scissors, penknife, 1 oval cut glass soap dish, scent bottle and pomade jar with electro-plated tops; size, $12 \times 6\frac{3}{4} \times 4\frac{1}{4}$ in.

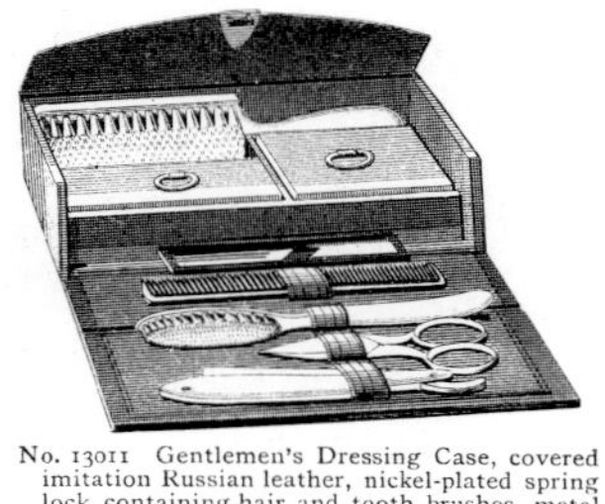

No. 13011 Gentlemen's Dressing Case, covered imitation Russian leather, nickel-plated spring lock, containing hair and tooth brushes, metal soap and brush box, comb, scissors, razor, mirror, &c.; size, $7\frac{1}{2} \times 3 \times 2\frac{1}{4}$ in.

No. 13012 As No. 13011, but fitted for Ladies' use, containing hair and tooth brushes, metal soap box, nail cleaner, metal brush box, scissors, tweezers, scoop, comb and mirror.

S&F.
London.

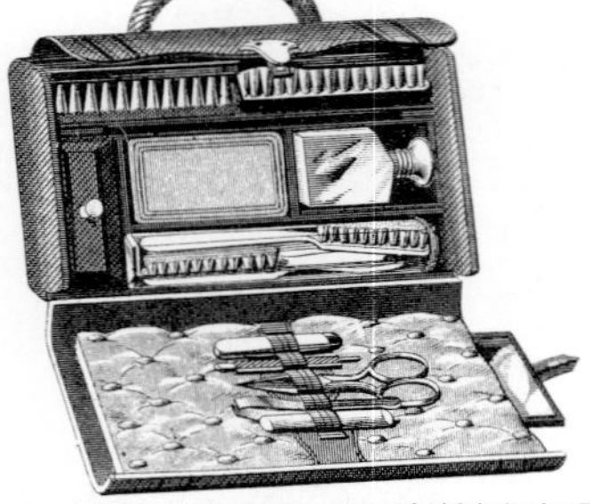

No. 13013 Ladies' Dressing Case, covered with imitation Russian leather, leather handle on top, lined with quilted satin, containing hair, cloth, tooth and nail brushes, comb, glass soap dish with metal top, cut glass scent bottle and jar for brushes, compartment for rings, &c., scissors, nail file, penknife, tweezers, needle case and bevelled edge mirror; size, $8 \times 5\frac{1}{2} \times 2\frac{3}{4}$ in.

No. 13014 As No. 13013, but fitted for Gentlemen's use, containing hair, cloth, tooth, nail and shaving brushes, glass soap dish with metal top, cut glass scent bottle and jar for brushes, comb, razor, penknife, nail file, scissors, tweezers and bevelled edge mirror

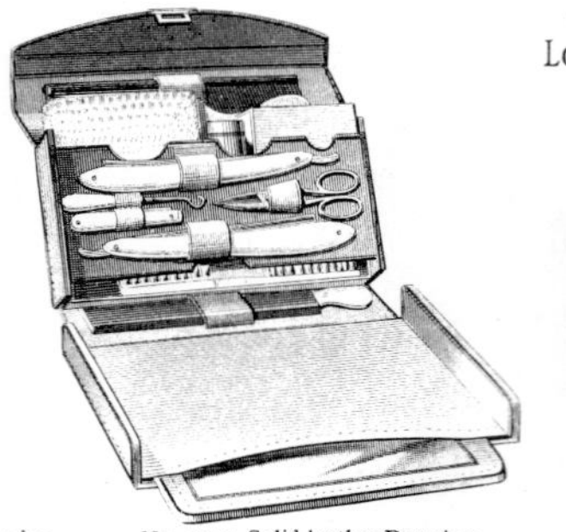

No. 13015 Solid-leather Dressing Case, with sliding handle and nickel-plated lock, fitted with hair brush, shaving brush, tooth and nail brushes in metal case, metal soap box, razor strop, comb, 2 razors, nail scissors, penknife, button hook and mirror; size, $7\frac{3}{4} \times 5\frac{1}{2} \times 2\frac{1}{2}$ in.

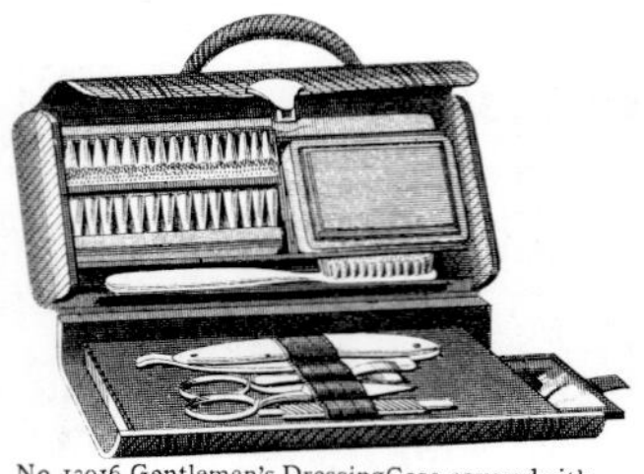

No. 13016 Gentlemen's Dressing Case, covered with imitation Russian leather, nickel-plated lock and key, leather handle on top, containing hair, cloth and tooth brushes, glass soap dish, razor, scissors, tweezers, nail file, comb and mirror; size, $7\frac{1}{2} \times 4 \times 2\frac{1}{2}$ in.

No. 13017 As No. 13016, but fitted for Ladies' use, containing hair, cloth and tooth brushes, glass soap dish, comb, needlecase, nail file, scissors, tweezers, scoop and mirror.

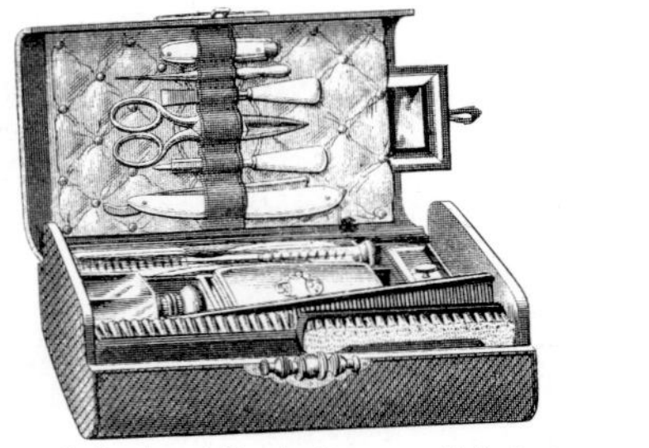

No. 13018 Gentlemen's Dressing Case, covered imitation Russian leather, with nickel handle, mounts and spring-lock, lined with quilted satin, containing hair, cloth, tooth, nail and shaving brushes, comb, glass soap dish, scent bottle, cut glass jar for brushes, all with metal tops, razor, nail file, scissors, tweezers, scoop, penknife and bevelled edge mirror; size $8 \times 5\frac{1}{2} \times 2\frac{1}{2}$ in.

No. 13019 As No. 13018, but fitted for Ladies' use, containing hair, cloth, tooth and nail brushes, comb, cut glass soap dish, scent bottle and glass jar for brushes, all with metal tops, compartment for rings, &c., scissors, penknife, tweezers, scoop, needlecase and bevelled edge mirror.

LADIES' AND GENTLEMEN'S FITTED "ETUI" CASES.

TRADE MARK

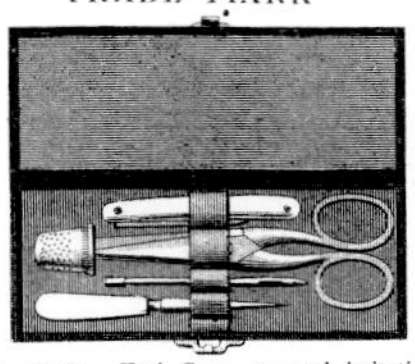

No. 13025 Etui Case, covered imitation leather, lined velvet and satin, containing pair of 4½ inch scissors, ivory knife, bodkin, stiletto and thimble; size 5¼ by 2¼ inch

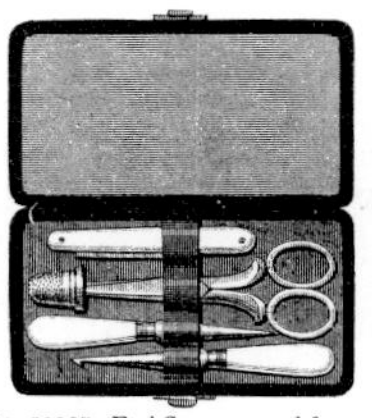

No. 13027 Etui Case, covered fancy leather, with patent fastener, lined velvet, containing 1 pair scissors, ivory handled penknife, stiletto and crochet needle, bodkin and thimble; size, 4¾ by 2⅜ inch

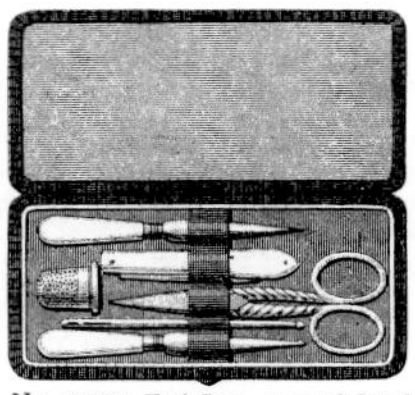

No. 13029 Etui Case, covered fluted leather, lined velvet and satin, containing 1 pair scissors, ivory handled penknife, stiletto and crochet needle, bodkin and thimble; size, 5½ by 2⅜ in.

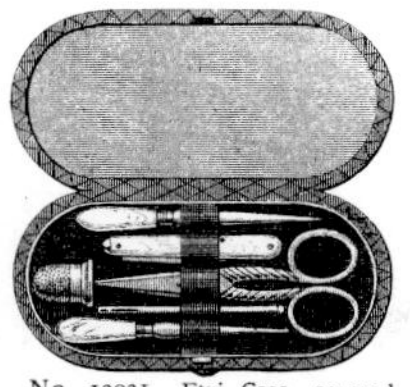

No. 13031 Etui Case, covered chequered leather, lined velvet and satin, containing 1 pair scissors, pearl handled penknife, stiletto and crochet hook, bodkin and thimble; size of case, 5¼ by 2⅜ inch

S&F.

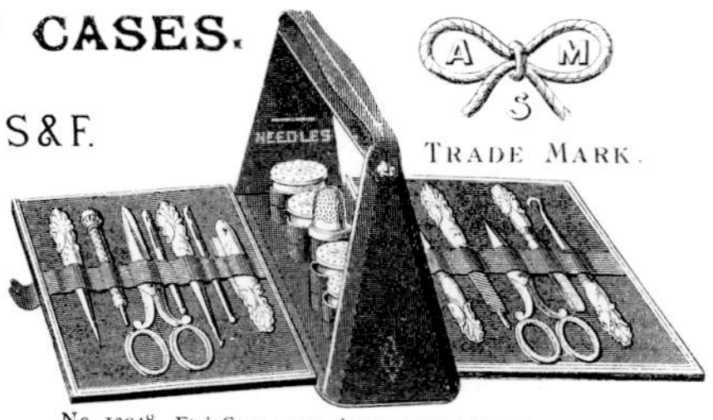

TRADE MARK.

No. 13048 Etui Case, camp shape, covered French morocco leather, gilt lines inside and out, containing 2 pairs scissors, carved pearl handled penknife, stiletto and crochet hook, corkscrew, nail file, tweezers and button hook, 2 bodkins, silver pencil case and thimble, and four carved pearl reels for silk, etc.; size, 6¼ by 4¼ inch

S&F.
London.

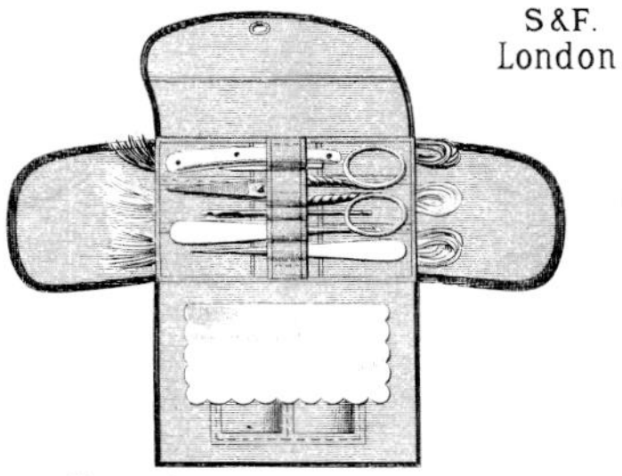

No. 13026 Etui Case, French morocco, folding, with nickel catch, containing a supply of silk, 2 packets of needles, scissors, ivory-handled knife, bodkin, stiletto and crochet needle; size when folded 4⅛ by 2½ inch

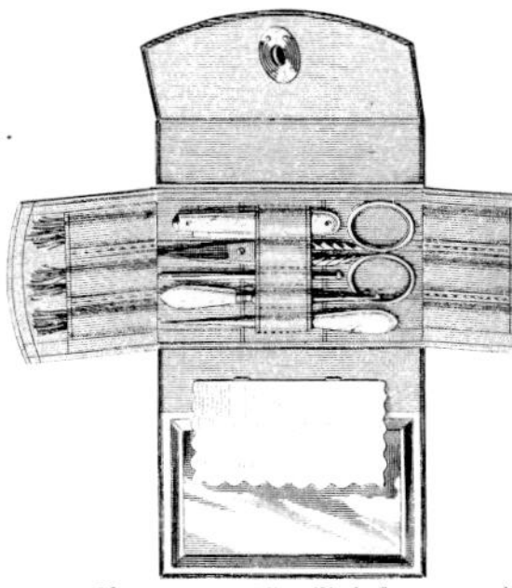

No. 13033 Folding Work Case, covered chequered Persian leather, lined imitation calf, with nickel-plated slide lock, containing 1 pair scissors, pearl handled penknife, stiletto, crochet hook, bodkin and a supply of fancy sewing silk, mirror in bottom fold of case; size, 4 by 2⅜ inch

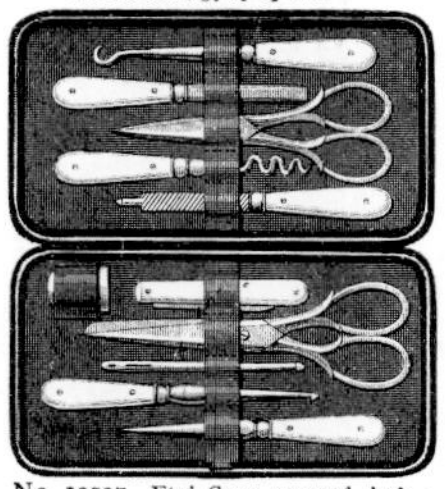

No. 13037 Etui Case, covered dark leather, with silver lines on top inside edges, lined velvet, containing 2 pairs scissors, penknife, stiletto, crochet needle, button hook, corkscrew, nail file and tweezers, all with ivory handles, bodkin and plated thimble; size, 6 by 3¼ inch

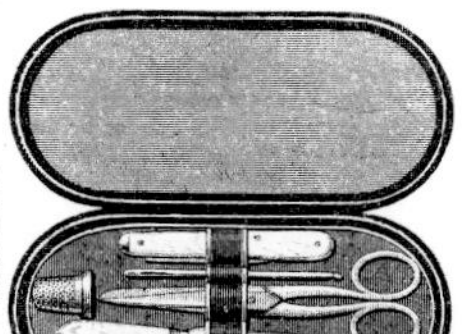

No. 13038 Etui Case, oval, covered French morocco leather, lined velvet and satin, gilt lines on inside and outside edges, containing 1 pair of gilt bow scissors, large pearl handled penknife, stiletto and crochet needle, bodkin and best plated thimble; size, 6¼ by 2¾ inch

TRADE MARK

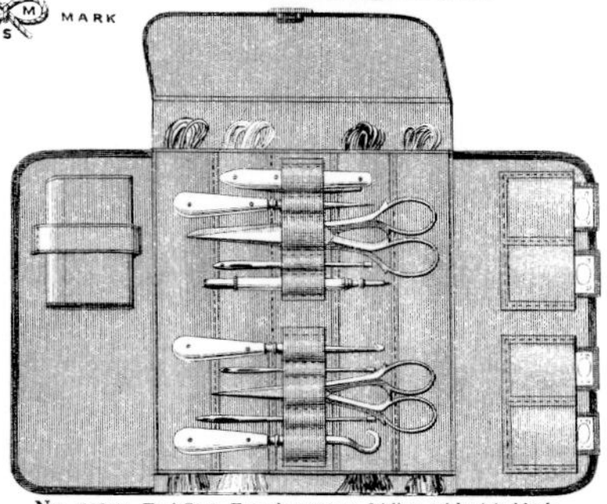

No. 13039 Etui Case, French morocco, folding, with nickel lock, containing a supply of silk, 4 packets of needles, 2 pairs of scissors, ivory knife, stiletto, crochet needle and button hook, pencil and 2 bodkins; size when closed 5¼ by 3¼ inch

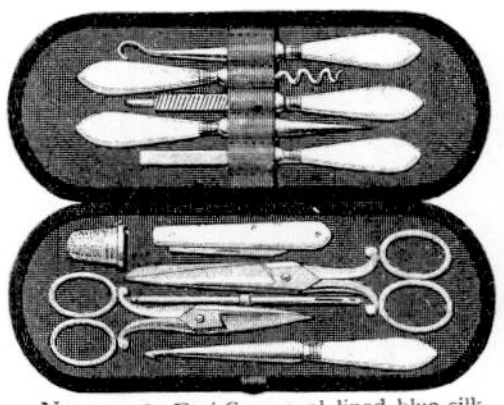

No. 13040 Etui Case, oval, lined blue silk velvet, containing 2 pairs scissors, penknife, stiletto, crochet hook, tweezers, nail file, corkscrew, and button hook, all with pearl handles, bodkin and plated thimble; size, 6¾ by 2⅜ inch

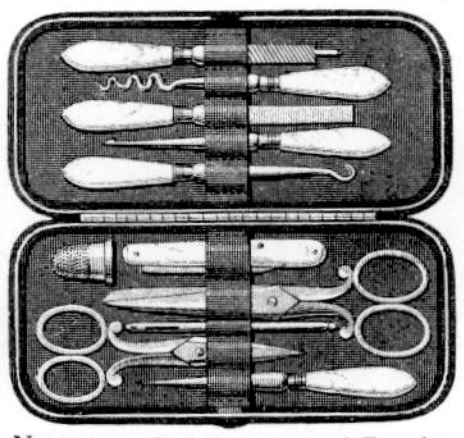

No. 13044 Etui Case, covered French morocco leather, gilt on top, lined silk velvet, containing 2 pairs scissors, penknife, stiletto, crochet needle, button hook, corkscrew, nail file, tweezers, all with pearl handles, bodkin and plated thimble; size, 6¾ by 3 inch

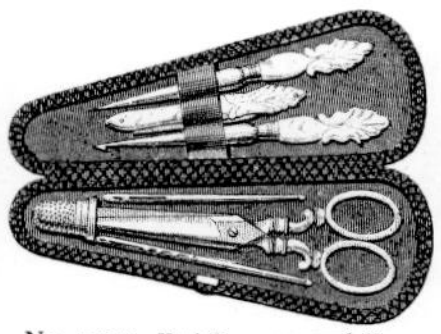

No. 13041 Etui Case, covered Russian leather, containing 2 pairs scissors (one under the other), carved pearl handled penknife, stiletto and crochet hook, 2 bodkins and plated thimble; size, 5¾ by 2¼ by 1 inch

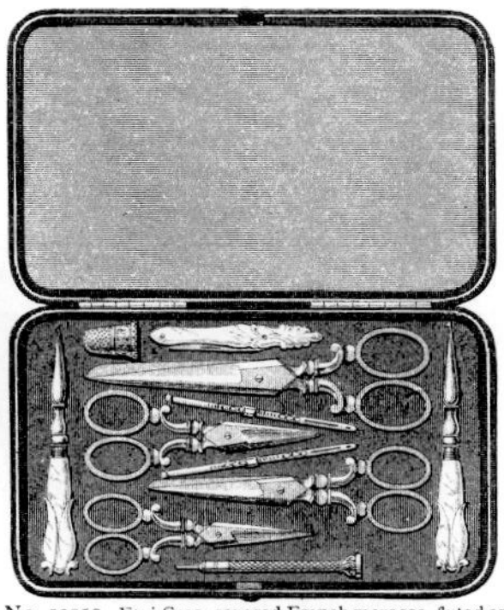

No. 13050 Etui Case, covered French morocco, fluted and gilt, lined silk velvet and satin, containing 4 pairs scissors, carved pearl handled penknife, stiletto, crochet needle, 2 bodkins, silver pencil case and thimble; size 7¾ by 5 in.

S&F.
London.

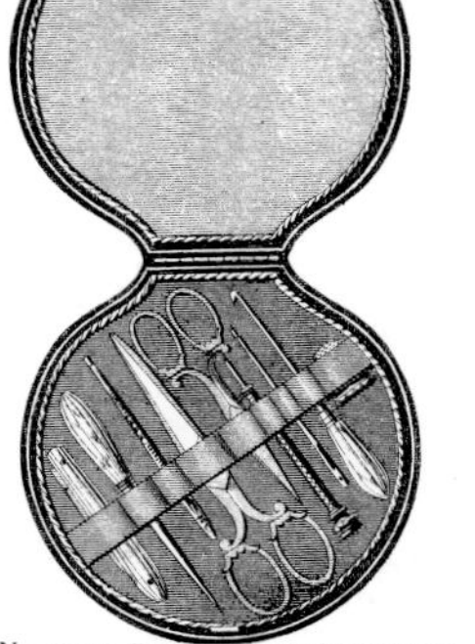

No. 13047 Etui Case, circular shape, covered Russia, lined silk velvet and satin, containing 2 pairs of best scissors, cut steel bodkin, best reeded pearl-handled knife, stiletto, crochet needle, silver pencil and silver thimble; size 5⅜ inch diameter

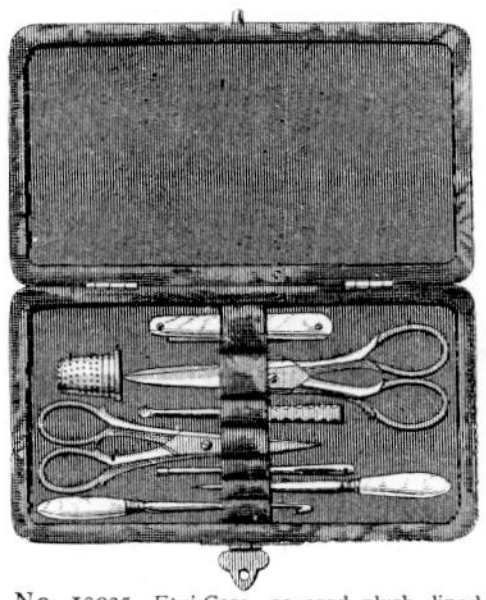

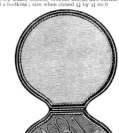

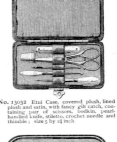

No. 13035 Etui Case, covered plush, lined plush and satin, with fancy gilt catch, containing 2 pairs of scissors, bodkin, steel tweezers, pearl knife, stiletto, crochet needle and best plated thimble; size 6⅛ by 3½ inch

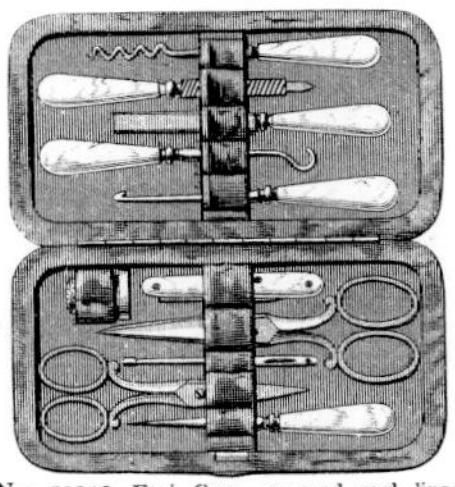

No. 13042 Etui Case, covered and lined plush, containing 2 pairs of scissors, bodkin, pearl knife, stiletto, crochet needle, button hook, corkscrew, nail file, tweezers and best plated thimble; size 6 by 3¼ inch

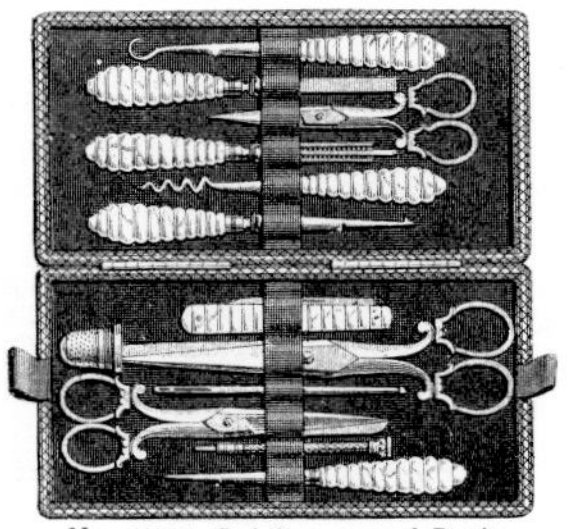

No. 13052 Etui Case, covered Russian leather, with tray inside, lined silk velvet, containing 3 pairs of best hard polished scissors, beaded pearl handled penknife, stiletto, crochet hook, corkscrew, nail file, tweezers and button hook, bodkin, silver pencil case and thimble; size, 6⅞ by 3⅜ by 1⅛ inch

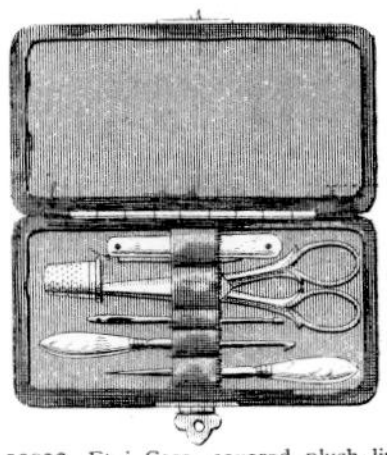

No. 13032 Etui Case, covered plush, lined plush and satin, with fancy gilt catch, containing pair of scissors, bodkin, pearl-handled knife, stiletto, crochet needle and thimble; size 5 by 2⅜ inch

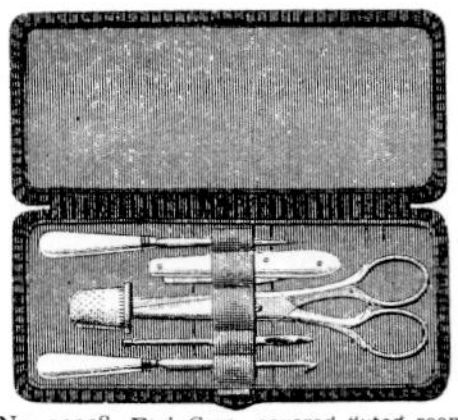

No. 13028 Etui Case, covered fluted roan, lined satin, containing 1 pair of scissors, bodkin, thimble, ivory-handled knife, stiletto and crochet needle; size 6 by 2⅜ inch

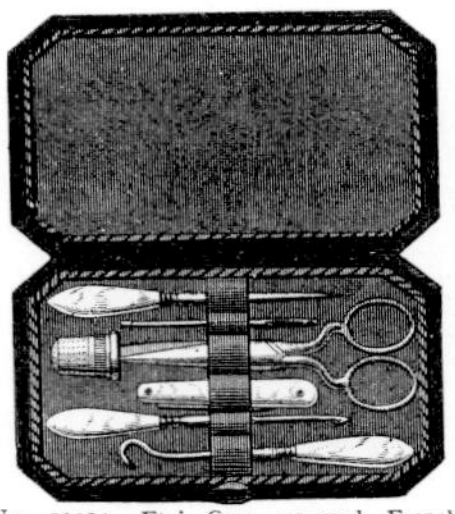

No. 13034 Etui Case, covered French morocco, lined silk velvet and satin, containing pair of scissors, bodkin, pearl-handled knife, stiletto, crochet needle, button hook and best plated thimble; size 5⅜ by 3¼ inch

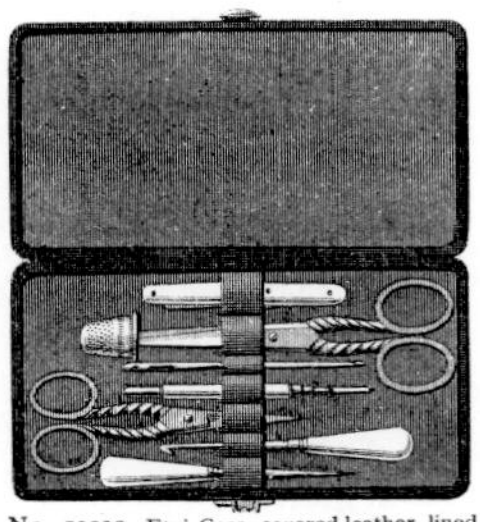

No. 13030 Etui Case, covered leather, lined velvet and satin, containing 2 pairs of scissors, ivory-handled knife, bodkin, bone pencil, stiletto, crotchet needle and thimble; size 6¼ by 3¼ inch

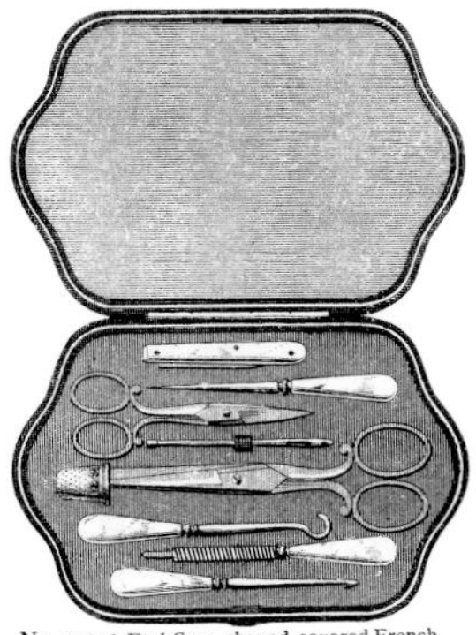

No. 13045 Etui Case, shaped, covered French morocco, lined silk velvet and satin, containing 2 pairs of scissors, bodkin, pearl-handled knife, stiletto, crochet needle, button hook, nail file and silver thimble; size 7 by 5 inch

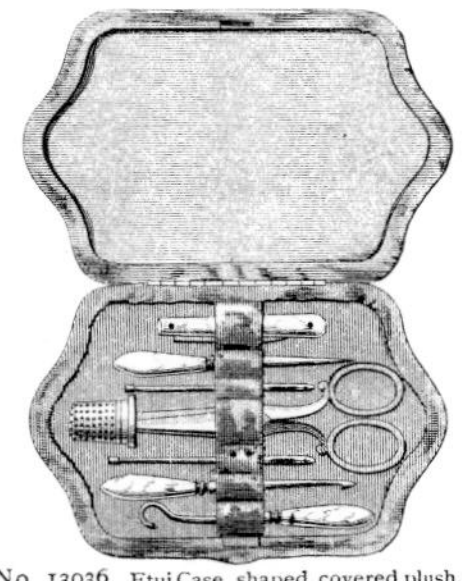

No. 13036 Etui Case, shaped, covered plush, lined plush and satin, containing pair of scissors, 2 bodkins, pearl-handled knife, stiletto, crochet needle, button hook and best plated thimble; size 5⅜ by 3⅛ inch

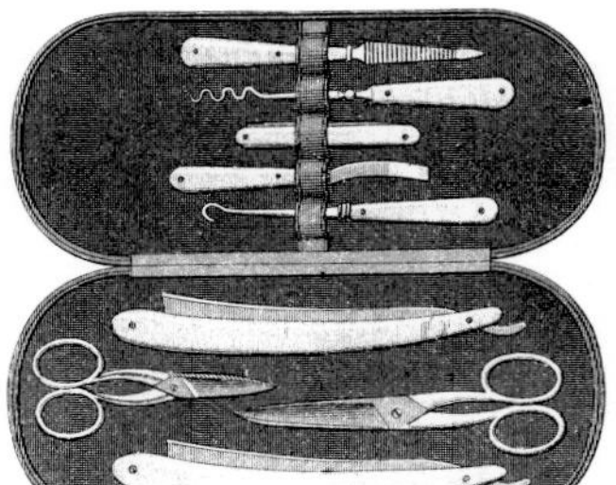

No. 13049 Gentlemen's fitted Etui Case, covered with morocco leather, lined with blue silk velvet, containing 1 pair ivory handled razors, 1 pair hair scissors, nail scissors, ivory-handled penknife, button hook, corkscrew, nail file and tweezers

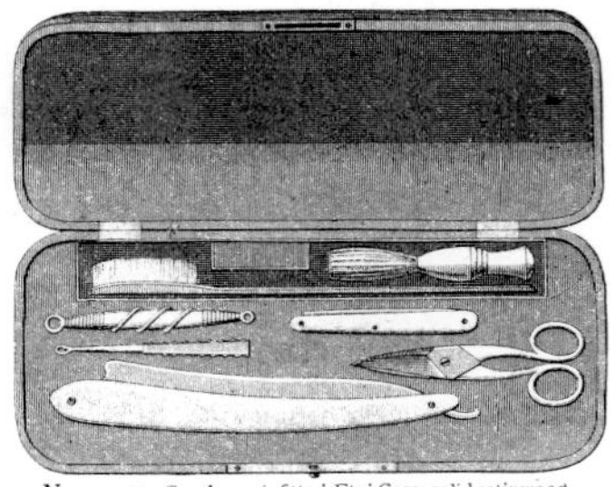

No. 13051 Gentlemen's fitted Etui Case, solid satinwood (spaces for fittings carved out), containing tooth and shaving brushes, 1 ivory handled razor, nail file, ivory handled corn knife, nail scissors, steel corkscrew and tweezers

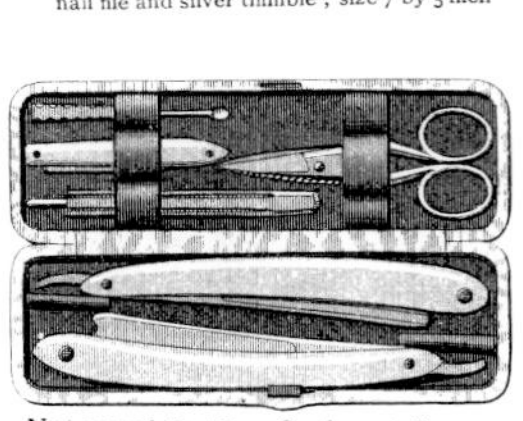

No. 13043 Etui Case, Gentleman's Companion, covered imitation crocodile leather, lined silk velvet, containing pair of "Rodgers'" ivory razors, nail scissors, penknife, steel nail file and tweezers

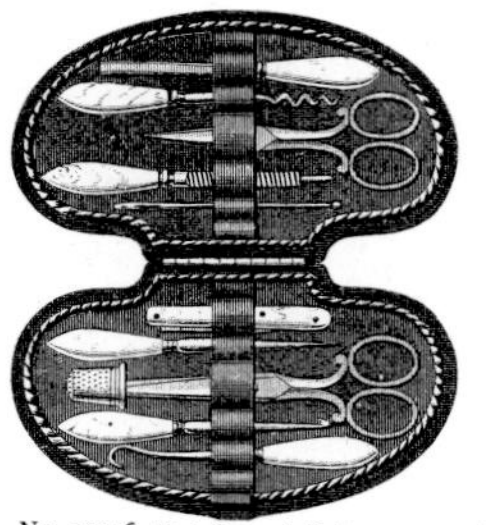

No. 13046 Etui Case, shell shape, covered French morocco, lined silk velvet, containing 2 pairs of scissors, bodkin, pearl-handled knife, stiletto, crochet needle, button hook, corkscrew, nail file, tweezers and best plated thimble; size 6¼ by 3¾ inch

No. 13060 Solid leather Purse, with elastic band

No. 13061 Solid leather Purse, with elastic band

No. 13062 Solid calf expanding Purse, with nickelled lock

No. 13063 Solid leather Purse, with nickelled lock

No. 13064 Solid leather expanding Purse, with tuck fastening

No. 13065 Solid leather Playing-card Case and Cribbage Board combined, for travellers' use

No. 13066 Solid leather Duplex Purse, with secret divisions for gold, nickelled locks

No. 13067 Solid leather Letter Case, with nickelled lock

No. 13068 Solid calf Purse, with new tuck fastening

No. 13069 Solid leather Portsea Purse, with nickelled lock

No. 13070 Solid leather Portsea Purse, with tuck fastening

No. 13071 Solid leather pull-out Fusee Case

No. 13072 Solid leather pull-out Fusee Case

No. 13073 Real pig-skin Wallet Pocket Book, with elastic band

No. 13074 Solid leather expanding Letter Case, patent tuck fastening

TRADE MARK

No. 13075 Solid leather Wallet Pocket Book, with elastic band

S&F. London.

No. 13076 Real pig-skin pull-out Fusee Case

TRADE MARK

No. 13077 Real pig-skin pull-out Cigarette Case

No. 13078 Real morocco pull-out Cigarette Case

No. 13079 Solid calf pull-out Cigarette Case, quite flat

No. 13080 Solid leather pull-out Cigar Case, with inside spring

No. 13081 Solid calf pull-out Cigar Case, quite flat

No. 13082 Real pig-skin pull-out Cigar Case

No. 13083 Solid leather Cigar Case, concave shape, to fit breast pocket

No. 13084 Real morocco leather pull-out Cigar Case

No. 13085 Solid leather pull-out Cigar Case, with gusset

No. 13086 Solid leather pull-out Cigar Case

CIGARETTE MAKERS, HOOKAHS, CIGAR HOLDERS, AND PIPE FITTINGS.

No. 13152.—Cigar Cutter, 1 hole.
No. 13153.—Cigar Cutter, 2 holes.
No. 13154.—Cigar Cutter, 3 holes.

No. 13155.—Cigarette Maker, Patent Automatic, with lid and tobacco box combined.

No. 13159.—Job Cigarette Paper.
No. 13160.—Real Job Cigarette Paper.
No. 13161.—Persan Cigarette Paper.
No. 13162.—Cosmopolite Cigarette Paper, gummed edges.
No. 13163.—La Mascotte Cigarette Paper, gummed edges.
No. 13164.—Pradon Cigarette Paper, gummed edges and amber tips.

No. 13156.—Cigarette Maker, Patent Rapid, simple and effectual.
No. 13157.—Cigarette Maker, Patent Express, with spring.
No. 13158.—Cigarette Maker, Patent Concinnum.

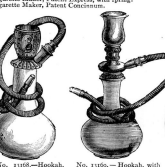

No. 13165.—Hookah, with meerschaum bowl and cigar holder, two flexible stems, real amber mouthpieces, and silver-plated mounts; céleste blue vase, richly decorated with floral designs and gilt, adapted for one or two smokers.

No. 13166. — Hookah, with meerschaum bowl and cigar holder, flexible stem, real amber mouthpiece, and silver-plated mounts; ruby-coloured vase, hand-painted decoration of flowers and ornamental designs.

No. 13167.—Hookah, with meerschaum bowl and cigar holder, flexible stem, real amber mouthpiece, and silver-plated mounts; crystal-coloured vase, hand-painted floral decoration, ruby and gilt.

No. 13168.—Hookah, with terra-cotta bowl, flexible stem, and real amber mouthpiece; alabaster-coloured vase.

No. 13169. — Hookah, with meerschaum bowl and cigar holder, flexible stem, real amber mouthpiece, and silver-plated mounts; opal white vase.

No. 13170.—Hookah, with meerschaum bowl and cigar holder, flexible stem, real amber mouthpiece, and silver-plated mounts; céleste-coloured vase, hand-painted decoration of flowers, &c.

No. 13171.—Hookah, with meerschaum bowl and cigar holder, flexible stem, real amber mouthpiece, silver-plated mounts; dark blue transparent glass vase, hand-painted decorations.

No. 13173.—Solid Amber Cigar Holder (finest quality), in case.

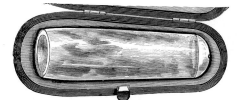

No. 13174.—Solid Amber Cigar Holder (finest quality), in case.

No. 13175.—Solid Amber Cigar Holder (finest quality), in case.

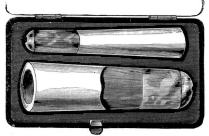

No. 13176.—Real Meerschaum Cigar and Cigarette Holder, in leather-covered companion case, with real amber mouthpieces.

No. 13172.—Hookah, with meerschaum bowl and cigar holder, three flexible stems, real amber mouthpieces, and silver-plated mounts; blue vase, profusely decorated with ornamental designs in colours, and gilt, adapted for one, two, or three smokers.

No. 13180.—3-inch.
No. 13181.—4-inch.
No. 13182.—6-inch.
No. 13183.—8-inch.
No. 13184.—10-inch.
No. 13185.—12-inch.
No. 13186.—14-inch.
No. 13187.—16-inch.

No. 13188.—Meerschaum Plugs, with Corks, assorted sizes.
No. 13189.—As No. 13188, but all meerschaum.
No. 13190.—Meerschaum Plugs, best make, pyramid shape.

CHERRY STEMS.

Finest Quality, with Horn Mouthpieces.

S. & F. LONDON.

TRADE MARK

No. 13191.—Real Amber Mouthpieces, with German silver mounts, assorted sizes.
No. 13192.—As No. 13191, (special line), 2 dozen on card.
No. 13193.—As No. 13192, but with engraved mounts.
No. 13194.—As No. 13193, but longer and stouter.
No. 13195.—As No. 13194, but with plain mounts.

No. 13196.—Bone and Metal Pipe Mounts, assorted sizes.
No. 13197.—As No. 13196, but fancy patterns.
No. 13198.—As No. 13196, but extra large.
No. 13199.—Black Horn and Metal Pipe Mounts, assorted sizes, bent and straight.
No. 13200.—Pipe Ferrules, German silver, ½ inch long, assorted sizes.
No. 13201.—As No. 13200, but engraved.
No. 13202.—As No. 13200, but 1 inch long.
No. 13203.—As No. 13202, but engraved.
No. 13204.—Pipe Ferrules, sterling silver, ½ inch long, assorted sizes, plain.
No. 13205.—As No. 13204, but engraved.
No. 13206.—As No. 13204, but ¾ inch long.
No. 13207.—As No. 13206, but engraved.
No. 13208.—As No. 13204, but 1 inch long.
No. 13209.—As No. 13208, but engraved.

No. 13177.—Solid Amber Cigarette Holder (finest quality), in case.

No. 13178.—Solid Amber Cigarette holder (finest quality), in case.

No. 13179.—Real Amber Cigar Holders, with black amber centres, in cases, assorted sizes.

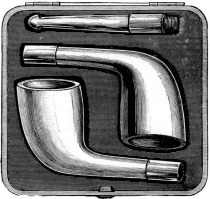

No. 13210.—Clay Companion, containing two pipes and one bone mouthpiece, German silver screw mounts, in leather-covered case.
No. 13211.—As No. 13210, but with real amber mouthpiece.

TRADE MARK

TRADE MARK

No. 13338.—Luncheon Basket, size 13 by 10 by 5½ inches, fitted for one person, with 1 tin, 1 pint bottle, 1 tumbler, 1 plate, and 1 knife and fork.

No. 13377.—The Royal Mail Luncheon Basket for two persons, fitted with 1 provision box, 2 tumblers, 2 condiment bottles, 1 wicker-covered bottle, 2 plates, fastened in lid with springs, and cutlery complete, with strap all round. Size of basket when closed, 13½ by 10½ by 8 inches. (See also illustration below.)

No. 13339.—Basket for two persons, fitted with 1 pint bottle, 2 glasses, 2 plates, 1 provision box, 2 knives and forks. Size of basket, 13 by 10 by 5½ inches.

S. & F.
LONDON
and
PARIS.

MANUFACTURERS,
IMPORTERS,
WAREHOUSEMEN,
& AGENTS.

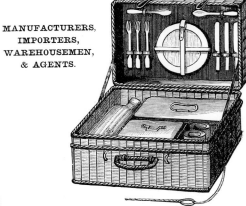

No. 13377.—The Royal Mail Luncheon Basket for two persons, fitted with 1 provision box, 2 tumblers, 2 condiment bottles, 1 wicker-covered bottle, 2 plates, fastened in lid with springs, and cutlery complete, with strap all round. Size of basket when closed, 13½ by 10½ by 8 inches. (See also illustration above.)

No. 13370.—Basket for two persons, fitted with 2 bottles, 1 covered china box, 2 tumblers, 2 condiment bottles, space for bread, 2 plates, cutlery, and padlock, and all metal fittings and cutlery are nickel plated. Size of basket, 14½ by 13 by 6 inches.

No. 13370A.—Basket for three persons, fitted with 1 bottle, 2 tins, 3 plates, 3 tumblers, 3 knives and forks, 2 spoons. Size of basket, 15½ by 12½ by 7½ inches.

SANDWICH OR FOWL BOX

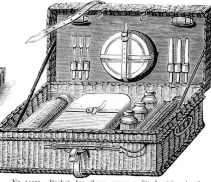

No. 13348.—Basket for six persons, fitted with 3 wicker-covered bottles, 1 sandwich box, 6 covered tumblers, mustard, pepper, and salt bottles, 6 wine glasses, space for 4 soda bottles, 6 enamelled plates, enamelled meat dish at end, 1 cold meat box on end, 1 soda water glass and spirit bottle fitted inside a bread tray, cutlery and corks complete. Size of basket, 33 by 18 by 12 inches.

No. 13372.—Basket for four persons, fitted with 2 large bottles, 1 large covered china box, 1 small ditto, 1 wicker-covered porcelain box for butter, 4 tumblers, 3 condiment bottles, 4 plates, padlock, and strap. Size of basket, 23 by 13 by 7 inches.

No. 13355.—Basket for three persons, fitted with 2 bottles, 3 glasses, 3 plates, 3 condiment bottles, 1 large japanned tin or a covered pie dish, strap round basket, and padlock. Size of basket, 17 by 11 by 7 inches.

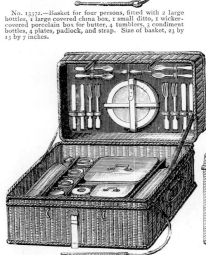

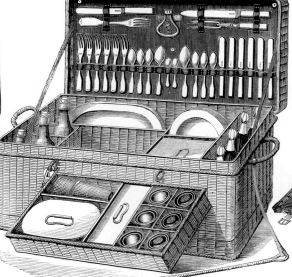

No. 13355A.—Basket for four persons, fitted with 2 bottles, 4 glasses, 4 plates, 2 provision boxes, 2 condiment bottles, 4 knives and forks, 2 spoons, and padlock. Size of basket, 19 by 12½ by 7½ inches.

No. 13375.—The "Expresss" Luncheon Basket, specially designed for railway travelling, fitted for two persons, with 2 bottles, 2 tumblers, 2 condiment bottles, 2 provision tins, 2 enamelled plates, open spaces for bread, and fall-down trays, straps, &c., and cutlery complete. Size, 14 by 7 by 15 inches.

No. 13350.—Basket for six persons, fitted with 1 large provision tin, 3 quart bottles, covered with fine wicker, 2 large enamelled iron dishes, 6 ditto plates, a large space for provisions, ditto for champagne, a movable tray, containing 6 covered tumblers, pepper, salt, and mustard bottles, 2 soda water tumblers, covered wicker, 1 large covered pie dish, 1 provision tin, and lock for lid of basket, cutlery and corks complete. Size of basket, 30 by 15 by 15 inches.

All Luncheon Baskets are made of best English Willow, and are of best workmanship.

SPECIALITIES IN LUNCHEON BASKETS, TEA & COFFEE BASKETS, AND GROG OR LIQUOR HAMPERS.

These Baskets are made of White Wicker and are of English manufacture. They can also be had in Brown Wicker, varnished, at a small extra charge.

S. & F.
London.

No. 13344.—Basket for 4 persons, fitted with 2 large tins, 2 quart bottles, 4 tumblers, 2 condiment bottles, 4 plates, knife and fork, and lock. Size of basket 16 by 10 by 8 inches.

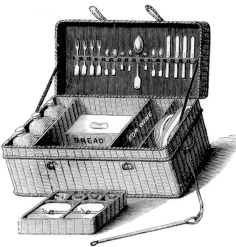

No. 13364.—Luncheon Basket for 4 persons, fitted with 3 large bottles, 1 provision tin, 4 plates, 1 meat dish, 1 movable tray containing 4 glasses, 2 covered pie dishes, 3 condiment bottles, spaces for provisions, champagne, &c., lock, and all cutlery complete. Size of basket 23 by 14 by 13 inches.

No. 13361.—Basket for 4 persons, fitted with 2 1½-pint bottles, 4 glasses, 4 plates, 1 china provision box and cover, 2 japanned provision boxes, 2 condiment bottles, 4 knives, 4 forks, 2 spoons, 2 condiment spoons, and padlock. Size of basket 22 by 12 by 8 inches.

No. 13389A.—Tea and Coffee Basket for 2 persons, fitted with portable cafetière, stove with spirit lamp, sponge spirit stove, boiler, 2 cups and saucers, 2 plates, 2 provision tins, tin bottle for water, tea pot, percolator, tin bottle for spirit, 2 condiment bottles, 2 egg cups, canisters, milk, 2 knives, 2 forks, 2 tea spoons, salt spoon, opener, and lock. Size of basket 16½ by 11 by 8 inches.

The Pannier Luncheon Basket may be carried on a man's back, or in pairs over a pony or horse, one fitted for luncheon (as drawing), the other, without fittings, to hold game.

No. 13384.—Pannier Luncheon Basket, for shooting or fishing parties, fitted for 4 persons, with 1 large meat tin, 4 wicker-covered tumblers with salt and pepper boxes fitted inside, 4 wicker-covered quart bottles, 4 iron enamelled plates and bread tray, 4 knives, 4 forks, 4 spoons, lined cover. Size of basket 23 by 14 by 16 inches.

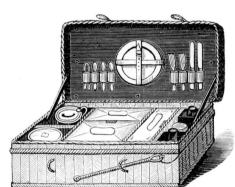

No. 13390.—Tea and Coffee Basket for 2 persons, fitted with patent spirit stove and boiler combined, tea kettle, saucepan, 2 spirit bottles, percolator, provision tin, tea and sugar canisters, tin of condensed milk, butter pot with patent lid, condiment bottle, 2 cups and saucers, 2 plates, 2 egg cups, large tin bottle, with screw-cap, for water, 2 knives, 2 forks, 2 tea spoons, opener, 2 condiment spoons, and lock. Size of basket 23 by 9½ by 10 inches.

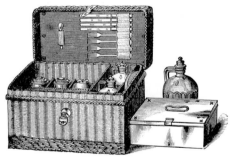

No. 13380.—Luncheon Basket for 4 persons, fitted with 2 1½-pint stone bottles (registered), 4 enamelled tumblers, 1 jar for butter or pickles, 1 provision box, 4 plates, 2 condiment bottles, space for bread, 4 knives, 4 forks, 2 plated top corks, salt spoon, and padlock. Size of basket 18 by 9 by 11 inches.

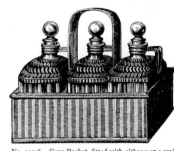

No. 13398.—Grog Basket, fitted with either 2 or 3 real Doulton ware bottles with nickel-plated corks, engraved "Brandy," "Whisky," &c., as required.

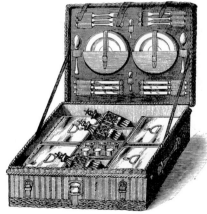

No. 13383.—Luncheon Basket, extra fine quality throughout, fitted for 6 persons, with 4 provision boxes, 3 large square glass bottles with patent corks, 6 cut glass tumblers, 3 condiment bottles, 6 ornamented enamelled plates, 6 knives, 6 forks, 2 spoons, mustard and salt spoons. Basket is lined with chamois leather, and is 22 by 10 by 8½ inches.

No. 13396.—As No. 13394, but fitted with 4 registered stone bottles.

No. 13403.—Basket for Brandy and Soda, fitted with 1 ½-pint registered brandy bottle, 1 cut soda glass, and a space for 1 soda water bottle.

No. 13394.—Grog or Liquor Basket, made of brown wicker, varnished, and fitted with 2 registered stone bottles, but can also be had fitted with 3 bottles.

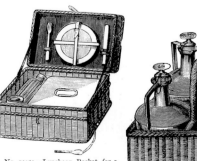

No. 13352.—Luncheon Basket for 1 person, fitted with 1 bottle, 1 wicker-covered glass, 1 enamelled iron plate, 1 provision tin, and cutlery. Size of basket 11 by 9 by 5¾ inches.

No. 13402.—Grog Basket, fitted with 4 1-pint antique bottles (brown); and can also be had with 2 or 3 bottles.

No. 13399.—Grog Basket, fitted with 4 real Doulton ware bottles, nickel-plated corks, engraved "Brandy," "Whisky," &c., as required.

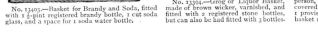

BUCKET CANTEENS, LINEN, WOOD, COAL, AND OTHER HOUSEHOLD BASKETS.

13406.
13405.   13406A.

No. 13404.—The "Etna" Canteen, for one person, fitted with wrought tinned iron saucepan, etna and spirit measure, tea strainer, frying pan, spirit bottle with brass screw cap, enamelled tea cup, plate, and tea spoon. Size of canteen 7 ins. by 4¾ ins.

No. 13405.—Oblong Wickered Bottles, with metal screw cap, 4 sizes, viz. ¾, 1, 1½, and 2 pints.
No. 13406.—Oval Wickered Bottles, with nickel-plated screw cap, 2 sizes, viz. 1 and 2 pints.
No. 13406A.—Round Wickered Bottles, without tops or stoppers, 2 sizes, viz. 1 and 2 pints.
No. 13407.—Wickered - covered Tumblers, four sizes.
No. 13407A.—Wickered Condiment Bottle, metal screw cap.

No. 13408.—Canteen, fitted with tea kettle, strainer, canister, wrought-iron tinned saucepan, frying pan, sugar canister, spirit bottle with screw cap, spirit stove, salt and pepper boxes, 2 enamelled cups and saucers, 2 plates, 2 knives, 2 forks, 2 spoons, and 2 tea spoons. The whole of the above fitting into a japanned box with strap and lock; movable lid can be used as tray. Size of Canteen 10 ins. by 9 ins. by 7½ ins.

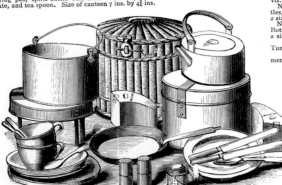

S. & F.
London.

No. 13409.—Bucket Canteen, containing strong fire stand, camp boiling pot, tea kettle, strainer, 2 canisters, pepper and salt boxes, 2 9-in. enamelled plates, 1 9-in. round enamelled pudding pan, 2 enamelled cups, 1 strong wrought-iron frying pan with folding handle, 2 knives, 2 forks, 2 spoons, and 2 tea spoons. All the above fitting into a strong galvanized iron bucket with straps and lid, which can be used as a wash-hand basin, and the whole fitting into a basket which may be used for marketing purposes.

No. 13410.—The Troop Regulation Bucket Canteen for 3 persons. Contents: 1 strong iron fire stand, camp boiling pot, 1 stew pan, 4 canisters for butter, tea, coffee, and sugar, saucepan, tea kettle, coffee pot, strainer, strong wrought-iron frying pan with folding handle, gridiron, mustard pot with screw top and glass lining, pepper and salt boxes, 3 enamelled cups, 3 9-in. soup plates, 3 knives, 3 forks, 3 spoons, cook's knife and sheath, cook's fork and spoon. The whole of the above fitting into a strong galvanized iron bucket with straps and lid, forming a wash-hand basin, and the whole fitting into a basket which may be used for marketing purposes.

No. 13411.—Basket for Game, white wicker, size 23 ins. by 14½ ins. by 16 ins.

No. 13412.—Children's Wicker Panniers, with single or double chair saddle, complete.

No. 13413.—Children's Wicker Panniers and Flounce, complete.

No. 13414.—Wicker Basket, to hold 6 wine bottles.

No. 13414A.—Wicker Basket to hold 12 wine bottles.

No. 13415.—Wicker Hampers for Linen (flat top), made in 2 qualities, and 7 sizes in each quality.

No. 13416.—Wicker Baskets for Wood, stained and varnished in ornamental work, red, brown, and black mixed, with balls on corners, made in 3 sizes, 23 ins. by 16 ins. by 14 ins., 20 ins. by 14 ins. by 13½ ins., 18 ins. by 12 ins. by 12½ ins.

No. 13417.—Wicker Parcels Cart, in 4 sizes, viz. 24 ins. by 18 ins., 29 ins. by 21 ins., 33 ins. by 24 ins., and 37 ins. by 28 ins.

No. 13418.—Baskets (tin lined) for clean plates, full size.

No. 13419.—Clothes Baskets (open), 8 sizes, viz. 22, 24, 26, 28, 30, 32, 34, and 36 ins.

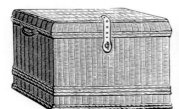

No. 13415A.—Wicker Hamper for Linen (trunk lid). Best quality only, with galvanized iron hasp and staple included, made in 7 sizes.

No. 13420.—Wicker Warehouse Basket (straight bar).

No. 13421.—Basket for Coal (unlined), made in 5 sizes and 2 qualities.

No. 13421A.—Coal Basket or Scuttle, lined with tin, made in 6 sizes.

No. 13422.—Basket for Dirty Plates (tin lined), 14, 16, 18, and 20 ins.

No. 13423.—Rustic Sauce Basket, stained and varnished, to hold 4 bottles, being the only basket that will take the Worcester Sauce bottle.

No. 13424.—Wood Basket, 2 sizes, 16 and 18 inches, in buff, wicker, ebonized, or ebonized and gilt.

No. 13245.—Grocer's Basket, with handle, 16, 18, 20, 21, 23, and 24 ins. across top.

No. 13126.—Linen Basket, round, with lid, 26 ins. high, 15 ins. diameter, and 29 ins. high, 16 ins. diameter.

No. 13427.—Linen Basket, vase shape.

No. 13428.—Linen Basket, barrel shape.

No. 13429.—Linen Basket, square shape.

CARRIAGES,

SADDLERY, HARNESS, HORSE CLOTHING,

WHIPS, STICKS, UMBRELLAS,

WATERPROOF CLOTHING, CARRIAGE RUGS AND APRONS,

BICYCLES AND TRICYCLES
(See Page 710).

GUNS AND PISTOLS,

POWDER FLASKS, GUN CASES,

AMMUNITION, Etc.

PHAETONS, WAGONETTES, DOG CARTS, AND BROUGHAMS.

THE "VICTORIA" PHAETON.

S. & F. London, Manufacturers, and Importers.

"MAIL" PHAETON.

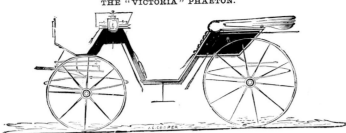

TRADE MARK.

No. 13430.—The "Victoria" Phaeton, a light carriage, hung on easy springs, is elegant in appearance and exceedingly easy for riding; painted any colour to order, and trimmed in best cloth or leather. Has break, lamps, apron, and head of best leather; mounted on Collinge's patent axles.

FOUR-WHEEL DOG CART.

No. 13431.—"Mail" Phaeton, a handsomely finished Carriage, with Collinge's axles, elliptic springs at front and back, trimmed in best cloth or leather, has leather dash and wings and leather head; lamps and break; can be painted and trimmed any colour to order.

LIGHT WAGONETTE.

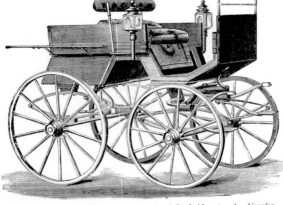

In the Manufacture of all Carriages sold by us the greatest care is exercised to use none but thoroughly seasoned timber.

S. & F. LONDON.

No. 13432.—Four-wheel Dog Cart. This carriage is fitted with seats and cushions for four persons; there is considerable space for luggage. It has lever break and lamps, and is mounted upon elliptic springs at front and back, Collinge's patent axles, cushions of horsehair covered on top with either cloth or repp, and leather on bottom; varnished or painted any colour to order. Usually made with wood dash and wings, but can be made with leather dash and wings at a small extra charge.

No. 13433.—Light Wagonette, a light carriage to carry six persons, mounted on elliptic springs at front and back, Collinge's patent axles, cushions of horsehair, covered on top with either cloth or repp, and leather on bottom; fitted with lever break, silver plated rein rail, and best lamps; varnished or painted any colour to order.

BROUGHAM.

TRADE MARK.

LIGHT WAGONETTE WITH HEAD.

No. 13434.—Brougham, to seat four inside, lined with cloth and finished in best style; has lamps and break; mounted upon elliptic springs at front and back, and Collinge's patent axles; painted any colour to order.

No. 13435.—Light Wagonette with Head, a handsomely-finished Carriage, to seat six persons, lined with cloth, and finished in best style. The framed cover has plate glass lights each side and at front, and door at back; this cover is made portable, and when taken off ordinary back rests can be fitted to the side seats. It has a crank axle at back to keep the body low to the ground, is fitted with easy springs, lamps, and lever break.

THE "PARISIAN" PHAETON.

Awarded Silver Medal, Birkenhead Show.

STANHOPE PHAETON, WITH SPRING DOOR AT BACK.

Estimates and designs can be furnished, at a few days' notice, of any special description of Carriage required.

No. 13436.—The "Parisian" Phaeton, a light four-wheel phaeton (under 4 cwt.) to seat four persons; fitted with Collinge's solid flap axles, wings over wheels, lamps, and cloth cushions; varnished or painted any colour to order.

No. 13437.—Stanhope Phaeton with spring door at back, a light phaeton, with easy springs, Collinge's axles, cushions, lamps, and break. Also made with door and step at back, the hind seat being attached to the door, thus giving a much better access to the hind seat than in the ordinary Stanhope.

LIGHT SPRING LUGGAGE VAN.

No. 13438.—Light Spring Luggage Van, suitable for carriage horse, is especially designed for carrying luggage, &c. Has springs, patent axles, brass oil caps, and wings over wheels, seat and cushions in front for two persons; varnished or painted any colour to order.

THE "GROSVENOR" DOG CART.

No. 13439.—The "Grosvenor" Dog Cart. Stylish and handsome dog cart of superior construction, with Collinge's axle, easy springs, double seats, cushions, best lamps, lancewood shafts, leather dash, and leather wings.

LIGHT VILLAGE CAR.

No. 13440.—Light Village Car. A light trap, has patent axle, lancewood shafts, springs and back springs, wings over wheels, movable seat, and floor-cloth on bottom.

THE "PRINCE OF WALES" CROYDON CAR.

No. 13441.—The "Prince of Wales" Croydon Car, as supplied to H.R.H. the Prince of Wales, Her Majesty the Ex-Empress of the French, &c., &c. Light low car, with patent axle, springs, lancewood shafts, and double seats for four persons.

THE "BRIGHTON" DOG CART.

No. 13442.—The "Brighton" Dog Cart. Useful dog cart, with lancewood shafts, lamps, double seats, easy springs, and cushions of repp; varnished or painted any colour to order.

S. & F. LONDON,

Manufacturers,

Importers,

Warehousemen,

and

Agents.

TRADE MARK.

THE "OXFORD" CAR.

No. 13443.—The "Oxford" Car. Handsome car, on patent axle and easy springs, has leather dash and wings, seats and cushions for four persons, and long lancewood shafts; varnished or painted any colour to order.

FOUR-WHEEL SHOOTING VAN.

No. 13444.—Four-wheel Shooting Van, mounted on patent axles, brass oil caps, springs, seats and cushions at front and back, portable boards fitted at top, front and back, dividing off the whole of the interior for dogs, guns, &c.; luncheon box at top, secured at each side by leather straps, and lock and key; pole for pair of horses.

FOR PARTICULARS OF

Axles, Springs, Coach Ironmongery, &c., see page 638a.

Harness, Horse Clothing, &c.,
see page 665.

Holsters, Valises, Bridles, &c.,
see page 666.

Saddles, see page 667.

Driving Whips, see page 668.

Riding Whips, see page 669.

Walking Sticks, see page 670.

Umbrellas and Sunshades, see
page 671.

Hose Pipe, Fire Buckets, &c.,
see page 672.

Leather Machine Belting, &c.,
see page 672a.

Saddlers' Ironmongery, Carriage Lamps, &c., see page
672b.

WAGONETTE CROYDON CAR.

No. 13445.—Wagonette Croydon Car. Light car, with springs and patent axle, lancewood shafts, wings over wheels, movable front seat, and two seats and door at back like an ordinary wagonette; cushions of repp, and varnished or painted any colour to order.

AMERICAN VICTORIA, WITH EXTENSION TOP.

No. 13446.—American Victoria, with extension top. A light carriage to seat four persons, fitted with Collinge's axles, elliptic springs, leather dash and leather wings, cloth cushions, and portable extension top that folds back when not in use, and is entirely removable.

THE "PARISIAN" PHAETON, WITH CANOPY.

No. 13447.—The "Parisian" Phaeton, with Canopy. Light carriage, shown with a connecting bar between front and hind axles, which is strongly recommended for use on rough roads; to seat four persons, fitted with Collinge's patent axles, wings over wheels, lamps, and cloth cushions; varnished or painted any colour to order.

TRADE MARK   TRADE MARK

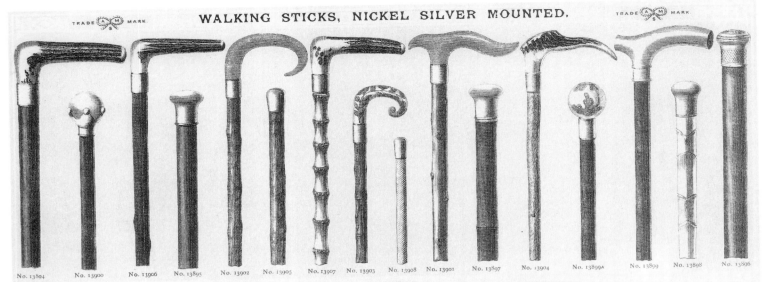

No. 13894 | No. 13900 | No. 13906 | No. 13895 | No. 13902 | No. 13905 | No. 13907 | No. 13903 | No. 13908 | No. 13901 | No. 13897 | No. 13904 | No. 13899A | No. 13899 | No. 13898 | No. 13896

WALKING STICKS, STERLING SILVER MOUNTED.

See Price List for Sword and Dagger Sticks, Pipe Sticks, African Chieftain Sticks, Constables' Truncheons, and Life Preservers of every description.

See Price List for Presentation Sticks of every description, with Sterling Silver or Gold Mounts.

Inscriptions, Monograms, &c., engraved to order.

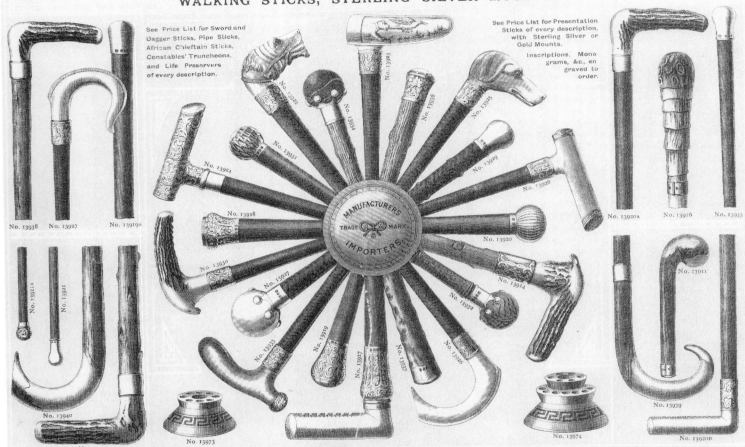

No. 13938 | No. 13927 | No. 13919A | No. 13922 | No. 13923 | No. 13936 | No. 13925 | No. 13920A | No. 13916 | No. 13935

No. 13931 | No. 13934 | No. 13929

No. 13924 | No. 13928

No. 13918 | No. 13920

No. 13921A | No. 13921 | No. 13930 | No. 13927 | No. 13914 | No. 13911

No. 13932

No. 13940 | No. 13933 | No. 13919 | No. 13917 | No. 13937 | No. 13926 | No. 13939

No. 13911B | No. 13973 | No. 13974 | No. 13920B

MANUFACTURERS TRADE MARK IMPORTERS

WALKING STICKS, NATURAL GROWTH, WITH CROOKS OR KNOBS.

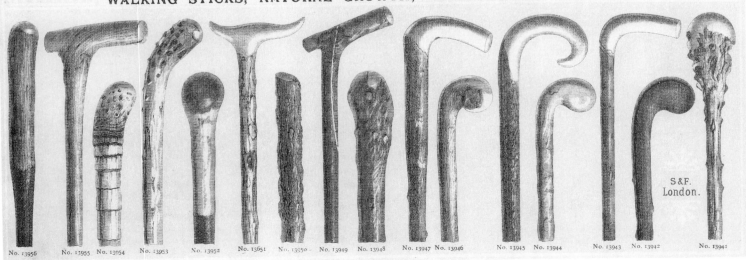

S&F. London.

No. 13956 | No. 13955 | No. 13054 | No. 13953 | No. 13952 | No. 13651 | No. 13950 | No. 13949 | No. 13948 | No. 13947 | No. 13946 | No. 13945 | No. 13944 | No. 13943 | No. 13942 | No. 13941

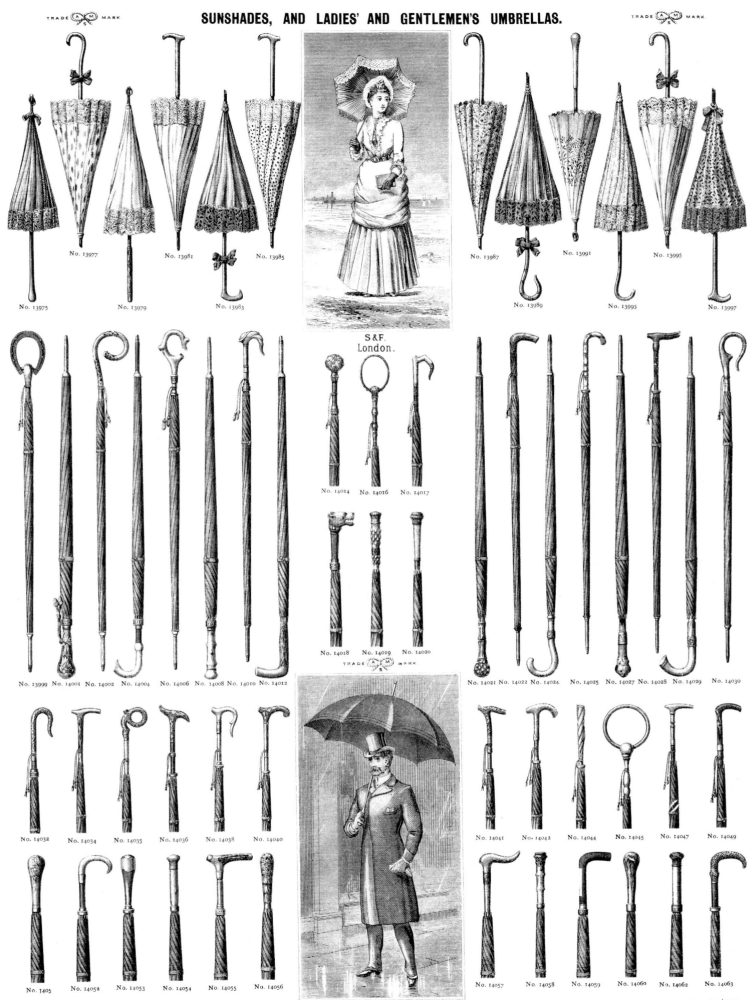

SUNSHADES, AND LADIES' AND GENTLEMEN'S UMBRELLAS.

No. 13975
No. 13977
No. 13979
No. 13981
No. 13983
No. 13985

S & F.
London.

No. 13987
No. 13989
No. 13991
No. 13993
No. 13995
No. 13997

No. 13999 No. 14001 No. 14002 No. 14004 No. 14006 No. 14008 No. 14010 No. 14012

No. 14014 No. 14016 No. 14017

No. 14018 No. 14019 No. 14020

No. 14021 No. 14022 No. 14024 No. 14025 No. 14027 No. 14028 No. 14029 No. 14030

No. 14032 No. 14034 No. 14035 No. 14036 No. 14038 No. 14040

No. 14041 No. 14042 No. 14044 No. 14045 No. 14047 No. 14049

No. 14051 No. 14052 No. 14053 No. 14054 No. 14055 No. 14056

No. 14057 No. 14058 No. 14059 No. 14060 No. 14062 No. 14063

Pawson & Brailsford, Engravers & Printers, Sheffield.

MANUFACTURERS, IMPORTERS, WAREHOUSEMEN AND AGENTS.

ENTERED AT STATIONERS' HALL.

CENTRE REEDED CUSHIONS.

No. 14281.—Centre Reeded Cushions. Sizes, 16 in. by 12 in., 16 in. by 14 in., 16 in. by 16 in., 18 in. by 13 in., 18 in. by 15 in., 18 in. by 18 in., and 18 in. by 20 in.

CIRCULAR REEDED CUSHIONS.

No. 14282.—Circular Reeded Cushions. Sizes, 15 in., 16 in., 17 in., 18 in., 19 in., 20 in., and 21 in.

SQUARE REEDED CUSHIONS.

No. 14283.—Square Reeded Cushions. Sizes, 16 in. by 12 in., 16 in. by 14 in., 16 in. by 16 in., 18 in. by 15 in., 18 in. by 18 in., 18 in. by 22 in., and 18 in. by 26 in.

PLAIN PILLOWS.

No. 14284.—Plain Pillows. Sizes, 18 in. by 13 in., 18 in. by 15 in., 18 in. by 18 in., 18 in. by 22, 18 in. by 24 in., 18 in. by 26 in., 18 in. by 28 in., and 18 in. by 30 in.

CIRCULAR PILLOWS.

No. 14285.—Circular Pillows. Sizes, 15 in., 16 in., 17 in., 18 in., 19 in., 20 in., 21 in., and 22 in.

CARRIAGE OR TRAVELLING CUSHIONS.

No. 14286.—Carriage or Travelling Cushions. Sizes, 16 in. by 12 in., 16 in. by 14 in., and 18 in. by 15 in.

INVALID CUSHIONS FOR CHAIRS.

AIR MATTRESSES.

No. 14287.—Air Mattresses. Sizes, 60 in. by 30 in., 66 in. by 33 in., 72 in. by 36 in., 78 in. by 39 in., 78 in. by 42 in., and 84 in. by 48 in.

BEDS, WITH OR WITHOUT RAISED PILLOW, AND WITH FILLING TUBE.

No. 14288.—Beds, with or without Raised Pillow, and with Filling Tube. Sizes, 72 in. by 24 in., 78 in. by 27 in., 84 in. by 30 in., 88 in. by 33 in., 88 in. by 36 in., and 88 in. by 39 in.

BELLOWS.

No. 14289.—Bellows for inflating beds, cushions, &c. Made in two sizes.

NECK PILLOWS.

No. 14290. — Neck Pillows. Sizes, 16 in. by 23 in., 16 in. by 25 in., and 18 in. by 25 in.

No. 14291.—Invalid Cushions for Chairs. Sizes, 16 in. by 12 in., 16 in. by 12 in., 16 in. by 14 in., 16 in. by 14 in., 16 in. by 16 in., 16 in. by 16 in., 18 in. by 15 in., 18 in. by 15 in., 18 in. by 18 in., 18 in. by 18 in., 18 in. by 18 in., 18 in. by 20 in., and 18 in. by 20 in.

LIFE OR SWIMMING BELTS.

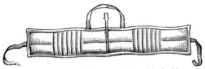

No. 14292.—Life or Swimming Belts. Sizes, 38 in. by 8 in., 42 in. by 8 in., 42 in. by 10 in., 44 in. by 11 in., 46 in. by 11 in., 48 in. by 11 in., 50 in. by 11 in., and 52 in. by 11 in.

THE NEW CIRCULAR BATH, WITH CASE.

OPENED.   CLOSED IN CASE

No. 14293.—Circular Folding Bath, in case complete. Sizes, 24 in., 27 in., 30 in., 33 in., 36 in., and 39 in.

SAUCER OR CAMP BATH, WITH CASE COMPLETE.

No. 14294.—Saucer or Camp Bath. Sizes 24 in., 27 in., 30 in., and 33 in.

WATERPROOF CARRIAGE AND DRIVING APRON.

WATERPROOF WALKING COATS OR ULSTERS.

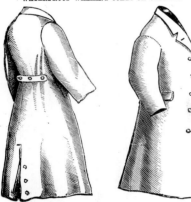

SHOWING BACK.   SHOWING FRONT.

No. 14295.—Waterproof Walking Coats or Ulsters. Made in a variety of textures and qualities.

LADIES' WATERPROOF MANTLES, WITH OR WITHOUT HOODS AND SLEEVES.

No. 14296.—Ladies' Waterproof Mantles, with or without hoods and sleeves.

WATERPROOF MILITARY COAT AND CAPE.

No. 14297.—Waterproof Military Coat and Military Cape.

WATERPROOF HUNTING COAT, WITH LEGGINGS ATTACHED.

No. 14298.—Waterproof Hunting Coat, with leggings attached.

No. 14299.—Waterproof Carriage and Driving Apron, lined imitation fur.

COWHIDE LEGGINGS.

LADY'S WATERPROOF RIDING JACKET.

No. 14300.—Lady's Waterproof Riding Jacket.

CIRJULAR WATERPROOF CAPE.

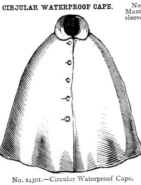

No. 14301.—Circular Waterproof Cape.

COACHMAN'S WATERPROOF DRIVING CAPE, WITH SLEEVES.

No. 14302.—Coachman's Waterproof Driving Cape, with sleeves.

HOT OR COLD WATER BAGS OR BOTTLES.

INDIA-RUBBER BED, FOR HOT OR COLD WATER.

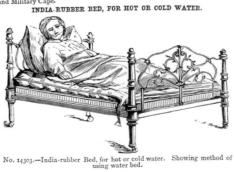

No. 14303.—India-rubber Bed, for hot or cold water. Showing method of using water bed.

WATER BED.

No. 14303.—Water Bed. Sizes, 27 in. by 30 in., approximate weight 8 lb.; 30 in. by 40 in., approximate weight 12 lb.; 36 in. by 48 in., approximate weight 15 lb.; 33 in. by 72 in., approximate weight 20 lb.; 36 in. by 72 in., approximate weight 23 lb.; 42 in. by 72 in., approximate weight 26 lb.; 48 in. by 72 in., approximate weight 30 lb.; 54 in. by 72 in., approximate weight 35 lb.

FISHING TROUSERS.

No. 14304.—Fishing Trousers, in various qualities and sizes.

FISHING STOCKINGS.

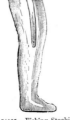

No. 14305.—Fishing Stockings, in various qualities and sizes.

No. 14306.—Hot or Cold Water Bottles. Sizes, 6 in. by 12 in., 7 in. by 10 in., 8 in. by 12 in., 8 in. by 14 in., 9 in. by 12 in., 10 in. by 12 in., 10 in. by 14 in., 10 in. by 16 in., and 12 in. by 16 in.

No. 14307.—Cowhide Leggings, "Napoleon," with tongue to cover instep.

Measurements necessary in ordering Waterproof Clothing are height of wearer and size round chest outside ordinary coat or dress.

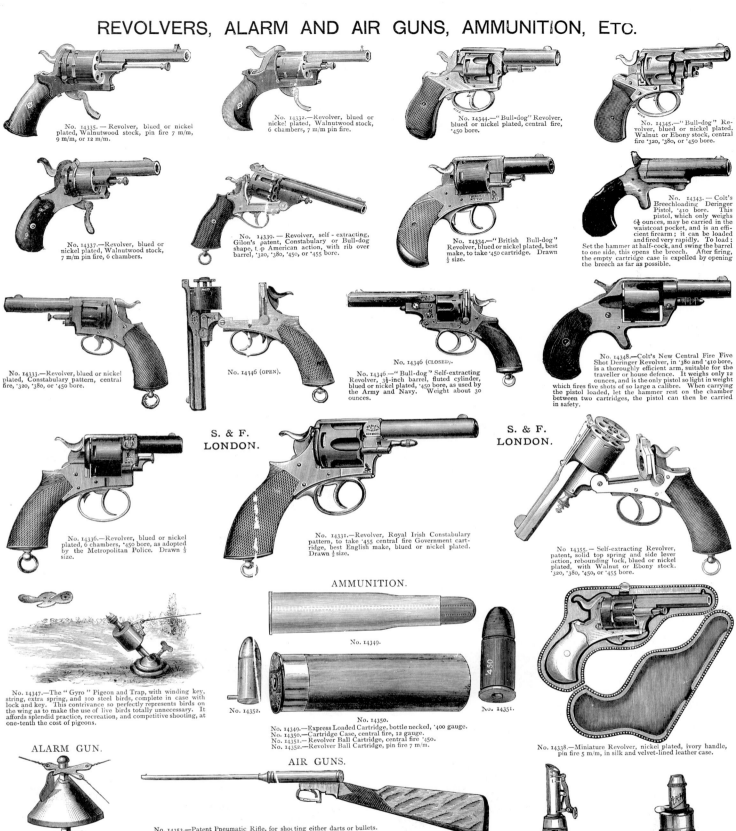

No. 14335. — Revolver, blued or nickel plated, Walnutwood stock, pin fire 7 m/m, 9 m/m, or 12 m/m.

No. 14332. — Revolver, blued or nickel plated, Walnutwood stock, 6 chambers, 7 m/m pin fire.

No. 14344. — "Bull-dog" Revolver, blued or nickel plated, central fire, ·450 bore.

No. 14345. — "Bull-dog" Revolver, blued or nickel plated, Walnut or Ebony stock, central fire ·320, ·380, or ·450 bore.

No. 14337. — Revolver, blued or nickel plated, Walnutwood stock, 7 m/m pin fire, 6 chambers.

No. 14339. — Revolver, self-extracting, Gilon's patent, Constabulary or Bull-dog shape, top American action, with rib over barrel, ·320, ·380, ·450, or ·455 bore.

No. 14334. — "British Bull-dog" Revolver, blued or nickel plated, best make, to take ·450 cartridge. Drawn ⅓ size.

No. 14343. — Colt's Breechloading Deringer Pistol, ·410 bore. This pistol, which only weighs 6½ ounces, may be carried in the waistcoat pocket, and is an efficient firearm; it can be loaded and fired very rapidly. To load: Set the hammer at half-cock, and swing the barrel to one side, this opens the breech. After firing, the empty cartridge case is expelled by opening the breech as far as possible.

No. 14333. — Revolver, blued or nickel plated, Constabulary pattern, central fire, ·320, ·380, or ·450 bore.

No. 14346 (OPEN).

No. 14346 (CLOSED).

No. 14346. — "Bull-dog" Self-extracting Revolver, 3½-inch barrel, fluted cylinder, blued or nickel plated, ·450 bore, as used by the Army and Navy. Weight about 30 ounces.

No. 14348. — Colt's New Central Fire Five Shot Deringer Revolver, in ·380 and ·410 bore, is a thoroughly efficient arm, suitable for the traveller or house defence. It weighs only 12 ounces, and is the only pistol so light in weight which fires five shots of so large a calibre. When carrying the pistol loaded, let the hammer rest on the chamber between two cartridges, the pistol can then be carried in safety.

S. & F. LONDON.

No. 14336. — Revolver, blued or nickel plated, 6 chambers, ·450 bore, as adopted by the Metropolitan Police. Drawn ⅓ size.

No. 14331. — Revolver, Royal Irish Constabulary pattern, to take ·455 central fire Government cartridge, best English make, blued or nickel plated. Drawn ⅓ size.

S. & F. LONDON.

No 14355. — Self-extracting Revolver, patent, solid top spring and side lever action, rebounding lock, blued or nickel plated, with Walnut or Ebony stock. ·320, ·380, ·450, or ·455 bore.

AMMUNITION.

No. 14347. — The "Gyro" Pigeon and Trap, with winding key, string, extra spring, and 100 steel birds, complete in case with lock and key. This contrivance so perfectly represents birds on the wing as to make the use of live birds totally unnecessary. It affords splendid practice, recreation, and competitive shooting, at one-tenth the cost of pigeons.

No. 14349.

No. 14352.

No. 14350.

No. 14351.

No. 14349. — Express Loaded Cartridge, bottle necked, ·400 gauge.
No. 14350. — Cartridge Case, central fire, 12 gauge.
No. 14351. — Revolver Ball Cartridge, central fire ·450.
No. 14352. — Revolver Ball Cartridge, pin fire 7 m/m.

No. 14338. — Miniature Revolver, nickel plated, ivory handle, pin fire 5 m/m, in silk and velvet-lined leather case.

ALARM GUN.

AIR GUNS.

No. 14353. — Patent Pneumatic Rifle, for shooting either darts or bullets. This rifle is simple, noiseless, quite harmless (when ordinary care is used), and can be managed by a child. Each rifle is fitted in a box, with a supply of darts, bullets, paper targets, and wrench.

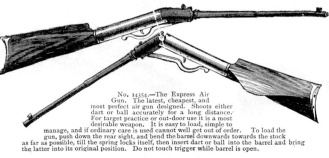

No. 14340. — Poachers' Alarm Gun, registered, breech-loading, for screwing in the ground. This is easily loaded or unloaded, no cleaning required after being discharged, there are no springs or complicated mechanism; no covering is required, as its construction excludes the wet.

No. 14354. — The Express Air Gun. The latest, cheapest, and most perfect air gun designed. Shoots either dart or ball accurately for a long distance. For target practice or out-door use it is a most desirable weapon. It is easy to load, simple to manage, and if ordinary care is used cannot well get out of order. To load the gun, push down the rear sight, and bend the barrel downwards towards the stock as far as possible, till the spring locks itself, then insert dart or ball into the barrel and bring the latter into its original position. Do not touch trigger while barrel is open.

No. 14341. — Shot Pouch, brown leather, with best brass lever charger.

No. 14342. — Powder Flask, bronzed copper, holding 8 ounces.

S. & F. LONDON.

S. & F. LONDON.

TRADE MARK.

TRADE MARK.

No. 14357.—WINCHESTER REPEATING RIFLE.

Express Model, with a reserve of 5 cartridges 500 bore, length 3 feet 7 inches, weight 8¾ lbs. It is sighted up to 300 yards, point blank to 150 yards, and shoots with great power and accuracy.

No. 14358.—WINCHESTER REPEATING CARBINE.

Model 1873, with a reserve of 12 cartridges 440 bore, length of barrel 20 inches, weight 7¼ lbs. This pattern is well suited for travellers or explorers, whether on foot, horseback, or in boats; also for house protection. It is light and handy, and shoots well up to 500 yards.

The principal advantage of this admirable weapon is, that below the barrel is a tube containing a reserve of cartridges, which are placed in the barrel one by one as the spent cartridge is ejected. This is done simply by the action of opening and closing the breech lever. The reserve cartridges may be kept intact if desired, and the weapon loaded for each discharge. These rifles are made in three different sizes and bores.

No. 14359.—Martini-Henry Sporting Rifles, short stocked, chequered hand and fore-end, with safety bolt, sporting sights.

No. 14360.—Martini-Henry Sporting Rifles, short stocked, chequered hand and fore-end, with safety bolts, military sights.

No. 14363.—Saloon Gun, with cartridge extractor, gun black rust-proof barrel, hardened mounting, chequered carved stock, &c.

**S. & F.
LONDON.**

No. 14361.—Muzzle-loading Single Barrel Gun, real twist barrel, back-action lock, walnut stock.

No. 14362.—Muzzle-loading Double Barrel Gun, real twist barrels, back-action lock.

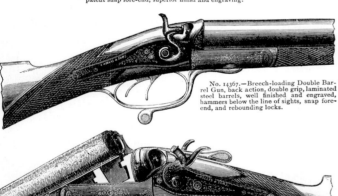

No. 14365.—Hammerless Breech-loading Double Barrel Gun, automatic safety bolts, Damascus barrels, patent snap fore-end, superior finish and engraving.

No. 14364.—Rook Rifle, hammerless, top lever, octagon barrel, superior filed action, pistol hand stock.

No. 14367.—Breech-loading Double Barrel Gun, back action, double grip, laminated steel barrels, well finished and engraved, hammers below the line of sights, snap fore-end, and rebounding locks.

No. 14366.—Breech-loading Rook Rifle, Martini, patent octagon barrel, safety bolts, platina-lined sights, pistol hand, superior finish.

No. 14369.—Breech-loading Double Barrel Gun, finely laminated steel barrels, hammers below the line of sights, solid strikers, top lever, patent snap fore-end, good figured stock, superior finish and engraving.

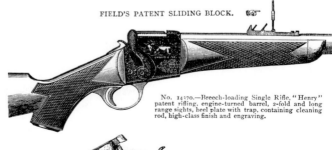

No. 14368.—Express Single Rifle, Field's patent, and Henry patent rifling, flat on top of barrel, improved pattern sights, high-class finish, and richly engraved. All these rifles are accurately sighted and shot.

FIELD'S PATENT SLIDING BLOCK.

No. 14371.—Breech-loading Double Barrel Gun, top lever, fine laminated steel barrels, well filed, 3-pin bridle rebounding lock, hammers below the line of sight, solid strikers, improved action, percussion fence, patent snap fore-end, good figured stock, superior finish and engraving.

No. 14370.—Breech-loading Single Rifle, "Henry" patent rifling, engine-turned barrel, 2-fold and long range sights, heel plate with trap, containing cleaning rod, high-class finish and engraving.

No. 14372.—Breech-loading Double Barrel Gun, top lever, Damascus barrels well bored, left barrel "choke," 4-pin bridle lock, hammers below the line of sight, superior filed action, treble bolts, extended rib, percussion fence, patent snap fore-end, handsome stock, high-class finish and engraving.

No. 14373.—Express Double Barrel Rifle, "Henry" patent rifling, Damascus barrel, 3-pin bridle rebounding lock, patent snap fore-end, file-cut rib, best improved sight, handsome stock, and richly engraved. The greatest attention is devoted to the sighting, &c., of the above rifles, and the utmost possible care exercised in testing them for accurate shooting.

GUN CASES, MAGAZINES & HOLSTERS, BREECH-LOADING GUN IMPLEMENTS, Etc.

No. 14387.—Cartridge Belt with patent spring clasps. This article is the lightest and most simple contrivance for carrying from 24 to 36 cartridges. It is worn under the coat, and requires no further cover. It fits very compactly into any gun case. Can be had in various sizes to carry 24, 27, 30, 33, or 36 cartridges.

No. 14390.—Combined Holster, Pouch, and Belt, leather, with buckle fastening.

No. 14388.—Sling Gun Case or Gun Bag, hide leather.

No. 14391.—The "Handy" Gun Case, solid leather.

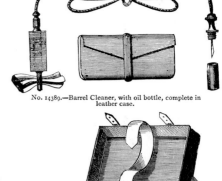

No. 14389.—Barrel Cleaner, with oil bottle, complete in leather case.

No. 14395.—Gun Case, black japanned canvas, lined cloth, short front straps and lock. This case is planned for the stock at bottom and barrels above. It has space for implements, ammunition, &c. It is most portable and compact for either breech or muzzle loaders.

No. 14396.—Cartridge Magazine, with regulating strap, recommended as being both convenient and portable, solid leather, made in different sizes to carry 200, 300, 400, 500, or 600 cartridges.

No. 14392.—Nipple Key, with polished wood handle.

No. 14393.—Turnscrew, with polished wood handle.

No. 14394.—Powder and Shot Measure combined, with ramming handle.

No. 14392.   No. 14393.   No. 14394.

No. 14399.—Cartridge Extractor, brass, for central fire cartridges.

No. 14400.—Cartridge Extractor, nickel silver, with dog whistle, for central fire cartridges.

No. 14401.—Wad Punch, steel.

No. 14399.   No. 14400.   No. 14401.

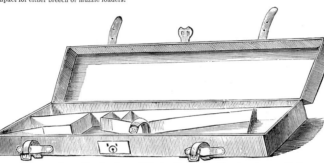

No 14397.—Compendium Gun Case, solid leather, lined green or blue, short straps, and lock.

No. 14398.—Cartridge Magazine, fitted with tubular trays, thus keeping each cartridge separate, solid leather, made in different sizes to carry 50, 100, 200, 300, or 400 cartridges.

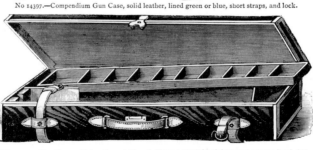

No. 14402.—Gun Case, with tray for cartridges (half-way across), black japanned canvas, lined cloth, covered tray, short front straps, and lock.

No. 14403. — Cartridge-closing Machine, with pusher out, for pin and central fire.

No. 14404.—Brass Funnel and Wood Rammer.

No. 14405.— Oil Bottle, glass, with brass top.

No. 14406.—Cartridge Extractor, brass, for central fire cartridge.

TRADE MARK.

A M S

No. 14407.— Re-capper and Expeller, polished brass.

S. & F., London.

No. 14408.—Cartridge Magazine, with regulating strap, flat shape, constructed to go under railway seat, solid leather, made in different sizes to carry 200, 300, 400, 500, or 600 cartridges.

No. 14409.—Folding Knife, Fork, and Spoon, with stag or ivory handles, in leather-covered case.

No. 14413.—Breech Cleaner, with brass cap for brush.

No. 14410.—Cartridge-filling, Ramming, and Closing Machine.

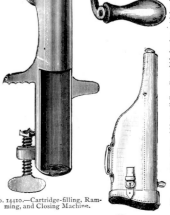

No. 14411.—The "Leg of Mutton" Gun Case, hide leather, with handle, brass furniture.

No. 14412.—Cleaning Rod, with implements.

No. 14411.   No. 14412.

S. & F., London.

PURSES, PORTEMONNAIES,

CIGAR AND CIGARETTE CASES, CARD CASES,
WALLETS, JEWEL CASES, TOURISTS' CASES,
ALBUMS, SCRAP BOOKS AND PHOTOGRAPH FRAMES,
MUSIC PORTFOLIOS, LADIES' COMPANIONS,
GLOVE AND HANDKERCHIEF BOXES,
FLASKS AND SANDWICH BOXES,
WRITING DESKS IN LEATHER AND WOOD,
LETTER BALANCES, CALENDARS,
WORK BOXES, DRESSING CASES, FITTED IVORY BRUSH CASES,
BRUSHES, COMBS, SOAP AND PERFUMERY,
BRACKETS, PAPIER-MACHÉ GOODS, TABLE MATS, CHAMOIS LEATHERS,
JAPANESE GOODS OF EVERY DESCRIPTION,
JUDSON'S DYES.

GAMES,
GYMNASTIC APPARATUS,
CRICKETING GOODS, LAWN TENNIS, FISHING TACKLE.

BICYCLES AND TRICYCLES,
PERAMBULATORS.

ENGLISH AND FOREIGN TOYS AND DOLLS.

ENGLISH AND FOREIGN BASKETS,
SHOW CASES AND FITTINGS.

CIGARS,
REAL HAVANA, CONTINENTAL, AND ENGLISH.
CIGARETTES.

PIPES,
MEERSCHAUM, BRIAR ROOT, AND SILVER MOUNTED.
GENERAL TOBACCONISTS' SUNDRIES.

PURSES, PORTEMONNAIES, WALLETS,

CIGAR, CIGARETTE, AND CARD CASES, JEWEL CASES, TOURISTS' CASES,
ALBUMS, SCRAP BOOKS, AND PHOTOGRAPH FRAMES,
WRITING DESKS, WORK BOXES, DRESSING CASES, FITTED BRUSH CASES,
BRUSHES, COMBS, SOAP AND PERFUMERY,
BRACKETS, PAPIER-MACHÉ GOODS, TABLE MATS, JAPANESE GOODS, Etc.
GAMES, BICYCLES AND TRICYCLES, PERAMBULATORS, ENGLISH AND FOREIGN TOYS AND DOLLS,
SHOW CASES AND FITTINGS.

The illustrations on the following pages give but a very inadequate representation of the assortment in each class of the Goods, named above, that we have always in stock, and which are more fully represented in the second volume of our General Catalogue published some little time ago. As the designs of many of these articles change very rapidly, and as even the best illustration gives but an imperfect idea of the goods, we recommend and invite our customers to visit our establishment as often as convenient, especially as we do not replace, when sold out, many of the novelties introduced or purchased by us every season.

When it is not convenient for our customers to make their own selections from our stock, we shall be happy to send them an assortment to such an amount as they may fix upon. We are convinced that the care and attention with which such orders are executed by us will lead to an increase of business to our mutual advantage.

Fancy goods of every description, whether of English or foreign manufacture, not enumerated in the following pages or in our former catalogues, can be procured for our customers when required. Our establishment in Paris and our connection on the Continent afford us special facilities for obtaining the latest novelties as soon as introduced, and also to purchase them at such prices as enable us to meet every fair competition. Owing to our large purchases we are frequently able to sell at lower prices than those which smaller buyers can obtain from the manufacturers. Estimates given for large quantities at the shortest notice.

CIGARS,

REAL HAVANA, CONTINENTAL, AND ENGLISH,
CIGARETTES, MEERSCHAUM AND BRIAR ROOT PIPES, TOBACCONISTS' SUNDRIES.

We think that we have the knowledge and means at our command requisite for the purchase of real Havana Cigars to the best advantage; the secret of success in this trade is to buy well, for cigars well bought are half sold.

Our Continental Cigars are in good repute, and have, without exception, given satisfaction to our customers for many years.

The sale of English Cigars is a recent addition to our Tobacco trade. The arrangements we have made are such as to render us confident in recommending these goods to our numerous customers.

Cigars in bond are sold in original cases of not less than 80 lbs. weight, or from 5,000 to 8,000 cigars in a case, according to the size of the cigars.

Original cases of Havana Cigars contain a fair proportion of light, medium, and dark colours. Should light colours only be desired, an advance of from 5 to 10 per cent. on quotations given will be charged.

No. 14421.—Lock Purse, imitation calf skin.

No. 14422.—Lock Purse, morocco leather, with paper knife.

No. 14424.—Lock Purse, real morocco leather, with expanding gusset.

No. 14425.—Lock Purse, real calf skin.

S. & F.
London.

No. 14426.—Lock Purse, Persian leather, with note book and pencil.

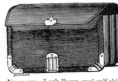

No. 14427.—Lock Purse, real calf skin, with expanding gusset, nickel silver mounts.

No. 14423.—Lock Purse, polished morocco leather.

No. 14428.—Lock Purse, "money-box purse," imitation crocodile.

No. 14437.—Lock Purse, calf skin, with ivory tablet.

No. 14436.—Lock Purse, calf skin, fitted with note book and pencil.

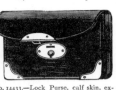

No. 14433.—Lock Purse, calf skin, expanding gusset, nickel silver mounts.

No. 14432.—Lock Purse, calf skin, with centre gold compartment.

No. 14430.—Lock Purse, calf skin, expanding gusset.

No. 14429.—Lock Purse, calf skin, treble opening.

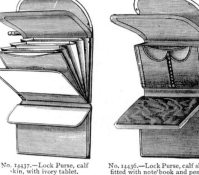

No. 14434.—Lock Purse, new secret spring, calf skin, expanding gusset.

No. 14439.—Lock Purse, calf skin, expanding gusset.

No. 14445.—Elastic Band Purse, morocco leather, with paper knife.

No. 14440.—Elastic Band Purse, with stamp pockets.

No. 14451.—Elastic Band Purse, Russia leather, with ivory tablet.

No. 14448.—Elastic Band Purse, Persian leather, expanding gusset.

No. 14438.—Lock Purse, calf skin, fitted with button-hook, stiletto, bodkin, and needle case.

No. 14443.—Elastic Band Purse, Persian leather, with note book and pencil.

No. 14441.—Elastic Band Purse, gilt lettered outside.

No. 14452.—Elastic Band Purse, striped Russia, with ivory tablet.

No. 14450.—Elastic Band Purse, calf skin, expanding gusset.

No. 14447.—Elastic Band Purse, Persian leather, with note book and pencil.

No. 14444.—Elastic Band Purse, Persian leather, with stamp pockets.

No. 14442.—Elastic Band Purse, real morocco leather.

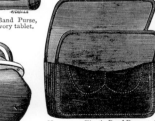

No. 14449.—Elastic Band Purse, calf leather, assorted colours.

No. 14446.—Elastic Band Purse, Persian leather, with card pocket outside.

No. 14463.—Bag Purse, kid leather, with gold compartment.

No. 14464.—Bag Purse, morocco leather, treble opening.

No. 14453.—Bag Purse, assorted leathers.

No. 14455.—Bag Purse, French morocco leather, steel frame.

No. 14469.—Presentation Purse, calf skin, silvered mounts, in satin-lined case.

No. 14465.—Bag Purse, morocco, embroidered flowers.

No. 14467.—Bag Purse, calf leather, centre pocket.

No. 14466.—Bag Purse, calf leather, ball fastening.

No. 14468.—Bag Purse, calf leather, with centre gold compartment.

No. 14456.—Bag Purse, French morocco, inside division.

No. 14458.—Bag Purse, French morocco, gilt frame, lined with rhamois leather.

No. 14459.—Bag Purse, morocco leather, double opening.

No. 14461.—Bag Purse, morocco leather, large size, double opening.

PURSES, CARD CASES, BILL CASES, &C.

No. 14471.—Portmonnaie, assorted plush, gilt mounts.

No. 14472.—Portmonnaie, assorted plush, nickel silver mounts.

No. 14474.—Portmonnaie, morocco leather, nickel silver mounts.

No. 14476.—Portmonnaie, morocco leather.

No. 14476A.—Portmonnaie, calf skin, nickel silver frame.

No. 14477.—Portmonnaie, calf skin, fancy frame.

No. 14478.—Portmonnaie, Russia leather.

No. 14479.—Portmonnaie, morocco leather.

No. 14484.—Portmonnaie, imitation tortoiseshell inlaid flowers.

No. 14486.—Portmonnaie, ivory sides, nickel silver frame.

No. 14481.—Portmonnaie, calf skin, riveted frame.

No. 14482.—Portmonnaie, calf skin, engraved frame.

No. 14488.—Portsea Purse, morocco leather.

No. 14489.—Portsea Purse, pigskin, with gusset.

No. 14491.—Portsea Purse, solid calf leather.

No. 14492.—Portsea Purse, solid calf leather, patent lock.

No. 14493.—Gold Purse, bag shape.

No. 14494.—Gold Purse, watch shape, nickel silver.

No. 14495.—Gold Purse, covered morocco leather, to hold sovereigns one end and half-sovereigns the other end.

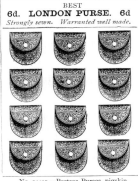

BEST
6d. LONDON PURSE. 6d
Strongly sewn. Warranted well made.

No. 14497.—Portsea Purses, pigskin, with division in centre.

THE EXPANDING
SOLID LEATHER PURSE.
One Shilling Each.

No. 14498.—Lock Purses, solid leather, lined leather, with nickel silver-plated locks.

THE USEFUL
1/6 each. CITY PURSE. 1/6 each.
Best make.

No. 14499.—Elastic Band Purses, Persian leather, large size, lined with leather.

BEST
1/ each. LONDON PURSE. 1/ each.
Russian Leather.

No. 14500.—Portsea Purses, Russia leather, with division in centre.

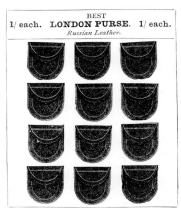

14507.—Card Case, calf leather, with sliding ivory tablet and pencil.

No. 14501.—Gentleman's Card Case, pull-off, scented Russia leather.

No. 14502.—Lady's Card Case, pull-off, scented Russia leather.

No. 14503.—Card Case, with spring, Persian leather.

No. 14504.—Lady's Card Case, calf leather.

No. 14505.—Lady's Card Case, morocco leather.

No. 14511.—Bill Case, cloth, without flap.

No. 14508.—Housewife, leather, fitted with cottons, &c.

No. 14506.—Card Case, morocco leather, with ivory tablet.

No. 14509.—Housewife, French morocco leather, tuck fastening.

No. 14515.—Bill Case for the pocket, roan leather, elastic band.

No. 14513.—Bill Case, black roan leather.

No. 14517.—Banker's Bill Case, roan leather.

WINE, SPIRIT, AND LIQUEUR CABINETS, ETC.

No. 14621.—The Combined Scent and Jewel Cabinet, in Brown Oak, with nickel mounts, mirror at back, fitted with 3 cut glass bottles and box in front for jewellery.

No. 14622.—The Patent Universal Liqueur Cabinet, in Oak, Walnut, or Coromandel wood, with 3 pint bottles and 10 glasses.

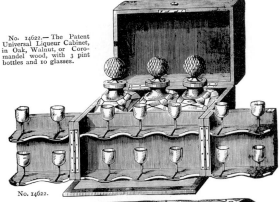

No. 14622.

TRADE MARK

No. 14623.—The "Excelsior" Scent Stand, in Brown Oak, with nickel mounts, fitted with 3 cut glass bottles and spring lock.

No. 14624.—The "Tantalus" Wine and Spirit Stand, in Brown Oak, with nickel handle and mounts, fitted with 3 richly cut bottles and Bramah lock.

No.14625.—Liqueur and Cigar Cabinet, in Brown Oak with nickel mounts, mirror at back, fitted with 3 richly cut bottles and box in front for cigars.

No. 14625.

No. 14626.—Wine and Spirit Cabinet, in Oak, with 4 cut crystal pint bottles.

No. 14627.—The Combined Brandy and Soda Water Cabinet, in Brown Oak, Walnut, or Coromandel wood, containing 4 cut crystal pint bottles, 2 tumblers, 2 soda water tumblers, and 8 glasses.

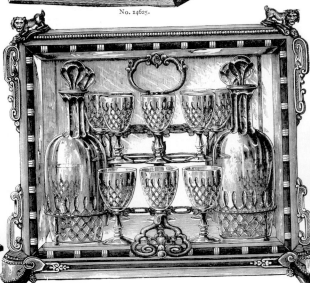

No. 14628.—Liqueur Cabinet. The sides, top, and bottom are of the best cut crystal bevelled glass, mounted in a frame of real bronze gilt, relieved with darkened bronze. The four feet representing the heads of elephants, as also the ornaments on top, are highly finished. The cabinet is fitted with a good lock and key, and holds in a movable frame 4 best cut decanters and 16 liqueur glasses to match. When open, the front and top are secured by a spring. Height 12½ inches, length 14¼ inches, width 12 inches.

S. & F.
LONDON.

S. & F.
LONDON.

No. 14629.—Liqueur Cabinet, ebonized wood finely polished and richly inlaid with brass buhl work, the sides being made to open as shown in the engraving, containing 4 cut crystal glass decanters and 16 glasses to match, with spring catch to fasten lid back, fitted with a good lock and key. Height 11 inches, length 12 inches, width 9 inches.

No. 14630.—Liqueur Stand, bronze frame richly gilt, fitted with mirrors at the back and bottom, containing 4 richly engraved crystal glass decanters and 16 glasses to match, the decanters and glasses being fitted into a framework. Height 15½ inches, length 13½ inches, width 8¾ inches.

No. 14631.—Liquor Cabinet, ebonized wood richly polished, handsomely inlaid with pearl and brass buhl work, the sides being made to open as shown in engraving, fitted with 4 richly cut crystal glass decanters, each decanter holding about 1½ pint. When open, the back is secured by a spring. Fitted with a good lock and key. Height 11 inches, length 12¾ inches, width 10½ inches.

No. 14632.—Liqueur Cabinet, ebonized wood with crystal glass top and sides, richly bevelled edges, fitted with a movable framework, holding 4 richly cut glass crystal decanters and 16 glasses to match. When open, the top is secured by a spring catch. Fitted with a good lock and key. Height 12¾ inches, length 14¼ inches, width 12¼ inches.

CIGAR, TOBACCO, SPIRIT, AND LIQUEUR CABINETS, Etc.

No. 14642.— Lava Tobacco Jar, decorated with floral designs on black ground. Height 5½ inches, diameter 3½ inches.

No. 14643.—Tobacco Jar, decorated with painted flowers, gilt lines, and with the word Tobacco printed in gilt letters on ivory coloured ground. Height about 5 ins., diameter about 3½ inches.

No. 14644.— China Tobacco Jar, decorated with blue floral designs and gilt on white ground. Height about 5 inches, diameter about 2¾ inches.

No. 14641.—Cigar Cabinet, ebonized wood richly polished and inlaid with ivory, pearl, and brass Buhl work, bound with solid brass, containing 4 Spanish mahogany trays, each to hold 12 cigars, and 1 drawer for tobacco; fitted with a good lock and key, and spring catch to fasten the lid back when open. Height 6½ inches, length 11½ inches, width 8¼ inches.

No. 14645.—Cigar Cabinet, ebonized wood richly polished, handsomely inlaid with pearl and brass Buhl work, solid brass edge to lid, containing 4 Spanish mahogany trays for cigars, and 1 drawer for tobacco; fitted with a good lock and key and spring catch to fasten lid back when open. Height 9 inches, length 11 inches, width 8½ inches.

No. 14646.—Cigar, Tobacco and Pipe Cabinet, in Walnutwood, drawers for cigars, cigarettes, and tobacco, with space for pipes, case on door to hold match box.

No. 14646.

No. 14647.—Cigar Cabinet, with three drawers, in Oak or Walnutwood, with spring Bramah lock, best finish.

No. 14649.—Cigar Cabinet, Walnutwood, inlaid fancy wood panels, 3 drawers, with brass sunken handles.

No. 14652.— Revolving Stand, ebonized, with gilt mounts, with gilt racks for cigars.

No. 14653.—Cigar Cabinet, in brown Oak, nickel handle on top, fall front, with drawer at bottom for pipes.

"THE JANITOR"

No. 14655.—The Patent Spring-opening Cigar and Cigarette Box, in Brown Oak.

No. 14656.—Cigar Cabinet, solid Oak, with two drawers and gilt handle on top.

No. 14664.—Cigar Lighter, with spirit lamp, electro-silver plated on nickel silver, or Britannia metal.

No. 14663. — The Janitor Wine and Spirit Frame, in Oak, Walnut, or Coromandel wood, with 4 richly cut bottles and nickel handle.

No. 14658.—China Ash Tray, leaf design, decorated with blue floral designs and gilt on white ground. Length 5 inches.

No. 14659.—China Ash Tray, leaf design, decorated with gilt lines on white ground. Length about 4 inches, width about 3 inches.

No. 14660.—China Ash Tray, leaf design, white, decorated with gilt lines. Length 5 inches.

No. 14661.—Wine, Spirit, and Cigar Cabinet, in Oak, Walnut, or Coromandel wood, fitted with 3 pint bottles, 4 tumblers, 6 glasses, and revolving cigar stand.

No. 14665.—New Patent Spirit and Cigar Cabinet, in brown Oak and nickel mounts, mirror in back, 3 richly cut bottles, 6 glasses, tray for cigars, and spring Bramah lock.

No. 14667.— The Tantalus Spirit Stand, in brown Oak, with nickel mounts, 3 richly cut bottles, and fitted with 12 glasses.

No. 14668.—The New Tantalus Spirit and Cigar Stand, in brown Oak, 3 richly cut bottles, and spring Bramah lock.

REAL BRIAR ROOT PIPES, POUCHES, CIGAR CUTTERS, &C.

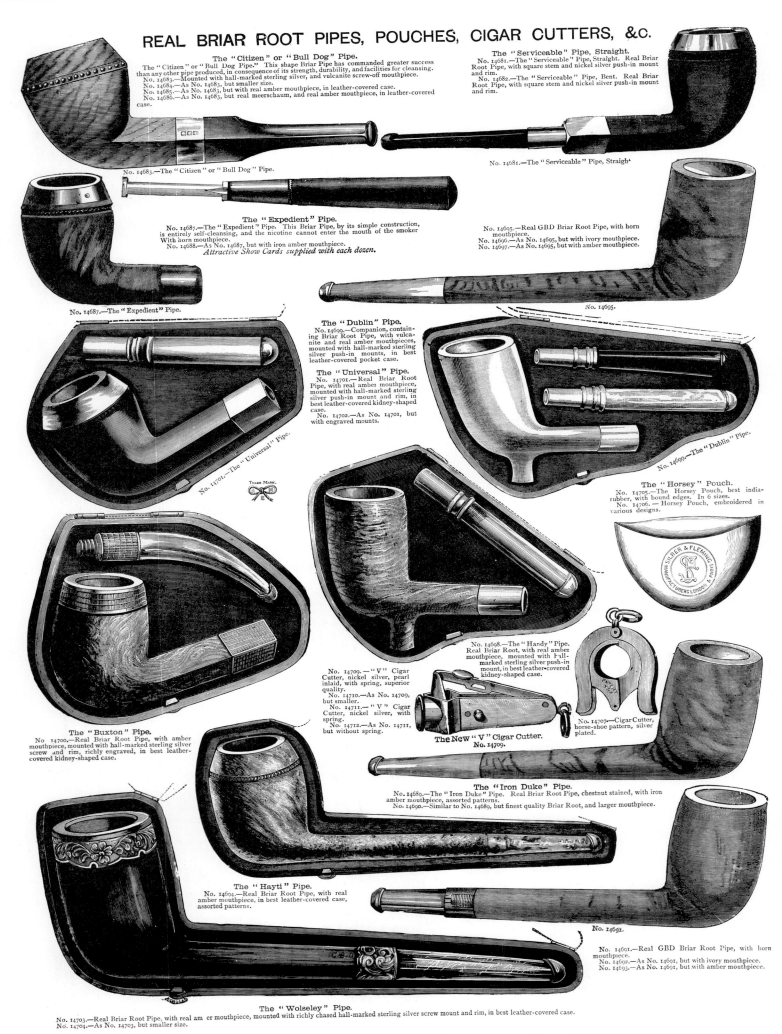

The "Citizen" or "Bull Dog" Pipe.
The "Citizen" or "Bull Dog Pipe." This shape Briar Pipe has commanded greater success than any other pipe produced, in consequence of its strength, durability, and facilities for cleansing.
No. 14683.—Mounted with hall-marked sterling silver, and vulcanite screw-off mouthpiece.
No. 14684.—As No. 14683, but smaller size.
No. 14685.—As No. 14683, but with real amber mouthpiece, in leather-covered case.
No. 14686.—As No. 14683, but real meerschaum, and real amber mouthpiece, in leather-covered case.

No. 14683.—The "Citizen" or "Bull Dog" Pipe.

The "Serviceable" Pipe, Straight.
No. 14681.—The "Serviceable" Pipe, Straight. Real Briar Root Pipe, with square stem and nickel silver push-in mount and rim.
No. 14682.—The "Serviceable" Pipe, Bent. Real Briar Root Pipe, with square stem and nickel silver push-in mount and rim.

No. 14681.—The "Serviceable" Pipe, Straight.

The "Expedient" Pipe.
No. 14687.—The "Expedient" Pipe. This Briar Pipe, by its simple construction, is entirely self-cleansing, and the nicotine cannot enter the mouth of the smoker With horn mouthpiece.
No. 14688.—As No. 14687, but with iron amber mouthpiece.
Attractive Show Cards supplied with each dozen.

No. 14687.—The "Expedient" Pipe.

No. 14695.—Real GBD Briar Root Pipe, with horn mouthpiece.
No. 14696.—As No. 14695, but with ivory mouthpiece.
No. 14697.—As No. 14695, but with amber mouthpiece.

No. 14695.

The "Dublin" Pipe.
No. 14699.—Companion, containing Briar Root Pipe, with vulcanite and real amber mouthpieces, mounted with hall-marked sterling silver push-in mounts, in best leather-covered pocket case.

The "Universal" Pipe.
No. 14701.—Real Briar Root Pipe, with real amber mouthpiece, mounted with hall-marked sterling silver push-in mount and rim, in best leather-covered kidney-shaped case.
No. 14702.—As No. 14701, but with engraved mounts.

No. 14701.—The "Universal" Pipe.

No. 14699.—The "Dublin" Pipe.

The "Horsey" Pouch.
No. 14705.—The Horsey Pouch, best india-rubber, with bound edges. In 6 sizes.
No. 14706. — Horsey Pouch, embroidered in various designs.

The "Buxton" Pipe.
No. 14700.—Real Briar Root Pipe, with amber mouthpiece, mounted with hall-marked sterling silver screw and rim, richly engraved, in best leather-covered kidney-shaped case.

No. 14698.—The "Handy" Pipe. Real Briar Root, with real amber mouthpiece, mounted with hall-marked sterling silver push-in mount, in best leather-covered kidney-shaped case.

No. 14709.—"V" Cigar Cutter, nickel silver, pearl inlaid, with spring, superior quality.
No. 14710.—As No. 14709, but smaller.
No. 14711.—"V" Cigar Cutter, nickel silver, with spring.
No. 14712.—As No. 14711, but without spring.

The New "V" Cigar Cutter.
No. 14709.

No. 14707.—Cigar Cutter, horse-shoe pattern, silver plated.

The "Iron Duke" Pipe.
No. 14689.—The "Iron Duke" Pipe. Real Briar Root Pipe, chestnut stained, with iron amber mouthpiece, assorted patterns.
No. 14690.—Similar to No. 14689, but finest quality Briar Root, and larger mouthpiece.

The "Hayti" Pipe.
No. 14694.—Real Briar Root Pipe, with real amber mouthpiece, in best leather-covered case, assorted patterns.

No. 14691.

No. 14691.—Real GBD Briar Root Pipe, with horn mouthpiece.
No. 14692.—As No. 14691, but with ivory mouthpiece.
No. 14693.—As No. 14691, but with amber mouthpiece.

The "Wolseley" Pipe.
No. 14703.—Real Briar Root Pipe, with real amber mouthpiece, mounted with richly chased hall-marked sterling silver screw mount and rim, in best leather-covered case.
No. 14704.—As No. 14703, but smaller size.

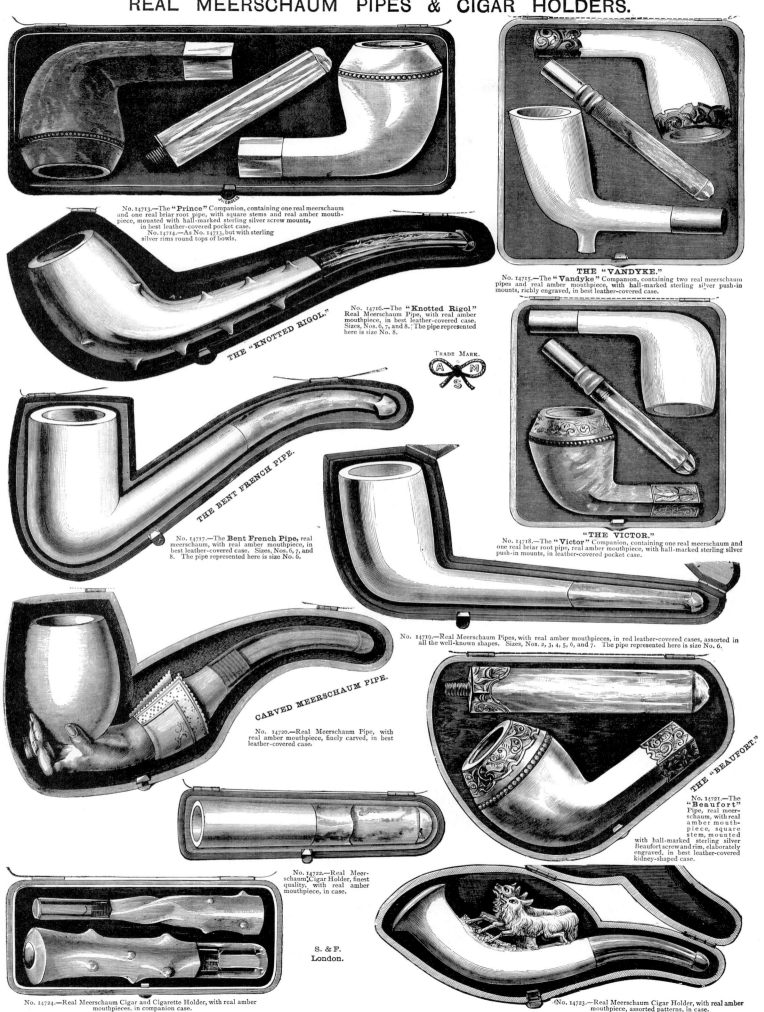

REAL MEERSCHAUM PIPES & CIGAR HOLDERS.

No. 14713.—The "**Prince**" Companion, containing one real meerschaum and one real briar root pipe, with square stems and real amber mouthpiece, mounted with hall-marked sterling silver screw **mounts**, in best leather-covered pocket case.
No. 14714.—As No. 14713, but with sterling silver rims round tops of bowls.

THE "KNOTTED RIGOL."

No. 14716.—The "**Knotted Rigol**" Real Meerschaum Pipe, with real amber mouthpiece, in best leather-covered case. Sizes, Nos. 6, 7, and 8. The pipe represented here is size No. 8.

THE "VANDYKE."
No. 14715.—The "**Vandyke**" Companion, containing two real meerschaum pipes and real amber mouthpiece, with hall-marked sterling silver push-in mounts, richly engraved, in best leather-covered case.

TRADE MARK.

THE BENT FRENCH PIPE.

No. 14717.—The **Bent French Pipe**, real meerschaum, with real amber mouthpiece, in best leather-covered case. Sizes, Nos. 6, 7, and 8. The pipe represented here is size No. 6.

"THE VICTOR."
No. 14718.—The "**Victor**" Companion, containing one real meerschaum and one real briar root pipe, real amber mouthpiece, with hall-marked sterling silver push-in mounts, in leather-covered pocket case.

CARVED MEERSCHAUM PIPE.

No. 14720.—Real Meerschaum Pipe, with real amber mouthpiece, finely carved, in best leather-covered case.

No. 14719.—Real Meerschaum Pipes, with real amber mouthpieces, in red leather-covered cases, assorted in all the well-known shapes. Sizes, Nos. 2, 3, 4, 5, 6, and 7. The pipe represented here is size No. 6.

THE "BEAUFORT."
No. 14721.—The "**Beaufort**" Pipe, real meerschaum, with real amber mouthpiece, square stem, mounted with hall-marked sterling silver Beaufort screw and rim, elaborately engraved, in best leather-covered kidney-shaped case.

No. 14722.—Real Meerschaum Cigar Holder, finest quality, with real amber mouthpiece, in case.

S. & F.
London.

No. 14724.—Real Meerschaum Cigar and Cigarette Holder, with real amber mouthpieces, in companion case.

No. 14723.—Real Meerschaum Cigar Holder, with **real amber** mouthpiece, assorted patterns, in case.

295

No. 14729.—Quarto Album, bound in best calf leather, handsomely embossed in gold.

No. 14730.—Quarto Album, solid olivewood cover, best morocco leather back, and superior nickel-plated corners, shield, and clasp, new floral interior.

No. 14731.—Quarto Album, extra large size, bound in best silk plush, cover mounted with superior gilt and bronze figure.

No. 14732.—Quarto Album, bound in best calf, cover inlaid with floral design. Superior illuminated floral interior.

No. 14733.—Quarto Album, bound in best morocco, extra large size, mounted with superior oxidised and gilt corners, shield, and clasp.

No. 14734.—Quarto Album, bound in best silk plush, and mounted on cover with bonnet made in fine silk, in which a portrait can be placed.

No. 14735.—Quarto Album, bound in best silk plush, mounted with best gilt ornament, shield, and clasp, the interior ornamented with superior floral decorations.

No. 14736.—Quarto Album, bound in best calf leather, mounted with superior nickel-plated corners and clasps, the interior decorated with new floral designs.

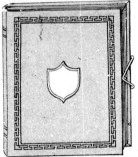

No. 14737.—Quarto Album, bound in leatherette, handsomely embossed, and mounted with nickel-plated shield and clasp.

No. 14738.—Quarto Album, bound in superior plush, mounted with best nickel-plated corners, shield, and clasp.

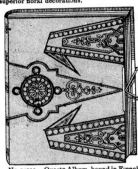

No.14739.—Quarto Album, bound in French morocco, padded cover, handsomely blocked in black and gold.

No. 14740.—Quarto Album, bound in best plush, padded cover, mounted with best nickel-plated shield and clasp, the interior decorated with superior floral illuminations.

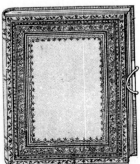

No. 14741.—Quarto Album, bound in French morocco, padded cover, handsomely embossed in black and gold, the interior decorated with views representing the principal castles of the kingdom.

No. 14742.—Quarto Album, bound in best calf, padded cover, handsomely blocked in black and gold, the interior ornamented with superior floral designs.

No. 14743.—Quarto Album, bound in French morocco, padded cover, handsomely embossed.

No. 14744.—Quarto Album, bound in best calf, padded, handsomely embossed in black and gold.

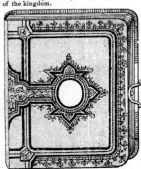

No. 14745.—Quarto Album, bound in Japanese morocco, padded, handsomely embossed in black and gold, the interior ornamented with superior floral designs.

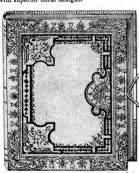

No. 14746.—Quarto Album, bound in French morocco, padded, handsomely embossed in black and gold, the interior ornamented with superior floral designs.

No. 14747.—Quarto Album, bound in leatherette, ornamented with handsome design in black and gold, the interior ornamented with superior floral designs.

No. 14748.—Quarto Album, bound in French morocco, padded, handsomely ornamented in black and gold, the interior ornamented with superior floral designs.

No. 14748.—Easel Album, bound in best silk plush, mounted with superior gilt and bronze figure, four bronze feet, and patent expanding clasp. Size about 14 by 11 inches, to contain 4 promenade, 14 cabinet, and 56 carte-de-visite portraits.

No. 14749.—Easel Album, bound in best silk plush, mounted with best nickel-plated mounts, and crystal glass in front for cabinet size photograph, also a nickel-plated clasp and hinges, and plush-covered folding leg rest, to contain 20 cabinet and 40 carte-de-visite portraits.

No. 14750.—Easel Album, bound in best silk plush, mounted with superior gilt and bronze plate, best oxidized clasp, to contain 4 promenade, 14 cabinet, and 56 carte-de-visite portraits.

No. 14751.—Easel Album, bound in best calf, padded, beautifully embossed in black and gold, fitted with patent spring clasp, the interior is of superior glazed marbled paper, to contain 4 promenade, 14 cabinet, and 48 carte-de-visite portraits.

No. 14752.—Easel Album, bound in best silk plush, fitted on cover with crystal glass for cabinet size photograph, and mounted with best nickel-plated clasp and hinges, so as to lay flat on table showing the back beautifully decorated with real ferns and flowers, To contain 20 cabinet and 40 carte-de-visite portraits.

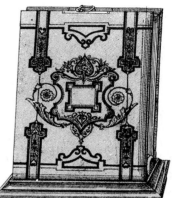

No. 14753.—Easel Album, bound in best morocco, beautifully embossed in black and gold, with padded cover, nickel-plated spring clasp, and beautifully decorated floral interior. Size about 13 by 11 inches. To contain 4 promenade, 16 cabinet, and 42 carte-de-visite portraits.

No. 14754.—Easel Album, bound in best silk plush, and beautifully mounted with flowers on raised silk, with best silk lining and nickel-plated clasp, to contain 16 cabinet and 64 carte-de-visite portraits.

No. 14755.—Photograph Stand or Screen, to stand on table, bound in best silk plush, with superior silk lining, and mounted with transparency decorated with real ferns and flowers, showing 8 cabinet photographs.

No. 14756.—Easel Album, bound in best calf, the cover beautifully embossed and hand painted, the interior ornamented with superior floral decorations, lined with best silk, and fitted with best nickel-plated clasp, to contain 15 cabinet and 58 carte-de-visite portraits.

No. 14757.—Easel Album, bound in best silk plush, with embossed plush centre, mounted with best gilt and nickel-plated ornaments and shield and patent clasp, lined with best silk, to contain 4 promenade, 14 cabinet, and 56 carte-de-visite portraits.

No. 14758.—Photograph Stand or Screen, bound in best silk plush, each end is mounted with glass transparency beautifully decorated with real ferns and flowers, to contain 6 cabinet and 24 carte-de-visite portraits.

No. 14759.—Easel Album, bound in best silk plush, the cover is padded and mounted with best gilt and nickel-plated ornaments and shield, fitted with best nickel-plated spring clasp, to contain 4 promenade, 14 cabinet, and 56 carte-de-visite portraits.

No. 14760.—Octavo Album, bound in leatherette, gold embossed nickel shield and clasp.

No. 14761.—Octavo Album, bound in leatherette, black and gold embossed, nickel clasp.

No. 14762.—Octavo Album, bound in superior calf, black and gold embossed, with extra stout nickel-plated clasp.

No. 14763.—Octavo Album, bound in superior calf, handsomely ornamented on cover, with Oxford pattern black and gold embossing, nickel-plated clasp.

No. 14764.—Octavo Album, bound in Japanese morocco, handsomely embossed on cover, the interior decorated with superior floral designs, nickel-plated clasp.

No. 14765.—Octavo Album, bound in French morocco, handsomely embossed in black and gold, with extra stout nickel-plated clasp.

No. 14766.—Octavo Album, bound in silk plush, with superior nickel-plated shield and clasp.

No. 14767.—Octavo Album, bound in leatherette, handsomely embossed in black and gold, nickel-plated clasp.

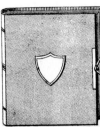

No. 14768.— Victoria Album, bound in silk plush, with superior nickel-plated shield and clasp.

No. 14769. — Victoria Album, bound in leatherette, handsomely blocked in black and gold, with nickel-plated clasp.

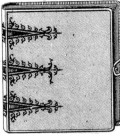

No. 14770. — Victoria Album, bound in best calf, soft padded cover, handsomely blocked in gold, with superior paper inside, and extra stout nickel-plated clasp.

No. 14771.—Victoria Album, bound in French morocco, handsome raised design on cover, with extra stout nickel-plated clasp.

No. 14772.—Victoria Album, bound in French morocco, with soft padded cover, handsomely blocked in black and gold, extra stout nickel-plated clasp.

No. 14773.—Victoria Album, bound in real morocco, handsomely blocked on cover, patent expanding screw clasp.

No. 14776.—Photograph Stand or Screen, bound in best silk plush, the interior decorated with superior floral relief designs; to contain 6 cabinet photographs.

No. 14777.—Best Silk Plush Bonnet Photograph Frame, with satin lining and bow.

No. 14775.—Quarto Album, bound in French morocco, handsomely blocked in black and gold, the interior decorated with handsome floral designs, and fitted with musical box, playing two popular airs.

No. 14778. — Bevelled Glass Cabinet Photograph Frame, gilt and chocolate border, with adjustable spring stand.

No. 14774. — Photographic Album, bound in French morocco, the interior handsomely decorated with new floral relief designs; to contain 16 cabinet photographs.

No. 14779. — Silk Plush Cabinet Photograph Frame, convex glass, square or oval mount.

No. 14780. — Velvet Horse Shoe Carte-de-Visite Frame, with brass mount.

No. 14781.—Imitation Blue and White China Cabinet Photograph Frame, convex glass.

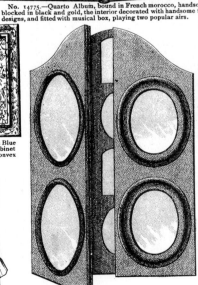

No. 14786.—Best Silk Plush Folding Photograph Screen, to hold 12 cabinet and 10 carte-de-visite photographs.

No. 14782.—Best Silk Plush Cabinet Photograph Frame, convex glass, square or oval mount.

No. 14783.—Best Silk Plush Photograph Frame, convex glasses, oval, square, or dome mounts, to hold 2 cabinet photographs.

No. 14784.—Best Silk Plush Cabinet Photograph Frame, with plush curtains, convex glass, dome or oval mount.

No. 14785.—Best Silk Plush Cabinet Photograph Frame, with satin curtains, convex glass, square or oval mount.

No. 14787.—Best Silk Plush Cabinet Photograph Frame, with folding doors, convex glass, oval or square mount.

No. 14788.—Stamped Brass Cabinet Photograph Frame.

No. 14789.—Gilt Moulded Cabinet Photograph Frame, with oval or dome flock mount.

No. 14791. — Best Silk Plush Photograph Frame, convex glasses ; to hold 4 carte-de-visite portraits.

No. 14790.—Velvet Cabinet Photograph Frame, with fall front, to hold 3 photographs.

No. 14792.—Best Silk Plush Cabinet Photograph Frame, convex glass, square, oval, or dome mount.

No. 14793.—Best Silk Plush Cabinet Photograph Frame, convex glass, oval, square, or dome mounts.

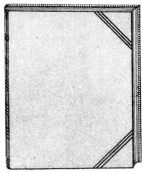

No. 14810.—Scrap Album, bound in half French morocco, superior gilt finish. Size 12½ inches by 10 inches.

No. 14811.—Scrap Album, bound in chequered Persian leather, finished in best style, gilt edges. Size 12½ inches by 10½ inches.

No. 14812.—Album for Postage Stamps, bound in cloth, handsomely blocked in black and gold. Size 11½ inches by 8 inches.

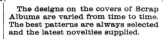

The designs on the covers of Scrap Albums are varied from time to time. The best patterns are always selected and the latest novelties supplied.

Special Scrap Books can be made to any size or number of leaves, and Photographs mounted in same to order.

No. 14813.—Scrap Album, bound in French morocco, extra gilt finish, gilt edges. Size 12½ inches by 10½ inches.

No. 14806.—Scrap Album, bound in cloth, decorated with designs in black and enamel. Size 10½ inches by 8½ inches.

No. 14807.—Album for Literary Scraps and Cuttings, bound in extra stout cloth and blocked with black and coloured designs. Size 8 inches by 10½ inches.

No. 14808.—Autograph Album, bound in cloth, the cover decorated with gold and enamel designs in various colours. Size 10½ inches by 8½ inches.

No. 14809.—Scrap Album, bound in cloth, handsomely decorated with designs in gold and various colours. Size 12½ inches by 10 inches.

No. 14794.—Scrap Album, bound in cloth, blocked with handsome gold and enamel design. Size 12½ inches by 9½ inches.

No. 14795.—Scrap Album, bound in cloth, handsomely blocked in black and gold, bevelled boards. Size 12½ inches by 10 inches.

No. 14796.—Scrap Album, bound in cloth, handsomely blocked in black and enamel. Size 12½ inches by 9½ inches.

No. 14797.—Scrap Album, bound in superior cloth, both sides alike, the cover decorated with raised designs in gold and enamel in variegated colours. Size 12½ inches by 10 inches.

No. 14798.—Scrap Album, for Christmas Cards, bound in cloth, superior design, handsomely blocked in gold and enamel, bevelled boards. Size 12½ inches by 10 inches.

No. 14799.—Scrap Album, bound in cloth, the cover decorated with superior designs inlaid with variegated colours and gold, bevelled boards. Size 12½ inches by 10 inches.

No. 14800.—Scrap Album, bound in cloth, the cover handsomely decorated with inlaid floral design in various colours. Size 12½ inches by 10 inches.

No. 14801.—Scrap Album, bound in cloth, handsomely decorated with black and gold design. Size 12½ inches by 9¾ inches.

No. 14802.—Scrap Album, bound in half morocco, handsomely decorated with inlaid gold and enamel design. Size 15 inches by 12½ inches.

No. 14803.—Scrap Album, bound in cloth, the cover handsomely decorated with designs in gold and various colours. Size 15 inches by 12 inches.

No. 14804.—Scrap Album, bound in cloth, bevelled boards, handsomely decorated with raised designs in black and gold. Size 15 inches by 12 inches.

No. 14805.—Scrap Album, bound in cloth, handsomely decorated with gold and enamel designs. Size 15 inches by 12 inches.

The "Princess" Jewel Case.

No. 14849.—Jewel Case, French morocco leather covered, gilt lines inside and outside, gilt handle, and strong lock, 11 inches long.

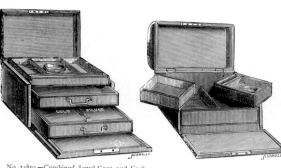

No. 14850.—Combined Jewel Case and Cash Cabinet, covered with French morocco leather, with handle on top, gilt lines, trays for jewellery, and drawers for cash, &c. (as shown in drawing). Sizes, 6 inches, 7 inches, 8 inches, 9 inches, or 10 inches long.

No. 14851.—Jewel Box, with swing trays, covered with French morocco leather, fitted with lock and key. Sizes, 6 inches, 7 inches, 8 inches, 9 inches, or 10 inches long.

No. 14852.—Jewel Box, covered with French morocco leather, with broad and narrow gilt lines, sunken gilt handle, Bramah lock, 2 trays lined with silk velvet. Sizes, 8 inches, 9 inches, 10 inches, 11 inches, or 12 inches long.

No. 14853.—Jewel Box, covered with French morocco leather, fitted with 1 tray, with gilt handle and gilt lines. Sizes, 6 inches, 7 inches, 8 inches, 9 inches, or 10 inches long.

No. 14854.—Jewel Box, covered with French morocco leather, with 2 trays, satin lined, nickel handle on top. Sizes, 7 inches, 8 inches, 9 inches, or 10 inches long.

No. 14855.—Jewel Box, covered with French morocco leather, velvet lined, with tray to lift out, lock and key. Sizes, 6 inches, 7 inches, 8 inches, or 9 inches long.

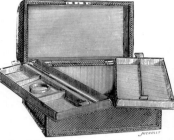

No. 14856.—Jewel Box, covered with Persian leather, 2 trays, satin lined, nickel-plated handle on lid. Sizes, 7 inches, 8 inches, 9 inches, or 10 inches long.

No. 14857.—Toilet Stand, covered rich silk plush, mounted with bevelled edge mirror, and 2 scent bottles.

No. 14858.—Scent Case, covered with French morocco leather, with nickelled plate on lid and nickel fastening, containing 2 cut glass bottles.

No. 14859.—Scent Case, covered with rich silk plush, nickelled mounts and handle, lock and key, lined with velvet and satin, and containing 3 cut glass bottles.

No. 14860.—Scent Case, covered with chequered Persian leather, with nickelled mounts and handles, lock and key, lined with velvet and satin, and containing 3 cut glass bottles.

No. 14861.—Scent Case, covered with Persian leather, bevelled plate glass top, nickelled mounts, lock and key, and containing 2 cut glass bottles.

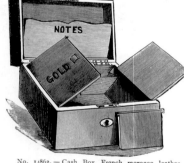

No. 14862.—Cash Box, French morocco leather covered, leather lined, gilt handle on top, fitted with lock and key, secret pocket at back for private papers, &c.

No. 14863.—Cash Cabinet, covered with French morocco leather, 4 drawers, and account books.

No. 14864.—Scent Case, oval, covered with rich silk plush, gilt mounts and handles, and containing 2 cut glass bottles.

No. 14865.—Scent Case, covered with chequered leather, nickelled mounts and fastening, containing 3 cut glass bottles.

The "Beatrice" Jewel Case.

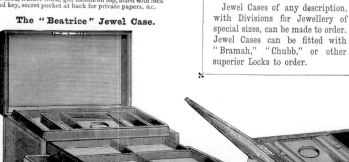

No. 14866.—Jewel Case, covered with French morocco leather, 2 trays, and 2 deep drawers for bracelets, &c., gilt lock and handle, gilt lines inside and outside, velvet and satin lined, 10 inches long.

Jewel Cases of any description, with Divisions for Jewellery of special sizes, can be made to order. Jewel Cases can be fitted with "Bramah," "Chubb," or other superior Locks to order.

No. 14867.—Combined Jewel and Writing Case, a most useful companion for travellers, covered with French morocco leather, silk and satin lined, 12 inches long.

TRADE MARK.

No. 14868.—Jewel Cabinet, covered with rich silk plush of the new stamped crocodile pattern, fall front, with 3 drawers and tray at top, lined with satin, nickel handle on lid. Size of case (when closed), length 7½ inches, width 6½ inches, height 8½ inches.

LEATHER-COVERED WRITING DESKS AND STATIONERY CASES.

No. 14900.—Register Desk, covered chequered leather, ornamented with gilt lines, containing note paper, envelopes, pen, pencil, inkstand, &c., and fitted with lock and key. Sizes, 8½ inches, and 10 inches.

No. 14900.

THE "ETON" WRITING CASE.
A VERY USEFUL AND PORTABLE DESIGN.

No. 14905.—"Eton" Writing Case, covered with French morocco leather, fitted complete, size 12 inches.

No. 14904.—Register Desk, covered with French morocco leather, with nickel or gilt handle, containing note paper, envelopes, pen, pencil, paper knife, inkstand, &c., lined with polished light wood and satin. Sizes, 8½ inches, 10 inches, and 12 inches.

No. 14904.

No. 14903.—Register Desk, covered chequered leather, with 4 nickelled corner mounts and handle on lid, lined with white polished wood, containing note paper, envelopes, pen, pencil, paper knife, inkstand, &c., fitted with lock and key. Sizes, 8½ inches, 10 inches, and 12 inches.

No. 14903.

No. 14907.—Register Desk, covered with chequered Persian leather, polished nickel handle, and fittings, lined with polished wood and watered silk, containing note paper, envelopes, pen, pencil, paper knife, and inkstand, and fitted with lock and key. Sizes, 10½ inches, 12 inches, and 14 inches.

No. 14907.

No. 14901.—Tray Desk, covered with French morocco leather, gilt handle, and ornamented with gilt lines, containing note paper, envelopes, pen, pencil, inkstand, &c., and fitted with lock and key. Sizes, 9 inches and 10 inches.

No. 14899.—Register Desk, covered with French morocco leather, lined with watered silk and satinwood, containing note paper, envelopes, pen, pencil, and inkstand, fitted with lock and key, size 8½ inches.

No. 14908.—Register Desk, covered French morocco leather, polished nickel handle, lined with mahogany and with leather, containing note paper, envelopes, pen, pencil, paper knife, and inkstand, and fitted with lock and key. Sizes, 10½ inches, 12 inches, and 14 inches.

TRADE MARK.

S. & F.
LONDON.

No. 14902.—Register Desk, covered with French morocco leather, mounted with nickel or gilt handle, lined with polished white wood, fitted as No. 14900. Sizes, 8½ inches, 10 inches, and 12 inches.

No. 14908.

No. 14906.—Alliance Desk, covered with French morocco leather, lined with imitation calf, nickel-plated handle and fittings, containing blotting case, note paper, envelopes, pen, pencil, paper knife, and inkstand, and fitted with lock and key. Sizes, 10½ inches, and 12 inches.

No. 14910.—Stationery Case, covered with French morocco leather, silk-lined flap.

Every description of leather-covered Writing Desks, Despatch Cases, Empty Despatch Boxes, &c., can be made to order on very short notice.
Basil Leather Cases, for protection of Desks, lined with swansdown, with strap and buckle, or lock and key, can also be supplied in all sizes.

No. 14912.—Improved Alliance Despatch Desk, covered with French morocco leather, lined with roan, fitted with quadrant hinges and Bramah lock, very strongly made, complete with stationery, cutlery, &c., as shown in drawing. Sizes, 12 inches, 14½ inches, and 16 inches.

No. 14912.

THE COMBINED DESPATCH BOX AND DESK.
Is specially arranged for holding a large supply of stationery, with convenience for letters, cash, notes, trinkets, &c.
No. 14911.—Covered with chequered Persian leather, and fitted complete. Sizes, 12 inches, 14 inches, and 16 inches.

No. 14909.—The "Wolseley" Despatch Desk, very compact and portable, covered with French morocco leather, lined with roan, fitted complete with stationery, cutlery, blotting cases, &c. Sizes, 12 inches and 14 inches.

No. 14911.

No. 14909.

TOURISTS' WRITING CASES, STATIONERY CASES, POST BAGS, ETC.

No. 14951. — Tourist Writing Case, French morocco leather, with nickelled double-action lock, fitted complete.

No. 14952.—Tourist Writing Case, French morocco leather, expanding gussets, fitted with strap and nickelled double-action lock.

No. 14953. — Tourist Writing Case, imitation alligator or crocodile leather, lined French morocco leather, expanding pockets, nickelled double-action lock.

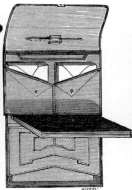

No. 14954. — Tourist Writing Case, French morocco leather, lined imitation calf, with satin-covered blotting book, and nickelled double-action lock.

No. 14955.—Tourist Writing Case, russian leather, lined French morocco, with nickelled double-action lock, leather-covered inkstand and pen box, fitted complete.

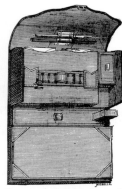

No. 14956.—Tourist Writing Case, russian leather covered, lined calf leather, with nickelled double-action lock, leather-covered inkstand and pen box, very superior quality and finish.

No. 14959. — Stationery Cabinet, of new, most convenient, and portable design, French morocco leather covered, with nickel handle and fittings, fully fitted with stationery, &c., 12 inches long.

No. 14962. — Stationery Case, covered with French morocco leather, polished nickel handle on lid, lined light leather, fitted with a good supply of stationery, blotting book, paper knife, pen, pencil, inkstand, &c. Size, 9½ ins. by 6½ ins. by 4½ ins.

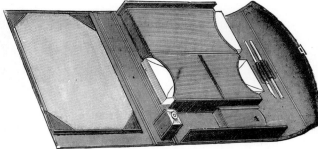

No. 14957.—Tourist Writing Case, quarto size, covered French morocco leather, with nickelled double-action lock, fitted with note paper, envelopes, pen box, inkstand, pen and pencil, blotting pad, &c. Size, 12½ ins. by 7½ ins. by 1½ ins.

The "Connaught" Stationery Case.

The special advantage of this case is that a large quantity of stationery, &c., is contained in a small space. Size when closed, 10 ins. by 6½ ins. by 3 ins.

No. 14965. Commercial Writing Case, with improved expanding lever lock and two keys, fitted with solid leather blotter, and contains pockets for envelopes, papers, stamps, pens, &c., and is stitched throughout. This case is more capacious than the ordinary 16-inch despatch box, and considerably less in size. 8vo, 10 ins. by 7 ins.; 4to, 12 ins. by 9 ins.; foolscap, 14 ins. by 9 ins.

No. 14969.—Solid Leather Post Bag, made in best brown or black leather.

EMPTY DESPATCH BOXES.

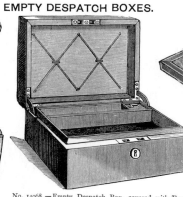

No. 14968. — Empty Despatch Box, covered with French morocco leather, roan lined, fitted with Bramah lock and gilt handle. Sizes, 12 inches, 14 inches, 16 inches, and 18 inches.

No. 14960.—Covered with French morocco, gilt handle and gilt lines, fitted with stationery, &c., lined with watered silk.

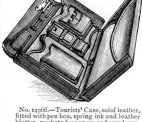

No. 14966.—Tourists' Case, solid leather, fitted with pen box, spring ink and leather blotter, pockets for papers and envelopes, stamps, &c., loops for pens, paper knife, &c., slide handle, double-action lock, all stitched throughout. 8vo, 9 ins. by 6½ ins ; 4to, 11 ins. by 9 ins.; foolscap, 14 ins. by 9 ins.

No. 14964.—Commercial Writing Case, solid hide inside and out, loops for pens and pencils, inside pockets, Bramah lock, 8vo size, 4to size, or foolscap size.

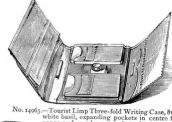

No. 14963.—Tourist Limp Three-fold Writing Case, 8vo, white basil, expanding pockets in centre for paper and envelopes, pockets for answered and unanswered letters, and flat metal screw top ink, strap round, or with double-action nickel lock. Size when closed, 9 ins. by 6½ ins. by 1 in.

The "Edinburgh" Stationery Case, Desk, and Cash Cabinet combined.

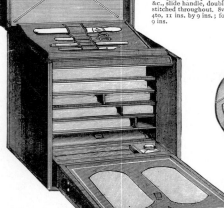

No. 14958.—Stationery Case, covered French morocco leather, fitted complete.

No. 14967.—A superior Tourists' Writing Case, made in best solid leather, either white or saffron, fitted with 2 spring inks, leather blotter, pockets for all necessary papers, envelopes, &c., loops for pens and paper knife, also polished pen box. No elastic whatever is used in this case, it is strongly stitched, has sliding handle on top, and Bramah lock. A most suitable case for hot climates. 8vo, 9 ins. by 6½ ins.; 4to, 11 ins. by 9 ins.; foolscap, 14 ins. by 9 ins.

No. 14961.—Covered with French morocco leather, gilt handle on lid, fitted with stationery, cutlery, inkstand, &c., 3 drawers for notes, gold, and silver, leather lined. Length 12 inches.

S. & F.
London.

TOURISTS' FLASKS (LEATHER COVERED), GLASS INKSTANDS, WRITING DESKS, BLOTTING CASES, Etc.

S. & F.
London.

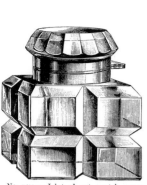

No. 15014.—Inkstand, cut crystal, square shape, richly cut on sides, with brass hinge and mounts, 1½, 2, and 2½ inches.

No. 15001.—Hunting Flask, flint glass, whole covered chequered russia leather, with slit to show contents, and fitted with electro-plated "Bayonet" cap.

No. 15002. — Dram Flask, best crystal glass, diamond cut, with best electro-plated cap and cup. Made in 3 sizes.

No. 15003. — Dram Flask, flint glass, half-covered morocco leather, with flat ends, and Britannia metal cup fitting over top. Made in 3 sizes.

No. 15004. — Dram Flask, all Britannia metal, with flat ends, cup fitting over top. Made in 3 sizes.

No. 15005.—Hunting Flask, flint glass, part covered russia leather; nickel-silver cup, electro-plated and gilt inside, with "Bayonet" cap.

No. 15015.—Inkstand, cut crystal glass, square shape, brass hinges and mounts, 1½, 1¾, 2, 2¼, 2½, 2¾, and 3 inches.

No. 15016.—Inkstand, two compartments, cut crystal glass, with brass hinges and mounts, 1½, 1¾, and 2 inches.

No. 15006.

No. 15006.—Dram Flask, flint glass, half-covered with leather, with Britannia metal cup and screw. Made in 4 sizes.

No. 15007.

No. 15007.—Dram Flask, all metal, without cup. Made in 4 sizes.

No. 15008.

No. 15008.—Dram Flask, best polished flint glass, half-covered russia leather; with nickel-silver cup, covered russia leather and gilt inside, with screw cap. Made in 6 sizes.

No. 15009.

No. 15009.—Dram Flask, flint glass, half-covered morocco leather, with slit to show contents; with hard metal fancy chased cup, electro-plated and gilt inside. Made in 4 sizes.

No. 15017. — Inkstand, cut crystal glass, octagon shape, with brass hinge and mount, 1½, 2, and 2½ inches.

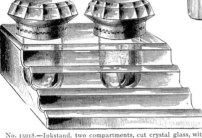

No. 15018.—Inkstand, two compartments, cut crystal glass, with 3 grooved steps for penholders, pencils, &c., with brass hinges and mounts, 1½, 1¾, and 2 inches.

No. 15010.—'Dram Flask, polished flint glass, half-covered russia leather, "Bayonet" cap; nickel-silver cup, plated and gilt inside. Made in 6 sizes.

No. 15011.—Dram Flask, flint glass, half-covered morocco, with slit; hard metal fancy chased cup and cap, electro-plated and gilt inside. Made in 4 sizes.

No. 15012.—Dram Flask, flint glass, half-covered morocco leather; with electro-plated cup, gilt inside, and screw cap. Made in 4 sizes.

No. 15013.—Dram Flask, flint glass, cut fluted bottle; nickel silver cup and screw cap, plated and gilt inside. Made in 4 sizes.

No. 15019.—Inkstand, two compartments, cut crystal glass, pyramid shape, with brass hinges and mounts, 3 inches long, 1½ inch wide.

No. 15020.—Spring Inkstand, round, covered with imitation russia leather, with double spring top, very secure, gilt inside.

No. 15033.—Pin Cushions, satin, with bevelled mirror, assorted patterns.

No. 15021.

No. 15021.—Spring Inkstand, japanned exterior, packed 1 doz. in box.

No. 15022.

No. 15022. — Spring Inkstand, leather covered, with patent secure fastening.

No. 15023.

No. 15023.—Spring Inkstand, best quality, morocco leather covered, with patent secure fastening.

No. 15024.

No. 15024.—Inkstand, cut crystal glass, 3 grooved steps for penholders, pencil, &c., with brass hinge and mount, 1½, 1¾, and 2½ inches.

No. 15025.—Spring Inkstand, round, covered with real russia leather, nickel-plated mounts, with double spring top.

No. 15026.—Blotting Book, with fancy Oleograph picture on cover, quarto size, 11 by 8½ inches.

No. 15027.—Blotting Book, French morocco leather covered, even edge, with broad and narrow gilt lines, octavo and quarto sizes.

No. 15034.—Pin Cushions, satin covered, assorted patterns.

No. 15028. — Cloth-covered Writing Desk, with spring top, fitted with envelopes, paper, pen, pencil, and inkstand. Size 9½ by 7½ inches.

No. 15032.—Horn Drinking Cup, plain tumbler shape. Made in various sizes.

No. 15031.—Blotting Book, French morocco leather covered, with 4 nickelled corner mounts and centre ornament, octavo and quarto sizes.

No. 15029.—Cloth-covered Writing Desk, superior quality, assorted colours, and mounted with pictures of dogs, horses, &c., in neat nickel rim.

TRADE MARK.

No. 15030.—Fitted Papeterie, cloth covered, hook-and-eye fastening, fitted with envelopes, paper, pen, pencil, inkstand, &c.

LADIES' WORK COMPANIONS, MUSIC CASES, GLOVE AND HANDKERCHIEF SETS, Etc.

THE NEW MUSIC "SAC."
(With Closed Ends.)

No. 15051.—The "Combination" Music Portfolio, French morocco, with nickel catch, leather handle, &c. This Portfolio is very compact; it bends the music once, and is not much larger than the ordinary music roll; the back is of moulded metal; the handle well secured.

No. 15052.—Music Case, French morocco, gilt double-action lock.

No. 15053.—Portfolio, very compact, with double-action lock, and handle, for music, drawings, legal and commercial papers, pamphlets, &c. Size 15 by 10½ inches.

No. 15054.—Music Case, fancy cloth, half music size, lettered in gilt "Music."

No. 15055.—Music Case, covered with fancy fluted roan, blind blocked, lacquered double-action lock, and fittings.

No. 15055.

No. 15056.—Handkerchief Box, covered chequered leather, lined quilted satin, with bevelled plate glass lid, fitted with lock and key.

No. 15058.

No. 15058.—Expanding Glove and Handkerchief Cases, Russia leather, with long glove case.

No. 15059.—Handkerchief Box, cloth covered, embossed, and top lettered in gold.

No. 15061.—Envelope and Blotting Case, covered Russian leather, lined with rich watered silk, and ornamented with gilt or nickel mounts.

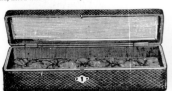

COMBINATION SET.
For Gloves, Handkerchiefs, Scent, Jewellery, &c.

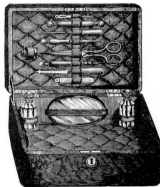

No. 15057.—Glove Box, covered chequered leather, lined quilted satin, with bevelled plate glass lid, fitted with lock and key.

No. 15063.—Collar Box, cloth covered, embossed, and top lettered in gold.

No. 15060.—Glove Box, cloth covered, embossed, and top lettered in gold.

No. 15064.—Combination Set, covered with calf skin, lined with quilted satin, containing 2 scent bottles with gilt tops, and fitted with lock and key.

No. 15065.—Combined Work Box and Writing Desk, covered French morocco leather, with gilt lines and gilt sunken handle on lid, lined quilted satin, and fitted complete with stationery, &c. Size 10 inches long.

No. 15066.—Lady's Work Box, covered rich silk plush of the newest colours, fitted with lock and key, mounted on lid, rich gilt engraved escutcheon, lined quilted satin, fully fitted with instruments, 2 gilt top perfume bottles, oval mirror, &c. Size 9¼ by 7½ by 4½ inches.

No. 15062.—Envelope and Blotting Case, covered French morocco leather, Gothic top, with broad and narrow gilt lines.

TRADE MARK.

S. & F.
LONDON.

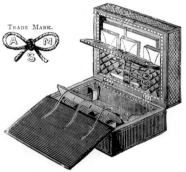

No. 15067.—Work Basket, covered chequered Persian leather, oval shape, lined best quilted satin throughout, trimmed edges and pockets, with handle on lid, gilt or nickel spring catch. Size 8½ inches long.

No. 15068.—Lady's Work Box, covered morocco leather, with bevelled plate glass lid, fitted with lock and key, lined quilted satin, and containing work instruments and scent bottles. Size 8½ by 6½ by 4 inches.

No. 15069.—Combined Work Box and Writing Desk, covered chequered Russian leather, with sunken brass handle and gilt lines on lid, lined quilted silk, and fitted complete with stationery, &c. Size 10 inches long.

No. 15070.—Combined Work Box and Writing Desk, covered chequered Persian leather, with gilt handle on lid and gilt lines, fitted complete with stationery, &c., and lined leather and silk. Size 10 inches long.

COLLAR BOXES.

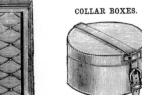

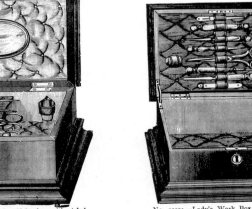

No. 15074.—Collar Box, round, solid leather, with buckle and strap.

No. 15071.—Lady's Work Box, covered calf leather, decorated with hand-painted floral bouquet on lid and sides, fitted with lock and key, lined quilted satin, complete with instruments, scent bottles, glove stretchers, and partitions for gloves and handkerchiefs. Size 14 by 11½ by 5 inches.

No. 15072.—Lady's Work Box, covered calf leather, with nickel handle and mounts, lock and key, lined quilted satin, complete with fittings. A 2-air musical box is concealed in a compartment underneath this case, which commences playing when the box is opened. Size 10 by 7 by 4½ inches.

No. 15073.—Lady's Work Box, ebonized wood, calf inlaid, mounted with brass handle and plate, fitted with lock and key, lined quilted satin, and containing scissors and other instruments, thimble, &c. Size 10¾ by 9 by 5½ inches.

COMBS AND BRUSHES.

HAIR BRUSHES.

Broad Oval.

No. 15100.—Polished satinwood backs, black, white, or unbleached hair.

Tortoiseshell and Pearl Backs.

No. 15102.—In a variety of designs and shapes.

Real Tortoiseshell Veneered Backs.

No. 15104.—Assorted shapes, fine white bristles.

Long Oval.

No. 15101.—Polished satinwood or rosewood backs, black, white, or unbleached hair.

Mirror Backs.

No. 15103.—Polished satinwood, with mirror backs.

Gentlemen's Military Oval.

No. 15105.—Satinwood backs, without handles.

No. 15108.—Best satinwood backs, screwed, white hair.

CLOTH BRUSHES.

Handle Cloth Brushes.

No. 15106.—Rosewood, pinned back, black bristles.

With Splash Brush on Back.

No. 15107.—Rosewood, pinned back, black bristles, with splash.

Roach Cloth Brushes.

No. 15109.—Polished satin or rosewood backs.

HAIR BRUSHES IN CASES.

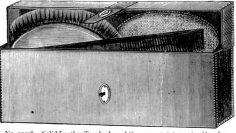

No. 15118.—Solid Leather Trunk-shaped Cases, containing pair of brushes and comb.

No. 15119.—Leather-covered Pull-off Cases, containing pair of hair brushes and comb.

No. 15120.—Solid Leather Cases, containing a pair of military oval hair brushes, satinwood backed, screwed.

HAT BRUSHES.

Velvet Back.

No. 15110.—Velvet back, assorted colours.

Curved Handle Hat Brush.

No. 15112.—Satinwood back.

Combination Hat and Cloth Brush.

No. 15113.—Rosewood handle.

FRENCH WHISK BRUSHES.

Without Handles.

No. 15114.—Polished wood or velvet backs, assorted colours.

With Handles.

No. 15116.—Polished wood backs.

No. 15121.—Leather-covered Cases, velvet-lined, with lock and key, solid ivory fittings, in great variety.

DRESSING COMBS.

No. 15129.—Imitation Tortoiseshell.

No. 15131.—White Horn.

No. 15134.—Roped-back Pattern.

No. 15135.—Roach Pattern.

No. 15136.—Rake Pattern.

MIRROR BRUSHES,

with Comb and Glass.

No. 15122.

LADIES' SMOOTHING BRUSHES.

Soft Bristles.

No. 15124.—Satinwood backs.

BONNET BRUSHES.

No. 15125.—Satinwood backs, long, white, soft bristles.

POCKET COMBS.

Pocket Combs in Cases.

No. 15137.

Shut-up Pocket Combs.

No. 15142.—Imitation Tortoiseshell.   No. 15146.—With Mirror.

SMALL TOOTH COMBS.

No. 15147.—Ivory.   No. 15150.—Buffalo.   No. 15151.—India-rubber.

TAIL COMBS.

No. 15152.

BOTTLE BRUSHES.

No. 15126.

FOREHEAD COMBS.

India-rubber, in a large variety of patterns.

No. 15153.   No. 15154.

No. 15155.   No. 15156.

305

FITTED IVORY BRUSH AND TOILET CASES, IVORY HAIR AND CLOTH BRUSHES, MIRRORS, ETC.

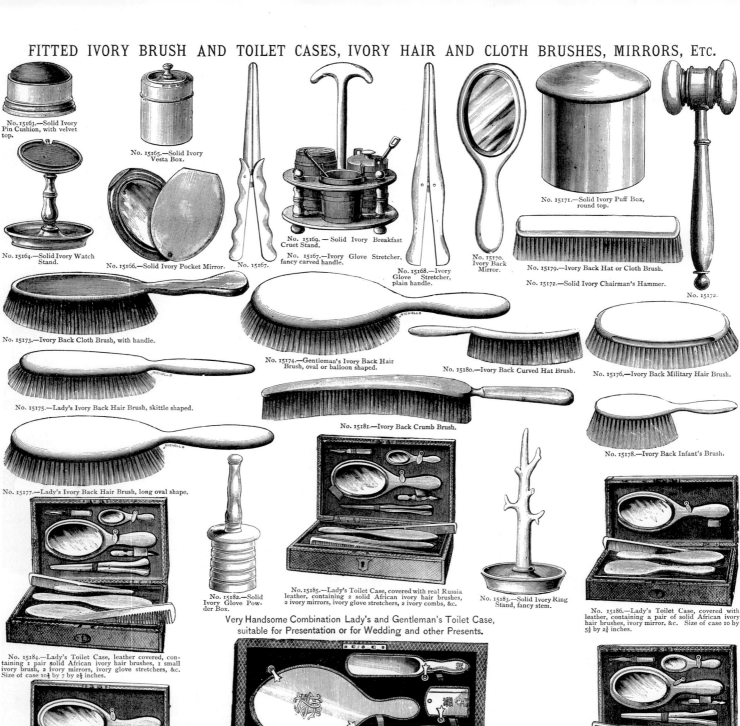

No. 15163.—Solid Ivory Pin Cushion, with velvet top.

No. 15165.—Solid Ivory Vesta Box.

No. 15164.—Solid Ivory Watch Stand.

No. 15166.—Solid Ivory Pocket Mirror.

No. 15167.

No. 15169.—Solid Ivory Breakfast Cruet Stand.

No. 15167.—Ivory Glove Stretcher, fancy carved handle.

No. 15168.—Ivory Glove Stretcher, plain handle.

No. 15170. Ivory Back Mirror.

No. 15171.—Solid Ivory Puff Box, round top.

No. 15179.—Ivory Back Hat or Cloth Brush.

No. 15172.—Solid Ivory Chairman's Hammer.

No. 15172.

No. 15173.—Ivory Back Cloth Brush, with handle.

No. 15174.—Gentleman's Ivory Back Hair Brush, oval or balloon shaped.

No. 15180.—Ivory Back Curved Hat Brush.

No. 15176.—Ivory Back Military Hair Brush.

No. 15175.—Lady's Ivory Back Hair Brush, skittle shaped.

No. 15181.—Ivory Back Crumb Brush.

No. 15178.—Ivory Back Infant's Brush.

No. 15177.—Lady's Ivory Back Hair Brush, long oval shape.

No. 15182.—Solid Ivory Glove Powder Box.

No. 15185.—Lady's Toilet Case, covered with real Russia leather, containing 2 solid African ivory hair brushes, 2 ivory mirrors, ivory glove stretchers, 2 ivory combs, &c.

No. 15183.—Solid Ivory Ring Stand, fancy stem.

No. 15186.—Lady's Toilet Case, covered with leather, containing a pair of solid African ivory hair brushes, ivory mirror, &c. Size of case 10 by 5½ by 2¼ inches.

Very Handsome Combination Lady's and Gentleman's Toilet Case, suitable for Presentation or for Wedding and other Presents.

No. 15184.—Lady's Toilet Case, leather covered, containing 1 pair solid African ivory hair brushes, 1 small ivory brush, 2 ivory mirrors, ivory glove stretchers, &c. Size of case 10½ by 7 by 2½ inches.

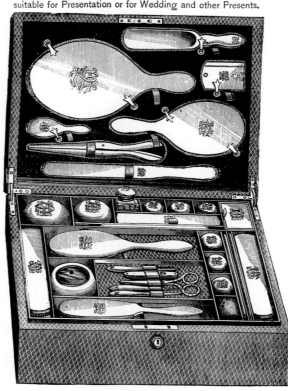

No. 15188.—Lady's Toilet Case, covered with chequered Russia leather, containing 2 solid African ivory hair brushes, 1 ivory hat and 1 ivory cloth brush, 2 ivory mirrors, glove stretchers, &c. Size of case 11 by 7⅜ by 2¼ inches.

No. 15187.—Lady's Toilet Case, covered chequered Russia leather, containing 1 pair solid African ivory hair brushes, ivory mirror, and 2 ivory combs. Size of case 10½ by 6½ by 2¾ inches.

No. 15189.—Lady's Toilet Case, leather covered, containing 1 pair solid African ivory hair brushes, ivory mirror, ivory glove stretcher, 2 ivory combs, &c. Size of case 11 by 6½ by 2½ inches.

No. 15190.—Very Handsome Combination Lady's and Gentleman's Toilet Case, covered with real Russia leather, containing 1 gentleman's and 1 lady's solid ivory hair brush, 1 ivory cloth and 1 ivory hat brush, 2 solid ivory puff boxes, 3 ivory mirrors, &c. Size of case 18¼ by 15⅜ by 5¼ inches.

No. 15191.—Lady's Toilet Case, covered with chequered Russia leather, containing 1 pair solid African ivory hair brushes, 2 ivory mirrors, ivory glove stretchers, &c. Size of case 11⅜ by 8½ inches.

FOR FULL DESCRIPTIONS AND CONTENTS OF TOILET CASES, SEE PRICE LIST.

PERFUMES, SOAPS, &c.

PERFUMES.

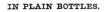

IN FANCY BOTTLES.

IN FANCY CHINA VASES.

IN PLAIN BOTTLES.   **IN FANCY CUT BOTTLES.**

Best Quality.

    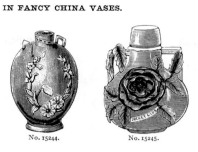   

No. 15238.   No. 15239.   No. 15240.   No. 15243.   No. 15244.   No. 15245.   No. 15246.   No. 15248.   No. 15250.   No. 15251.

FANCY CABINETS OF PERFUMES.

PERFUMED WATERS FOR TOILET USE.

EAU DE COLOGNE.   **LAVENDER WATER.**   **TOILET VINEGAR.**

FOUNTAIN PERFUMES.

No. 15254.—Size when closed 11½ inches by 8 inches.

No. 15257.—Wicker Flask.   No. 15258. Sprinkling Top.   No. 15261.—Octagon shape.   No. 15262. Panel shape.   No. 15264.—Barrel shape.   No. 15265. Sprinkling Top.   No. 15267. Square shape.   No. 15269.—In Fancy Papers, all sizes.

POMADES.

LIME JUICE AND GLYCERINE.

SMELLING SALTS.

ROSE LEAF FACE POWDER.

No. 15272.—Best quality Pomade.   No. 15273.—In round glass bottles.   No. 15275.—In oval glass bottles, with metal caps.   No. 15276.—Pomade, in fancy shaped glass jars.   No. 15277.—In round bottles.   No. 15278.—In flat bottles.   No. 15279.—In moulded glass bottles.   No. 15280.—In cut glass bottles.   No. 15281.—In cut glass bottles, with gilt decorations.   No. 15283.—Tinted pink for the complexion.

TOOTH PASTE AND POWDER.

FANCY SOAPS.

No. 15285.—Areca Nut Tooth Paste, in pots.   No. 15288.—Tooth Powder, in glass bottles.   No. 15290.—Tooth Powder, in wooden boxes.

No. 15294.—Brown Windsor Soap, in squares.   No. 15295.—Glycerine Soap, in tablets.

MARKING INK.

No. 15292.—Marking Ink (prepared by the daughter of the late John Bond), blue wrapper.

No. 15297.—Coal Tar Soap in oval tablets.   No. 15298.—Egg Shape Tablets, assorted Honey, Brown Windsor, and Glycerine Soap, in ½-gross wood boxes.

GOFFERING IRONS.

CURLING TONGS.

GLOVE STRETCHERS.

No. 15303.—Goffering Irons.   No. 15301.—Curling Tongs.   No. 15300.—Glove Stretchers, polished wood, or bone handles.

SHAVING BRUSHES.

No. 15305.—Wooden handle with bone socket.

No. 15307.—Bone handle, white hair.

Turnback, for Travelling.

OPEN.

SHUT.

No. 15309.

No. 15309.

NAIL BRUSHES.

Wooden Backs, Fibre.

Bridge Nail Brushes.

No. 15312.—Roach shape.

No. 15316.—Bone handles.

Concave Nail Brushes.

Long Handled Nail Brushes.

No. 15319.—Bone handle.

Nail Brushes, with wings.

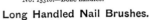

No. 15318.—Bone or wooden handle.

No. 15322.—Bone handle.

TOOTH BRUSHES.

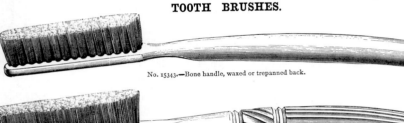

No. 15343.—Bone handle, waxed or trepanned back.

No. 15344.—Assorted fancy handles.

Double Tooth Brushes.

No. 15345.—Buffalo or Transparent Horn Handle Tooth Brush and Palate Brush combined.

The "Holdfast" Tooth Brush.

No. 15346.—The "Holdfast" Tooth Brush. Can be used with confidence and pleasure, the discomfort hitherto unavoidable consequent upon bristles coming out in the mouth being entirely obviated.

CHEST AND LUNG PROTECTORS.

No. 15375.—Single Chest Protector.

No. 15379.—Double Chest Protector.

SOAP BOXES.

No. 15381.—Metal or porcelain.

Waterproof Sheeting and Nursing Aprons of all kinds.

INFANTS' HAIR BRUSHES.

No. 15323.—Bone back.

No. 15324.—Tortoiseshell back.

No. 15325.—Pearl back.

No. 15326.—Pearl and tortoiseshell back.

PUFFS.

No. 15338.—Kid top.

No. 15339.—Bone top.

S. & F.
LONDON.

FEEDING BOTTLES.

No. 15341.

No. 15342.

WATERPROOF BATHING CAPS.

No. 15357.—Round shape.

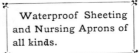

No. 15358.—Hood shape.

INFANTS POWDER BOXES.

No. 15329.—Plain wood. No. 15330.—Tartan. No. 15331.—Plain metal.

No. 15333.—Fancy metal. No. 15334.—Fancy metal. No. 15332.—Coloured metal.

No. 15335.—Tortoiseshell. No. 15336.—Pearl.

VIOLET POWDERS
IN FANCY PACKETS.

SUPERFINE VIOLET POWDER

No. 15340.

SPONGES.

Sponges on Strings.

Sponges on Cards.

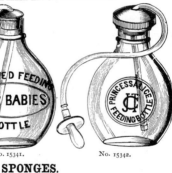

SUPERIOR TURKEY HONEYCOMB SPONGES

No. 15350.

No. 15347.—Fine Turkey.

No. 15348.—Honeycomb.

Waterproof Sponge Bags.

Sanitary Sponges.

No. 15349.—Sanitary Sponge, bone handle.

No. 15351.

TRADE MARK.

No. 15390.—Dressing Case (Lady's), Walnut or Rosewood, silk velvet lined, reversible mirror in lid, 5 deep cut crystal bottles for scents, oils, pomades, &c., 2 small cut glass jars for tooth powders, 3 cut crystal trays for tooth and nail brushes, good brushes and comb, and English cutlery. Size, 12 by 9 by 7 inches.

No. 15402.—Dressing Case (Lady's) Walnutwood, round top, silk velvet lined, reversible mirror in lid, 4 deep-cut crystal bottles for scents, &c., 2 small glass jars for pomade, 3 cut crystal trays for soap, tooth and nail brushes, jewel drawer in front opened by a spring in interior of case. Size, 12 by 9 by 7 inches.

No. 15407.—Dressing Case (Gentleman's), Walnut or Rosewood, brass bound and strapped, fitted with cut crystal bottles and jars, brushes, comb, and cutlery. Size, 12 by 9 by 6 inches.

No. 15391.—Dressing Case (Lady's), Walnut or Rosewood, silk velvet lined, with 4 deep cut crystal bottles for scent, &c., and two small jars for pomades, fitted with brushes, comb, and cutlery.

No. 15397.—Dressing Case (Lady's), Walnutwood, fall-down front, with best silver-plated tops to bottles, trays, and jars, also contains brush and jewel drawers, brushes, comb, and best English cutlery, fitted complete. Size 12 by 9 by 7 inches.

S. & F.
London.

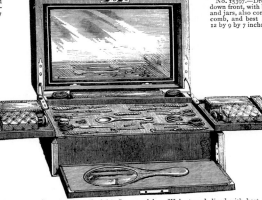

No. 15403.—Dressing Case (Lady's), Coromandel or Walnutwood, lined with best silk velvet, the wings are fitted with richly cut bottles, which are mounted, like the trays and jars, with sterling silver mounts, hall marked. The case also contains 2 richly cut bottle jars, 1 tooth brush tray, and ivory hand mirror, a complete set of cutlery, hair brushes, combs, &c.

No. 15400.—Dressing Case (Lady's), Walnut or Rosewood, silk velvet lined, 5 deep cut crystal bottles for scents, &c., 2 small cut glass jars for tooth powder, 3 cut crystal trays for soap, &c., reversible mirror in lid, jewel drawer in front opened by a spring in interior of case, good brushes, comb, and cutlery. Size 12 by 9 by 7 inches.

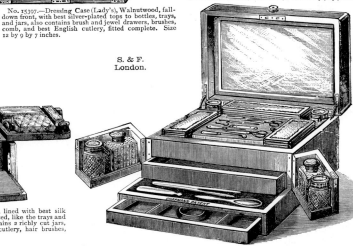

No. 15405.—Dressing Case (Lady's), Coromandel or Walnutwood, with solid brass edges; lined best silk velvet. The fittings are all mounted in stout engraved sterling silver (hall marked), the two drawers open with springs, reversible mirror in lid, fitted with best brushes, combs, and cutlery. The case also contains ivory glove stretcher, mouth mirror, and shoe lift. Size 12 by 9 by 8 inches.

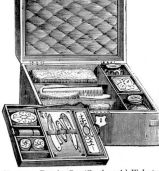

No. 15412.—Workbox, Walnutwood, round top, gilt mounted, basket lined, fitted with cutlery and thimble complete. Length 12 inches.

No. 15411.—Workbox, Walnutwood, round top, inlaid tulipwood panel, with pearl corners and centre, lined best satin. Length 12 inches.

No. 15404.—Dressing Case (Lady's), Walnutwood, with two spring drawers, fitted with 5 deep cut crystal bottles, 2 small cut crystal jars, 3 cut crystal trays, brushes, comb, and cutlery complete. Size 12 by 9 by 7 inches.

No. 15410.—Workbox, Olivewood, basket lined, best finish, fitted with cutlery and thimble complete. Size 12 by 9 by 7 inches.

No. 15415.—The New Wing Combination Cabinet, in Coromandel or Walnutwood. The wings contain 4 richly cut perfume bottles, in the inner front are 3 drawers, the upper one fitted with glove stretcher and space for gloves, the lower drawers are fitted for handkerchiefs and bracelets, the upper part is arranged for watches, rings, &c.; fitted with best cutlery.

No. 15417.—Workbox, Walnutwood, inlaid fancy straps, lined Persian silk.

No. 15432.—Workbox, Walnutwood, round top, large pearl plate, honeycombed in lid, satin lined. Length 12 inches.

No. 15427.—Workbox, Walnutwood, inlaid fancy panel, flat top, lined best satin, puckered in lid.

No. 15425.—Workbox, Walnutwood, round top, inlaid fancy panel, lined satin, puckered in lid.

No. 15441.—Desk (Gentleman's), Walnutwood, solid brass-edged, polished inside, and secret drawers.

No. 15470.—Victoria (Workbox and Desk combined), Walnutwood, satin lined. Size 12 by 9 by 7 inches.

No. 15456.—Desk (Lady's), Walnutwood, round top, large Oxford pattern pearl plate, lined with silk velvet, best finish.

No. 15450.—Desk (Gentleman's), Walnutwood, solid brass-edged, 2 brass lines round edges, lock flap, Bramah lock, best finish.

No. 15479.—Desk (Gentleman's), Walnutwood, 8 brass corners, 4 brass caps, Bramah lock, secret drawers, lined leather, very best finish, polished inside.

No. 15458.—Desk (Lady's), Walnutwood, round top, polished inside, best finish, lined with silk velvet.

No. 15482.—Papeterie, black Walnutwood, arranged for paper and envelopes.

No. 15480.—Papeterie, Walnutwood, nickel mounts, leather-covered slope for writing.

No. 15483.—Papeterie, Walnut and Blackwood, arranged for paper and envelopes, desk shape.

Presentation Desks, in Walnut, Hungarian Ash, Thuya, Maple, Amboyna, Olive, and other Fancy Woods, always in stock.

No. 15476.—Victoria (Workbox and Desk combined), Walnutwood, puckered satin in lid, the desk lined with silk velvet. Size 12 by 9 by 7 inches.

No. 15465.—Desk (Lady's), Walnutwood, round top, with envelope range and secret drawers, polished inside, lined with silk velvet.

No. 15460.—Desk (Lady's), Walnutwood, round top, inlaid fancy straps, silk velvet lined, polished inside.

No. 15445.—Desk (Gentleman's), Mahogany, Rosewood, or Walnutwood, 8 brass corners, 4 brass caps, and brass straps, polished inside, and with secret drawers.

No. 15454.—Desk (Gentleman's), Mahogany, Rosewood, or Walnutwood, 4 brass corners, 4 brass caps, lined with velvet.

No. 15481.—Papeterie, Walnutwood, to hold small post octavo paper, and No. 4 and court-shape envelopes.

No. 15443.—Desk and Stationery Case combined, in Walnut, Coromandel, or Olivewood, with nickel or gilt mounts, fitted with double-action spring lock, and 2 cut glass ink bottles. Size 15 by 11 by 9½ inches.

No. 15468.—Desk (folding), Walnutwood, with stationery rack in top, lined with satinwood throughout, desk lined with silk velvet. Length 14 inches.

TRADE MARK.

No. 15475.—The Princess (Workbox and Desk combined), Walnutwood, lined with satin, polished inside, best finish. Size 12 by 9 by 7 inches.

No. 15467.—Desk (folding), Walnutwood, round top with spring, stationery rack, lined with silk velvet, polished inside, fitted with stationery and 2 ink bottles.

No. 15491.—Lamp Bracket, maroon bronzed. 10½ inches by 5½ inches.

No. 15492.—Lamp Bracket, maroon bronzed. 7 inches by 4 inches.

No. 15493.—Lamp Bracket, maroon bronzed. 7 inches by 5 inches.

No. 15494.—Lamp Bracket, maroon bronzed. 5 inches by 4 inches.

No. 15500.—Pen Rack, maroon bronzed. 5 inches by 2 inches.

No. 15495.—Wall Bracket, polished and maroon bronzed. 10 inches by 4½ inches.

No. 15496.—Wall Bracket, polished bright brass or copper colour. 11 inches by 6½ inches.

No. 15497.—Wall Bracket, polished electro-brass and relieved, with folding shelf. 10 inches by 5 inches.

No. 15498.—Wall Bracket, maroon bronzed. 10 inches by 4 inches.

No. 15499.—Wall Bracket, polished and maroon bronzed. 8½ inches by 3½ inches.

No. 15501.—Wall Bracket, maroon bronzed. 5 inches by 4 inches.

No. 15504.—Match Safe, 2 divisions, maroon bronzed. 6 inches by 4½ inches.

No. 15502.—Wall Bracket, polished brass and relieved, Japanese design. 12 inches by 6½ inches.

No. 15503.—Wall Bracket, polished bright brass or copper colour, with saucer for holding lamp, &c. 11 inches by 7 inches.

No. 15507.—Letter Rack, maroon bronzed, tasteful design. 6½ inches by 4 inches.

No. 15506.—Corner Bracket, maroon bronzed. 10 inches by 4½ inches.

S. & F.
London.

No. 15509.—Wall Bracket, polished, bright brass and relieved, best finish. 12½ inches by 8 inches. (Drawn half size.)

No. 15508.—Wall Bracket, maroon bronzed. 10 inches by 4½ inches.

No. 15511.—Bronzed Match Safe, with 2 divisions, the top division having a folding lid. 6½ inches by 5 inches.

No. 15512.—Electro-bronzed Candlestick, to affix to wall, &c., relieved and finished in the best style. 8 inches by 5 inches.

No. 15513.—Electro-bronzed Candlestick, to affix to wall, &c., relieved and finished in the best style. 7 inches by 5½ inches.

No. 15510.—Polished electro-brass Candlestick, relieved, tasteful design. Height 8 ins.

No. 15514.—Bronzed Inkstand and Pen Rack, with revolving ink bottle.

No. 15515.—Maroon Bronzed Pen Rack.

No. 15516.—Maroon Bronzed Inkstand and Pen Rack, with porcelain or glass well.

No. 15517.—Japanned Hat or Coat Rail, with 14 hooks, expanding, supplied with nails, complete.

No. 15518.—Maroon Bronzed Inkstand and Pen Tray, with 2 wells. 7 inches by 5 inches.

No. 15519.—Electro-bronzed Candlestick, to affix to wall, &c., relieved and finished in the best style. 10 inches by 4½ inches.

No. 15524.—Papier-maché Workbox, floral decoration, satin-lined tray.

No. 15528.—Papier-maché Inkstand with 2 bottles and stamp box.

No. 15534.—Papier-maché Work & Jewel Cabinet with folding doors, very superior decoration. Height 13 inches, width 11½ inches, depth 9 inches.

No. 15536.—Papier-maché Inkstand and Envelope Case, with drawer.

No. 15539.—Papier-maché Writing Desk, fancy pearl decoration. Length 12 inches, depth 9 inches.

No. 15540.—Papier-maché Crumb Brush & Tray.

No. 15541.—Papier-maché Inkstand & Stationery Rack, with 2 bottles and stamp box. Length 12½ inches, depth 9 inches, height at back 5 inches.

No. 15542.—Papier-maché Oval Inkstand, gold ground, with pen rack.

No. 15545.—Papier-maché Clock Bracket, black ground, painted roses and birds. Height 11½ in., width of shelf 13 in., depth 6½ in.

No. 15546.—Papier-maché Pipe Rack, Japanese rose decoration, with 7 holes for pipes, length 12 inches.

No. 15547.—Papier-maché Wall Bracket, Japanese rose decoration. Height 14 in., width of shelf 10 in., depth 5 in.

No. 15548.—Papier-maché Corner Bracket, with 2 shelves, Japanese rose decoration. Height 15 in., depth of top shelf 9 in.

No. 15548.

No. 15553.—Papier-maché Parlour Bellows, best finish.

No. 15553.

No. 15550.—Papier-maché Fan-shaped Bracket. Extreme length 21 inches, length of shelf 10 inches, depth of do. 4½ inches.

No. 15558.—Papier-maché Bookslide, painted floral decoration, with fancy gold border.

No. 15554.—Set of Papier-maché Glove & Handkerchief Boxes with lock and key.

No. 15562. Papier-maché Card Basket, on gilt stand, painted birds and flowers. Diameter 12 inches.

No. 15563.—Papier-maché Pillar Wall Bracket, with 2 shelves and bevelled mirror, painted floral decoration. Height 18½ inches, width 10 inches, depth 4½ inches.

No. 15563.

No. 15564.—Papier-maché Wall Bracket with Mirror, black ground, gold decoration. Height 13 inches, width 9½ inches.

No. 15559.—Set of 4 Papier-maché Occasional Tables, the 2nd size forming a Chess Board.

No. 15565.—Papier-maché Blotting Case, 12 by 9 in., fancy blue ground, painted bird and sprig.

No. 15565.

No. 15566.—Papier-maché Blotting Case, 8 in. by 5 in., black ground, painted flowers.

No. 15567.—Set of 3 Papier-maché Round Trays, Japanese rose decoration. Diameters 8 in., 10 in., 12 in.

No. 15567.

No. 15569.—Four-fold Papier-maché Fire Screen, shaped top, painted birds and flowers on black ground. Height 24 inches, width 27 inches.

No. 15569.

S. & F. London.

HOUSEHOLD SUNDRIES, SEWING MACHINES, SALT BOXES, TABLE MATS, CHAMOIS LEATHERS, ETC.

S. & F. London.

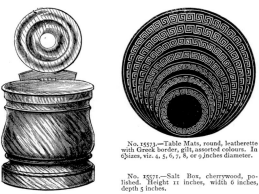

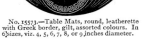

No. 15571.

No. 15571.—Salt Box, cherrywood, polished. Height 11 inches, width 6 inches, depth 5 inches.

No. 15573.—Table Mats, round, leatherette with Greek border, gilt, assorted colours. In 6 sizes, viz. 4, 5, 6, 7, 8, or 9 inches diameter.

No. 15575.—Table Mats (folding), wood, brown and white strips, polished, oval shape. 6 mats in set, viz. 2 each 8 ins. by 5½ ins., 10 ins. by 7 ins., and 12½ ins. by 10 ins.

No. 15576.—Table Mats, morocco leather, with Greek border, gilt. 8 mats in set, viz. 2 each 10, 12, 14, or 16 inches long.

No. 15577.—Wood Box, brown and white strips, polished, to hold salt, tobacco, sugar, &c. Height 9 inches, width 5 inches, depth 4 inches.

No. 15578.—Table Mats, Indian straw, colours and patterns well assorted. 6 mats in set, viz. 2 each 9½ ins. by 6 ins., 11 ins. by 7½ ins., and 13½ ins. by 9 ins.

No. 15579.—Flower Pot Covers, expanding wood, packed in boxes of 1 doz., assorted as follows: 4 each 6, 7, and 8 inches high.

No. 15580.—Table Mats (folding), wood, brown and white strips, polished, oblong shape. 6 mats in set, viz. 2 each 8 ins. by 5½ ins., 10 ins. by 7 ins., and 13 ins. by 9 ins.

No. 15581.—Biscuit Box, brown and white wood strips, polished. Height 6 inches, diameter 5 inches.

No. 15582.—Spice Box, made of cherrywood, polished, to hold spices, cloves, nutmegs, &c. Height 9 inches, width 6½ inches, depth 3 inches.

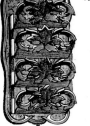

No. 15583.—Letter Rack, brown wood carved, 12 ins. high, 4 ins. wide.

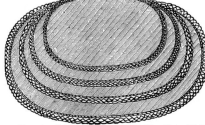

No. 15584.—Lamp Shades, made of perforated paper, assorted fancy designs.

No. 15585.—Table Mats, made of fine white willow, with fancy edge. 8 mats in set, viz. 2 each 9 ins. by 7 ins., 10 ins. by 7½ ins., 12 ins. by 9 ins., and 14 ins. by 10 ins.

TRADE MARK.

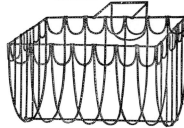

No. 15586.—Sponge Rack, galvanized wire. In 2 sizes viz. 7 inches long and 10 inches long.

CHAMOIS LEATHERS.

No. 15588.—Chamois Leathers, 1st quality. Can be supplied in dozens or in original kipps of 30 leathers.

No. 15592.—Table Mats, white wicker, in sets of 8, viz. 2 each 9 ins. by 7 ins., 10 ins. by 7½ ins., 12 ins. by 9 ins., and 14 ins. by 10 ins.

No. 15589.—Crumb Tray and Brush, papier-maché, decorated with Chinese figures. Size of tray 10 inches square.

No. 15587.—Crumb Tray and Brush, in olivewood or oakwood, with ebonized edges, polished. Size of tray 10 inches square.

No. 15587.

No. 15589.

No. 15591.

No. 15591.—The Wanzer "A" Lock Stitch Hand Sewing Machine, with all fittings and attachments, including Instruction Book, packed in strong deal case.

No. 15594.—The Wanzer "B" Lock Stitch Hand Sewing Machine, has all the latest improvements, and is the easiest running and most silent machine in the market, with all appliances and packed in deal case.

No. 15594.

No. 15590.—Flower Pot, papier-maché, with floral decorations. Made in 2 sizes, viz. 6½ inches high, 6½ inches diameter, and 7½ inches high, 7½ inches diameter.

PERFORATED METAL CAMPHOR BOXES FILLED WITH FINEST CAMPHOR

No. 15593.—Metal Box filled with Camphor, for the prevention of moth in furs, &c.

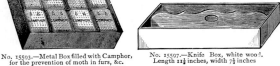

No. 15597.—Knife Box, white wood. Length 11½ inches, width 7½ inches

No. 15598.—Knife Box, cherrywood, polished, with 3 divisions. Length 18 inches, width 11 inches.

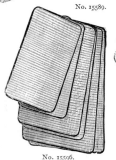

No. 15595.—Table Mats, made of papier-maché, black ground with gold decorations, oblong or oval shape. 6 mats in set, viz. 2 each 9 ins. by 6 ins., 11½ ins. by 8½ ins., and 14 ins. by 10 ins.

No. 15596.

No. 15596.—Table Mats, white willow, the edges bound with cloth of assorted colours. 6 mats in set, viz. 2 each 9 ins. by 6 ins., 10½ ins. by 7 ins., and 12 ins. by 8 ins.

No. 15599.—China Plates in wire frames, to hold fruit or flowers, assorted patterns. In 2 sizes, viz. 7 ins. and 9 inches diameter.

No. 15599.

No. 15600.—Smokers' Table, fitted with cigar rack, tobacco box, match case, cutter, &c., in ebonized, walnut, and other woods. Height about 36 inches, assorted patterns.

No. 15600.

JAPANESE CHINA VASES, TEA SETS, PLATES, ETC., AND LACQUERED GOODS.

No. 15668.—Shell Tray, with bark covering outside, to hold ash, &c. Length 5 inches, width 3½ inches, height 1½ inches.

No. 15669.—Lacquered Ash Trays, assorted brown and black. Diameter 4 inches.

No. 15670.—Round Cups, lacquered, in nests of six, with lid for outside cup. Diameter of largest cup 4 inches.

No. 15664.—Japanese Paper Umbrella on bamboo frame, a large variety of patterns. Extreme length 30 inches.

No. 15663.—Benares Vases, made of finest brass, the engraving being different on each vase.

No. 15666.—Lacquered Bread Trays, red inside. Length 12 inches, width 6 inches.

No. 15667.—Bamboo Basket, 40 pieces in a case, of which there are scarcely two alike. A very saleable line for bazaars, &c.

No. 15671.—Bamboo Waste Paper Basket, in nests of three. Size of outside basket 15 inches high, 9 inches diameter.

No. 15665.—Lacquered Cabinet for jewels, cash, &c., in a great variety of designs. Size about 5 inches long, 3 inches wide, 4 inches deep.

No. 15653.—Imari Plates for wall decoration or table use. Diameter about 8 inches. Patterns well assorted.

No. 15650.—Imari Teté-a-Teté set of five pieces, various tasteful decorations.

No. 15672.—Satsuma Plates, richly ornamented, various designs, on ivory coloured ground. Diameter 8 inches.

No. 15649.—Imari Tea Cup and Saucer, assorted patterns and colours.

No. 15652.—Fine Kaga Jar, with lid, handsomely decorated. Height 8½ inches.

No. 15651.—Blue and White China Fern Pots, round or octagon.

No. 15661.—Lacquered Trays, round, assorted gold decorations, and in five sizes, viz. 10 inches, 12 inches, 14 inches, 16 inches, and 18 inches diameter.

No. 15656.—Lacquered Handkerchief Box, with gold decorations, assorted, 7 inches by 7 inches.

No. 15654.—Imari Bowls, in nests of three, viz. one bowl each, 6 inches, 7 inches, 8 inches diameter, designs well assorted.

No. 15647.—Imari Vases, height about 7 inches, in a great variety of patterns.

No. 15646.—Awata Vases, assorted patterns. Height about 3½ inches.

S. & F. London.

TRADE MARK

No. 15673.—Satsuma Vases, with cover and ornamental figure on top, and very finest workmanship and finish, in a great variety of designs. Total height about 9 inches.

No. 15648.—Kaga Vases, height about 7 inches, designs and shapes well assorted.

No. 15655.—Imari Jar, with lid, height about 6 inches, assorted decorations.

No. 15657.—Lacquered Glove Boxes, with gold decoration, 9½ inches long, 3½ inches wide.

No. 15660.—Lacquered Trays, gold decorations, assorted, oval or oblong, in eight sizes, viz. 8 inches, 10 inches, 12 inches, 14 inches, 16 inches, 18 inches, 21 inches, 24 inches.

No. 15658.—Lacquered Cabinet, with gold decorations. Height 14 inches, width 12 inches, depth 6 inches. Patterns well assorted.

No. 15662.—Lacquered Trays, square, extra fine quality, and thick gold edges.

No. 15659.—Lacquered Boxes, in nests of three, viz. one each 5 by 3½ by 2 inches, 5½ by 4¼ by 2¾ inches, 6½ by 5 by 3½ inches.

HOUSEHOLD JUDSON'S SPECIALITIES

SIMPLE. JUDSON'S DYES. *EFFECTIVE.*

(LIQUID)

Packed one dozen in attractive Card Box (14 bottles to the dozen, 6d. size).

No. 15706, 6d. size.
No. 15707, 1s. „
No. 15708, 1/6 „
No. 15709, 2/6 „
No. 15710, 5s. „

POWDER DYES.

No. 15711, 6d. size
No. 15712, 1d. „

In attractive boxes.

MAHOGANY (glass sliding lid).

Show Case gratis, containing 6 dozen **6d.** Dyes, assorted.
1 dozen **6d.** Dyes, Black.
Show Frames gratis with this case.

Judson's Gum.

"The Stickiest Sticker extant."

No. 15718, **2s.** size. Stock Gums, quarts.
No. 15719, **4d.** size. One dozen in box, with cap and brush, a most complete article.
No. 15720, **1d.** size. The best Penny Gum out; square bottles, packed with economy, clean, sweet, and adhesive, half-gross boxes.
No. 15721, **6d.** size. Dry Gum, specially prepared for export.
No. 15722, **1s.** size. Dry Gum, specially prepared for export.
No. 15723, **1s.** size. The Commercial Gum, with boxwood cap and superior brush, one dozen in a box.
No. 15724, **1s.** size. The pint of Refill-Gum, in strong bottles, "capsuled," one dozen in a box.
No. 15725, **6d.** size. The Commercial Gum, with boxwood cap and superior brush, well secured for export, "capsuled," one dozen in a box.
No. 15726, **6d.** size. The half-pint, or Economic Gum, for re-filling, "capsuled," one dozen in a box.

Judson's Black-All,

An Enamel Varnish for Stoves, &c.

Imparts a brilliant and lasting polished surface, resembling polished Black Marble, to Stoves, Fenders, Fire Irons, and all kinds of Iron Work.

DRIES QUICKLY.

"BLACK-ALL" should be applied with a small painter's brush or paste brush.

A Mahogany Show Case, sloping glass top, gratis with an order for 20/ worth of Black-All.

No. 15713, **6d.** size.
No. 15714, **1s.** size.

In good bottles with attractive labels.

Judson's A | Marking Ink, Warranted.

A most reliable ink for marking linen, &c.

A good-sized bottle, well corked, in a beautifully polished boxwood box to prevent evaporation. Box may be used for holding needles, bodkin, &c., &c. Price 1s. per bottle, including a linen stretcher; smaller size, 6d. per bottle, without stretcher.

No Heat required.

Jet Black.

Carded, or in mahogany glass-top cases.

3 dozen of either size.

No. 15715, **1s.** size. One dozen bottles in boxwood boxes, and 12 stretchers.
No. 15716, **1s.** size. Without stretcher.
No. 15717, **6d.** size. One dozen bottles in boxwood boxes.

Judson's Furniture Polish.

No. 15727, **6d.** size.
No. 15728, **1s.** „

CLEANS AND POLISHES.

JUDSON'S FURNITURE POLISH is simply magical in the results it produces, and that without waste of time or labour. It is made from the recipe of one of the leading pianoforte manufacturers, and every one knows how brilliant a piano always looks when first sent in. Give it a trial; do not pass over this page and say, "Mine is good enough," but try it once, and you will always continue to use it.

"Krokum," the Great Insect Destroyer.

TRADE MARK.

No. 15729, **1s.** size. Glass Castor.
No. 15730, **6d.** size. Glass Castor.
No. 15731, **6d.** size. Boxwood Castor.

No. 15732, **3d.** size. Glass Castor.
No. 15733, **3d.** size. Boxwood Castor.
No. 15734, **1d.** size. Glass Castor.

"Krokum" is perfectly harmless to human beings and all animals.

Judson's Gold Paint.

BOXED.

For re-gilding picture frames, gilding lamp stands and gas fittings, artistic cabinet or basket work, illuminating on paper, silk, or leather, renewing ormolu ornaments, and for a thousand useful purposes.

No. 15750, **6d.** size. 1 Bottle Gold Powder, 1 bottle mixing liquid, 1 mixing bowl, and 1 brush.
No. 15751, **1s.** size. 1 Bottle Gold Powder, 1 bottle mixing liquid, 1 mixing bowl, and 1 brush.
No. 15752, **1/6** size. 1 Bottle Gold Powder, 1 bottle mixing liquid, 1 mixing bowl, and 1 brush.
No. 15753, **3/6** size. Equal to 4 at 1/6, 2 bottles, bowl and brush, each set in separate box.
No. 15754, **10/6** size. Equal to 4 at 3/6, with brush only, each in box.
Six sets on a card or each set in card box.

Cement of Pompeii

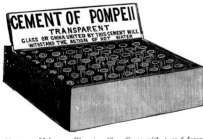

No. 15735. Mahogany Glass-top Show Cases, with 3 or 6 dozen **6d.** size.
No. 15736. Mahogany Glass-top Show Cases, with 6 dozen **3d.** size.
No. 15737, **1s.** size. Cement of Pompeii, superior bottle and brush, large size. 1 dozen on card.
No. 15738, **6d.** size. Cement of Pompeii, white, clear, withstands fire and water; for mending china, glass, meerschaum, leather, wood, &c., it is not to be equalled, each bottle with brush. 1 dozen on card.
No. 15739, **3d.** size. Cement of Pompeii, same quality as above in every respect, good value for the money. 1 dozen on card.

Judson's Sponges on Cards.

It is a well-known fact that retailers of sponges (who buy them by the case) very often lose money by them, or at best do not know what they make out of them.

We are therefore laying ourselves out to supply sponges of various sizes, mounted on attractive cards, showing a good profit to both wholesale and retail.

These sponges, mounted on cards (lithographed in red and black), have a striking effect when displayed in a window.

No. 15740, **1d.** size. 1 dozen on card.
No. 15741, **2d.** size. 1 dozen on card.
No. 15742, **3d.** size. 1 dozen on card.
No. 15743, **4d.** size. ½ dozen on card.
No. 15744, **6d.** size. ½ dozen on card.
No. 15745, **1s.** size. ½ dozen on card.
No. 15746, **1/6** size. ½ dozen on card.
No. 15747, **2s.** size. ½ dozen on card.
No. 15747A, **3s.** size. The Carriage Sponge, one on card.
Superior Sponges can be had from 5/ each.

Judson's Artists' Black,

For Picture Frames, Woodwork, &c.

Applied with a soft brush, it imparts a rich lustrous black polish to any hard substance, and dries in a few minutes. Ornaments may then be picked out with "Judson's Gold Paint." The expenditure of a few shillings and a little labour will be amply repaid by the result.

No. 15755, **1s.** size. Bottle and Brush, packed in separate boxes or on cards.
No. 15756, **2/6** size. Larger and more economical.

Judson's Gold and Silver Invitation Ink.

Price 6d. and 1s. per bottle.

This elegant preparation is used with an ordinary pen. The writing is clear and brilliant, and the effect most attractive.

It is admirably adapted for complimentary correspondence, writing invitations, ruling Oxford borders, writing names and dates in photographic albums and on cartes-de-visite, illuminating texts, and imitating gold jewellery in photographic paintings, &c.

No. 15748, 1 dozen 6d. size, on card.
No. 15749, 3 dozen 6d. size, in mahogany glass-top case.

Not less than ½ gallon supplied in bulk. Bottles, 1s. per gallon returnable.
Names of Stains—Oak, Antique Oak, Ebony, Maple, Satinwood, Mahogany, Antique Mahogany, Rosewood, Walnut.

Judson's Wood Stains.

For Staining, Improving, Preserving, and Imitating every known kind of Wood, whether hard or soft, with or without grain.

Judson's Wood Stains require neither sizing nor knotting before or after use, being *all three combined*, thus necessitating only one operation instead of four, and above all, the articles may be varnished at once, thus saving *time*, labour, dirt, and annoyance.

Very attractively got up, each Bottle in coloured Box.

No. 15757, **6d.** size.
No. 15757A, **1s.** „
No. 15757B, **2s.** size.
No. 15757C, **4s.** „

S. & F.
London & Paris.

ARCHERY.

Bows.

No. 15901.—Bows, polished, 3 feet 3 inches, 3 feet 9 inches, 4 feet.
No. 15902.—Bows, stained and polished, 4 feet 9 inches, 5 feet 6 inches, 6 feet.
No. 15903.—Bows, horn tip, 4 feet, 4 feet 6 inches, 5 feet, 6 feet.
No. 15904.—Bows, superior plush handles, 4 feet, 4 feet 6 inches, 5 feet 6 inches, 6 feet.
No. 15905.—Bows, best lancewood, made to weight, 4 feet, 5 feet, 5 feet 3 inches, 6 feet.
No. 15906.—Bows, ladies', lancewood, 5 feet 3 inches.
No. 15907.—Bows, gentlemen's, lancewood, 6 feet.
No. 15908.—Bows, ladies', lance or hickory wood, 5 feet 3 inches.
No. 15909.—Bows, gentlemen's, lance or hickory wood, 6 feet.
No. 15910.—Bows, ladies', fancy wood backed, 5 feet 3 inches.
No. 15911.—Bows, gentlemen's, fancy wood backed, 6 feet.
No. 15912.—Bows, ladies', three piece, 5 feet 3 inches.
No. 15913.—Bows, gentlemen's, three piece, 6 feet.
No. 15914.—Bows, ladies', snakewood, 5 feet 3 inches.
No. 15915.—Bows, gentlemen's, snakewood, 6 feet.
No. 15916.—Bows, best yew.

Tassels.

No. 15927.—Tassels, Ladies' green.
No. 15927A.—Tassels, red, white and blue.
No. 15927B.—Tassels, Gentlemen's green.
No. 15927C.—Tassels, red, white and blue.

No. 15927D.—Wooden Tablets.
No. 15927E.—Ivory Tablets.
No. 15927F.—Wooden Spring Prickles.
No. 15927G.—Ivory Spring Prickles.
No. 15927H.—Wooden Grease Cups, with lid.
No. 15927J.—Ivory Grease Cups, with lid.
No. 15927K.—Flemish Bowstrings, whipped ready for use.
No. 15927L.—Best White Bowstrings, whipped ready for use.
No. 15927M.—Baize Bow Case.
No. 15927N.—Waterproof Bow Case.

No. 15918.—Targets, 12, 15, 18, 21, 24, 30, 36, 42, 48 inches.
No. 15919.—Stands for Targets.

Quivers, Ladies' and Gentlemen's.

No. 15926.—Quiver, to hold 12 arrows.
No. 15926A.—Quiver, to hold 24 arrows.

Gentlemen's Arm Guards.

No. 15923.—Gentlemen's Arm Guard, plain, elastic band.
No. 15923A.—Gentlemen's Arm Guard, lined and stitched.
No. 15923B.—Gentlemen's Arm Guard, best, lined and stitched.

Ladies' Quiver Belts.

No. 15924.—Ladies' Quiver Belt, plain.
No. 15924A.—Ladies' Quiver Belt, with slides.
No. 15924B.—Ladies' Quiver Belt, stitched.

Gentlemen's Quiver Belts.

No. 15925.—Gentlemen's Quiver Belt, plain.

Ladies' Arm Guards.

No. 15922.—Ladies' Arm Guard, plain green.
No. 15922A.—Ladies' Arm Guard, lined and stitched.
No. 15922B.—Ladies' Arm Guard, silk lined.
No. 15922C.—Ladies' Arm Guard, plain brown.
No. 15922D.—Ladies' Arm Guard, lined and stitched.

Lawn Tennis Shoes.

Pyramid, Corrugated, or the "Registered Diamond" India-rubber soles.
No. 15926/2.—Ladies' Canvas or Twill Uppers.
No. 15926/3.—Ladies' Superior Kid Uppers.
No. 15927.—Gentlemen's Canvas or Twill Uppers.

Arrows.

No. 15917.—Arrows, 12-inch, 16-inch.
No. 15917A.—Arrows, 20-inch, sharp points, glued feathers.
No. 15917B.—Arrows, 21-inch, three feathers.
No. 15917C.—Arrows, 21-inch, painted and polished.
No. 15917D.—Arrows, 24-inch, polished.
No. 15917E.—Arrows, 24-inch, painted and polished.
No. 15917F.—Arrows, 25-inch, half knocks, painted and polished.
No. 15917G.—Arrows, 21-inch.
No. 15917H.—Arrows, 28-inch.
No. 15917J.—Arrows, 25-inch, three-quarter knocks.
No. 15917K.—Arrows, 28-inch, three-quarter knocks.
No. 15917L.—Arrows, 22-inch, youths', best pine wood, painted and gilt.
No. 15917M.—Arrows, 25-inch, ladies' ditto.
No. 15917N.—Arrows, 28-inch, gentlemen's.
No. 15917P.—Arrows, 25-inch, ladies', old deal, painted and gilt, and painted feathers.
No. 15917R.—Arrows, 28-inch, gentlemen's.
No. 15917S.—Arrows, 25-inch, ladies', pine wood footed.
No. 15917T.—Arrows, 28-inch, gentlemen's.
No. 15917V.—Arrows, 25-inch, ladies', old deal footed.
No. 15917W.—Arrows, 28-inch, gentlemen's.

Ladies' Gloves.

No. 15920.—Ladies' Gloves, plain, elastic bands.
No. 15920A.—Ladies' Gloves, plain, elastic bands, round top.
No. 15920B.—Ladies' Gloves, plain, lace tips.
No. 15920C.—Ladies' Gloves, spring.
No. 15920D.—Ladies' Gloves, knuckle tips.
No. 15920E.—Ladies' Gloves. screw tips.

Gentlemen's Gloves.

No. 15921A.—Gentlemen's Gloves, plain, elastic bands.
No. 15921B.—Gentlemen's Gloves, plain, round top.
No. 15921C.—Gentlemen's Gloves, plain, round lace tips.
No. 15921D.—Gentlemen's Gloves, spring laced.
No. 15921E.—Gentlemen's Gloves, knuckle tips.

No. 15927.

No. 15926.

LAWN TENNIS.

No. 15928.—Four French bats, 4 balls, 2 portable poles, net lines and runners, mallet for driving in poles, and rules, in box complete.
No. 15929.—Four English bats, net 33 feet by 4 feet, painted poles, 6 balls, guy ropes, pegs, runners and mallet, in box complete.
No. 15930.—Four English bats, net 42 feet by 4 feet, painted poles, 6 balls, guy ropes, runners, mallet, and book of rules, in box complete.
No. 15931.—Four superior English bats, net 42 feet by 4 feet, polished ash poles, 6 regulation balls, guy ropes, pegs, runners, mallet, and book of rules, in box complete.
No. 15932.—Four superior English bats, net 42 feet by 4 feet, polished ash poles, 12 felt-covered regulation balls, guy ropes, pegs, runners, mallet, in polished box complete.
No. 15933.—The "Club" set (see drawing), polished dovetail box with lock and key, containing 4 best-shaped lawn tennis bats, net 42 feet by 4 feet, best quality ash poles, 12 best covered regulation balls, polished press for 4 bats, guy ropes, tent pegs, runners, mallet, and book of rules, complete.
No. 15934.—The "Registered Garden Seat" lawn tennis set, containing 4 bats, balls, poles, net, and all the requisites for the game, fitted inside with racks, and forming an excellent seat for the lawn.
No. 15935.—The "Oxford and Cambridge" lawn tennis set, containing 4 best English bats, 6 covered and 6 plain balls, 2 painted poles with flags, tanned net, lines, runners, hammer and drill, racket press, with illustrated diagram and rules, complete, in polished and painted box.
No. 15936.—The "Oxford and Cambridge" lawn tennis set, in polished oak or birch box, superior finish, fitted with 4 best English bats, extra stout polished ash poles, best net, extra balls, pegs, ropes, and runners, with ball carriers and the latest improvements.
No. 15937.—The "Army and Navy" tennis, containing 4 best English bats, 6 covered and 6 plain balls, 2 painted poles with flags, tanned net lines and runners, hammer and drill, racket press, with illustrated diagram and rules, complete in polished and painted box.
No. 15938.—As No. 15937, but in polished oak, birch, or mahogany box, brass bound, superior finish, fitted with four best carriers and the latest improvements.

LAWN TENNIS SETS.
(Complete.)

No. 15933.

By Her Majesty's Royal Letters Patent.

THE "CAXTON" LAWN TENNIS MARKER.

No. 15953.

THE ROTARY TENNIS COURT MARKERS.

No. 15952.

No. 15952A.

THE
"CHAMPION" RACQUET.

No. 15949.

THE
"EXCELSIOR" RACQUET.

No. 15951.

THE
"EGYPTIAN" RACQUET.

No. 15950.

LEGGINGS.

No. 15996.—Men's yellow chamois.
No. 15996A.—Men's coloured chamois, cane and cork.
No. 15996B.—Men's white lambskin.
No. 15996C.—Men's chamois.
No. 15996D.—Men's buckskin, bordered and sewn.
No. 15996E.—Youth's yellow chamois.
No. 15996F.—Youth's white chamois.

POLISHED CRICKET BATS.

Half-cane Handles.

All-cane Handles.

Whalebone and Cane Handles.

No. 15970.—Youths' polished Bats.
No. 15971.—Youths' oiled Bats.
No. 15972.—Youths' plain Bats.
No. 15973.—Men's polished Bats.
No. 15974.—Men's plain Bats.

No. 15975.—Men's polished, dovetailed.
No. 15976.—Men's plain, dovetailed.
No. 15977.—Men's half-cane handle Bats.
No. 15978.—Youth's half-cane handle Bats.
No. 15979.—Men's all-cane handle Bats.
No 15980.—Youth's all-cane handle Bats.
No. 15981.—Men's whalebone and cane handle Bats.
No. 15982.—Men's india-rubber and cane handle Bats.
No. 15983.—Men's ash tongue handle Bats.

POLISHED STUMPS.

(Brass-bound ebony tops.)

No. 15995.—Men's polished Stumps, ash, brass-bound ebony tops.
No. 15995A.—Men's polished lancewood Stumps, ebony tops.
No. 15995B.—Men's polished lancewood Stumps, ebony top.
No. 15995C.—Men's polished lancewood Stumps, ebony balls.
No. 15995D.—Men's beech Stumps, iron shoes.
No. 15995E.—Men's beech Stumps, lancewood shoes.
No. 15995F.—Men's beech Stumps, solid brass top, iron shoes.

POLISHED STUMPS.

No. 15991.—Youths' polished Stumps.
No. 15992.—Youths' plain Stumps.

POLISHED STUMPS.

(Brass-bound.)

No. 15993.—Men's plain Stumps.
No. 15994.—Men's polished Stumps.

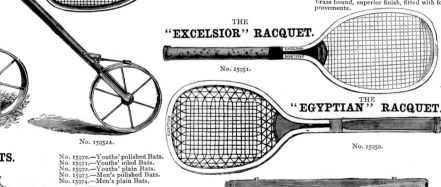

THE
PRESENTATION-SET
OF
CRICKET

CRICKET

No. 16000.—Presentation Set of Cricket, each set in a strong box, and consisting of two bats, one ball, one set of polished stumps, and book of rules.

CRICKET BAGS.

No. 15984.—Carpet Cricket Bag, tapestry.
No. 15985.—Carpet Cricket Bag, best Brussels.
No. 15986.—Marylebone do., Green, Navy Blue, or Crimson.

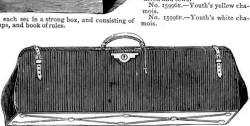

No. 16101.—Nursery Yachts, length from 60 inches to 84 inches, made in beech or birchwood.

No. 16102.—Rocking Horse with glass eyes, ordinary quality. Length of rocker 3 feet to 7 feet 5 inches, height of horse to saddle 1 foot 8 inches to 3 feet 9 inches.
No. 16102E.—Best quality Rocking Horse, extra strong, length of rocker 4 feet 6 inches to 7 feet 5 inches, height of horse 2 feet 2 inches to 3 feet 9 inches.

No. 16103.—Varnished Pinewood Cart. Length from 22 inches to 30 inches, width from 11 inches to 12½ inches.

No. 16104.—Toy Perambulator, painted wood. Height from 12 inches to 36 inches.
No. 16105.—Wicker Perambulator. Height from 12 inches to 36 inches.

No. 16106.—Shaped Pole Horse, painted and varnished, on green painted stand. Length from 16 inches to 34 inches, height from 12 inches to 24 inches.

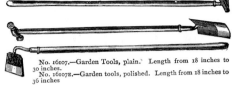

No. 16107.—Garden Tools, plain. Length from 18 inches to 30 inches.
No. 16107E.—Garden tools, polished. Length from 18 inches to 36 inches

Ladies' Sets of Floral Tools.

No. 16110.—Juvenile Tool Chest.

No. 16111.—Barrel or Castle Money Boxes. Height 2½ inches to 4½ inches, diameter 2 inches to 3½ inches.
No. 16112.—Money Boxes, assorted, wood. Length from 5½ inches to 7 inches, width from 2½ inches to 3½ inches.

No. 16111.

No. 16119.—Schooner, painted bottom, superior finish. Length from 15 inches to 30 inches.

No. 16116.—Open Boat, painted or varnished. Length from 10 inches to 18 inches.

No. 16117.—Lifeboat, with sail, complete. Length from 8 inches to 13 inches.

No. 16108.—Set of Floral Tools, comprising hoe, rake, spade, steel trowel, packed in box.
No. 16109.—As No. 16108, but smaller size, packed in box.

TRADE MARK.

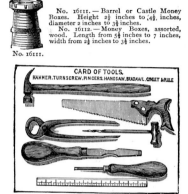

CARD OF TOOLS.
HAMMER, TURNSCREW, PINCERS, HANDSAW, BRADAWL, GIMLET & RULE

No. 16113.—Card of Tools. Length from 10 inches to 14 inches, width from 6 inches to 10 inches.
No. 16114.—The New Household Card of Tools.

No. 16120.—Schooner, with topsails, complete, painted and bronzed bottom. Length from 20 inches to 36 inches.

No. 16118.—Open Boat, with sails. Length from 10 inches to 18 inches.

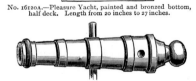

No. 16120A.—Pleasure Yacht, painted and bronzed bottom, half deck. Length from 20 inches to 27 inches.

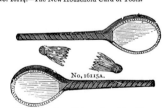

No. 16115A.

No. 16115.—Drum Bat, parchment or vellum.
No. 16115A.—Shuttlecocks.

No. 16121.—Mechanical Screw Steamboats, each packed in deal box, with directions, complete. Length 10 inches, 20 inches, and 27 inches.

No. 16125.—Painted Iron Pail.
No. 16126.—Wooden Spade.

No. 16126.

No. 16124.—Brass Cannon, 1½ inches, 1¾ inches, 2½ inches, 3 inches, 3¼ inches, and 4 inches.

No. 16130.—Berlin Wool Elephant, white or brown.

No. 16122.—Mechanical Paddle Steamboats, each packed in deal box, with directions complete. Length 12 inches, 20 inches, and 27 inches.

No. 16128.—Transparent Slate, white frame.

No. 16127.—Painted Horses and Carts, assorted patterns. Hay Carts, Dust Carts, Musical Carts, Chaises, Drays with painted barrels, Pickford's Loaded Carts.

No. 16123.—Model of Eighty-one Ton Gun, mounted on solid wood carriage, 2¾ inches, 3 inches, 3¾ inches, and 4¼ inches.

No. 16129.—Brass Anchor, 1½ inches, 2½ inches, 3¼ inches, and 4½ inches.

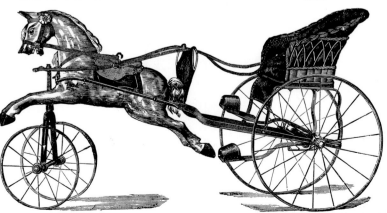

No. 16131.—Wicker Velocipede Carriage with Horse, Harness, Reins, &c., adjustable chair, lined seat.

"The Club Racer" Bicycle.

No. 16151.

SPECIFICATION.—Enamelled plain black, plain hollow steel front and back forks, elliptical backbone, neat Stanley head with improved long centres and deep neck, improved adjustable single ball bearings to front and back wheels, improved new section hollow felloe, ⅞-inch best red rubber tyres, steel hubs with direct spokes, 24-inch to 26-inch hollow handle bar, head, hubs, handle bar, and cranks plated; adjustable rat-trap ball pedals. Weight of 55-inch machine, 23 lbs. complete.

The "Club" Tandem.

No. 16152.

The advantages of the "Club" Tandem over all others are :—

1st. The front rider steers, and thus has an uninterrupted view of the road.

2nd. The steering being the same as in an ordinary front steerer, it is as easy to steer two riders as one.

3rd. Perfect safety. It is as safe as a sociable. Impossible to tilt.

4th. More space between the two riders than is usual with other machines.

In its single form this Tricycle is a central-geared front steerer.

To convert into a tandem it is merely necessary to fix three bolts. The attachment is jointed, so as to allow for inequalities of the road. Can be made to steer from the back if required.

"The Club Sociable" Tricycle.

No. 16153.

"The Club Sociable" will be found, both in design and material, to be of our usual standard quality. It is specially adapted to ladies' use, as the Patent "Cheylesmore" gear can be fitted to one of the cranks.

SPECIFICATION.—Steel tube frame, front steerer, double spoon brake, all bright parts plated, ball bearings to driving wheels and cranks, painted in two colours. Width 4 feet 11 inches.

The "Rover."

No. 16154.

Specially constructed for gentlemen requiring a light machine with vertical or bicycle position, very easy, comfortable, perfectly safe, and the best hill-climber yet made.

Open front, fitted with Starley's patent automatic double-driving gear, ball bearings to all wheels, adjustable handles and seat, safe yet effective band brake, plated parts, hubs, handles, brackets, seat, and steering rod, &c.

The Lady's "Cheylesmore" Tricycle.

No. 16155.

SPECIFICATION.—Open fronted, double driver. patent automatic clutch action, finest steel tube frame, ball bearings to driving wheels, steering wheel and crank shaft; steel hubs with direct butt-ended spokes, all the bright parts nickel plated and polished, improved patent swing lever double spoon brake applied simultaneously to both driving wheels, painted in three colours, ⅞-inch or ¾-inch best moulded tyres. Width of 44-inch machine, 3 feet 2 inches; 48-inch machine, 3 feet 4 inches.

The "Imperial Club" Tricycle No. 1.

No. 16156.

SPECIFICATION.—Finest steel tube frame, improved patent balance gearing, band brake, ball bearings to all wheels and cranks, all the bright parts plated, patent noiseless steering, painted in three colours. Width 3 feet 4 inches. Standard size 48 inches.

For ordinary roads we recommend this machine geared level, but we can supply it geared up to 54 inches where great speed is required, or down to 42 inches for very hilly country.

For Ladies' use 46-inch driving wheels, geared down to 42-inch, are advised.

The "Club" Semi-Racer.

No. 16157.

SPECIFICATION.—Plain hollow front and back forks, elliptical steel backbone, Stanley head, and improved long centres, improved adjustable single-ball bearings to front and back wheels, steel hubs with direct spokes, 24-inch and 26-inch handle bars.

The "Club" Bicycle.

No. 16158.

SPECIFICATION.—Very easy sliding spring with rubber cushions in front, plain hollow forks, elliptical backbone, adjustable single-ball bearings to back wheel, ⅞-inch or ¾-inch best rubber tyres, 24-inch to 26-inch handle bar with horn ends.

The "Coolie" Cycle.

No. 16159.

This machine is of quite a novel construction, and is built specially for use in India and other warm climates ; it is made for four persons, two of whom sit at rest in front in a comfortable seat, while two coolies, perched on saddles behind, drive the machine by means of endless chains connecting the crank shafts and the driving wheel. The Cheylesmore clutch gear is used, so that the cranks remain stationary while descending hills. The machine is so arranged that the steering as well as the brake can be managed by the front as well as by the back riders.

SPECIFICATION.—It is a double driver, patent Cheylesmore automatic clutch action being used, hollow steel tube frame, ball bearings to driving wheels and crank shafts, steel nuts with patent lock-nutted spokes, all the bright parts nickel plated, and double spoon brake applied simultaneously to both wheels.

No. 16201.—Single Perambulator, flat back shape, mounted on common springs, round spoke wheels, apron straps, &c., complete.
No. 16201A.—Double Perambulator, similar to No. 16201.

No. 16210.—Single Perambulator, Albert shape, birch-wood body, mounted on best elliptic springs, steel fronts, 18-inch carriage wheels, movable cushion.
No. 16210A.—Double Perambulator, similar to No. 16202.

No. 16202.—Single Perambulator, flat back shape, mounted on shackle springs, carpet on footboard.
No. 16202A.—Double Perambulator, similar to No. 16202.

No. 16207.—Single Perambulator, spider shape, on imitation elliptic steel springs, round spoke wheels.
No. 16207A.—Double Perambulator, similar to No. 16207.

No. 16213.—Single Perambulator, circular back, on best elliptic springs, steel fronts, 18-inch carriage wheels, movable cushion, &c.
No. 16213A.—Double Perambulator, similar to No. 16213.

No. 16221.—Wood or Wicker Bassinette, carriage springs, lined American cloth, loose cushion beds, hood, complete, 20, 22, or 24-inch wheels, india-rubber tyres, superior cloth lined.

No. 16217.—The "Barouche," 24-inch wheels, india-rubber tyres, best steel springs, lined American cloth, hood, apron, and straps.

TRADE MARK.

No. 16213B.—"Double Double" Perambulator, circu-lar back, partition in centre, same underwork and finish as No. 16213.

The Bassinette or Sociable Vis-a-Vis

is fitted with the newly-invented hood, which, being constructed to work on a centre piece, may be used at either end without the trouble of removing, and which, when used at the back, can be raised so that the infant can be seen. A movable cushion is provided for the centre when it is required to use the carriage as a bassinette.

Superior Fur Rugs, mounted on blue, brown, or red cloth, for Single, Double, and Bas-sinette Perambulators.

Vis-a-Vis Wicker Bassinette.
No. 16243.—Carriage springs, loose cushion bed, hood, complete, superior quality, 24-inch wheels, india-rubber tyres, brass jointed hood.

Vis-a-Vis Circular Backs.
No. 16244.—A very elegant carriage-built perambulator, painted and finished throughout in the best style, upholstered in carriage cloth, mounted on the best 24-inch bicycle wheels, india-rubber tyres, and steel springs, brass-jointed hood.

Canopies and Hoods.

Reversible Perambulator.
No. 16245.—Body of carriage and wheels made of seasoned wood; seat, cushion, and back well stuffed, covered with American cloth; the hood is made of the same material, and lined. Single.

Revolving Metallic Bassinette.
No. 16246.—Well-finished, lined American cloth, substantial apron and first-class knuckle-jointed hood, wood wheels.
No. 16246A.—As No. 16246, but with iron wheels, ariel india-rubber tyres.

Vis-a-Vis Panel Backs.
No. 16247.—Nicely painted and lined, upholstered in carriage cloth. jointed hood, bicycle wheels.

No. 16216.—Folding (Trotman's patent), mounted on steel springs, carriage wheels, brick apron, &c., single.

No. 16216.

No. 16231.—American Cloth Hoods, lined with chintz, single and double.

No. 16228.—3-wire Holland Canopies, single or double.

No. 16235.—Patent Fan-opening Canopy in satin cloth, 4-inch fringe, drab, blue, brown, black, or green; single.

FOREIGN TOYS, ETC.

No. 16251.—Brass Cornets, with china mouth-pieces, varying from 6 to ro inches in length, 3/6, 4/6, 7/6, 9/, 12/, 14/, 16/ per dozen.

No. 16252. — Brass Trombones, with china mouthpieces, varying from 6 to 14 inches in length, 3/6, 4/6, 7/6, 9/, 12/, 14/, 16/ per dozen.

No. 16253.—Brass Bugle Horns, with china mouthpieces, varying from 6 inches high by 6 inches wide, to 8 inches high by 8 inches wide, 4/6, 7/6, 9/, 12/, 16/ per dozen.

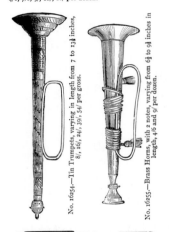

No. 16254.—Tin Trumpets, varying in length from 7 to 13½ inches, 8/, 16/, 24/, 39/, 54/ per gross.

No. 16255.—Brass Horns, with 2 notes, varying from 6½ to 9½ inches in length, 4/6 and 9/ per dozen.

No. 16256.—Musical Pop Guns, varying in length from about 6 to 14 inches, 1/4, 2/, 2/6, 3/, 4/6, 6/, 7/6 per dozen.

No. 16257.—Musical Cup and Ball, varying from 9 to 17 inches in length, 2/6, 3/, 4/, 5/, 6/, 7/6 per dozen.

No. 16258.—Accordions, with tin keys, varying from 3½ to 8½ inches in length, 3/, 4/, 5/, 6/, 8/ per dozen.

No. 16259.—Horn Horns, 1/9, 3/3, 4/, 6/ per dozen.
No. 16259A.—Horn Horns, nickel mounted, with china mouthpieces, 2/9, 3/3, 3/6, 4/6 per dozen.

No. 16260.—Toy Concertinas, varying from 3½ to 4½ inches across, 4/3 and 8/6 per dozen.

No. 16261.—Skipping Ropes, 1/9, 2/9, 3/6, 4/6, 9/ per dozen.
No. 16261A.—Gilt corded rope and polished handles, 9/ per dozen.

No. 16262.—Cube Games, length from about 6 to 19 inches, width from about 4 to 14 inches, 4/6, 9/, 14/6, 18/ per dozen ; 2/, 2/6, 4/6, 6/, 8/6, 9/6 each.

No. 16263.—Toy Pianos, length from about 7½ to 14 inches, width in proportion, 4/6, 9/, 12/, 18/, 27/ per dozen.

No. 16264.—Metalaphons, 11 by 4 inches, 4/6 per dozen.
No. 16264A.—Metalaphons, 17 by 6 inches, 9/ per dozen.

No. 16265.—Colour Boxes, white, 9d., 1/6, 2/, 3/, 4/6, 6/ per dozen.
No. 16265A.—Colour Boxes, mahogany, 9/, 15/, 24/ per dozen.
No. 16265B.—Colour Boxes, fancy inlaid, 19/6 and 32/ per dozen.

No. 16266.—Noah's Arks, painted, varying in length from about 9 to 24 inches, 9/, 10/6, 18/, 21/, 27/ per dozen, 4/, 5/6, 7/6, 10/6, 14/ each.

No. 16267.—Noah's Arks, white wood, varying in length from 8 to 21 inches, 4/6, 9/, 13/, 27/ per dozen ; 3/, 4/6, 6/, 7/6, 10/6 each.

No. 16269.—Stables, varying in length from 11 to 24 inches, 9/, 12/, 18/, 24/, 36/, 48/, 60/, 72/ per dozen.

No. 16270.—Boxes of Bricks, plain, 4/3, 8/6, 14/, 24/, 36/, 48/ per dozen.
No. 16270A.—Boxes of Bricks, Gothic, 4/3, 8/6, 14/, 21/, 24/, 36/, 48/ per dozen, 5/6, 7/6 each.
No. 16270B.—Boxes of Bricks, hard wood, varying from 6 to 23 inches in length, 4/, 6/, 9/, 12/, 14/, 16/ each.

No. 16271.—Box Toys, Bedroom Furniture, varying in length from about 6 to 18 inches, and width from 4 to 9 inches, 4/6, 9/, 18/, 24/, 30/, 36/, 48/ per dozen.
No. 16271A.—Drawing Room Furniture, varying in length from about 6 to 18 inches, and width from 6 to 12 inches, 2/, 3/, 4/, 5/6, 8/, 10/, 14/, 18/, 24/ per set.
No. 16271B.—Dining Room Furniture, varying in size from 8 by 6 inches to 1. by 9 inches, 2/6, 3/6, 4/6, 5/6, 7/6, 8/6 9/6, per set.

No. 16272.—Guns with springs and firing percussion caps, varying in length from 18 to 36 inches, 4/6, 9/, 14/6, 21/, 24/, 27/, 30/ per dozen.
No. 16272A.—Guns with Bayonets, 12/, 18/, 24/ per dozen.

No. 16273.—Swords with Scabbards, 4/6, 9/, 14/6, 21/, 24/, 27/, 36/, 42/, 48/, 54/, 60/ per dozen.

No. 16274.—Magnetic Toys, assorted fish, birds, and animals, in boxes with glass tops, varying in length from about 6 to 12 inches, 4/6, 9/, 14/6, 21/, 24/, 27/, 30/ per dozen.
No. 16274A.—Magnetic Boats, 4/6, 9/, 14/6 per dozen.
No. 16274B.—Magnetic Ducks, 4/6, 9/ per dozen.
No. 16274C.—Magnetic Fish, 4/6, 9/ per dozen.

S. & F.
LONDON
AND
PARIS.

No. 16275.—Box Toys, in oval chip boxes, varying in length from about 6 to 12 inches, 8d., 1/4, 2/, 3/, 4/, 8/ per dozen.

No. 16276. — Masks, assorted newest patterns, 8d., 1/4, 2/, 2/9, 3/ 4/6, 8/ per dozen.
No. 16276A.—Masks, with whiskers and caps, 12/, 18/, 27/ per dozen.
No. 16276B.—Animal heads, 4/6, 8/, 12/ per dozen.

No. 16277.—Skittles, in square wooden boxes, varying from 9 to 24 inches, 4/, 8/, 12/, 16/, 24/, 36/, 48/ per dozen.

No. 16278.—Watches and Chains, 9d., 1/4, 2/, 2/9, 3/6, 4/6, 6/, 8/, 12/, 16/, 18/, 24/ per dozen.

No. 16279.—Targets, with Guns, various patterns and designs, 9/, 18/, 24/, 36/ per dozen.

No. 16280.—Bellows Heads, 9d., 1/9, 2/, 3/, 4/, 6/ per dozen.

No. 16281.—Chinese Lanterns, globe shape, 8d., 1/4, 2/, 3/, 4/, 6/, 8/ per dozen.
No. 16281A.—Chinese Lanterns, fancy, in various shapes, 3/3, 4/6, 9/, 12/, 18/, 27/, 36/ per dozen.
No. 16281B.—Chinese Lanterns, long, 9d., 1/6, 2/, 3/, 4/6, 6/, 9/, 12/ per dozen.

No. 16268.—China Tea Sets, in cartoon boxes, 4/6, 9/, 14/, 21/, 27/, 36/, 48/, 54/ per dozen.
No. 16268A.—China Tea Set, in cartoon box, coloured and gilt decoration, containing 6 cups, 6 saucers, cream jug, sugar basin, and tea pot, 4/9 per set.
No. 16268B.—China Tea Set, in cartoon box, decorated with flowers and gold, 6 cups, 6 saucers, 2 bread-and-butter plates, cream jug, sugar basin, and tea pot, 6/9 per set.
No. 16268C.—China Tea Set, in cartoon box, decorated with flowers and gold, containing 6 cups, 6 saucers, cream jug, sugar basin and tea pot, spoons and tongs, 7/9 per set.

No. 16282.—Lead Soldiers, Horse and Foot, in glass-top boxes, varying from 3½ to 14 inches in length, 9d., 1/6, 2/3, 4/6, 9/, 14/, 21/, 33/ per dozen.

TOYS, BOATS, MARBLES, ETC.

No. 17001.

No. 16300.—Tin Toys, Cabs, 2/, 2/3, 4/6 per doz.
No. 16301.—Tin Toys, Gigs, 1/4, 2/3, 3/3. 4/6, 9/ per doz.
No. 16302.—Tin Toys, Carriages, 4/6, 6/, 14/6, 24/. 36/, 48/, 60/ per doz.
No. 16303.—Tin Toys, Canoes on Wheels, 4/6, 9/ per doz.
No. 16304.—Tin Toys, Carts, assorted, 9/ per doz.
No. 16305.—Tin Toys, Animals, 12 kinds, in box, 8/ per doz. bozes.
No. 16306.—Tin Toys, Engines and Carriages, 5 pieces, 4/6 ; 9 pieces, in box, 9/ per dozen boxes.
No. 16307.—Tin Toys, Magic Lanterns, with slides complete, 4/6, 9/, in box, 14/6, 21/, 27/, 36/, 48/, 60/ per doz. boxes.
No. 16308.—Tin Toys, Metal Pop Pistols, 1/4, 2/, 3/, 4/, 6/, 8/ per doz.
No. 16309.—Tin Toys, Scales in Glass Top Boxes, 3/3, 4/6, 9/ per doz.

MARBLES.

No. 16287.   No. 16288.   No. 16289.   No. 16290.   No. 16291.

No. 16287.—Marbles, Polished Stone, 1/10 per 1000.
No. 16288.—Marbles, China, 2/, 3/, 3/9, 6/, 9/, 13/6, 20/, 27/ per 1000.
No. 16289.—Marbles, Glass, 7/, 9/6, 12/, 15/6, 21/, 30/, 45/, 54/ per 1000.
No. 16290.—Marbles, Blood Alleys, 6/ per 1000.
No. 16291.—Marbles, Agate, best quality, 16/ per 100.

No. 16293.—Mechanical Clockwork 2-horse Gigs, about 5½ inches in length, 9/ per doz.

No. 16298—Mechanical Clockwork Girl with Perambulator, about 5 inches in length, 9/ per doz.

No. 16296.—Mechanical Clockwork Velocipede and Rider, about 4½ inches in length, 9/ per doz.

No. 16295.—Mechanical Clockwork Chariot with horse, about 5¼ inches long, 9/ per doz.

No. 16294.—Mechanical Clockwork Omnibus, with two horses, about 5¾ inches in length, 9/ per doz.

No. 16284.—India-rubber Toys.—Dogs and other Animals, 4/6, 9/, 16/, 21/, 36/, 48, and 60/ per dozen ; figures on assorted animals, 10/6, 15/6, 21/, 27/, and 30/ per dozen ; rattles, with rings, 4/6 and 6/ per dozen ; boy in chair, 4/6 per dozen ; large figures, assorted, 12 in a box, 4/6 per box ; large figures, superior quality, 9/ per box.

No. 16325.—Mechanical Walking Poodle Dogs, natural movement, fitted with best and strongest clockwork movement, 18/6 each.

No. 16297.—Mechanical Clockwork Mice, in glass top boxes, from 2 inches to 3 inches in length, 4/6, 6/, 7/6, 9/, 10/6, 12/ per doz.

TRADE MARK

SPECIAL NOVELTY.

No. 16324.—Doll in Perambulator. The perambulator is made of wicker, handsomely enamelled in fine colours, silk apron and lace canopy, 13 inches long, 6 inches wide, 18½ inches high. The doll is finely modelled, turns and cries "mamma" when the perambulator is pushed along. 8/6 each.

No. 16324.

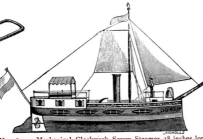

No. 16310.—Mechanical Clockwork Screw Steamer, 18 inches long, 4½ inches wide, 15 inches high to top of mast, height of stern 7½ inches, made of metal, beautifully painted in colours, one funnel, fully rigged, highly finished, 24/ each.

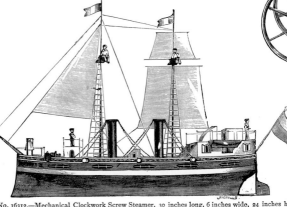

No. 16312.—Mechanical Clockwork Screw Steamer, 30 inches long, 6 inches wide, 24 inches high to top of mast, height of stern 8 inches, made of metal, beautifully painted in colours, two funnels, fully rigged, men sitting on the yards, armed with six brass cannons, highly finished, 60/ each.

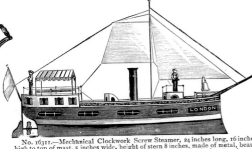

No. 16311.—Mechanical Clockwork Screw Steamer, 24 inches long, 16 inches high to top of mast, 5 inches wide, height of stern 8 inches, made of metal, beautifully painted in colours, one funnel, fully rigged, highly finished, 32/ each.

No. 16324.—Child's Folding Perambulator, made of iron and wood, the seat is fancy canvas, the table and foot-board grained and varnished wood. The ironwork is painted blue, with other colour decoration ; the spokes and tyre of wheels are iron. Height from ground to handle 28 ins., height of seat from ground 15 ins., height of table from ground 22 ins. ; width 15 ins. This is a very strong and useful perambulator. 7/6 each.

No. 16322.—Mechanical Elephant, walks and raises its trunk ; skin covered, and fitted with best and strongest clockwork movement, 27/6 each.

No. 16323. — Mechanical Bear playing drum, the figure is skin covered, and fitted with best and strongest clockwork movement, 22/6 each.

No. 16292.—Mechanical Clockwork Engine and 3 Carriages, 9/ and 12/ per doz. ; superior (as drawing), from 13 inches to 31 inches in length, 2/, 2/8, 3/6, 4/6, 6/, 11/6, 15/6, 22/, 33/ each.

No. 16286. — The New Mechanical Revolving Kaleidoscope Charmer, produces an endless variety of colours and designs, with brass movement, mounted on turned polished stand. Height from about 11 inches to 14 inches, length from about 8 inches to 11 inches, 5/9, 6/9, and 7/9 each.

No. 16315.—LITTLE TOT'S A B C, 4 large cubes in box, prettily decorated, 24/ per doz.

No. 16316.—LITTLE PET'S A B C, half cubes, in boxes, 42/ per doz.

No. 16317.—BABY BUNTING A B C, 8 large cubes in prettily decorated box, 42/ per doz.

No. 16318.—MOTHER GOOSE, a dissected puzzle, 12 varieties, 15/ per doz.

No. 16319.—MAMMOTH A B C, containing 7 cubes, each fitting in the other, 45/ per doz.

No. 16320.—DOLL'S TROUSSEAU. The box contains dressed doll on spring gilt chair. 4/, 6/6, 7/6 each.

No. 16321.—Boys' sets of SOLDIERS' OUTFITS on cards, containing swords, guns, helmets, &c., 4/, 6/6, 8/6, 10/6, 12/6, 14/6 per set.

No. 16285.—Stoves, 4/6, 9/, 14/, 21/, 36/ per dozen ; 4/, 6/, 8/, 10/, 15/, 18/, 27/ each.
Varying from about 4 inches to 24 inches in height.

No. 16313.—Clockwork Omnibuses, superior quality, 4/, 5/6, 6/, 7/6, 8/6, 12/, 14/6, 17/6 each.
No. 16313A.—Clockwork Tram Cars, from 8 inches to 21 inches, 4/6, 6/, 8/6, 10/6, 12/6, 16/, 18/6 each.
No. 16313B.—Clockwork Jockeys riding on Horse, from 4 inches to 7 inches in length, 9/, 14/6, 20/, 33/, 48/ per doz.

DOLLS.

No. 16330.—Indestructible Doll, painted black hair.

No. 16333.—Indestructible Doll, with fur wig and fancy worked shirt; this doll has the appearance of wax, but is made of a very strong material, which is not affected by any climate.

No. 16336.—Nankeen Doll.

No. 16339.—India-rubber Doll, wool dressed.

No. 16340.—Biscuit China Doll.

No. 16345.—Doll, with china head, hair, and natural eyes; the body is jointed so that the doll can be placed in any position; white shirt, trimmed with lace.

No. 16345.

No. 16331.—Model Crying Doll, with head-dress, fancy worked shirt, and painted boots.

No. 16333.

No. 16337.—Model Crying Doll, wax head, natural eyes, assorted head-dresses, wax arms and feet, white shirt trimmed with coloured print.

No. 16342.—Model Crying Doll, dressed, with fancy head-dress, assorted patterns.

No. 16346.—Fine Model Crying Dolls, assorted boys and girls, wax head, with natural eyes, wax arms and feet, with stockings, sitting body, fancy shirt, inserted hair.

No. 16334.—Half Model Crying Baby Doll, cap and shirt, natural eyes, composition arms and legs.

No. 16341.—Half Model Crying Doll, with fancy head-dress, fancy fronted shirt, and painted boots.

No. 16343.—Model Crying Doll, with cap, wax head, natural eyes, composition arms and feet, plain shirt trimmed with lace.

No. 16332.—"Mamma" and "Papa" Doll, wax head, natural eyes, fur wig, wax arms and feet, white shirt with lace; the doll is made to cry by raising its hands.

No. 16335.—Model Crying Doll, wax head, fine eyes (known as "natural eyes"), wax arms and feet, long flowing hair, Prince Charlie's model, best made body, each packed in separate box.

No. 16338.—"Mamma" and "Papa" Baby Doll, wax head, natural eyes, wool cap, white shirt with lace, wax arms and feet, with stockings; the doll cries "mamma" and "papa" on the arms being raised.

No. 16344.—Model Crying Doll, wax head, natural eyes, fur wig, fine model limbs, fancy worked shirt, &c.

No. 16347.—Model Boy Doll, wax head, natural eyes, inserted hair, stockings and boots, best sitting body, wax arms and feet, fancy worked shirt.

No. 16347.

BABY, PLATE, KNIFE, BUTCHER, PALM, AND WASTE PAPER BASKETS, WASHSTAND SCREENS, AND CANE WINDOW BLINDS.

No. 16381.—Baby Baskets, made of fine white wicker, in nests of 4, size of outside basket 18 ins. long and 15 ins. wide. Can also be had in open work in nests of 3.

No. 16382.—Baize-lined Plate Baskets, in 5 sizes, viz. 12 by 8 ins., 14 by 8½ ins., 16 by 9 ins., 17 by 10 ins., and 18 by 12 ins.

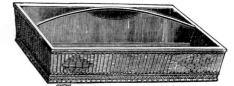

No. 16383.—Tin-lined Basket for Dirty Knives, in 2 sizes, viz. 12 by 7½ ins., and 16 by 9½ ins.

No. 16384.—Butchers' or Garden Baskets, white wicker, in nests of 3, size of outside basket 17 by 14 by 7 inches.

No. 16385.—Palm Baskets, in nests of 3, oval. Size of outside basket 14 by 8 by 7 inches.
No. 16385A.—As No. 16385, but square shape.

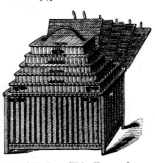

No. 16386.—Brown Wicker Hampers, fine quality, with leather handles and fastenings, in 5 sizes, viz. 7, 8, 9, 10, 12, and 14 inches in length.

No. 16387.—White Wicker Wall Tidies, in 9 sizes, viz. 7½, 9, 11, 13½, 16, 18, 19, and 21 inches high.

No. 16388.—White Wicker Waste Paper Baskets, in 3 sizes, viz. 9, 10, and 11 inches high.

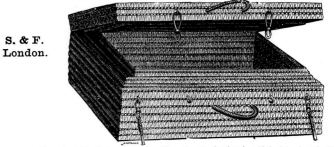

S. & F. London.   S. & F. London.

No. 16389.—Palm Basket, Portmanteau Shape, in nests of 3, size of outside basket 17 by 12 by 8 inches.

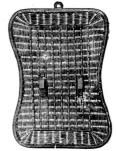

No. 16390. — White Wicker Screens for Chair Backs, 27 inches high, 18 inches wide.

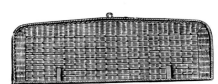

No. 16391.—White Wicker Washstand Screens, in 9 sizes, viz. 2 feet 6 inches, 2 feet 9 inches, 3 feet, 3 feet 3 inches, 3 feet 6 inches, 3 feet 9 inches, 4 feet, 4 feet 3 inches, and 4 feet 6 inches long, width in proportion.

No. 16392.—White Willow Washstand Screens, woven border and floral centre in colours, 3 sizes, viz. 18 by 36 ins., 20 by 40 ins., and 24 by 44 ins.

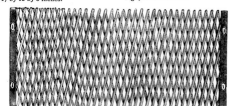

No. 16393.—Expanding Window Blinds (white wood), 3 sizes, viz. 15, 18, and 21 inches high.

WINDOW BLINDS, MADE OF BLACK AND WHITE CANE, CAN BE MADE TO FIT ANY SIZE WINDOW.

No. 16394.

No. 16395.

No. 16396.

No. 16397.

No. 16398.

No. 16399.

The Prices of Cane Blinds are quoted at per square foot, and in sending measurement please give exact width between beads of window sash, also exact height from bottom rail to extreme top of centre ornament.

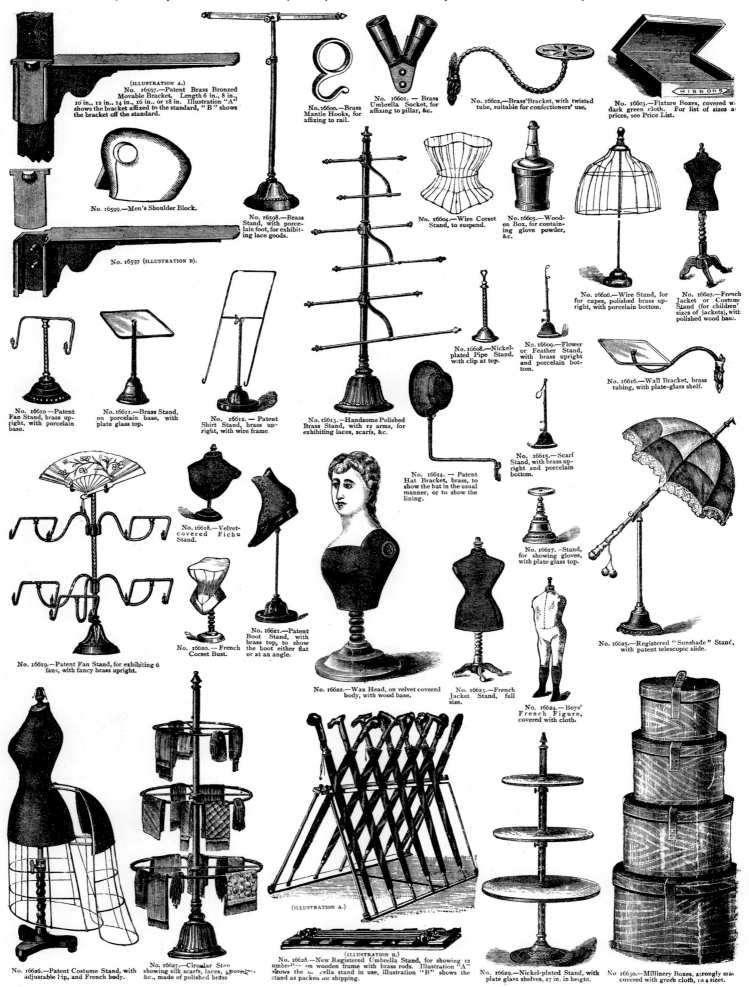

(ILLUSTRATION A.)

No. 16597.—Patent Brass Bronzed Movable Bracket. Length 6 in., 8 in., 10 in., 12 in., 14 in., 16 in., or 18 in. Illustration "A" shows the bracket affixed to the standard, "B" shows the bracket off the standard.

No. 16599.—Men's Shoulder Block.

No. 16597 (ILLUSTRATION B).

No. 16598.—Brass Stand, with porcelain foot, for exhibiting lace goods.

No. 16600.—Brass Mantle Hooks, for affixing to rail.

No. 16601.—Brass Umbrella Socket, for affixing to pillar, &c.

No. 16602.—Brass Bracket, with twisted tube, suitable for confectioners' use.

No. 16603.—Fixture Boxes, covered with dark green cloth. For list of sizes and prices, see Price List.

No. 16604.—Wire Corset Stand, to suspend.

No. 16605.—Wooden Box, for containing glove powder, &c.

No. 16606.—Wire Stand, for fur capes, polished brass upright, with porcelain bottom.

No. 16607.—French Jacket or Costume Stand (for children's sizes of jackets), with polished wood base.

No. 16610.—Patent Fan Stand, brass upright, with porcelain base.

No. 16611.—Brass Stand, on porcelain base, with plate glass top.

No. 16612.—Patent Shirt Stand, brass upright, with wire frame.

No. 16613.—Handsome Polished Brass Stand, with 12 arms, for exhibiting laces, scarfs, &c.

No. 16608.—Nickel-plated Pipe Stand, with clip at top.

No. 16609.—Flower or Feather Stand, with brass upright and porcelain bottom.

No. 16616.—Wall Bracket, brass tubing, with plate-glass shelf.

No. 16614.—Patent Hat Bracket, brass, to show the hat in the usual manner, or to show the lining.

No. 16615.—Scarf Stand, with brass upright and porcelain bottom.

No. 16617.—Stand, for showing gloves, with plate glass top.

No. 16618.—Velvet-covered Fichu Stand.

No. 16620.—French Corset Bust.

No. 16621.—Patent Boot Stand, with brass top, to show the boot either flat or at an angle.

No. 16619.—Patent Fan Stand, for exhibiting 6 fans, with fancy brass upright.

No. 16622.—Wax Head, on velvet covered body, with wood base.

No. 16623.—French Jacket Stand, full size.

No. 16624.—Boys' French Figure, covered with cloth.

No. 16625.—Registered "Sunshade" Stand, with patent telescopic slide.

No. 16626.—Patent Costume Stand, with adjustable hip, and French body.

No. 16627.—Circular Stand, showing silk scarfs, laces, gloves, &c., made of polished brass.

(ILLUSTRATION A.)

(ILLUSTRATION B.)

No. 16628.—New Registered Umbrella Stand, for showing 12 umbrellas on wooden frame with brass rods. Illustration "A" shows the umbrella stand in use, illustration "B" shows the stand as packed for shipping.

No. 16629.—Nickel-plated Stand, with plate glass shelves, 27 in. in height.

No. 16630.—Millinery Boxes, strongly made, covered with green cloth, in 4 sizes.

No. 12305 Plain Black Compasses

No. 12306 Best Wing Compasses

No. 12307 Brass Drawing Compasses

No. 12308 In and Out Callipers

No. 12309 Best Egg Callipers

No. 12310 Spring Dividers

No. 12311 Steel Callipers, to pass inside and out

No. 12312 Measuring Tape, metallic

No. 12313 Round Brad Punch

No. 12314 Gun Wad Punch

No. 12315 Saddlers' Punch

No. 12316 Tool Pad, containing various tools in handle

No. 12317 Improved Cutting Gauge

No. 12318 Cutting Gauge

square or oval heads inlaid edges

No. 12319 Marking Gauge

No. 12320 Joiners' Name Stamp for Wood

No. 12321 Name Stamp for Steel

TRADE MARK

No. 12322 Carpenters' Rule, 2-fold, measuring 2 feet

No. 12323 Gouge Slip, Grecian

No. 12326 Hone or Oilstone

No. 12324 Long Chalk Line Reel

No. 12325 Flat Chalk Line Reel

No. 12327 Cased Oilstone

No. 12328 Spokeshave, Beech or Boxwood

No. 12329 Improved Sliding Bevel, Rosewood or Ebony handle

No. 12330 Engineers' Oil Can, with copper spout

No. 12331 Coopers' Straight Stave Knife

TRADE MARK.

No. 12332 Combination Mitre and Square

No. 12334 Scraper Blade

No. 12336 Best Plated Square, Rosewood or Ebony

No. 12333 Best Plated Mitre Square Rose or Ebony

No. 12335 Japanned Iron Bull Nose Plane

No. 12337 Brass Stocked Sash Square

No. 12338 Bench Claw or Stop

No. 12339 Double Smoothing Cast-steel Plane

No. 12340 Spirit Level, double-plated

No. 12341 Rebate Plane, skew or square mouth

No. 12342 Beading or Grooving Plane

TRADE MARK

No. 12343 Plough Plane, cap'd and wedged, with screwed stems

No. 12344 Sash Fillister Plane, cap'd stems and wedged

S&F. London.

No. 12345 Jack Plane, Cast-steel

No. 12346 Trying Plane. Cast-steel double irons

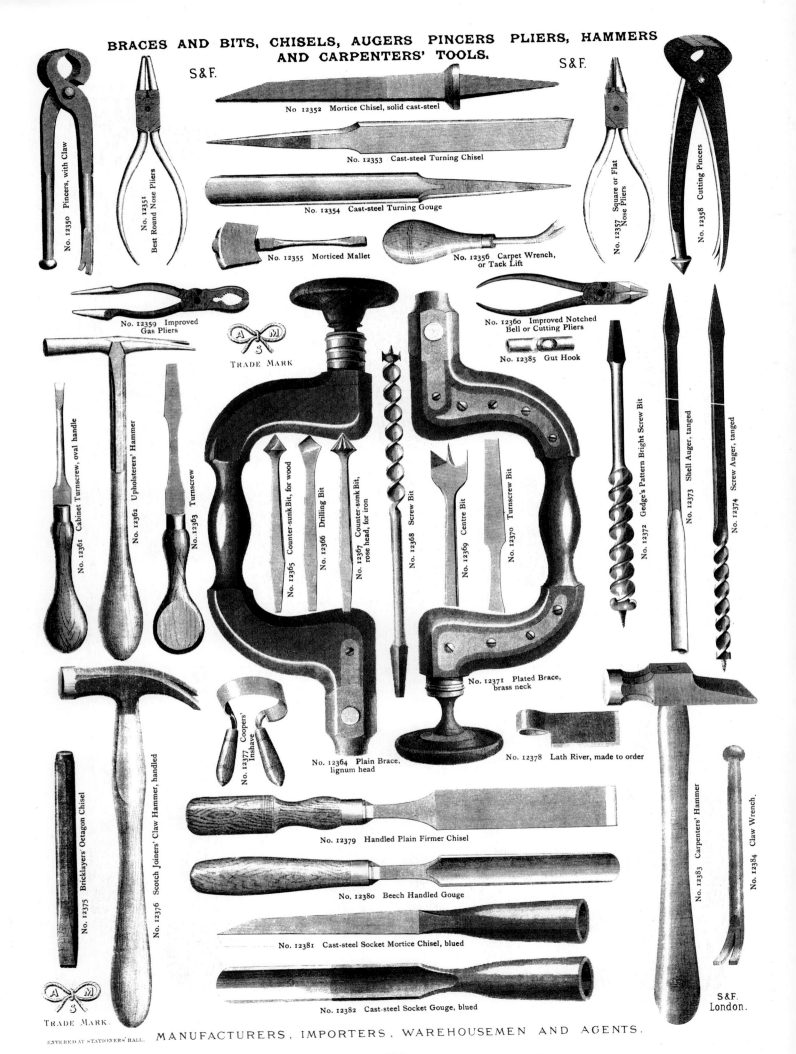

BRACES AND BITS, CHISELS, AUGERS PINCERS PLIERS, HAMMERS AND CARPENTERS' TOOLS.

S&F.

S&F.

No. 12350 Pincers, with Claw

No. 12351 Best Round Nose Pliers

No 12352 Mortice Chisel, solid cast-steel

No. 12353 Cast-steel Turning Chisel

No. 12354 Cast-steel Turning Gouge

No. 12355 Morticed Mallet

No. 12356 Carpet Wrench, or Tack Lift

No. 12357 Square or Flat Nose Pliers

No. 12358 Cutting Pincers

No. 12359 Improved Gas Pliers

TRADE MARK

No. 12360 Improved Notched Bell or Cutting Pliers

No. 12385 Gut Hook

No. 12361 Cabinet Turnscrew, oval handle

No. 12362 Upholsterers' Hammer

No. 12363 Turnscrew

No. 12365 Counter-sunk Bit, for wood

No. 12366 Drilling Bit

No. 12367 Counter-sunk Bit, rose head, for iron

No. 12368 Screw Bit

No. 12369 Centre Bit

No. 12370 Turnscrew Bit

No. 12372 Gedge's Pattern Bright Screw Bit

No. 12373 Shell Auger, tanged

No. 12374 Screw Auger, tanged

No. 12371 Plated Brace, brass neck

No. 12377 Coopers' Inshave

No. 12364 Plain Brace, lignum head

No. 12378 Lath River, made to order

No. 12375 Bricklayers' Octagon Chisel

No. 12376 Scotch Joiners' Claw Hammer, handled

No. 12379 Handled Plain Firmer Chisel

No. 12380 Beech Handled Gouge

No. 12381 Cast-steel Socket Mortice Chisel, blued

No. 12383 Carpenters' Hammer

No. 12384 Claw Wrench.

No. 12382 Cast-steel Socket Gouge, blued

TRADE MARK.

ENTERED AT STATIONERS' HALL.

S&F. London.

MANUFACTURERS, IMPORTERS, WAREHOUSEMEN AND AGENTS.

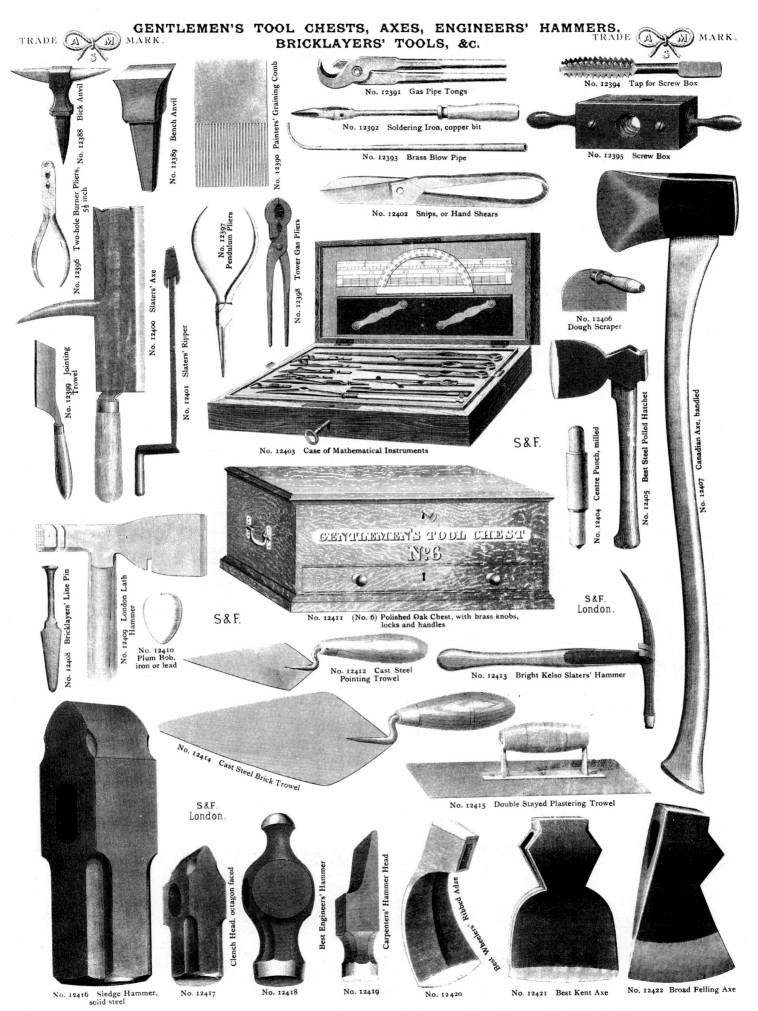

TRADE MARK. TRADE MARK.

Bick Anvil, No. 12388

No. 12389 Bench Anvil

No. 12390 Painters' Graining Comb

No. 12391 Gas Pipe Tongs

No. 12392 Soldering Iron, copper bit

No. 12393 Brass Blow Pipe

No. 12394 Tap for Screw Box

No. 12395 Screw Box

No. 12396 Two-hole Burner Pliers, 5½ inch

No. 12397 Pendulum Pliers

No. 12398 Tower Gas Pliers

No. 12400 Slaters' Axe

No. 12401 Slaters' Ripper

No. 12399 Jointing Trowel

No. 12402 Snips, or Hand Shears

No. 12403 Case of Mathematical Instruments

S&F.

No. 12406 Dough Scraper

No. 12404 Centre Punch, milled

No. 12405 Best Steel Polled Hatchet

No. 12407 Canadian Axe, handled

No. 12408 Bricklayers' Line Pin

No. 12409 London Lath Hammer

No. 12410 Plum Bob, iron or lead

S&F.

No. 12411 (No. 6) Polished Oak Chest, with brass knobs, locks and handles

No. 12412 Cast Steel Pointing Trowel

No. 12413 Bright Kelso Slaters' Hammer

S&F. London.

No. 12414 Cast Steel Brick Trowel

No. 12415 Double Stayed Plastering Trowel

S&F. London.

No. 12416 Sledge Hammer, solid steel

No. 12417

Clench Head, octagon faced

No. 12418

Best Engineers' Hammer

No. 12419

Carpenters' Hammer Head

Best Wheelers' Ribbed Adze

No. 12420

No. 12421 Best Kent Axe

No. 12422 Broad Felling Axe

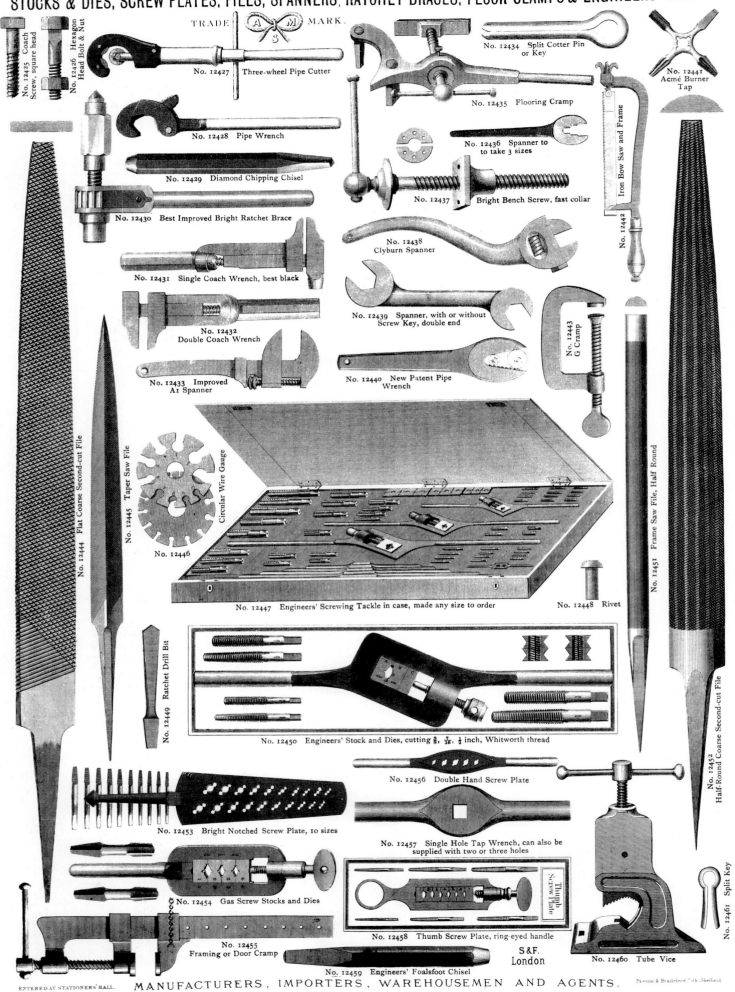

TRADE MARK.

No. 12425 Coach Screw, square head

No. 12426 Hexagon Head Bolt & Nut

No. 12427 Three-wheel Pipe Cutter

No. 12434 Split Cotter Pin or Key

No. 12441 Acmé Burner Tap

No. 12428 Pipe Wrench

No. 12435 Flooring Cramp

No. 12436 Spanner to take 3 sizes

No. 12429 Diamond Chipping Chisel

No. 12430 Best Improved Bright Ratchet Brace

No. 12437 Bright Bench Screw, fast collar

No. 12431 Single Coach Wrench, best black

No. 12438 Clyburn Spanner

No. 12442 Iron Bow Saw and Frame

No. 12432 Double Coach Wrench

No. 12439 Spanner, with or without Screw Key, double end

No. 12443 G Cramp

No. 12433 Improved A1 Spanner

No. 12440 New Patent Pipe Wrench

No. 12444 Flat Coarse Second-cut File

No. 12445 Taper Saw File

No. 12446 Circular Wire Gauge

No. 12451 Frame Saw File, Half Round

No. 12447 Engineers' Screwing Tackle in case, made any size to order

No. 12448 Rivet

No. 12449 Ratchet Drill Bit

No. 12450 Engineers' Stock and Dies, cutting $\frac{3}{8}$, $\frac{7}{16}$, $\frac{1}{2}$ inch, Whitworth thread

No. 12452 Half-Round Coarse Second-cut File

No. 12456 Double Hand Screw Plate

No. 12453 Bright Notched Screw Plate, 10 sizes

No. 12457 Single Hole Tap Wrench, can also be supplied with two or three holes

No. 12454 Gas Screw Stocks and Dies

Screw Plate

No. 12461 Split Key

No. 12455 Framing or Door Cramp

No. 12458 Thumb Screw Plate, ring-eyed handle

S&F. London

No. 12460 Tube Vice

No. 12459 Engineers' Foalsfoot Chisel

MANUFACTURERS, IMPORTERS, WAREHOUSEMEN AND AGENTS.

Pawson & Brailsford Lith. Sheffield